U.S. MARINES IN VIETNAM

AN EXPANDING WAR

1966

by

Jack Shulimson

HISTORY AND MUSEUMS DIVISION
HEADQUARTERS, U.S. MARINE CORPS
WASHINGTON, D.C.

1982

A Marine from Company G, 2d Battalion, 4th Marines, holds his rifle chest-high as he crosses a stream. The battalion is moving to link up with the 3d Battalion, 4th Marines, in Helicopter Valley, in July 1966.

Foreword

This is the third volume in a planned 10-volume operational and chronological series covering the Marine Corps' participation in the Vietnam War. A separate topical series will complement the operational histories. This particular volume details the continued buildup in 1966 of the III Marine Amphibious Force in South Vietnam's northernmost corps area, I Corps, and the accelerated tempo of fighting during the year. The result was an "expanding war."

The III Marine Amphibious Force had established three enclaves in I Corps during 1965. Employing what they believed was a balanced strategy—base defense, offensive operations, and pacification—the Marines planned to consolidate their base areas in 1966. At the beginning of 1966, the 1st Marine Division reinforced the 3d Marine Division and 1st Marine Aircraft Wing in Vietnam. By the end of the year, the III Marine Amphibious Force had nearly doubled in size. Two separate events, however, were to dash the high hopes held by the Marines in 1966. An internal political crisis in the spring halted the Marine pacification campaign south of the large Da Nang Airbase. In July, the North Vietnamese Army launched an incursion through the Demilitarized Zone and Marines went north to counter the enemy thrust. By December 1966, Marine units were stretched thin along the 265-mile length of I Corps. As one Marine commander observed, "too much real estate—do not have enough men."

Although written from the perspective of III MAF and the ground war in I Corps, the volume treats the activities of Marine advisors to the South Vietnamese Armed Forces, the Seventh Fleet Special Landing Force, and Marines on the staff of the U.S. Military Assistance Command, Vietnam, in Saigon. There are separate chapters on Marine air, artillery, and logistics. An attempt has been made to place the Marine role in relation to the overall effort.

The author, Mr. Jack Shulimson, is the senior Vietnam historian in the History and Museums Division. He has been with the division since 1964 and is the author of several earlier classified histories and co-author of *U.S. Marines in Vietnam, 1965: The Landing and the Buildup*. Mr. Shulimson has a bachelor of arts degree from the University of Buffalo and a master of arts in history from the University of Michigan. He is at present a candidate for a doctoral degree in American studies at the University of Maryland.

E. H. SIMMONS
Brigadier General, U.S. Marine Corps (Ret.)
Director of Marine Corps History and Museums

Other Volumes in the Marine Corps
Vietnam Operational Histories Series

U.S. Marines in Vietnam, 1954-1964, The Advisory and Combat Assistance Era, 1977

U.S. Marines in Vietnam, 1965, The Landing and the Buildup, 1978

U.S. Marines in Vietnam, 1967, now in preparation

U.S. Marines in Vietnam, January-June 1968, scheduled for preparation

U.S. Marines in Vietnam, July-December 1968, scheduled for preparation

U.S. Marines in Vietnam, 1969, now in preparation

U.S. Marines in Vietnam, 1970-1971, now in preparation

U.S. Marines in Vietnam, 1971-1973, now in preparation

U.S. Marines in Vietnam, 1973-1975, now in preparation

Preface

U.S. Marines in Vietnam: An Expanding War, 1966 is largely based on the holdings of the Marine Corps Historical Center. These include the official unit monthly command chronologies, Marine Corps messages and journal files, the Oral History Collection of the History and Museums Division, comment files of the division, and previously classified studies prepared by members of the division. Especially useful in the latter category were Captain Moyers S. Shore III, "Marines in Vietnam, January-June 1966," and Lieutenant Colonel Ralph F. Moody and Major Thomas E. Donnelly, "Introduction of North Vietnamese Regulars," parts III and IV of a then-projected single-volume history of the war. Two other former members of the division, Major Jack K. Ringler and Mr. George W. Garand, worked on preliminary drafts covering the 1966 period.

The author has supplemented the above sources with research in the records of the other Services and pertinent published primary and secondary sources. Although none of the information in this history is classified, some of the documentation on which it is based still has a classified designation. More than 135 reviewers, most of whom were participants in the events depicted in the history, read a comment edition of the manuscript. Their comments, where applicable, have been incorporated into the text. A list of all those who commented is included in the appendices. All ranks used in the body of the text are those ranks held by the individual in 1966.

The production of this volume, like its predecessors, has been a cooperative effort. All of the Vietnam historians, past and present, in the Histories Section, History and Museums Division, especially two former members, Lieutenant Colonel Lane Rogers and Dr. Graham A. Cosmas, have reviewed the draft manuscript. Access to Marine Corps documents has been facilitated by Mrs. Joyce Bonnett and her assistant, Mrs. Linda Benedict, of the division's Archives Section. Miss Evelyn Englander, head librarian, and her assistant, Mrs. Pat Morgan, have been most helpful in obtaining needed references. The Reference Section, headed by Mrs. Gabrielle M. Santelli, and her successor, Mr. Danny J. Crawford, made its files available and answered numerous queries cheerfully and professionally. Gunnery Sergeant William K. Judge and Mrs. Regina Strother of the Center's former Still Photo Depository, now a part of the Defense Audio Visual Agency, assisted in photographic research. The Head, Oral Histories Section, Mr. Benis M. Frank, was equally supportive in making his collection available.

Mrs. Vivian A. Lyon and Miss Faye A. Grant typed numerous card entries for the Index, and Major Edward F. Wells provided excellent assistance to the author in organizing it.

Mr. Robert E. Struder, head of Publications Production Section, and his predecessor, Mr. Paul D. Johnston, adeptly guided the manuscript through the various production phases. Maps were produced by Staff Sergeant Jerry L. Jakes and Mr. Richard A. Hillman. Mr. Hillman also did the design and layout of the book. The manuscript was typeset first, for the comment edition, by Corporal Paul W. Gibson. Final typesetting was accomplished by Corporals Gibson and Joseph J. Hynes, with Miss Catherine A. Stoll contributing significant technical expertise, and assistance in final stages from Lance Corporal Mark J. Zigante.

Special thanks are due Brigadier General Edwin H. Simmons, Director of Marine Corps History and Museums, who established the guidelines for the Vietnam series and made available his personal notebooks for 1966 when he commanded the 9th Marines; Colonel John E. Greenwood, former Deputy Director for Marine Corps History, who closely supervised the comment edition and gave wise counsel; his successor, Colonel Oliver M. Whipple, Jr., who pushed the project to completion; and Mr. Henry I. Shaw, Jr., Chief Historian, who provided me with the benefit of his long experience in writing Marine Corps history, encouragement when it was needed, and general editorial direction. I am indebted to my colleagues in the historical offices of the Army, Navy, and Air Force, who freely exchanged information and made documents available for my examination. I must express my gratitude also to all those who reviewed the comment edition and provided corrections, personal photographs, and insight available only to those who took part in the events. Finally, however, the author is responsible for the contents of the text, including opinions expressed and any errors in fact.

JACK SHULIMSON

Table of Contents

Page

Foreword III
Preface V
Table of Contents VII
Maps X

PART I THE MARINE BASE AREAS IN EARLY 1966 1

Chapter 1 A Larger Force for a Growing War, III MAF in January 1966 3
    III MAF, I Corps, and the Three Marine TAORs 3
    Command Relations 6
    Planned Deployment of the 1st Marine Division 9
    The Enemy Buildup 9
    The Marine Counterguerrilla War Versus the MACV Perspective 11
    Marine Mission and Future Plans 14
Chapter 2 Expanding War in Southern I Corps 17
    The Chu Lai TAOR 17
    Operation Double Eagle 19
Chapter 3 The War In Central I Corps 37
    The Da Nang TAOR 37
    Honolulu and the Reemphasis on Pacification 44
Chapter 4 A New Threat in Northern I Corps 50
    The Buildup at Phu Bai 50
    The Fall of A Shau 56
    The Aftermath of A Shau 64
    Continuing Reinforcement of Phu Bai and Operation Oregon 65

PART II CRISIS AND WAR IN CENTRAL I CORPS, SPRING 1966 71

Chapter 5 A Troubled Spring 73
    The Beginnings of the Political Crisis 73
    Restructuring the Command 74
    The Beginnings of the Da Nang Offensive 75
    "Keep Out . . . Da Nang Has Troubles" 81
Chapter 6 The Advance to the Ky Lam 92
    April Actions and Operation Georgia 92
    The May Ky Lam Campaign 96
    Operation Liberty 102

PART III SPRING FIGHTING IN SOUTHERN I CORPS 107

Chapter 7 "They're Not Supermen," Meeting the NVA in Operation Utah 109
    First Contact with the NVA 109
    Operation Utah Expands 115
Chapter 8 Further Fighting and an Expanding Base of Operations,
Chu Lai, March-June 1966 120
    A Bloody March 120
    Expansion at Chu Lai 128
    Operation Kansas 131

PART IV THE DMZ WAR 137

Chapter 9 The Enemy Buildup in the North 139
 Speculation About the Enemy's Intentions 139
 Reconnaissance at Khe Sanh, Operation Virginia 140
 Marine Operations in Thua Thien, April-May 1966 143
 Contingency Planning and Reconnaissance at Dong Ha 145
 Politics and War 147
 Heavy Fighting in Thua Thien Province 149
 Further Reconnaissance in the North 156

Chapter 10 Marines Turn North, Operation Hastings 159
 Finding the Enemy 159
 Reactivation of Task Force Delta and Heavy Fighting Along the DMZ,
  12-25 July 1966 161
 Hastings Comes to an End, 26 July-3 August 1966 174

Chapter 11 The DMZ War Continues, Operation Prairie 177
 Reconnaissance in Force, 3 August-13 September 1966 177
 Assault from the Sea, Deckhouse IV 188
 The Continued Fighting for Nui Cay Tre (Mutter) Ridge and the Razorback 189
 The Opening of Khe Sanh and the 3d Marine Division Moves North 195

PART V THE UNRELENTING WAR IN CENTRAL AND
SOUTHERN I CORPS, JULY-DECEMBER 1966 199

Chapter 12 The Struggle for An Hoa, Operation Macon 201
 The First Clash 201
 The Operation Expands 204
 Macon Continues 207
 Macon Ends but Little Changes 210

Chapter 13 The Continuing War 211
 Operations Washington and Colorado 211
 The September Election 220
 The Marine TAORs, July-December 1966 222

PART VI PACIFICATION: THE ELUSIVE GOAL 229

Chapter 14 Marine Corps Pacification 231
 County Fair and Golden Fleece 231
 Combined Action 239
 Personal Response 243
 Kit Carson 245
 Psychological Warfare 247
 Civic Action 247
 The I Corps Joint Coordinating Council 249

Chapter 15 Pacification, the Larger Perspective 251
 Pacification Receives Priority 251
 Reorganization and Support of Revolutionary Development 255
 Measurements of Progress 257

PART VII SUPPORTING THE TROOPS ... 259

Chapter 16 Marine Aviation in 1966 ... 261
    Wing Organization and Expansion ... 261
    The Pilot Shortage ... 262
    Marine Aircraft: The New and the Old ... 263
    Relations with the Seventh Air Force ... 268
    Marine Air Control Systems ... 269
    Air Defense ... 269
    Air Operations ... 271

Chapter 17 Artillery Support in 1966 ... 276
    Organization and Employment, January-June 1966 ... 276
    The Guns Move North and Restructuring the Command, July-December 1966 ... 278

Chapter 18 Men and Material ... 283
    Manpower ... 283
    Logistics, Medical Support, and Construction ... 285

PART VIII THE SLF, ADVISORS, OTHER MARINE ACTIVITIES, AND A FINAL LOOK AT 1966 ... 295

Chapter 19 The SLF of the Seventh Fleet ... 297
    The SLF, Double Eagle, and Doctrinal Debates ... 297
    The Okinawa Conference ... 299
    Changes in Command and Composition ... 299
    Further Operations and Changes in Commands and Units ... 300
    The May Conference ... 303
    The SLF to the End of the Year ... 304

Chapter 20 Other Marine Activities ... 307
    Staff and Security in Saigon ... 307
    Marine Advisors to the VNMC ... 308
    Rung Sat Marines ... 310
    Marine I Corps Advisors ... 310
    Air and Naval Gunfire Liaison ... 311

Chapter 21 At the End of the Year ... 312
    Plans for Reinforcing the Marines in I Corps ... 312
    Planning the Barrier ... 314
    Conclusion ... 319

NOTES ... 321

APPENDICES
    A. Marine Command and Staff List, January-December 1966 ... 342
    B. Glossary of Terms and Abbreviations ... 352
    C. Chronology of Significant Events ... 357
    D. Medal of Honor Citations, 1966 ... 359
    E. List of Reviewers ... 365
    F. Distribution of Aircraft, Fleet Marine Force, Pacific ... 367
    G. Distribution of Personnel, Fleet Marine Force, Pacific ... 369

INDEX ... 374

Maps

Location of Major U.S. Marine and ARVN Headquarters in I Corps, January 1966 .. 4
Communist Military Regions and Suspected NVA Divisions
    in Northern and Central South Vietnam, January 1966 12
Chu Lai TAOR, January 1966 16
Double Eagle I Landing and Area of Operations............................. 20

Double Eagle II Operating Area, February 1966............................. 36
Da Nang TAOR and Unit Positions, January 1966 39
Operation Mallard, 10-17 January 1966 42
Da Nang Pacification Campaigns 46
Phu Bai TAOR and Operation New York, February 1966 53

Operation Troy, 2-3 March 1966 55
A Shau in Relation to Da Nang, Hue, and Phu Bai 57
Enemy Assault on A Shau Special Forces Camp, 9-10 March 1966 60
Entry of Forces into Operation Oregon, 19-21 March 1966 66
Phu Bai TAOR and Location of Infantry Units, 31 March 1966 68

Ky Lam Area and King's Operating Area, March 1966 77
Da Nang City Area 82
Georgia Area, April-May 1966... 94
9th Marines Ky Lam Campaign Plan, May 1966 98
1/9 Area of Operations, 10-15 May 1966 101

Operation Liberty, June 1966..103
3d Marine Division Regimental TAORS After June Adjustments 105
Operation Utah, Assembly of Forces, 4-7 March 1966 116
Operation Texas, March 1966 122
Operation Kansas, June 1966..133

4th Marines Operations, April-June 1966 144
III MAF Enemy Order of Battle, Northern I Corps, 1 June 1966 151
Operation Jay, June 1966...153
Assault into the Ngan Valley, Operation Hastings, 15 July 1966 162
Operation Hastings, Days 3-5, 18-20 July 1966 170

Prairie Area of Operations, 30 November 1966..............................178
Actions in Operation Prairie, 8 August-4 October 1966.....................180
Beginning of Operation Macon, 4-6 July 1966 203
Operation Washington Area of Operations..................................212
Operation Colorado, 6 August 1966 215

Marine Units in Operation Chinook 225
Golden Fleece Area of Operations 235
SLF Operations 1966 302

PART I
THE MARINE BASE AREAS
IN EARLY 1966

CHAPTER 1

A Larger Force for a Growing War, III MAF in January 1966

III MAF, I Corps, and the Three Marine TAORs — Command Relations — Planned Deployment of the 1st Marine Division — The Enemy Buildup — The Marine Counterguerilla War Versus the MACV Perspective — Marine Mission and Future Plans

III MAF, I Corps, and the Three Marine TAORS

The III Marine Amphibious Force (III MAF) began 1966 with reason for optimism. From its origin as the 5,000-man 9th Marine Expeditionary Brigade (9th MEB) in March of 1965, III MAF had developed into a potent combined arms force consisting of the reinforced 3d Marine Division, 1st Marine Aircraft Wing, and supporting components. Major General Lewis W. Walt, the burly and much decorated III MAF commanding general, now had more than 41,000 men under his command.

The Marines were located in the northernmost of South Vietnam's four military regions, I Corps Tactical Zone (I CTZ). To the north the Demilitarized Zone (DMZ), immediately north and south of the Ben Hai River, separated North and South Vietnam. Bordered by Laos to the west, the South China Sea to the east, and II Corps Tactical Zone (II CTZ) to the south, I Corps extended 265 miles from north to south and varied in width from 30 to 70 miles east to west, encompassing 10,000 square miles.

The heavily forested Annamite mountain chain dominated western I Corps. East of the Annamites, the terrain gradually descended into densely vegetated hill masses, interlaced by river valleys and stream beds. A rich alluvial coastal plain characterized eastern I Corps, with occasional ridges, running from the mountains to the sea, compartmentalizing the region.

I Corps was not only a military and political division, but also a significant cultural and economic area. Its five provinces, Quang Tri, Thua Thien, Quang Nam, Quang Tin, and Quang Ngai, contained 2.6 million people. Two of South Vietnam's major cities were located in I Corps: Hue, the ancient imperial and cultural capital of Vietnam, and Da Nang, formerly called Tourane by the French, a large seaport, second in size only to Saigon. The bulk of the population lived in the coastal region and fertile river valleys where most made their living as rice farmers or fishermen.

In 1966, two Army of the Republic of Vietnam (ARVN) divisions were in I Corps. The 1st ARVN Division, with its headquaters at Hue, was responsible for the two northern provinces of Thua Thien and Quang Tri. In southern I Corps, the ARVN 2d Division, headquarted at Quang Ngai City, was deployed in Quang Tin and Quang Ngai Provinces. An independent regiment, the ARVN 51st, protected the approaches to Da Nang in Quang Nam Province.

With the deterioration of South Vietnamese Government control in the spring of 1965 and subsequent American intervention, the 9th MEB established an eight-square-mile base at the Da Nang Airfield. By January 1966, Marine forces, now III MAF, were operating from three enclaves in I Corps which contained 800 square miles and held over 400,000 South Vietnamese civilians. The large Da Nang tactical area of responsibility (TAOR) consisted of more than 530 square miles.* Over a quarter of a million South Vietnamese lived within its limits, largely in the fertile coastal plain between the air base and the junction of the Thu Bon and Ky Lam Rivers.

Fifty miles south of Da Nang along the coast was the Marines' second largest base, Chu Lai. By the

---

*According to present U.S. military usage, a TAOR is, "A defined area of land for which responsibility is specifically assigned to the commander of the area as a measure for control of assigned forces and coordination of support." See Joint Chiefs of Staff, *Department of Defense Dictionary of Military and Associated Terms*, JCS Pub 1 (Washington, 3Jan72), p. 295. Colonel Robert J. Zitnik, who commanded Marine Observation Squadron (VMO) 6 during 1965 and early 1966, emphasized that when his unit arrived in Vietnam in August 1965 the term TAOR referred to much more than tactical operations. "It seemed to imply the Civic Action Program, pacification, charitable works and many other human kindnesses. . . ." Col Robert J. Zitnik, Comments on draft MS, dtd 6Jun78 (Vietnam Comment File).

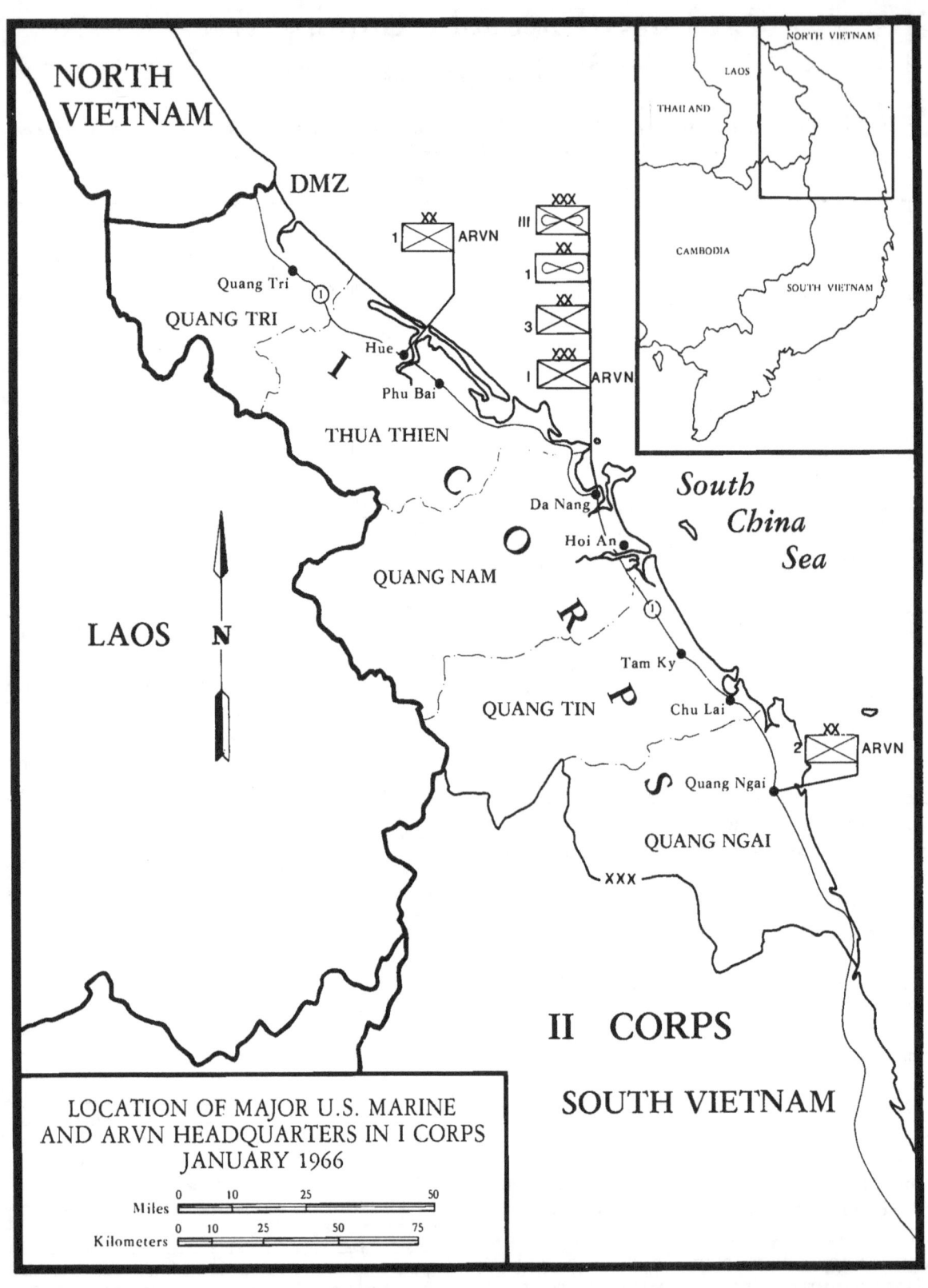

Marine Corps Photo A186662

The American and South Vietnamese flags fly in front of the 3d Marine Division Headquarters at Da Nang. This massive bunkered structure reinforced by timbers and concrete was indicative of the growing Marine presence in I Corps.

beginning of 1966, the Chu Lai TAOR contained 205 square miles of Quang Tin and Quang Ngai Provinces and over 100,000 persons, who lived in the numerous fishing and farming hamlets in the area.

Phu Bai in Thua Thien Province, the third Marine base, was approximately 35 miles northwest of Da Nang and eight miles southeast of Hue. The Phu Bai TAOR was the smallest of the three, only 76 square miles in area with 36,000 persons living in the six villages surrounding the small airstrip there.

Da Nang, the central and largest of the three bases, was the site of the headquarters of III MAF, the 3d Marine Division, and the 1st Marine Aircraft Wing. Two infantry regiments, the 3d and 9th Marines, with a total of six infantry battalions, were also in the Da Nang TAOR. An artillery regiment, the 12th Marines, which had its headquarters and two battalions at Da Nang, supported the infantry.

The rest of the 3d Division was divided proportionately between the other two bases. Two regiments, the 4th and 7th Marines, consisting of five infantry battalions supported by a two-battalion artillery group, were at Chu Lai. At Phu Bai, the Marines positioned an infantry battalion, the 2d Battalion, 1st Marines, supported by an artillery battalion, the 4th Battalion, 12th Marines, both under the operational control of the 3d Marines at Da Nang.

The 1st Marine Aircraft Wing also was widely dispersed. One fixed-wing group, Marine Aircraft Group (MAG) 11, was based at Da Nang and another, MAG-12, at Chu Lai. The Marine

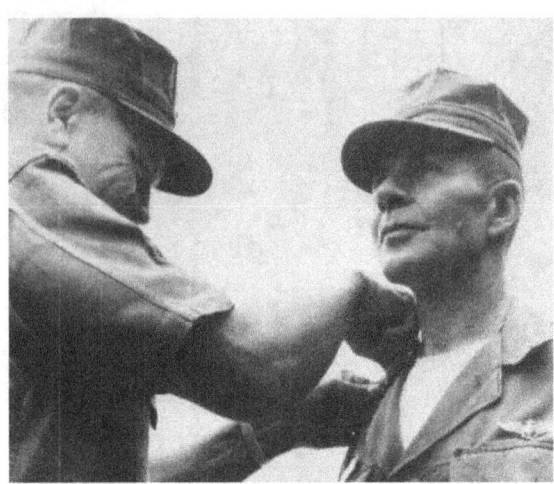

Marine Corps Photo A194585

MajGen Lewis W. Walt, Commanding General, III MAF (left), pins the second star on his newly promoted deputy, MajGen Keith B. McCutcheon. Gen McCutcheon is also the commander of the 1st Marine Aircraft Wing in Vietnam.

helicopter groups were deployed in the same manner; MAG-16 was stationed at the Marble Mountain Air Facility in the Da Nang enclave, and MAG-36 was located at the Ky Ha Air Facility in the Chu Lai TAOR. Marine Medium Helicopter Squadron (HMM) 163 from MAG-16 was assigned to Phu Bai, while still another MAG-36 squadron, HMM-363, was at Qui Nhon in II Corps under the operational control of the U.S. Army command, Field Force, Vietnam.

General Walt was the commanding general of both III MAF and the 3d Marine Division. Walt, an all-conference guard in football at Colorado State University and an honors graduate of the ROTC unit, accepted a Marine commission upon his graduation in 1936. As a member of the 1st Raider Battalion on Guadalcanal during World War II, he earned the Silver Star and Purple Heart as well as a battlefield promotion to lieutenant colonel. Later in the war, he was awarded two Navy Crosses, one at Cape Gloucester, where a key terrain objective became known as "Walt's Ridge," and the second at Peleliu, which also had its "Walt's Ridge." During the Korean War, he commanded the 5th Marines in 1952-53 and then became the G-3 of the 1st Marine Division. On 4 June 1965, as the junior major general of the Marine Corps, General Walt assumed command of III MAF.[1]

Major General Keith B. McCutcheon, the commanding general of the 1st Marine Aircraft Wing, was also the III MAF deputy commander.* McCutcheon, a slight, deceptively soft-spoken man, had had a brilliant, innovative career in Marine aviation. He played a leading role in the development of Marine close air support doctrine during World War II and in the postwar development of helicopter tactics. During the Korean War, he commanded HMR-161, the Marine helicopter squadron which supported the 1st Marine Division. Prior to assuming command of the 1st MAW in May 1965, McCutcheon had served as the operations officer on the staff of Admiral Ulysses S. Grant Sharp, Commander in Chief Pacific Command (CinCPac), who was responsible for all U.S. forces in the Pacific, including Vietnam.[2]

To help him with the widely scattered forces, logistics, and construction effort, General Walt had two assistant division commanders in the 3d Marine Division. Brigadier General Jonas M. Platt coordinated activities at Chu Lai, while Brigadier General Lowell E. English assisted Walt at Da Nang. This arrangement lasted until mid-March, when Walt was relieved of his direct responsibility for the 3d Marine Division.**

Command Relations

Command relations in the Vietnam War were complicated by the very nature of the war and the way the United States entered the conflict. Starting with a strength of a few thousand when it was established on 8 February 1962, the United States Military Assistance Command, Vietnam (USMACV) was committed to the training of the South Vietnamese Armed Forces (RVNAF) to fight a counterinsurgency war. As the dimensions of the struggle increased through the succeeding years, the American involvement correspondingly expanded. In 1965, the first major U.S. combat units deployed to Viet-

---

*At the beginning of 1966, General McCutcheon was still a brigadier general. He received his second star in a formal promotion ceremony at Da Nang on 22 January. See 1st MAW ComdC, Jan66.

**See Chapter 4 for the restructuring of the III MAF command relations in March.

nam and by the beginning of 1966, MACV totaled nearly 185,000 men.

General William C. Westmoreland, a former airborne commander and West Point superintendent, who had assumed command of MACV in June 1964, combined several command functions in his person. He not only headed the military advisory effort to the South Vietnamese Armed Forces, but also was a subordinate unified commander under CinCPac. In this latter capacity, he had operational control of all U.S. forces in Vietnam, including III MAF, Field Force, Vietnam, and the U.S. Air Force 2d Air Division, and was responsible for the overall U.S. military conduct of the war, with the exception of the bombing of North Vietnam and the limited air and air-ground operations in Laos. Admiral Sharp retained personal direction of the air campaign in the north while General Westmoreland shared responsibility with the U.S. Ambassador in Laos for the U.S. operations conducted in that country.[3] Westmoreland also functioned as the Army component commander and as such was the Commanding General, U.S. Army, Vietnam, the Army's logistic, administrative, and support command within South Vietnam.*

General Walt's command responsibilities were almost as diverse as General Westmoreland's. Not only was he commander of both III MAF and the 3d Marine Division, he was also ComUSMACV's Naval Component Commander, Vietnam (NCC), having under his operational control the Naval Mobile Construction Battalions (Seabees) in I Corps. In his role as NCC, Walt was concerned with common item supply for U.S. forces in I Corps, base construction in the northern provinces, and the running of all ports, beaches, and depots from Quang Ngai Province in southern I Corps to the DMZ. As the commander of both III MAF and the Naval Component,

General Walt served directly under the MACV commander. For purely Marine administrative and Marine logistic considerations, however, he reported to the Commanding General, Fleet Marine Force, Pacific (CGFMFPac), Lieutenant General Victor H. Krulak.

As NCC, with operational control of Naval Support Activity, Da Nang, Walt had a direct link to the Commander in Chief Pacific Fleet (CinCPacFlt), Admiral Roy L. Johnson. This occurred because Johnson retained command of Naval Support Activity, Da Nang, exercising it through Vice Admiral Edwin B. Hooper, Commander, Service Force, Pacific Fleet. General Walt also held one other position that was distinct and separate from his responsibilities as CG III MAF. Since August 1965, he had been the Senior U.S. Advisor for I Corps and directed the U.S. advisory effort in the five northern provinces. Thus, in one capacity or another, General Walt directed the activity of nearly all U.S. forces in I Corps.**

Political considerations limited the authority of the U.S. military in Vietnam. General Westmoreland did not have command of the South Vietnamese Armed Forces, and his military advisory functions often overlapped those of the U.S. civilian assistance program under the U.S. Ambassador, Henry Cabot Lodge, Jr., who then was serving his second tour in that position. Westmoreland's relationship with both the South Vietnamese and the U.S. Embassy was one of close consultation and coordination. He was a member of the U.S. Mission Council, chaired by Ambassador Lodge, which developed and coordinated U.S. policy within South Vietnam. Moreover, General Westmoreland was the senior

---

*According to U.S. military doctrine, "With the exception of the commander of a unified command and members of his joint staff, the senior officer of each Service assigned to a unified command and qualified for command by the regulations of his own Service is the commander of the component of his Service...." JCS, *Unified Action Armed Forces* (UNAAF), JCS Pub. 2 (Washington, D.C., Nov59), p. 40. As a subordinate unified commander, General Westmoreland could have designated another Army general to head the Army component command, but decided to retain responsibility for this function in his own person.

**Vice Admiral Hooper commented that these complex command relations were not "widely understood. Yet from them stem much of the effectiveness and flexibility of the Navy and Marine Forces. The exercise of responsibility and authority up the Navy's chain of command was one of the secrets of the notable success of the logistic support provided by the Navy." VAdm Edwin B. Hooper, Comments on draft MS, n.d. [May 1978] (Vietnam Comment File). Lieutenant General Hugh M. Elwood, who became assistant wing commander of the 1st MAW in April 1966, was less sanguine about command relations, remarking that "CGFMFPac, in his Op Order, applied the term 'Command less OpCon' to III MAF. This made command relations sticky indeed since it gave CG III MAF two masters...." LtGen Hugh M. Elwood, Comments on draft MS, dtd 4Jun78 (Vietnam Comment File).

U.S. advisor to the South Vietnamese Joint General Staff, which according to the former MACV commander, gave him "defacto control over the broad scope of operations."[4]

General Walt developed similar procedures with the South Vietnamese authorities and U.S. civilian agencies in I Corps. He and the Regional Director of the U.S. Operation Mission (USOM) in the I Corps Sector, Marcus J. Gordon, initiated the organization of the I Corps Joint Coordinating Council. The council consisted of senior representatives from the Marine command, the Navy, the U.S. civilian assistance program, and the Vietnamese Government who met once a month under the chairmanship of General McCutcheon. It had no command responsibility, but under its auspices the various American and South Vietnamese civilian and military authorities could meet, discuss their programs, coordinate policy, and smooth out misunderstandings.*

As significant as the development of the Council, and perhaps even more so, was the close relationship that General Walt established with the volatile I Corps commander, Lieutenant General Nguyen Chanh Thi. Thi, who as a paratroop brigade commander had led an abortive coup against the Ngo Dinh Diem regime as early as 1960, played a large role in the inner circle of "young Turk" military commanders who dominated South Vietnamese politics following the fall of Diem in 1963. As I Corps commander, Thi controlled both the South Vietnamese civilian and military apparatus in I Corps. Although not openly defiant of Saigon, he carefully selected the directives which he chose to obey. In the South Vietnamese capital, one often heard rumors that Thi was about to lead a coup against the flamboyant Air Marshal Nguyen Cao Ky and the more reticent General Nguyen Van Thieu, who, respectively, as the Commissioner in Charge of the Executive Branch and the Chairman of the Joint Directorate, the official name for the ruling military junta, governed South Vietnam.[5]

General Walt did not concern himself with the machinations of Vietnamese politics, but rather with the establishment of a working partnership with General Thi. The Marine general respected the courage and military competence of the Vietnamese I Corps commander and recognized that Thi also had political responsibilities. Walt later commented, "We sometimes find that this political purpose and military purpose get on collision courses, but always to date we [Thi and himself] have been able to sit down and talk this out." Acknowledging that Thi was an ambitious man, Walt nevertheless believed that the Vietnamese general's ambition lay in making I Corps an example for the rest of the country.[6]

During 1966, the existing command relations were to become even more complex as the war, and the American role in it, expanded. As hope for any peaceful solution to the conflict diminished and the American "peace" offensive, inaugurated in late 1965 by a temporary suspension of the bombing of the north, proved futile, the war increased in intensity and dimension. With the accelerated arrival of U.S. combat forces, MACV planned further alterations of its component commands. The one that directly affected the Marine Corps was the proposed change in the NCC.

Both General Westmoreland and Rear Admiral Norvell G. Ward, commander of the Naval Advisory Group, believed that the increased naval participation in the war required a naval component commander to be in Saigon, directly under ComUSMACV. General Wallace M. Greene, Jr., the forceful Commandant of the Marine Corps, who was in Vietnam on an inspection trip in January, met with General Westmoreland and Admiral Ward in Saigon and received their assurances that an independent NCC would not alter command relations between MACV and III MAF. Although agreeing to the need for a large naval role in Vietnam, Greene suggested that the proposal receive further study in order to determine its possible ramifications. When he asked General Walt for his opinion a few days after the Saigon meeting, the latter replied that he had no objection to the transfer of his NCC responsibility to the Navy, as long as Marines had a "strong representation on the policy and working level."[7]

---

*Colonel Sumner A. Vale observed that whatever the successes of the Joint Coordinating Council it did not create a "unity of effort"—U.S. and Vietnamese, civil and military—comparable to what the British found essential for counterinsurgency operations in Malaya. Col Sumner A. Vale, Comments on draft MS, dtd 18Jul78 (Vietnam Comment File).

Planned Deployment of the 1st Marine Division

With the continuing buildup of U.S. forces, increasing responsibility was spread among the various component services of MACV. In late 1965, Secretary of Defense Robert S. McNamara recommended to President Lyndon B. Johnson the doubling of U.S. forces in Vietnam during the new year. For the Marine Corps, this involved the further deployment of both ground and air units to Vietnam and the establishment of a force structure for III MAF consisting of 18 infantry battalions, 21 aviation squadrons, and other supporting units, totaling approximately 70,000 troops.[8]

The major deployment for the Marines during the first half of the year was to be the movement of the 1st Marine Division from Okinawa to Vietnam. Major General Lewis J. "Jeff" Fields, the division commander, an experienced artillery and staff officer who had served with the 11th Marines during both World War II and Korea, had transferred the headquarters of the division from Camp Pendleton, California, to Camp Courtney, Okinawa, in August 1965. He held a rear echelon, including the 5th Marines, at Pendleton under his assistant division commander, Brigadier General William A. Stiles. Even before the establishment of the division forward headquarters at Courtney, one of its regiments, the 7th Marines, sailed from Okinawa for Vietnam with its 1st Battalion. The other two battalions had already departed Okinawa; the 2d Battalion was inserted at Qui Nhon in II Corps and the 3d Battalion became the Seventh Fleet's Special Landing Force (SLF) battalion. By the end of the year, all three 7th Marines battalions and a supporting artillery battalion from the 11th Marines were at Chu Lai. Two other infantry battalions from the division were also in Vietnam at this time, the 1st Battalion, 1st Marines at Da Nang and the 2d Battalion, 1st Marines at Phu Bai. These two battalions represented no further reinforcement for III MAF, but were "in country" as a result of an FMFPac intratheater rotation system. Under this policy, the 2d Battalion, 3d Marines and the 3d Battalion, 4th Marines rotated from Vietnam with the former battalion slated to become the SLF with the Seventh Fleet and the latter returned to Okinawa for rest and refitting.[9]

Under the new deployment authorized by the President, the division headquarters, the regimental headquarters of the 1st, 5th and 11th Marines, the remaining infantry and artillery battalions, and division support elements were scheduled to reinforce III MAF. Lieutenant Colonel Roy E. Moss, the 1st Marine Division embarkation officer, related that he learned about the decision at a December conference at FMFPac Headquarters in Honolulu at which a tentative schedule for moving the division to Vietnam was drawn up. Moss arrived back on Okinawa at 0200, the morning of 27 December and five hours later briefed General Fields. According to Moss, the general asked, "Roy, how do we get all of our units moved to Vietnam . . . ?" Moss replied that the tentative schedule called for 30 ships, staggered over a two and a half month period, to accomplish the mission. General Fields approved and sent Moss to Subic Bay in the Philippines to discuss the matter with representatives of Task Force 76, the Seventh Fleet Amphibious Force. At the U.S. Naval Base at Subic, the Navy agreed that with "judicious scheduling [it] could meet the needs of the division."[10]

The Enemy Buildup

The American buildup did not occur in a vacuum, but because of the South Vietnamese inability to cope with the increase in strength of the Communist-led forces within South Vietnam. Allied intelligence estimates of the total enemy strength in South Vietnam had risen from a possible 138,000 in March 1965 to over 226,000 men by the end of the year. MACV believed that these forces consisted of more than 110,000 guerrillas, 39,000 political cadre, 18,000 combat support troops, and approximately 70,000 men organized in regular formations, inculding 19 regiments ranging from 2,000 to 2,500 men in strength. Seven of these regiments were positively identified as North Vietnamese.[11]

Although Communist North Vietnam had long provided the insurgency in the south with leadership, inspiration, and logistic support, it was not until late 1964 that regular North Vietnamese Army [NVA] units began to infiltrate into South Vietnam, and it was not until the autumn of 1965 that the first major encounter between allied forces and North Vietnamese troops occurred. In October, the U.S. 1st Cavalry Division (Airmobile) defeated elements of two NVA regiments, the *32d* and *33d*, during the battle of the Ia Drang Valley in the II Corps Central Highlands. The following month, the South Viet-

North Vietnamese Army troops parade in Hanoi. By the beginning of 1966, North Vietnamese regulars were infiltrating into South Vietnam at the rate of 12 battalions per month.

namese 37th Ranger Battalion repulsed the *NVA 18th Regiment's* attack of the Thach Tru outpost, 16 miles south of Quang Ngai City. Despite the allied victories in these two engagements, the growing North Vietnamese presence in the south alarmed both the South Vietnamese and American commands. General Westmoreland later stated that the North Vietnamese were infiltrating at the rate of 12 battalions a month at the end of the year and more than 26,000 NVA soldiers had come south during 1965.[12]*

Larger enemy formations continued to appear in South Vietnam in 1966, especially in the Central Highlands, southern I Corps, and the border region between I Corps and II Corps. By early 1966, three North Vietnamese divisions were operating in these areas: the *1st NVA Division*, consisting of the *33d, 32d,* and *66th NVA Regiments*, was in the Central Highland provinces of Pleiku and Kontum; the *2d NVA Division*, consisting of the *21st NVA, 3d NVA* and *1st Viet Cong (VC) Regiments*, was in Quang Tin and Quang Ngai Provinces; and the *3d NVA Division*, consisting of the *18th NVA, 22d NVA,* and *2d VC Regiments*, was in Quang Ngai and Binh Dinh Provinces. The allies also received reports of a substantial North Vietnamese unit buildup just north of the DMZ.

The Communists made several administrative changes in their command and control organization which reflected the increasing North Vietnamese role in the war, especially in northern South Vietnam. Since 1961, the headquarters of *Military Region 5 (MR-5)*, which extended from Quang Tri Province in the north to Dar Loc and Khanh Hoa Provinces in the south, had been responsible for both military operations and the political ad-

---

*U.S. Air Force historians commented that Rand Corporation analysts in a 1968 study of infiltration raised the estimate of North Vietnamese moving into South Vietnam during 1965 to 36,000 personnel, "roughly a three-fold increase over the total for 1964." Office of Air Force History, Comments on draft MS, dtd 28Jul78 (Vietnam Comment File).

ministrative process in this sector. Although *MR-5* received both military and political direction from North Vietnam, the headquarters was ostensibly subordinate to the *Central Office of South Vietnam (COSVN)*, the Viet Cong military high command and politburo. The North Vietnamese partially discarded the facade of subordination to *COSVN* when they established two new commands. In the Central Highland provinces of Kontum, Dar Loc, and Pleiku, they formed the *B-3 Front* which was directly under North Vietnamese military control, while in I Corps, they detached the two northern provinces of Quang Tri and Thua Thien from *Military Region 5*. These two provinces then became the *Tri-Thien-Hue Military Region* under the direct control of *Military Region 4*, the administrative and military subdivision for southern North Vietnam.

The Marine Counterguerrilla War Versus the MACV Perspective

Despite the buildup of enemy main force units and North Vietnamese intervention, the major concern of the Marine command in I Corps was with the tightly knit VC political and guerrilla substructure. Of the 30,000 estimated Viet Cong and NVA in I Corps, approximately half were believed to be irregulars, subordinate to local village and hamlet level VC organizations. At Da Nang, for example, III MAF estimated no more than 2,000 main force and local force VC troops to be within a 25-mile radius of the airbase, yet the Communist political and guerrilla apparatus permeated the southern portion of the TAOR.[13] General Walt estimated that this VC local "infrastructure" controlled one-third of the population living in I Corps and influenced, largely through terror, still another third of the populace.[14]

Confronted with this situation, the Marines had emphasized small-unit counterguerrilla tactics through 1965 rather than multibattalion operations against the enemy's main force units. Operation Starlite, south of Chu Lai in August, and Operation Harvest Moon, in the Que Son Valley along the border between Quang Nam and Quang Tin in December were notable exceptions, but the emphasis was on pacification. General Walt stressed that the objective of the war was to win the loyalty of the populace to the government, and the only way to

Marine Corps Historical Collection
General Nguyen Chi Tranh, who in 1966 was Commander-in-Chief, "Liberation Army of South Vietnam," and Chief of the Viet Cong Central Office for South Vietnam, is seen reading a book in his South Vietnam headquarters. Tranh was also a general in the North Vietnamese Army and a member of that government's National Defense Council.

obtain this objective was to eradicate the Viet Cong in the villages and hamlets. This was what the Marines sought to do. In describing this pacification effort, one former Marine staff officer, Colonel George W. Carrington, Jr., the 3d Marine Division G-2 in January 1966, later wrote that:

> . . . to reassure the villagers that they were safe, supported and protected, U.S. Marines undertook a most demanding pattern of intensive, multiple, day-and-night, tedious patrol activity. The incredible total of man-hours devoted to this end and the sincere, compassionate, and dedicated manner in which thousands of Marines did their duty were never understood or appreciated by outsiders.[15]

General Krulak, the FMFPac commander, was a strong advocate of the III MAF concept of operations. Known since his Naval Academy days as the "Brute," partially as a jesting reference to his small stature, but also in deference to his commanding and forthright personality, Krulak had served earlier

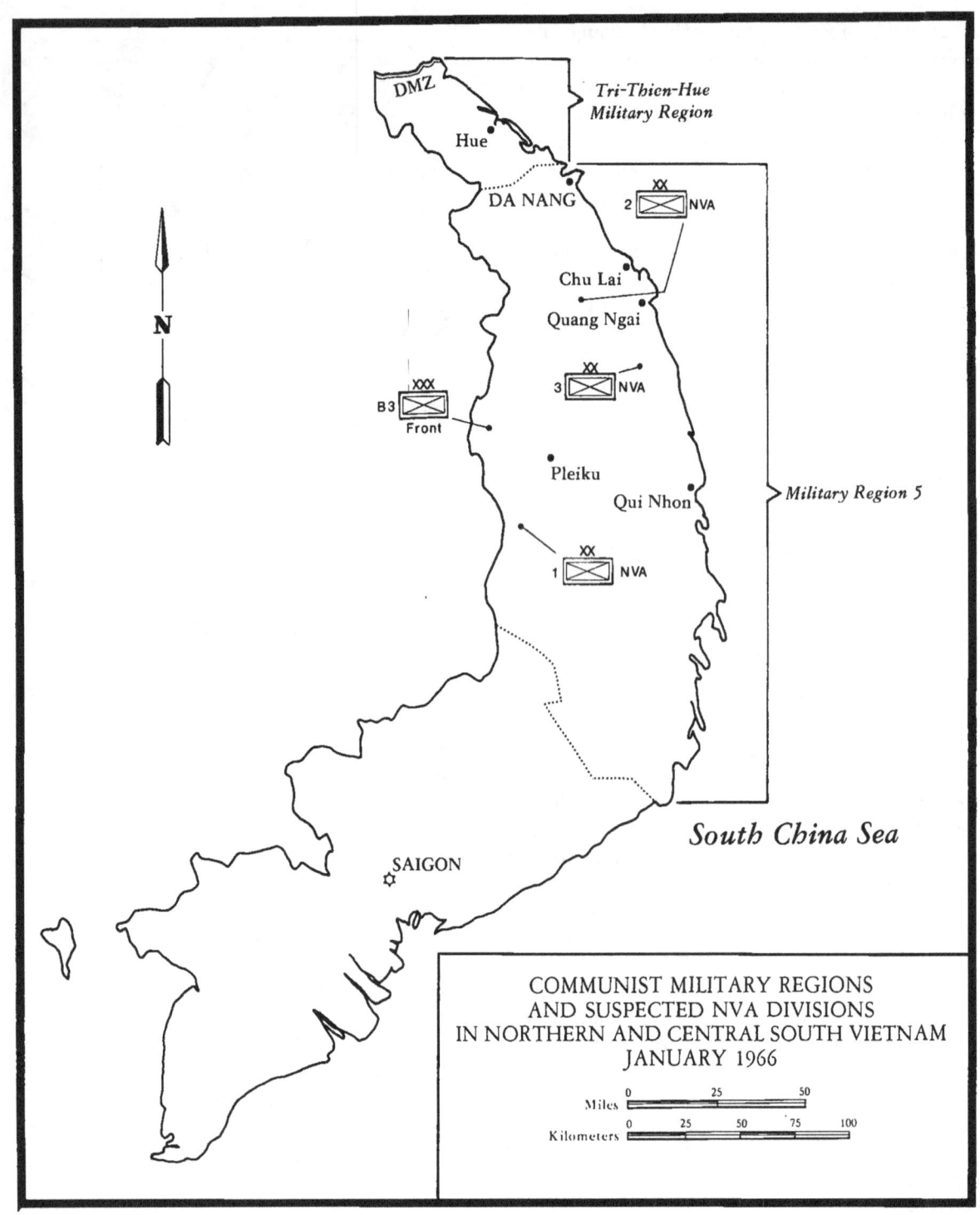

A LARGER FORCE FOR A GROWING WAR

as a special assistant for counterinsurgency to the Joint Chiefs during the Kennedy administration. According to General Krulak, Admiral Sharp used him as a personal advisor "on *all* Marine matters," and he [Krulak] sought to persuade:

> CinCPac . . . that there was no virtue at all in seeking out the NVA in the mountains and jungle; that so long as they stayed there they were a threat to nobody, that our efforts should be addressed to the rich, populous lowlands. . . . [16]

Krulak argued:

> It is our conviction that if we can destroy the guerrilla fabric among the people, we will automatically deny the larger units the food and the intelligence and the taxes, and the other support they need. At the same time, if the big units want to sortie out of the mountains and come down where they can be cut up by our supporting arms, the Marines are glad to take them on, but the real war is among the people and not among these mountains.[17]

General Westmoreland had a different perspective. He contended that the introduction of North Vietnamese Army units into the south created an entirely new situation. The MACV commander's opinion was that the Communists wanted to develop multidivision forces in relatively secure base areas, while at the same time continuing extensive guerrilla action to tie down allied forces. His intelligence staff section stated that the enemy planned to mount major offensives in 1966 in the provinces northwest of Saigon and in the Central Highlands. According to MACV, the enemy hoped to achieve control of the Pleiku-Qui Nhon axis and thus isolate I Corps from the rest of Vietnam. General Westmoreland viewed 1966 as a year of transition in which he was building up his troop strength and "a widespread logistical infrastructure (ports, airfield, supply storage areas, etc.)." He believed that in order to protect his vulnerable base areas, he had to husband his forces and resources and use in concert the intelligence available, the tactical mobility, and the shock action his troops possessed to launch spoiling attacks and keep the enemy's main forces off-balance.[18]

The MACV commander, moreover, had some reservations about the thrust of the Marine Corps pacification campaign. He recalled that in 1964, the ARVN 22d Division in the populated, coastal Binh Dinh Province had concentrated on small-unit operations against the guerrilla forces, and as:

> . . . progess began to become evident, two main-force enemy regiments debouched from the hills and virtually destroyed the spread-out South Vietnamese units in detail, making a shambles of the pacification program. It took well over a year to recover what was lost.[19]

General Westmoreland's staff reinforced his doubts about the Marine Corps concentration on the small-unit counterguerrilla campaign south of Da Nang. On 15 November 1965, Brigadier General William E. DePuy, the MACV J-3, reported to General Westmoreland after a visit to III MAF that he was "disturbed by the fact that all but a tiny part of the I Corps area is under the control of the VC who have freedom of movement east and west—north and south—outside the Marine enclaves." DePuy stated that the Marines were "stalled a short distance south of Da Nang," because the Vietnamese were unable to "fill in behind Marines in their expanding enclaves." Although impressed with the Marine professionalism and concern for the "security of the people and the pacification process," General DePuy believed that III MAF should use part of its force "as a mobile element throughout the Corps." He recommended to General Westmoreland that the Marines "be directed" to launch large-unit offensive operations against VC base areas "with two to three battalion forces during at least two weeks out of every month."[20]

General Westmoreland agreed with his operations officer's analysis of Marine operations. As he later wrote: "I believed the Marines should have been trying to find the enemy's main forces and bring them to battle, thereby putting them on the run and reducing the threat they posed to the population." Although General Westmoreland wanted the Marines to form mobile strike forces, he "had no wish to deal so abruptly with General Walt" that he would "precipitate an interservice imbroglio." He recognized that "as a senior regional commander, General Walt had a mission-type order which by custom afforded him considerable leeway in execution." Westmoreland explained, "Rather than start a controversy, I chose to issue orders for specific projects that as time passed would gradually get the Marines out of their beachheads."[21]

From the III MAF perspective, the differences with MACV were more in emphasis than in substance. General Walt did not consider his "ink blot strategy," with its gradual extension of the

Marine Corps Photo A186695

Gen Wallace M. Greene, Jr., Commandant of the Marine Corps, holds a news conference at Da Nang during a visit there in January 1966. Gen Walt is seated to his right.

Marine enclaves as manpower became available, necessarily in conflict with General Westmoreland's advocacy of highly mobile "search and destroy"* operations aimed at the enemy's main force units. Colonel Edwin H. Simmons, the III MAF operations officer, later observed:

> Westmoreland's view was, "Yes, we accept the Marine Corps' concern about pacification, but we want you to do more." He wanted the Marines to experiment with lighter battalions and new tactics. General Walt's position was, 'Yes, I will engage the enemy's main force units, but first I want to have good intelligence."[22]

At FMFPac Headquarters, General Krulak viewed

---

*General Westmoreland believes that the term "search and destroy," which was later abandoned, had been distorted by critics to imply "aimless searches in the jungle and the random destroying of villages and other property." Westmoreland states that this was not the case, and that "search and destroy" was nothing more than an operational term for a tactic . . . ," synonymous with "sweeping operations or reconnaissance in force." Westmoreland, *A Soldier Reports*, p. 83. General Wallace M. Greene, Jr., the Commandant of the Marine Corps in 1966, observed in his comments: "Search and destroy means traversing the same terrain repeatedly against a nebulous foe—while the people were untended." Gen Wallace M. Greene, Jr., Comments on draft MS, dtd 5May78 (Vietnam Comment File).

the Marine differences with MACV as more basic. He recalled in 1978 that he differed with General Westmoreland, ". . . not in a limited, but in a profound way." Krulak declared, "Our effort belonged where the people were, *not* where they weren't. I shared these thoughts with Westmoreland frequently, but made no progress in persuading him."[23]

In Washington, the Commandant perceived the disagreement between the Marines and MACV in much the same way as General Krulak. General Greene later stated that General Westmoreland and his commanders were preoccupied with the large unit war and that, "From the very beginning the prime error had been the failure to make the population secure—to stamp out the VC hidden in town and hamlet." Greene contended that:

> I Corps was ideally established geographically (the bulk of the population in a narrow coastal strip) to do this—and to initiate security operations from the sea against key points along the coast.

He declared that he had advocated such a strategy:

> . . . in a presentation to the Joint Chiefs and to General Westmoreland. The Chiefs were interested but Westmoreland wasn't and being CG MACV his views of the "big picture," the "broad arrow," prevailed. . . .[24]

Marine Mission and Future Plans

Despite the differences over pacification and the big-unit war between MACV and the Marines, the basic directives which governed III MAF operations were broad enough to incorporate both approaches. According to the 21 November 1965 MACV Letter of Instruction (LOI) to General Walt, the mission of III MAF was to:

> Conduct military operations in I ARVN Corps Tactical Zone (CTZ) in support of and in coordination with CG, I ARVN Corps, and in other areas of RVN [Republic of Vietnam] to defeat the VC and extend GVN [Government of South Vietnam] control over all of Vietnam.

In order to carry out this assignment, the Marines were to defend and secure the base areas of Phu Bai, Da Nang, and Chu Lai; to conduct search and destroy missions against VC forces which posed an immediate threat to these bases; to launch other search and destroy operations against more distant enemy base areas; to extend clearing operations in selected areas contiguous to the major bases; and finally to execute any contingency plan in I CTZ or elsewhere in Vietnam as directed by ComUSMACV.[25]

These all-encompassing objectives were reinforced by the U.S./GVN Combined Campaign Plan for 1966 which was promulgated by General Westmoreland and the South Vietnamese Joint General Staff on 31 December 1965. American forces were to secure their base areas and conduct clearing operations in the vicinity of the base, and all "friendly forces were to conduct operations against VC forces in heretofore 'safe havens, areas, and bases.'"[26]

Working within these very general guidelines, General Walt's III MAF 1966 campaign plan maintained a balance among mutually supporting activities. This "balanced approach" consisted of a three-pronged effort comprised of search and destroy missions, counterguerrilla operations, and pacification.* With the aim of extending government control throughout I Corps, the Marines were to concentrate first on the coastal region between Da Nang and Chu Lai. Once the linkup of these two TAORs was accomplished, the Marine command was to focus its attention on the coast north of Da Nang to the DMZ and south of Chu Lai to the II Corps' boundary. III MAF believed that it could secure the entire coastal plain from Quang Tri to Quang Ngai by the end of 1966 and could make considerable progress in the populated inland river valleys.[27]

General Walt based his concept of operations on several contingency factors, the two most important being the arrival of additional allied forces and no North Vietnamese buildup except in southern I Corps. With the arrival of the remainder of the 1st Marine Division and the possibility of obtaining operational control of the South Korean Marine Brigade, then in II Corps, the III MAF commander had hopes of having 21 infantry battalions under his command by midyear. He required 10 battalions to develop and defend the base areas, which would allow 11 battalions for more mobile operations.[28]

During 1966, the implementation of III MAF plans was different at each of the Marine enclaves; the military situation at each base was dissimilar and called for various approaches. With only one infantry battalion at Phu Bai, the northern Marine enclave was primarily concerned about base defense. At Da Nang, major emphasis was on pacification because of the highly concentrated population south of the airbase. Although not neglecting the pacification aspects, the proportionately stronger Marine forces in the less settled Chu Lai region were able to mount operations against the enemy's regular force buildup in southern I Corps.

---

*General Krulak commented in 1978 that this "'balanced approach' was a compromise with Westmoreland and not a balance, that every man we put into hunting for the NVA was wasted...." The former FMFPac commander further maintained that he had sought to persuade CinCPac that this approach was "a mutation strategy... designed to pacify all shades of strategic thought; that if we persisted in such a compromise, we would bleed ourselves—which we did." LtGen Victor H. Krulak, Comments on draft MS, n.d. [May 1978] (Vietnam Comment File).

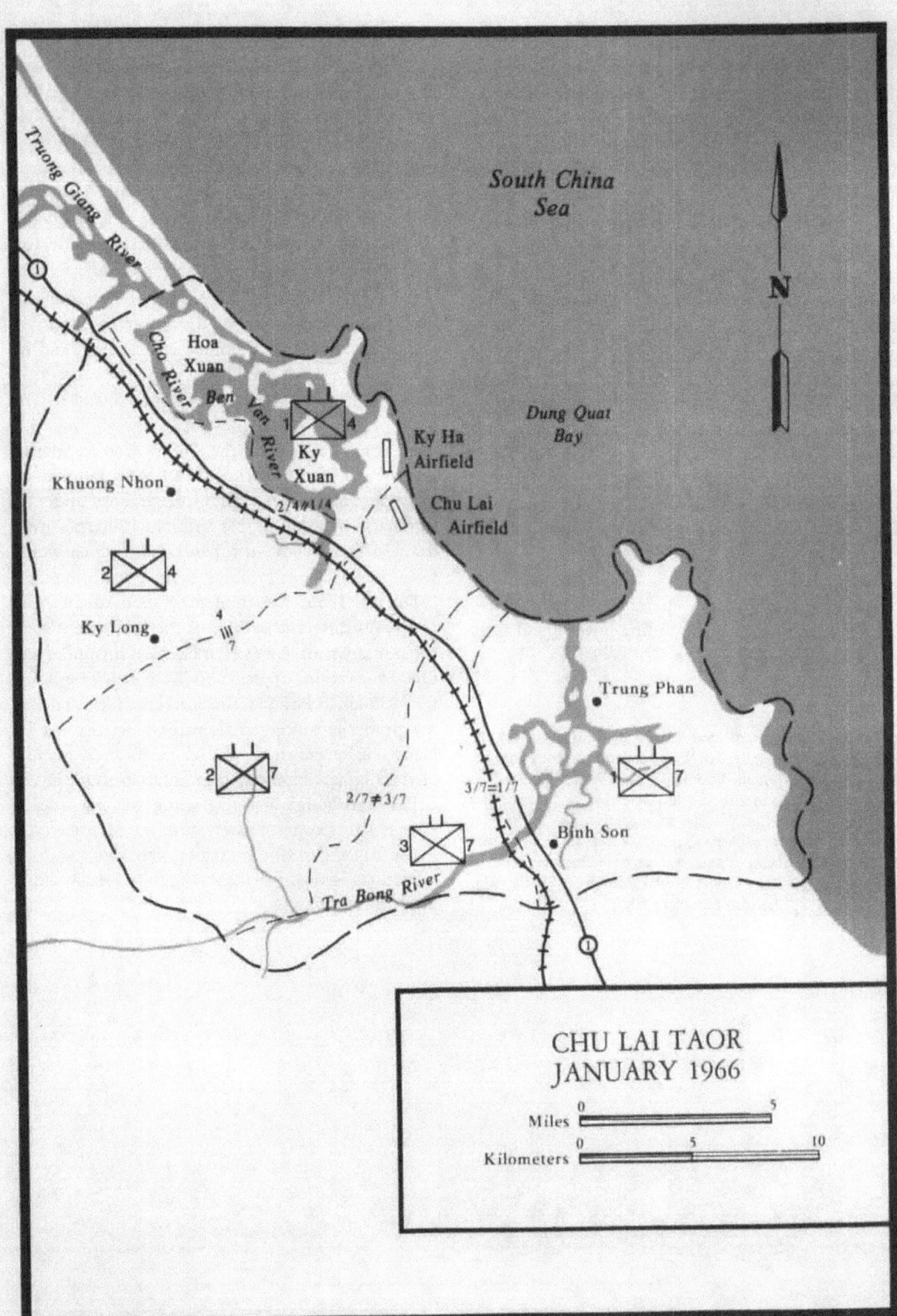

CHAPTER 2
Expanding War in Southern I Corps
The Chu Lai TAOR—Operation Double Eagle

The Chu Lai TAOR

In January 1966, the Chu Lai TAOR, which straddled the Quang Tin and Quang Ngai Province boundary, stretched from Hoa Xuan Island in the north to just below the town of Binh Son in the south, a distance of 17 miles. The eastern portion of the TAOR bordered the South China Sea and the western sector extended 15 miles inland at its widest point. Route 1, the major north-south highway, bisected the TAOR, paralleling the coast and connecting Chu Lai to Da Nang, 57 miles to the northwest, and Quang Ngai City, 20 miles to the south.

In the Chu Lai region, the Annamite chain reaches within four miles of the sea and the coastal plain is relatively narrow, limiting the amount of arable land. Several rivers provide drainage, the most important being the Truong Giang, the Cho, the Ben Van, and the Tra Bong. With the South China Sea, these waterways form islands, peninsulas, coves, and bays along the coast which provide an excellent livelihood for the inhabitants of the several fishing villages in the region.

Selected in 1964 as a possible site for a supplementary airbase to Da Nang, Chu Lai became a major Marine base in May 1965. Immediately after landing, Marines and Seabees began work on a short airfield for tactical support (SATS) inland from Dung Quat Bay, aligned with the prevailing winds, northwest to southeast. Within a month, MAG-12's Douglas A-4 Skyhawk attack aircraft were flying from Chu Lai. Soil stabilization was a continuous problem throughout 1965, but at least half the 8,000-foot runway was always operational. In addition, III MAF had contracted with a U.S. commerical firm for the construction of a permanent 10,000-foot concrete runway, 2,000 meters west of the SATS field.* Northwest of the SATS field, the Marines and Seabees had already built a helicopter air facility on Ky Ha Peninsula, which, since September 1965, had been the base of operations for MAG-36.

With the buildup of Marine forces at Chu Lai during the summer of 1965, General Walt appointed Brigadier General Frederick J. Karch, one of his two assistant division commanders (ADC), the base coordinator. In November 1965, newly promoted Brigadier General Jonas M. Platt relieved Karch at Chu Lai after the latter had completed his overseas tour. Platt was responsible for the 14,000 Marines at Chu Lai, the defense of the base, and all tactical ground operations. He had operational control of two reinforced infantry regiments, the 4th and 7th Marines, and the artillery group, consisting of the 3d Battalion, 11th Marines and the 3d Battalion, 12th Marines. As the Chu Lai Base Coordinator, General Platt directed the security arrangements for the two Marine aircraft groups, Colonel Leslie E. Brown's MAG-12 and Colonel William G. Johnson's MAG-36, as well as for the Chu Lai Logistic Support Unit.

The two infantry regiments shared the responsibility for the defense of the base. Colonel James F. McClanahan's 4th Marines had two battalions on line for the protection of the northern and central portions of the TAOR. His northernmost, the 1st Battalion, 4th Marines, defended the northern coastal approaches and the Chu Lai vital areas.

---

*In the strict sense, Chu Lai was not a true SATS field. "A SATS is a type of shore-based carrier deck complete with catapult and arresting gear. The Chu Lai field was longer than a true SATS and a catapult was not installed until April 1966, but it did use SATS components." LtGen Keith B. McCutcheon, "Marine Aviation in Vietnam, 1962-70," *Naval Review*, 1971, pp. 129-130. For additional information concerning the building of the airfield and 1965 operations, see Chapter 18 and Jack Shulimson and Major Charles Johnson, *U.S. Marines in Vietnam, 1965* (Washington: His&MusDiv, HQMC, 1978), Chapters 3 and 12.

Marine Corps Photo A186377
Two Marines relax outside their defensive positions on the outskirts of a hamlet in the western sector of the Chu Lai Tactical Area of Responsibility (TAOR). The men are from the 2d Battalion, 4th Marines.

Marine Corps Photo A186383
Marines of the 2d Battalion, 4th Marines cross a flooded rice paddy in the western Chu Lai sector. The troops are after local guerrillas who have fired upon them.

Lieutenant Colonel Ralph E. Sullivan, the battalion commander, maintained his command post and two companies on Ky Ha Peninsula, and his other two companies were on Ky Xuan and Ky Hoa Islands which controlled the access into the inland waterways of the northern TAOR. Lieutenant Colonel Rodolfo L. Trevino's 2d Battalion, 4th Marines manned the defenses in the central portion of the TAOR, operating west of the airfield and Route 1. The battalion's area of operations centered around the farming villages of Khuong Nhon and Ky Long in the western sector of the TAOR.

Colonel Oscar F. Peatross' 7th Marines had all three battalions on line to secure the southern sector defenses. Lieutenant Colonel James P. Kelly's 1st Battalion, 7th Marines, on the coast, had a company-size combat base on the Trung Phan Peninsula and tied in with the 3d Battalion, 7th Marines on its western flank. The 3d Battalion, under the command of Lieutenant Colonel Charles H. Bodley, was responsible for most of the sector in Quang Ngai province immediately to the west of Route 1. Lieutenant Colonel Leon N. Utter's 2d Battion, 7th Marines, flanked by the 4th Marines on the north and Bodley's battalion to the east, was responsible for the southwestern portion of the TAOR.

During the first weeks of January, securing TAORs was the main objective of both the 4th and 7th Marines, with the exception of Lieutenant Colonel Bodley's battalion which participated in the 3d Marines' Operation Mallard from 10-17 January in the An Hoa region south of Da Nang. The two regiments had established several civil affairs programs in conjunction with the Vietnamese authorities. These included such diverse activities as the distribution of food and clothing, medical assistance programs, and school and market place construction. Nevertheless, the major emphasis of the Marine battalions at Chu Lai was in aggressive small-unit patrolling designed to eliminate the VC guerrillas.

Contact was sparse throughout most of January in the 7th Marines TAOR. Only the company stationed at the combat base on the Trung Phan Peninsula had any significant combat. It accounted for 10 of the 13 VC killed by the regiment during the month. According to Colonel Peatross, the VC tactics consisted of small-scale probes, harassment of patrols, and extensive use of land mines.¹

In the 4th Marines TAOR, Lieutenant Colonel Trevino's 2d Battalion found and destroyed more than 40 mines and booby traps. Although reporting a marked increase in reconnaissance and probing activity by the *VC A-19* and *A-21 Local Force Companies,* the thinly spread 1st Battalion, 4th Marines to the northeast found itself hard pressed to engage the VC in significant numbers, killing only one VC and capturing seven while sustaining nine casualties, including five dead.² Lieutenant Colonel Sullivan, the battalion commander, later stated that his main concern during the period "was that the VC would bring 120mm mortars onto Hoa Xuan Island," located just northwest of Ky Hoa Island, and thus bring the Ky Ha airfield within mortar range. He explained that since he "was 'two-hatted,'" serving also as the Ky Ha defense commander, and that two of his companies "were tied by order to manning the 'swath' on Ky Ha during hours of darkness, we were too 'troop poor' to occupy Hoa Xuan." Sullivan declared that his requests for a fifth company "to 'sit on top' of the *A-19* and *A-21 VC LF Companies,* who were active on Hoa Xuan, were denied." The battalion commander several years later remarked:

> Hoa Xuan, according to my mission, had to be patrolled each week. It made no difference if I sent a platoon up there, or exercised the whole battalion, Hoa Xuan was exerting an average toll of one KIA and several WIA each week . . . The island was literally nickel and diming us to *death* whenever we set foot on the place.

He contended: "Occupation of Hoa Xuan, I remain convinced, would have cut our casualties, and virtually eliminated the northern 120mm mortar threat to the Ky Ha Peninsula and the airfield at Chu Lai."³

The war for the Chu Lai Marines intensified with the incremental deployment of 1st Marine Division units to Vietnam and the continuing buildup of regular forces in southern I Corps. On 17 January, Colonel Bryan B. Mitchell's 1st Marines Headquarters arrived at Chu Lai, followed a little over a week later by Lieutenant Colonel James R. Young's Battalion Landing Team (BLT)* 3/1. Young's battalion remained on board its amphibious shipping in preparation for the pending multibattalion Double Eagle operation in southern Quang Ngai Province. These reinforcements allowed the Marines to mount large mobile operations and provided more flexibility at Chu Lai.

In the 7th Marines' sector, Colonel Peatross ordered his battalions to advance 4,000 to 5,000 meters toward the forward edge of the regimental TAOR. Lieutenant Colonel Utter's 2d Battalion, on the western flank of the regiment, began its displacement on 20 January, followed by the other two battalions on the 24th and 25th. Upon the completion of the movement, the 7th Marines established new defensive positions along the Tra Bong River and the 1st Battalion's positions extended as far south as Binh Son across the river.⁴

The major change in troop dispositions occurred in what had been the 4th Marines sector. On 20 January, the 1st Marines assumed operational control of the two battalions of the 4th Marines. Six days later, the 1st Battalion, reinforced by a 7th Marines company, took over responsibility for the 2d Battalion's TAOR. Lieutenant Colonel Trevino's 2d Battalion was assigned to the reactivated Task Force Delta, essentially the 4th Marines Headquarters and maneuver battalions from Chu Lai. Operation Double Eagle, one of the largest search and destroy missions in South Vietnam up to that time, was about to begin.⁵

Operation Double Eagle

Double Eagle planning began the previous month. On 7 December 1965, General Westmoreland ordered III MAF and Field Force, Vietnam to initiate a coordinated offensive against the enemy buildup in the region of the I and II Corps border during late January. By the beginning of the year, General Walt had received approval of a general concept for a multibattalion operation in southern Quang Ngai Province.⁶

On 6 January, General Walt ordered General Platt to reactivate Task Force Delta Headquarters for planning. General Platt had commanded Task Force Delta during Operation Harvest Moon in December, but closed out the headquarters upon completion of the operation. A task force organization allowed the Marines a large degree of leeway in both composition and command for operations outside the major enclaves. Its size was limited only by its mission, and

---

*A Marine infantry battalion reinforced by artillery and other supporting elements to permit independent operation; the basic unit for amphibious operations.

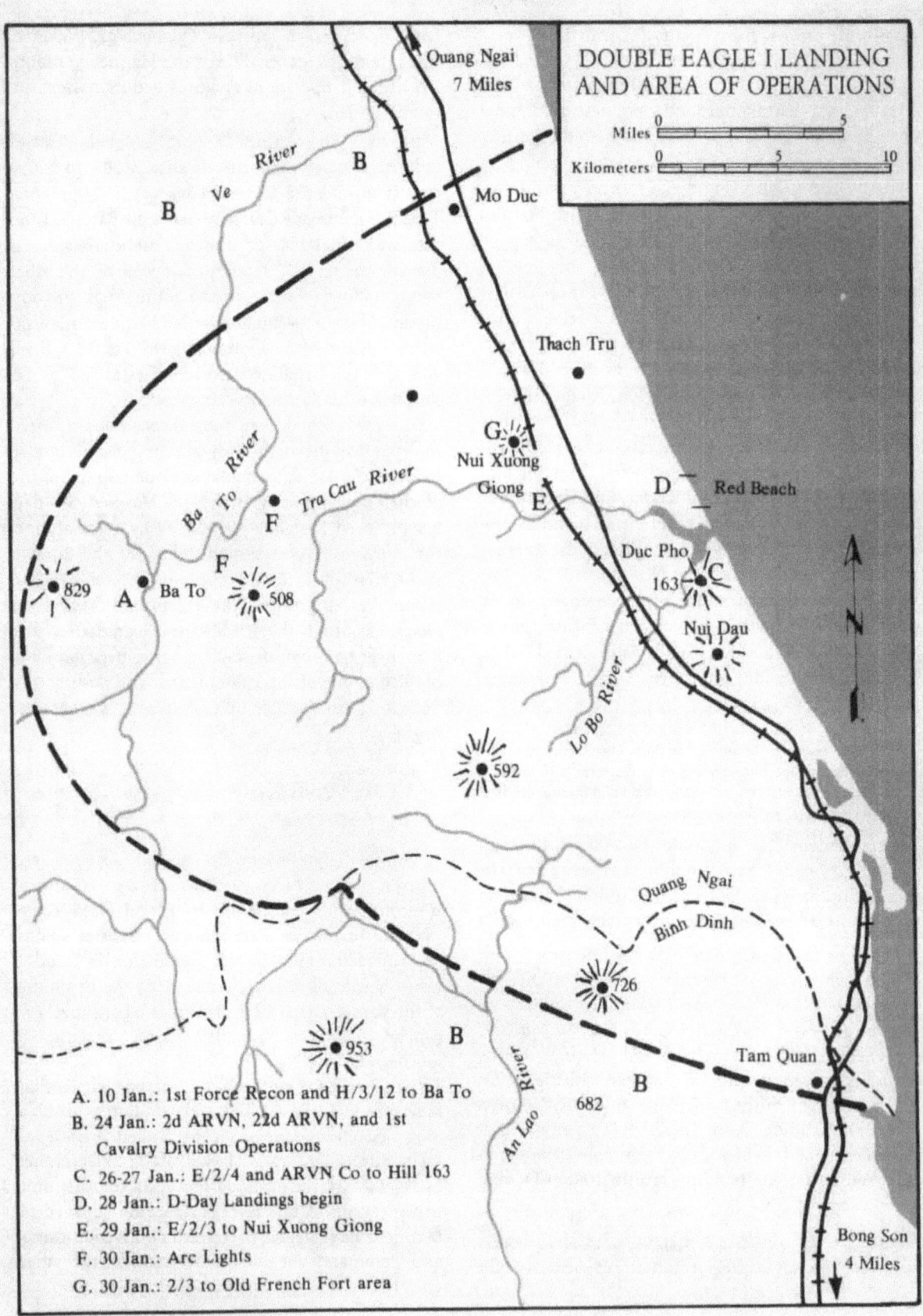

its formation permitted the employment of air and ground components under a single commander. Equally important, this ad hoc organization permitted the least disruption of the command structure of units remaining in the TAORs. Normally a Marine task force was of such size to merit a general officer as commander. According to Colonel Peatross, "This was a strong factor in getting the Vietnamese generals into the field."[7]

General Platt and Brigadier General Hoang Xuan Lam, the South Vietnamese 2d ARVN Division commander, had established excellent personal relations since working together during Harvest Moon. They also discovered they had a common interest in tennis and played when they had the opportunity. Generals Lam and Platt soon became good friends. On a professional level, the Marines found Lam very cooperative and respected his military judgment.[8]

Similar personal friendships facilitated coordination between III MAF and the South Vietnamese I Corps military commanders. General Walt stated that for large operations, "General Thi and I talk it over—we come up with a concept and we put the concept to our staffs, who get together" and work out the details.[9]

The working out of details for Double Eagle was somewhat more complicated. It involved coordination not only with I Corps but with MACV, Seventh Fleet, Field Force, Vietnam, and the Vietnamese authorities in II Corps. General Walt's original concept involved a two-battalion amphibious landing in southern Quang Ngai Province near Duc Pho and a helicopter landing of another battalion in the vicinity of the U.S. Special Forces camp at Ba To, 18 miles inland. Field Force, Vietnam and RVN II Corps commands were to launch a supporting operation in Binh Dinh Province to the south while an ARVN task force under General Lam was to block the enemy's avenues of retreat to the north.

General Walt established liaison with the Seventh Fleet very early in the planning phase.* On 6 January, the commander of the Seventh Fleet Amphibious Ready Group (ARG), Captain William J. Maddocks, and the Marine commander of the Special Landing Force, Colonel John R. Burnett, visited III MAF to discuss the operation. By the next day, General Walt's staff and the amphibious commanders had adopted a tentative concept of operations for the proposed landing. Shortly after the departure of Maddocks and Burnett from Da Nang, Admiral Sharp approved the plans and the assignment of two battalions for the landing, BLT 2/3, the SLF battalion, and BLT 3/1, which at that time was on board Seventh Fleet amphibious shipping for its previously planned move to Chu Lai. On 12 January, Vice Admiral John J. Hyland, Commander of the Seventh Fleet, issued his initiating directive for the operation, designating Captain Maddocks commander of the amphibious task force, and Colonel Burnett commander of the landing force. In accordance with amphibious doctrine, the amphibious commander was to transfer operational control of the ground forces to the III MAF ground commander for the operation, General Platt, once all the troops were ashore.[10]

The morning after Admiral Hyland issued his directive, General Thi, the I Corps commander, hosted a conference at his Da Nang headquarters, which included the senior U.S. and South Vietnamese commanders in both I and II Corps. General Thi explained that the purpose of the meeting was to develop an overall concept for operations in southern Quang Ngai-northern Binh Dinh Provinces. After a two-hour discussion, the conference reached a general agreement. Most of the conferees believed that the NVA and VC main force units were in Quang Ngai Province, but that their base areas were located in the Tam Quan coastal region and the An Lao River Valley in Binh Dinh Province. The III MAF task force, buttressed by 2d ARVN Division units, was to destroy the enemy main force units while the 1st Cavalry Division (Airmobile), in a

---

*III MAF was under the operational control of MACV while the Seventh Fleet was a component command of CinCPacFlt. Both ComUSMACV and CinCPacFlt were subordinate to CinCPac. When General Walt wanted Seventh Fleet amphibious forces committed in I Corps he had to submit his request through MACV which, assuming concurrence, forwarded the request to Admiral Sharp for his approval. Despite this seemingly lengthy command chain, the amphibious forces were normally readily available for in-country use when requested. Vice Admiral Hooper, former ComServPac, pointed out the reason for this arrangement in commenting on the draft manuscript: "Seventh Fleet under CinCPacFlt, had responsibilities throughout the entire Far East and western Pacific. Its forces, including TFs 76 and 79, had to react to crises, and sometime multicrises . . . not just in Vietnam." VAdm Edwin B. Hooper, Comments on draft MS, n.d. [May 78](Vietnam Comment File).

separate but coordinated operation supported by the ARVN 22d Division, was to go after the base areas.

General Walt viewed "these operations as a converging effort to entrap" the enemy. On the other hand, Major General Stanley R. Larsen, the Field Force, Vietnam commander, was less sanguine than Walt and declared "that we should not think in terms of entrapping and annihilating large bodies of VC, but should consider ourselves highly successful to destroy one battalion." Both commanders did agree that the Corps boundaries "were not inviolate—they could be crossed by I Corps and II Corps forces as required to exploit the situation."[11]

During the next two weeks the Marines refined their plans for the operation. On 15 January, III MAF published its operation order which directed Task Force Delta to be prepared to deploy two reinforced battalions by helicopter or amphibious shipping to an objective area near Thach Tru in Quang Ngai Province. General Platt was to coordinate the date of D-Day with the Seventh Fleet, Field Force, Vietnam, and the ARVN commanders. A reconnaissance effort was to precede the operation and U.S. Air Force Strategic Air Command Boeing B-52 Stratofortresses were to fly bombing missions against suspected enemy positions further inland subsequent to the landing. The SLF battalion, BLT 2/3, was to remain on board amphibious shipping, ready to land on order to exploit the situation. III MAF modified its order the following day to provide for two BLTs, BLT 3/1 and BLT 2/4, to land over the beach on D-Day. Later, on 16 January, General Walt established D-Day for the operation as 28 January, so BLT 3/1 and the SLF BLT could conduct a practice landing in the Philippines.[12]

General Platt and his staff expedited final planning for the operation. His ADC command group, reinforced by the Headquarters Company of the 4th Marines as well as members of the 3d Marine Division and 7th Marines staffs, provided the personnel for the Task Force Delta Headquarters. Colonel Donald W. Sherman, the former 3d Division Chief of Staff who had relieved Colonel McClanahan on 24 January 1966 as commander of the 4th Marines, became General Platt's Chief of Staff for the operation. After establishing liaison with the Seventh Fleet, General Platt and Colonel Johnson, whose MAG-36 was to provide helicopter support for the operation, visited General Lam at his headquarters in Quang Ngai to coordinate with the 2d ARVN Division. On 24 January, the task force commander published his operation order and briefed General Walt the next day on the final plan.[13]*

Task Force Delta's operating area consisted of 500 square miles, the center of which was approximately 20 miles south of Quang Ngai City and about 10 miles west of Duc Pho. The southern boundary encompassed a small portion of northern Binh Dinh Province in II Corps. Red Beach,** the site selected for the landing, was a 1,000-meter stretch of flat sand about three and a half miles northeast of Duc Pho. Inland from the beach, the assault elements would have to place heavy reliance on helicopters and amphibian tractors for movement in a region partially inundated by numerous rivers, streams, and marshes. To the west lay a mountainous area of jagged peaks criss-crossed by valleys and trails. Despite heavy foliage, there were numerous sites suitable for helicopter landing zones, but the lush jungle vegetation, precipitous hills, and intertwining valleys seriously impeded overland movement from these zones. In short, it was the sort of terrain which

---

*Several commentators remarked on various initiatives taken during the planning phase of the operation. Colonel Noble L. Beck, who was the executive officer of the 4th Marines in 1966, recalled that "General Platt had learned on Operation Harvest Moon that command control of several infantry battalions and supporting air simply couldn't be managed by an inadequately staffed task force headquarters. Accordingly he tasked me (then) . . . Deputy Chief of Staff designate for Task Force Delta for Operation Double Eagle to come up with the Task Force headquarters T/O . . . this Task Force T/O proved-out on Double Eagle and became standard for the expeditionary task force operations which followed." Col Noble L. Beck, Comments on draft MS, n.d. [Aug 78](Vietnam Comment File). According to Colonel Zitnik, Colonel Johnson, the MAG-36 commander, was made the tactical air commander for the operation. "Colonel Johnson and one or two of his Sqdn. COs and Staff Officers were involved in all the ground planning." Col Robert J. Zitnik, Comments on draft MS, dtd 6Jun78 (Vietnam Comment File). Colonel Nicholas J. Dennis, the commander of the 3d Engineer Battalion in January 1966, stated that unlike the planning for other operations his battalion supported, General Platt at the Double Eagle briefing, "had each unit commander provide a resume of what role his unit would perform." Col Nicholas J. Dennis, Comments on draft MS, n.d. [Jun 78](Vietnam Comment File).

**Marine Corps documentation refers to the landing beach for Double Eagle as Red Beach while Navy documentation refers to Blue Beach. See TF Delta AAR Double Eagle I and II, 28Jan-1Mar66, dtd 15Mar66 and TG 76.6 OpO 304-66, dtd 24Jan66.

favored the enemy's highly mobile light infantry and hit-and-run tactics.

General Platt's intelligence section estimated the enemy strength to be 6,000 regulars, reinforced by approximately 600 guerrillas. Two NVA regiments, the *18th* and *95th*, were supposedly located in the mountains roughly 10 miles southwest of Red Beach, while the *2d VC Main Force Regiment* was thought to be four miles north of the NVA regiments. Additionally, the 300-man *38th Independent Battalion* and 11 separate companies, ranging from 90 to 150 men each, normally operated in this area. The remaining enemy units consisted of scattered guerrilla bands and support troops including the *Binh Son Transportation Battalion* with 250 permanent personnel and about 1,000 laborers.

The 5,000-plus Marines of Task Force Delta approximated the size of the enemy's regular units. Ultimately, General Platt would have four Marine battalions under his command, including three BLTs, initially BLTs 2/3, 3/1, and 2/4. The fourth battalion, Lieutenant Colonel William F. Donahue, Jr.'s 2d Battalion, 9th Marines from the Da Nang TAOR, would consist of only a command group and two of its four rifle companies. Supporting forces were organized into provisional commands. These were Lieutenant Colonel Leslie L. Page's artillery group with a total of 26 pieces ranging from 4.2-inch mortars to 155mm guns and howitzers, a provisional reconnaissance group, an engineering company, an amphibian tractor company, and a shore party group.

The Marine concept of operations called for three distinct phases: reconnaissance, landing, and exploitation. Marine reconnaissance units and an artillery battery were to be inserted at the Special Forces camp at Ba To well before D-Day. From this location, the reconnaissance Marines were to provide information on enemy positions and movement in the western portion of the Double Eagle area of operations. The artillery battery would not only support the reconnaissance missions, but would be in position to cover the amphibious landing forces as they moved inland beyond the range of naval guns. After the establishment of the Ba To contingent, one company of the 2d Battalion, 4th Marines was to conduct a reconnaissance of the landing beach in conjunction with the 2d ARVN Division two weeks before the landing. On D minus 1 (27 January), another company from the battalion, with a company from the 4th ARVN Regiment, was to secure Hill 163, which overlooked Red Beach from the south. At H-Hour on 28 January, BLTs 3/1 and 2/4 were to land across Red Beach and secure immediate objectives north and west of the landing beach. Once the landing force had secured the beachhead, the Delta command group was to land, at which time the amphibious task group commander would pass operational control to General Platt. BLT 2/3 was to remain on board amphibious shipping as the

Reconnaissance Marines at the U.S. Special Forces camp at Ba To protect themselves from the rain with their ponchos. Inserted by helicopter into various landing zones, reconnaissance teams monitored enemy movement in the western sector of the Double Eagle operating area.

Marine Corps Photo A186724

task force reserve while the 2d Battalion, 9th Marines was airlifted from Da Nang to Quang Ngai City for the final phase of the operation.

Since General Platt wanted to create the impression that his forces were ashore only to conduct limited sweeps close to the coast, the 2d Battalion, 9th Marines was to stay at Quang Ngai and the SLF battalion to remain on board its shipping out of sight over the horizon. The exploitation phase was to be the main effort, signaled by B-52 strikes against suspected enemy troop concentrations and marshalling areas. These B-52 missions or Arc Lights, the codename for all B-52 strikes in Vietnam, were scheduled for D plus 2. Following this intensive bombardment, the Marine infantry was to move inland by helicopter to cut off any enemy forces attempting to escape.[14]

The reconnaissance phase began in early January. On 7 January, General Walt ordered the establishment of the 3d Marine Division reconnaissance base at Ba To Special Forces Camp. Three days later, six U.S. Air Force Sikorsky CH-3C helicopters ferried four 105mm howitzers and crews from Battery H, 3d Battalion, 12th Marines and two platoons of the 1st Force Reconnaissance Company from Chu Lai to the camp. After establishing his base on 12 January, Captain William C. Shaver, the commanding officer of the reconnaissance company, sent out his first patrols.[15]

For the next two weeks, the reconnaissance Marines reported the movements of small groups of VC. One 14-man patrol, led by 1st Lieutenant Richard F. Parker, Jr., encountered a significant enemy force near Hill 829, approximately 4,000 meters northwest of the Ba To Camp. Lieutenant Parker and an advance party reached the top of the hill at 1400 on 21 January and halted for the day because of poor visibility. Three hours later, Parker's Marines heard yelling and firing from the vicinity of their rear base on the lower slope of the mountain. By the time Parker and his group reached the patrol's rear party it had already repulsed four or five attacks. In the confusion, 1st Lieutenant James T. Egan, Jr., a forward observer from the artillery battery, had disappeared. Parker and his men searched the immediate area, but found no sign of the missing lieutenant.

At 0745 the next morning, the reconnaissance Marines began the difficult climb down the mountain to continue their mission. About two and a half hours later, 50 to 60 enemy soldiers suddenly attacked from the rear. Lieutenant Parker wryly remarked in his after action report, "the entire descent was made under conditions of heavy contact and was not a controlled movement."[16] The patrol leader and five of his men escaped into a densely vegetated draw and set up an ambush. They were joined one-half hour later by three other Marines from the patrol. Lieutenant Parker then called for an artillery mission on suspected enemy positions. After the battery stopped firing, four helicopters from MAG-36, two Sikorsky UH-34s escorted by two Bell UH-1E gunships, picked up the patrol, the nine men in the draw, and three other Marines stranded nearby. One Marine, Lance Corporal Edwin R. Grissett, was missing. The 1st Force Reconnaissance Company, which had come under the operational control of Task Force Delta on 21 January, conducted other patrols in the vicinity of Hill 829 several days after Parker's men returned to Ba To, but never found Lieutenant Egan or Lance Corporal Grissett.*

While the reconnaissance Marines continued their patrolling in the Ba To region during mid-January, the preparations for the coordinated allied offensives in Quang Ngai and Binh Dinh Provinces entered the final stages. On 13 January one of the companies from Lieutenant Colonel Trevino's 2d Battalion, 4th Marines conducted a surveillance mission with the Reconnaissance Company, 2d ARVN Division in the initial objective area at Red Beach and the immediate coastal region. Ten days later, BLTs 2/3 and 3/1, conducting Exercise Hill Top III, landed on the island of Mindoro in the Philippines as a dress rehearsal for Double Eagle. With the completion of the exercise the following day, 24 January, both battalions embarked on their amphibious shipping and sailed for the South China Sea where they were to rendezvous with the rest of the amphibious task force.**

---

*On 3 February 1978, the Marine Corps officially changed the status of by then Major Egan from missing in action to killed in action. HQMC, Report of Casualty 2866A66 Final JNL/1fr, dtd 3Feb78, Subj: Egan, James Thomas, Jr., Maj USMCR. Lance Corporal Grissett was captured by the enemy and died of malnutrition in December 1968 while in captivity. Information provided by GySgt William A. Hoffman, Casualty Section, Personnel Affairs Branch, HQMC, 13Mar75.

**The two BLTs were embarked in the attack transports *Paul Revere* (APA 248) and *Montrose* (APA 212); the dock landing ships *Catamount* (LSD 17) and *Monticello* (LSD 35); and the am-

On the 24th, four battalions of the 1st Cavalry Division began Operation Masher near Bong Son in the coastal region of Binh Dinh Province, 50 miles north of Qui Nhon. Six ARVN airborne battalions and six infantry battalions from the 22d ARVN Division reinforced the airmobile division during Operation Thang Phong II, the South Vietnamese companion operation to Masher in Binh Dinh. Further north in I Corps, General Lam's 2d ARVN Division prepared to launch Operation Lien Ket-22. With the two-battalion South Vietnamese Marine Task Force Bravo attached to his command, General Lam planned a five-battalion advance from a line of departure eight miles south of Quang Ngai City to blocking positions in the Song Ve Valley and the coastal region north of the U.S. Marines in Double Eagle. The combined allied forces for Masher/Thang Phong II and Double Eagle/Lien Ket-22 were the equivalent of three divisions; the area of operations covered more than 2,000 square miles.

On 26 January, Task Force Delta undertook the last of the preliminary operations before the amphibious landing. Nine UH-34Ds from HMM-261 carried 190 troops of Captain Brian D. Moore's Company E, 2d Battalion, 4th Marines from Ky Ha Airfield at Chu Lai to the Nui Dau ARVN outpost, eight miles south of the Double Eagle landing beach. At Nui Dau, Major Ernest L. Defazio, the executive officer of the Marine battalion, assumed command of a combined force, consisting of Company E, 4th Marines and the 2d Company, 3d Battalion, 4th ARVN Regiment. Shortly after midnight, the combined unit left the outpost, Company E in the lead followed by the ARVN company. The force was to move to the beach and then travel along the coast and secure Hill 163. According to Defazio, it took over six hours in the darkness to cross the one mile of rugged terrain from Nui Dau to the beach.

---

phibious assault ship *Valley Forge* (LPH 8). Other ships assigned to, or supporting, the amphibious task group for Double Eagle included: the attack transport *Navarro* (APA 215); the dock landing ship *Fort Marion* (LSD 22); the tank landing ships *Tom Green County* (LST 1159), *Tioga County* (LST 1158), *Windham County* (LST 1170), and *Westchester County* (LST 1167); the high speed transport *Weiss* (APD 135); the gasoline tanker *Elkhorn* (AOG 7); the salvage vessels *Safeguard* (ARS 25) and *Bolster* (ARS 38); the attack cargo ship *Skagit* (AKA 105); the guided missile light cruisers *Oklahoma City* (CLG 5) and *Topeka* (CLG 8); and the destroyer *Barry* (DD 933).

Marine Corps Photo A186776
Marines from Company E, 2d Battalion, 4th Marines scale rocks along the shore line as they begin ascent to secure Hill 163 on 27 January prior to D-Day for Double Eagle. From Hill 163, the company had a ringside seat for the amphibious landing the following day.

Slowed by the loose sand, intense heat during the day, and heavy packs, the combined task unit did not reach the top of Hill 163 until 1300 on 27 January. The Marines and South Vietnamese soldiers prepared defensive positions on the hill which had a commanding view of Red Beach. Major Defazio remarked that he had a "ringside seat" for the amphibious landing the next day.[17]

D-Day, 28 January, was a dismal day with low overcast and light rain. Despite the heavy seas, the first wave of Lieutenant Colonel James R. Young's BLT 3/1 landed at 0700 as planned. Offshore, a destroyer, the USS *Barry* (DD 933), and a cruiser, the USS *Oklahoma City* (CLG 5) provided naval gunfire coverage, while eight Douglas A-4 Skyhawks from MAG-12 and eight McDonnell F-4B Phantoms from MAG-11 were on station overhead. The only opposition encountered by the assault troops occurred late that day. Companies I and M were exposed to occasional small arms fire; one Company I Marine was wounded. Shortly after Lieutenant Colonel Young's men secured their objectives, five 105mm

Marines clamber down net from the transport into landing craft for the assault across Red Beach in Double Eagle. This operation was the largest extended amphibious operation of the war.

howitzer-equipped amphibian tractors (LVTH-6) moved ashore to provide artillery support for the infantry battalion. Company B from the 3d Engineer Battalion was also on the beach to establish various water points. Lieutenant Colonel Nicholas J. Dennis, the battalion commander, remembered that "The beach assault took a toll of operational engineer equipment and generators."[18]

At midmorning the surf began to build rapidly. Swells, six to eight feet in height, held up the debarkation of Lieutenant Colonel Trevino's 2d Battalion, 4th Marines. Nevertheless, by noon, the battalion was ashore, as were the forward elements of Task Force Delta's Headquarters and Lieutenant Colonel Page's provisional artillery command group. Battery H, 3d Battalion, 11th Marines also landed and reinforced the LVTH-6 platoon in support of the infantry.

Weather hampered the operation for the rest of the day. Although General Platt arrived at Red Beach from Chu Lai by midafternoon, he was unable to assume operational control of the Double Eagle forces because high seas and pounding surf prevented the landing of sufficient communication equipment. As a result, the command of forces ashore remained with the amphibious task force commander, Captain Maddocks, and with the commander of the landing force, Colonel Burnett, the SLF commander. General Platt received the concurrence from Captain Maddocks "to coordinate actions

Marines from the 2d Battalion, 4th Marines move across Red Beach. Ships of the amphibious task force and landing craft approaching the shore can be seen in the background.

Marines unload LST on Red Beach. Rough seas, as seen in the background, hampered the bringing of additional equipment and supplies ashore.

ashore in the event of emergency," which in practical terms would give operational control to Platt.[19]*

High seas also curtailed the artillery and logistic buildup. Supplies slowly accumulated at the beach support area (BSA) while the rest of the artillery remained on board ship. These units included the 3d 155mm Gun Battery; the 107mm Mortar Battery, 3d Battalion, 12th Marines; Battery M, 4th Battalion, 11th Marines; and a platoon from the 4.2-inch Mortar Battery, 11th Marines.

The weather, typical of the second half of the northeast monsoon season, continued to plague the operation on the following day, 29 January. Low overcast and periodic rain squalls prevented any sizeable helicopter operations until late afternoon and restricted both infantry battalions to operations within 6,000 to 8,000 meters of the landing beach. The Marine infantry did receive some reinforcements during the day. Captain Moore's Company E left its positions on Hill 163 and rejoined its parent battalion, the 2d Battalion, 4th Marines. That same afternoon, HMM-362, the SLF helicopter squadron, assisted by six MAG-36 UH-34s which arrived at the BSA from Chu Lai, flew Company E, BLT 2/3 from the USS *Valley Forge* (LPH 8) to Nui Xuong Giong, a 180-meter peak west of Red Beach. The Marine company was to provide security for a detachment of the task force communications platoon which was to establish a radio relay station on the hill to insure reliable communications for the planned operations in the mountains and Song Ve Valley to the west.

Lieutenant Colonel Robert J. Zitnik, the commanding officer of VMO-6, later remarked that his UH-1Es accompanied the SLF squadron's UH-34s to Nui Xuong Giong. He recalled:

> The landing . . . was to be unopposed, but at the last

---

*See Chapter 19 for a further discussion of command relations during the amphibious portion of Double Eagle.

minute VMO-6 was assigned to escort the helos on this mission. . . . As the H-34s were landing on the hilltop the lead pilot . . . of my second section observed what he described as a military training unit with some uniformed VC. . . . a uniformed soldier (with rifle) was shedding his uniform while running and as we were trying to get permission to fire we heard the firm order "Do not fire." . . . all the VMO-6 pilots on this flight experienced . . . frustration at not being allowed to pursue what appeared to be, and eventually proved to be, the only few enemy in the area.[20]

The VMO-6 commander conceded that he never was able to pinpoint the originator of the message but believed "that it was either from afloat or an enemy transmission." Zitnik concluded: "This incident occurred before the transfer of control ashore and contributed to frustrations in General Platt's headquarters as well as with the UH-1E pilots."[21]

Although General Platt had not as yet received operational control of the units ashore, preparations for the exploitation phase were well under way on 29 January. Air Force Lockheed C-130 Hercules transports lifted Lieutenant Colonel William F. Donahue's 2d Battalion, 9th Marines command group and two rifle companies from Da Nang Airbase to Quang Ngai Airfield, 2,000 meters west of Quang Ngai City. From the airfield, which the Marines were using as a helicopter staging area, MAG-36 UH-34s were to helilift the battalion into the Song Ve Valley to exploit B-52 Arc Light missions.

The Marine command attempted to postpone the B-52 strikes for a day, but MACV replied that the missions would either have to be flown on the 30th as scheduled or canceled altogether.[22] Flying high above the low-lying clouds on 30 January, the Stratofortresses struck three target areas in the Song Ve Valley. Despite some improvement in the weather, poor visibility prohibited helicopter operations in the mountains and Marine ground exploitation of the Arc Light missions.

Task Force Delta took advantage of the calm seas on the 30th to bring more forces ashore. The remaining artillery batteries and other supporting units arrived in the BSA. Later that afternoon, 28 helicopters from three MAG-36 helicopter

Marines from BLT 2/3, part of the Special Landing Force (SLF) on the carrier Valley Forge (LPH 8), *run to board helicopters for movement ashore on D plus 1 (29 January 1966) of Double Eagle. Some of the troop-laden helicopters are already airborne and can be seen flying above the ship.*

Marine Corps Photo A186769

squadrons and 12 UH-34s from HMM-362 transported Lieutenant Colonel William K. Horn's BLT 2/3 command group and his remaining three companies from the *Valley Forge* to an old French fort northwest of Company E's position, eight miles inland. After the lift was completed at 1730, most of the helicopters returned to the Quang Ngai Airfield since Colonel Johnson, the MAG-36 commander, thought it unnecessary to risk the aircraft overnight in a forward area when they could easily return in the morning.[23]

On the afternoon of 30 January, MAG-36 did establish a forward operating base in the Double Eagle BSA, located 400 meters inland from Red Beach and known as "Johnson City." In addition to the logistic support area* and task force headquarters, "Johnson City" contained an expeditionary airfield complete with a tactical air fuel dispensing system (TAFDS), maintenance facilities, tower, runway, and airfield lights. As the tactical air commander for the operation, Colonel Johnson established his MAG-36 combat operations center 100 yards from General Platt's command post and adjacent to the mobile direct air support center (DASC) from Marine Air Support Squadron 2. This collocation allowed the air commander to tie in the DASC with the fire support coordination center (FSCC). According to Johnson, the close proximity of the Task Force Delta air and ground commanders "permitted the detailed and continuous planning which enabled us to react expeditiously throughout Double Eagle."[24]**

On 31 January, the weather finally cleared in the objective area and the tempo of operations increased. At 1210, General Platt assumed operational control of the landing force and began to move inland. Two USAF CH-3C helicopters and a Marine Sikorsky CH-37 Mojave lifted the six 105mm howitzers from Battery H, 3d Battalion, 11th Marines from the "Johnson City" support area to the old French fort so that the artillery could support operations to the west. Shortly after noon, Marine UH-34s transported Company E, 2d Battalion, 4th Marines to Hill 508, five miles southwest of the fort. The Marine company was to provide protection for another detachment from the communications platoon, whose mission was to relay radio transmissions from Lieutenant Colonel Trevino's 2d Battalion which was to operate in this rugged terrain. At 1600 that afternoon, MAG-36 completed the helilift of Trevino's command group and his remaining three companies into a landing zone in the Song Ve-Song Ba To Valley, 2,000 meters northwest of Hill 508. The Marine battalion advanced rapidly to exploit one of the Arc Light targets on the high ground to the northeast. During the day, 14 Marine jets, 6 A-4 Skyhawks, 2 F-4B Phantoms, and 6 Chance Vought F-8E Crusaders, provided helicopter landing zone preparations and air cover for the infantry.

The next day, 1 February, General Platt moved his forces deeper into the interior of the Double Eagle area of operations. Helicopters from MAG-36 lifted Lieutenant Colonel Donahue's 2d Battalion, 9th Marines command group and two rifle companies to a landing zone on the high ground east of the Song Ve, 7,000 meters northwest of where the 2d Battalion, 4th Marines had landed the previous day. At the same time, Lieutenant Colonel Horn's 2d Bat-

---

*Major General Oscar F. Peatross, who in 1966 commanded the 7th Marines, remarked, "that although Task Force Delta was self-supportive, some critical supplies were flown by helicopter from the Logistic Support Unit, Chu Lai . . . into the Logistics Support Area." He recalled that he only visited the Task Force headquarters a few times, but that "each time I rode down in a helicopter taking supplies from Chu Lai and on three occasions the helicopter was loaded with among other things . . . radios that had been picked up the evening before, repaired overnight, and returned the next morning." According to General Peatross, Lieutenant Colonel William L. Nelson, the commanding officer of the Logistic Support Unit, Chu Lai, visited the TF Delta Headquarters each day and "brought back a critical list every day, filled it every night, and criticals were flown back the next morning." MajGen Oscar F. Peatross, Comments on draft MS, dtd 1Jun78 (Vietnam Comment File).

**Colonel Zitnik in his comments reinforced Colonel Johnson's remarks. Zitnik observed: "Aircraft were requested and provided as needed. There became a new kind of relationship between the planners on the spot and the [Wing Tactical Air Command Center (TACC)]. . . . Even though the TACC was not 100 percent up to date, when the word came to them that MAG-36 and the ARVN or Marines, or both, were being committed there appeared a remarkable spirit of cooperation and trust on the part of the TACC . . . they never questioned the need for fixed-wing or helo support just because a request came that did not appear on the pre-planned schedule." Col Robert J. Zitnik, Comments on draft MS, dtd 6Jun78 (Vietnam Comment File).

Gen Walt together with LtGen John A. Heintges, USA, Deputy Commander, U.S. Military Assistance Command (USMACV), visit Task Force Delta Headquarters during Double Eagle. From left to right: Gen Heintges; Gen Walt; BGen Jonas M. Platt, the Task Force Delta commander; and an unidentified U.S. Army colonel.

A Marine 60mm mortar section from the 2d Battalion, 4th Marines provides fire support for the advancing infantry. Apparently feeling relatively secure, the troops have placed their rifles against the right side of the Vietnamese structure in the picture.

talion, 3d Marines made an overland sweep west of the fort area in the valley of the Tra Cau River.

During the succeeding days, despite the extensive commitment of Marine units, there was no heavy fighting. Marine units encountered only small guerrilla bands. According to Captain James R. Hardin, Jr., company commander of Company F, 2d Battalion, 3d Marines, the Viet Cong "would hit us—pull out. Hit us and pull out. They wouldn't stick around for firefights."[25] Although firefights were the exception the Marines did take a heavy toll of the enemy's local forces. In two engagements on 2 February, Lieutenant Colonel Young's 3d Battalion, 1st Marines accounted for 31 enemy dead in the coastal region north of Red Beach. On 3 February, General Platt began to move most of his forces south toward Binh Dinh Province to trap the NVA and VC main force regiments between the Marines and the 1st Cavalry Division.

In contrast to the Marines, the 1st Cavalry troopers encountered North Vietnamese regulars early in their operation. In heavy fighting which lasted from 28 January through 3 February, the Cavalry's 3d Brigade engaged the *18th NVA Regiment* in the coastal region of Binh Dinh Province eight miles

Marines move through densely jungled terrain after a B-52 strike. The broken tree limbs and fallen trees are a result of the heavy carpet bombing of the area.

An Air Force CH-3C helicopter lifts a Marine 105mm howitzer from the beach support area further inland. The rapid deployment of the guns permitted the Marine artillery to keep the advancing infantry within the artillery fan.

A heavily-laden Marine 81mm mortar section trudges forward to a new firing position during Double Eagle. The first man carries the mortar bipod and an extra round while the third man totes the mortar tube.

Marine Corps Photo A421241
Marine in the foreground directs an UH-34 into a landing zone during Operation Double Eagle. Gen Platt had the use of two-thirds of the III MAF helicopters for the operation.

"Johnson City" support area. The task force commander took full advantage of the fact that he had two-thirds of III MAF's helicopters available for his use and ordered a series of small search and destroy missions. His improvised maneuver elements would land in an area, search it, and reboard the helicopters for further movement south. The infantry units accomplished 17 battalion and 19 company helilifts during the operation. Lieutenant Colonel Page's provisional artillery group displaced 47 times, including two small amphibious landings further south along the coast, in order to support the fast advancing infantry.[27]

During the advance, the Marines seized hills both for the purpose of providing supporting artillery fire and to maintain better voice communication with the infantry battalions. The Task Force Delta communications platoon established three relay stations

Marine Corps Photo A186718
Marine infantrymen advance through a gulley with razor-sharp punji stakes protruding on both embankments. Local Viet Cong guerrillas employed such crude, but effective, impediments to hinder the Americans during the operation.

north of Bong Son. During that six-day period, Colonel Harold G. Moore, the brigade commander, reported that his troops killed over 600 enemy by body count, captured 357 NVA soldiers, and recovered 49 individual weapons and six crew-served weapons. The Army brigade suffered 75 KIA and 240 wounded. After being reinforced by the 2d Brigade of the 1st Cavalry near Bong Son, Moore's brigade moved into the rugged interior of the An Lao region to link up with the Double Eagle Marines with the aim of smashing the *18th NVA Regiment* once and for all.[26]

As Task Force Delta deployed into the southern portion of the Double Eagle area of operations, General Platt split his battalions into smaller elements, each consisting of a command group and two rifle companies reinforced by an 81mm mortar section. This provided Platt with six to seven maneuver elements in the field while at the same time enabling him to provide security for the

on mountain tops to keep radio contact with the widely dispersed maneuver elements. According to General Platt, the task force communications capability was stretched to the absolute limit and the newly distributed AN/PRC-25 radios proved indispensable and reliable, often reaching distances of 20 to 25 miles.[28]

On 4 February, Company G, 2d Battalion, 4th Marines, accompanied by a small communication platoon detachment, secured Hill 726, 1,000 meters south of the I Corps boundary, and linked up with Battery B, 1st Battalion, 30th Artillery, 1st Cavalry Division.* While the Marines provided security and radio communication, the Army battery fired in support of Marine units in Quang Ngai Province and the 1st Cavalry Division in Binh Dinh. Through the next week, neither the Marine infantry nor the cavalry brigades encountered enemy main force units, only light resistance from local guerrillas. On 11 February, Task Force Delta maneuver elements began to redeploy north toward the "Johnson City" support area, using the same tactics in the retrograde movement as they had in the advance.

During this period, the most significant sighting of enemy forces was made by Captain James L. Compton's provisional reconnaissance group, which consisted of a command group, Company B, 3d Reconnaissance Battalion, and Captain Shaver's 1st Force Reconnaissance Company. While Shaver's men patrolled a 11,500-meter circle around Ba To, the Company B reconnaissance Marines operated throughout the Double Eagle area. The task force reconnaissance group primarily employed four- to five-man teams, who could call artillery and air missions on targets of opportunity.

On 12 February, two UH-34 helicopters inserted two four-man teams from Company B into the mountainous terrain 11,000 meters northwest of Ba To. Shortly after landing, one of the teams observed 31 armed men to their front dressed in green uniforms carrying two mortars. The Marines called an artillery mission which killed 10 enemy. After the artillery had fired another mission, 80 more enemy soldiers appeared. The team asked to be extracted and 15 minutes after its departure, 1st MAW jets, controlled by radar, dropped 39 250-pound bombs on the enemy concentration. The next day, a UH-1E from VMO-6 took out the second team, which had come under heavy fire and suffered one man dead.[29]

During the entire operation, the Marine reconnaissance group conducted more than 40 patrols and sighted nearly 1,000 enemy soldiers. The reconnaissance Marines called for 20 artillery and naval gunfire missions which resulted in at least 19 known enemy dead.[30] Battery H, 3d Battalion, 12th Marines at Ba To fired more than 1,900 rounds in support of the 1st Force Reconnaissance Company alone.[31]

Gradually, it became apparent that most of the North Vietnamese units had left the Double Eagle operating area. According to one prisoner report, the main force enemy units withdrew from Quang Ngai Province a few days before D-Day. The Army's Operation Masher, redesignated White Wing on 5 February because of criticism in certain U.S. Government circles that the U.S.-named operations sounded too brutal, turned out to be the main show instead of a side event when the 1st Cavalry Division encountered the *18th NVA Regiment* in Binh Dinh Province. Even during Masher/White Wing, nearly half of the 2,000 enemy casualties claimed by the operation occurred during the first heavy fighting. Thereafter, until the end of the operation on 6 March, the cavalry troopers met the same pattern of

---

*Although uneventful for the Marines of Company G, the helilift of the company from its former positions in the Lo Bo Valley, 12,000 meters north of Hill 726, caused some excitement for the helicopter pilots. A Marine aircraft reported taking ground fire from one of the villages near the pickup point and UH-1E gunships were assigned to escort the UH-34 troop transports. Colonel Zitnik, at the time VMO-6 commander and the flight leader of the gunships, recalled, "I directed the troop carrier helos around a burning village from which 50 caliber or heavier fire was observed. I called for A-4 support but could not get it in time (this was an on-call mission laid on late in the day) to help the troop carriers, so I commenced a rocket run towards the village and immediately received fire causing my helo to crash." Zitnik's wingman, 1st Lieutenant William L. Buchanan, landed in the darkness next to the wrecked aircraft and loaded onboard the five-man crew, who all survived the crash. According to Zitnik, "the trip out was memorable," as Buchanan's aircraft, with now nine men on board, "staggered into the air along and between the burning villages in the dark of the night." Task Force Delta sent a reinforced Marine infantry platoon and maintenance men to protect and repair the downed aircraft. An Air Force CH-3C lifted the UH-1E out of the crash site the next morning. See: Col Robert J. Zitnik, Comments on draft MS, dtd 6Jun78 (Vietnam Comment File); MAG-36 AAR, Double Eagle, dtd 28Mar66, encl MAG-36, ComdC, Mar66; 2/4 AAR 5-66, Operation Double Eagle, encl, 2/4 ComdC, Feb66; MASS-2, Report of Double Eagle DASC Opns, dtd 17Mar66 in 1st MAW, Double Eagle Folder, Jan-Mar66.

sporadic resistance that the Marines faced during Double Eagle.

Generals Platt and Lam ended their coordinated operations in Quang Ngai Province in mid-February. South Vietnamese Marine Task Force Bravo closed out Lien Ket-22 on 12 February, having found only a few enemy in its zone of operations.[32] By 17 February, all Task Force Delta forces, including the reconnaissance and artillery elements that were at Ba To, were on board amphibious shipping, or had already returned to their respective base areas. During the operation, the U.S. Marines killed 312 enemy soldiers and captured 19. General Platt's men also captured 20 tons of rice, 6 tons of salt, and 4 tons of miscellaneous supplies including barley, copra, corn, concrete, and fertilizer. In addition, the Marines captured 18 weapons and 868 rounds of ammunition. These results were achieved at the cost of 24 Marines killed and 156 wounded.[33]

Although Task Force Delta ended its operations in southern Quang Ngai Province on 17 February, Double Eagle entered an entirely new phase 50 miles to the north, a development not called for in the original plans. Major General McCutcheon, acting CG III MAF* at that time because General Walt was in Washington, had received intelligence that the *1st Viet Cong Regiment* had entered the Que Son Valley near the border of Quang Nam and Quang Tin Provinces west of Tam Ky, the area where the Marines had previously conducted Operation Harvest Moon. McCutcheon ordered General Platt to redeploy Task Force Delta and launch Double Eagle II in this region.

Retaining his basic task organization, but replacing the 2d Battalion, 4th Marines with Lieutenant Colonel Leon N. Utter's 2d Battalion, 7th Marines, a unit which had participated in Harvest Moon, General Platt began the operation on the morning of 19 February. Elements of four battalions, employing both helicopters and trucks, converged on the objective area. The 3d Battalion, 1st Marines moved by

---

*During General Walt's one month absence from Vietnam, 10Feb-9Mar66, General McCutcheon was both CG 1st MAW and acting CG III MAF. Brigadier General Lowell E. English, the 3d Division ADC, was the acting CG 3d Marine Division. According to English, "Keith McCutcheon and I had an agreement while Gen Walt was back in the States. Keith said: 'You run the ground war and I'll run the air war.'" MajGen Lowell E. English, Comments on draft MS, dtd 12Jun78 (Vietnam Comment File).

Marine Corps Photo A186586
Marines from Task Force Delta confiscate VC rice and salt during Double Eagle. During the operation in southern Quang Ngai Province, the Marines captured or destroyed 26 tons of rice and salt belonging to the enemy.

truck from Chu Lai to north of Tam Ky where it dismounted. As Lieutenant Colonel Young's 3d Battalion moved into blocking positions, helicopters carried the 2d Battalion, 7th Marines; BLT 2/3 of the SLF; and the 2d Battalion, 9th Marines into landing zones further to the southwest in the Que Son sector. The helilifted battalions then attacked in a northeasterly direction towards the 3d Battalion.

The *1st VC Regiment* was not there. Interrogation of prisoners revealed that the Viet Cong unit had withdrawn long before the Marines arrived. For the next 10 days, the Marines swept through numerous villages, cleared out isolated guerrilla bands, and uncovered enemy supplies, but found no major VC units. Task Force Delta accounted for 125 enemy dead and 15 captured. Marine losses were six killed and 136 wounded. The Marines also captured or destroyed caches including 28 tons of rice, 500 pounds of sweet potatoes, 53 weapons, and 450 rounds of ammunition.[34]

On the next-to-last day of the operation, the 2d Battalion, 7th Marines entered the hamlet of Ky Phu, west of Tam Ky, where the battalion had encountered the *80th VC Battalion* during Harvest Moon in December. This time the Marines found a concrete marker on which was inscribed the Viet Cong claim that they had defeated the Americans. According to Captain Alex Lee, the acting S-3 of the battalion, "While many desired to use demolitions on this sign, it was Lieutenant Colonel Utter's decision to let it stand for the lie it was."[35]

Task Force Delta began returning to Chu Lai the afternoon of 27 February, but the VC made one last attempt to disrupt the Marine forces before the closeout of the operation. In the early morning hours of 28 February, a VC squad attacked the Task Force Delta command post perimeter, just outside of Tam Ky. A Marine platoon from Company E, 2d Battalion, 7th Marines repulsed the enemy. Captain Edwin W. Besch, who was at the time the Task Force Delta Headquarters Commandant, remembered that the VC were led by a man "who had dressed in ARVN uniform and sauntered up in a friendly manner to Marines who had taken him into their . . . CP for coffee the night before. . . ."[36] Another Task Force Delta Headquarters staff officer, Colonel Glen E. Martin, recalled that the Marines stopped the VC assault "just short of General Platt's tent."[37] Captain Lee later wrote that "five naked VC with explosives strapped around their bodies stumbled directly into a 2/7 machine gun position . . . ."[38] As a result of the early morning action, the Marines killed two VC for sure, possibly another two, and took one wounded VC prisoner. The Marines suffered casualties of one man dead and another wounded. The last elements of Task Force Delta departed Tam Ky at 1300 on 1 March and Double Eagle II was over.[39]

While neither of the Double Eagle operations produced the desired results, General Platt believed that they both achieved an element of success. Although the Marines had not encountered any sizeable enemy formations, they had taken a heavy toll of local guerrilla forces in these areas. Moreover, General Platt argued that the people residing in both the Que Son Valley and southern Quang Ngai Province learned that neither area was "the VC private backyard because U.S. Marines trampled over a huge area with little or no significant opposition."[40]

General Krulak, on the other hand, insisted, several years later, that the lessons of the Double Eagle operations were largely negative. He pointed

A UH-34 lifts off after bringing Marines into a landing zone during Double Eagle II. Double Eagle II took place in the Que Son Valley, 50 miles to the north of the site of Double Eagle I.

Marine Corps Photo A186763

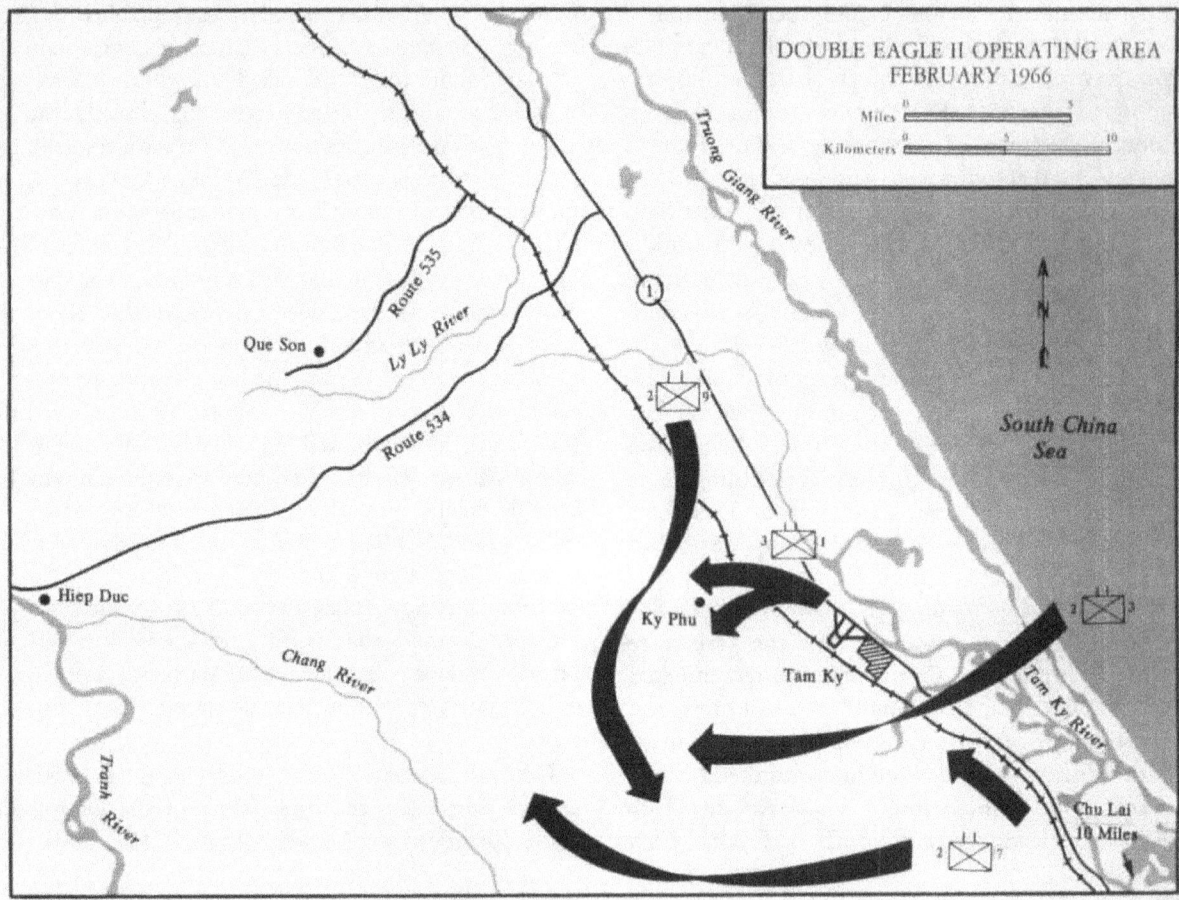

out that the operations failed primarily because the VC and NVA had been forewarned. Furthermore, and even more important, Krulak contended that both operations taught the people in the area that the Marines "would come in, comb the area and disappear; whereupon the VC would resurface and resume control."[41]

The displacement of two Marine battalions and supporting elements from Chu Lai for such an extensive period placed a heavy strain on the remaining units in the TAOR. For example, on 27 February, a VC raiding party hit a squad outpost of the thinly stretched 1st Battalion, 4th Marines. They killed five Marines before being repulsed.[42] In February, the 7th Marines reported that the local VC initiated more than 60 incidents in its sector.[43] The Marines had conducted a major, mobile operation, but they had yet to secure their base areas.

CHAPTER 3
The War in Central I Corps
The Da Nang TAOR—Honolulu and the Reemphasis on Pacification

The Da Nang TAOR

The Marine buildup was well under way in the extensive Da Nang TAOR at the beginning of 1966. Two infantry regiments, the 3d and 9th Marines, were reinforced by air, artillery, and a large logistic facility. The four fixed-wing squadrons of Colonel Emmett O. Anglin, Jr.'s MAG-11 were stationed at the main airbase, while three of the helicopter squadrons of Colonel Thomas J. O'Connor's MAG-16 were located across the Da Nang River at the Marble Mountain Air Facility on the Tiensha Peninsula. The headquarters and the 1st and 2d Battalions of the 3d Marine Division's artillery regiment, Colonel James M. Callender's 12th Marines, were at Da Nang. One infantry battalion, Lieutenant Colonel William W. Taylor's 3d Battalion, 9th Marines, was the Base Defense Battalion, under direct operational control of III MAF. Including the personnel of the Naval Support Group, the Seabees, and Colonel Mauro J. Padalino's Force Logistic Support Group, there were over 24,000 Marines and sailors at Da Nang.

Colonel John E. Gorman's 9th Marines was responsible for the southern and eastern sectors of the Da Nang TAOR, an area of approximately 250 square miles. Bounded by three major rivers, the Cau Do on the north, the Yen on the west, and the Ky Lam on the south, the regiment's zone of action was cut up by numerous streams. Except for a narrow sandy strip along the coast, the area consisted of rich, densely populated farm lands interspersed with heavy vegetation. Lieutenant Colonel William F. Doehler, who on 5 January assumed command of the 1st Battalion, 9th Marines from Lieutenant Colonel Verle E. Ludwig, was responsible for the eastern portion of the TAOR extending from Route 1 to the coast. The 2d Battalion, 9th Marines, under the command of Lieutenant Colonel William F. Donahue, Jr., occupied the sector of the TAOR between Route 1 and the main north-south railroad. Lieutenant Colonel Joshua W. Dorsey III's 3d Battalion, 3d Marines, under the operational control of the 9th Marines, secured the regiment's western flank by occupying the key terrain between the railroad and the Song Yen. Although the 9th Marines' TAOR extended as far south as the Ky Lam and Thu Bon Rivers, the regiment confined most of its activities, with the exception of some patrolling, to that area north of the Thanh Quit and La Tho Rivers.

The 3d Marines, commanded by Colonel Thell H. Fisher, protected the more sparsely populated northern and western sectors of the 3d Division TAOR. Lieutenant Colonel Harold A. Hatch's 1st Battalion, 1st Marines, attached to the 3d Marines, tied in with the 9th Marines sector at the Yen River and occupied the strategic high ground west of the airbase. The 1st Battalion, 3d Marines, commanded by Lieutenant Colonel Robert R. Dickey III, defended the northern and northwestern approaches, including the Cu De River Valley, where the Marines had first begun their pacification efforts.

Pacification continued to be the principal concern of the regiments at Da Nang. In mid-1965, the Marines first experimented with population security in the village complex of Le My, seven miles northwest of the airbase in the 3d Marines sector. Here the regiment's 2d Battalion, later relieved by the 1st Battalion, occupied defensive positions around the village. Behind this security shield, the Marines instituted a civic action program with the assistance of the local Vietnamese authorities. Le My, at least initially, set the pattern for the Marine pacification campaign.

This system worked well in the lightly populated 3d Marines sector, but the problem was more complex in the 9th Marines area south of Da Nang. A quarter of a million people lived in the villages and hamlets in the 15-mile stretch of land between the airbase and the Ky Lam River. Many were sympathetic to, or dominated by, the Viet Cong; the

Two men of the 3d Battalion, 3d Marines move past a Buddhist tomb while on patrol in the southern part of the Da Nang area of operations. As evidence of Viet Cong influence in the region, the scrawled sign in Vietnamese on the building in the picture reads: "Long Live the People's Revolution."

South Vietnamese Government controlled only a thin belt of territory paralleling Route 1.

During the latter half of 1965, the South Vietnamese began the Ngu Hanh Son Campaign, a pilot pacification program, within the 9th Marines TAOR. The campaign was slated for a 20-square mile, rice-rich, alluvial plain in southern Hoa Vang District containing 38 hamlets. The South Vietnamese divided the target area into two sectors, one consisting of a five-village complex west of Route 1 and the other consisting of a four-village complex east of the highway.

In November 1965, the South Vietnamese assigned a 60-man Rural Reconstruction, or *Can Bo*,* Platoon, to the five-village sector west of Route 1, thus inaugurating the Ngu Hanh Son Campaign. Part of

A Marine from the 2d Battalion, 9th Marines, pulls the nails from his boot after stepping on a punji trap in the contested sector south of Da Nang. The nails went through the side of the boot but were stopped by the punji liner in the boot.

---

*The word *Can Bo* is of Chinese origin and during World War II the Communist Viet Minh used the term to designate highly motivated individuals who operated clandestinely against the Japanese and Vichy French. It was their mission to first indoctrinate and then organize the local populace against colonial rule. According to the MACV historian, the South Vietnamese Government attempted to capitalize "on the position of honor and respect these Can Bo occupied in what became a historic and successful revolution . . . and so designated those lower level government employees who worked at the village and hamlet levels." MACV Comd Hist, 1966, p. 502.

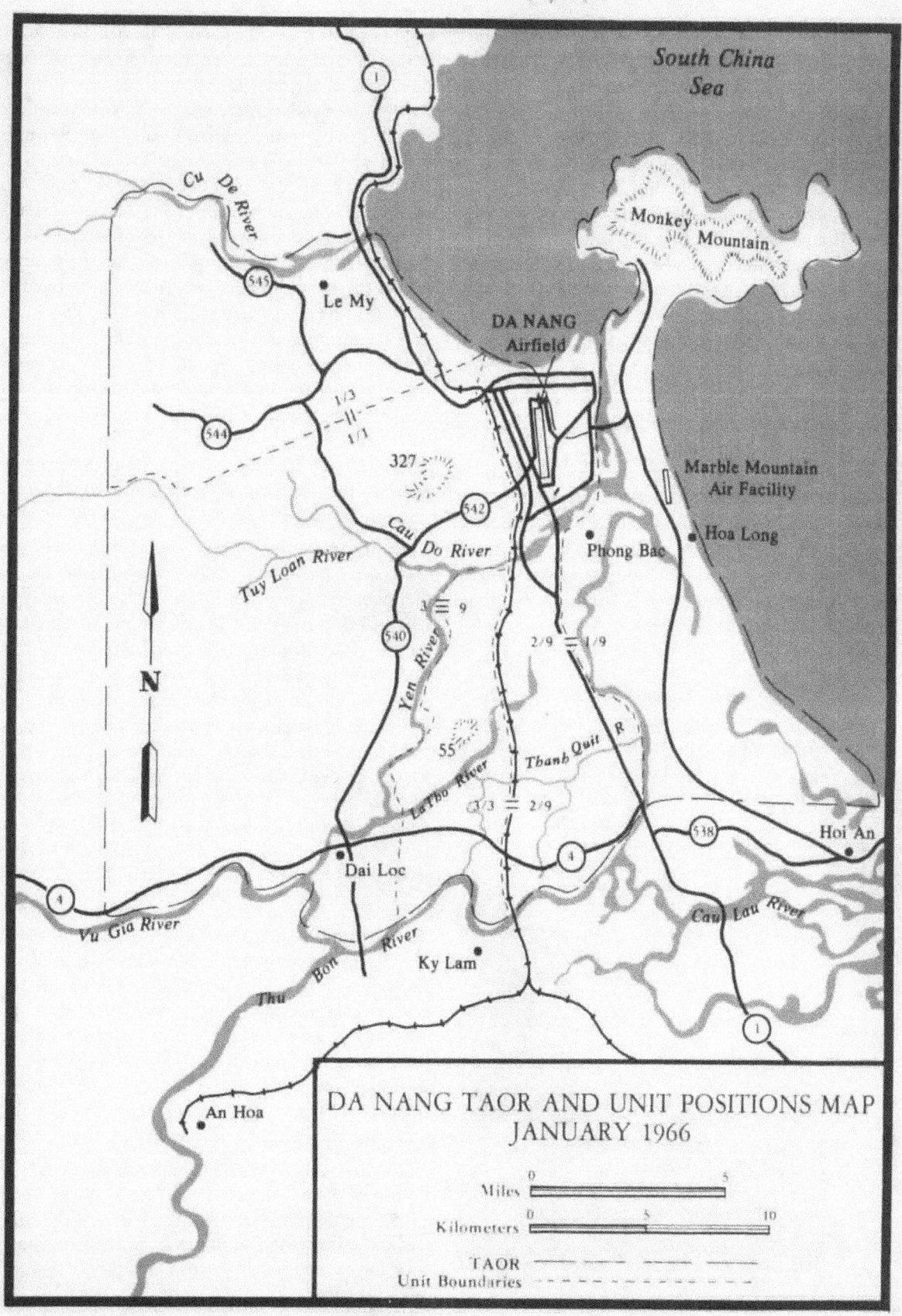

the platoon furnished limited security within the hamlets, while the other members assisted the villagers in building up the local economy and meeting community needs. Supplementing the Rural Reconstruction cadre were the 59th Regional Force Battalion (RF) and Popular Force (PF) units. The RF were locally recruited militia who operated directly under the province chief and could be assigned anywhere in the province while the PF personnel operated directly under the district chief and normally remained in their native hamlets. The battalions of the 9th Marines were to provide the forward protective screen for the five villages undergoing pacification.[1]

Although there was some initial progress, the Ngu Hanh Son Campaign was in difficulty by the beginning of 1966. Both the Marines and the South Vietnamese had overestimated the ease with which they would be able to eradicate enemy influence. One problem the program faced was that nearly 20 percent of the 9,000 families, living in the five villages, were estimated to have Viet Cong relatives. Complicating the situation even further, confusion prevailed among the Vietnamese as to who was responsible for the campaign. The demarcation of authority between the commander of the Quang Nam Special Sector, who had operational control of ARVN forces and military responsibility for pacification in Quang Nam, and the Quang Nam Province Chief, who also was responsibile for pacification as well as political administration within the province, was vague and a cause for some friction. Nevertheless, the basic factor for the lack of success in the Ngu Hanh Son Campaign was the lack of security within the hamlets. The Viet Cong simply avoided the Marine battalions and attacked the understrength South Vietnamese militia and Rural Reconstruction cadre. Over 15 percent of the latter quit their positions. Instead of building up the PFs and RFs, the South Vietnamese removed the province chief, Lieutenant Colonel Le Trung Tuong, who had originated the concept, from the chain of command. The program continued to flounder through January.[2]

Another area, the An Hoa region just south of the Da Nang TAOR, was to play a significant role in Marine pacification efforts during 1966. An Hoa lies nestled in a fertile plain 20 miles from Da Nang immediately southwest of the confluence of the Thu Bon and Vu Gia Rivers. To the west, the terrain rises into the foothills of the Annamite mountain range while another series of mountains, the Que Sons, rises to the south and southeast. This small triangular area possesses all the basic ingredients for industrialization. The rivers and small streams in the region form a natural basin with hydroelectric potential. The only coal mine in South Vietnam is located seven miles to the southwest at Nong Son.

The South Vietnamese Government had realized the economic possibilities of this region. In 1962, the Diem regime selected An Hoa as one of its strategic hamlets and started establishing an industrial complex to consist of hydroelectric, water purification, and chemical fertilizer plants. By 1964, the factory equipment was either in Saigon or awaiting shipment to Vietnam. The project engineer, Le Thuc Can, had chosen the sites for the buildings and construction had begun.

It was then the Viet Cong struck, isolating An Hoa from government influence. In late 1964 and early 1965, enemy troops severed the roads in the area leading to Da Nang and the coast. At the same time, they forced the South Vietnamese to halt all con-

Marines from the 3d Battalion, 7th Marines engage VC in a firefight during Operation Mallard. The operation took place northwest of the An Hoa region, later called the "Arizona Territory" after the western badlands.

Marine Corps Photo A186547

struction of a railroad spur to link An Hoa with the main north-south railway.

Despite these setbacks, the French-educated Can was determined to continue the project. At An Hoa, he had gathered together several Vietnamese engineers and established training schools to teach the young Vietnamese peasants the rudiments of mechanics, electronics, and other useful industrial skills. When the roads were cut, Can had supplies flown into the small An Hoa airfield. Eventually, he found it necessary to lengthen the 1,500-foot runway to 3,000 feet in order to accommodate larger aircraft.[3]

Security continued to be a problem. To protect the industrial area, the hard-pressed ARVN 51st Regiment maintained an infantry company, reinforced by two 105mm howitzers, in the hills to the south. Despite the government presence, the VC *R-20 [Doc Lap] Main Force Battalion* controlled the area surrounding the complex. Colonel Edwin H. Simmons, the III MAF G-3, recalled: "My own feelings at the time [1966] were that an accommodation had been reached between the VC and local ARVN commander. . . ."[4]*

The 3d Marines' Operation Mallard during January 1966 was the first large III MAF penetration into the An Hoa region. Acting on intelligence that the *R-20 Battalion* had been reinforced by the *5th VC Main Force Battalion*, the Marine regiment, supported by a composite artillery battalion, conducted a two-battalion operation in the area. On 10 January, Air Force C-130 transports flew two 105mm howitzer batteries from the Da Nang airfield to the An Hoa airstrip where the 1st Battalion, 12th Marines established an artillery fire base. The following day, Lieutenant Colonel Dickey's 1st Battalion, 3d Marines, reinforced by Company G from the 2d Battalion, 9th Marines, crossed the Vu Gia River in LVTs and began to search for the VC in the area northwest of An Hoa, later commonly known as the

---

*Colonel George W. Carrington, Jr., in his comments, agreed with Colonel Simmons' view that an accommodation existed between the ARVN and the VC and further remarked on the incongruities there: "There were tremendous anachronisms and inequities that stick in my memory. . . . I seem to recall that there were French resident engineers in An Hoa, who continued to live in very comfortable homes and enjoyed speedboating and water skiing on the lake there." Col George W. Carrington, Jr., Comments on draft MS, dtd 15May78 (Vietnam Comment File).

Marine Corps Photo A186548

A Marine takes time to relax and eat during Operation Mallard. C-Rations were the basic staple of the Marines in the field.

"Arizona Territory" after the Western badlands. A 155mm howitzer battery north of the Vu Gia also supported the operation. On 12 January, MAG-16 helicopters lifted Lieutenant Colonel Bodley's 3d Battalion, 7th Marines, which had arrived two days previously at the Da Nang airfield from Chu Lai, into landing zones in the mountains west of An Hoa to exploit a B-52 raid.

The heaviest action occurred during the early morning hours of 14 January in the 1st Battalion, 3d Marines sector. A four-man fire team from Company G, 9th Marines, leaving its platoon's patrol base on the west side of the Thu Bon some 4,000 meters northwest of An Hoa, surprised about 40 VC "deployed in skirmish line with four 60mm mortars on line."[5] According to the fire team leader, Corporal Mark E. DePlanche:

> We moved along this trail when all of a sudden I saw something white move . . . It appeared as though there was a hedgerow along the trail and suddenly two more bushes started moving and I yelled, "Oh God" and started spraying the area to my left. . . .[6]

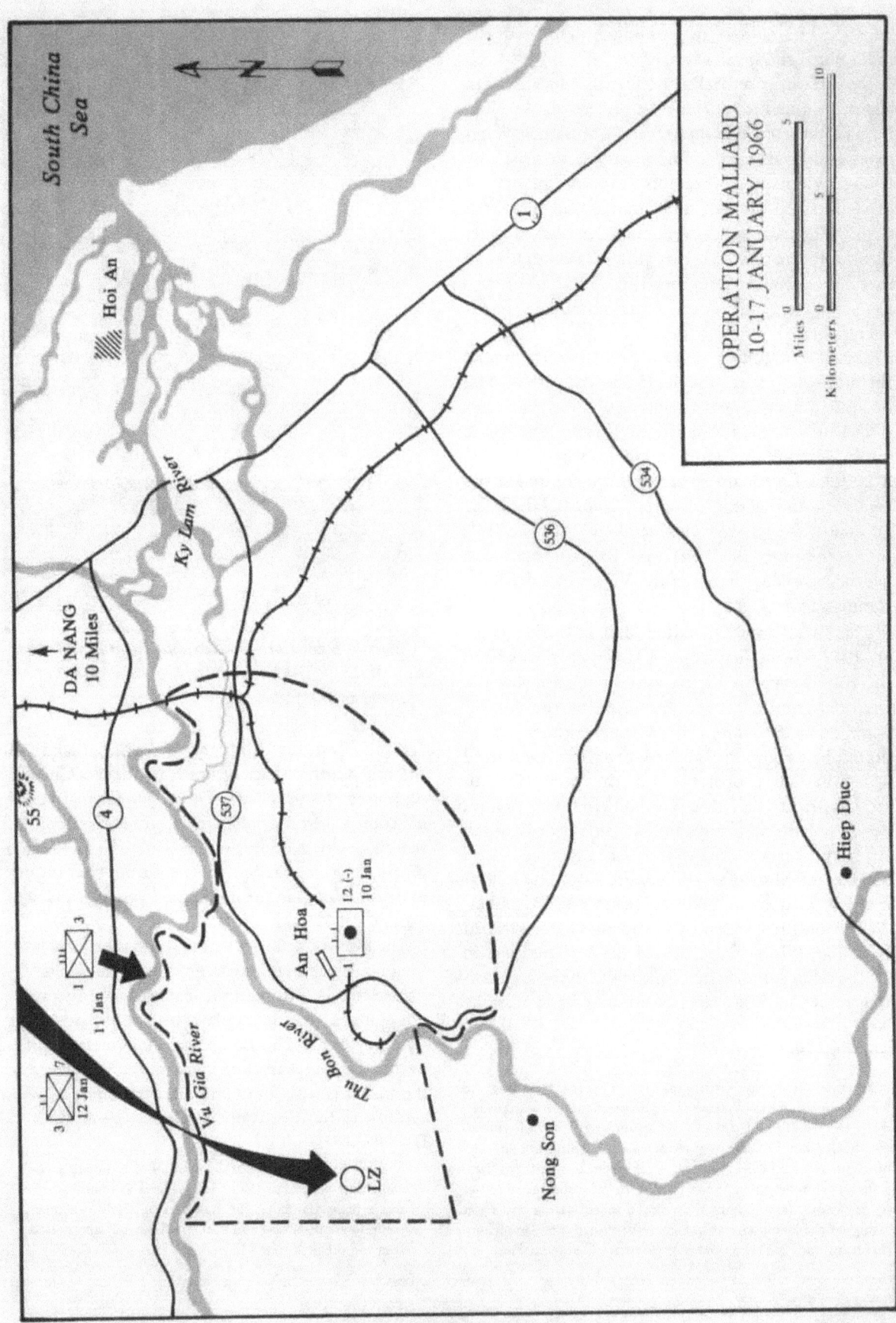

The three other members of the Marine fire team also opened fire and the startled VC "became disorganized and dispersed," leaving behind the mortars.[7] A number of the enemy withdrew to a nearby small hill and began throwing down grenades at the Marines. Maintaining radio contact with its platoon, the fire team was soon reinforced and the VC broke contact. Policing the battlefield, the Marines found four dead VC, captured the four mortars, and 80 60mm mortar shells, and recovered 15 enemy packs and a quantity of assorted small arms ammunition. Corporal DePlanche was the only Marine casualty, sustaining a slight wound to his right hand from an enemy grenade. He was later awarded the Navy Cross and the other three members of the team received Silver Stars for the action.

The military results of Operation Mallard, nevertheless, were minimal if measured with the enemy casualty yardstick. Viet Cong units simply fled west into the mountains upon the approach of the Marines. The important aspect of the operation, which ended on 17 January, was the response of the An Hoa population. More than 300 villagers asked to be evacuated to more secure areas. According to the Dai Loc District Chief, these people wanted to live in their own hamlets "but not until the VC had been driven out. . . . the people wanted the Marines to come back into their area, drive the VC out, and stay there to make security."[8] General Walt met Le Thuc Can for the first time and was impressed with what the man had accomplished under adverse circumstances and promised that the Marines would return to An Hoa.[9]

The lack of South Vietnamese Government cohesion in I Corps and Viet Cong strength in the Da Nang area prevented General Walt from carrying out his promise to Can for several months. On 25 January, the enemy forces demonstrated their capabilities. Employing 120mm mortars, the VC brazenly shelled the Da Nang Airbase, firing from positions within the Ngu Hanh Son area. Although the attack resulted in the death of one Marine and the wounding of seven others, the mortar rounds caused only minor damage to the base itself.* Again

---

*This was the second reported attack during the month in which the enemy employed 120mm mortars. In an earlier attack, the enemy shelled the U. S. Army Special Forces camp at Khe Sanh in northwestern Quang Tri Province. Sharp and Westmoreland, *Report on the War*, p. 115.

A Marine attempts to make friends with a puppy during Operation Mallard. The interior of the Vietnamese house in the picture is typical of those in the villages surrounding Da Nang.

Marine Corps Photo A186549

Marine Corps Photo A186559
Marines escort villagers who asked to leave their homes for a more secure area during Operation Mallard: Gen Walt promised that the Marines would return to the An Hoa region.

American Embassy in Vietnam, Admiral Sharp's CinCPac staff, and their Washington counterparts met secretly in Warrenton, Virginia, to review the course of the war. The conferees examined the South Vietnamese Rural Reconstruction Program, the label for pacification at the time, as well as the structure of the American civilian assistance organization in South Vietnam. The most important result of the conference was its general focus and direction. William J. Porter, the U. S. Deputy Ambassador to South Vietnam, commented that the watchword in Washington was to become "pacification."[10]

The truth of this particular statement became evident the following month at the Honolulu meeting between President Johnson and the Vietnamese Chief of State, Nguyen Van Thieu, and Prime Minister Nguyen Cao Ky. On 8 February 1966, the U.S. and South Vietnamese Governments issued the "Honolulu Declaration." President Johnson renewed the American pledge to support the South Vietnamese in their struggle against the Communists, while Ky and Thieu promised renewed dedication to the eradication of social injustices, building of a viable economy, establishment of a true democracy, and the defeat of the Viet Cong and their allies.[11] President Johnson stated that as a result of this conference both governments were committed to winning the "other war," an euphemism for pacification. He quoted Henry Cabot Lodge, the U. S. Ambassador to South Vietnam: "We have moved ahead here today in the fight to improve the lot of the little man at the grassroots. That is what this is all about."[12]

Despite its emphasis on pacification, the conference was by no means a repudiation of General Westmoreland's large unit strategy. At the conclusion of the conference, Secretary of Defense Robert S. McNamara and Secretary of State Dean Rusk provided the MACV commander with a memorandum of understanding as to the consensus of the meeting. The memorandum approved an increase in South Vietnamese and U.S. regular forces and directed "intensified offensive operations against major VC/PAVN [People's Army of Vietnam] forces, bases, and lines of communications—almost doubling the number of battalion-months of offensive operations from 40 to 75 a month." In effect, Honolulu endorsed the so-called "balanced approach." As General Westmoreland recently commented: "It was not a matter of either pacification or

on 15 February, the Viet Cong revealed the vulnerability of government control in the Da Nang sector when an assassination team killed the Le My village chief during a ceremony in one of the Le My hamlets. These instances demonstrated that continued emphasis upon pacification and security in support of pacification was still sorely needed.

Honolulu and the Reemphasis on Pacification

At two high-level conferences early in 1966, U.S. policymakers stressed that pacification in Vietnam should receive greater priority. In January, representatives from General Westmoreland's staff, the

actions to thwart enemy main force operations, it was both."[13]

Still, the Honolulu Conference gave a renewed impetus to the country-wide South Vietnamese pacification program. On 21 February, General Nguyen Duc Thang, the Minister for Rural Construction, became the Minister of Revolutionary Development, and the Rural Reconstruction cadre became Revolutionary Development teams, although retaining the Vietnamese designation *Can Bo*. General Thang designated national priority areas to be targeted for an extensive pacification effort in each of the four corps areas.[14]

In I Corps, the Ngu Hanh Son area was expanded to include all of Hoa Vang and parts of Hieu Duc and Dien Ban Districts and was redesignated as National Priority Area 1 (NPA 1). Lieutenant Colonel Lap, commander of the 51st ARVN Regiment, was placed in charge of both the security and pacification aspects of the program.[15]

Lap's appointment promised both a more vigorous Vietnamese pacification effort and better coordination with the 9th Marines, the regiment largely responsible for supporting the South Vietnamese effort in NPA 1. Colonel Simmons, who relieved Colonel Gorman as commander of the 9th Marines on

Marine Corps Photo A801847

MajGen McCutcheon, Commanding General, 1st Marine Aircraft Wing and Deputy Commander, III MAF, congratulates Col Edwin H. Simmons upon the latter's assumption of command of the 9th Marines. Col Simmons, the former operations officer of III MAF, relieved Col John E. Gorman.

At the Honolulu Conference, President Johnson (at right center) speaks across the table to Vietnamese Chief of State Nguyen Van Thieu (leaning forward) and Prime Minister Nguyen Cao Ky (seated to the left of Thieu). To the right of the President is the U.S. Secretary of Defense, Robert S. McNamara.

Marine Corps Historical Collection

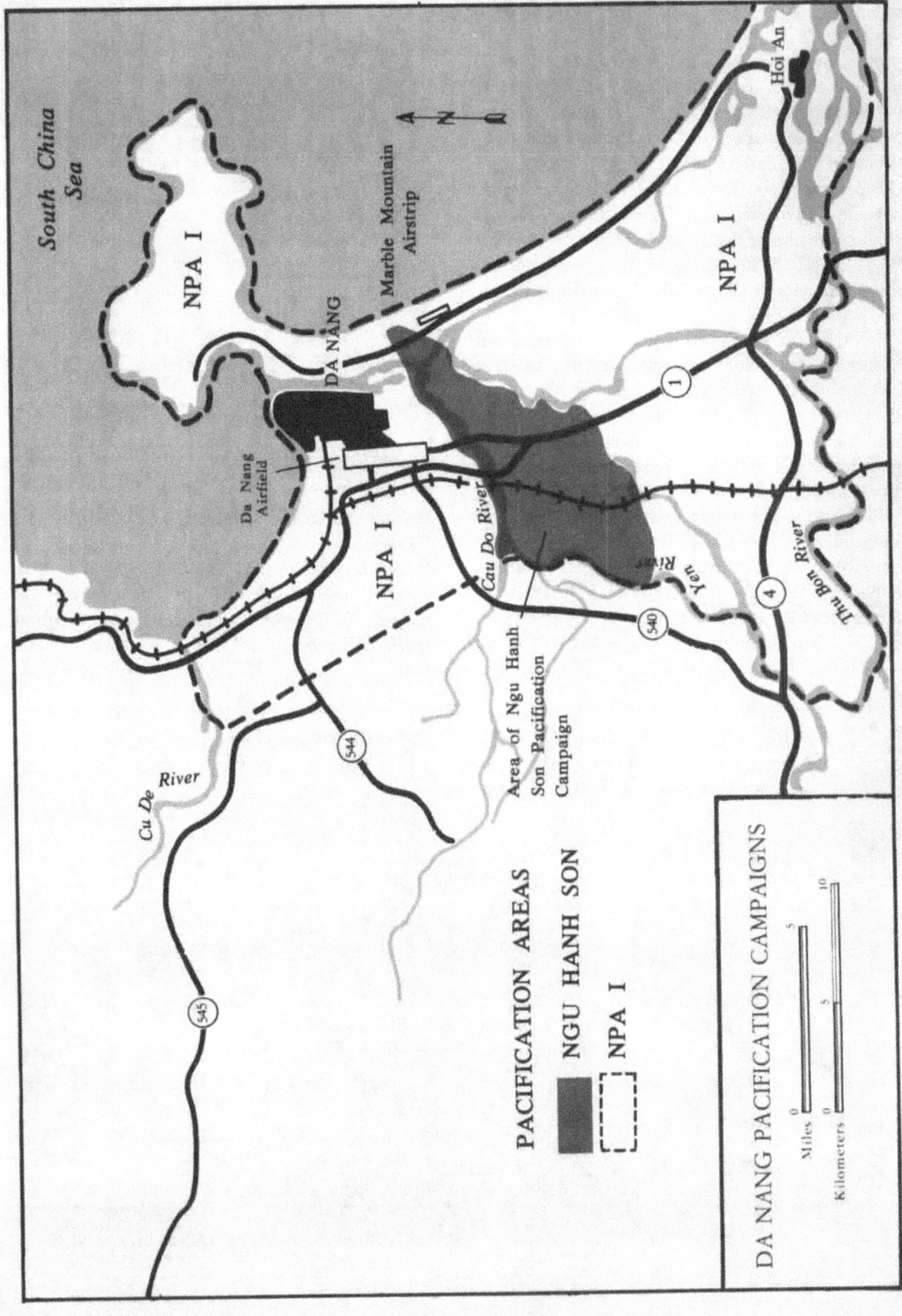

18 February, described Lap as a "compassionate man, brought up in the classical Confucian ethic, [who] had an affinity with the people and a maturity of judgment which previously had been lacking."[16]

The Marines for their part continued to experiment with techniques of cooperating in pacification with the local South Vietnamese forces. The 3d and 9th Marines each had an RF company under their command. Lieutenant Colonel "Woody" Taylor's 3d Battalion, 9th Marines, the Base Defense Battalion, had eight PF platoons under its operational control, seven in the vicinity of the main airfield and the eighth in the village of Hoa Long south of the Marble Mountain helicopter facility.

In January, General Walt received permission from General Thi to extend the combined action company program to all Marine enclaves including Da Nang. The program had begun the previous year in the Phu Bai TAOR under Lieutenant Colonel Taylor, then commanding the 3d Battalion, 4th Marines. Under its concept, a Marine squad was integrated with a PF platoon on the premise that while the Marines provided training for the local forces they themselves gained knowledge about the local populace and countryside. This, it was hoped, would create a bond of mutual interest among Marines, PFs, and villagers. Although Taylor initated the training program at Da Nang, Lieutenant Colonel Doehler's 1st Battalion, 9th Marines relieved the 3d Battalion as the Base Defense Battalion on 17 February and established the first formal combined action unit in the TAOR at the Hoa Long Village complex.[17]

In the 9th Marines sector, Lieutenant Colonel Dorsey's 3d Battalion, 3d Marines, in conjunction with South Vietnamese troops and local administrative and police officials, conducted a sophisticated cordon and search operation in the hamlet of Phong Bac on 24-25 February. While the Marines provided limited administrative and infantry support and attempted to remain as unobtrusive as possible, South Vietnamese officials screened and registered the villagers. Although the regiment had experimented with this technique in 1965, this was the first operation to have the full cooperation of the local officials and to bear the title, "County Fair."*

---

*See Chapter 14 for further discussion of the combined action and County Fair programs.

Marine Corps Photo A187590
Vietnamese villagers in the hamlet of Phong Bac drink water from Marine lister bags during 9th Marines "County Fair" operations on 24 February 1966. The County Fair concept employed a sophisticated cordon and search technique in which the Marines provided limited administrative and infantry support while South Vietnamese officials screened and registered the villagers.

The design of the program was "to convince the people that the GVN (Government of Vietnam) was an effective government that was interested in the welfare of the people and that a GVN victory against the VC was inevitable."[18]

During February, the 9th Marines concentrated on plans to eradicate the guerrilla forces in its TAOR. Colonel Simmons reminded his officers that General Walt's highest priority was the pacification effort south of Da Nang.[19] The regimental commander anticipated a gradual, coordinated advance of his battalions from their base areas south of the La Tho and Thanh Quit Rivers to the Ky Lam and Thu Bon Rivers. Despite the fact that Lieutenant Colonel Donahue's 2d Battalion, 9th Marines command group and two of his rifle companies participated in the Double Eagle operations during most of the month, the remaining regimental units maintained a high level of small unit patrolling in preparation for the clearing operation.*

To sustain mobility and flexibility, the regiment stationed a reinforced rifle squad of 22 men at Marble Mountain which could be rapidly helilifted to exploit a VC contact. According to a III MAF special report, this concept, codenamed Sparrow Hawk, gave a battalion commander "a small, effective air-ground unit able to respond . . . in a rapid manner without tying down large forces of either infantry or helicopters." The report concluded that although the 9th Marines had not as yet killed any large number of VC, "the use of this fast-acting force has undoubtedly prevented a number of friendly casualties."[20] In an incident on 25 February, Lieutenant Colonel Donahue's Company E, one of the battalion's rifle companies remaining in the Da Nang TAOR during Double Eagle, engaged 30 Viet Cong in the hamlet of La Tho Bac (1), 1,000 meters east of the railroad and 2,000 meters north of the La Tho River. Captain Robert J. Driver, Jr., the company commander, requested and was reinforced by the Sparrow Hawk squad. According to the 9th Marines situation report for the day, "At 1200 all major units involved linked up (at the river south of the hamlet). . . . Total of 11 VC KIA (body count)."[21]**

The greatest difficulty the 9th Marines encountered during February was not with Viet Cong troops, but with mines and booby traps. Over 70 percent of the regiment's casualties for the month, 12 of the 17 killed and 120 of the 173 wounded, were a result of these explosive devices.[22] Extensive enemy use of mines was best exemplified on Hill 55. The hill, 3,000 meters northeast of the confluence of the Yen, the Ai Nghia, and the La Tho Rivers, was the dominant terrain feature in the 9th Marines TAOR. It had to be occupied before any advance could be made to the Ky Lam and Thu Bon Rivers.

In late January, Lieutenant Colonel Dorsey's 3d Battalion began mine clearing operations when Captain Grady V. Gardner's Company I secured the hill. During February, the battalion, supported by mine-clearing LVTE-1s from the 1st Amphibian Tractor Battalion and engineers from the 3d Engineer Battalion, started the difficult and dangerous task of removing the mines and constructing the forward battalion CP on the low-lying hill. Lieutenant Colonel Dorsey recalled that on 4 February, he personally briefed General Krulak "on top of the only engineer constructed bunker there at that time."[23]

During the month, the engineers lost a road grader and a light crane to mines while constructing a road and bunkers on the hill. The LVTE-1s expended 31 line charges which caused 99 secondary explosions. Lieutenant Colonel Nicholas J. Dennis, the commanding officer of the 3d Engineer Battalion, remembered that his engineers employed man-pack line charges together with transistorized mine detectors in addition to the engineer tractors to detonate the enemy explosive devices.*** By the end of February, the infantry and engineers had completed most of their mine clearing mission on Hill 55, but as Lieutenant Colonel Dennis later observed, "No sites were ever considered 'cleared' since the VC would remine and booby trap locations we previously had cleared."[24]

In the 3d Marines sector, Colonel Fisher, an experienced combat veteran of both World War II and Korea, expressed the same concern about the enemy mines and booby traps. Although reporting only light contact with enemy units in February, he

---

*Colonel Nicholas J. Dennis, the commanding officer of the 3d Engineer Battalion in early 1966, observed in his comments that the deployment of rifle units from Da Nang during Double Eagle "resulted in a quasi-reaction force being organized from service and service support units in the Da Nang TAOR to meet any contingency." Col Nicholas J. Dennis, Comments on draft MS, n.d. [Jun78] (Vietnam Comment File).

**Variations of the Sparrow Hawk technique existed in other sectors as well. Colonel Zitnik commented that "Marines in the Chu Lai sector also operated in a manner similar to Sparrow Hawk, except the designated troops remained in their battalion area and were picked up en route to the target area. Upon initial insertion of the small unit, the parent company (and battalion if necessary) prepared to reinforce its unit again with a larger helo lift." Col Robert J. Zitnik, Comments on draft MS, dtd 6Jun78 (Vietnam Comment File).

***In his comments, Colonel Dennis remarked that the man-pack units "were not a normal item of issue," for a Marine engineer battalion. Prior to coming to Vietnam, he had seen both the man-pack units and the "new" transistorized mine detectors on a visit to the Army's Fort Belvoir. When he later assumed command of the 3d Engineer Battalion, he requested both items "for 'testing.'" Col Nicholas J. Dennis, Comments on draft MS, n.d. [Jun78] (Vietnam Comment File).

A Marine from the 3d Battalion, 3d Marines uses a flamethrower to clear obstacles near Hill 55. This small hill was the dominant terrain feature in the 9th Marines area of operations and was later to be the site of the command post for the regiment.

observed that the number of mine incidents during the month represented a 110 percent increase over January and a 350 percent increase over the preceding four months. All told there were 52 mining incidents in the 3d Marines TAOR during February, the worst occurring near the Cu De River when an amphibian tractor hit a mine, exploded, and caught fire, resulting in the death of five Marines and one ARVN soldier, and the wounding of 20 other Marines and one Navy corpsman. Colonel Fisher concluded that the increasing incidence and sophistication of the enemy explosive devices reflected a determined organized attempt of the VC to restrict the freedom of Marine patrol activity in the Da Nang TAOR.[25]

With the expanding small-unit war in the enclave, the Marine infantry buildup at Da Nang continued. After the completion of Double Eagle II at the end of February, Lieutenant Colonel Horn's 2d Battalion, 3d Marines, the former SLF battalion, rejoined its parent regiment at Da Nang. The battalion relieved the 1st Battalion, 1st Marines in the 3d Marines southern sector. Lieutenant Colonel Hatch's 1st Battalion went into division reserve with its command post at Marble Mountain and prepared to act as a mobile force wherever needed.

CHAPTER 4
A New Threat in Northern I Corps

The Buildup at Phu Bai—The Fall of A Shau—The Aftermath of A Shau—Continuing Reinforcement of Phu Bai and Operation Oregon

---

The Buildup at Phu Bai

At the beginning of 1966, the Phu Bai enclave, centered around the airfield located there and eight miles southeast of Hue in Thua Thien Province, was the smallest and northernmost of the three Marine base areas. The Phu Bai forces consisted of Lieutenant Colonel Robert T. Hanifin, Jr.'s reinforced 2d Battalion, 1st Marines supported by a Marine artillery battalion and helicopter squadron. Lieutenant Colonel Edwin M. Rudzis' 4th Battalion, 12th Marines artillery pieces included 105mm howitzers, 107mm howtars (a combination of a howitzer and mortar), and both towed and self-propelled 155mm howitzers.* HMM-163 under Lieutenant Colonel Charles A. House was the UH-34 helicopter squadron at the base. Rounding out the defensive forces at Phu Bai and attached to Hanifin's battalion, were a platoon each of tanks and Ontos, a platoon of reconnaissance troops, and a platoon of engineers. A small logistics support unit provided the material support for the Phu Bai units. Although the 2d Battalion was under the operational control of the 3d Marines at Da Nang, Lieutenant Colonel Hanifin, as the base coordinator, was responsible for the 2,000-plus Marines at Phu Bai and the defense of both the airfield and the U.S. Army's 8th Radio Research Unit facility based there.

Hanifin accomplished his defensive tasks by extensive patrolling throughout the 76-square-mile TAOR. The terrain to the west consisted of low rolling hills. Lack of vegetation and very little population permitted easy spotting of any movement in this area. North and east of the airstrip, an extensive built-up area, consisting of a series of hamlets and ricelands, extended to the waterways. Three rivers, the Dai Giang to the north and east, the Nong to the east and south, and the Ta Trach on the west, formed a semicircle around the Marine enclave, roughly defining the boundaries of the entire TAOR. The combined action company, which was formed at Phu Bai in August 1965, provided the defensive force for the built-up area, called Zone A. Six combined action platoons were in this sector, one in each of the hamlets of Thu Duong, Thuy Tan, Phu Bai, and Loc Ban, and two guarding Route 1 and the railroad bridges. Roving combat patrols kept the enemy off-balance and maintained the security of the base.

Through 1965 and into January 1966, the enemy threat in the Phu Bai area was largely guerrilla in nature. Enemy units confined themselves to night harassment of the Marine perimeter, minelaying, and intelligence gathering. According to the Marine enemy order of battle, only one VC battalion was in the area, the 360-man *810 VC Main Force Battalion*, located in the mountains 14 kilometers south of the base. During January, the Marines mounted three combined operations with the ARVN outside of the TAOR, but accounted for only 22 enemy dead, largely as a result of Marine artillery and air. At the end of the month, the Marines' major concern was with the VC's increased use of mines throughout the TAOR, and not with any major buildup of enemy forces.[1]

---

*The 4th Battalion, 12th Marines was made up of Hq Btry, 4/12; 107mm Mortar Battery, 1/11 with six howtars; Battery B/1/11 with six 105mm howitzers; Battery M/4/12 with six M109 155mm howitzers (SP); and Yankee Battery, a provisional battery, with six 155mm towed howitzers. Colonel Rudzis explained the reason for the existence of the provisional battery when he commented: ". . . in September 1965 when the M109s . . . were brought into Vietnam as replacements for the towed 155mm howitzers, nothing was known about their capabilities in combat, such as durability, maintenance problems and ability to fit into the scheme of tactical maneuvers. Therefore by stretching the personnel assets of the battalion, instead of providing just one six-howitzer medium artillery battery, two were provided consisting of the M109s and the provisional battery of six towed 155mm howitzers." Col Edwin M. Rudzis, Comments on draft MS, dtd 26May78 (Vietnam Comment File).

With the relatively small level of enemy activity in the Phu Bai area, General Walt planned to keep the Phu Bai forces at the same strength until July. At that time, he hoped to obtain operational control of the South Korean Marine Brigade and position the Korean Marines at Phu Bai. The U.S. Marine reinforcements arriving during the spring of 1966 would either go to Da Nang or Chu Lai.[2]

General Westmoreland and his staff, however, perceived a much larger threat in the northern two provinces than did III MAF. In January, MACV intelligence estimates placed 22 Communist battalions in Quang Tri and Thua Thien Provinces as opposed to nine identified by the Marine command. At the urging of General Westmoreland, III MAF at the end of January, prepared contingency plans to counter any Communist thrust in the north. These plans called for the entire 3d Marines to deploy north in the event of an enemy attack or major buildup in the north.[3]

In contrast to January, all signs during February pointed to a marked increased in the presence of enemy main force units in Thua Thien Province, especially near Phu Bai. At the end of the month, Colonel Fisher, the 3d Marines commander, reported, "For the first time since the occupation of the Hue/Phu Bai TAOR, there appears to be considerable enemy interest in that area."[4] He believed a general Communist main force buildup was in progress. Marine intelligence sources in mid and late February identified two VC regiments, the *1st Provisional* and the *6th VC*, reinforced by two separate battalions, the *803d* and the already identified *810th*, within striking distance or 35 miles of Phu Bai. These same reports indicated that the enemy was planning to attack the Marine base at the beginning of March.[5]

Reacting to this intelligence, the Marine command refined its plans for the reinforcement of Phu Bai and for the possible activation of a battalion-sized task unit, under Lieutenant Colonel Hanifin, at the base. This task unit, designated Hotel, would have the mission of supporting the hard-pressed ARVN 1st Division. Hanifin would be given operational control of two additional infantry companies which were to arrive from either Da Nang or Chu Lai or both. These companies would provide the 2d Battalion commander enough forces to defend the Phu Bai base area in the event Task Unit Hotel was activated and committed outside the TAOR. Other plans called for further reinforcement.[6]

With the approval of Brigadier General English, acting 3d Marine Division commander in the absence of General Walt, who was still on leave, Lieutenant Colonel Hanifin on 26 February activated Task Unit Hotel, "for the purpose of providing a reserve for CG 1st ARVN Division."[7] At this time, the 1st Division was committed to three operations and thinly spread. In Lam Son-234, the Vietnamese were operating in Quang Dien District northwest of Hue and called for Marine assistance. On the afternoon of 26 February, Hanifin attended a briefing at 1st ARVN Division Headquarters at Hue and Brigadier General Nguyen Van Chuan, the 1st Division's commanding general, assigned the Marine battalion an objective area in the Pho Lai village complex, some seven kilometers northwest of Hue. According to allied intelligence, a 100-man local force VC company was in the vicinity of the village.[8]

Returning to Phu Bai, Hanifin hurriedly made his plans for the operation, codenamed New York. He assembled, under Task Unit Hotel, three infantry companies, Companies F and G from his own battalion, and Company K from the 3d Marines. The 3d Marines company and Company F from the 9th Marines had arrived at Phu Bai that day from Da Nang. This reinforcement permitted Hanifin to leave three companies behind to cover the base area together with most of the Marine artillery. One Marine battery, the provisional 155mm towed-howitzer battery from the 4th Battalion, had already been committed to Lam Son-234 since 21 February and was in position to provide general support to Task Unit Hotel.[9]

The first phase of Operation New York went as planned except the enemy simply was not in the objective area. Companies F and G of the 2d Battalion moved by truck into jumpoff positions southwest of Pho Lai, arriving at their destination in the late afternoon and early evening of 26 February. About the same time, HMM-163 brought Company K, 3d Marines into blocking positions northeast of the village. Establishing his command group with Companies F and G that evening, Lieutenant Colonel Hanifin ordered the two companies into the attack. Companies F and G advanced through Pho Lai without opposition and reached Company K's blocking positions at 2215 that night. Task Unit Hotel remained in the Pho Lai vicinity through the next morning, but failed to encouter any enemy. The Marine units of Task Unit Hotel were back at Phu Bai by 1815 on the 27th.

Lieutenant Colonel Hanifin and Task Unit Hotel were to have little rest. An hour and a half after his return to Phu Bai, Hanifin received another call for assistance from General Chuan. The 1st Battalion, 3d ARVN Regiment and a small group of Popular Force and Regional Force troops had engaged the *810th VC Battalion* on the supposedly pacified Phu Thu Peninsula located almost immediately to the east of the Phu Bai TAOR. After returning from another briefing at 1st Division Headquarters and receiving permission from III MAF, Hanifin decided to order at 2100 a night helicopter landing of the same forces that he had used in the Pho Lai village area to relieve the pressure on the South Vietnamese battalion. He realized that his men were not fresh, "but they were all that was available. The anticipation of engagement with a VC force boxed in on a peninsula overcame physical handicaps on the part of the troops."[10]

Lieutenant Colonel House's HMM-163 landed the three infantry companies of Task Unit Hotel into landing zones just north of the peninsula, completing the entire helilift at 0200 the next morning. Supported by the Marine artillery at Phu Bai on 28 February, Companies F, G, and K advanced abreast toward the southeast. While the South Vietnamese blocking forces from the 1st Battalion moved into position on the enemy's flanks, the Marine companies made a frontal assault against the well-prepared VC defenses, "at which time the VC broke contact and withdrew in small disorganized groups." The Marines continued the cleanup phase of the operation, meeting occasional enemy resistance, until 3 March. Task Unit Hotel during the one-week operation, also called New York, killed 120 of the enemy, captured 7 more, and seized 69 weapons. The Marines suffered casualties of 17 dead and 37 wounded.[11]

While the Marines conducted Operation New York on the Phu Thu Peninsula, evidence of a growing enemy presence in southern Quang Tri and Thua Thien Provinces continued to mount. In Lam Son-235, 1st ARVN Division units operating east and south of Quang Tri City accounted for over 240 enemy troops, but sustained losses of 23 killed and 158 wounded, including two U.S. advisors, through the end of February. Further south, Communist main force troops on 28 February ambushed a 1st Division unit conducting Operation Lam Son-236 in Phong Dien District of Thua Thien Province, 17 miles north of Hue. As a result of this action, the South Vietnamese suffered casualties of 15 killed and 22 wounded, and lost 56 weapons. Closer to Phu Bai, an ARVN unit reported contact on 1 March with a small Communist force at the Truoi River Bridge on Route 1, six miles south of where Task Unit Hotel had engaged the *810th VC Battalion* the day before. Other intelligence revealed that a VC company from the badly mauled *810th*, carrying its

In Operation New York, the 2d Battalion, 1st Marines advances on the enemy under cover of Marine air strikes. The Phu Bai-based Marines engaged the 810th VC Battalion *on the Phu Thu Peninsula, located just east of the Marine base.*

Marine Corps Photo A186946

A NEW THREAT IN NORTHERN I CORPS

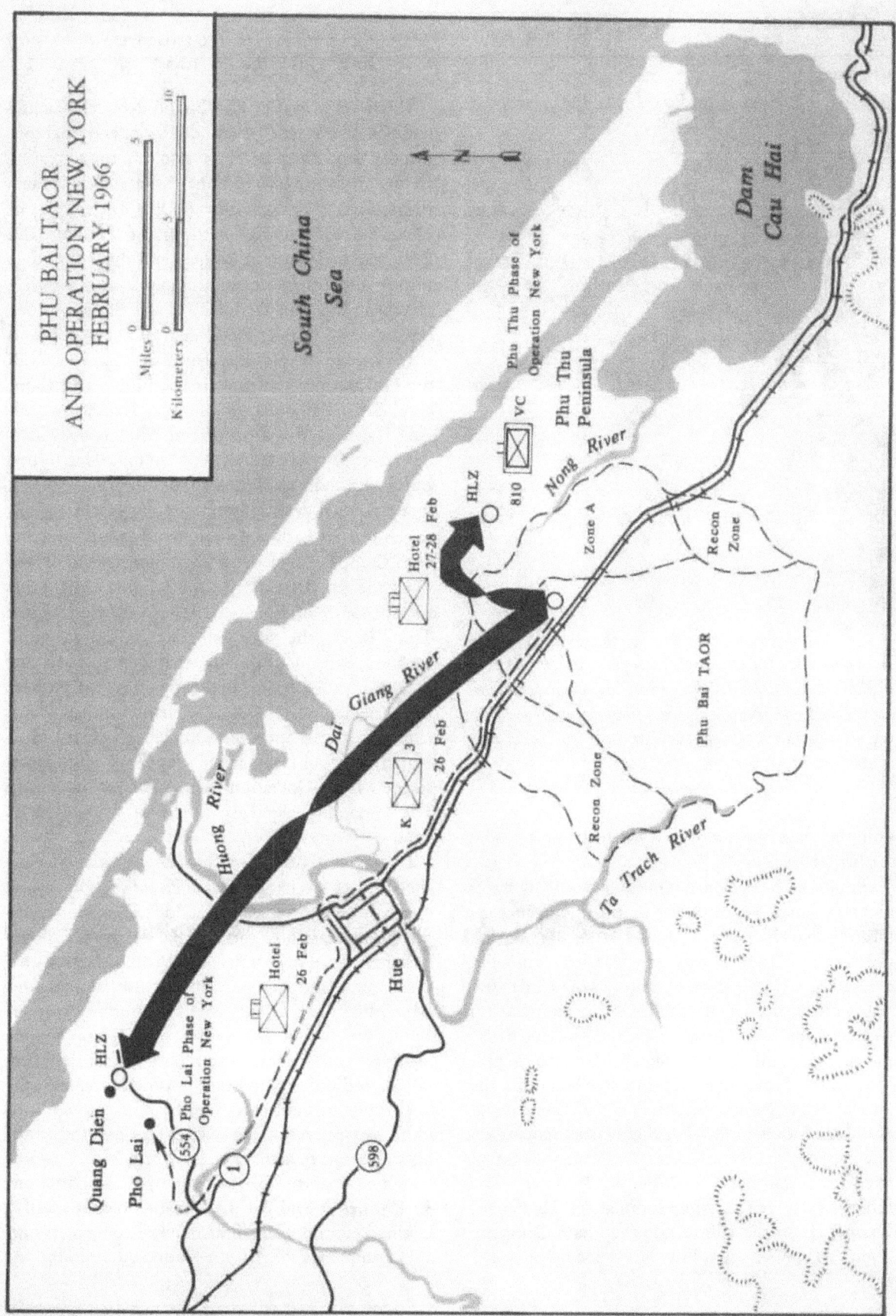

Marine Corps Photo 187628

A Vietnamese student places a lei around the neck of a Marine from the 2d Battalion, 1st Marines at Phu Bai. The Vietnamese awarded their Cross of Gallantry to 32 Marines from the battalion for their participation in Operation New York.

wounded, was moving toward Route 1 just north of the bridge.[12]

Influenced by the general buildup of enemy forces and also wanting to capitalize on the intelligence indicating that the remnants of the *810th* were fleeing toward the Truoi Bridge, the Marine command decided to reinforce its northern enclave. While alerting additional units at both Da Nang and Chu Lai and with the concurrence of General McCutcheon, the acting CG III MAF, on March 1 General English ordered the deployment of his reserve battalion, the 1st Battalion, 1st Marines, to Phu Bai. Company A of the 1st Battalion, which had only been relieved on line earlier that day, departed Da Nang on Marine fixed-wing transports at 1700 on 1 March. The following day, the battalion commander, Lieutenant Colonel Hatch, his command group, and Company C joined Company A at Phu Bai. Colonel Fisher, the 3d Marines commander, also arrived at Phu Bai on 2 March to look over the situation.[13]

Upon his arrival at Phu Bai on 2 March, Lieutenant Colonel Hatch came under the operational control of the 3d Marines. Hoping to trap the retreating elements of the *810th*, Colonel Fisher ordered Hatch to conduct an operation in the Phu Loc District of Thua Thien Province, southwest of the Phu Thu Peninsula and south of Route 1 and the Truoi River Bridge. One of the reserve companies of Task Unit Hotel at Phu Bai, Company F, 2d Battalion, 9th Marines, already had established blocking positions at the bridge the previous day. Assuming control of the 9th Marines company at the bridge and Company E, 2d Battalion, 1st Marines, Lieutenant Colonel Hatch prepared his scheme of maneuver for a three-company operation. At 1230 on 2 March, one and a half hours after the battalion commander first received his orders, helicopters from HMM-163 inserted the 1st Battalion's command group, together with Company E of the 2d Battalion and Company C of the 1st Battalion, into a landing zone 3,000 meters south of Route 1. Remaining west of the Truoi River, the two companies advanced north without encountering any resistance toward the blocking positions of Company F at the bridge. With negligible results, Lieutenant Colonel Hatch closed out the operation, designated Troy, on 3 March, at about the same time Task Unit Hotel secured from Operation New York further north. The remaining elements of the *810th* had made good their escape.[14]

During this time, Generals English and McCutcheon, after receiving Colonel Fisher's report on the enemy buildup in the area, decided to continue with the augmentation of the Phu Bai defenses. Colonel Fisher returned to Phu Bai at 0815 on 3 March with a small command group from the 3d Marines and established Task Group Foxtrot, assuming responsibility for the Phu Bai enclave. Task Group Foxtrot included both infantry battalions, the artillery battalion, and other supporting forces. Lieutenant Colonel Hatch had only a forward headquarters and two of his own infantry companies at Phu Bai, the rest of his command remaining at Da Nang. Hatch assumed operational control of Company K, 3d Battalion, 3d Marines at Phu Bai. Lieutenant Colonel Hanifin retained control of his four infantry companies and also Company F of the 9th Marines. Rounding out

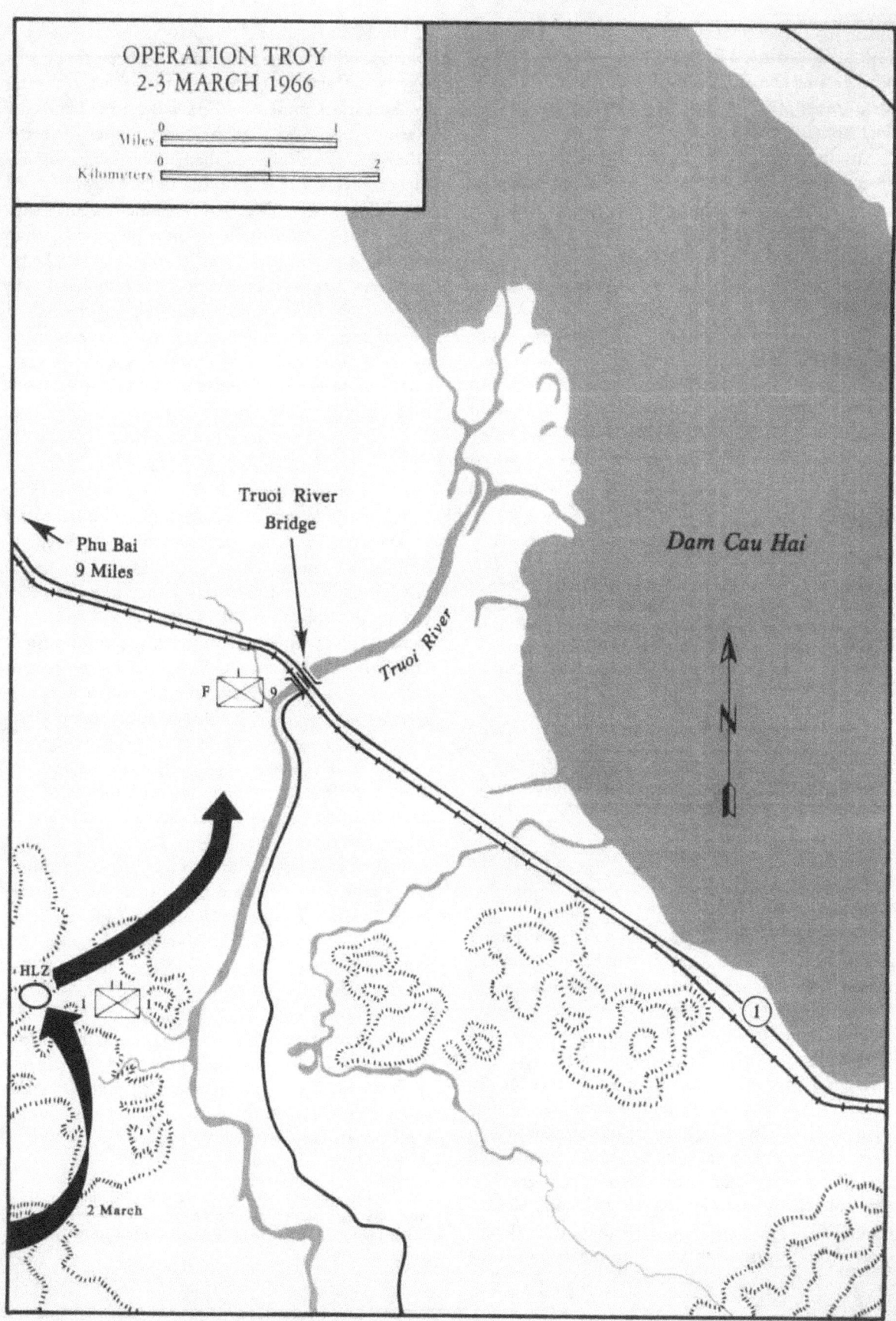

the new reinforcements, Battery C, 1st Battalion, 12th Marines arrived from Da Nang with six 105mm howitzers on the afternoon of 3 March and brought the number of artillery pieces under Lieutenant Colonel Rudzis to 30.[15]

Although intelligence reports continued to speak of a buildup of VC forces near Hue and the likelihood of an attack against the Phu Bai base, the enemy remained quiescent for the next few days. Task Group Foxtrot spent the time consolidating its defenses and planning the extension of the Phu Bai TAOR.

The Marines were confident that they were in control of the situation. On 4 March, General McCutcheon radioed General Krulak that III MAF in Operation New York and the ARVN 1st Division in Operations Lam Son-234, -235, and -236 had killed over 700 of the enemy. Comparing these operations to the French experience in Vietnam, McCutcheon observed:

> This overall campaign took place essentially in the area of the "Street without Joy" where the French in 1953 used about 20 battalions against a Viet Minh Regiment. Contrary to their actions we and the ARVN used about 8 battalions to engage about 6 VC battalions and of these the *806th, 808th,* and *810th Battalions* were rather severely mauled. Although it was not a perfect operation by any manner or means it did result in victory.[16]

McCutcheon concluded:

> Furthermore, I believe it substantiates our concept and strategy that the primary battleground is close to the sea because that is where the people are and the people are the primary object for both sides . . . we can act swiftly in strength to good intelligence and engage the enemy on our own terms rather than merely react to his actions or waste our efforts beating the bushes in the hinterlands chasing shadows.[17]

McCutcheon's message touched on the continuing debate between MACV and III MAF concerning offensive operations. Since returning from the Honolulu Conference, General Westmoreland placed even more pressure on his command to take the offensive against the enemy main force units. At a high-level MACV commander's conference on 20 February, Westmoreland told the assembled officers that the U.S. had enough troops in Vietnam to step up the tempo of operations "by going out after the Viet Cong rather than sitting around base areas."[18] On 3 March, Westmoreland visited General McCutcheon at Da Nang and reiterated that 50 to 75 percent of the Marine units should be engaged with the enemy at all times and to "Leave defense of bases to logistic and headquarters types."[19] McCutcheon succinctly defined the MACV philosophy as "defend less and attack more . . . ."[20] On the other hand, the Marines countered that they were "indeed, on the offensive," pursuing simultaneously their antiguerrilla campaign and large unit actions. They promised to redouble their efforts to demonstrate that they were "doing more offensive work per capita than anybody else and, moreover, that it . . . [was] being done on a balanced basis with some tangible results to show" for their effort.[21] Despite all of the talk of the offensive, the American command, as evidenced by the Marine buildup at Phu Bai, was largely reacting to unforeseen circumstances and the corresponding buildup of the enemy's forces.

The Fall of A Shau

While the Marines reinforced their Phu Bai forces in response to what they perceived as a major buildup in eastern Thua Thien Province, the *95th NVA Regiment* completed its preparations for an attack on the isolated A Shau Special Forces outpost in western Thua Thien, some 33 miles southwest of Phu Bai. Manned by a U.S. Special Forces detachment and a South Vietnamese Civilian Irregular Defense Group (CIDG),* this allied camp was ideally situated to monitor enemy movement through the A Shau Valley. The valley, itself, was a major Communist infiltration route about two miles from and parallel to the Laotian border. Surrounded by steep, jungle-covered mountains, this key artery extended along a northwest-southeast axis for about 15 miles. One branch ran westward and joined the elaborate Ho Chi Minh Trail network. Other tributary trails led eastward from A Shau through the mountains into the populated area around Hue and Phu Bai. During 1965, the allies had manned three CIDG bases in the valley, A Loui, Ta Bat, and A Shau. The South Vietnamese had abandoned two of the camps, A Loui and Ta Bat, on 8 December 1965, leaving only the A Shau base in the southern portion of the valley, 13 miles south of A Loui and eight miles south of Ta Bat.

---

*The CIDG forces, mostly Montagnards, the nomadic tribes which populate South Vietnam's highlands, normally manned the isolated outposts along the borders and were advised by U.S. Army Special Forces.

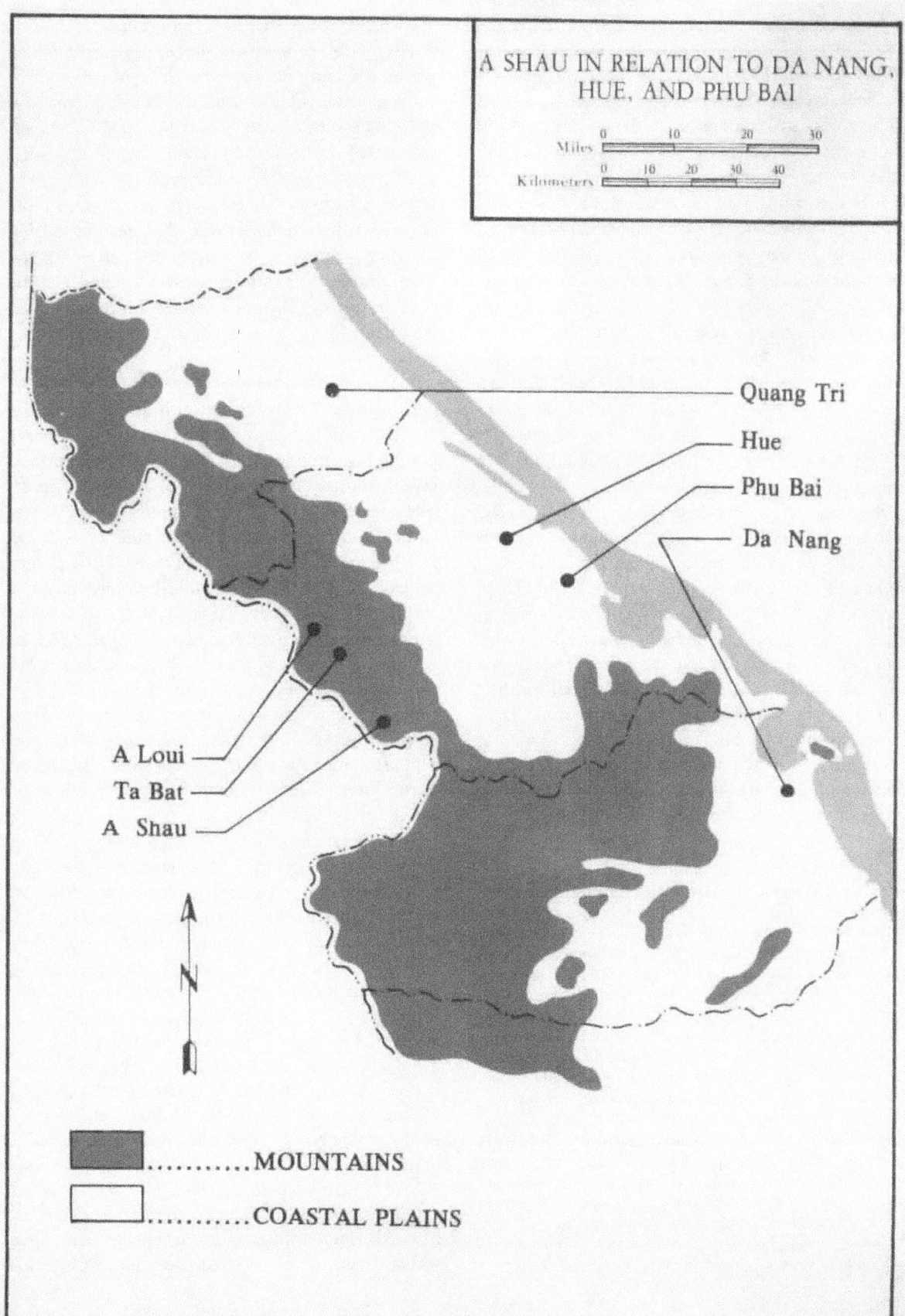

In late February and early March, the A Shau garrison obtained intelligence on the presence of the *95th Regiment, 325th NVA Division* in the area. On 28 February, the Special Forces captured an NVA soldier who had maintained a diary. According to the soldier's account, the NVA regiment had left "the friendly country," probably a reference to North Vietnam, on 29 December 1965. Seven days later, 5 January 1966, the unit arrived in the A Shau. Through January and February, enemy patrols reconnoitered the Special Forces camp. The prisoner recorded in his diary that on two occasions, he "had crawled through the first row of barbed wires, surrounding the camp."[22] On 5 March, two more North Vietnamese soldiers surrendered to the A Shau defenders. Claiming to be officers from the *325th NVA Division*, the two deserters reported that the enemy planned to attack the A Shau Camp on 11 or 12 March.[23]

Reacting to this intelligence, the A Shau CIDG commander asked the South Vietnamese I Corps command for reinforcements. With the 1st Division spread thin in eastern Quang Tri and Thua Thien Provinces and the 2d ARVN Division heavily engaged in Quang Ngai Province, the South Vietnamese had few if any additional forces to send to the isolated outpost. From Nha Trang, the commanding officer of the 5th U.S. Special Forces Group (Airborne) committed one of his mobile strike force companies to A Shau. It arrived at the base on 7 March and increased the allied defenders' strength to approximately 400 men.[24]*

---

*Mobile strike forces were small battalion-size units used as reserve or reaction forces. Each mobile strike force consisted of a headquarters and three companies, a total strength of 594 men. The mobile forces were trained to a tactical competence beyond that of a regular CIDG company. A detachment of U.S. Special Forces troops was normally assigned to the strike force. See Kelly, *U.S. Army Special Forces*, p. 92. There is no evidence that the Special Forces called upon III MAF for reinforcements prior to the attack and the command relations between the Marines and the Special Forces were rather tenuous. General Simmons recalled: "Westmoreland specifically told Walt that he had authority and responsibility over and for the outposts and the Special Forces. However, the Special Forces covertly resisted this authority." BGen Edwin H. Simmons, Comments on draft MS, dtd 9Sep74 (Vietnam Comment File). Colonel Roy C. Gray, Jr., the 1st Wing operations officer, recalled in 1978 that he was never overly impressed with the military efficiency of the Special Forces and "never too sure of the accuracy of their intelligence reports or combat action reports." Col Roy C. Gray, Jr., Comments on draft MS, dtd 20July78 (Vietnam Comment File).

Believing that an attack was imminent, the A Shau garrison commander on the night of 8 March placed the camp on a general alert. At 0300 on the early morning of the 9th, the North Vietnamese opened up with a heavy two-and-one-half hour mortar barrage, inflicting 50 casualties on the defenders and destroying several buildings. Under cover of the mortar attack, two enemy companies probed the camp's southern defenses with the apparent mission of cutting through the wire and determining the camp's firepower. Throughout the remainder of the day, the enemy continued pressure on the base, but refrained from launching a full-scale ground assault.[25]

A Shau was beyond the range of friendly artillery, enabling the enemy to take full advantage of the weather and surrounding mountains. A heavy ground fog shrouded the valley and a 100-foot cloud ceiling limited the effectiveness of allied air support. The nearest Marine Air Support Radar Team (ASRT), equipped with TPQ-10 radar, was at Da Nang, 60 miles away and out of range. Ground controllers could not conduct radar bombing missions around the perimeter. General McCutcheon, the wing commander, directed the Chu Lai ASRT to deploy to Phu Bai, where on subsequent days it was able to provide TPQ support for the camp.[26]

North Vietnamese gunners, on the 9th, shot down an Air Force AC-47 "Puff the Magic Dragon" ground support plane. An Air Force helicopter was able to rescue three of the crewmen from the wreckage at the crash site north of A Shau.

While weather hampered the fixed-wing pilots on the first day of fighting, a few helicopters were able to reach the camp. Two Marine helicopter crews, on search and rescue alert at the small Quang Tri City airstrip, took off for A Shau to evacuate wounded. The two UH-34s from HMM-363, piloted by Lieutenants Richard A. Vasdias and David E. Brust, respectively, skimmed under the overcast. When it attempted to land at the camp, Vasdias' aircraft was hit in the oil line and crashed within the compound. Brust quickly touched down, picked up the downed Marine crewmen, and flew to Marble Mountain Air Facility at Da Nang. The crashed helicopter was later destroyed by U.S. forces.

Shortly after noon on the 9th, the A Shau defenders radioed: "We suspect we are heavily infiltrated, don't think the camp will last the night without reinforcement."[27] At this point, I Corps informed III MAF that a CIDG company would arrive at Phu Bai from Nha Trang to be helilifted into A Shau. The Marines also placed two companies of the 1st Battalion, 1st Marines on alert at Phu Bai, but also told the I Corps command not to expect any helicopter support unless the weather conditions cleared up.[28]

That afternoon, Brigadier General Marion E. Carl, the assistant wing commander and one of the Marine Corps' first helicopter pilots, flew his own UH-1E from Da Nang to Phu Bai. According to Carl, he then discussed the A Shau situation with Lieutenant Colonel House, the HMM-163 commander.[29] House later commented that General Carl stopped off at Phu Bai to refuel his aircraft, but did not talk to him. The squadron commander remarked in 1978, "We anticipated commitment, so recon'd the route."[30] In any event, General Carl took off from Phu Bai to look over the objective area for himself. He later recalled that the weather "would come down, go up, go down . . . ."[31] At 1500, III MAF informed MACV that the helilift of the CIDG company into A Shau would begin at 1620, but shortly afterward had to postpone the lift because of the weather and the enemy's concentrated antiaircraft guns surrounding the camp. By 1700, it was clear that the reinforcements could not be flown in that evening. All the Marines at this point could accomplish was to monitor the radio communications and prepare plans for the next morning.[32]

In the early morning hours of 10 March, the North Vietnamese began their final assaults on the besieged camp. Initiating the action at 0400 with an intensive mortar and recoilless rifle bombardment which lasted for about an hour, the enemy followed up with a heavy ground attack which breached the southern and eastern defenses. With the enemy troops surging into the compound, the defenders either retreated across the runway into the communications bunker or into hastily-built fighting positions along the northern wall. Some of the South Vietnamese irregulars fought bravely while others surrendered en masse to the North Vietnamese. According to Captain John D. Blair IV, USA, the Special Forces detachment leader, the CIDG camp commander hid "in various bunkers making no effort to lead or command during the entire battle." At 1000, Blair requested that the camp with the exception of the communication bunker and the northern wall be bombed and strafed.[33]

Despite heavy cloud cover and the steep mountains surrounding the valley, Marine and U.S. Air Force aircraft had been providing close air support since the early morning. In one of the missions, the

An aerial view of the A Shau Special Forces Camp near the Laotian border in western Thua Thien Province before the assault on the camp by the 95th NVA Regiment. The surrounding mountains combined with heavy clouds to hinder allied relief and evacuation efforts.

U.S. Air Force Photo 96256

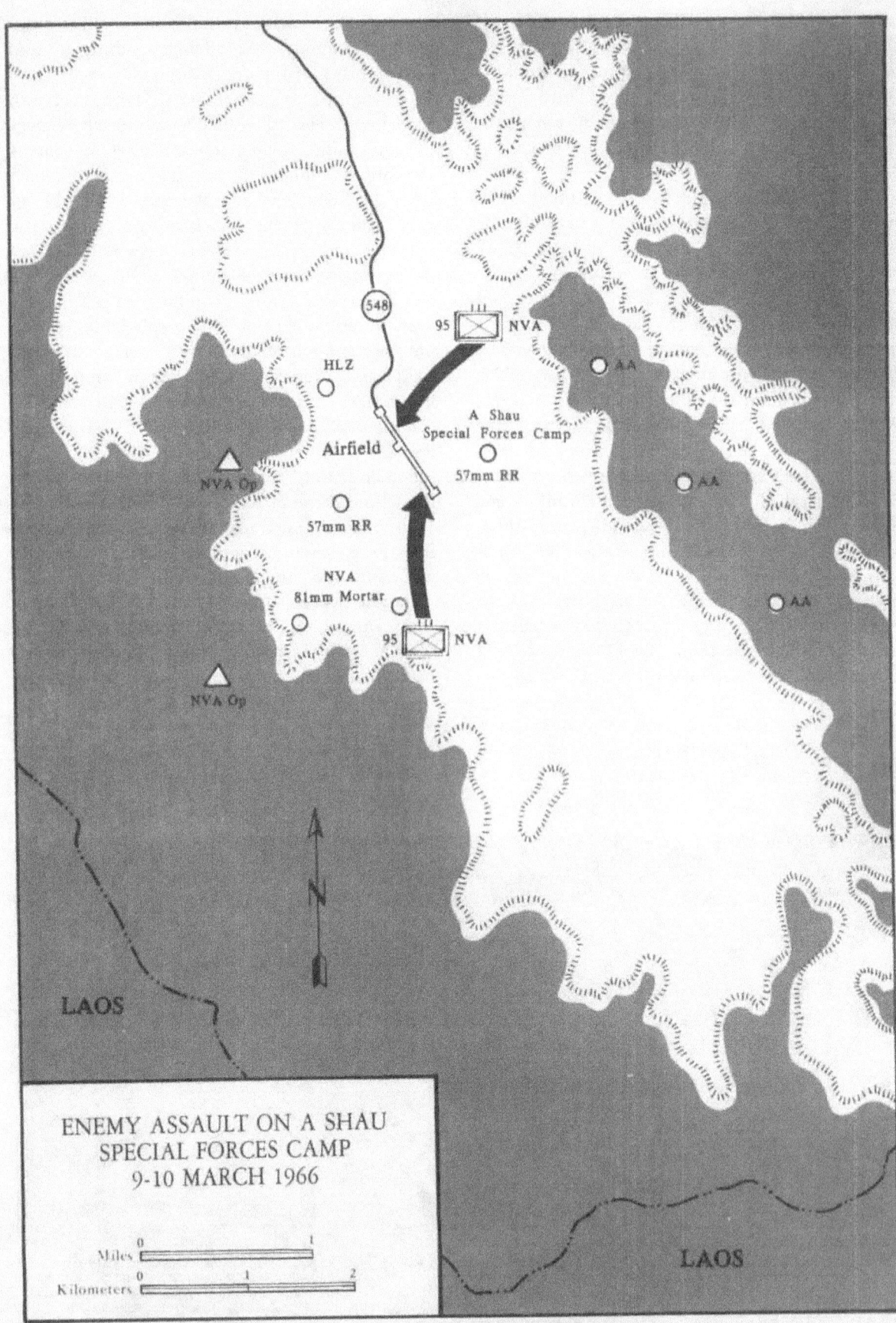

ENEMY ASSAULT ON A SHAU
SPECIAL FORCES CAMP
9-10 MARCH 1966

Marines lost an A-4 Skyhawk from MAG-12. The pilot, 1st Lieutenant Augusto M. Xavier, the leader of a two-plane flight from Chu Lai, arrived over the camp in predawn darkness and ordered his wingman to orbit above the cloud cover. Xavier descended through the overcast under the glow of parachute flares dropped by an Air Force C-123. He maneuvered his Skyhawk around the mountains and made a low-level bombing pass on the enemy positions. In the face of heavy ground fire, he made a second pass, this time strafing the NVA with 20mm cannon fire. Xavier failed to pull out and crashed into the side of a mountain. For his actions, Lieutenant Xavier was posthumously awarded the Silver Star. The commander of MAG-12, Colonel Leslie E. Brown, later commented: "Xavier's performance on this mission might indeed be termed a classic in an aviator's determination to support the man on the ground."[34]

An Air Force aircraft was also lost while supporting the camp on 10 March, but the pilot was saved in an unusual rescue. Major Bernard F. Fisher from the 1st Air Commando Squadron at Pleiku led a flight of Douglas A-1E Skyraiders over A Shau. One of the Skyraiders, piloted by Major Dafford W. Myers, suffered heavy damage from ground fire. Major Myers made a forced landing on the dirt strip at A Shau and escaped seconds before the plane exploded. Major Fisher immediately called for a rescue helicopter, but then saw that the air strip below him was swarming with enemy soldiers. He then decided to rescue the downed pilot himself. Fisher landed his A-1E on the shell-cratered runway and Myers quickly scrambled into the cockpit with him. While the NVA fired at the aircraft, Fisher gunned his engine and successfully took off. For his action, Major Fisher was later awarded the Medal of Honor.

Despite the heroics of the Marine and Air Force aviators, the situation on the ground for the A Shau defenders continued to deteriorate. Shortly after noon, they radioed "Need reinforcements—without them kiss us goodby," and 20 minutes later sent the message "Do not have area where they can land reinforcements."[35] The options open to the allied command in response to these appeals were limited. Given the miserable weather, marginal flying conditions, mountainous terrain, and concentrated enemy antiaircraft and ground strength in the area, the helilifting of reinforcements into the camp was now out of the question. Two choices remained: to attempt a helicopter evacuation of the trapped garrison, or to tell the defenders to break out and escape the best they could.

Later in the afternoon of 10 March, General Walt, recently promoted to lieutenant general and just back from leave, chaired an emergency meeting at III MAF Headquarters on the A Shau situation. All of Walt's senior officers were present at the conference; Lieutenant General John A. Heintges, Deputy Commander, USMACV, represented General Westmoreland, and General Chuan was the Vietnamese I Corps command representative. Brigadier General Carl, who earlier in the day had made another reconnaissance flight over A Shau in his UH-1E and, in fact, had been 20-minutes' flying time from A Shau when Major Fisher made his dramatic rescue, recommended the immediate evacuation of the camp. Having witnessesed the low overcast and heavy antiaircraft fire in the area, he warned that the Marines stood the chance of losing one out of every four helicopters in the evacuation attempt but believed "we could not abandon the troops encircled there."[36] Colonel Roy C. Gray, Jr., the 1st Wing operations officer, who was also at the meeting, remembered:

> The weather was lousy and there was not too much daylight left for an evacuation attempt. . . . Everything considered it was decided to have HMM-163 make an attempt to get under the weather into the valley for one last attempt. As I recall we merely called the Phu Bai squadron on the land line phone and asked them to give it a try, explaining the situation as best we could and advising that if the Special Forces types had to "bug out" they would be outside the camp over the north wall.[37]*

---

*As previously noted, General Carl and Lieutenant Colonel House have differing recollections on the events that led to the decision to order the helicopter evacuation of the camp. General Carl recalled that on the morning of the 10th he had stopped off at Phu Bai and discussed with Lieutenant Colonel House the feasibility of flying into the Special Forces camp. According to Carl, House responded that the weather had not improved and recommended against any further flights into the valley, but "would make the effort if so ordered." Carl then took off in his UH-1E and made his own reconnaissance of the area. Carl Comments, 1969. Lieutenant Colonel House, on the other hand, denied that he had any discussion with General Carl on 10 March. According to House, "I was told to go by Wing G-3, but said I would only go if ordered by the Wing Commander. Later, I received another call, 'It's an order.'" LtCol Charles A. House, Comments on drafts MS, n.d. [Jun 78] (Vietnam Comment File).

At A Shau, the defenders on the 10th continued to hold out the best they could. Under cover of the American air support, Captain Blair's forces made several unsuccessful counterattacks on North Vietnamese positions on the southern wall, but finally had to give up the attempt to dislodge the heavily entrenched enemy. At 1415, American aircraft broke up an enemy concentration east of the camp, but the North Vietnamese continued to place heavy fire on the allied defenders on the northern wall and in the communication bunker. By 1500, the end was in sight. According to Blair's account, "Almost all friendly crew-served weapons were destroyed. Very little ammunition remained. No food and water had been available for 36 hours."[38] At 1530, the defenders received word that the Marine helicopters would arrive in about an hour and a half to take them out. At approximately 1730, Blair ordered the evacuation of the camp and the establishment of a helicopter landing zone, about 300 meters north of the camp. The plan was for the able-bodied Special Forces troops and the irregulars to fight a rearguard action while the wounded were placed first on the aircraft.[39]

Shortly after 1730, Lieutenant Colonel House led 16 UH-34s from his squadron, supported by six UH-1Es from VMO-2 and fixed-wing aircraft, into the valley. According to one account, a North Vietnamese machine gun on a hill just north of A Shau opened fire on House's aircraft as he approached the camp. Veering away from the fire, the squadron commander, "noticed the survivors pouring over the parapets on the north side. . . ."[40] House then turned around and began his descent into the improvised landing zone.

There was chaos on the ground. The South Vietnamese irregulars had panicked and abandoned the wounded. They clambered over one another in order to get into the helicopter. House later stated in a television interview: "So many people wanted to get out, they hung on the cables, almost pulled the helicopters into the zone." Attempting to create a semblance of order, the Special Forces troops clubbed some of the able-bodied South Vietnamese off the aircraft with their rifle butts. When this failed, the Americans fired into the hysterical men. House observed during the television interview:

> . . . it was a hell of a thing to have to do; some of them had to be shot in order to maintain control. . . . I know of no other answers in a case of this nature. It was either that or sacrifice everybody. That's the only decision to be made.[41]*

As House's aircraft began to rise, a North Vietnamese recoilless rifle round struck its tail section, causing the helicopter to crash 200 meters from the landing zone. House and his crew then joined the Special Forces on the ground. The North Vietnamese also shot down House's wingman, 1st Lieutenant William J. Gregory. Gregory, his copilot, and crew chief survived and made their way to another helicopter, but the gunner was forced to hide in the bush. In addition to the two downed aircraft, three Marine F-4Bs, two A-4s, two UH-1Es, and three other UH-34s sustained damage, but returned to Phu Bai. With approaching darkness and deteriorating weather, the wing halted the evacuation of the camp. Only one flight had been able to get into the landing zone, but the helicopters succeeded in taking out 69 of the defenders, including four of the U.S. Army advisors.[42]

With the end of the evacuation attempt on the 10th, the survivors of the camp escaped into the jungle to avoid capture. Lieutenant Colonel House took command of a ragtag group, including his crew, the gunner from Gregory's aircraft, South Vietnamese irregulars, and Army advisors. Shortly after noon on the 11th, Marine pilots from HMM-163, searching for the evacuees, spotted House and his men in a small clearing, approximately 3,000 meters northwest of the previous landing zone. As the helicopters landed, there was once more difficulty with the CIDG, who rushed pell-mell to get on board the aircraft. House later claimed that the Special Forces had to shoot about 13 of the irregulars.[43] The Special Forces, on the other hand, denied killing any of the South Vietnamese, but declared they and some of the CIDG maintained

---

*The evidence is unclear who initiated and took part in the shooting of the Vietnamese troops. House declared in the aforementioned interview that the Special Forces troops took the initiative: "They knew the men more and they were well aware that was the only way the situation could be solved." See Transcript of Intvw, Current News, dtd 15Mar66, p. 4. The Special Forces, on the other hand, reported that Lieutenant Colonel House ordered his crew to shoot the Vietnamese. See 5th Special Forces Group AAR, Battle for A Shau, dtd 28Mar66 (Acc. No. 69A729). In a message to Washington, MACV declared that the helicopter crew chief and a Special Forces sergeant were involved in the shooting of the CIDG. See ComUSMACV msg to SecDef OASD PA, dtd 16 Mar66 (III MAF Msg & Jnl Files).

control, "by using butt strokes and firing" in front of the feet of the terror-stricken men.⁴⁴ The UH-34s succeeded in taking out about 60 of the group, including House, six other Marines, and one Special Forces soldier.⁴⁵

On the following morning, seven aircraft from HMM-163 and two from VMO-2 flew through extensive ground fire and evacuated 34 more survivors, including two Marine crewmen and five Army advisors. On the ground, the CIDG panicked and fought among themselves. One of the South Vietnamese threw a grenade, killing 10 of the struggling troops. According to the Special Forces, "U.S. personnel . . . witnessed the action, but did not participate in the shooting."⁴⁶ All of the Marine aircraft returned safely to Phu Bai, but many sustained severe damage. Captain Wilbur C. McMinn, Jr. nursed his crippled UH-34 back to base with 126 bullet holes in the aircraft. According to Lieutenant Colonel House, 21 of the 24 helicopters of this squadron eventually had to be replaced as a result of the three-day evacuation operation.⁴⁷

Following House's return to Phu Bai, CBS Correspondent John Laurence conducted an interview with the squadron commander that appeared on national television and caused some furor. In addition, syndicated columnist Jim Lucas wrote an article relating to the performance of the CIDG troops at A Shau. At the request of the Office of the Secretary of Defense, MACV and III MAF completed an investigation into the "unfavorable TV and press releases in the U.S. . . . ."⁴⁸ Lieutenant Colonel House had the dubious distinction of receiving a Navy Cross and a letter of reprimand for his part in the A Shau evacuation. According to General Carl, who presided over the invesigation, House's difficulty arose out of his statement to the press.⁴⁹ Colonel Thomas J. O'Connor, commanding officer of MAG-16 and House's immediate superior, wrote in 1978:

> I had flown with Chuck House on several missions and knew him to be a dedicated Marine. Unfortunately upon his return from A Shau he made some rather emotionally charged statements to authority about the wisdom and futility of the mission, thus the anomalous results of both a citation and disciplinary action.⁵⁰

Colonel Roy C. Gray, Jr., the wing G-3, recalled that Lieutenant Colonel House in conversation with both reporters and with senior commanders "ex-

Marine Corps Photo A194536
LtCol Charles A. House, the commander of HMM-163, whose helicopter was shot down during the evacuation of A Shau, poses at Phu Bai with U.S. Army Special Forces soldiers and South Vietnamese irregulars who survived the enemy overrunning of the base. Capt John D. Blair IV, USA, who commanded the Special Forces detachment is to the right of LtCol House.

pressed considerable bitterness and criticism of the Wing and how the mission was handled." Gray then declared that House was "probably right, but in retrospect I don't know what else there was to do except either forget A Shau or make an attempt for the pickup of survivors as was done."⁵¹

With the end of the helicopter evacuation of A Shau on 12 March, those survivors who escaped the enemy attack and missed the airlift had little choice but to try to make the long trek over the mountains to friendly lines. For the allies, the battle had been costly. In addition to aircraft lost during the fighting, 248 out of the total garrison of 434 were either missing or dead, including five U.S. Special Forces soldiers. Marine helicopters, mostly from HMM-163, flew 131 sorties from 9-12 March and brought back 161 of the 186 survivors, including 10 of the 12 Army advisors who got out. The fall of the A Shau Camp opened the way for increased enemy infiltration of men and material through the valley into central I Corps.⁵²

The Aftermath of A Shau

During and immediately after the fall of A Shau, the allied commanders in I Corps evaluated the idea of launching a combined operation into the valley. On the morning of 10 March, General Chuan, the 1st Division commander, gave serious consideration to the insertion of one of the I Corps reserve battalions, reinforced by Marines, to relieve the embattled garrison. With one battalion, the 1st Battalion, 1st Marines, on three-hour alert at Phu Bai since 9 March, III MAF on 10 March placed the 1st Battalion, 4th Marines on one-hour standby at Chu Lai for possible air movement to Phu Bai.[53]

Despite the decision of the meeting at III MAF Headquarters on the afternoon of the 10th not to send infantry reinforcements into A Shau, the Marines continued to maintain the two battalions on an alert status and strengthened the forces at Phu Bai. At 2000 on the 10th, the rear elements of the 1st Battalion, 1st Marines at Da Nang, hampered by rain and darkness, began loading their equipment on 41 trucks for movement to Phu Bai. The truck convoy departed Da Nang at 0630 on the 11th and arrived at its destination at 1330 that afternoon. The following night, III MAF ordered the deployment of the battalion command group and two companies of the 1st Battalion, 4th Marines to Phu Bai. Lieutenant Colonel Ralph E. Sullivan, the battalion commander, his headquarters, and his Companies A and B arrived at Phu Bai by KC-130 transports on 13 March. Colonel Fisher, Commanding Officer, Task Group Foxtrot, now had the principal elements of three Marine infantry battalions under his command at Phu Bai.[54]

During the next few days, the South Vietnamese pressed for a large search and destroy operation in the A Shau Valley and the reestablishment of a Special Forces camp in the area. On 15 March, General Chuan, who had just relieved General Thi as a result of a falling out between Thi and Premier Ky, urged the South Vietnamese Joint General Staff to intercede with MACV for such a course of action. Explaining that he already had committed most of his reserve forces into strategic areas near Hue that were now threatened because of the fall of the camp, Chuan wanted the Marines to make up the bulk of the attacking forces into the A Shau Valley itself.[55]

Despite Chuan's recommendation, the allied commanders finally rejected the idea of a direct assault at this time into the valley. Both Lieutenant Colonel Hatch, commanding officer of the 1st Battalion, 1st Marines, and Lieutenant Colonel Sullivan, now at Phu Bai with the two companies of his battalion, remembered that their units remained on alert for several days for an operation into the valley. Sullivan described A Shau "as a place for disasters to occur in . . ." and recalled:

> After an aerial recon, and talking to Chuck House and others, I became convinced that if two bob-tailed battalions were to be sent into A Shau, that someone had better have a string on a regiment in case we stepped in defecation. Fisher agreed, and the operation was called off.[56]

American and South Vietnamese intelligence during this period continued to show a buildup of enemy units in the two northern provinces. The U.S. Army senior advisor to the 1st ARVN Division reported to General Walt that despite the relative quiet in the division's sector, the available intelligence indicated the movement of enemy units and the possibility of a major enemy campaign in the northern two provinces. He pointed to an enemy regiment with three battalions massing near Quang Tri City and another two battalions, the *802d* and *804th* of the *1st VC Provisional Regiment*, in the Co Bi-Thanh Tan area about 15 miles west of Hue, and moving toward Route 1 and the coast. As yet, the allied commanders had no hard evidence of the intentions of the *95th Regiment*, which had just overrun the A Shau Camp.[57]

In order to obtain such information, the South Vietnamese brought into I Corps a special long-range reconnaissance group called Project Delta. The Project Delta forces consisted of six-man reconnaissance teams made up of four South Vietnamese Special Forces troops and two U.S. Army Special Forces advisors; five-man CIDG road patrols, nicknamed "roadrunner" teams; and a reaction force of South Vietnamese Army ranger companies. From 17 March through 29 March a total of 10 Project Delta reconnaissance teams, 3 roadrunner teams, and 2 ranger companies shuttled in and out of an approximately 150-square-mile operating area extending southwest of Hue to the Quang Nam-Thua Thien border. Although not entering the A Shau Valley itself, the teams penetrated the most significant infiltration corridors leading from the valley into the coastal region. Enemy gunners shot down, during the course of the inserts and extractions, two Army helicopters, and Communist antiaircraft fire forced the aborting of several missions. The reconnaissance teams spotted several enemy concentrations and called either artillery or air strikes on various occasions against such forces. Nevertheless, the teams accounted for only four confirmed enemy dead and one wounded. The results of the extended intelligence operation were tentative. Despite finding some enemy units, the teams obtained little evidence of a major NVA buildup in the area southwest of Hue. The North Vietnamese plans to exploit their A Shau victory remained obscure.[58]

Continuing Reinforcement of Phu Bai and Operation Oregon

While the deliberations over returning to A Shau continued and the Project Delta forces operated southwest of Hue, General Walt made new plans for the reinforcement of Phu Bai. In a discussion on 12 March with Marine Brigadier General William K. Jones, the director of the MACV Command Center, whom General Westmoreland had sent to Da Nang to discuss the situation with III MAF, Walt declared that he decided to position four battalions permanently at Phu Bai. Two of the battalions would be from the Korean Marine Brigade, slated to arrive later in the spring.[59] Two days later, the III MAF commander began to implement his decision to build up his northern base. He ordered Colonel Donald W. Sherman, the commanding officer of the 4th Marines, whose headquarters personnel provided most of the staff for the Chu Lai ADC command group, to prepare to move his headquarters to Phu Bai and assume control of the TAOR from Task Group Foxtrot. At the same time, Walt requested the Seventh Fleet to land BLT 3/4, which had embarked on amphibious shipping on Okinawa for return to Vietnam, at Hue/Phu Bai instead of Da Nang as originally scheduled. The same ships would then be used to reembark Lieutenant Colonel Sullivan's headquarters group and two companies for return to Chu Lai. When the ships arrived at Chu Lai, the 4th Marines Headquarters would then embark for movement to Phu Bai.[60]

On 19 March, Lieutenant Colonel Sumner A. Vale's 3d Battalion, 4th Marines debarked from amphibious shipping and arrived at Phu Bai, ending for the time being the intratheater battalion rotation program between Okinawa and Vietnam. But once more events altered Marine plans. Instead of returning to Chu Lai with the arrival of the ships, Lieutenant Colonel Sullivan's command was committed to an operation 20 miles north of Hue.

Earlier, on 17 March, General Chuan had requested III MAF to provide a Marine company for a combined operation with a South Vietnamese unit in an area south of Phong Dien, the district capital where the ARVN had killed about 50 enemy troops from the *804th VC Battalion*. General Walt, on the following day, directed Colonel Fisher, the Task Group Foxtrot commander, to make liaison with the ARVN 1st Division. That afternoon, Fisher visited the division headquarters in Hue where he learned that the target area was in the coastal plain between Route 1 and the sea some 8,000 meters north of Phong Dien, rather than south of the town as originally indicated.[61]

With the concurrence of Walt and the South Vietnamese, Colonel Fisher decided upon a battalion-size operation and to hold in reserve both a Marine and a South Vietnamese battalion. His plan for Oregon, as the operation was named, called for the helicopter insertion on the morning of 19 March of Lieutenant Colonel Sullivan's command group and Companies A and B into two landing zones, designated Eagle and Robin, located north and south respectively of Route 597, which roughly paralleled Route 1. The two Marine companies were to advance to the southeast on either side of the road and clear the hamlets of Ap Phu An and Ap Tay Hoang, some 4,000 meters from the landing zones. Allied intelligence placed two companies of the *VC 802d Battalion* with some VC local force units at an approximate strength of 250 men in the two hamlets. If Sullivan's companies made contact with the enemy, Fisher planned to reinforce the battalion with Hanifin's 2d Battalion, 1st Marines and if need be with the 3d ARVN Regiment. Other ARVN units were conducting Lam Son-245 to the north and west of the proposed Marine area of operations. Marine air and artillery and Navy gunfire were available to support the Marine infantry.[62]

Delays plagued the operation from the very beginning. Heavy cloud cover, rain, and winds on 19 March forced Colonel Fisher to cancel the helilift of Sullivan's battalion and to reschedule it for the following morning. On the 20th, heavy fog caused the task group commander to hold up the helicopter

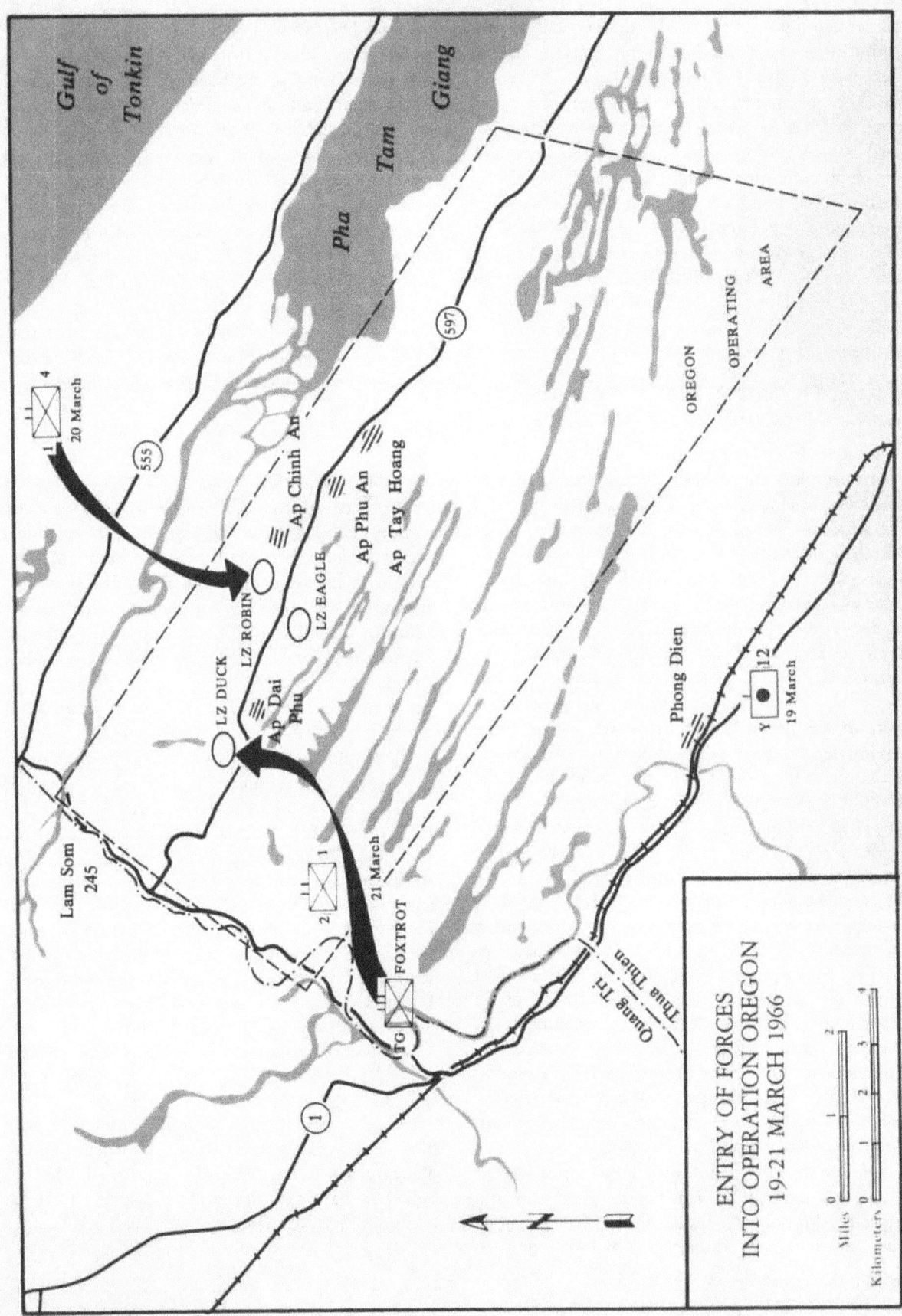

assault for two hours. At 1015, the helicopters from HMM-163 arrived in the objective area, but enemy antiaircraft fire prevented the aircraft from landing. Fisher then requested Marine artillery and air to soften up the landing zones. Provisional Battery Y, 4th Battalion, 12th Marines with six towed 155mm howitzers, which had moved by truck the morning of the previous day from Phu Bai to forward firing positions just outside of Phong Dien, responded to the request. Because of the low ceiling, Marine fixed-wing aircraft were not available until 1145. After the artillery and air bombardment, HMM-163, finally, at 1255, started to bring Lieutenant Colonel Sullivan's command group and both companies into Landing Zone Robin.[63]

Based on South Vietnamese intelligence that a large force of VC had moved east from the Lam Son-245 sector into the Marine area of operations and from the location of the enemy antiaircraft fire, Colonel Fisher ordered Lieutenant Colonel Sullivan to clear out the hamlet of Ap Dai Phu, about 1,000 meters to the west of LZ Robin before advancing to the south. After consolidating his positions around the landing zone, Sullivan was about to carry out his new orders when his Company A opened fire on two VC. The enemy soldiers evaded the Marines and escaped into some heavy brush to the east of the landing zone. According to the battalion commander, this action initiated "one of the Battalion's fiercest and hardest fought battles. . . ."[64]

Unknown to the Marines, the *802d Battalion*, with two infantry companies, supported by a heavy weapons company, had fortified the tree-shrouded hamlet of Ap Chinh An, 800 meters east of LZ Robin. Camouflaging their bunkers as simple straw houses, the enemy carefully laid out fields of fire for their automatic weapons. They surrounded the village with barbed wire and a minefield. While extending its perimeter outward from the landing zone, Company B entered the minefield and detonated a mine which wounded one Marine. Still unaware of the extent of the enemy defenses and the size of the enemy force, Sullivan attempted to maneuver both his companies to take the hamlet. The enemy countered with 61mm and 82mm mortars and heavy machine gun fire. Forced to fall back, the battalion commander requested supporting arms. Marine artillery, air, and naval gunfire from the destroyer USS *Richard B. Anderson* (DD 786) bombarded the Communist positions, but the enemy, well dug-in, continued to hold out. At the request of Lieutenant Colonel Sullivan, Colonel Fisher reinforced the battalion with Company E from the 1st Marines, which arrived in LZ Robin at 1649. After repeated unsuccessful assaults and after sustaining casualties of nine killed and 41 wounded, Lieutenant Colonel Sullivan decided to halt the attack that evening and wait for reinforcements the following morning.[65]

Colonel Fisher on the night of 20 March developed his plans for the next day. He directed an artillery command group and a battery of 105mm howitzers to join the 155mm howitzers at Phong Dien. After a massive artillery and air bombardment, Lieutenant Colonel Sullivan would renew his assault on Ap Chinh An. Fisher planned to helilift Lieutenant Colonel Hanifin's 2d Battalion, 1st Marines into a landing zone, called LZ Duck, some 3,000 meters west of Robin. Hanifin's battalion would first clear the village of Ap Dai Phu and then reinforce Sullivan's attack on Ap Chinh An.[66]

A dense morning fog prevented air strikes in the objective area on 21 March, but Marine artillery laid down a heavy barrage on suspected enemy positions. After the artillery fire lifted, Lieutenant Colonel Sullivan's 1st Battalion finally took Ap Chinh An against minor enemy resistance. Taking advantage of the darkness and fog, the bulk of the enemy force had moved out of the hamlet, leaving only a small rear-guard to harass the Marines. The fog also delayed the arrival of Lieutenant Colonel Hanifin's battalion into LZ Duck until 1115. Hanifin's battalion met no opposition and was able to clear its objectives without incident. Colonel Fisher arrived in LZ Duck later in the day and established his CP with the two Marine battalions.[67]

For the next two days, Task Group Foxtrot and its two Marine battalions, reinforced on the 22d by two South Vietnamese battalions, remained in the Oregon objective area. The 2d Battalion operated in the northwest sector while Sullivan's battalion advanced to the southeast, as originally planned, toward blocking positions established by the South Vietnamese battalions. Encountering only an occasional straggler, neither battalion met with any serious resistance. The operation officially came to end at 1130 on 23 March. Colonel Fisher and Hanifin's battalion returned to Phu Bai while Sullivan's unit remained in the Operation Oregon sector for a few more days.

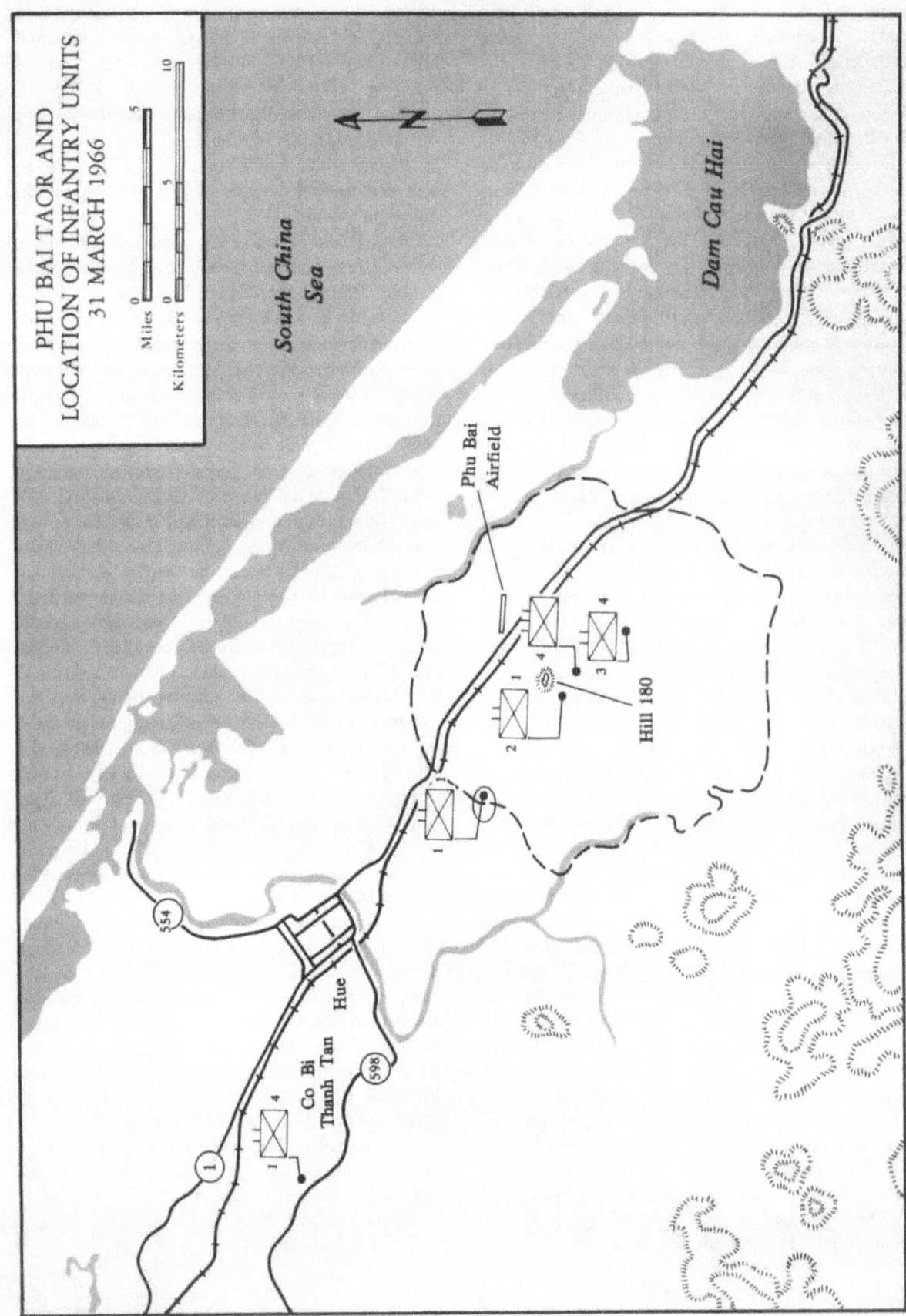

For the four-day operation, the Marines sustained casualties of 11 dead and 45 wounded while killing at least 48 of the enemy and taking eight prisoners. Estimates of enemy dead were as high as 100. All of the Marine casualties occurred in the heavy fighting for Ap Chinh An. Supporting arms accounted for most of the enemy dead. Lieutenant Colonel Rudzis, the commanding officer of the 4th Battalion, 12th Marines, recalled several years later that his provisional 155mm battery during the operation fired on a VC machine gun bunker "and scored a direct hit on the first volley of fire."[68] In his analysis of the operation, Colonel Fisher observed that the weather was a large factor, denying the Marines the advantage of surprise. Fisher also remarked that the lightness of Sullivan's assault battalion limited the Marines' maneuverability once contact was made.[69] Moreover, the Marines had encountered a seasoned and well-trained foe. Lieutenant Colonel Sullivan grudgingly complimented his enemy, declaring, "The tactics they utilized were not uncommon to good soldiering."[70]

With the completion of Operation Oregon, the new changes in command at the Phu Bai enclave were about to take place. As planned, on 28 March, Colonel Sherman, whose 4th Marines Headquarters had arrived from Chu Lai, opened his command post at Phu Bai. Colonel Fisher dissolved Task Group Foxtrot and returned to Da Nang and the 3d Marines. At about the same time, Lieutenant Colonel Leslie L. Page's 3d Battalion, 12th Marines Headquarters assumed control of the Phu Bai artillery from Lieutenant Colonel Rudzis' 4th Battalion. Lieutenant Colonel Rudzis and his headquarters personnel departed on 29 March for Da Nang where he established his new CP. The Marines had reinforced Phu Bai with two reconnaissance companies, B and D, from the 3d Reconnaissance Battalion, which on the 28th formed Provisional Reconnaissance Group B, under the Company B commander, Captain James L. Compton. By the end of the month, the Marine forces at Phu Bai numbered nearly 6,400 men including four infantry battalions, a helicopter squadron, the artillery battalion, the reconnaissance group, and other supporting units.[71]

Responsible for the defense of the northern base, Colonel Sherman assigned three of the battalions within the TAOR, and one outside, protecting the northwestern approaches. The 1st Battalion, 1st Marines was in the western sector; the 2d Battalion, 1st Marines had the defense of the Phu Bai vital area; and the 3d Battalion, 4th Marines operated in the southern portion of the TAOR. On 27 March, Lieutenant Colonel Sullivan's battalion had moved from the Oregon area to the Co Bi-Thanh Tan region west of Hue. From there, the battalion, together with two artillery batteries located 2,500 meters to the south of its postion, was able to support and provide a quick reaction force for the Marine reconnaissance teams operating northwest of Phu Bai.[72]

Despite the Marine buildup at Phu Bai, III MAF and MACV still differed about the extent of the enemy threat in the northern two provinces. General Walt believed that the successful operations earlier in the month together with the buildup of his northern forces had combined to contain the enemy.[73] Although A Shau had fallen, there was no apparent attempt by the *95th NVA Regiment* to move toward the coast. On the other hand, General Westmoreland's intelligence staff spoke of a major enemy offensive in the north, referring to the formation of a new enemy division and other units and a "known plan to attack Phu Bai."[74] In a meeting with General Walt on 24 March at Chu Lai, Westmoreland expressed his concern that the fall of A Shau exposed the I Corps western flank to the enemy. He also pointed to reports of NVA troops in the DMZ and near the Khe Sanh Special Forces Camp in northwestern Quang Tri Province as evidence that the enemy was on the move.[75] The Marines continued their close watch over developments in the north.

PART II
CRISIS AND WAR IN CENTRAL I CORPS, SPRING 1966

CHAPTER 5
A Troubled Spring

The Beginnings of the Political Crisis—Restructuring the Command—The Beginnings of the Da Nang Offensive—"Keep Out . . . Da Nang Has Troubles"

The Beginnings of the Political Crisis

The increasing threat from the north during the spring of 1966 was a major concern, but an internal South Vietnamese political crisis in I Corps overshadowed the Communist buildup. Beneath the outward facade of national unity, several groups were dissatisfied with the military regime in Saigon. Deposed and disgruntled politicians maneuvered to restore civilian authority. Various Buddhist leaders criticized the National Leadership Committee or Directorate and demanded a national assembly. Within the government itself, military factions jockeyed for position. Compounding these rivalries were the traditional schisms between "northerners" and "southerners," and between Catholics and Buddhists. These elements of disharmony threatened the delicate fabric of South Vietnamese political cohesiveness.

Until the end of February, Premier Ky managed to keep his political opponents off-balance by granting piecemeal concessions. He promised a constitution to be approved by a referendum, followed by creation of a representative government; this reform process would take over a year to implement. The referendum on the constitution was not to be held until October 1966, and elections to any resulting national assembly would not take place until sometime in 1967. In effect, Ky was offering his rivals the possibility of power sometime in the future, while he and his supporters remained at the helm for an indefinite period.

The South Vietnamese Premier viewed General Thi, the I Corps commander, as his most dangerous potential rival. Born of peasant stock and native to the region, Thi was popular with both his troops and the people of I Corps. He capitalized on this sentiment, as well as the population's traditional distrust of Saigon, and carved out his own power base, centered in Hue where he maintained his residence. During 1966, Thi continued to consolidate his position in I Corps by appointing officials personally loyal to him, including a new mayor of Da Nang, a civilian physician with little administrative experience, Dr. Nguyen Van Man.

After his return from the Honolulu Conference, General Ky viewed the existing political situation in I Corps with increasing alarm. On 3 March, the premier flew to Hue in order personally to investigate allegations that Thi was directing agitation against the government. In a lively confrontation, Ky and the I Corps commander exchanged charges and countercharges; Premier Ky promptly returned to Saigon and called for a special meeting of the National Leadership Council to settle the dispute.

At the extraordinary session of the Council which assembled on 10 March, Ky asked his military colleagues for a formal vote of confidence. He further

LtGen Nguyen Chanh Thi, the South Vietnamese I Corps commander, presents a captured enemy weapon to Gen Wallace M. Greene, Jr., Commandant of the Marine Corps, during the latter's visit in January 1966. The removal of Gen Thi in March was to trigger the spring political crisis.

Marine Corps Photo A186694

stated that he would resign if Thi was not stripped of his command. In a secret ballot the majority of the Council backed the premier and called for Thi's dismissal on grounds of insubordination. The deposed I Corps commander, present during the proceedings, accepted the decision gracefully. On 11 March, a government spokesman announced that General Thi had requested sick leave because of "sinus trouble." Brigadier General Nguyen Van Chuan, the 1st ARVN Division commanding general, became the new I Corps commander and Brigadier General Pham Xuan Nhuan replaced Chuan as division commander.[1]

The removal of General Thi caused an immediate shock wave throughout I Corps. On the announcement of his removal, approximately 2,000 persons, including soldiers, marched through the streets of Da Nang in protest. Soon afterward, elements loyal to the ousted general and other factions opposed to the government, including several Buddhist groups, joined forces. A number of anti-Ky coalitions were formed in the northern cities. The one in Da Nang assumed the title of the "Military and Civilian Strug-

A Marine MP searches a South Vietnamese worker employed at the Da Nang Airbase as he departs the base. Political tensions, which included strikes by Vietnamese employees of the Americans, increased security precautions.

Marine Corps Photo A187177

gle Committee for I Corps," while a group in Hue called themselves the "Popular Forces to Struggle for the Revolution."

The "Struggle Force," as the dissident forces came to be known, immediately applied economic and political pressure on the Saigon regime. On 13 March the Struggle Committee in Da Nang called a general strike which practically paralyzed the city. No policemen reported for duty; shops, port facilities, and schools closed; and approximately 90 percent of the civilian workers at the Da Nang Airbase failed to show up for work. Large numbers of protesters held mass meetings and conducted more demonstrations.

On 15 March, Premier Ky made an unsuccessful attempt to placate the insurgents. He allowed General Thi to return to I Corps for a brief visit. Supposedly the former I Corps commander was to announce publicly that he accepted his dismissal as being in the best interest of the country. Upon his arrival, Thi was received by large enthusiastic crowds both in Da Nang and Hue. In his somewhat ambiguous addresses to the throngs, Thi expressed several reservations about the central government. Furthermore, instead of a brief visit, Thi moved into his official residence in Hue for an "extended rest." He remained in I Corps for almost two months, thus adding to the political ferment by his presence.

Restructuring the Command

Despite the internal Vietnamese political crisis, the United States continued its planned buildup in Vietnam and revamped the command structure to accommodate the needs of the growing American force. During March, the Secretary of the Navy approved the establishment of U.S. Naval Forces, Vietnam while the Air Force moved to transform the 2d Air Division into the Seventh Air Force. These two new MACV component commands were established on 1 April 1966. In the interim, General Westmoreland made some changes in his Army combat forces. On 15 March 1966, he redesignated Lieutenant General Stanley R. Larsen's command in II Corps from Field Force, Vietnam to I Field Force, Vietnam. In III Corps, he established II Field Force, Vietnam under Lieutenant General Jonathan O. Seaman. Generals Larsen and Seaman were responsible directly to General Westmoreland in his capacity as ComUSMACV for all U.S. ground operations in their respective corps operating areas.

In I Corps, similar changes were occurring in the Marine command. Throughout the first three months of 1966, units of the 1st Marine Division continued to arrive in Vietnam. Major General Fields planned to move his headquarters from Okinawa to Chu Lai at the end of March. The 1st Division was to assume responsibility for the Chu Lai TAOR while the 3d Marine Division was to retain control of the Phu Bai and Da Nang enclaves.

In March, General Walt began to restructure his command to conform to the planned transformation of III MAF into a two-division ground force supported by a large aircraft wing. On the 15th, he established the Force Logistic Command (FLC), which assumed control of the force logistic support groups at Da Nang and Chu Lai and the logistic support unit at Phu Bai. The III MAF commander named his former Chief of Staff, Colonel George C. Axtell, Jr., as the FLC commander. General Walt then abolished the 3d Marine Division command group at Chu Lai. Colonel Peatross, as the senior officer there, temporarily assumed command of the enclave awaiting the arrival of General Fields and the 1st Division Headquarters. The former assistant division commander at Chu Lai, General Platt, then replaced Colonel Axtell as the III MAF Chief of Staff.

On 18 March, General Walt relinquished direct command of the 3d Marine Division so that he could devote more time and energy to his duties as Commanding General, III MAF. Recently promoted Major General Wood B. Kyle, winner of two Silver Stars during World War II, became the new commanding general of the division. Brigadier General Lowell E. English continued as the assistant commander of the 3d Marine Division.* He assumed responsibility for Task Force Delta operations outside the Marine enclaves and later moved his headquarters to Phu Bai.

---

*Brigadier General English arrived at Da Nang in late December 1965 on very short notice from the U.S. Strike Command as the replacement for Brigadier General Melvin D. Henderson. He later wrote that he moved out of the Strike Command "with 48 hours notice to HQMC (16 Dec) and Da Nang (20 Dec)." MajGen Lowell E. English, Comments on draft MS, dtd 12Jun78 (Vietnam Comment File).

General Walt also prepared to give up his functions and responsibilities as MACV's Naval Component Commander to Rear Admiral Norvell G. Ward, who was to head the U.S. Naval Forces, Vietnam, a command that was to be established effective 1 April 1966. The Naval Support Activity, Da Nang would then come under Ward's operational control although remaining under the command of the Commander in Chief, U.S. Pacific Fleet and continuing to provide common item supply and other supporting services to III MAF.[2]

These structural changes in the command and staff had little effect on III MAF's basic mission. It remained all-inclusive. The Marines would continue to conduct military operations in I Corps "in support of and in coordination with CG, I ARVN Corps and in other areas of RVN as directed by ComUSMACV, in order to assist the GVN to defeat the VC/NVA and extend GVN control over all of South Vietnam."[3]

The Beginnings of the Da Nang Offensive

During early and mid-March, the 3d Marine Division units in the Da Nang enclave made some progress in extending government control within the TAOR. Although Colonel Fisher and many of his 3d Marines staff were attached to Task Group Foxtrot at Phu Bai during much of this period, both his 1st and 2d Battalions maintained a high level of small-unit activity at Da Nang.

In the 3d Marines northern sector, Lieutenant Colonel Robert R. Dickey III's 1st Battalion, 3d Marines conducted extensive patrols throughout its area of operations. One company operated north of the Cu De River while two companies sent out long-range patrols to the western edge of the battalion's TAOR. The remaining company maintained security for the battalion CP.

On 14 March, Lieutenant Colonel Dickey issued his operation order for Golden Fleece II, an operation to protect the spring rice harvest in his TAOR. The 1st Battalion, 9th Marines had originated the designation for this type operation during the previous fall harvest season.** Under the Golden

---

**See Shulimson and Johnson, *Marines in Vietnam, 1965*, Chapter 9.

Fleece concept, a Marine battalion protected the Vietnamese villagers harvesting their crop "by conducting day and night patrols in areas suspected to be used by VC for access to rice harvest areas; assisting local PF units to guard rice harvesters and rice storage areas as requested by village chiefs."[4] Dickey's Marines provided protection for the harvesters and the crop through the remainder of the month. Contact with the VC was minimal.

In the regiment's southern area of operations, Lieutenant Colonel William K. Horn's 2d Battalion, 3d Marines conducted more than 550 squad patrols and established over 530 night ambushes during the month of March alone. More than half of the patrols were conducted at night. Like Dickey's battalion, Horn's Marines made only limited contact with the VC. The 2d Battalion suffered casualties of six killed and 31 wounded, while killing one VC and capturing one prisoner. Despite the low-grade combat in his area of operations, Lieutenant Colonel Horn observed in his monthly chronology, ". . . numerous reports indicate VC units are moving eastward," into the 9th Marines sector.[5]

Colonel Simmons' 9th Marines was responsible for the southern approaches to Da Nang. At the beginning of March, he prepared plans for offensive operations against local VC forces that were literally entrenched within his TAOR. The regimental commander compared the VC "infrastructure" in his sector to a cancerous growth with its tentacles embedded in the hamlets. Simmons believed that the only way the Marines could root out the "cancer" was to "scrub" the hamlets clean. He observed that mere patrolling and ground sweeps would not do the job. It was:

> . . . not a matter of going from here to there. We can march from Dien Ban to Dai Loc any time of the day we want to. This didn't mean anything. You had to take apart each one of these hamlets bit by bit and see what was in there and put it together again.[6]

Simmons' concept of operations for his March offensive south of Da Nang required the regiment to continue its "vigorous clearing action down to the La Tho and Thanh Quit River line," employing County Fair search and cordon tactics. Later in the month, the 9th Marines would extend its "scrubbing" operations southward. The regiment first would concentrate its efforts around Route 4 where the ARVN maintained a number of outposts, and then gradually advance south of the confluence of the Thu Bon and Ky Lam Rivers. In these phases of the offensive, the Marines would take a 1,000-meter square or a complex of hamlets as an objective, using one or two companies to "work this area until we find what was there."[7]

At the beginning of March, the battalions of the 9th Marines started their clearing operations south of Da Nang. On the regimental western flank, Lieutenant Colonel Dorsey's 3d Battalion, 3d Marines on 5 March established its forward headquarters on Hill 55, which was later to become the regimental command post for the southward advance. The Viet Cong, nevertheless, continued to resist the battalion's clearing efforts on this important site as exemplified in the following excerpts from Lieutenant Colonel Dorsey's diary:

> On 10 March two VC killed as they attempted to infiltrate the defensive wire on Hill 55.
> On 12 March Hill 55 came under mortar attack.
> On 17 March three engineers were KIA at the water point just to the east of Hill 55 (. . .back-to-back chewings by Gen Walt and Col Simmons re security at W.P. . . .)[8]

In the 9th Marines' eastern zone of operations, Lieutenant Colonel Taylor's 3d Battalion, 9th Marines, acting on intelligence that a guerrilla platoon was in the vicinity of the Can Bien River, conducted a three-company operation at the Hoa Long village complex south of Marble Mountain. Although the Marines encountered no VC, they found evidence of recent guerrilla activity. The village chief, who accompanied the Marines, pointed out the house of a local VC and assisted in the screening of the villagers. Lieutenant Colonel Taylor observed that the presence of the village chief not only assisted in the questioning of the suspects, but also exposed the population "to a local GVN official." The battalion commander also asked that RFs or PFs be attached to his unit for such operations as these Vietnamese would ". . . remove the image of 'American occupation,' that is generated by the extended use of U.S. forces only on such operations."[9]*

---

*Colonel Carrington recalled an incident involving Lieutenant Colonel Taylor that graphically illustrated the frustrations the U.S. forces faced in telling friend from foe in the hamlets south of Da Nang. Taylor had personally been involved in a "chase to catch some enemy suspects, but had to admit that he could not prove them such after they had abandoned their weapons and were without identifying uniforms." Carrington quotes Taylor explaining to General Walt, "'Yeah. There they were, General, sweating like whores in Church.'" Col George W. Carrington, Jr., Comments on draft MS, dtd 15Jun78 (Vietnam Comment File).

A TROUBLED SPRING

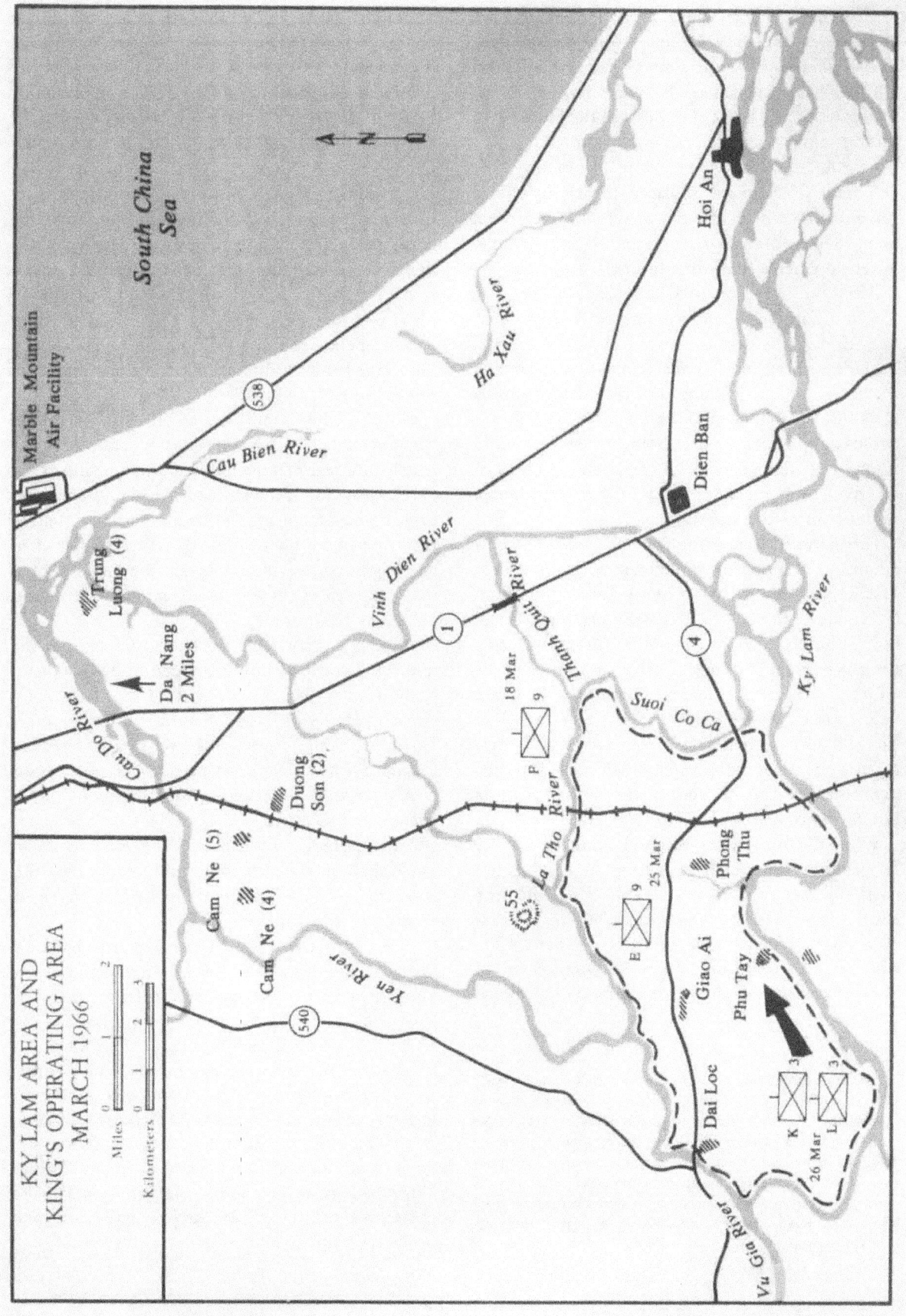

Lieutenant Colonel Donahue's 2d Battalion, 9th Marines, in the 9th Marines central sector, conducted the month's first County Fair operation on 7-8 March in the hamlet of Duong Son (2), 2,500 meters below the Cau Do and east of the railroad. In this combined operation, the Marines killed five VC. According to a captured enemy document, "The U.S. and GVN forces displaced the villagers to a general area where our cadre were isolated from them. Some of our cadre and guerrilla fighters were forced to emerge from their hiding places. . . ."[10]

After the operation in Duong Son (2), the 9th Marines' battalions conducted three more County Fairs during the next 10 days. Lieutenant Colonel Taylor's 3d Battalion, 9th Marines carried out one in the hamlet of Trung Luong (4), on a small peninsula 2,500 meters southwest of Marble Mountain. In this two-day operation, 14-15 March, Marines and ARVN officials registered 1,397 persons and provided them with identity cards. They held three suspects for further questioning.

Further west, Lieutenant Colonel Dorsey's 3d Battalion, 3d Marines, in conjunction with the ARVN 51st Regiment, held two County Fairs in the Cam Ne village complex, the scene the previous year of the notorious Zippo lighter incident.* During County Fairs on 17 March, Dorsey's Marines and the ARVN troops netted some measurable results in the hamlets of Cam Ne (4) and (5). They killed two Viet Cong, held 13 persons for further questioning, captured a VC nurse, confiscated over a ton of hidden rice, found several VC documents, and, as an extra bonus, discovered two ARVN deserters.[11]

While the 9th Marines was conducting the County Fair cordon and search operations in the hamlets north of the La Tho and Thanh Quit line, the Marine command was perfecting plans for the advance to the Ky Lam-Thu Bon Rivers. General Kyle, who assumed command of the 3d Division on 18 March, was in complete agreement with Colonel Simmons' desire to "scrub" the area south of Da Nang. He ordered his division staff to prepare an operational order for a regimental operation to relieve enemy pressure on the ARVN outposts along Route 4. The mission of the 9th Marines was to conduct "search and destroy operations in south central Quang Nam Province . . . and to provide Golden Fleece and/or Rural Construction operations as required or requested." Although officially designated as a search and destroy mission to satisfy MACV demands for battalion days in the field, the operation, codenamed Kings, was obviously intended to be a long-term occupation of the area. The Kings area of operations extended from the La Tho-Thanh Quit Line southward to the Ky Lam, with the main target the area south of Route 4.[12]

On 18 March, Company F, 9th Marines, under Captain Carl A. Reckewell, was conducting a routine search and clear mission on the northern bank of the La Tho just east of the railroad. At 1630 the Marines came under 81mm and 60mm mortar fire. After the mortar bombardment, a VC company launched three ground assaults. Captain Reckewell's men repulsed each of the enemy attacks and later found 10 enemy bodies nearby.

Although it had been scheduled for later in the month, Colonel Simmons decided to begin Operation Kings at once. He designated Lieutenant Colonel Donahue's 2d Battalion as the controlling unit. Donahue, whose command post was located in Duong Son (2), asked for permission to move his headquarters to Hill 55 to ensure "a central location and good observation of the area" for the operation. When approval was given, the 2d Battalion established its forward headquarters on the hill, temporarily displacing the command post of the 3d Battalion, 3d Marines.[13]

From 19 March through the 23d, the battalion systematically worked over the eastern sector of the Kings area of operations, extending from the La Tho River south to the Ky Lam and from the railroad east to the Suoi Co Ca River. Although reinforced by two companies of the 3d Battalion, 9th Marines, Donahue employed no more than three companies in Kings at any one time. On 23 March, as the companies moved into the 3d Battalion, 3d Marines sector west of the railroad track, Lieutenant Colonel Dorsey assumed command of the operation and also operational control of Company E, 9th Marines and his own Company M.[14]

---

*See Shulimson and Johnson, *Marines in Vietnam, 1965*, Chapter 4. The Cam Ne area continued to be a trouble spot for the Marines. Colonel Dennis commented that the Cam Ne villages were located along the Marine main supply route which "required mine-booby trap clearing at least daily—sometimes twice or three times daily. In fact, one bridge along this route was destroyed four times, including burning and dismantling." Col Nicholas J. Dennis, Comments on draft MS, n.d. [June 78] (Vietnam Comment File).

Marine Corps Photo A187763

Marines of Company H, 2d Battalion, 9th Marines search a house in a Vietnamese hamlet south of Da Nang during Operation Kings. The Marines' objective was to eliminate the VC power base in the area south of Da Nang by taking "apart each one of these hamlets bit by bit and see what was in there and put it together again."

The heaviest action occurred in the early morning of 25 March. Captain Robert J. Driver, Jr.'s Company E had established defensive positions for the night, 3,500 meters west of the railroad and 1,000 meters north of Route 4. At 0030, the Marines at a listening post heard a small force of VC, using water buffalo as a screen, attempting to infiltrate the company's perimeter. In the resulting exchange of small arms fire, the Marines killed two VC. Another listening post reported enemy movement to its front at about the same time and a Marine threw a grenade at the suspected VC. One-half hour later, a 75-round mortar barrage hit the company position. The Viet Cong followed the mortar attack with a two-company assault. Simultaneously, other enemy units placed a heavy volume of small arms fire on night positions of Company M, 9th Marines to the southwest, preventing these Marines from coming to Driver's assistance. Company E bore the brunt of repeated VC ground attacks for the next hour. With the help of 1,000 105mm rounds of supporting fire from the 2d Battalion, 12th Marines, Driver's men repulsed the VC with heavy losses. Although the enemy attack ended shortly after 0200, Marine artillery continued to fire interdiction missions, and a Marine flare plane illuminated the battlefield until 0500. As a result of the fighting, Company E suffered five killed and 19 wounded, but the Marines killed at least 40 of the enemy.[15]

The Marines identified the attacking enemy unit as the *R-20* or *Doc Lap Battalion*, which had been harassing the ARVN outposts on Route 4 since mid-February. In its March chronology, the 9th Marines made the following observations about the attack on 25 March:

> The preliminary contacts, sequence of attacks, scheme of maneuver, large-scale employment of mortars, use of a diverting force, speed and ferocity of attack once battle was joined and the very evident seeking out of the specific key targets and objectives during the attack, all indicate that this was a well-planned, deliberately executed, and hard fought action conducted by seasoned well-trained Main Force Viet Cong troops.[16]

The operation continued for three more days. On the morning of 26 March, Boeing CH-46 Sea Knight helicopters from newly arrived HMM-164 brought two companies from the 3d Battalion, 3d Marines into landing zones south of Route 4.* After artillery and fixed-wing preparation, Captain William F. Lee's Company L landed at 0730 just north of the Ky Lam River and approximately 3,700 meters southwest of where Company E had been attacked by the *Doc Lap Battalion*. Company K under Captain Lyndell M. Orsburn landed two hours later, 1,500 meters north of Company L's landing zone. The two companies then advanced along a northeasterly axis toward Route 4. At about 1400, Captain Lee's company met heavy resistance from VC, who fought from well-prepared positions near Phu Tay (3). Lee asked for close air support; Marine jets from MAG-11 and MAG-12 responded, dropping general purpose bombs and napalm on the VC entrenchments and then strafing them with 20mm fire. Enemy opposition ended.[17]

On 27 March, the two 3d Battalion companies renewed their advance toward Route 4, experiencing the same pattern of fighting as that of the previous day. Both companies met stiff resistance from well-entrenched VC and called in air support to destroy the enemy. After the air missions, the Marine companies proceeded with their "scouring" action south of the highway. In the meantime, Companies E and M of the 9th Marines were withdrawn from Operation Kings at midday, after completing a similar operation north of Route 4. The following day, the 28th, the entire operation came to an end when the two 3d Battalion, 3d Marines companies reached Route 4, their final objective. Eight Marine companies had participated in Kings, although no more than four during any given period.[18]

The results of Operation Kings were more significant than the resulting kill ratio. The 9th Marines killed at least 58 enemy, while the regiment suffered eight Marine dead and 60 wounded. The most important result was the Marine penetration for an extended period of an area that had long been dominated by the Viet Cong. Colonel Simmons later observed that, "we moved back and forth during Kings with rather good results."[19] According to the 9th Marines monthly report, the regiment cleared out:

> ... a substantial portion of the ... enemy fortification's defenses, extended the boundaries of the battalion's zones of operation, and went far toward preparing the region for the reassertion of GVN influence and control.[20]

By the end of March, the 9th Marines had made a significant enlargement of its zone of operations south of the Cau Do and its operations now extended below Route 4. Lieutenant Colonel Dorsey had moved his battalion command post back to Hill 55 and, on 29 March, Marine engineers had begun constructing the regimental command post there.

The Marines believed they had made vital progress in pacification, both as a result of Operation Kings and the County Fairs conducted during the month. Furthermore, Lieutenant Colonel Taylor's 3d Battalion, in the 9th Marines eastern sector, began its rice harvest protection mission, similar to the one conducted by the 3d Marines and also called Golden Fleece II. On 4 April, General Kyle issued an operation order which extended Golden Fleece II to all rice harvesting areas in 3d Marine Division sectors.

At this point the bubble of optimism about pacification progress suddenly burst. During the period 5-12 April, the dispute over the removal of General Thi almost caused open combat between armed factions of South Vietnamese forces. South of Da Nang, elements of the 51st ARVN Regiment, including the attached 39th Ranger Battalion, abandoned their Giao Ai and Phong Thu outposts along Route 4. At Phong Thu, the rangers left behind, unguarded, 13 tons of ordnance, including small arms ammunition, mortar rounds, and 700 antipersonnel mines. The Viet Cong helped themselves to this material. Necessarily, the 9th Marines halted all offensive operations and assumed a defensive stance.[21] The effect upon pacification was readily apparent in the I Corps National Priority Area.

An American civilian official assigned to the sector during this period, Paul Hare, commented that the Marine County Fair operations were one of the most successful security measures and ". . . probably the only way to break the back of the local VC infrastructure, but to be effective it must be a continuing operation. Needless to say, none have taken place in the last ten days or so." Hare pointed out that other factors, such as the confusing command structure, were also responsible for some of the difficulties in the National Priority Area. He wryly remarked:

---

*HMM-164, under Lieutenant Colonel Warren C. Watson, arrived in Vietnam on 7 March. It was the first CH-46 squadron assigned to Vietnam. The twin-engine, tandem-rotor Sea Knight aircraft carried almost twice the load of the UH-34s. For further discussion of the 46s, see Chapter 14.

› Basic to the problem is the relationship of Major Nhat (... Pacification Leader) and Captain Hoa (District Chief of Hoa Vang). Cadre generally speak to Major Nhat; village and hamlet chiefs to both; ARVN to Colonel Lap; RF to nobody; and the PF and (Revolutionary Cadre) to anyone who happens to talk to them. The situation is confusing to the extreme.

This, compounded with the fact that ARVN security forces now "focused on the political intrigues of Da Nang," brought pacification to a standstill.²²

"Keep Out . . . Da Nang Has Troubles"

Following General Thi's return to I Corps, the political situation deteriorated. The deposed corps commander's presence in Hue provided the "Struggle Forces" with a living symbol of their confrontation with the Saigon regime. On 23 March, they held crippling strikes in Da Nang and Hue, which seriously impeded the flow of supplies to III MAF. The Buddhist leaders demanded that the military junta resign in favor of a civilian assembly and for the first time attacked Premier Ky by name. Students seized the Hue radio station and used it to support their antigovernment agitation. Statements of dissidents began to take on anti-American overtones. While expressing gratitude for U.S. assistance, they accused the Americans of interfering in internal South Vietnamese politics by supporting the Ky administration.

General Walt attempted to keep his forces out of any involvement in the dispute, but minor incidents between the Marines and the "Struggle Forces" occurred. In one such incident on 26 March, a Marine lance corporal from the 3d Battalion, 4th Marines, assigned to the Marine security guard at the Hue City LCU ramp, tore down an anti-American banner put up by some students on a nearby wall. The student leader went to the American consulate and warned that if he "did not receive an apology within two hours," the students would destroy the United States Information Service Building. At that point, Colonel Fisher, who was still at Phu Bai as Commander, Task Group Foxtrot, arrived at the consulate to discuss the matter with the student leader, Buu Ton, and consular and other U.S. and South Vietnamese officials there. Colonel Fisher told Buu Ton that he would investigate the affair, and that if Marines were responsible, he would apologize.

Fisher insisted that the tearing down of the banner in no way reflected U.S. policy. Buu Ton was unwilling to accept Colonel Fisher's explanation and demanded to go to the LCU ramp and identify the Marine.²³

The group at the consulate, including Buu Ton and Colonel Fisher, departed for the LCU ramp area where they confronted the hapless Marine responsible for the incident. The young lance corporal apologized for his action to the student leader, but the latter refused to acknowledge it. Buu Ton had further demands. He wanted the Marine to make his apology publicly over the Hue radio and then replace the banner "in public view." Moreover the American officials were to issue orders to all U.S. personnel not to interfere or participate in South Vietnamese politics. Buu Ton then left the U.S. and South Vietnamese officials and returned to his headquarters.²⁴

After arriving back at the consulate, the American officials received instructions from the U.S. Embassy in Saigon on how to deal with the situation. There was to be "no public apology;" the Marine "would not replace the banner . . . [and] The man would be punished within the framework of U.S. military justice;" but Buu Ton "would be assured that there would be no further occurrences of this nature."²⁵

In another meeting with the student leader and South Vietnamese officials later that day, Colonel Fisher informed Buu Ton that the "Act was by an individual contrary to orders and U.S. policy and that appropriate disciplinary action would be taken by III MAF authorities." Buu Ton was still not satisfied. He stated that he had to have something "in writing to show his followers." At that stage, Colonel Geoffrey H. Boston, the U.S. Army senior advisor to the 1st ARVN Division and the subarea coordinator, entered the discussion. He promised Buu Ton "a written assurance that he would do what he could to prevent such acts in the future." Buu Ton received his letter the following day, thus ending this particular episode.²⁶

On 30 March, there occurred another incident which further inflamed relations between the U.S military and the dissident groups in I Corps. A Marine driver in Da Nang scraped the fender of a civilian vehicle on one of the city's narrow streets. The dissidents claimed two Vietnamese died in the accident and demanded that "top U.S. officials come to Da Nang within 48 hours or we will not be

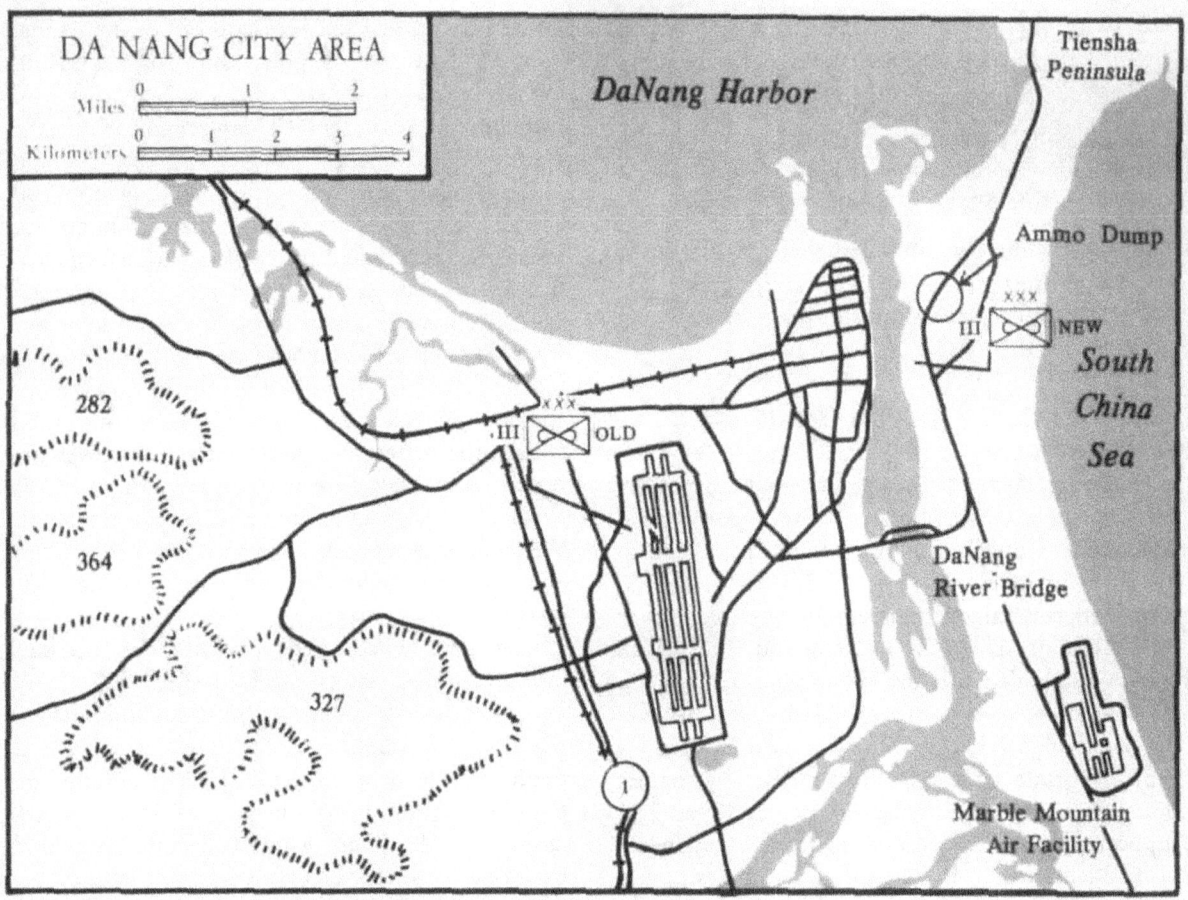

responsible for the lives and property of U.S. residents." Both the Embassy and MACV ignored the ultimatum, but it was indicative of the increasing militancy of the Struggle Forces.[27]

Since the dissidents held many of the centers of political power in I Corps, Premier Ky decided to reassert his authority. At a press conference on 3 April, he stated: "I consider Da Nang to be in the hands of the Communists and the government will organize an operation to retake . . . [the city]." The next night, Ky, accompanied by two members of the Directorate and three Vietnamese Marine battalions, flew to Da Nang on board U.S. Air Force transport aircraft. The Marines were held at the airfield and did not attempt to enter the city. General Chuan, the I Corps commander, visited Ky at the airbase on the morning of 5 April and apparently convinced the premier to change his mind about moving against the insurgents. Ky made a radio broadcast that afternoon in which he stated that the city was not under Communist control as he had first believed. Ky left for Saigon that night, but the Vietnamese Marine battalions stayed behind.[28]

With the three Vietnamese Marine battalions poised at Da Nang Airbase and the rebels in control of the city, General Walt was in a very uncomfortable position. Although not wanting to appear to be meddling in South Vietnam's internal politics, the III MAF commander wanted to keep the antagonists apart. He feared that the crisis would not only interrupt the war against the Communists, but, more importantly, that U.S. forces would become embroiled if fighting broke out between the two factions.[29]

The situation came to a climax on 9 April. Colonel Dam Quang Yeu, commander of the Quang Nam Special Sector, who openly supported the Struggle Movement, led an armored convoy of antigovernment ARVN forces equipped with four 155mm howitzers north along Route 1 from Hoi An toward Da Nang. About 1030, General Kyle directed Colonel Simmons to block the highway as close to Dien Ban as possible. The 9th Marines commander decided that the Thanh Quit Bridge, nine miles south of the airbase, was the best place to stop the convoy. An hour later, Captain Reckewell, the commander of Company F, 9th Marines, stationed one of his platoons supported by two Ontos on the northern side of the bridge. The Marines purposely had stalled a 2½-ton truck on the bridge itself. In somewhat of an understatement, the 9th Marines reported, "This block effectively served its purpose by stopping northbound vehicular traffic."[30]*

The dangers of a serious confrontation at the bridge remained. Armed American Marines faced the heavily armed South Vietnamese convoy. Colonel Yeu emplaced his 155mm howitzers and trained them on the airfield. When General Walt learned of the situation, he sent the III MAF G-3, Colonel John R. Chaisson, who had relieved Colonel Simmons when the latter assumed command of the 9th Marines, to talk over the situation with Colonel Yeu. Chaisson, a 1939 Harvard graduate, a veteran of two previous wars, and a highly articulate officer, arrived at the bridge site to meet with the South Vietnamese commander. He warned Yeu that if the latter's troops continued their advance or shelled the base, the Americans would consider it an attack upon themselves and would react accordingly. As Chaisson spoke, a flight of Marine F-8E Crusaders, armed with bombs and rockets, circled overhead. General Walt ordered Marine artillery to lay one 155mm battery and two 8-inch howitzers on the rebel positions, but to fire only on his personal command.

While the situation remained tense, Colonel Chaisson apparently convinced Colonel Yeu that aggressive action by the rebels would not be in anyone's best interests. Yeu contented himself with a show of force. Thirty minutes after Chaisson left to report back to General Walt, the ARVN commander

---

*According to one Marine officer, Captain Reckewell later told him that Colonel Yeu had threatened to use his howitzers, but Reckewell had replied: "I'll see those 155's and raise you two F-8's." General Simmons recently wrote that not finding the battalion commander, he personally led Reckewell's "company to the bridge that day." Col Paul C. Trammell, Comments on draft MS, dtd 12Jun78 and BGen Edwin H. Simmons, notation on Trammell Comments, dtd 16Jun78 (Vietnam Comment File). The battalion commander, Lieutenant Colonel Donahue, had been called earlier to the III MAF CP for a briefing on the evacuation of U.S. nationals from Da Nang.

Marine Corps Photo A187321
Marines from the 9th Marines stand outside the Hotel Da Nang as they prepare to evacuate U.S. civilians from the city during the political crisis. Using loudspeakers, radios, and telephones they directed people to the evacuation sites.

ordered his artillery unit to return to Hoi An, but Yeu and the ARVN infantry stayed where they were.[31]

Prior to the confrontation at the Thanh Quit Bridge, the Marines evacuated American civilians, U.S. military personnel, and foreign nationals from the city of Da Nang in accordance with orders from MACV. Lieutenant Colonel Donahue, the 2d Battalion, 9th Marines commander, later recalled that he was helilifted at 0200 on the morning of 9 April to the III MAF CP to attend a briefing on the planned evacuation by Colonel Chaisson "and a representative of the State Department."[32] At 0740, helicopters from MAG-16 landed two of his companies, E and H, in the northeastern sector of the city. The Marines, using radios, telephones, and loudspeakers, directed the people to the evacuation site. Marine helicopters and Navy landing craft brought 700 evacuees from Da Nang to Marine positions on the Tiensha Peninsula. By 1620, the evacuation operation was over.[33]

During the following week, there was a considerable lessening of tension in I Corps. On 10 April, General Ton That Dinh replaced General Chuan as the I Corps commander and the newly appointed officer quickly took steps to defuse the situation. He ordered all ARVN troops back to their units and moved one of the Vietnamese Marine battalions

Marine Corps Photo A421624

A Marine carries a baby for its mother as they hurry to board a waiting helicopter. During the evacuation, the Marines brought out 700 people from Da Nang City.

to Quang Ngai. On 12 April, the remaining Vietnamese Marines returned to Saigon. At the conclusion of a government-sponsored national political congress on 14 April, Chief of State Thieu announced that general elections would be held in three to five months. This decree satisfied many of the dissidents. Even the outspoken Thich Tri Quang, who had led the 1963 Buddhist revolt and was still a key Buddhist leader in Central Vietnam, called for a moratorium on strikes and demonstrations. The head of the Buddhist Institute, the moderate Tam Chau, also agreed that the Ky government should stay on until the formation of a national assembly. In Da Nang and Hue, shops reopened, civilian laborers reported for work, and governmental functions returned to normal.

This uneasy calm was short-lived. On 15 April, General Thi demanded that the Saigon government step down immediately. Mayor Man supported the demand and the rebel-controlled Da Nang and Hue radio stations repeated the verbal attacks against the Ky regime. In a move reminiscent of the 1963 Revolution against Diem, the radical Buddhist leaders announced that 60 monks and nuns were prepared to immolate themselves if Ky did not resign.

At a press conference on 7 May, Ky provided further provocation. He announced that the constituent assembly, which the government had promised within five months, would not be transformed into a national assembly. Instead that body would simply draft a constitution and be dissolved until a national assembly was elected some time in 1967. Ky's statement drew an immediate reaction. Tri Quang led a chorus of protests, and demonstrations once more broke out in Da Nang and Hue. The premier remained adamant and replaced the Director General of the National Police, a Thi supporter, with Colonel Ngoc Loan, a man loyal to Ky.

Early on the morning of 15 May, Premier Ky moved swiftly to put down the revolt in Da Nang once and for all. Charging that the Struggle Forces had committed acts of terror the previous night, Ky airlifted two Vietnamese Marine battalions and two airborne battalions to the Da Nang Airbase in South Vietnamese transport aircraft. The sudden arrival of the four battalions came as a surprise for III MAF Headquarters, especially since the city had been quiet that night. Ky had made the move without consulting any of his American advisors. Whether an actual threat to the inhabitants of Da Nang did exist at that point was immaterial. In short order government forces controlled most of the city. They secured Vietnamese I Corps Headquarters, the police station, the city hall, the ARVN garrison barracks, and the radio station, and arrested Mayor Man and several Struggle Movement leaders. The rebels still occupied the Da Nang soccer field, several pagodas, and most of Tiensha Peninsula across the river from the city. General Dinh, the I Corps commander who had been attempting to negotiate with the Struggle Forces, was not a party to the government's move. In fact, he fled from his quarters only minutes ahead of a government armored column to the asylum of III MAF Headquarters.[34]

As during the April crisis, III MAF was caught in the middle and General Walt once more attempted to mediate. He radioed Major General William B. Rosson, the MACV Chief of Staff, about the situation in Da Nang since General Westmoreland at the time was visiting CinCPac Headquarters in Honolulu. Walt told Rosson that General Dinh had the support of most of the ARVN forces in I Corps and that he recommended that the government be urged to withdraw its Marine and airborne forces from Da Nang city. Later that morning, III MAF

A TROUBLED SPRING

received the MACV reply; Deputy Ambassador William J. Porter had relayed Walt's message to Premier Ky. MACV directed Walt, to "continue to do what we are doing. . . . Use good offices to prevent bloodshed."[35]

Several incidents involving South Vietnamese aircraft and U.S. Marine ground units occurred during the morning of 15 May. Two Vietnamese Air Force aircraft strafed ARVN units on Highway 1 north of Da Nang, near Marine positions. Later that morning, a small Vietnamese Air Force observation aircraft buzzed Marine ground positions near the strategic Nam O Bridge across the Cu De River north of Da Nang. It also dropped a cannister near a Marine truck on Highway 1 which contained the message, "Keep out of Da Nang because Da Nang has troubles." In response, General Platt, the III MAF Chief of Staff, radioed the U.S. advisor with the Vietnamese Air Force units at Da Nang, "Tell VNAF from General Walt that these dangerous incidents must cease and desist. VNAF's provocative actions can lead to bloodshed. III MAF does not want bloodshed." The III MAF warning, for the time being, halted Vietnamese flights over Marine positions.[36]

The South Vietnamese Government was in no mood to compromise with the dissidents in I Corps. The Directorate rejected General Walt's advice to support the I Corps commander and to withdraw its forces from Da Nang, but on the morning of 16 May, Premier Ky replaced the I Corps Commander, General Dinh, with Major General Huynh Van Cao. Cao was not only a Catholic but had been the IV Corps commander under President Diem. His appointment hardly served to placate the militant Buddhist leaders of the Struggle Force.

The new I Corps commander soon learned the extent of dissident support in I Corps when he visited the 1st ARVN Division Headquarters in Hue on 17 May. Brigadier General Pham Xuan Nhuan, the division commander, had refused to commit himself to the government's side and conveniently was sick

South Vietnamese infantrymen supported by tanks enter Da Nang to put down the "Struggle Movement" in May. They arrested the mayor of the city and several of the leaders of the movement.

Marine Corps Photo A193990

on the 17th so that he could not meet with Cao. After leaving Nhuan's headquarters where he was briefed by the division staff, General Cao, accompanied by Colonel Archelaus Hamblen, the senior U.S. Army advisor in I Corps, and General Platt, prepared to depart for Da Nang. An angry crowd had broken into the division compound so the trio hastily boarded the U.S. Army helicopter waiting for them. As the aircraft lifted off, an ARVN lieutenant fired two pistol shots at it at point blank range. Although not hitting any of the occupants, both rounds struck the helicopter. After the second shot, the U.S. Army helicopter gunner fired a six-round burst killing the ARVN lieutenant and wounding two other Vietnamese soldiers. The Struggle Forces immediately made the dead lieutenant a "martyr" to their cause and accused the Americans of blatant interference in South Vietnamese internal affairs.

The most dramatic confrontation between the American and the dissident forces occurred the following day, 18 May, at Da Nang and involved General Walt himself. By that morning the Vietnamese Marines had pushed to the western edge of the Da Nang River Bridge which connected Da Nang with the Tiensha Peninsula. When they attempted to cross, they were fired on by Struggle Force troops entrenched on the other side. The leader of the dissident forces sent a message to General Cao that he had wired the bridge with demolitions and would destroy it if the Vietnamese Marines continued their advance. Cao relayed the message to General Walt. The bridge was a single span over which III MAF received much of its logistic support.

Indeed, all of the bridges in the Da Nang area were important. Da Nang is essentially an island city. Every exit from the city to the south, east, and northwest is by way of a major bridge and any force that controlled these points, controlled the city. General Walt, therefore, wanted to keep the Da Nang River Bridge intact and ordered Colonel Chaisson to work out a compromise between the government and the Struggle Forces.

Arriving at the bridge, the III MAF operations officer asked the Vietnamese Marine commander to pull back and allow American Marines to occupy their former positions. The Vietnamese commander readily agreed to Chaisson's proposal and Company M from the 3d Marines, then part of the airfield defense battalion, replaced the Vietnamese Marines on that side of the river. Before crossing the river to talk with the rebel leader, Chaisson asked for a reinforced squad from the 3d Battalion to meet him on the eastern side.

Colonel Chaisson then flew across the river in a Marine helicopter and began negotiations with the Struggle Force commander. He was unable to persude the Vietnamese to abandon their positions on the eastern bank. Chaisson then ordered Captain William F. Lee, the commanding officer of Company L, 3d Marines who had accompanied his reinforced squad to the other side, to move his troops into the dissident ARVN troop formation. The Americans advanced directly into the midst of the rebels and simply sat down; they made no attempt to dislodge the Vietnamese. Colonel Chaisson then boarded his helicopter and reported to General Walt.

Walt and Chaisson then returned to the bridge in Walt's staff car. According to Colonel Chaisson:

> Walt and I went back down to the west side . . . in his car and we got out. He walked out on the bridge and I went out with him. And as we got to the east side this [Vietnamese] warrant officer walked out and told him to stop. This warrant officer showed that he was going to blow it up—take the whole three of us out.

The III MAF commander tried unsuccessfully to convince the Vietnamese officer to remove the demolitions. Chaisson vividly described the confrontation between the large Marine general and the small Vietnamese officer in the following manner:

> Walt really gave him hell and was trying to initimidate him. The guy wasn't intimidating very much and so Walt said, "Well, I'm going to stay right here and send for a platoon of Marines." So he called this platoon of Marines . . . and this warrant officer . . . was holding his hand up as though he was going to give the signal to blow it and Walt stood right in there.[37]

General Walt in 1978 recalled:

> . . . the Vietnamese warrant officer said in a very commanding voice, "General we will die together." He brought his raised arm down sharply to his side. There was no doubt that he expected the bridge to blow on his signal. I shall never forget the expression on his face when his signal did not blow up the bridge and us with it.[38]

The incident ended in somewhat of an anticlimax. Chaisson later related:

> This platoon of Marines came from the west side and just came right across and went right through . . . an Army lieutenant, who'd been the advisor with this engineer outfit, went [alone] over the rail and went underneath and pulled off whatever the stuff was. And they did have it wired. Then Walt got back in his car and drove away. But

he really showed them it was a showdown and he called it and they did it.[39]

III MAF laconically reported to MACV: "After considerable debate ARVN engineers succeeded in removing the demolitions from bridge. . . . It is planned to use the bridge for civilian and U.S. military traffic commencing 19 May."[40]

Once the bridge incident was over, the focus of attention returned to the fighting in the city itself. The Struggle Forces had barricaded themselves in several pagodas and refused to surrender. The main point of resistance was the Tinh Hoi Pagoda where about 350 heavily-armed rebels held out against government troops. General Cao did not want unnecessary casualties and would not order a direct assault on the pagodas. The National Police Chief, Colonel Loan, went to the I Corps Headquarters where, according to Cao, the colonel pulled a gun and threatened his life unless Cao gave the order to attack. General Cao made a hasty retreat to the III MAF compound and asked General Walt for "asylum and transport to the United States."[41] Premier Ky did not relieve Cao; he simply named Brigadier General Du Quoc Dong as the acting I Corps commander. The following day, Ky recalled Colonel Loan to Saigon and directed the government forces not to attack the pagodas. The government troops were to encircle each stronghold and starve out the defenders.

On the Tiensha Peninsula, the situation remained tense. The Struggle Forces continued to control the eastern bank of the Da Nang River and exchanged shots with government forces on the western bank. A large ARVN ammunition dump was adjacent to the new III MAF Headquarters compound being constructed on the peninsula. Captain Dinh Tan Thanh, the commanding officer of the 519th ARVN Ordnance Company, which controlled the supply point, threatened to blow up the dump if government troops crossed the river.

To prevent this, on 20 May, General Walt told the 9th Marines to move Lieutenant Colonel Paul X. Kelley's 2d Battalion, 4th Marines, which had arrived at Da Nang from Chu Lai the previous month, to the new III MAF compound. The battalion was to occupy the site and be prepared to seize the ammunition dump which was just across the road.

Lieutenant Colonel Kelley loaded two rifle companies on trucks at Marble Mountain and, supported by a platoon of tanks, headed north. After a brief delay at a Struggle Forces' roadblock, the Marines reached their destination. While the Marines were preparing defensive positions, Captain Thanh paid a visit to Lieutenant Colonel Kelley. Thanh vaguely hinted that if the Marines would guarantee his safety and that of his men he would consider turning the dump over to the Marines. The battalion commander relayed the gist of this conversation to III MAF Headquarters.

Lieutenant Colonel Kelley had reason to be concerned about the safety of his troops. Firing across the river continued all night and into the morning of 21 May. Shortly after sunrise, a Vietnamese A-1 Skyraider made two strafing passes on the Marine positions, but no one was injured. Minutes later, two more Skyraiders fired into the compound with 20mm cannon and 2.75-inch rockets, wounding seven Marines. Apparently the Vietnamese Air Force pilots were after a rebel truck parked outside the perimeter fence, but missed their target.

General Walt warned the Vietnamese Air Force that if any further air attacks occurred, Marine jets would shoot down the Vietnamese planes. He later remembered that after the strafing incident he ordered four Marine A-4s to fly as a combat air patrol (CAP) over the four Vietnamese Skyraiders. The Vietnamese air commander then ordered:

An aerial view of the bridge connecting Da Nang with the Tiensha Peninsula. The bridge was the site of a dramatic confrontation between Gen Walt and dissident forces.

Navy Photo K-52114

> ... four more Skyraiders above our jets. I then ordered four more A-4's to fly CAP over the top of the second layer of Skyraiders. For over an hour I sat in the III MAF command center with two phones in my hand—one to the Marine air commander and the other to the Vietnamese air commander.

According to Walt, he cautioned the Vietnamese air commander:

> ... that if his planes fired one round, one rocket or dropped one bomb we would shoot all his planes out of the sky. On the other phone I told my Marine air commander to be prepared to immediately carry out my order. Finally having been convinced I meant what I said the Vietnamese commander gave orders for his planes to land at the airfield and the crisis was past.[42]

There were no further air strikes, but later that morning the 2d Battalion came under mortar attack from the rebel side. Eight more Marines were wounded. Lieutenant Colonel Kelley warned the insurgents that he would retaliate if there were any more provocations. There were none.

During the next two days, the Marines attempted to convince the ARVN dissidents to surrender the ammunition dump to the Americans. Finally at 0200 on 23 May, Captain Thanh, fearing the Vietnamese Marines were preparing to attack, told Lieutenant Colonel Kelley that he was willing to turn over the dump. For the next two hours, the officers ironed out the details of a 15-point agreement. Thanh was extremely meticulous and insisted that every word be approved by other members of the local Struggle Force committee. Kelley only insisted that the Marines be able to bring tanks into the dump, a point which Thanh conceded. After completing the final draft of the document, the two men conducted a tour of the installation. At 0530, Lieutenant Colonel Kelley brought the text of the agreement to General Walt, who gave it his approval. At 0800, two M-48 tanks followed by a Marine company entered the dump.[43]

Although not related to the incident at the ammunition depot, the entire Struggle Movement in Da Nang collapsed on 23 May. At 1400, the dissidents in the Tinh Hoi Pagodas surrendered; the loyalist troops disarmed 325 rebels, removed 33 bodies, and recovered over 1,300 weapons. All ARVN troops sympathetic to the Struggle Movement returned to their former units. The Directorate appointed Lieutenant Colonel Le Chi Cuong to replace the imprisoned Nguyen Van Man as mayor of Da Nang and by the evening of the 23d, the city had returned to normal. All told, about 150 Vietnamese on both sides were killed during the fighting in Da Nang and another 700 wounded. American casualties were 23 wounded, including 18 Marines.[44]

The end of the Struggle Movement in Da Nang apparently convinced General Thi to abandon any hope for a return to power. He conferred with General Westmoreland on 24 May and reluctantly agreed to meet with Premier Ky to discuss their differences. Three days later the two met at Chu Lai.* Thi stated that he only wanted what was best for the Vietnamese people and that he was not a puppet of the Buddhists. According to Thi, the Struggle Forces lacked discipline and he offered to cooperate fully with the premier. Ky decided that the former Corps commander would be most "helpful" if he left I Corps and shortly after the meeting Thi left for Da Lat to await reassignment. Later in the year, General Thi and his family went into exile in Washington, D.C.

Before leaving I Corps, Thi tried to persuade General Cao at Da Nang to return to I Corps Headquarters and work for a final settlement. General Cao refused since he still feared for his personal safety and that of his family. Indeed, he wrote a letter to General Westmoreland:

> ... asking for asylum in the United States where he would like "to become an American citizen, to join the Marines or the Army, to fight against the Communists. ... My wife and children will be safe in your country, and I will do my best to serve freedom and the United States."[45]

In any event, recognizing that Cao was unacceptable to Ky, the Directorate named the loyal 2d ARVN Division commander, Brigadier General Hoang Xuan Lam, I Corps commander.

Despite Thi's departure, the situation in Hue continued to deteriorate. The most radical of the Buddhist leaders had taken control. The day before the

---

*Lieutenant Colonel Alex Lee, who at the time, as a captain, commanded Company F, 7th Marines, recalled that Companies E and F of the 2d Battalion had the assignment to guard the Chu Lai strip during the meeting. According to Lee, there was "an unending stream of rumors and counterrumors concerning possible VC attack, NVA attack, and possible RVN unit attack. None of these rumors came true; however, it was a hot dusty and very tense time to wait developments with little or nothing in the way of valid information." LtCol Alex Lee, Comments on draft MS, dtd 26May78 (Vietnam Comment File).

Gen Walt (right) greets MajGen Hoang Xuan Lam (left), upon his arrival at Da Nang to assume command of I Corps. Lam, the former Commanding General, 2d ARVN Division, was the last in a rapid succession of I Corps commanders after the removal of Gen Thi.

Chu Lai conference, an estimated 10,000 people filed through the streets of Hue in a massive funeral procession for the young Vietnamese officer who had fired on General Cao's helicopter. After the funeral, 300 students marched on the United States Information Services Library. While police and ARVN soldiers watched, the mob smashed windows, set books and furniture ablaze, and even pried the brass lettering off the face of the library. All that remained of the modern, two-story structure was a burned-out shell.

On 29 May, the radicals employed a familiar but most gruesome tactic. A Buddhist nun sat down in front of a pagoda in Hue, doused her robe with gasoline, and set herself on fire. That night, another nun followed suit in front of the Saigon Buddhist Institute and next morning a monk did the same in Da Lat. In a press conference, Tri Quang stated that President Johnson was responsible for the fiery suicides and several days later he began a much-publicized hunger strike to protest American support of the Vietnamese Government.

On 1 June, the protests were once more aimed at the Americans. Intelligence reports indicated that a mob planned to attack the U.S. consulate at Hue. The staff therefore destroyed all classified material and evacuated the building. Before leaving, the U.S. consul contacted General Nhuan and asked for troops to protect the building. The 1st ARVN Division commander complied, but his guards hastily departed when a mob of 800 protesters stormed the mission. After first stoning the building, the mob broke down the door and set the consulate on fire with barrels of gasoline. It then moved next door where it sacked and burned the residence of the U.S. administrative assistant. The homes of the Thua

Thien province chief and other Vietnamese officials also went up in flames.

As a result of the increasing violence, the government granted additional concessions to the Buddhists. At a meeting of the Armed Forces Council on 6 June, the Directorate was enlarged to include 10 civilian members, two of whom were Buddhists. A week later, Premier Ky established a predominantly civilian 80-man People-Army Council to advise the government on political, economic, and social matters. These changes in Saigon did not satisfy the dissidents. Those Buddhists who had been installed in the government were not official representatives of the Buddhist Insitute and both Tam Chau and Tri Quang continued to voice their opposition to the existing administration.

The Buddhists also employed a nonviolent harassing tactic. In Da Nang, Hue, Quang Tri, and Qui Nhon, they began placing family altars and statues in the streets. All U.S. personnel were ordered not to touch the religious figures since the desecration of one could precipitate an incident. In Da Nang, the cluttered streets snarled traffic and General Walt restricted the use of vehicles. The movement of supplies from the piers came to a halt. The I Corps commander, General Lam, ordered the police to remove all shrines; this was accomplished in Da Nang. In Hue, however, the 1st ARVN Division troops and National Police refused to touch the altars.*

At this time, Premier Ky decided to act. He ordered General Lam to rectify the situation in Hue. On 10 June, Lam airlifted 300 riot control police to the old imperial capital. Two days later, the first of four government battalions arrived and the National Police Chief, Colonel Loan, took command of final operations against the rebels.

This time the government forces acted with restraint and there was little fighting. While clearing the streets, the Vietnamese policemen bowed three times and then carefully removed each altar. Those demonstrators who refused to disperse were quickly hustled into waiting trucks and rushed off to jail. In breaking up the few last protest marches, ARVN troops used tear gas instead of bullets. The main areas of resistance were located in the Citadel and near two Buddhist pagodas, but by the evening of 18 June Colonel Loan's unit had neutralized these strongholds. With the arrest of key rebel leaders and the ousting of General Nhuan as the 1st ARVN Division's commander, the Struggle Movement disintegrated. By morning, the government had reestablished its control of Hue.

Throughout the crisis period, General Westmoreland and Ambassador Lodge backed Premier Ky and the Directorate. Their cooperation, especially during April when the Vietnamese Marines arrived at Da Nang, placed General Walt in a difficult position. He viewed the situation differently than MACV. Walt had an extremely close relationship, both professionally and personally, with General Thi. The Marines considered Thi a good, competent commander who had been effectively prosecuting the war in I Corps. His removal was a disappointment to III MAF.[46]**

The Marines were not anti-Ky. Their main interest was to get on with the war, and each move by the government, be it a troop deployment, an inflammatory public announcement, or a removal of a key

---

*Several Marine commanders stationed near Phu Bai during this period remarked in their comments on the inconvenience caused by the Buddhist demonstrations. Colonel Samuel M. Morrow, then a major and commanding officer of the 3d Battalion, 12th Marines, remembered that ". . . the Buddhists would set shrines down the middle of Highway 1 making the passage of trucks and self-propelled artillery virtually impossible for fear of knocking one of them over. . . ." Col Samuel M. Morrow, Comments on draft MS, dtd 23May78 (Vietnam Comment File). On the other hand, Colonel Sumner A. Vale, then commanding officer of the 3d Battalion, 4th Marines, recalled that the altars ". . . were not placed in the center of the highway but enough off-center so that a 2½-ton truck could still use the road." Col Sumner A. Vale, Comments on draft MS, dtd 12Jul78 (Vietnam Comment File). Lieutenant Colonel Ralph E. Sullivan, who commanded the 1st Battalion, 4th Marines, commented that during the Buddhist difficulties in Hue, ". . . nearly all our resupply was by helo. Since ammo had first priority, we frequently got only one meal of C's per day. We made up the other two meals from captured rice, sweet corn, and peanuts." LtCol Ralph E. Sullivan, Comments on draft MS, dtd 9May78 (Vietnam Comment File).

**One veteran Marine commander observed in his comments: ". . . it would appear that the natural (and healthy) differences and professional rivalry between [U.S.] Marine and [U.S.] Army sort of played into the hands of the political differences between Ky and Thi in this one instance. Of course the geographic separation of Walt from Westmoreland, coupled with the proximity of Thi to the former and Ky to the latter, also aggravated the situation. I think it's even more to General Walt's credit that he managed this situation so expertly." Col Leon N. Utter, Comments on draft MS, dtd 13Jul78 (Vietnam Comment File).

Struggle leader, caused reverberations throughout I Corps. The parade of corps commanders through Da Nang, finally ending with the appointment of Lam, also complicated the Marine task. Colonel Chaisson, much later, expressed the fears of the Marine command when he stated:

> If we'd got ourselves in a position with the government forces fighting the local forces up there, and particularly if we had been caught in the middle of it and there'd been any significant U.S. casualties, I have a feeling that the U.S. Government would have probably pulled out of the war right then and there.[47]

The fact of the matter was that the Saigon forces put down the revolt without a full civil war, thus, Ky and the Directorate achieved temporary solidification of their government at the expense of a certain amount of instability in I Corps.

CHAPTER 6
The Advance to the Ky Lam

April Actions and Operation Georgia—The May Ky Lam Campaign—Operation Liberty

---

April Actions and Operation Georgia

The spring political crisis caused a serious disruption of Marine offensive operations at Da Nang. With the sudden arrival of Vietnamese Marine battalions at the Da Nang Airbase in April, the U.S. Marine regiments in Quang Nam Province suddenly found themselves with a new mission. They not only had to fight a war against the Communists, but also to prevent one between government troops and the Struggle Forces. Colonel Simmons compared the role of his regiment to that of the "ham in the sandwich," the filler to absorb the shock of the confrontation between the two opposing sides.[1]

This situation could only benefit the Communists. The 9th Marines had to revert to the defensive because of the threat to the security of Da Nang created by the polarization of the ARVN forces into hostile factions. With the abandonment of several government outposts along Route 4 and vast amounts of ammunition, the VC not only rearmed at GVN expense, but reentered the area the Marines had just cleared during Operation Kings.*

On 16 April, an old enemy, the *R-20 "Doc Lap" Battalion,* attacked one of the companies from Lieutenant Colonel Donahue's 2d Battalion, 9th Marines in position north of the abandoned 39th Ranger outpost at Phong Thu. Company H, commanded by Captain Everette S. Roane, had established defensive positions north of Route 4, and put a squad ambush south of the road. Suddenly, at 0400, the enemy opened up with recoilless rifle and mortar fire. Simultaneously, the enemy launched two company-size assaults, one from the southeast and the other from the southwest. The attack from the southwest, about 100 men, ran into a Marine ambush and stalled. According to the Marine squad leader, his men "shot 12-15 VC for sure—most likely more." At dawn the following morning, the squad found two enemy bodies in front of its position.[2]

The approximately 150-man force attacking from the southeast reached the north side of Route 4, but was unable to penetrate the Marine company's perimeter. As soon as the attackers crossed the road:

> The VC were like ducks in a shooting gallery. Many VC were shot as they crossed the road and went down into the paddy in front of the 2d Platoon. At one point, 22 VC bodies could be counted in that vicinity. Other VC were shot as they attempted to remove bodies. During the lulls in illumination, as bodies would be removed and more VC would cross the road, there would be more bodies.[3]

Marine aerial observers arrived overhead and as Marine artillery responded, the enemy's supporting mortars and recoilless rifles fell silent. The VC ground assault dissipated, and the attacking force broke up into small groups. Enemy probes continued along the Marine company perimeter, but, "this most likely was to cover the collection of VC casualties and the withdrawal of the main force."[4]

At first light, the Marines counted 12 enemy bodies, but estimated killing another 63. Company H had not gone unscathed, suffering seven dead and 37 wounded, largely as a result of the enemy's recoilless rifle and mortar attack.[5]

In mid-April the 9th Marines resumed the initiative, following the temporary standoff of the political crisis. Originally, the regiment planned to follow Kings with a one-battalion operation beginning on 10 April in the An Hoa region south of the Ky Lam and Thu Bon. Thus, the Marines would

---

*Colonel Nicholas J. Dennis, the commanding officer of the 3d Engineer Battalion in early 1966, commented that he vividly recalled "a request . . . for engineers to clear mines and booby traps from one of the abandoned ARVN encampments on Route 4." He and his engineers came under a night attack from the VC before the job was done and his engineers sustained four casualties, including one man killed. Col Nicholas J. Dennis, Comments on draft MS, n.d. [Jun 78] (Vietnam Comment File).

carry out General Walt's promise to Mr. Can, the An Hoa project leader, that III MAF would protect the industrial complex there. Though unable to meet the original date, the 9th Marines completed its revised order for Operation Georgia by 14 April. The mission was assigned to Lieutenant Colonel Taylor's 3d Battalion, 9th Marines.[6]

With the completion of the planning, the 9th Marines battalions began preliminary preparations for the operation. On 18 April, Lieutenant Colonel Kelley's 2d Battalion, 4th Marines, which had arrived at Da Nang three days earlier, relieved the 3d Battalion on the eastern flank of the 9th Marines area of operations. Both Lieutenant Colonel Donahue's 2d Battalion and Taylor's 3d Battalion then reentered the former Kings area of operations in conjunction with ARVN and Vietnamese militia forces. Their assignment was not only to eradicate the VC but to determine suitable LVT river-crossing sites and assembly and resupply points for the forthcoming operation.

Although the operation had not officially begun, Lieutenant Colonel Taylor established a forward base at the An Hoa airstrip on 20 April. Helicopters from MAG-16 lifted the command group and Company L from Marble Mountain while Air Force C-123s, as in Operation Mallard, flew in an artillery battery, Battery F, 12th Marines.

On the 21st, the designated date for the start of the operation, the rear headquarters and two rifle companies, supported by a platoon of LVTHs from Company B, 1st Amphibian Tractor Battalion, moved overland toward the objective area. A third company, Company I, 9th Marines, arrived at An Hoa by helicopter and Air Force transports brought in a second 105mm battery, Battery B, 12th Marines. Both fixed-wing transports and helicopters continued to fly in supplies for the An Hoa buildup. On 22 April, Company L linked up with the LVT convoy after it had crossed the Thu Bon River.

With the establishment of the An Hoa base, the battalion began the second phase of the operation. Lieutenant Colonel Taylor had divided the An Hoa region into 20 well-defined, company-size TAORs and the Marines, with local ARVN and South Vietnamese Popular Forces, began a series of actions, using tactics similar to those used during Operation Kings. Combining County Fair and Golden Fleece techniques, the Marines attempted to secure the

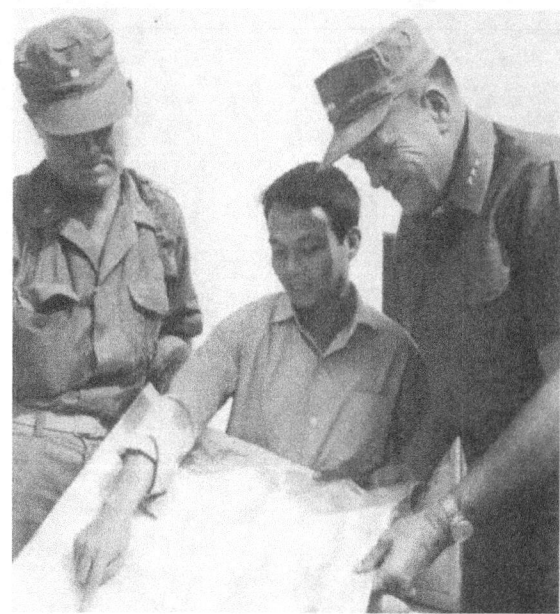
Marine Corps Photo A186933
Le Thuc Can, project leader of the An Hoa Industrial Complex (center), discusses plans with Gen Walt and LtCol William W. Taylor (left), Commanding Officer, 3d Battalion, 9th Marines. The battalion is about to reenter the An Hoa region in Operation Georgia.

hamlets surrounding the An Hoa base in order that the industrial complex there could become a reality.

Despite intelligence reports indicating the presence of the *VC V-25 (5th VC) Battalion* in the western sector of the Georgia zone of action, that area between the Vu Gia and Thu Bon Rivers, the Marines encountered little opposition through the end of April, only harassing fire and mines. Marine aerial observers and a platoon from the 3d Reconnaissance Battalion, supporting the operation, accounted for most of the VC sightings at this stage. Air observers and reconnaissance Marines "frequently detected movement of small enemy forces at long range and directed artillery fire at the VC with telling effect."[7] Major Samuel M. Morrow, commander of the provisional artillery group at An Hoa, commented that although some:

> . . . very fine targets were observed and some excellent missions . . . fired, there was a tendency on the part of these untrained observers [the reconnaissance Marines] to enter fire for effect too early and attempt to "chase the target" rather than reenter the adjustment phase. . . .[8]

Yet the reconnaissance outposts on the southern and

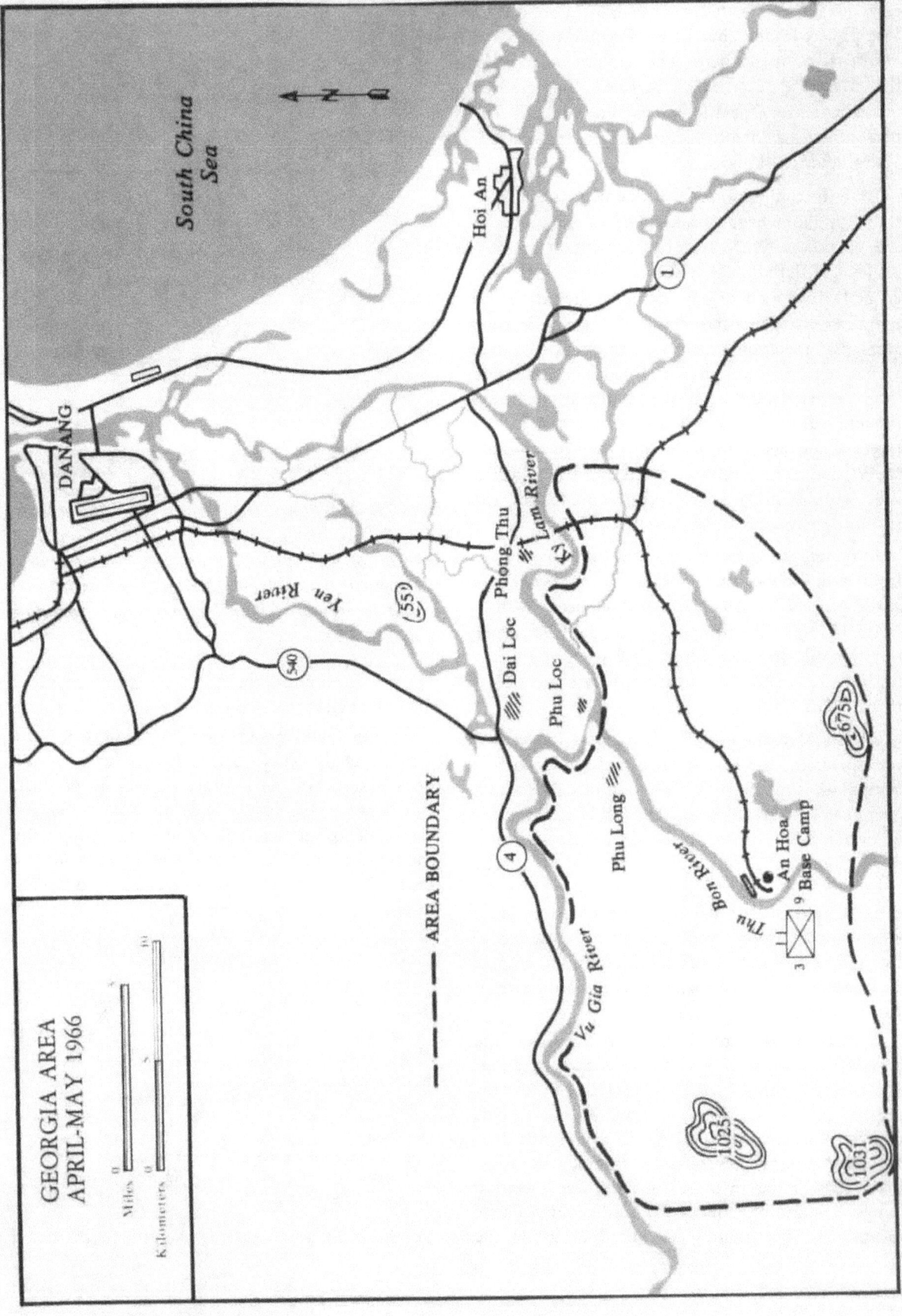

western fringes of the Georgia operating area controlled 36 artillery missions and six air strikes, resulting in an least 30 enemy dead.[9] Lieutenant Colonel Paul C. Trammell, who relieved Lieutenant Colonel Taylor in early May as the commanding officer of the 3d Battalion, later recalled that although Major Morrow expressed his doubts about the "effectiveness of the recon teams in fire adjustment," the artillery commander afterwards "conceded that the concept worked well."[10]

The heaviest action of Operation Georgia occurred on 3 May. Captain George R. Griggs' Company M, 9th Marines, which had just relieved another company during the operation, prepared to cross the Thu Bon. Its objective was the hamlet of Phu Long (1) on the northern bank of the river in the north-central sector of the Georgia area. During the river crossing, an estimated one- to two-company enemy force, later identified as being from the ubiquitous *R-20 Battalion*, opened fire on the Marine company in LVTs. In a four-hour firefight lasting through the afternoon, Griggs' company, reinforced by two other Marine companies and supported by air and artillery, finally secured Phu Long (1). LVTHs, which accompanied the Marines in the river crossing, brought direct fire upon the enemy positions and

Marine Corps Photo A187160
A 60mm mortar team from the 3d Battalion, 9th Marines in Operation Georgia has just fired off a round at a VC sniper.

A Marine appears to be watching over a pastoral scene during Operation Georgia. Smoke, however, can be seen rising where Marines have destroyed a VC bunker.
Marine Corps Photo A187042

Marine Corps Photo A187050

Marines from the 3d Battalion, 9th Marines engage the VC in a firefight during Operation Georgia. The Marine on the left appears to be reaching for a clip to reload his M14 rifle.

As Marines from the 3d Battalion watch, a VC suspect raises his hands in surrender and comes out of his bunker. The Viet Cong made effective use of bunkers, fighting holes, and underground tunnels.

Marine Corps Photo A187024

were "instrumental in neutralizing enemy fire and preventing more casualties."[11] During the engagement, the Marines suffered five dead and 54 wounded. They killed 15 of the VC and estimated that they had inflicted another 100 casualties.

Although technically ending on 10 May, Georgia, like Kings before it, was in reality an extension of the Marine area of operations. Lieutenant Colonel Trammell held his command post and two rifle companies, reinforced by an artillery battery from the 12th Marines at the An Hoa base. The final reports of Georgia indicated that a favorable kill ratio had been achieved, 103 confirmed VC dead at a cost of nine Marines killed and 94 wounded.

The May Ky Lam Campaign

Taking advantage of the truce in the political situation, on 4 May, Colonel Simmons published a plan for a renewed offensive above the Ky Lam River. The Ky Lam Campaign, named after the river, was to be a three-phased advance "to clear the regimental zone of action of organized resistance south to the line of the Thu Bon-Ky Lam-Dien Binh-Cau Lau-Hoi An Rivers."[12] At the end of May, the forward battalions were to reach Phase Line Brown, a line which extended from below Dai Loc in the west and followed the La Tho-Thanh Quit Rivers eastward, with the exception of a 2,000 meter-wide horseshoe-shaped salient extending south 5,000 meters along both sides of Route 1 to just above Dien Ban. In June, the regiment was to begin the second phase of the operation, securing all of Route 4 west of Route 1 and extending the Marines' lines down to the Ky Lam. During July, the 9th Marines, in the final phase of the campaign, was to advance southward in the region east of Route 1 and incorporate the city of Hoi An in its area of responsibility.[13]

The concept of operations for the offensive required the same "scrubbing" tactics used in Kings and Georgia. Battalions were "to deploy their companies in a diamond configuration, terrain permitting, and to employ all supporting arms imaginatively and vigorously."[14] Colonel Simmons later explained that the failure to use air and artillery in the past had resulted in needless Marine casualties. He believed that the American command had to take a realistic attitude toward civilian casualties. The selective employment of supporting arms did not by itself increase the number of civilians killed and wounded, but did cause the inhabitants of contested hamlets to abandon their homes, thus becoming refugees. Simmons viewed the refugee from his perspective as an asset, "a person who had made his election physically to move over to our side." The removal of refugees from the hamlets in the uncleared area made the Marine task of identifying and eradicating the VC that much easier. The cost of housing, feeding these refugees, and rebuilding their hamlets, if necessary, was considered a minimal price to pay.[15]

For the Ky Lam Campaign, Colonel Simmons had four infantry battalions under his operational control. These were the 2d Battalion, 4th Marines and all three 9th Marines battalions, including the 3d Battalion in An Hoa. Lieutenant Colonel William F. Doehler's 1st Battalion, 9th Marines, which had been the Da Nang Base Defense Battalion, became available for the campaign when relieved by Lieutenant Colonel Dorsey's 3d Battalion, 3d Marines. Doehler's battalion inherited Dorsey's responsibility for the 9th Marines' western sector.

The heaviest fighting in the early stages of the campaign was in Doehler's zone of action. On 10 May, he had established the battalion's forward command post in Dai Loc. His Company B, commanded by Captain Norman E. Henry, was on the eastern bank of the Vu Gia, 3,500 meters south of Dai Loc to provide a covering force for units leaving the Georgia area of operations. That morning, Company A, 9th Marines, which had been under the operational control of the 3d Battalion during Operation Georgia, crossed the Vu Gia in LVTs and rejoined its parent battalion at Dai Loc. After the river crossing, Company A prepared for a clearing operation around the town of Dai Loc, while Henry's company made preparations for a similar operation in southern Dai Loc District above the Thu Bon. Allied intelligence sources indicated that the *R-20 Battalion* had reinfiltrated this area. A report received on 11 May stated that a company of the battalion was in the hamlet of Do Nam near a small finger lake, 2,000 meters northeast of Company B's position.[16]

On the morning of 12 May, one of Henry's patrols unexpectedly came upon the enemy. The 14-man squad had left the company CP at 0630, moving east. One hour later, the patrol reported that it had come under small arms fire and captured a VC suspect. Encountering no further resistance, the Marines continued their patrol. At 0830, the squad leader radioed back that a water buffalo was in its path. Captain Henry ordered the squad to avoid the animal, but "if threatened by it, they were given permission to shoot." In the squad's next report, about 30 minutes later, the Marines stated that they had wounded the buffalo and were giving chase to finish it off. Fifteen minutes after that, the patrol reported harassing fire and seeing Viet Cong fleeing to the east "and that the patrol was giving physical pursuit." The patrol leader asked for supporting mortar fire. Company B's mortar section fired an 81mm ranging round, but the patrol was unable to observe its impact. Captain Henry ordered his mortars to cease firing, fearing that they might hit his own men. About that time, the company lost radio contact with the patrol.

The company commander sent out a second squad to follow the route of the first patrol. The second

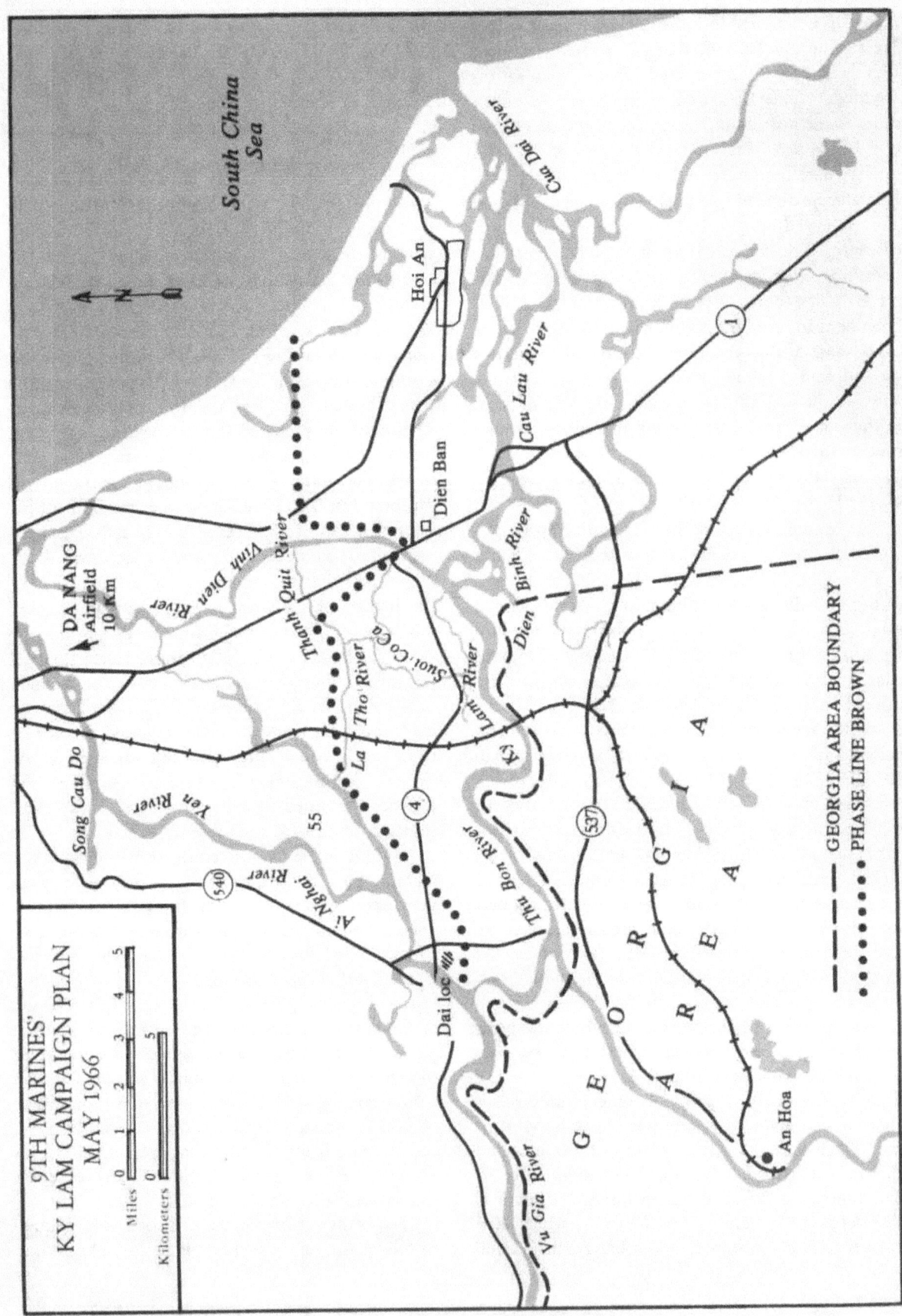

squad came under small arms and mortar fire itself. The Marines countered with mortar fire from the company base area which silenced the enemy's weapons. About 1030, the squad leader reported hearing a "heavy volume of small arms fire, mortars, M79s, and hand grenades due east of their position," near the village of Do Nam. Believing that he had found the missing Marines, he asked for an aerial observer.

Although no Marine observation aircraft was available, "an Army AO [aerial observer] happened into the area and reported an apparent firefight" in the vicinity of the action recently reported by the second squad. The Army aircraft dropped a red smoke grenade in the village of Do Nam and fired four rockets into a trenchline in front of the Marines. Making another pass, the Army AO threw out two messages to the Marines below, informing them that there were 20 VC in the trench line.

By this time, Captain Henry decided to move the rest of his company to support his embattled Marines. By 1145 he had established a 500-meter defensive line near the village of Hoa Tay, 500 meters southwest of the second squad's position. The company commander then ordered the squad, which had suffered five heat casualties, to pull back to the company lines. By 1230, the entire company was heavily engaged. The company's 81mm and 60mm mortars failed to silence the enemy's weapons and Henry asked for artillery and air support. After an artillery mission fired by the 2d Battalion, 12th Marines, the action died down for about 20 minutes. At noon, the enemy opened up again with small arms and mortars, but by this time F-4Bs from VMFA-542 were overhead. The jets' first runs on the entrenched VC in Do Nam once more temporarily silenced the enemy.

Following the air strikes, about 1320, Captain Henry's men spotted two Marines crossing an open field toward their lines. Henry ordered "a base of fire and mortar fire" to cover the two men. Both Marines were from the first patrol and badly wounded. The company commander asked them, before they went under sedation, where the rest of the squad was. The men vaguely pointed in a general direction to the northeast and said that they were all dead. Before being overrun, the wounded men claimed that the patrol had killed 30 of the enemy.

Despite poor communications, Lieutenant Colonel Doehler had been able to follow the course of the Company B action. Through "fragments of information which had sifted through," the Marine battalion commander believed that his company had encountered the *R-20 Battalion*. He had just received an intelligence report that two companies of the *R-20* had reinforced the enemy company already in the area "to ambush Marine units operating in the area." Doehler ironically remarked later that since Company B was heavily engaged at the time, "it was considered to be an accurate if not timely report."

Shortly after 1330, the 1st Battalion commander decided to reinforce his Company B. After some initial problems in obtaining helicopter support, he moved Company D and a platoon from Company A to link up with Henry's company. By 1815, the three Marine units were consolidated in a 360-degree defensive perimeter around the hamlet of Hoa Tay.

By this time, Marine air and artillery had broken the back of enemy resistance. F-4Bs, F-8s, and A-4s from VMFA-542, VMF(AW)-235, and VMA-214, respectively, joined UH-1E gunships from VMO-2 in 27 close air support missions. Nine airstrikes were run at half-hour intervals. Marine artillery had fired 242 supporting rounds. The combination of air and artillery apparently inflicted heavy casualties on the VC. According to Doehler, the supporting arms disorganized the enemy, forcing them to break up into small groups. Later interrogation of the villagers revealed that these small bands of VC had slipped back across the Thu Bon during the night of 12 May. They had forced civilians in the hamlets to carry their dead and wounded.

On the morning of 13 May, Lieutenant Colonel Doehler moved his CP into Hoa Tay and prepared to conduct a two-company search and clear operation. That afternoon Company B recovered the bodies of the 12 missing Marines near the western tip of the small finger lake. For the next two days the battalion carried out a series of cordons and searches in the area of southern Dai Loc Distrct containing the hamlets of Hoa Tay, Hoa Nam, and Giao Thuy (2) and (3).

This entire sector contained a series of heavily fortified hamlets interspersed among large, open fields. Lieutenant Colonel Doehler described the village defenses as formidable, observing:

> A complex network of trenches surrounded each of the villages. In many cases, communication trenches extended from village to village. These trenches typically were four

Marine Corps Photo A187064
Marines from Company B, 1st Battalion, 9th Marines recover the bodies of the men from the unit's lost patrol. The VC had overrun the Marine squad, killing 12 of its 14 members.

to six feet deep with firing positions located every few meters. At the bottom of the trenches, tunnels were dug back into the ground to provide overhead cover. . . . In some places bamboo-lined bunkers were found, some of which were underground and some above ground.

The Marines found the villagers of Hoa Nam and Giao Thuy "cooperative and fairly talkative as long as they were alone with an interpreter and an interrogator." They told what they knew about VC movements in the area and in several cases volunteered the names of VC guerrillas living in their hamlets.

The Marine battalion was unable to take advantage of this intelligence. The renewal of the political crisis on 15 May, signaled by the arrival of the South Vietnamese Marines at Da Nang, forced Lieutenant Colonel Doehler to cut short the operation on that date. Once more the ARVN units south of Da Nang divided into opposing factions and abandoned their outposts along Route 4. Lieutenant Colonel Doehler moved his CP back to Hill 55, and his battalion was again on the defensive.

During the first two weeks in May, the other 9th Marines' battalions conducted similar scrubbing actions in their respective sectors, but encountered only harassing fire and mines. With renewed political troubles in Da Nang, they too returned to their former positions. The regiment's offensive ground to a halt. Nevertheless, in the three-day period from 12-15 May, Doehler's battalion claimed to have killed 57 of the enemy. One later intelligence source indicated that the VC casualties may have been as high as 150 dead. The Marine battalion suffered 15 killed, 17 wounded, and 10 nonbattle casualties.*

With the Marines on the defensive south of Da Nang, the enemy tried to exploit the chaotic situation caused by the political crisis. On 21 May, Lieutenant Colonel Doehler's 1st Battalion, 9th Marines met the *R-20 Battalion* again. The enemy unit had infiltrated the hamlet of An Trach, a former model village for Marine Corps civic action, located north of Hill 55. At 1115 a Company C squad made contact with 40 to 50 VC 500 meters across the Yen River from An Trach (1). The fighting escalated into a fierce engagement extending across both banks of the river. In a seven-hour battle, Companies A and C, reinforced by Sparrow Hawk squads, M-48 tanks, and supported by air and artillery, defeated two companies of the *R-20*. According to the 3d Marine Division account:

> In the initial stages of the contact, the Viet Cong fought from trenches until they were overrun by Marines. Later, Viet Cong were seen attempting to run from the Marines, even digging frantically, to evade contact with Marine units. During the later stages . . . the Viet Cong became very confused and appeared to be without leadership.[17]

In the day's fighting, the battalion killed 53 enemy and possibly another 83, but suffered 12 dead and 31 wounded.[18]

Colonel Simmons observed that all of the regiment's significant contacts during May resulted from VC initiative. The enemy would begin the action when the Marines were at a disadvantage, either because of numbers or terrain, and in some cases because of both. The Marines, nevertheless, eventually attained the upper hand. For the entire month, the 9th Marines killed more than 270 of the enemy; 75 Marines died, 328 were wounded. Over 50 percent of the Marine casualties in May were caused by enemy mines and explosive devices, many of them made from equipment abandoned by the

---

*Colonel George W. Carrington, Jr., who during this period was the 3d Marine Division G-2, recalled, ". . . they told Bill Doehler to confirm body counts . . . he replied there is not a damn, single [enemy] body out here. We had to pause for about three full days in counting bodies, in order to allow the totals to catch up with what [was] already reported." Col George W. Carrington, Jr., Comments on draft MS, dtd 15May78 (Vietnam Comment File).

THE ADVANCE TO THE KY LAM

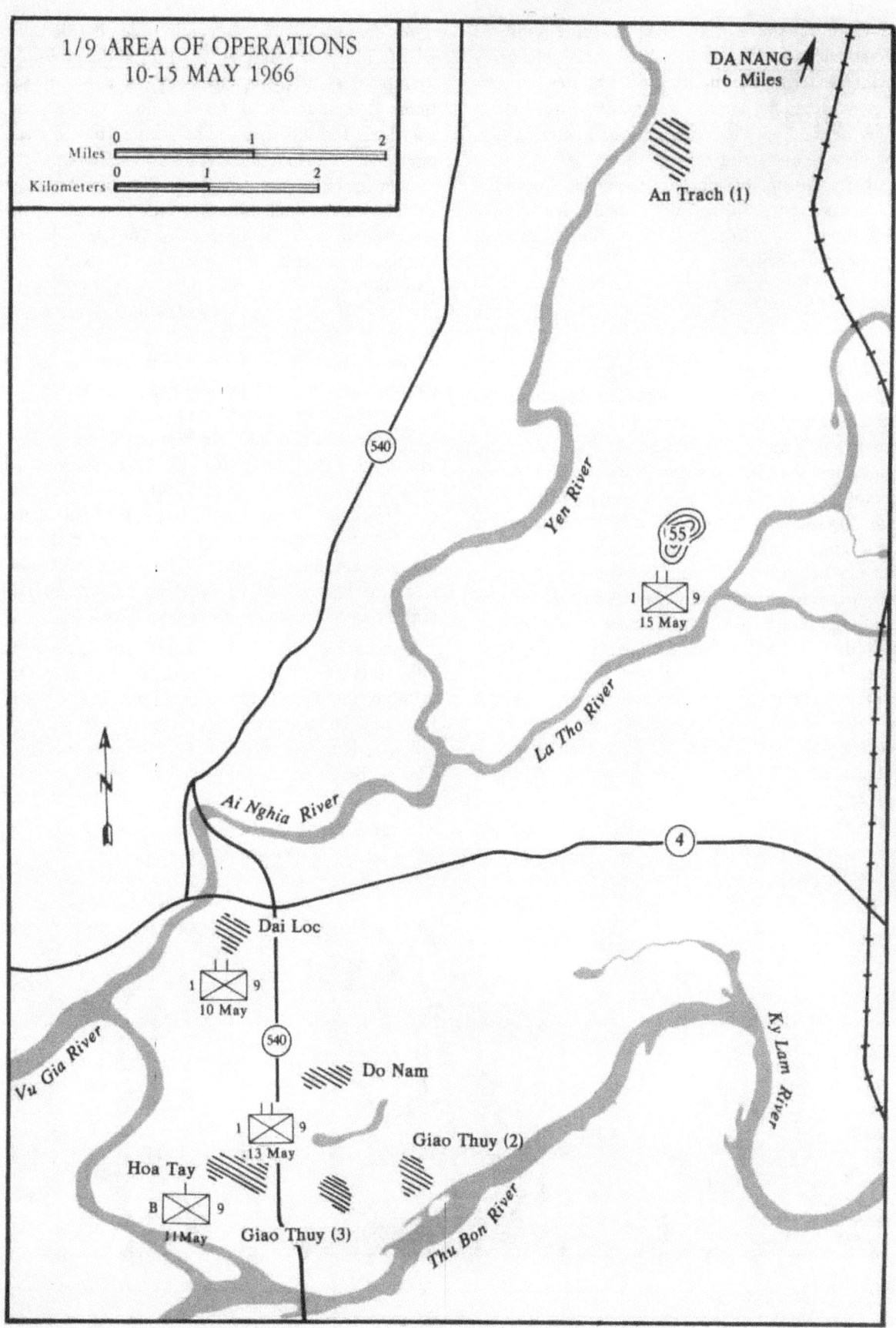

ARVN forces south of Da Nang. Colonel Simmons remarked upon the considerable increase of enemy incidents during the month, declaring that this upsurge was largely due to "the increased freedom of movement enjoyed by the Viet Cong in many outlying areas as the result of diminished GVN military activities during the periods of political instability . . . ." As a result, the regiment failed to reach Phase Line Brown on 31 May and the Ky Lam Campaign was behind schedule.[19]

Operation Liberty

With the surrender of the Struggle Forces at Da Nang and the restoration of some stability there, the 9th Marines once more renewed its offensive, coordinated with the South Vietnamese. On 2 June, Colonel Lap, who had replaced Colonel Yeu as the Quang Da Special Sector commander, visited Colonel Simmons at his CP. The South Vietnamese commander wanted the 9th Marines to resume County Fair operations in the five-village pacification area. He assured Simmons that at least one battalion from the 51st ARVN Regiment would be committed to the pacification campaign. Following Lap's visit, Colonel Simmons revised portions of his previous orders. On 5 June, he ordered his battalions to renew County Fair operations with the Vietnamese and extended the deadline for the attainment of Phase Line Brown from 31 May to 20 June.[20]

At this juncture, General Kyle decided to transform the 9th Marines Ky Lam Campaign into a division-size offensive, involving "a conventional linear type attack of all forward units to push the frontlines forward in a deliberate search and clear operation to include the cordon and search of every hamlet in the zone. . . ." He divided the Da Nang TAOR into three sectors: the cleared, the semicleared, and the uncleared. The cleared area formed an irregular arc around the Da Nang Airbase, delineated by the South China Sea to the east, the Cau Do to the south, the foothills to the west, and the Cu De River to the north. Extending the arc outward from the cleared area boundary, the semicleared sector reached the Thanh Quit River to the south, three to five kilometers into the high ground to the west and the Hai Van Pass to the north. The uncleared region consisted of the area between the La Tho-Thanh Quit Rivers and the banks of the Ky Lam-Thu Bon. Phase Line Green, the final phase line, paralleled the latter two rivers. The 3d Marine Division commander ordered that only minimum forces be held in the rear and set 30 June as the target date for reaching Phase Line Green.[21]

Continuing arrival of Marine reinforcements allowed General Kyle to make this all-out effort. On 28 May, the 1st MP Battalion arrived at Da Nang from the United States and relieved the 3d Battalion, 3d Marines of its airfield security mission. The 3d Battalion then returned to the operational

Marines of the 1st Battalion, 9th Marines sit in a captured Viet Cong barracks and training site in Dai Loc District south of Da Nang. The site is near where the Marine lost patrol was overrun.

Marine Corps Photo A187072

THE ADVANCE TO THE KY LAM

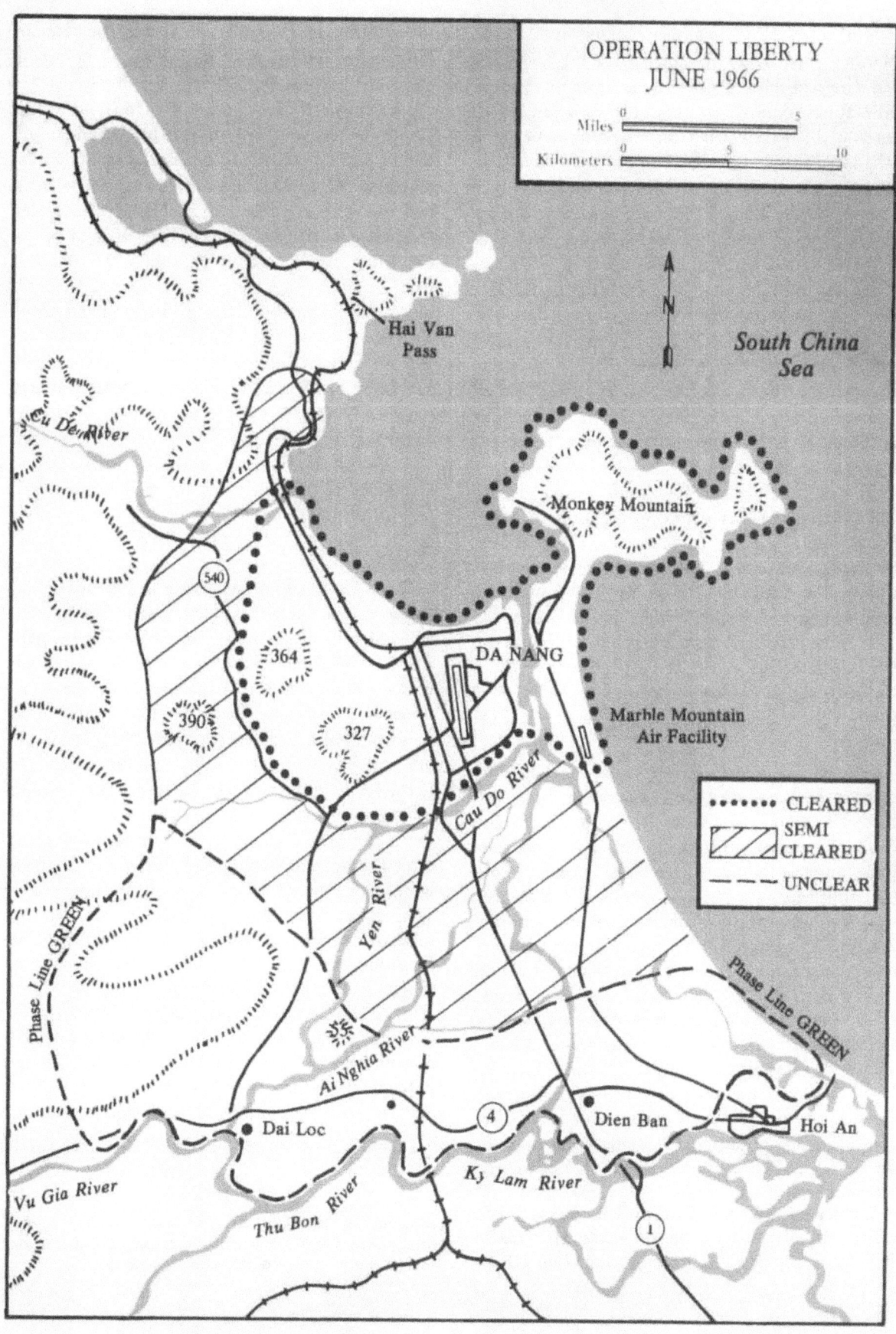

control of its parent regiment, taking over the 3d Marines western TAOR. Colonel Harold A. Hayes, Jr., who had relieved Colonel Fisher on 16 April as 3d Marines commander, at last had command of all three of his battalions. Other reinforcements were scheduled to arrive at Da Nang, or were already in place. Colonel Bryan B. Mitchell was slated to transfer his 1st Marines Headquarters from Chu Lai to Da Nang in June. In fact, two of his battalions had already moved by the end of May. The 3d Battalion, 1st Marines arrived at Da Nang on 22 May while the 1st Battalion arrived on 31 May. Both battalions were temporarily placed under the operational control of the 9th Marines. The 3d Battalion became the regimental reserve; the 1st Battalion relieved the regiment's eastern flank battalion, the 2d Battalion, 4th Marines, which rejoined its parent regiment at Phu Bai.

By mid-June General Kyle could expect to have three Marine infantry regiments consisting of eight battalions at Da Nang. He planned to reduce the extensive 9th Marines TAOR by assigning the 1st Marines to the eastern flank while the 3d Marines took over that part of the 9th Marines TAOR west of the Yen River. In effect, Kyle visualized a shoulder-to-shoulder advance to the Ky Lam. The operation, codenamed Liberty, was scheduled to begin on 7 June, with the 9th Marines bearing the brunt of the campaign in its initial stages.

Colonel Simmons divided his TAOR into company-size objective areas. His reserve battalion, the 3d Battalion, 1st Marines, was to concentrate on combined operations with ARVN and Vietnamese local forces in the five-village pacification region in the semicleared area. The 3d Battalion, 9th Marines was to continue its two-company holding action in the An Hoa region. All the remaining infantry companies were assigned to the three forward battalions, the 1st Battalion, 1st Marines on the eastern flank, the 2d Battalion, 9th Marines in the center, and the 1st Battalion, 9th Marines on the western flank. Thus each forward battalion was to consist of five infantry companies instead of the usual four, with three companies deployed to the front and two to the rear. The advancing battalions were to secure Route 4 by 20 June and reach the Ky Lam by the end of the month.[22]

Lieutenant Colonel Van D. Bell, Jr.'s 1st Battalion, 1st Marines, on the division's left, had its heaviest engagement just before Operation Liberty started. During the evening of 5 June, the battalion commander and his small mobile command group, embarked in three Ontos,* found themselves stalled on the northern fringes of Phong Ho (2), a hamlet 10,000 meters south of the Marble Mountain Air Facility and in an area "noted for their hostility toward ARVN soldiers and their allies." Bell's vehicle had run out of gas and the group had just been resupplied by helicopter. As the aircraft took off for the return trip to Marble Mountain, VC weapons from positions approximately 1,000 meters to the southwest opened fire. Using his command group with its Ontos as a blocking unit, Lieutenant Colonel Bell ordered reinforcements from his Company B, supported by LVTs and tanks, brought up from the south of Phong Ho (2). According to the battalion commander, "the result was a sound thrashing of the VC" with 11 dead enemy left on the battlefield and a number of captured weapons. Bell remembered several years afterward, "This area was never pacified and later was leveled, and the villagers removed and relocated."[23]

On 7 June Operation Liberty began with heavy preparatory artillery fires. Marine artillery neutralized 35 objective areas in front of the advancing infantry.[24] Initially, the enemy countered the Marine offensive with only small arms fire and mines. The mines were the more deadly of the two. The most significant mine incident occurred on 11 June in the 9th Marines central sector. Captain Carl A. Reckewell's Company F, 2d Battalion, 9th Marines, walked into a large minefield in a grassy plot just south of the La Tho River. Two detonations killed three Marines and wounded 21. While the wounded were being evacuated, four to five additional explosions occurred and the grass caught fire, but fortunately there were no further Marine casualties. The following day, the artillery fired a destruction mission which caused seven secondary explosions in that same field.[25]

On 15 June, the division completed its planned realignment of regiments in the TAOR. Colonel Mitchell assumed operational control of his two 1st Marines battalions and took over responsibility for

---

*The Ontos was a full-tracked, lightly armored, mobile carrier, mounting six 106mm recoilless rifles, four .50 caliber spotting rifles, and one .30 caliber machine gun. It had a crew of three and was the primary weapon of the antitank battalion.

THE ADVANCE TO THE KY LAM

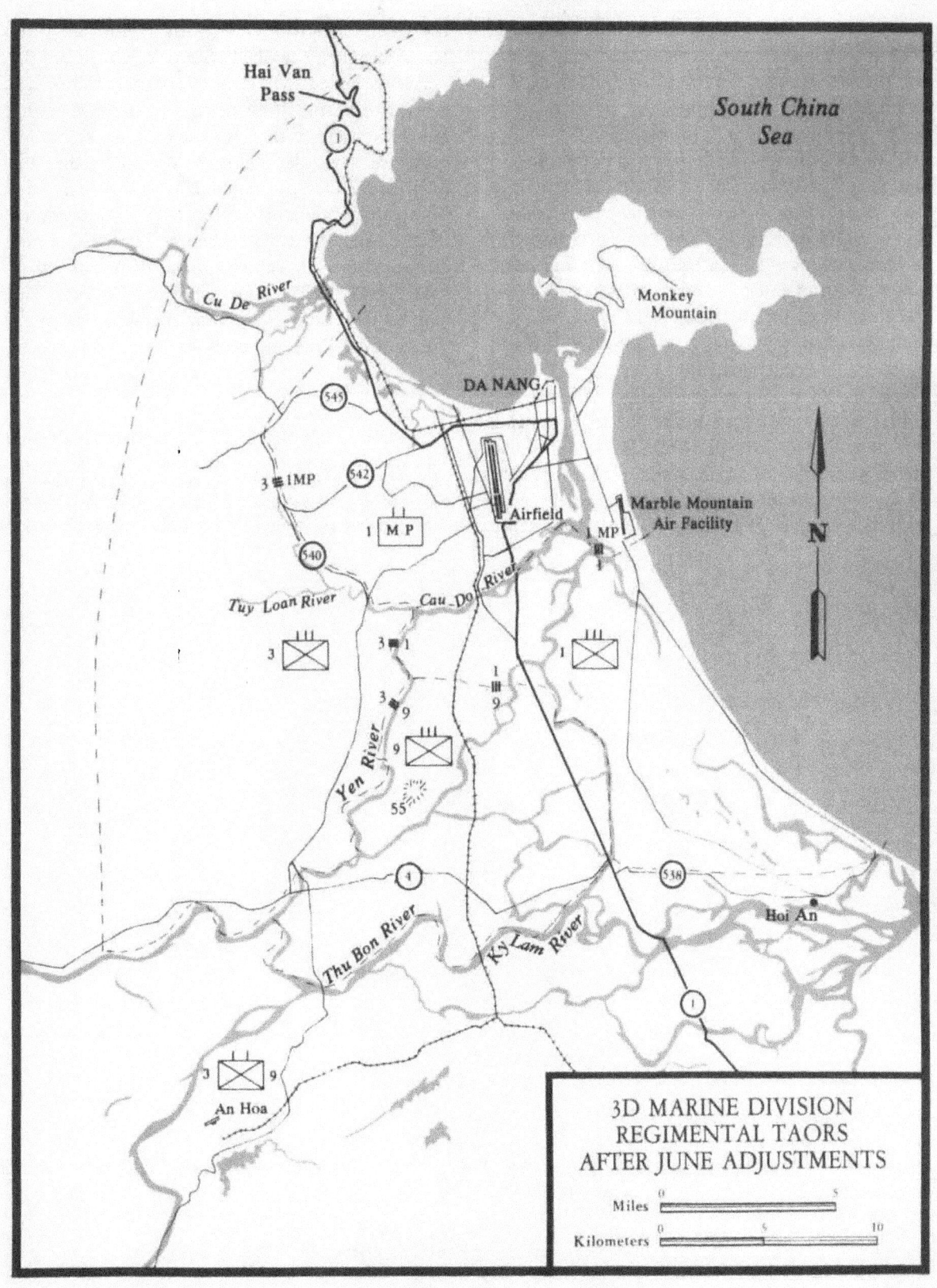

the division's eastern flank from the 9th Marines. With a corresponding reduction in the western sector, the 9th Marines' TAOR now consisted of only 134 square miles, the regiment having given away nearly 100 square miles in the exchange.

With the adjustment of forces and sectors, the 3d Marine Division continued its "scrubbing" actions in Operation Liberty. The only serious enemy opposition occurred in the 9th Marines zone of action. On 18 June, Company C, 9th Marines, operating 2,000 meters south of Dai Loc, came under heavy mortar and small arms fire, suffering eight wounded. The company asked for supporting air and artillery which ended the enemy resistance. Lieutenant Colonel Donahue's 2d Battalion, 9th Marines underwent a similar attack on 22 June in the hamlet of La Hoa (1), immediately east of the railroad and 4,000 meters north of the Ky Lam. Marines once more called upon supporting arms, including naval gunfire from the destroyer USS *Marton* (DD 948), to silence the enemy.* By the end of the month, all three Marine regiments reached Phase Line Green and the operation ended. VC resistance to the Marine advance had been scattered and ineffective. The 9th Marines observed that the lack of major enemy resistance gave plausibility to the thesis that the momentum of Operation Liberty prevented them from gaining any degree of initiative and uprooted them "from what had been a relatively secure operating area."[26] That regiment alone claimed to have recovered 40 square miles from the VC. The Marines were once more optimistic about pacifying the extensive Da Nang enclave.

---

*According to U.S. Navy historians, "Between four and nine ships including destroyers, cruisers, and rocket ships were available for gunfire support in Vietnam at any one time and more than half the missions supported Marines in I Corps." NHD, Comments on draft MS, dtd 19Jun78 (Vietnam Comment File).

PART III
SPRING FIGHTING IN SOUTHERN I CORPS

CHAPTER 7

"They're Not Supermen," Meeting the NVA in Operation Utah, March 1966

First Contact with the NVA — Operation Utah Expands

First Contact With the NVA

In contrast to the extended antiguerrilla small-unit war waged in the Da Nang TAOR, the Marines in southern I CTZ fought a series of sharp engagements during the late winter and early spring against North Vietnamese regulars. The first heavy fighting occurred during Operation Utah, early in March. Planning for Utah began when Colonel Bruce Jones, USA, senior advisor to the 2d ARVN Division, visited General Platt on 3 March, just after Platt returned to his CP at Chu Lai following Operation Double Eagle. Jones told Platt that the ARVN division had obtained intelligence that the *21st NVA Regiment* had recently moved into a region seven miles northwest of Quang Ngai City.

With the concurrence of both Generals McCutcheon and English, who were acting CG III MAF and CG 3d Marine Division, respectively, during General Walt's visit to Washington, General Platt decided to mount a coordinated attack with the 2d ARVN Division. Platt ordered his senior regimental commander, Colonel Peatross, the commanding officer of the 7th Marines, to meet with the 2d Division commanding general, who was still General Lam. Colonel Peatross, who, like General Platt, had worked closely together with General Lam during previous operations, flew that evening together with Colonel William G. Johnson, the commanding officer of MAG-36, to the 2d Division Headquarters at Quang Ngai City. There, the American and South Vietnamese commanders agreed to launch a combined operation using one ARVN and one Marine battalion.

According to the concept of operations, the two battalions were to land near the hamlet of Chau Nhai (5), 15 kilometers northwest of Quang Ngai City. The ARVN battalion was to land first and secure the landing zone, followed by the Marine battalion. Then both battalions were to advance southeastward paralleling Route 527 and then due east to Route 1, a distance of seven miles. The ARVN battalion was to operate north of Route 527, while the Marines were to deploy south of the road.

The planning period was very brief. Arriving back at Chu Lai late on the night of 3 March, Colonel Peatross and Colonel Johnson, who had been designated tactical air commander, met with Lieutenant Colonel Leon N. Utter, the commanding officer of the 2d Battalion, 7th Marines, at the 7th Marines CP and told him about the forthcoming operation. By morning, the 2d Battalion had three companies staged at Chu Lai for helicopter movement. Captain Alex Lee, the battalion's assistant operations officer, characterized the preparations as "nothing more than get on your horse and go."[1]

The objective area consisted of paddy lands and the hamlets of the Chau Nhai village complex. Hills 97 and 85 overlooked the landing zone from the southwest. Doughnut-shaped Hill 50 was the dominant terrain feature to the northeast. The hamlet of Chau Nhai (5), the first objective of the ARVN battalion, southwest of that hill was to be the scene of extensive fighting during the next few days.

On the morning of 4 March, Marine A-4s from MAG-12, F-4s from MAG-11, reinforced by USAF Martin B-57 Canberra bombers, strafed and bombed the objective area to prepare for the helicopter landings. Despite this aerial bombardment, the MAG-36 helicopters carrying the first elements of the 1st ARVN Airborne Battalion were taken under 12.7mm antiaircraft fire as they began to land at 0900. Within 10 minutes, all four of the accompanying armed UH-1Es from VMO-6 were hit. Enemy gunners downed one of the Hueys, but its crew was evacuated. Marine jets overhead attacked while the tactical air commander increased the landing intervals between successive helicopter waves. Enemy ground fire shot down one F-4 from VMFA-531 while it was making a napalm run, but the crew was rescued after ejecting and landing in the South China Sea.

Despite the intensity of the antiaircraft fire, the MAG-36 helicopters continued landing. Ten of the 20 UH-34s from HMM-261 and HMM-364 in the first lift were hit. Major Michael J. Needham, the HMM-364 strike leader, was forced to relinquish control of the landing when his aircraft was hit in the fuel line. Colonel Johnson later recalled: "the role of strike leader was then passed from aircraft division [usually four planes] to aircraft division as each division came in to land its troops." As the tactical air commander for the operation with access to 1st Wing support assets, the MAG commander was airborne in a command and control helicopter on his way from Chu Lai to the Quang Ngai Airfield at the time of the insertion of the ARVN airborne troopers. When hearing of the heavy resistance encountered in the landing zones, he "ordered by radio all MAG-36 helos to report to Quang Ngai for a briefing." This order caused an interruption of all planned missions and "consternation in air command and control agencies, but was effective." Sixteen UH-34s from the group's remaining transport squadron, HMM-363, soon joined the HMM-261 and HMM-364 aircraft to lift the remaining ARVN airborne troops from the Quang Ngai field to the landing zone.[2]

By 1030 that morning, the last elements of the 1st ARVN Airborne Battalion were in the zone. The Marine helicopter group had completed the lift of more than 400 men of the battalion under most adverse circumstances. Colonel Johnson expressed the opinion that:

> The North Vietnamese did not think we would continue the lift in the face of that automatic weapons fire. We did continue the lift and we kept the automatic weapons under almost constant attack by fixed-wing aircraft while we were going in there. And this enabled us to get in.[3]

In contrast to the heavy opposition that the Marine pilots encountered, the South Vietnamese troops met little resistance on the ground as they attacked northeast toward Hill 50.

With the completion of the landing of the South Vietnamese battalion, the MAG-36 helicopters returned to Chu Lai to bring Lieutenant Colonel Utter's battalion into the objective area. By 1040, the first elements of the battalion were on their way. Once more enemy gunners challenged the landing. The first wave, the 1st Platoon of Company F, landed under heavy fire. The platoon was isolated for 15 minutes until the helicopters could bring in the rest of the company. By 1130, both Companies F and G, and the battalion command group, were on the ground, meeting only light resistance as they secured the immediate area, but the intensity of the enemy antiaircraft fire delayed the arrival of Company H until after 1300.

Marine Corps Photo A186813
Marines from Company F, 2d Battalion, 7th Marines meet resistance after arriving in the landing zone during Operation Utah. Marine on the right is firing a M79 grenade launcher.

During the two-and-one-half hour lift, Colonel Johnson's helicopters, reinforced by a squadron from MAG-16, moved more than 600 men of the 2d Battalion, 7th Marines from Chu Lai into the Utah area of operations. In the course of landing the Marine battalion, several more UH-34s were hit and one crashed in the landing zone. One platoon from Company H remained in the LZ to provide security for the downed craft. Lieutenant Colonel Utter had to send a platoon from Company G 1,500 meters southwest of the landing zone to guard the UH-1E downed earlier, thus further reducing his effective strength. His Company E was already lost to him for the operation because it had been assigned to accompany Battery M, 4th Battalion, 11th Marines which had displaced to firing positions near Binh Son, 7,000 meters northeast of Utter's position.

While the 2d Battalion was arriving in the battle area, the Marine command began preparations to expand the operation. Colonel Peatross had accompanied Colonel Johnson to Quang Ngai. He was present when Lieutenant Colonel Robert J. Zitnik, the commanding officer of VMO-6, reported to Colonel Johnson after leading his gunships in the pre-H-hour preparation of the landing zones. According to Peatross, Zitnik stated something to the effect that "we have a tiger by the tail." Agreeing with the VMO commander that the heavy antiaircraft fire indicated the presence of a sizeable enemy force, Colonel Peatross left his operations and intelligence officers at the 2d ARVN Division command post and returned to Chu Lai to give General Platt a firsthand report and to alert additional Marine forces.[4]

At this point, approximately 1130, General Platt decided to reactive Task Force Delta. Colonel Peatross was assigned as Chief of Staff and personnel from the 7th Marines and 4th Marines Headquarters made up the rest of the staff. By late afternoon, a Marine truck convoy had moved most of the Task Force headquarters personnel and equipment to a command post near Quang Ngai, close to the 2d Division CP. According to General Platt, the two headquarters were "literally collocated. . . . I was very close to General Lam. Our 2s and 3s were only a few feet apart." Both CPs were about 2,000 meters northeast of Quang Ngai City on a 101-meter height named Nui Thien An, meaning "Mountain of Heavenly Peace," but called "Buddha Hill" by the Marines because of a nearby Buddhist temple. General McCutcheon, the acting III MAF commander, later compared the hill to "Little Round Top" at Gettysburg as it overlooked the southern sector of the developing battle seven miles to the northwest.[5]*

---

*Captain Edwin W. Besch, who at the time was the Task Force Delta Headquarters commandant, recalled that both the TF Delta and 2d Division CP were virtually without any security the first night, while located "about 50 yards from a Regional/Popular Forces triangular-shaped fortified company outpost which had been *annihilated* by a Main Force unit" a month before. According to Besch, security was later provided by a variety of units, including a South Vietnamese airborne company, ". . . only 38 men strong, but looking extremely confident (cocky) and armed with a mixture of M-14 rifles, captured AK-47s . . . Thompson & M-3 submachine guns, etc. . . . a Marine rifle company in reserve, and an ARVN 105mm battery, and a small unit of . . . Nung mercenaries." Capt Edwin W. Besch, Comments on draft MS, dtd 12Jun78 (Vietnam Comment File).

Marine Corps Photo A332583 (MajGen Oscar F. Peatross)
Col Oscar F. Peatross, Commanding Officer, 7th Marines visits the 2d Battalion, 7th Marines command post during Operation Utah. Col Peatross became the TF Delta Chief of Staff under BGen Jonas M. Platt.

A view of Utah area of operations as seen from Buddha Hill, the TF Delta command post. Because it overlooked the developing battle, MajGen McCutcheon compared Buddha Hill to "Little Round Top" at Gettysburg.

Marine Corps Photo A332571 (MajGen Oscar F. Peatross)

Shortly after 1300, Lieutenant Colonel Utter's battalion secured Hills 97 and 85 and began advancing south. Although the Marine companies encountered only very light resistance, the airborne battalion to the northeast ran into heavy opposition in the vicinity of Chau Nhai (5) and then Hill 50. About 1330, the ARVN commander asked for help from the Marine battalion. Utter received permission to stop his advance and ordered his companies to wheel about to reinforce the southern flank of the Vietnamese battalion. In Utter's words:

> We went cross-country and found the airborne battalion engaged in an argument with the enemy over a small hill [Hill 50] that dominated the surrounding terrain. . . . I met a real soldier . . . when I sought out the American advisor Captain Pete Dawkins [Captain Peter Dawkins of West Point football fame] and I met his counterpart, the airborne battalion commander . . . we agreed to attack to the east. Airborne on the left, Marines on the right.[6]

The Marines were forced to make some late-minute adjustments to their original plan. Lieutenant Colonel Utter received a radio message from Dawkins that the ARVN airborne battalion commander planned "to work completely around Hill 50" before attacking. Utter then ordered Captain Jerry D. Lindauer, who had recently assumed command of Company F on the battalion's northern flank, to maneuver his company toward the ARVN right and then hold this line until Company G moved abreast. In effect, the Marine battalion was to make a pivoting movement and tie in with the ARVN flank.[7]

The ARVN battalion did not move, which initially did not alarm the Marines. Captain Lindauer, the Company F commander, several years later recalled that he spoke to Captain Dawkins, "to let him [Dawkins] know we were moving forward," and remembered: "It was a mutal understanding that the ARVN would remain in the vicinity of Hill 50" until the ARVN wounded were evacuated.[8]

The Marine battalion then advanced in a general easterly direction: Company F on the left, Company G in the center, and Company H in an echelon formation to protect the open southern flank. According to Lieutenant Colonel Utter:

> We got off to a good start. It was fairly even ground, we had a nice even line with good contact, there was enough excitement to keep everyone on his toes, air was on station and artillery was within range and in position. I wasn't even too concerned about being minus one company and short a platoon from each of two others.[9]

The Marines had only pushed forward a few hundred meters in this fashion when they came under heavy fire from what Lieutenant Colonel Utter later estimated to have been two battalions of the *21st NVA Regiment*. The enemy fought from well prepared positions and took full advantage of the ground. They were too close to the Marines for Utter to call in artillery and air. He had very little choice but to continue the attack. Utter later explained, "we were in a frontal attack pure and simple, with everything committed from the outset."[10]

His Company G, under Captain William D. Seymour in the battalion center, penetrated the enemy positions in two places, but Utter did not have the reserves to exploit these minor gains. According to one of the battalion's staff officers, the Marines "employed fire and maneuver taking cover behind rice paddy dikes" but that the "NVA heavy machine gun fire . . . was delivered at so close a range it actually destroyed sections" of these dikes.[11]

Company H on the battalion right had made some progress, when the enemy counterattacked. An estimated NVA company maneuvered to the south and attacked the Marine company from that direction. Using his 81mm mortars to good effect, the company commander, a West Point graduate, 1st Lieutenant James Lau, directed the defense. Company H repulsed the enemy attack.

The growing gap on the Marine battalion's left flank between it and the ARVN battalion posed the greatest danger to the Marines. Lieutenant Colonel Utter requested Captain Dawkins, the U.S. Army advisor, to ask the Vietnamese battalion commander to attempt to close this gap between the two battalions but the Vietnamese commander "refused to do so."[12]

According to Utter:

> This meant our left flank was wide open, with nothing to put there. But the PAVNs [Peoples Army of Vietnam] had plenty of people, so they poured through. . . . and back to the south the enemy was going at it again with "H" Company. And there we were, taking it from three sides, the front, and both flanks, and from an enemy who was literally hugging us so we wouldn't use our supporting arms.[13]

Captain Lindauer's Company F on the exposed left flank was most vulnerable to the enemy attack. Lindauer, who was 200 meters behind his lead platoons, the 1st and the 2d, when the enemy struck, moved forward ". . . to get a firmer grasp of the situation." He managed to reach the 2d Platoon, but the 1st Platoon, further north, was cut off from the rest of the company, and the entire company was taking heavy casualties. Lindauer, who had been wounded himself, recalled that, "other than the fact that I was damned mad about the situation, I was lucid and able to make decisions."[14]* He radioed the battalion executive officer, reported the situation, and remonstrated about delays in artillery and medical evacuation helicopters. Lindauer later apologized, explaining that he "was somewhat distraught with all the dead and wounded" around him and that he "expected miracles in that field," but now realized that the battalion was doing all that was possible, under the circumstances. In fact, shortly after speaking to the executive officer, as Lindauer recalled:

> Air came up on Bn Tac [battalion tactical net] and asked me to mark the target. I had a yellow smoke thrown and told him to take a 90 degree azimuth 100-200 meters from it and keep hitting it. Simultaneously Arty said they were ready to fire, so I told air to stand by until completion of the fire mission, and if Arty was on, to hit the same area. You can tell Jim Black [Captain James O. Black, Commander, Battery M, 4th Battalion, 11th Marines] he was right on the money, and then the air started a continual attack which took a lot of pressure off us. . . .[15]

Learning that Lindauer had a badly shattered arm, Lieutenant Colonel Utter sent his assistant operations officer, Captain Lee, to take over the command of Company F. Lee made his way through heavy fire and finally reached the company's CP about 1700 and relieved Lindauer. The new company com-

---

*Captain Lindauer, a retired lieutenant colonel in 1978, bitterly recalled the refusal of the ARVN battalion to reinforce the Marines: ". . . I received no support from the ARVN and my supporting arms requests to the left flank were denied as too close to the ARVN. During that entire day, I am not aware that the ARVN Airborne Battalion did anything except view our critical situation as detached observers from the vantage point of Hill 50, and even allowed the NVA to come in behind us." Lindauer stated that Captain Dawkins "endeavored to get . . . [the battalion commander] to move but to no avail." LtCol Jerry D. Lindauer, Comments on draft MS, dtd 12Jun78 (Vietnam Comment File). Lieutenant Colonel Utter in his after action report was more charitable to the ARVN commander. He declared that he was not aware of the ARVN situation nor of the "ability of the ARVN commander to respond to this request." Utter suggested that, "The answer could have been a single commander on the spot to coordinate and direct both forces, based on the engagement of each." 2/7 AAR, Opn Utah, dtd 12Mar66. In any event it is not clear that the ARVN ever secured Hill 50. If they did, they soon abandoned it.

Marine Corps Photo A186812
Marines from 2d Battalion, 7th Marines take cover and return fire as they come under attack during Operation Utah. The Marines engaged two battalions of the 21st NVA Regiment.

mander reported to Utter that Company F's situation was still serious and that they were running out of ammunition. At this point the battalion received reinforcements; the platoon from Company H, left behind in the landing zone to protect the damaged helicopter, arrived at the battalion command group's position, the helicopter having been repaired and flown back to Chu Lai. According to Utter, ". . . the decision was made for me—they [the Company H platoon] had to go to that open left flank." This assistance enabled Lee to solidify his positions and close the gap between his 1st and 2d Platoons.[16]

By this time, all of Utter's companies were reporting shortages of ammunition. The battalion S-4, Captain Martin E. O'Connor, had organized a group of 81mm mortarmen to distribute ammunition to the frontline elements.** Although the group ac-

---

**Captain O'Connor recalled in his comments that the ammunition which was distributed had been brought in by two helicopters, which "landed under fire and jettisoned their badly needed cargo." LtCol Martin E. O'Connor, Comments on draft MS, dtd 24May78 (Vietnam Comment File).

complished this mission and also evacuated the seriously wounded to a more secure area, the battalion's position remained precarious. Lieutenant Colonel Utter decided to order his companies to fall back. He later explained:

> . . . darkness coming . . . up against superior numbers . . . no reserve; the enemy increasing his fire and his movement around us; wounded and dead on our hands; and fast running out of ammunition. I had nothing to lose but my pride in ordering a withdrawal—so I ordered one.[17]

The Marine battalion disengaged under heavy pressure. According to Utter, "We made the first 50 to 100 yards—painfully. Then we rolled in the air. Under cover of bombs, rockets, napalm, and strafing runs we made 200 more rather easily." As Company H began to pull back, it came under 60mm mortar fire and enemy infantry advanced toward the Marines. The company repulsed the North Vietnamese attack and continued its withdrawal to Chau Nhai (4), where the battalion was establishing night defensive positions. The last elements of the battalion reached the new perimeter two hours after dark.[18]

General Platt had already begun to take measures to reinforce the 2d Battalion. His main concern at that stage was that the North Vietnamese might evade the allied force as they had done during Double Eagle. He had ordered the deployment of another 155mm battery to Binh Son and Lieutenant Colonel James R. Young's 3d Battalion, 1st Marines to establish blocking defenses north of Utter's battalion. Shortly after 1800, Young's battalion was in position on the high ground south of the Tra Bong River, 5,000 meters west-southwest of Binh Son. Because of the heavy resistance encountered by Utter's battalion, General Platt alerted yet another battalion, Lieutenant Colonel Paul X. Kelley's 2d Battalion, 4th Marines still at Chu Lai, for helicopter movement the following morning to a landing zone 2,500 meters south of Utter's night perimeter.[19]

During the night of 4-5 March, the enemy continued to harass Utter's battalion in Chau Nhai (4). The North Vietnamese became especially active when helicopters arrived. Because of the intensity of the enemy fire, Lieutenant Colonel Utter had called off helicopter missions during the day, but about 2130, MAG-36 once more renewed flights. During the next seven hours the helicopter pilots brought in much needed supplies and evacuated 70 casualties, despite some NVA fire.* Lieutenant Colonel Utter remarked:

> As we tried resupply and evacuation, we received .50 caliber and mortars on each bird. But this disclosed a trenchline to our right rear and "H" Company took it in a night assault—killing twenty. After that the birds worked all night—while my Marines gleefully used their fresh ammunition on the enemy. . . .[20]

During that night Marine supporting arms also played a large role. An Air Force AC-47 arrived on station and dropped flares. Marine jets continued to strike at suspected enemy positions with bombs, rockets, and napalm, while A-4s from MAG-12 made high altitude, radar-controlled bombing strikes on enemy trail networks leading into the bat-

A Marine jet streaks in to provide close air support during Operation Utah. Marine infantry can be seen advancing in the foreground.

Marine Corps Photo A186942

---

*General Peatross commented on the difficulty of resupplying the committed units during the night of 4 March. Although observing that no unit actually ran out of ammunition, "we had to be selective as to which units to resupply. . . . as it generally happens, the units that needed it most were the most difficult to get to. Nevertheless, in total darkness, helicopters flew into the area . . . and hovered as low as was practical—50 to a 100 feet above—and dropped the ammunition and other items of supply." MajGen Oscar F. Peatross, Comments on draft MS, dtd 1Jun78 (Vietnam Comment File).

tle area. Colonel Leslie E. Brown, the MAG-12 commander, recalled:

> We were just in a long stream of bombing and coming back and rearming and going back as fast as we could . . . you were not necessarily flying with the same squadron that you left with. You came back and joined up and the next two to four airplanes off became a flight . . . the level of proficiency was so high that it didn't matter who was leading.[21]

Artillery kept pace with the air effort during the night and early morning hours of 4-5 March. Both 155mm howitzer batteries at Binh Son, Batteries K and M, 4th Battalion, 11th Marines, fired in support of the Marines and the ARVN airborne battalion further north. The Marine artillerymen expended so many rounds that two ammunition resupply truck convoys from Chu Lai were required to replenish the stock.*

Just as the second convoy arrived at Binh Son shortly after 0500, the North Vietnamese launched a major attack against the 1st ARVN Airborne Battalion's defensive position near Hill 50. Major Elmer N. Snyder, at that time Task Force Delta operations officer, asked the artillery liaison officer to call for ". . . maximum fires on the four grid squares that comprised the battlefield. . . ." In the largest single fire mission yet conducted in the Chu Lai area, the two Binh Son batteries, reinforced by a 155mm gun battery at Chu Lai, fired 1,900 rounds in two hours.[22]

At 0730 on the 5th, General Platt ordered Lieutenant Colonel Young to advance south from his blocking positions south of the Tra Bong River to secure the northern flank of the 1st ARVN Airborne Battalion. Young's 3d Battalion, with Company L on the right, Company M on the left, and the command group and Company I following, met only slight resistance during the first two hours as it pushed forward to relieve enemy pressure on the South Vietnamese troopers.

Operation Utah Expands

While the 3d Battalion, 1st Marines moved to link up with the ARVN airborne troopers, Generals Lam and Platt brought additional forces into the battle. Having found that the *21st NVA Regiment* was more than willing to stand and fight, both commanders wanted to take advantage of the opportunity to surround and destroy the enemy unit. During the early morning, General Lam ordered the 37th Ranger Battalion, supported by his Strike Company** and an APC troop, to move from Quang Ngai to form blocking positions, 1,500 meters west of the railroad track and 3,000 meters east of Chau Nhai (4). The South Vietnamese Airborne Task Force Alfa command group and the 5th ARVN Airborne Battalion was to be airlifted from Saigon to Quang Ngai. On its arrival, General Lam planned to land the 5th ARVN Airborne in the same landing zone where the 1st ARVN Airborne Battalion and the 2d Battalion, 7th Marines had landed the previous day. From there, the newly inserted ARVN unit was to attack northeast, joining the 1st ARVN Airborne. Utter's 2d Battalion, 7th Marines was to secure the landing zone for the Vietnamese unit, clear its battlefield of the previous day, and serve as the Task Force Delta reserve battalion. General Platt also had alerted Lieutenant Colonel James P. Kelly's 1st Battalion, 7th Marines command group for movement to Binh Son and had inserted "P. X." Kelley's 2d Battalion, 4th Marines into the southern Utah area to close out any avenue of escape for the enemy regiment.[23]

The 2d Battalion, 4th Marines began landing shortly after 0830 on a small hill near An Tuyet (1), 3,000 meters north of the Tra Khuc River. Despite air preparation of the landing zone, Communist gunners contested the helicopter landing of the Marine battalion. Heavy machine gun fire put several MAG-36 helicopters out of commission and

---

*According to Colonel Paul B. Watson, Jr., who commanded the 3d Battalion, 11th Marines in March 1966, "the convoys consisted of supply trucks, a 105mm howitzer battery, and the command group from 3d Battalion, 11th Marines. . . . they departed Chu Lai at 0200. Upon arrival at the Binh Son artillery positions, the ammunition trucks were backed up to the gun positions and unloaded one round at a time directly into the weapons chambers." Both Colonel Watson and General Peatross suggested that this was "the first Marine convoy to have ventured out of either the Da Nang or Chu Lai enclaves at night." Col Paul B. Watson, Jr., Comments on draft MS, n.d. [June 78] (Vietnam Comment File). See also MajGen Oscar F. Peatross, Comments on draft MS, dtd 1Jun78 (Vietnam Comment File).

**The Strike Company of the 2d ARVN Division was an elite infantry unit directly under the operational control of the division commander.

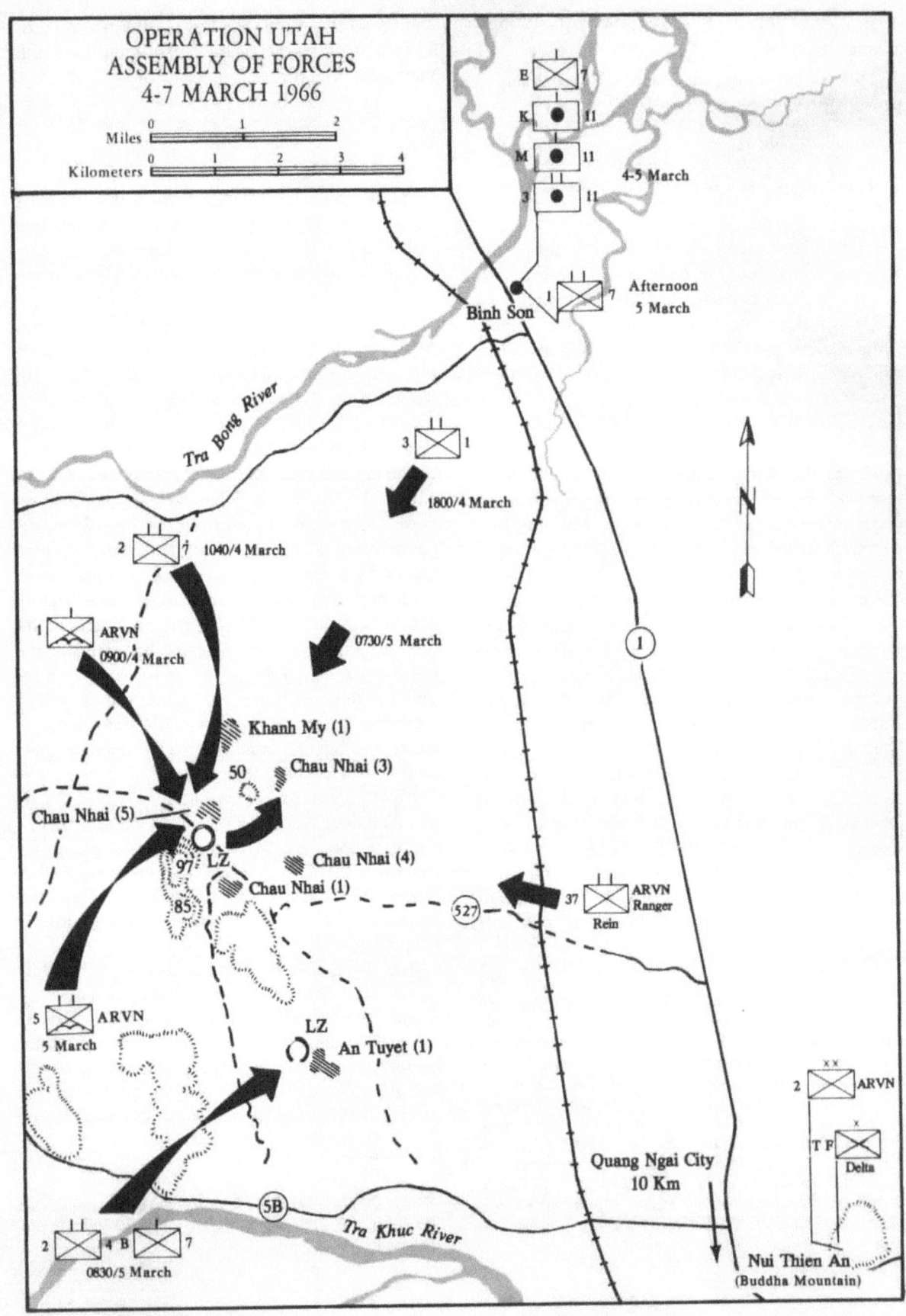

caused repeated transfers of leadership during the lift. Lieutenant Colonel Mervin B. Porter, Commanding Officer, HMM-261, the first flight leader, was hit several times on his third trip into the landing zone and was forced to retire. Major David A. Spurlock then became flight leader, but the enemy gunfire forced his aircraft down in the landing zone. Captain James P. Kenny from HMM-261 took over as leader, and with eight other pilots completed the battalion lift, but not before another UH-34 crashed in the LZ. Major Snyder, the Task Force Delta operations officer, wrote:

> American advisors to the 2d ARVN Div had warned me when planning 2/4's lift into the LZ selected that a VC Battalion (Provincial Force) had long operated in that area and that we might receive substantial trouble. What with the tempo of operations, it was determined that this was a necessary calculated risk.[24]

Lieutenant Colonel Kelley's battalion met stiff resistance on the west and in the villages northwest and southwest of the landing zone. Two of Kelley's companies were engaged at close quarters until 1100. At that time, General Platt ordered the battalion commander to continue the original mission of closing the southern flank of the objective area. Kelley disengaged the two companies, G and H, from the firefight and began a sweep to the north. Company B, 1st Battalion, 7th Marines, attached to Kelley's command for the operation, remained in the landing zone to provide security for the downed helicopters. The battalion's forward companies and command group reached Lieutenant Colonel Utter's battalion without incident and established night defensive positions.[25]

While these events were going on in the southern Utah area, Lieutenant Colonel Young's battalion in the north encountered major enemy opposition shortly after 1030 while trying to link up with the 1st ARVN Airborne Battalion. Company M on the 3d Battalion's eastern flank came under heavy fire just north of Chau Nhai (3). Company L skirted the Company M fight and one of its platoons was ordered to "join the ARVN" on Hill 50. As the 3d Platoon moved to carry out these orders, it soon became clear that the NVA not the ARVN held Hill 50. The enemy confronting both companies had the advantages of prepared positions and terrain; they held the high ground. Bamboo fences and hedgerows masked the enemy position from the Marines. Having constructed an extensive tunnel

Marine Corps Photo A186762
BGen Jonas M. Platt, Commanding General, Task Force Delta, visits site of captured NVA command post on Hill 50 during Utah. Capt Charles W. Latting, the commanding officer of Company M, 3d Battalion, 1st Marines, gestures as he describes the action to Gen Platt.

network which connected bunkers and spider traps, the enemy lay in wait in elaborate entrenchments protected by minefields and booby traps.

Despite these formidable defenses, the Marine battalion pressed the attack. Eventually reinforced by the 1st ARVN Airborne, Company L succeeded in taking Hill 50 after a three-and-a-half-hour engagement. Near Chau Nhai (3), Company M, however, made little headway against an estimated NVA battalion. With Company M stopped, Lieutenant Colonel Young sent his reserve company, Company I, into the action; it passed around Company M's positions and tried to push into Chau Nhai (3) from the east. At the same time, the 5th ARVN Airborne Battalion advanced toward Young's battalion in a pincer movement from the southwest. Plans called for them to relieve Company L on Hill 50. As darkness fell, both Companies L and M withdrew well to the north, while Company I consolidated its position on the eastern edge of Chau Nhai (3). Lieutenant Colonel Young's battalion's casualties were 32 killed and 90 wounded during the day's fighting.[26]

At this point, Generals Lam and Platt believed they had the enemy regiment surrounded and could tighten the ring the next morning. In addition to the two ARVN airborne battalions and the 3d Battalion,

1st Marines closing in on the Hill 50 area, the two generals had moved other units into blocking positions to the east and south. The 2d Battalions of the 7th and 4th Marines were to the south and the 1st Battalion, 7th Marines was to the northeast. A 2d Division task force, consisting of the 37th Ranger Battalion and 1st Battalion, 5th ARVN Regiment, was along the railroad due east of the battle area. General Platt had already reinforced the artillery at Binh Son with the command group of the 3d Battalion, 11th Marines and a 105mm howitzer battery.

Company B, 1st Battalion, 7th Marines, far from the previous fighting, was still providing security for one of the downed helicopters near An Tuyet (1). Paradoxically, the heaviest action of the night and early morning hours of 5-6 March occurred at this relatively isolated position. At 2300, Captain Robert C. Prewitt, the company commander, reported to the 2d Battalion, 4th Marines that he was under mortar and heavy small arms attack.* According to Lieutenant Colonel Kelley, "Prewitt advised me that he was dangerously low on ammunition." The battalion commander informed General Platt of the situation and asked for an emergency resupply for the company. The task force commander approved the mission and two HMM-364 helicopters took off from Quang Ngai to deliver the needed ammunition.[27]

---

*General Peatross commented on the rationale for leaving Prewitt's company behind to guard the downed helicopters. He declared that the question "To leave or not to leave a helicopter had been a subject as old as the first helicopter in the testing stage, in the Marine Corps Schools, in writing of the manual Helicopterborne Operations, in training exercises . . . and other operations." Peatross recalled that General McCutcheon during a visit to the Task Force Delta CP suggested destroying the aircraft, but that "I felt otherwise. We discussed that matter in . . . detail and concluded that we should not leave one unless the helicopter was already destroyed beyond repair." According to Peatross, there were two major reasons for this decision: The first was to keep up the morale of the helicopter crews who knew they and their craft would be protected and "the other point was that a downed helicopter almost invariably drew enemy action near it or to it everytime one went down. . . . as we were constantly searching for the enemy in our daily activities in Vietnam, why leave the helicopter when we knew that the enemy was going to come to it." Peatross remembered General McCutcheon calmly stating that if it "did not interfere with pursuit of the bigger enemy force, to do what we saw fit about the downed helicopter. This we did." MajGen Oscar F. Peatross, Comments on draft MS, dtd 1Jun78 (Vietnam Comment File).

As the aircraft approached the landing zone, they both came under heavy fire and were unable to land. According to Major Snyder, who was in radio contact with Company B, the lead pilot, First Lieutenant Terril J. Richardson, radioed Prewitt:

> . . . and regretfully announced that they would not be able to land. After Prewitt informed him of the severity of the need (less than 100 rds of rifle ammo left in the company) the pilot [Richardson] said in effect that they would get the ammo in somehow. The result was that the two helos came across the zone a few feet off the ground and at about 10-20 mph while the crewmen kicked the ammo boxes out the doors. Both aircraft were hit by ground fire, but managed to flounder back to Quang Ngai.[28]

On the ground, Prewitt's company came under increasing pressure. Supported by mortars and automatic weapons, two North Vietnamese companies closed in on the Marine perimeter. About 0130, the enemy attacked the Marine positions from three directions—north, south, and west. With the help of Marine artillery at Binh Son and an ARVN 105mm battery at Quang Ngai, the newly replenished Marines repulsed the NVA attack. Even after the attack failed, the North Vietnamese continued to subject the Marine company to heavy mortar, small arms, and automatic weapons fire until early morning.

At 0745 6 March, General Platt ordered the 2d Battalion, 4th Marines to return to the landing zone and relieve Company B. The battalion left the blocking positions that it had established the night before, leaving the 2d Battalion, 7th Marines in place. By midafternoon, Kelley's battalion had moved overland and seized the high ground west of the landing zone. There was only light enemy resistance to the move; the main enemy force had withdrawn, but not without heavy losses. Captain Prewitt confirmed 38 enemy dead and estimated that at least twice that figure had been carried away. Major Snyder observed that "Bravo Company was too busy fighting for its life to worry about sophisticated estimates."[29]

The heavy fighting anticipated in the northern Utah area never developed. The night of the 5th was relatively quiet. On the morning of 6 March, Company I pulled back to join Companies L and M, and the two ARVN airborne battalions pulled back from forward positions to allow for the employment of supporting arms. After an intensive two-and-one-half-hour air and artillery bombardment, which lasted until 1240, the three battalions advanced. The North Vietnamese were no longer there.

The North Vietnamese regiment had sustained heavy losses during the three-day fight. Lieutenant Colonel Young's Marines found 100 enemy bodies when the 3d Battalion reoccupied Hill 50 on 6 March. Later that afternoon, the battalion found an enormous cave complex, which apparently had served as the NVA regimental command post. The extensive tunnel network, still largely undamaged despite the allied bombardment, contained weapons, supplies, and documents. Earlier, Lieutenant Colonel Utter's battalion had discovered a similar defensive complex in its sector, consisting of "caves, trenches, foxholes, wire barricades, and deep, deep shelters." Utter remarked that some of the shafts went straight down for 15-to-20 feet and then swerved off in two to four directions. The 2d Battalion, 7th Marines found 43 enemy bodies in one of these tunnels. During Utah, allied forces claimed to have killed nearly 600 North Vietnamese soldiers and captured five prisoners and 49 weapons, including three 12.7mm machine guns and two mortars. Marine casualties were 98 dead and 278 wounded, while ARVN forces lost 30 killed and 120 wounded.[30]

Operation Utah ended on 7 March after Lieutenant Colonel Young's battalion, assisted by

Marine Corps Photo A332584 (MajGen Oscar F. Peatross)
BGen Hoang Xuan Lam (wearing beret), Commanding General, 2d ARVN Division, inspects one of the captured enemy 12.7mm machine guns that had been used so effectively against the Marines and ARVN in Operation Utah. Gen Platt, the Task Force Delta commander, is on the right of the picture.

Marine engineers, destroyed the enemy's defensive complex. Lieutenant Colonel Utter characterized the NVA enemy by saying, "they're not supermen. But they can fight. And they will fight when cornered or when they think they have you cornered."[31]

CHAPTER 8

Further Fighting and an Expanding Base of Operations, Chu Lai, March-June 1966

A Bloody March—Expansion at Chu Lai—Operation Kansas

A Bloody March

A few weeks after Operation Utah ended, the Marines engaged another Communist regiment in the Binh Son/Son Tinh region. Unknown to the allies, the *1st VC Regiment* had moved south from the Que Son area north of Chu Lai into northern Quang Ngai Province. On the night of 18-19 March, the enemy regiment overran a remote outpost on Hill 141 about 2,000 meters south of the Tra Bong River and 12,000 meters west-southwest of Binh Son District town. The position was known as the An Hoa outpost taking its name from a nearby village.*

When radio contact was lost with the outpost, manned by the 936th Regional Force (RF) Company, and after learning that a 15-man patrol returning to the camp had come under heavy small arms fire from inside the camp, General Lam, on 19 March, decided to send a 2d ARVN Division reaction force to An Hoa. A 10-helicopter detachment from HMM-261, led by Major Robert P. Guay, picked up 120 ARVN soldiers at Quang Ngai and flew toward the outpost. As the helicopters approached the landing zone, enemy heavy machine guns opened fire, hitting eight of the 10 aircraft. Only three of the UH-34s were able to land, discharge their passengers, and take off. At this point, General Lam and the wing decided to "abort" the mission. Two Phantom jets from VMFA-542 bombed and strafed the former RF outpost so that the Marine helicopters could take out the 30 ARVN troops stranded in the nearby landing zone. HMM-261 completed the evacuation shortly after 1630.[1]

Faced with the fact that, An Hoa position was now in enemy hands, General Lam asked III MAF for assistance in retaking the outpost. General Kyle, the 3d Marine Division's commanding general, ordered Colonel Peatross, the 7th Marines commander and senior officer at Chu Lai since General Platt's departure to become the III MAF Chief of Staff, to establish liaison with the 2d ARVN Division. On the afternoon of the 19th, Lam and Peatross had agreed to a concept of operations similar to that used for the Utah operation. Marine helicopters were to land a Marine and an ARVN airborne battalion about 4,000 meters west of An Hoa. Both battalions then were to close in on the former RF camp on top of Hill 141. Marine artillery was to support the operation and other infantry units were to be committed as required. The two commanders alerted their respective assault forces, the 3d Battalion, 7th Marines and the 5th ARVN Airborne Battalion, for the combined operation, codenamed Texas.[2]

By early morning on 20 March, Colonel Peatross and Colonel Johnson had established the forward command posts of the 7th Marines and MAG-36 at Binh Son.** Colonel Johnson was once more the tactical air commander for the operation. The 2d ARVN Division also collocated its forward headquarters with the Marines. A battalion artillery group formed around the headquarters of the 3d Battalion, 11th Marines, and consisting of a 105mm howitzer battery and a 155mm howitzer battery, moved into firing positions 5,500 meters southwest of Binh Son. After fixed-wing strikes in the objective area, the 155mm howitzer battery, Captain James O. Black's Battery M, 4th Battalion, 11th Marines, started firing the landing zone preparation mission at 0730.

---

*This An Hoa should not be confused with the An Hoa basin southwest of Da Nang.

**Colonel Zitnik, the commanding officer of VMO-6 in March 1966, recalled that he dropped off Colonel Peatross and a few of his officers at Binh Son sometime around 2200 on the night of 19 March. Col Robert J. Zitnik, Comments on draft MS, dtd 6Jun78 (Vietnam Comment File).

Following the air and artillery bombardment, MAG-36 helicopters landed Lieutenant Colonel Charles H. Bodley's 3d Battalion, 7th Marines and the ARVN 5th Airborne Battalion. The two units moved east with the ARVN battalion on the left flank and the Marines on the right. Neither unit met any serious opposition. The 3d Battalion's Company I was helilifted to the top of Hill 141 where the Marines found the bodies of 31 of the outpost defenders; the other 85 were missing. The enemy had departed.

That afternoon, Lieutenant Colonel "P. X." Kelley, whose 2d Battalion, 4th Marines had been designated the backup force for Operation Texas, decided to visit Binh Son to check the course of the battle. After an unscheduled stopover at the positions of the 3d Battalion, 7th Marines, he arrived at the 7th Marines command post. Discussing the situation with the regimental staff, he learned that the allies believed that the enemy force, suspected to be the *NVA 21st Regiment,* had escaped to the west and that his battalion "would most likely not be committed."[3]

According to Kelley:

> I then talked with Colonel Bruce Jones, the senior advisor to the 2d ARVN Division and suggested that the VC might have moved towards the Vinh Tuy Valley, an area which had considerable activity in the past. My original suggestion at the time was to have 2/4 land there. After considerable discussion, I mentioned the fact that possibly the VC may have done the reverse of the obvious—that they may have moved in an easterly direction from Hill 141, towards the coastal plain. I then suggested the possibility of 3/7 changing its axis of advance to the Vinh Tuy Valley, and once it had passed through the valley it could join with 2/4 for a two-battalion sweep eastward to National Route 1.[4]

Colonel Jones and Kelley decided to present this concept to Colonel Peatross. Kelley later recalled that Colonel Peatross agreed in principle, but wanted to discuss the new plan with General Lam. The three officers then boarded a helicopter, piloted by Lieutenant Colonel Zitnik, commander of VMO-6, and Colonel Johnson, and flew to Quang Ngai City where they ". . . received General Lam's blessing." On the return flight to Binh Son, their course took them over Phuong Dinh (2) hamlet, 4,500 meters southeast of the An Hoa outpost. Colonel Peatross and Lieutenant Colonel Kelley, with the concurrence of Colonel Johnson, selected a large open field 1,000 meters west of the hamlet as the landing zone for the 2d Battalion, 4th Marines on the following day.[5] Lieutenant Colonel Zitnik several years later observed that this close coordination between the senior air and ground officers permitted the air commander with a nod of his head to indicate to the ground commander that "their plans were supportable and they could proceed."[6]

The allies planned for the ARVN and Bodley's battalion to attack southeast from An Hoa on 21 March, while Kelley's battalion landed near Phuong Dinh (2) further to the south. General Lam reinforced the 5th ARVN Airborne Battalion with the 4th ARVN Regimental Headquarters; the 2d Battalion, 5th ARVN Regiment; and an APC company. This ARVN task force was to advance until it reached Route 527 and then follow the road until it linked up with another ARVN battalion, the 3d Battalion, 5th ARVN Regiment, in blocking positions west of Route 1. Operating west and southwest of the ARVN forces, Lieutenant Colonel Bodley's battalion was to march through the Vinh Tuy Valley and tie in with Kelley's battalion at Phuong Dinh (2). In the event of sizeable contact, Colonel Peatross would then commit his reserve, Lieutenant Colonel Young's 3d Battalion, 1st Marines.[7]

On the 21st, both Kelley's and Bodley's battalions encountered large enemy forces in strongly fortified positions. For Kelley's 2d Battalion, 4th Marines, the battle began as UH-34s from MAG-36 carrying the battalion's lead elements approached the landing area. The enemy reacted with small arms and machine gun fire. Company F, which landed first, repulsed attacks from north, east, and south of the landing zone. While the company maneuvered to secure the area, MAG-12 A-4s struck Phuong Dinh (2). Armed UH-1Es from VMO-6 flew suppressive fire missions while controlling the MAG-12 jets.

By 1115, the battalion command group, Company D, 1st Battalion, 4th Marines, attached to the 2d Battalion for the operation, and Company E had joined Company F on the ground. At this time, Kelley called for artillery bombardment of Phuong Dinh (2) from where most of the enemy resistance was coming. Once the artillery fire ended at 1230, the 2d Battalion began its assault on Phuong Dinh (2). Company D maneuvered toward the slightly higher ground north of the hamlet, while Companies E and F, with Company E in the lead, attacked due east. Aerial observers overhead detected no movement in Phuong Dinh (2). Five minutes after

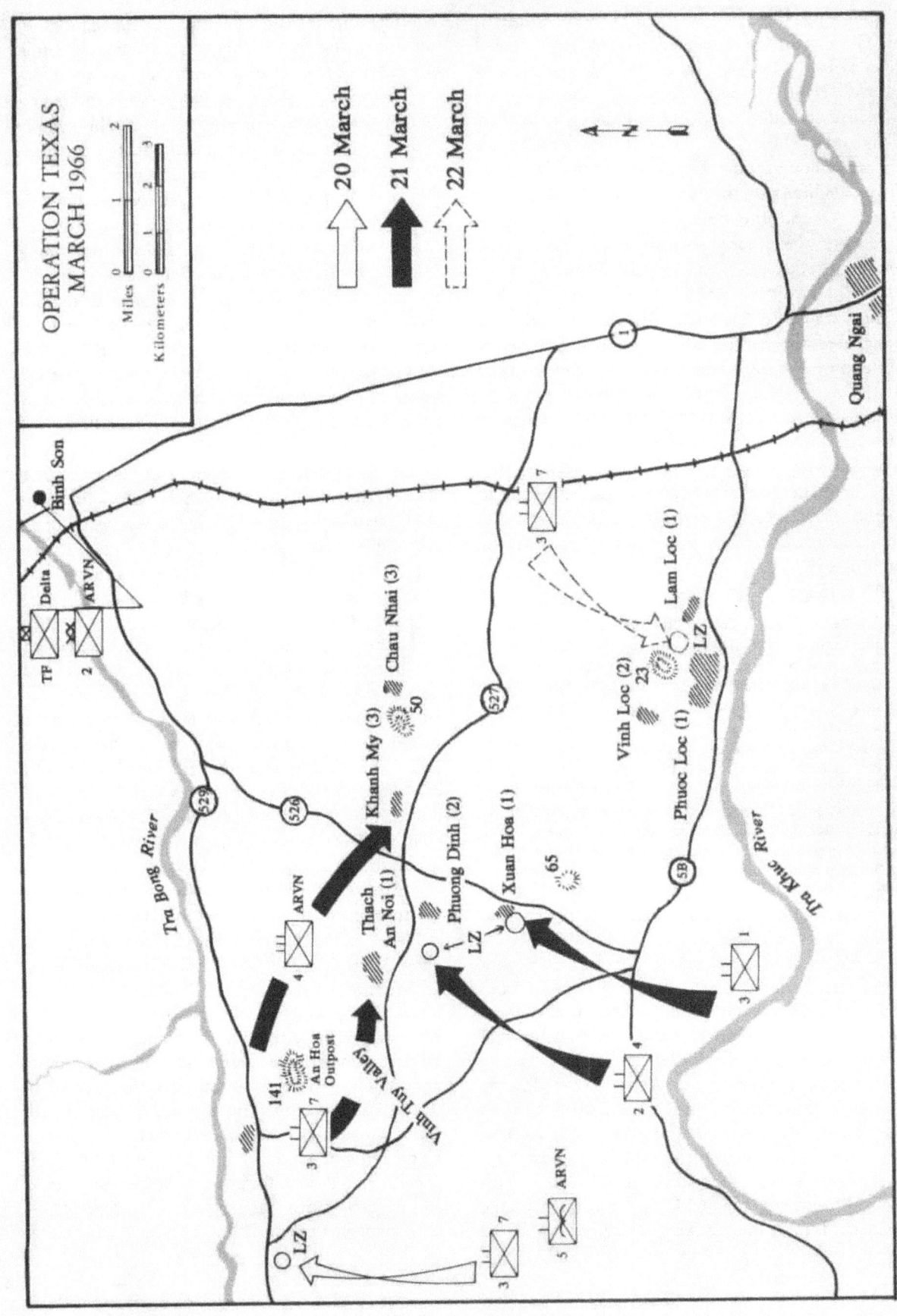

the attack started, one of the pilots from VMO-6 radioed Lieutenant Colonel Kelley exclaiming, "My God, I can't believe it! They're erupting from the ground! There are hundreds of them."[8]

Simultaneously, the advance elements of Company E were hit by massed enemy infantry weapons fire. While the rest of the Marine company established a heavy base of covering fire, one platoon fought its way through the hamlet's outer defenses, only to discover three more interior defensive perimeters, including mutually supporting bunkers and three bands of tactical wire entanglements. Commenting on the situation, Lieutenant Colonel Kelley later wrote:

> Since ammunition was running low, I ordered Company E to withdraw to a covered position near the line of departure so that more artillery and air could be delivered on the target. At the same time, I ordered Company D to . . . establish a base of fire to relieve the pressure on Company E.[9]

Company D also ran into heavy enemy resistance and was unable to advance, but the company was able to place enough fire upon the enemy to afford some relief for Company E. At this time, Lieutenant Colonel Kelley and his command group were on a small rise about 50 meters west of the hamlet, caught in a cross fire. Fourteen Marines in this group were killed or wounded. The situation for the 2d Battalion was so critical that Kelley called in air strikes which dropped napalm unusually close to his frontlines.[10]

Marine air and artillery engaged in an all-out effort to support the stalled infantry. Lieutenant Colonel Paul B. Watson, Jr., the commanding officer of the 3d Battalion, 11th Marines, added two new batteries, one 105mm howitzer and one 155mm howitzer, to the battalion artillery group supporting the operation. The original two batteries fired 1,346 rounds in support of the 2d Battalion, 4th Marines during one continuous firing mission lasting from 1330 to 1500. Marine jets at the request of Colonel Johnson supplemented the artillery effort. By 1600, A-4s and F-4s had flown 51 strikes against the enemy. The 1st MAW Tactical Air Control Center (TACC) reported that it had diverted all Marine jets to the Texas operation. Lieutenant Colonel Zitnik remembered that the requests caused some disruption "at the TACC, but all were provided and utilized."[11]

With this support and the arrival of additional

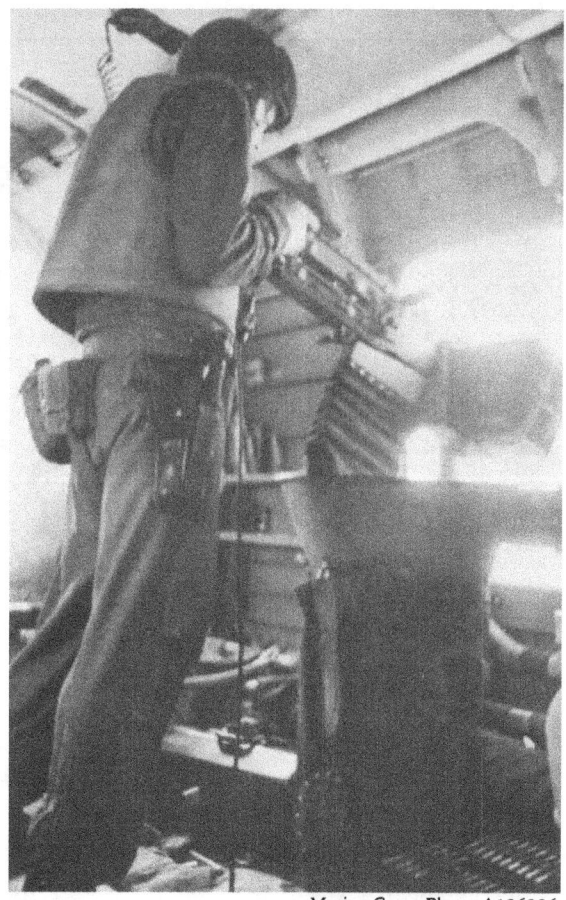

Marine Corps Photo A186286
A Marine helicopter crew member mans a machine gun during Operation Texas. The helicopters bringing in the 2d Battalion, 4th Marines came under fire as they approached the landing zone.

supplies by 1800, the 2d Battalion was able to consolidate its positions west of Phuong Dinh (2). Kelley later recalled:

> I seriously considered a night attack, but with the average company strength down to 80-90, and pitted against a numerically superior enemy in well dug-in positions, with no reserve battalion to back up, I opted to continue the attack by fire.[12]

About 2,000 meters to the north of Phuong Dinh (2), the 3d Battalion, 7th Marines had encountered another fortified hamlet. As the battalion moved through the Vinh Tuy Valley the morning and early afternoon of 21 March, it passed through several nearly abandoned villages which displayed telltale signs of Viet Cong control. Only a few old men, women, and children appeared in fields abounding

Marine Corps Photo A186822

Marines prepare to evacuate killed and wounded from battle area in Operation Texas. The troops are collecting extra ammunition and equipment from the casualties.

in unharvested rice and other grains, while Marines found abandoned enemy defenses such as spider traps and tunnels. About 1515, near Thach An Noi (1), enemy machine guns and AK-47s began firing. As at Phuong Dinh (2), the enemy troops fought from well-prepared positions and showed a high degree of battle discipline. An overcrowded radio net caused delay in obtaining supporting air and artillery, but after three hours of close fighting in the hamlet, the Communist force, an estimated two companies, broke contact.[13]

With two of his battalions heavily engaged on the afternoon of 21 March, Colonel Peatross decided to commit his reserve. He selected the hamlet of Xuan Hoa as the target, 1,500 meters southeast of Phuong Dinh (2). The helilift of Lieutenant Colonel Young's 3d Battalion, 1st Marines, reinforced with the 2d ARVN Division Strike Company, began at 1600. Lieutenant Colonel Zitnik remembered that his Hueys from VMO-6 had controlled fixed-wing air strikes all afternoon and he had "thought we had neutralized . . . " the area. The transport helicopters carrying Young's battalion flew "low over open fields" toward the objective hamlet, situated at the foot of a low-lying hill. Zitnik recalled seeing some uniformed VC heading toward Xuan Hoa and calling down strikes on the hamlet. According to the VMO-6 commander:

> The hamlet was almost totally destroyed when the helos appeared, but . . . a few large mm tracers were fired at the flight and hit their mark. The A-4D pilots quickly took the position under attack and quieted the fire, but not until after one helo was hit.[14]

The helicopter from HMM-163 "rolled, inverted, and crashed," exploding and burning on impact. Seven 3d Battalion Marines and three crew members died in the wreckage. The pilot, 1st Lieutenant Noah M. Kraft, was thrown clear, but later died of injuries.[15]

On the ground, the Marine infantry battalion and ARVN company encountered only sporadic resistance until reaching the outskirts of Xuan Hoa. Once more, the Marines and ARVN met well-entrenched VC who had organized their defenses within a tree line and bamboo fence which surrounded the hamlet. By nightfall, after two hours of close-quarter combat, Young's battalion had advanced 150 meters into Xuan Hoa. At this time, the estimated enemy company disengaged and retreated, pursued by Marine artillery and Huey gunships.[16]

In the northern Texas area on 21 March, the ARVN 4th Regimental Task Force reached Route 527 and advanced east toward Route 1, without incident, at first. The 1st Battalion, 5th ARVN Regiment was on the regimental left flank while the 5th ARVN Airborne Battalion was on the right. Outside Khanh My (3), 2,000 meters west of the Chau Nhai complex where Operation Utah had taken place, the 5th Airborne Battalion and its supporting APC company ran into an enemy battalion. Twice, the ARVN airborne troops attacked the hamlet, supported by artillery and air, and twice, the Communists drove them back. Nine of the 12 tracked vehicles supporting the ARVN airborne were hit by mortars and grenades. Fighting continued into the night.[17]

By this time, General Lam had moved to his forward headquarters at Binh Son and very early on 22 March, Brigadier General Lowell E. English, the 3d Marine Division assistant division commander, assumed command of the Marine forces in Operation Texas as Commanding General, Task Force Delta. This reactivation of Task Force Delta was in line with General Walt's policy of having Marine generals in command of major operations in the field with their Vietnamese counterparts. According to Colonel Peatross, the reactivation of Task Force Delta was a change of designation not the establishment of a new headquarters. The 7th Marines staff became the Task Force Delta staff; the only thing that changed was the name. He later wrote:

> General English did fly into the CP and remain until the operation was over. . . . There was no question in my mind but that he was in command, but he brought no staff with him, no aide, no runner nor any communications. . . . Technically he was in command and I was the chief of staff; but, I continued to run the operation and kept him informed.[18]

The allied plan of action for 22 March was to continue the attack. ARVN forces were to advance toward Route 1, while the Marine battalions cleared their respective sectors in the southern area of operations. If the 2d Battalion, 4th Marines and the 3d Battalion, 7th Marines met further resistance in Phuong Dinh (2) and Thach An Noi (1), Lieutenant Colonel Young's battalion was to attack north, otherwise it was to seize Hill 65, 2,000 meters southeast of Xuan Hoa, and then advance to the northeast.[19]

As planned, the allied battalions renewed their attacks at daybreak, but encountered little opposition. The Communist forces had slipped away during the night. The 4th ARVN Regimental Task Force secured Khanh My (3) and continued, uncontested, eastward along Route 527. Lieutenant Colonel Kelley's 2d Battalion took Phuong Dinh (2) and began searching the hamlet and destroying the enemy's defenses. Further south, Lieutenant Colonel Young's 3d Battalion met only scattered resistance as it seized Hill 65 at 1700 that afternoon and then moved to the northeast to set up night defenses. Bodley's 3d Battalion, 7th Marines also successfully carried out its mission, advancing through Thach An Noi (1), and then eastward until it reached a line 2,000 meters east of the hamlet.

When it became apparent that strong enemy forces were no longer in the original Texas objective area, General English and Colonel Peatross decided to extend the operation further south. They ordered the helilift of Bodley's battalion from Thach An Noi (1) to a new area near the Phuoc Loc village complex,

Marine Corps Photo A186816
MajGen Wood B. Kyle, Commanding General, 3d Marine Division, walks with LtCol Paul X. (P. X.) Kelley, Commanding Officer, 2d Battalion, 4th Marines after the battalion secured Phuong Dinh. The strain of battle is reflected on the faces of the exhausted Marines on each side of the path.

9,000 meters to the southeast just above the Tra Khuc River.[20]

The helicopter landing of Bodley's battalion took place without incident and by 1815 the battalion had secured Hill 23, 500 meters north of Phuoc Loc (1). With the command group remaining on the hill and Company I in blocking positions to the west, Companies K and L advanced on the hamlet. The Marines soon found themselves in the same type of combat that characterized the fighting in Phuong Dinh (2) and Thach An Noi (1) the day before. The enemy force, about two battalions, was firmly entrenched in the hamlet. As the Marine companies closed in on Phuoc Loc (1), the VC opened fire and stopped the Marine advance. Heavy fighting continued until after dark, but the Marine battalion remained unable to penetrate the enemy's defenses.

Soon after making contact, the Marines called for air and artillery support. The artillery response was immediate; the task force artillery group fired almost 2,000 155mm rounds in support of the 3d Battalion. When the artillery was not active, jets from both MAG-11 and MAG-12 bombed and strafed the objective area.

The 1st MAW had made some adjustments to bring in fixed-wing support for the operation. When Task Force Delta was activated, General McCutcheon sent Lieutenant Colonel Richard A. Savage from MAG-11 to Chu Lai to be the assistant tactical air commander for the operation. Savage placed the fixed-wing support aircraft on ground alert, rather than on combat air patrols. By keeping the jets on 15-minute ground alert and by close monitoring of the tactical situation, he could scramble the ". . . aircraft when it became apparent that they would be needed."[21]

On the morning of 23 March, the 3d Battalion, 7th Marines secured Phuoc Loc (1). Again the VC had slipped out during the night. Bodley's battalion remained in the hamlet to destroy the extensive fortifications there. In their search, the Marines discovered an outer and inner ring of trenches and over 300 fighting holes. The Marine battalion also uncovered two intricate tunnel networks which explained how the enemy was able to get out of Phuoc Loc. According to the villagers, the VC had divided into two groups, one of which crossed the Tra Kruc River by boat while the other escaped on foot to the west.

Questioning the residents of Phuoc Loc (1) with the assistance of an ARVN intelligence officer and local authorities, the Marines learned that the enemy force had suffered substantial casualties. Apparently anticipating a battle, the VC had taken 30 men of the hamlet to serve as stretcher bearers on the afternoon of 22 March. They later returned and impressed 80 more people, including old men, women, and children, to haul away the dead and wounded. One old couple told the Marines that they had counted 30-32 dead and about 100 wounded VC being carried past their house. A 56-year old farmer stated that he had seen another 36 bodies shuttled toward the river. Some villagers provided distorted figures

Marine rifleman escorts a prisoner taken in the fighting for Phuong Dinh. The prisoner is 16 years old.

Marine Corps Photo A194538

obviously to please the Americans; one estimate was 500 dead. Most of the inhabitants of the hamlet remained in their family shelters during the fighting and could not have seen anything. Although finding no enemy bodies in Phuoc Loc (1), Lieutenant Colonel Bodley, as a result of an analysis of the interrogations, reported 60 enemy dead. The Marine battalion lost seven men killed and 56 wounded in the same engagement.[22]

On the morning of 23 March, the 4th ARVN Regimental Task Force encountered a VC force just west of the railroad on Route 527, killing 40 of the enemy. This engagement was the last significant action of the combined operation. The Marines continued Operation Texas for two more days in order to complete mopping up in Phuoc Loc (1) and Phuong Dinh (2).

On 24 March, General English deactivated Task Force Delta, and the 7th Marines reassumed control of the operation.* The Marines closed out Texas the following day. From captured enemy documents, the allies determined that they had encountered elements of three battalions, the *60th* and *90th* from the *1st VC Regiment* and the *11th* from the *21st NVA Regiment*. The Marines reported killing 283 enemy troops while sustaining casualties of 99 dead and 212 wounded. Lieutenant Colonel Kelley's 2d Battalion found 168 of the enemy dead in Phuong Dinh (2).[23]

A few days later, Kelley offered the following analysis of his battalion's experience in Operation Texas, which for the most part held true for the other Marine battalions which participated in the operation:

> The overriding problem in Operation Texas was one which had plagued the Marine Corps for many years: how to inflict maximum loss on a determined, well-entrenched enemy with complex defensive positions at a minimum loss to one's own forces. In the case of Phuong Dinh (2) over 2,500 rounds of artillery and innumerable air strikes with napalm and heavy ordnance were called. The net result, however, indicated that the enemy in well-constructed bunkers, in holes with overhead cover and 20-feet deep tunnels was not appreciably hurt by our preparatory fires and had to be killed in his positions by infantry action at close quarters.[24]

---

*General Peatross commented that the deactivation of Task Force Delta merely consisted of General English flying back to Da Nang. MajGen Oscar F. Peatross, Comments on draft MS, dtd 1Jun78 (Vietnam Comment File).

Marine Corps Photo A186818
Gen William C. Westmoreland, ComUSMACV (center), attends briefing on Operation Texas. Col Oscar F. Peatross (on the right of the picture) holds the briefing charts while BGen Lowell E. English, Commanding General, Task Force Delta (to the left and rear of Westmoreland), and Gen Hoang Xuan Lam, Commanding General, 2d ARVN Division (left), look on.

General Westmoreland visited Phuong Dinh (2) on 24 March and observed the extent of the enemy defenses. He had Colonel Peatross assemble the two battalions in the area and thanked them personally for their performance. Later, he sent a congratulatory message to General Walt. The MACV commander complimented the Marine units in the operation for their aggressive spirit and close coordination. General Walt added his "well done."[25]

There was a short epilogue to Texas—Operation Indiana. Early on the morning of 28 March, the 3d Battalion, 5th ARVN Regiment, which had remained in positions near the hamlet of Lam Loc (1) approximately 1,500 meters east of Phuoc Loc (1), repulsed several attacks by an estimated Communist regiment. The Marine command reinforced the ARVN forces when Marine helicopters brought Lieutenant Colonel James P. Kelly's 1st Battalion, 7th Marines into a landing zone 2,000 meters northwest of Lam Loc (1) late that afternoon. The 1st Battalion was to establish blocking positions 2,000 meters to the southwest on the northern bank of the

Tra Khuc, but Kelly's Company C ran into an estimated enemy battalion in the hamlet of Vinh Loc (2), about 500 meters northwest of the landing zone. Shortly after 1900, after taking heavy casualties, the company fell back, so that Marine supporting arms could hit the enemy forces.

On the following day, Kelly's 1st Battalion renewed the assault on Vinh Loc (2) while Lieutenant Colonel Utter's 2d Battalion, 7th Marines deployed into blocking positions 3,000 meters north of Vinh Loc (2). By this time the enemy units had disengaged and escaped during the night. Kelly's battalion captured one VC and 19 weapons in Vinh Loc (2). The Marines killed 69 of the enemy while the ARVN forces claimed another 100 Communist dead. Marine losses were 11 dead and 45 wounded, nearly all from the 1st Battalion's Company C. The 7th Marines ended Indiana on 30 March.[26]

Colonel Peatross observed that his battalions fought these March battles largely as integral units. Headquarters and support personnel filled in the gaps in the Chu Lai defenses left by the infantry. Paymaster personnel logged more time in the defense than any other unit at Chu Lai. Peatross later wrote that his 7th Marines had two distinct advantages over other regiments during his tour in Vietnam: "it had one regimental commander and no changes in the battalion commanders, and these units were always together...."[27]* In any event, the month of March had proven to be a bloody one for both the allies and Communist forces in southern I Corps.

---

*Colonel Leon N. Utter, who commanded the 2d Battalion, 7th Marines during this period, reinforced Colonel Peatross' observations on the importance of unit integrity: "Platoons, companies and battalions are *not* interchangeable parts of identical machines. . . . As a battalion commander, I frequently was directed to provide a platoon or a company to someone else's headquarters for operations. My answer was, invariably, 'Assign me the mission and let me take my own people! While this required the replacement of 'my own people' on the line—we went to the field as 2/7. We *knew* each other, how to *communicate*; we had our common experiences and lessons learned and mistakes made; we could anticipate one another. While we frequently distressed administrators and logisticians by wanting to fight *as a unit*, it is my not-too-humble opinion that our tactical successes proved, repeatedly, the validity of the concept and justification of the effort." Col Leon N. Utter, Comments on draft MS, dtd 13Jul78 (Vietnam Comment File).

Expansion at Chu Lai

Between August 1965 and January 1966, the headquarters and battalions of the 1st and 7th Marines had entered Vietnam incrementally, while the division's support and combat support elements had arrived in small echelons, often bumping against the total in-country personnel ceiling established by Washington. In February the last units of the 1st Marine Division departed Camp Pendleton for Okinawa, and on 9 March the division officially closed its rear headquarters at the California base. By the end of March, nearly all of the division, including the aforementioned two infantry regiments, the 11th Marines with three of its four artillery battalions, the 1st Tank Battalion, the 1st Motor Transport Battalion, the 1st Engineer Battalion, the 1st Medical Battalion, and the 1st Shore Party Battalion, was in Vietnam. Only the 5th Marines; the 2d Battalion, 11th Marines; and a few support units remained on Okinawa. A few days before he and his headquarters left for Vietnam, Major General Lewis J. Fields, the division commander, received the following message from General Krulak: "You met every deadline and every shipping date and when your unit sailed they were ready to fight. No one could ask more."[28]**

On 29 March, General Fields arrived at Da Nang. After a brief meeting with General Walt, he went on to Chu Lai where he established the division command post. That afternoon he assumed operational control of all Marine ground forces at Chu Lai and also became the deputy commander of III MAF. In this capacity General Fields was the Chu Lai installation coordinator responsible for the security of all

---

**There had been some thought given to retaining a division rear headquarters on Okinawa under the assistant division commander, Brigadier General William A. Stiles, who had arrived from Camp Pendleton in mid-February. It was decided, however, in order to avoid administrative and fiscal complications, not to establish an official division rear. Instead Brigadier General Stiles, with a small personal staff, was assigned on 30 March as a double-hatted commanding general of both Task Force 79 and the newly established 9th Marine Amphibious Brigade (9th MAB) on Okinawa. General Stiles was relieved of these temporary assignments and assumed his duties as assistant division commander at Chu Lai on 15 April 1966. 1st Mar Div ComdCs, Feb-April 1966. See Chapter 18 for further discussion of the 9th MAB.

A joint honor guard of the 1st and 3d Marine Divisions passes in review at a ceremony at Da Nang marking the arrival of the 1st Marine Division in Vietnam. The 1st Marine Division Headquarters was established at Chu Lai while the 3d Division retained control of Marine units at Da Nang and Phu Bai.

organizations and facilities located within the TAOR. To meet these requirements, he activated the Chu Lai Defense Command and tasked it with the defense of vital areas on Ky Ha Peninsula, the SATS airfield, and the supply complex. This command consisted of two rifle companies from one of the infantry battalions and two platoons each from the tank and antitank battalions. An additional 400 personnel from the ground elements of the two aircraft groups augmented the defenses.

Colonel Glen E. Martin, who had been Chief of Staff of the former ADC group at Chu Lai, recalled the initial nervousness of some of the newly arrived troops, who had taken over security of the division CP area. He remembered that "About midnight a few rounds were fired, followed by several explosions from hand grenades. Then firing became continuous by the CP Security Group." Martin "finally brought an end to the firing by going to each security point in a jeep with the lights on, putting the lights on the security point, and walking in the lights to the Marine sentry on duty." The colonel then identified himself and advised "the Marine there were better things to do than fire at his fellow Marines." The firing finally stopped and Martin and another officer went to the 7th Marines "regimental mess for coffee."[29]

There was some modification in the disposition and control of the Chu Lai infantry regiments and battalions. The 7th Marines, with all three of its battalions under its operational control, continued to be responsible for the southern half of the TAOR, but received a new commander. On 7 April, Colonel Eugene H. Haffey relieved Colonel Peatross, whose

Marine Corps Photo A801960

The photo depicts an aerial view of the Chu Lai base area in April 1966, looking south. The 1st Division Headquarters is located approximately in the middle of the picture.

tour in Vietnam was about to come to an end. Colonel Haffey had been the 1st Marine Division comptroller and according to General Fields, "a most valued member" of his staff.³⁰

The major changes at Chu Lai were made in the 1st Marines sector as the battalions of the 5th Marines arrived. On 13 April, the 2d Battalion, 5th Marines landed at Chu Lai and on the following day it replaced the 2d Battalion, 4th Marines in the 1st Marines sector. The latter battalion, which had been under the operational control of the 1st Marines, moved to Da Nang. Colonel Byran B. Mitchell, the 1st Marines commander, now had his own 3d Battalion and the 2d Battalion, 5th Marines, under his control. On 22 May, the 3d Battalion, 1st Marines also displaced to Da Nang and was replaced in the 1st Marines northern sector by the 1st Battalion, 5th Marines, which had been relieved earlier in the month by BLT 3/5 as the SLF battalion. Finally on 27 May, Colonel Charles F. Widdecke, a holder of both the Navy Cross and Silver Star earned in World War II, brought the 5th Marines' Headquarters from Okinawa to Chu Lai. On 3 June, Widdecke's headquarters assumed control of the 1st and 2d Bat-

The 1st Battalion, 7th Marines debark from UH-34s in an unopposed landing south of Chu Lai in April 1966. From April through June, the 1st Division units at Chu Lai conducted 10 battalion-size operations.

Marine Corps Photo A373657

Marine Corps Photo A369046
The 7th Marines display U.S. manufactured weapons captured during Operation Hot Springs. The weapons include Browning automatic rifles in the foreground, .30 and .50 caliber machine guns, and 106mm recoilless rifles.

talions, 5th Marines, while the 1st Marines Headquarters transferred to Da Nang.

In June 1966, the 1st Marine Division at Chu Lai consisted of over 17,000 men in two infantry regiments of three and two battalions respectively, an artillery regiment of four battalions, and other supporting units including engineer, tank, amtrac, antitank, and reconnaissance battalions, as well as separate detachments. Future plans called for the deployment to Chu Lai of the 3d Battalion, 5th Marines and reinforcement by the Korean Marine Brigade later in the summer.

The Chu Lai TAOR had expanded from 205 square miles at the beginning of the year to 340 square miles at the end of June. The 1st Battalion, 5th Marines established its command post on Hill 54, some 10 miles north of the airfield and only six miles south of Tam Ky, the capital of Quang Tin Province. The Marines planned that the Da Nang and Chu Lai TAORs would meet at Tam Ky, a point equidistant between the two enclaves, by the end of the year.

In the Chu Lai TAOR, the division continued to use the same combination of battalion and independent small-unit actions that had characterized earlier operations. From April through June, 1st Marine Division units at Chu Lai launched 10 battalion-sized operations outside the division TAOR. In one, Operation Hot Springs in April, the 7th Marines again engaged the *1st VC Regiment* in the same general area where Utah, Texas, and Indiana had taken place. The Marines killed over 150 of the enemy and captured 23 weapons, including 6 that were crew-served. Although carefully planned and executed, the other nine large operations had minimal contact with the NVA and VC. On the other hand, the small-unit actions within the TAOR increased during this period. Marine patrols and ambushes rose from 2,285 in April, resulting in 11 enemy dead, to nearly 2,900 in June resulting in 72 enemy dead.[31]

Operation Kansas

At the beginning of June, the 1st Marine Division turned its attention toward the Do Xa Region, a suspected enemy base area, 30 miles southwest of Chu Lai near the western border of I Corps. MACV placed the headquarters of the enemy *Military Region V* in the Do Xa and for some time had wanted the Marines to mount an operation there. Since late April and shortly after his arrival at Chu Lai, the 1st Division assistant division commander, Brigadier General William A. Stiles, a 1939 Naval Academy graduate and seasoned campaigner, commanded a special task force headquarters, Task Force X-Ray, to plan a reconnaissance in force in the Do Xa. After some postponements and some problems with coordination, Stiles and his staff had completed their plans for the Do Xa when disturbing reports reached III MAF that the enemy's *2d Division*, also known as the *620th NVA Division*, with all three regiments, the *3d NVA*, the *21st NVA*, and the *1st VC*, had entered the Que Son Valley straddling the Quang Tin-Quang Nam provincial boundaries northwest of Chu Lai.[32]

Control of the Que Son Valley was important to both sides, and it had been the area of operations for both Double Eagle II in February and Harvest Moon the preceding December. Bounded by mountains on the north, south, and west, the valley extends some 24 miles east to west from Route 1 to Hiep Duc. The Ly Ly River and Routes 534 and 535 traverse most of its length. Supporting a population of 60,000 persons, the valley contains some of the best farmland in Vietnam as well as rich salt deposits. General Thi, the former I Corps commander, once described the Que Son area as one of the keys to the struggle for I Corps.[33]

Faced with the reported incursion of North Vietnamese units into the strategic Que Son Valley, Generals Walt and Fields had little choice but to postpone the Do Xa operation. On 13 June, they ordered an extensive reconnaissance campaign between Tam Ky and Hiep Duc and directed General Stiles' Task Force X-Ray Headquarters to begin planning for a combined operation with the 2d ARVN Division. The concept of operations for the reconnaissance effort called for the insertion of six teams from the 1st Reconnaissance Battalion and a seventh team from the 1st Force Reconnaisance Company into selected landing zones to determine the extent of the NVA penetration. On the 13th, the 1st Reconnaissance Battalion's command group, which was to control the reconnaissance operation, and a 13-man reconnaissance team were to be helilifted to Nui Loc Son, a small mountain in the center of the Que Son Valley and some seven miles northeast of Hiep Duc. Another 18-man reconnaissance team, on the same date, was to be landed on the Nui Vu hill mass that dominates the terrain approximately 10 miles west of Tam Ky. These initial landings were to be followed on the next day by the insertion of the remaining teams—two to the higher ground just south of the valley, two to the northwest of the valley, and one to the south of Hiep Duc. The last group, a 13-man team from the 1st Force Reconnaissance Company, was to make a parachute drop on Hill 555 just east of the Tranh River.[34]

The insertion of the reconnaissance teams went much as planned. During the early evening of 13 June, the first two reconnaissance teams had landed on Nui Vu and Nui Loc Son and Lieutenant Colonel Arthur J. Sullivan, the commanding officer of the 1st Reconnaissance Battalion, had established his command post at Nui Loc Son. On the night of 13-14 June, the 1st Force Reconnaissance Company team made a successful parachute drop from an Army transport into their objective area. Their only casualty was one man who slightly twisted his ankle on landing. Marine helicopters brought the four remaining teams from the 1st Reconnaissance Battalion into their respective landing zones without incident late on the evening of 14 June, thus completing the first phase of the operation.[35]

The team from the 1st Force Reconnaissance Company was the first to be extracted from its zone of action. Upon landing, the men had buried their parachutes and climbed Hill 555, where they established their observation post. The team during the course of the morning and afternoon of the 14th spotted approximately 40 armed enemy dressed in khaki or "black pajamas" and wearing sun helmets, some of whom were apparently undergoing tactical training. At about 1830, two woodcutters with a dog came across the spot where the team had hidden its parachutes. The dog apparently detected an unfamiliar scent and the woodcutters found one of the chutes and immediately departed. About a half hour later, the Marines observed the two woodcutters accompanied by nine armed men moving along the eastern bank of the Tranh River, obviously looking for someone. At this point, 1st Lieutenant Jerome T. Paull, the patrol leader, asked that his men be extracted from their position. Shortly afterward, a Marine helicopter brought the men back to Chu Lai.[36]

Of the remaining patrols, the 18-man team led by Staff Sergeant Jimmie L. Howard on Nui Vu was to have the sharpest encounter with the enemy forces. After their insertion on the 13th, Howard's men found the 1,500-foot hill an excellent observation platform and for the next two days reported extensive enemy activity in the region. Supported by an ARVN 105mm battery located at the Tien Phuoc Special Forces Camp, seven miles south of Nui Vu, the Marines called artillery missions on targets of opportunity.[37]

Although Howard had taken the precaution to call the fire missions only when an American spotter plane or helicopter was in the area, the enemy by the 15th had become aware of the patrol's presence in the area. Late that night, a patrol from the Special Forces camp reported an enemy battalion moving toward Nui Vu from the southeast. Between 2130 and 2330, Howard called for artillery support as the Marines heard North Vietnamese troops massing at the bottom of the hill. Shortly after midnight, the Communists probed the Marine defenses and then followed with a three-sided, all-out attack. According to the Navy corpsman with the Marines, the enemy forces," . . . were within 20 feet of us. Suddenly there were grenades all over. Then people

FURTHER FIGHTING AND AN EXPANDING BASE OF OPERATIONS

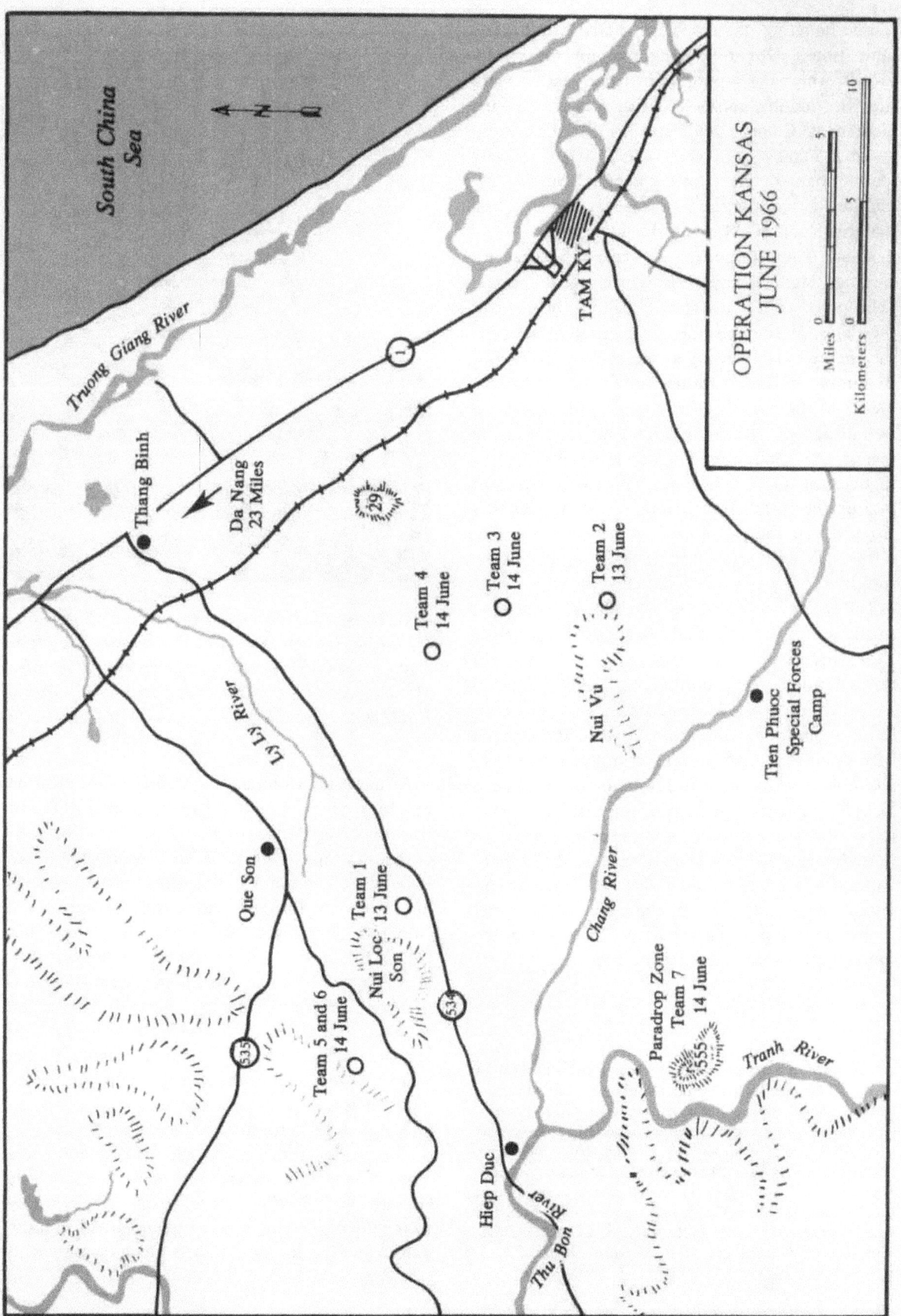

started hollering. It seemed everybody got hit at the same time." Despite the intensity of the enemy assault, which was supported by heavy machine gun fire, the Marine perimeter held. Howard radioed Lieutenant Colonel Sullivan, his battalion commander, "You've gotta get us out of here . . . There are too many of them for my people." Sullivan attempted to reassure the patrol leader and told him that assistance would be on the way.[38]

About 0200, supporting air arrived overhead including Marine and Air Force flare planes, helicopters, and attack aircraft. Under the light of the flares, Marine jets and Huey gunships attacked the enemy forces massing at the bottom of the hill. At times, VMO-6 gunships strafed to within 20 meters of the patrol's perimeter and the fixed-wing aircraft dropped bombs and napalm as close as 100 meters. At 0300, enemy ground fire drove off a flight of MAG-36 helicopters which were trying to pick up the patrol. Lieutenant Colonel Sullivan told Howard that the patrol could not expect any reinforcements until dawn and to hold on as best he could.*

The action on and around the hill was reduced to small, scattered, individual fire fights. Wary of the U.S. aircraft orbiting overhead, the Communist forces decided against another mass assault, but continued to fire at the Marines throughout the night. Running short of ammunition, Howard and his men fired single shots and threw rocks at suspected enemy positions, hoping that the NVA would mistake the rocks for grenades. The fighting was exacting a heavy toll on the reconnaissance patrol; each man had been wounded at least once and six were dead. Sergeant Howard was struck in the back by a ricochet, temporarily paralyzing his legs. Unable to use his lower limbs, Howard pulled himself from hole to hole, encouraging his men and directing fire.

---

*Colonel Zitnik commented on the extensive effort by VMO-6 to support Howard's patrol: "Huey availability was down to three aircraft during these early hours, yet continuous TAC(A) [tactical air controller (airborne)] and gunship support was provided with the TAC(A) working without his gunship escort. Helicopters refueled at Ky Ha where they returned with gauges indicating near zero each flight. . . . Crews *were not* rotated as there was no time to brief new crews. They merely reported while the aircraft were refueling and returned to the scene." Col Robert J. Zitnik, Comments on draft MS, dtd 7Jun78 (Vietnam Comment Files).

Marine Corps Photo A414461
SSgt Jimmie C. Howard is seen wearing his Medal of Honor and other medals. Sgt Howard's platoon stood off a NVA battalion on Nui Vu, later called "Howard's Hill," near the Que Son Valley north of Chu Lai.

At dawn on 16 June, MAG-36 UH-34s, escorted by Huey gunships, safely landed Company C, 1st Battalion, 5th Marines near the base of Nui Vu. One of the gunships, however, piloted by Major William J. Goodsell, the commanding officer of VMO-6, was hit by enemy fire and crash landed. Both Major Goodsell and his copilot were evacuated, but Goodsell later died of his wounds. Lieutenant Colonel Zitnik, who had commanded the squadron until March, remembered that Colonel Johnson, the commanding officer of MAG-36, was the TAC(A) for the mission and observed an enemy soldier "throw a grenade into the downed helo but elected not to divert forces from the primary rescue mission of Sergeant Howard."[39]

The Marine company on the ground met some resistance as it advanced up Nui Vu to relieve Howard's patrol. When the relief force finally reached the top of the hill, Howard greeted them with the warning, "Get down . . . There are snipers right in front of us." First Lieutenant Marshall B. "Buck" Darling, the Company C commander, remembered that he found Howard's men mostly armed with AK-47s taken from dead North Vietnamese. The North Vietnamese, later identified as a battalion from the *3d NVA Regiment*, continued to battle the Marines for control of the hill until noon, and then disengaged. They left behind 42 dead and 19 weapons while Company C suffered two dead and two wounded.[40]*

By this time, General Stiles and his Task Force X-Ray Headquarters had completed the planning for a combined operation with the ARVN, codenamed Kansas, in the Que Son region. These plans called for a force of eight infantry battalions, four from III MAF and four from the 2d ARVN Division, supported by air and artillery, to take part in the operation. Two battalions from the 5th Marines and two Vietnamese Marine Battalions, attached to the 2d ARVN Division for the operation, were to make up the initial assault force. The Task Force X-Ray and 2d ARVN Division Headquarters were to be collocated at Tam Ky.[41]

In anticipation of Kansas, III MAF on 16 June deployed artillery units from both Da Nang and Chu Lai into forward firing positions on Hill 29, just west of the railroad some seven miles north of Tam Ky, and near Thang Binh, nine miles further north on Route 1. The 3d Battalion, 1st Marines with a command group and two companies accompanied the artillery from Da Nang and provided security for the gun positions at both Hill 29 and Thang Binh. Battery K, 4th Battalion, 12th Marines with six 155mm howitzers (towed) and the 4th Battalion, 11th Marines Headquarters were in position on Hill 29 and Provisional Battery Y, 4th Battalion, 12th Marines was near Thang Binh with two 155mm howitzers (towed).[42]

Shortly after General Stiles established his forward headquarters at Tam Ky on 17 June, General Walt reduced the scope of the proposed operation. That morning, General Lam, the I Corps commander, had informed Walt that the two Vietnamese Marine battalions would not be available for Kansas because of the political situation in Hue. The I Corps commander was sending one of the battalions to that city and wanted to keep the other at Da Nang in case the trouble spread there. General Walt agreed to delay the operations, and, at the same time decided to change the Kansas plan of action. Instead of a multibattalion heliborne operation in the Que Son Valley, Walt elected to continue the reconnaissance effort of the 1st Reconnaissance Battalion supported by the Marine artillery already deployed in the field. The 5th Marines would remain in the Chu Lai TAOR, but remain ready to exploit the situation in the event the reconnaissance teams came across a sizeable body of enemy troops. General Stiles' headquarters with the 5th Marines would control the operation.[43]

During the next few days, the Marines reinforced the artillery and repositioned some of the guns to provide better coverage for the reconnaissance teams. On 18 June, Battery K, 4th Battalion, 11th Marines with four 155mm howitzers (SP), joined the 4th Battalion Headquarters on Hill 29, and, at the same time, the provisional battery from the 12th Marines deployed to new firing positions, some 6,000 meters southwest of Thang Binh. The following day, Battery K of the 12th Marines moved from Hill 29 and linked up with the provisional battery further north. On the 19th as well, two especially prepared CH-46 helicopters lifted two 105mm howitzers from Battery D, 2d Battalion, 11th Marines, from the Chu Lai TAOR to the Tien Phuoc Special Forces Camp, a distance of some 30 miles. The 3d Battalion, 1st Marines, which came under the operational control of the 5th Marines on 17 June, provided security for the artillery near Route 1 while the ARVN provided the security for the Marine and South Vietnamese 105mm batteries at Tien Phuoc.[44]

With the supporting arms largely in position, Lieutenant Colonel Sullivan, the reconnaissance battalion commander, had moved his forward CP on 18 June from Loc Son to the Tien Phuoc Special Forces Camp. From the 19th through 28 June, the reconnaissance battalion, reinforced by two platoons of the 1st Force Reconnaissance Company and the 2d ARVN Division Reconnaissance Company, continued to conduct extensive patrolling throughout the Que Son region. Beginning with the initial entry on 13 June, 25 reconnaissance teams took part in the operation. With the exception of the parachute drop

---

*For this action, 15 men of Howard's platoon were awarded the Silver Star and two more the Navy Cross. Staff Sergeant Howard was awarded the Medal of Honor.

and two other patrols that walked into their target areas from forward bases, Marine helicopters inserted and extracted the Marine reconnaissance teams.[45]

Operation Kansas, which officially began on 17 June and ended on the 22d when General Stiles closed his Tam Ky headquarters, never expanded much beyond the reconnaissance stage. The Marine infantry participation, with the exception of the relief of Howard's platoon, was confined to a one-company exploitation of a B-52 Arc Light strike on 21 June in rugged terrain 3,500 meters east of Hiep Duc. Shortly before 0900, Marine helicopters landed Company E, 2d Battalion, 5th Marines in the landing zone near the B-52 bomb impact area. Although encountering some minor resistance near the landing zone, the Marine company found little evidence of any large body of enemy forces. By 1015, the last elements of the company had reembarked on board helicopters for the return flight to Chu Lai.[46]

Despite the official end of Kansas on 22 June, both the Marine artillery and reconnaissance teams remained deployed in and around the Que Son Valley for six more days. Throughout the entire period from 13 June through 27 June, the reconnaissance teams made 141 sightings and observed a total of 763 enemy troops. The teams had a direct communication link with the fire direction center with the 4th Battalion, 11th Marines on Hill 29 and could call upon artillery and air. Marine jets flew, and the artillery batteries fired, an equal number of missions, 43 each, in support of the reconnaissance Marines. In addition, the USS *Morton* (DD 948) provided naval gunfire support, firing 384 rounds of naval gunfire at suspected enemy positions. In one of the more successful actions, a Marine reconnaissance outpost brought artillery fire upon a small force of NVA, killing all seven of the enemy. The Marines then asked "the guns to remain laid on this position." Soon afterward, more NVA arrived to remove the bodies and the Marines called artillery down upon this new group, inflicting another 10 casualties on the North Vietnamese. Exclusive of the enemy killed in the fight for Nui Vu, the Marine reconnaissance teams by calling upon supporting arms accounted for 85 enemy dead as well as 40 elephants and 10 water buffalo. The Marines sustained casualties of nine killed and 20 wounded. All of the Marine dead and 14 of the wounded were as a result of the NVA attack on Nui Vu.[47]

More significant than the comparative casualty ratio was the fact that a relatively few reconnaissance Marines, supported by air and artillery, prevented the NVA from massing their forces and penetrating the Que Son Valley in strength. As Lieutenant Colonel Sullivan observed:

> Whatever his [the enemy's] intentions for forming in that area, this recon effort supported by fire broke up his formations, caused him to move, and inflicted casualties upon him and his logistic buildup. . . . He is particularly vulnerable to observed fire and air strikes.[48]

The experience of the 1st Reconnaissance Battalion in Operation Kansas was an exceptional one. Usually it fell to the infantry to tramp the rough terrain on both large operations and small-unit patrols to seek out the illusive enemy and destroy him in sharp fire fights. In Kansas the Marines did it a different way.

By the end of June, III MAF reported substantial progress against the enemy in southern I Corps and in the pacification of the Chu Lai TAOR. In contrast to Da Nang and Phu Bai, the spring political crisis had little impact on the Chu Lai base. The 2d ARVN Division, which operated in this area, had remained loyal to the government, and its commander, General Lam, had become the I Corps commander. The extensive Marine operations in Quang Ngai and Quang Tin Provinces and the reconnaissance campaign in the Que Son Valley had succeeded in keeping the enemy's large units out of the coastal populated areas. Moreover, statistics compiled by the Marines and pacification teams showed that nearly 30,000 of the 160,000 people in the Chu Lai TAOR lived in villages that scored more than 80 percent on Marine pacification indices. There was every reason for optimism by midyear.[49]

PART IV
THE DMZ WAR

CHAPTER 9
The Enemy Buildup in the North

Speculation about the Enemy's Intentions—Reconnaissance at Khe Sanh, Operation Virginia—Marine Operations in Thua Thien, April-May 1966—Contingency Planning and Reconnaissance at Dong Ha—Politics and War—Heavy Fighting in Thua Thien Province—Further Reconnaissance in the North

Speculation About the Enemy's Intentions

Throughout the period of political unrest and the expansion of the Marine base areas at Da Nang and Chu Lai, General Westmoreland continued to be concerned about northern I Corps and speculated about Communist intentions there. As early as February at the Honolulu Conference, he told President Johnson that if he were an enemy general he would attempt to "capture Hue." The MACV commander made the point that the former imperial capital was a "symbol of a united Vietnam," and its loss would have a traumatic effect upon the allied war effort. He periodically referred to the military advantages for the enemy to make a thrust in the north. Westmoreland argued that such a move not only shortened the lines of communication for the NVA, but that the mountain spur north of Da Nang effectively isolates the two northern provinces of Thua Thien and Quang Tri from the rest of South Vietnam and made them particularly vulnerable to an enemy attack. Any allied reinforcements along Route 1 and the railroad, the only north-south arteries, had to wend their way through the narrow confines of the strategic Hai Van Pass, which was subject to enemy harassment. The Marines only kept the pass open through extensive patrolling and armed "Rough Rider" road convoys. Through March, the enemy effectively closed the railroad between Da Nang and Hue 50 percent of the time.[1]

Intelligence reports and events reinforced Westmoreland's belief that the enemy was staging his forces in the north for a major offensive. He contended that the fall of A Shau may have been only a prelude for a later attack on Hue itself. Allied intelligence estimates placed the enemy infiltration into South Vietnam as averaging 7,000 men a month during the period January through March of 1966. Several sources reported the massing of North Vietnamese units in Laos opposite the border with Quang Tri and Thua Thien Provinces. In early April, MACV received information that the North Vietnamese had begun to move their *324B Division* from Ha Tinh, 180 kilometers north of the DMZ, into southern North Vietnam. The MACV enemy order of battle carried three enemy regiments and indicated the possible existence of a fourth in the two northern provinces of South Vietnam. In addition, other intelligence revealed the establishment of a

A view of the Royal Palace in Hue as photographed in February 1966. Hue was the former imperial capital of Vietnam and stood as a "symbol of a united Vietnam."

Marine Corps Photo A187610

major enemy headquarters in north central Thua Thien Province, some 20 miles west of Hue. At first, allied intelligence officers believed the headquarters to be that of a division, but later identified it as that of the newly formed *Tri-Thien-Hue Military Region*, which reported directly to the North Vietnamese command.[2]

In contrast to MACV, General Walt and his staff read the intelligence data differently. Although acknowledging some buildup of enemy forces in the two northern provinces, they saw little evidence of any major enemy all-out offensive. The III MAF intelligence section, in comparison to the MACV J-2, was relatively conservative in giving credence to the establishment of enemy regimental organizations in northern I Corps. As opposed to the three and possibly four enemy regiments carried by MACV, III MAF officially placed the third regimental headquarters, the *6th NVA*, in its order of battle only on 15 April. Moreover, the Marines contended that since the arrival of the 4th Marines at Phu Bai in late March, contact with the enemy had been sparse. Although throughout April reports reached the 4th Marines of the movement of large Communist forces into the area, an extensive reconnaissance effort "failed to confirm a significant buildup in the approaches leading into Hue-Phu Bai."[3] Commenting on the failure of the enemy to react to the Marine reinforcement of its northern base, Colonel Donald W. Sherman, the commander of the 4th Marines, later stated, "I don't think the enemy was planning anything against Phu Bai at the time."[4] Further north, the 1st ARVN Division, with the exception of two relatively small engagements on 28 March and 10 April, also encountered few Communist forces. Even General Westmoreland remarked on the lull in enemy activity, but quickly observed that he believed the Communists were preparing the battlefield.[5]

At a MACV commanders' conference on 21 April, Westmoreland asked General Walt if the III MAF commander had any reason to doubt the number of major NVA units in I Corps that were being carried by the MACV J-2. Walt replied that his forces in extensive long-range reconnaissance operations had been unable to verify the existence of any large body of enemy troops. He then declared, "If they [the NVA] were there, that they were hiding in the mountains not far from the Laos border."[6] Throughout this period, the Marines resisted, as one III MAF staff officer remembered, every effort to "get us extended" and away from the pacification campaign further south.[7]

Reconnaissance at Khe Sanh, Operation Virginia

Despite such reluctance, the Marines in April, at the insistence of General Westmoreland, conducted a one-battalion operation near the isolated Special Forces camp at Khe Sanh in the northwestern corner of Quang Tri Province. General Westmoreland placed a very high priority on the strategic location of Khe Sanh. Surrounded by high hills and mountains and located 4 miles from the Laotian border, 14 miles south of the DMZ, and 55 miles northwest of Phu Bai, the Khe Sanh base overlooked Route 9, the most feasible entry into Quang Tri Province from the west. Using the base to monitor enemy infiltration and for special reconnaissance operations into Laos, the MACV commander also viewed Khe Sanh as "an eventual jump-off point for ground operations to cut the Ho Chi Minh Trail" if he ever received permission from Washington. He continually stressed to General Walt "the critical importance of the little plateau."[8]

In January 1966, the Communists employed 120mm mortars against the Khe Sanh base, but failed to follow up with a ground assault. Intelligence reports, nevertheless, persisted through the following months of an enemy buildup in the area. At the same time that A Shau fell, the Khe Sanh commander informed MACV that enemy units were staging in the area north of the camp. Fearing that a similar fate awaited Khe Sanh as had befallen A Shau, MACV urged upon the Marines a battalion search and destroy mission in the Khe Sanh sector. III MAF planned such an operation, codenamed Virginia, for mid-March, but circumstances, including the Marine commitment to Operation Oregon in northeastern Thua Thien Province, forced the Marine command to postpone the operation. In his meeting with General Walt at Chu Lai on 24 March, General Westmoreland continued to emphasize the dangers in the north.[9]

On 27 March, General Kyle, the 3d Marine Division commander, ordered the 4th Marines at Phu Bai to deploy one battalion, reinforced by a 105mm howitzer battery and a mortar battery, to Khe Sanh. Colonel Sherman selected the 1st Battalion, 1st

Marines to carry out the operation. Lieutenant Colonel Van D. Bell, Jr., who was to assume command of the battalion on 1 April from Lieutenant Colonel Hatch, several years later recalled that he flew to Khe Sanh at the end of March to establish liaison with the Special Forces commander and to get a feel for the terrain. Bell remembered that he found the Special Forces troops "very nervous." According to the Marine officer, the Special Forces were not patrolling, but "trusted this important mission to the Nungs and some ARVN . . . ," who often brought in false intelligence. Bell related:

> Surprisingly, the Special Forces commander believed their reports. . . . During the S-2 briefing, I was shown the enemy contact profile and it appeared that they had the Special Forces camp surrounded.[10]

After the completion of his visit, Lieutenant Colonel Bell returned to Phu Bai and, on 3 April, issued his operation order for Virginia, scheduled to begin two days later. An advance party consisting of the battalion's executive officer, logistic support personnel, and a rifle platoon from Company C arrived at Khe Sanh on 4 April, but bad weather together with the uncertainties of the South Vietnamese political crisis caused a delay in the beginning of the operation for more than a week. On 17 April, Marine KC-130 aircraft from VMGR-152 began to fly the main body of the Marine battalion into the small airfield at Khe Sanh. Once more weather conditions hindered the operation and forced the Marines to stop the airlift after nearly 50 percent of the Marine force had landed. Finally on the next day, the transports completed the lift of the battalion and its supporting forces to Khe Sanh.[11]

Lieutenant Colonel Bell established his main base at a coffee plantation just north of the Special Forces camp. His plan called for a three-phased operation within a 10-kilometer radius of Khe Sanh. The Marines were to first search the northeast quadrant, then move to the northwest, and finally to the southwest sector of the area of operations. An ARVN battalion was to secure the southeast quadrant.

On 18 and 19 April, Bell with the assistance of Marine helicopters from HMM-163 moved his forward headquarters, his mortars, an attached reconnaissance platoon, and Company C to a blocking position about six kilometers north of the base camp. Later on the 19th, the Marine helicopters

Marine Corps Photo A193997
LtCol Van D. Bell, Jr., Commanding Officer, 1st Battalion, 1st Marines (sitting right), briefs his company commanders at Khe Sanh in April 1966 during Operation Virginia. Khe Sanh at this time was a Special Forces camp in northwestern South Vietnam near the Laotian border.

lifted the battalion's remaining companies, A and B, into a landing zone some nine kilometers further to the east.* According to plan, the two companies then pushed westward along parallel axes toward the blocking positions. Encountering no resistance, except from the dense vegetation, the attacking companies reached their objective on 21 April. The Marine battalion returned to its base camp two days later.

At this point, the Marines decided to modify their plans for Virginia. Based on negative reports from his reconnaissance patrols in the northwestern sector of the battalion's area of operations, Bell cancelled the second phase of the operation. At the same time, staff officers at both the division and MAF levels wanted to expand the operation to determine, if

---

*The battalion's fourth company, Company D, was still at Da Nang under the operational control of the 3d Marines.

out. So he marched out Highway 9, which was allegedly the first major force that had ever come along Highway 9 in something like eight or nine years.[13]

In preparation for the march, Lieutenant Colonel Bell prepositioned three 105mm howitzers, together with a second command group under his executive officer and a security force, at Ca Lu, 15 miles east of Khe Sanh on Route 9, to cover the infantry. At the same time, the Marine command moved the 3d Battalion, 4th Marines command group and two companies from Phu Bai to Dong Ha, the eastern terminus of Route 9, from where it could provide a reaction force if Bell's battalion ran into trouble. Outside of difficulty with an attached recalcitrant ARVN company and the heat, the 1st Battalion's trek was uneventful. The battalion reached Cam Lo, some 30 miles from Khe Sanh, at the end of the month. On 1 May, the foot-weary troops rode Marine trucks the remaining eight miles to Dong Ha, where they were greeted by both Generals Walt and Westmoreland. The artillery and the second command group had already been retracted.[14]

Despite the dramatic flourish closing out the operation, Virginia's results were inconclusive except to invalidate the reports of the supposed enemy buildup around Khe Sanh. The size of the enemy's

Marine Corps Photo A187001
Marines from the 1st Battalion, 1st Marines scale a steep cliff in Operation Virginia. The photo gives a good depiction of the rugged terrain surrounding Khe Sanh.

possible, the validity of the claims of an enemy buildup in the north. Colonel George W. Carrington, Jr., the 3d Marine Division G-2, later wrote that he suggested Bell march his battalion "along Route 9 from Khe Sanh east to the sea. It was territory hitherto untouched in the war, but it was important to learn if there was infiltration from the north, across the DMZ."[12] Colonel Chaisson, the III MAF G-3, remembered:

> Old "Ding Dong" [Bell] only had one shot fired at his unit in the whole [period] he was up there [at Khe Sanh] . . . But in order for just a little bravado and to do it a little differently from anyone else up there, we let him march

The 1st Battalion, 1st Marines is seen crossing a bridge along Route 9 during its march from Khe Sanh to Dong Ha. The Marine unit was the first allied force to use this route in several years.

Marine Corps Photo A187769.

forces in the north and his intentions remained a matter of conjecture. As Lieutenant Colonel Bell pointed out in his after-action report:

> ... it is difficult to draw any conclusions about the extent of enemy presence along the route of march. The failure of the enemy to attack, or even to harass, the march column could have been inspired by either (1) inadequate forces, (2) fear of excessive punishment by Marine supporting arms and aircraft, or (3) a desire to inspire overconfidence in the area later—or any combination of these or lesser factors.[15]

Marine Operations in Thua Thien, April-May 1966

Throughout April, the enemy avoided any contact with the Marines in Thua Thien Province. At Phu Bai, with the departure of Bell's battalion for Khe Sanh, Lieutenant Colonel Hanifin's 2d Battalion, 1st Marines took over from the 1st Battalion the western sector of the TAOR while still providing security for the Phu Bai Vital Area. The 3d Battalion, 4th Marines under Lieutenant Colonel Vale continued to operate in the southern portion of the TAOR while Lieutenant Colonel Sullivan's 1st Battalion, 4th Marines remained in the Co Bi-Thanh Tan area. All the Phu Bai battalions conducted Golden Fleece rice protection operations while Sullivan's battalion also provided security for Marine reconnaissance teams northwest of Phu Bai. In the only large unit operation in Thua Thien during the month, the SLF battalion of the Seventh Fleet, BLT 1/5, in Operation Osage, made an amphibious landing on 27 April in Phu Loc District, north of the Hai Van Pass. The SLF Marines failed to engage any major enemy unit and reembarked on board their ships on 6 May.

During May, the 4th Marines increased the number of named operations in the Phu Bai area. This increase may have been influenced by the continuing debate with MACV over the statistical measure "battalion days in the field," as much as by intelligence indicating a sharp influx of enemy units in the sector. Since "battalion days in the field" did not include Marine pacification efforts within the TAORs, III MAF compared unfavorably in the number of "battalion days" it attained as opposed to those accumulated by Army units in less densely populated regions. As one Marine officer on the MACV staff, Colonel Francis F. Parry, observed: "It looks as if the Marines are standing on their hands." Parry recalled that he suggested to III MAF that the Marines should play the statistical game "more realistically." He specifically recommended that three of the four battalions at Phu Bai:

> ... should be considered on operations all the time. . . . [This] may seem a little dishonest, but it is something we have to do in self-defense. As long as we are in a statistical war in which the analysts back in the Pentagon are going to look at these statistics every week, we have to put ourselves in as favorable a light as possible.[16]

Whatever the Marine rationale may have been, General Westmoreland, on 1 May, remarked that he "was delighted to see that the Marines are planning more operations on a sustained basis."[17]

In the first operation, Operation Cherokee, 5-7 May, Colonel Sherman moved a regimental command group into the Co Bi-Thanh Tan region and reinforced the 1st Battalion, 4th Marines already there with two other battalions, the 1st Battalion, 1st Marines (back from Virginia) and the 3d Battalion, 4th Marines, and supporting units. During the three-day operation, the Marines accounted for nine VC while sustaining losses of one Marine killed and 17 wounded. Then acting on intelligence that the *804th VC Battalion* was in Phu Loc District, some 10 miles south of the Phu Bai Airfield and only one mile south of the TAOR, the 4th Marines on 10-12 May conducted Operation Wayne with the 1st Battalion, 1st Marines, and its own 3d Battalion, supported by artillery and engineers, in the area southwest of Route 1 in this sector. The results were similar to Cherokee; the Marines killed five VC and suffered 11 wounded. After the completion of the operation, Lieutenant Colonel Vale's 3d Battalion remained in this area and on 15 May began Operation Athens just northeast of the Wayne area of operations with the mission of keeping Route 1 open. This operation continued into June with only minor enemy resistance.

Based on several sightings and contacts with VC units by Marine reconnaissance patrols in the Co Bi-Thanh Tan area in mid-May, the 4th Marines planned a combined operation in that sector with the 1st ARVN Division. The continuing political turmoil in I Corps at this time, however, prevented any such undertaking with the South Vietnamese. The only change that the Marines made in the Co Bi-Thanh Tan area at this point was to replace the 1st Bat-

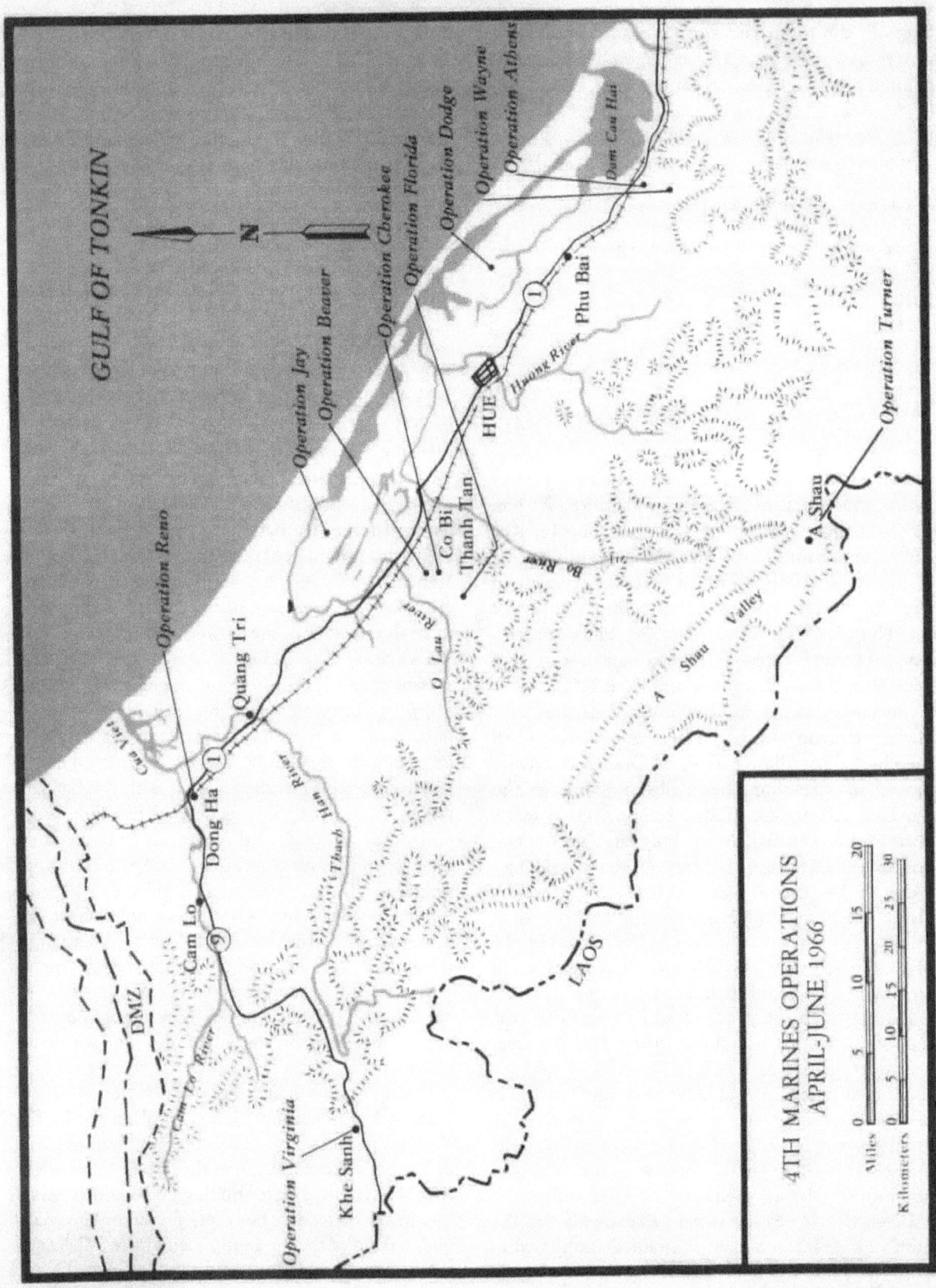

talion, 4th Marines there on 25 May with the 2d Battalion, 1st Marines. Lieutenant Colonel Sullivan's 1st Battalion then took over the protection of the Phu Bai Vital Area. Recalling his battalion's activities in the Co Bi-Thanh Tan area, Lieutenant Colonel Sullivan later wrote: "I'd bet that of all the VC-NVA mortar ammo expended in I Corps during this period, 1/4 was on the receiving end of nearly half of it. As someone once observed, 'Few things in life are as exhilarating as to be shot at with very little result.' "[18]

Contingency Planning and Reconnaissance at Dong Ha

Through this period, General Westmoreland continued to insist on the development of contingency plans to meet any enemy offensive. At the April commanders' conference, he asked that all subordinate commands "work up detailed scenarios of what the enemy might do." In preparing such studies, the MACV commander suggested that the U.S. planners assume that the Communists "will try to suck us into a fight on a field of their choosing," and that it was "necessary to wargame in order to avoid barging into battle at a disadvantage." He further told the assembled commanders that they could not depend upon MACV for reserves since the enemy might strike in more than one place and that they should plan accordingly.[19]

Other U.S. commands, outside of MACV, were also preparing contingency studies. Earlier in the month, the U.S. Army Pacific presented a plan to CinCPac that called for the establishment of a two-division Army corps which would be deployed north along the DMZ and extend into Laos. According to the Army planners, such a move would take "the war out of the south," and bring it "to the north, where we can fight better and make the enemy mass near the DMZ."[20]

Although General Westmoreland was reluctant to move any Army troops into I Corps and opposed at the time to the insertion of another command there not under III MAF, he looked favorably at the establishment of a corps-sized contingency force under his control. At the April commanders' conference, he brought up the idea of the establishment of a corps-size "strike" force, consisting of three divisions, that would be "capable of moving anywhere in South Vietnam to confront any strong enemy thrusts." The MACV commander cautioned that this idea was still in a conceptual stage and that none of the major command and control or logistic problems posed by such a force had as yet been addressed. Westmoreland was not even sure whether such a "strike force" would be based in Vietnam or on Okinawa, or possibly split between the two. In any event, during the next month or so, both the Westmoreland "strike force" and the U.S. Army Pacific plans continued to be discussed among senior U.S. commanders, but without any resolution.[21]

While the American commands prepared their various contingency plans, evidence began to mount of an enemy buildup in the eastern DMZ sector. In mid-May, U.S. reconnaissance aircraft observed increased truck traffic in southern North Vietnam moving south along Route 1. On 19 May, NVA units, in early morning assaults, attacked two ARVN outposts, Gio Linh and Con Thien, just south of the Demilitarized Zone. At both outposts, the South Vietnamese sustained heavy losses, 43 dead and 54 wounded at Gio Linh and 20 casualties at Con Thien. On the same date, a North Vietnamese surrendered to the ARVN and told his captors the *324B NVA Division* had infiltrated through the DMZ into South Vietnam. Three days later, 22 May, the 2d Battalion, 2nd ARVN Regiment, in a search and destroy mission about eight kilometers north of Dong Ha, located a VC company, killing 35 and capturing three of the enemy, at a cost of seven ARVN dead.[22]

Based on additional intelligence that indicated the presence of a North Vietnamese force, possibly of regimental size, east and west of Dong Ha with the mission of taking that city and later attacking Quang Tri, MACV alerted III MAF on 28 May that the situation might require the movement of a Marine battalion to the Dong Ha Air Facility. In anticipation of the proposed operation, the Marine command designated Lieutenant Colonel "P. X." Kelley's 2d Battalion, 4th Marines at Da Nang for the move north. Kelley's battalion was already slated to join its parent regiment at Phu Bai and exchange TAORs with Lieutenant Colonel Bell's 1st Battalion, 1st Marines which was scheduled to go to Da Nang.*

---

*The 1st Battalion, 1st Marines moved to Da Nang from Phu Bai on 31 May and came under the operational control of the 9th Marines. See Chapter 6.

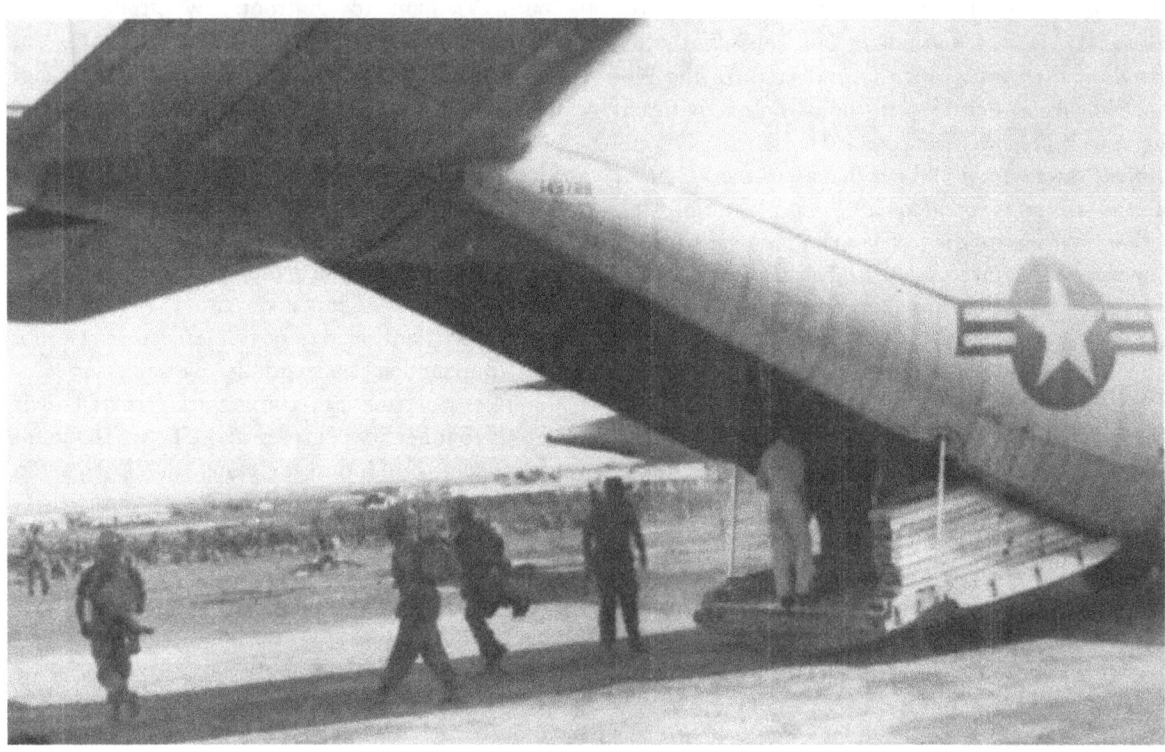

Marine Corps Photo A187155

Marines from the 2d Battalion, 4th Marines arrive at Dong Ha by Marine KC 130 to begin Operation Reno. The battalion remained in the Dong Ha sector for 11 days but encountered few enemy.

On 29 May, General Kyle, the 3d Marine Division commander, made liaison arrangements with the 1st ARVN Division and issued his operational order for the Dong Ha operation, codenamed Reno. The following day, he placed Kelley's battalion under the operational control of the 4th Marines and Marine KC-130s flew the 2nd Battalion's command group, two infantry companies, an attached artillery battery, and support troops to Dong Ha.[23]

From 30 May through 8 June, Kelley's battalion, in coordination with the ARVN, conducted a reconnaissance in force within an eight-kilometer radius of Dong Ha. During this 11-day period, the only enemy activity was an ambush of a six-man U.S. Air Force survey team from the Air Force radar detachment based at the Dong Ha Air Facility. The team

The U.S. radar site at the Dong Ha Air Facility pictured here was manned by U.S. Air Force personnel. It provided early warning of any air threat from the north.

THE ENEMY BUILDUP IN THE NORTH

had departed the airfield in a jeep on the morning of 5 June after refusing an offer by Kelley to provide security. An air observer at 1500 that afternoon spotted a burning vehicle four miles south of Dong Ha and a Marine reaction force, arriving at the scene 20 minutes later, found all six men of the survey team shot to death. There was no sign of the VC. The ambushers apparently stopped the jeep with a grenade, killed each of the Air Force men with a bullet to the head, and then burned the vehicle.[24] Despite this incident, the 2d Battalion found little evidence of any major enemy unit in the Dong Ha sector. With the closeout of Operation Reno on 8 June, the Marine battalion departed Dong Ha. During the operation, the Marines killed three NVA with no casualties of their own. The enemy's intentions in the north still remained unclear.[25]

Politics and War

Although South Vietnam was confronted with a possible buildup of enemy forces in the north, the political confrontation between the Struggle Forces and the central government during this period had a larger impact on the war effort in the two northern provinces. It particularly had an erosive effect upon the morale of the 1st ARVN Division which was responsible for the northern sector. Recruited locally, the troops and several commanders were personally loyal to the former commander of I Corps, General Thi, who had once commanded the division and made his home in Hue. Division Buddhist chaplains led the men in demonstrations against the government. Brigadier General Pham Xuan Nhuan, the division commander, refused to commit himself to either side and conveniently became ill or disappeared at strategic moments. After the burning of the U.S. Information Center Building in Hue on 1 June, the new I Corps commander, General Lam, briefly considered employing the division to put down the disorders in the city, but finally decided against such a move. The division had become politicized and was no longer a dependable fighting force.[26]

The 4th Marines maintained a "hands-off" policy, but attempted to keep open the lines of communication between Phu Bai and the LST ramp in Hue. In the Co Bi-Thanh Tan area, Lieutenant Colonel Hanifin's 2d Battalion, 1st Marines conducted Operation Beaver from 1-7 June. The battalion met only scattered resistance, but confiscated 25,000 pounds of rice. Hoping to get the 1st ARVN Division back into the war, Generals Walt and Lam scheduled a combined operation in this region.[27]

On 5 June, Colonel Sherman with members of his staff visited the 1st Division Headquarters at Hue to coordinate the operation, codenamed Florida, with the South Vietnamese. Based on intelligence that the *6th NVA* Regimental Headquarters and the *800th VC Battalion* were in the Co Bi-Thanh Tan area, the planners selected a 54-square-mile area sandwiched between the two rivers, the O Lau on the west and the Bo on the east. Two Marine battalions, the 2d Battalion, 1st Marines already in the area, and Kelley's 2d Battalion, which was to be helilifted from Dong Ha to the Co Bi-Thanh Tan sector, were to attack south from Route 1. Colonel Sherman was to move his forward headquarters into the objective area and the 3d Battalion, 12th Marines was to provide artillery support. In a companion operation, Doan Ket, the 1st ARVN Division with two of its own battalions, a Vietnamese Marine Corps battalion, and two airborne battalions, was to secure the high ground to the south, the Marines rear to the north, and the Marine left flank to the east. Marine reconnaissance teams were to screen the area west of the Song O Lau.[28]

First on, then off, and then on again, the operation was beset with problems at the outset. The tense political situation caused the allies to postpone the operation, originally scheduled to begin on the 7th. Dissidents clogged the streets of Hue and Route 1 with Buddhist altars, blocking both military and civilian traffic. Brigadier General English, the 3d Marine Division assistant commander, and Colonel Sherman went to Hue on the 7th to discuss the situation with the South Vietnamese authorities. Because of General Lam's reluctance to delay the operation further, the allied commanders decided to test the situation on the following day by sending two Marine convoys down Route 1. One supply column, which had been stuck at the LST ramp in Hue, would try to travel south to Phu Bai. The second convoy consisting of Battery B, 1st Battalion, 12th Marines, which had been in support of Kelley's battalion in Reno, would attempt to move from Dong Ha south to the 2d Battalion, 1st Marines CP in the Co Bi-Thanh Tan sector. ARVN troops would escort both convoys.[29]

The test proved inconclusive. Although stopped

Marine Corps Photo 532569 (Capt Edwin W. Besch [Ret.])

Col Donald W. Sherman (in center of group in right front of picture) responds to a newspaperman's question during Operation Florida. Buddhist demonstrators had halted a 4th Marines column by placing religious altars in the Marines' path.

for a time south of Quang Tri, the artillery column from Dong Ha reached its destination on 8 June with few complications. The supply convoy from Hue ran into more difficulty. More than 2,000 statues and altars were strewn along Route 1 between Hue and the Marine base. At one point when the Marine vehicles could not move, ARVN soldiers demolished a concrete culvert to make a by-pass. A "friendly monk" then guided the trucks "around the altars . . . and there was no unpleasant incident." The convoy arrived at Phu Bai at 2100 that evening. The allied commanders, nevertheless, elected to go with the operation on 9 June.[30]

Again, on the 9th, Buddhist roadblocks delayed the beginning of the operation. Although both infantry battalions supported by two 105mm batteries were already in the Florida operating area, the 4th Marines command group, the artillery command group, and a 155mm battery were to move by convoy along Route 1 from Phu Bai into the Co Bi-Thanh Tan sector. The operation was scheduled to start at 0730, but Buddhist altars on a bridge halted the Marine column from Phu Bai. Buddhist and student demonstrators refused to remove the items and the ARVN escort was apparently under orders not to disturb the religious artifacts. At 1100, after failing to resolve the impasse with the dissidents, Colonel Sherman decided to return to Phu Bai and forego the support of the medium artillery battery for the operation.* MAG-16 helicopters lifted the two Marine command groups from the Phu Bai Airfield into the operational area.[31]

Operation Florida finally got underway at 1630 on 9 June. As could be expected with the fits and starts that characterized the beginning of the operation, any enemy unit in the area had long left. The Marines and the South Vietnamese ended Florida/Doan Ket on 12 June with only minimal military results. At a cost of four wounded because of mines and booby traps, the two Marine battalions in Florida accounted for 15 VC dead. Yet there was

---

*Captain Edwin W. Besch, who at the time of Florida commanded Headquarters Company, 4th Marines, remembered that later the altars "were smashed by Vietnamese Marines." Capt Edwin W. Besch, Comments on draft MS, dtd 12 Jun 78 (Vietnam Comment File).

another aspect to the operation that Colonel Sherman pointed out:

> It is considered that from the ARVN standpoint, the primary operation was political in nature and was achieved, that objective being the displacement of the 1st ARVN Division out of the city of Hue and into the field.[32]

The denouement of the political situation soon followed. With the arrival of additional police at Hue and the massing of Vietnamese Marines and airborne troops at Phu Bai, the government was about to make its move. On 14 June, General Lam told the American command that he planned to go into Hue, "with whatever force required, arrest the leaders of the Struggle Group, clear the streets of the Buddhist altars, and reestablish government control."[33] Although the dissident leaders called for demonstrations and for South Vietnamese troops to stop fighting, only two battalions of the 1st Division heeded the call. On 17 June the battalions left an ARVN operation and headed for Hue, but stopped before reaching their destination after being strafed by Vietnamese aircraft. The following day, a South Vietnamese airborne brigade and a two-battalion Vietnamese Marine task force entered the city and occupied key positions. At the same time, the Vietnamese Joint General Staff replaced the equivocating General Nhuan as commander of the 1st Division with the airborne commander, Colonel Ngo Quang Truong. By morning on the 19th, Hue was quiet.[34]

Despite the aborted mutiny of the two battalions, the 1st Division recovered remarkably fast from its embroilment with the "Struggle Movement." Shortly after the breakup of the dissident group in Hue, the division, with two of its own battalions together with two South Vietnamese Marine battalions and supported by its armored troops and U.S. Marine air, defeated the *808th NVA Battalion*. Apparently emboldened by the political crisis, the enemy unit, one of the battalions of the *6th NVA Regiment*, had entered the Quang Tri coastal plain from its mountainous base area on a rice-gathering mission and was willing to take on the South Vietnamese in a stand-up fight. In a two-day engagement, lasting from 21-23 June, seven kilometers northeast of Quang Tri City, the ARVN division killed 312 of the enemy while sustaining casualties of 37 killed and 104 wounded. In addition, the South Vietnamese captured 40 NVA troops including one company commander. The 1st Division had returned to the war with a vengeance.[35]

Heavy Fighting in Thua Thien Province

In Thua Thien Province, following Operation Florida, the 4th Marines made some adjustments in its units. As directed by the 3d Division, Colonel Sherman ordered Hanifin's 2d Battalion, 1st Marines out of the Co Bi-Thanh Tan area and back to Phu Bai where it took over the TAOR formerly manned by Bell's 1st Battalion. Lieutenant Colonel Sullivan's 1st Battalion, 4th Marines remained responsible for the Phu Bai Vital Area, while Vale's 3d Battalion continued with Operation Athens, south of the TAOR, against very light enemy resistance until 25 June. After its participation in Operation Florida, Lieutenant Colonel Kelley's 2d Battalion, 4th Marines, on 17 June, began Operation Dodge, five miles north of the base. During the operation which lasted until 23 June, the battalion encountered few enemy, but confiscated 4,000 pounds of rice.[36]

During this period, a small 4th Marines force made a daring, if uneventful, sortie into the abandoned A Shau Special Forces Camp. After the fall of the camp in March, the *95th NVA Regiment* apparently returned to its base area in Laos without any major attempt to clean up the battlefield. In May, a Special Forces patrol entered the camp to recover the allied dead left behind during the evacuation. Much to the patrol's surprise none of the bodies had been disturbed or boobytrapped and a great deal of ammunition and weapons lay strewn around the camp. Upon the return of the Special Forces detachment with the bodies, it reported its findings to higher headquarters.[37]

Based on the Special Forces' report, General Walt, on 1 June, decided to send a Marine demolitions team later in the month into the former camp to destroy the ammunition. He ordered General Kyle to come up with a plan.[38] On 10 June, the 3d Marine Division reported back to III MAF with a tentative concept of operations. It called for a ground force of some 70 Marines, to include a reinforced rifle platoon, demolition personnel, and an engineer detachment, supported by eight to 10 CH-46 helicopters and fixed-wing close air support. General Kyle suggested that it might be better to accomplish the destruction mission with air strikes rather than risk a ground operation.³⁹ III MAF, nevertheless, insisted on the ground force, and the division, in turn, gave the assignment to the 4th Marines.⁴⁰

Working with the 3d Division concept, Colonel Sherman's staff developed the plans for the operation, codenamed Turner. A platoon from Company I, 3d Battalion, 4th Marines, reinforced with a machine gun team, a forward air control team, and demolitions and engineer personnel, was to carry out the mission. With the attack force divided into two groups, one element was to destroy the ammunition within the compound while the second exploded two pallets of small arms ammunition that had been airdropped southwest of the camp during the March fighting. The remaining platoons of Company I would stay at Phu Bai as a reserve reaction force.⁴¹

After extended rehearsals and one or two postponements, Operation Turner went off smoothly. On 23 June, under cover of Marine fixed-wing aircraft and armed Hueys from VMO-2, six CH-46s from HMM-164 lifted the attack force into A Shau. Arriving at their destination prior to 0700, both groups completed their missions and were once more airborne within two hours. The Marines were back at Phu Bai by 0915, having seen no sign of any enemy force in the objective area.⁴²

If the *95th NVA* had become a phantom regiment, the allies had little difficulty in locating the battalions of the *6th NVA* which had moved into the coastal region of southern Quang Tri and northern Thua Thien Provinces. As a result of their contact with the *808th Battalion* in Lam Son-283 north of Quang Tri City, the South Vietnamese learned that the remaining two battalions of the enemy regiment, the *806th* and *812th*, were in Quang Dien District in Thua Thien. On 23 June, an ARVN patrol in the district, operating just north of the O Lau River ran into a strong enemy force and sustained heavy casualties. After looking at the available intelligence, U.S. advisors to the 1st Division and the 4th Marines staff believed that both the *806th* and *812th* had entered the old Operation Oregon* area and were deployed along Route 597.⁴³

Acting on this information, Colonel Sherman and his staff on 24 June visited the 1st ARVN Division Headquarters at Hue where they worked out a concept for a combined operation. Quickly approved by the various echelons of command, the resulting plan called for the helilift of two Marine battalions into an area of operations bounded by the O Lau River on the north and west, and Route 1 to the south. The 2d Battalion, 4th Marines would land in the northwest sector and attack along Route 597 toward blocking positions established by the 2d Battalion, 1st Marines, approximately 6,000 meters to the southeast. The 4th Marines command group together with the artillery battalion, the 3d Battalion, 12th Marines, and other support forces would move by road convoy along Route 1 into the southern portion of the operational area, just north of Phong Dien. Company I, 3d Battalion, 4th Marines was the regimental reserve for the operation and the 3d Batttalion remained ready to provide additional companies if needed. The 1st ARVN Division in the companion operation, Lam Son-284, was to establish blocking positions to the north of the Marine operation, across the O Lau River. A Navy destroyer stood offshore to provide naval gunfire while the 1st Marine Aircraft Wing would furnish both fixed-wing and helicopter air support.⁴⁴

By 0730 on the morning of 25 June, the operation, codenamed Jay, was ready to begin. Colonel Sherman had opened his forward CP in the objective area and the 3d Battalion, 12th Marines artillery, consisting of a 105mm battery and a 155mm battery, was in place. To the north, two ARVN battalions were in position across the O Lau. At 0800, under clear skies, the first wave of 19 CH-46s from MAG-16, carrying the lead elements of the 2d Battalion, 4th Marines, started their descent into Landing Zone Raven, approximately 8,000 meters north of the 4th Marines' command post. After some delay, the Marine helicopters completed the lift of the remainder of Kelley's battalion without incident at 0945. One-half hour later, the battalion crossed its line of departure with Company F on the north side of Route 597, Company H on the south of the road, and the command group and Company E following in trace.

The terrain in the objective area consisted of dry paddy land interspersed with several streams and lagoons. Despite the relatively flat, open ground in the region, paddy dikes and thick stands of bamboo, hedgerows, and scrub growth, as well as extensive tree lines surrounding the hamlets, provided excellent cover and concealment for any defending enemy force.

---

*See Chapter 4 for a description of Operation Oregon.

THE ENEMY BUILDUP IN THE NORTH

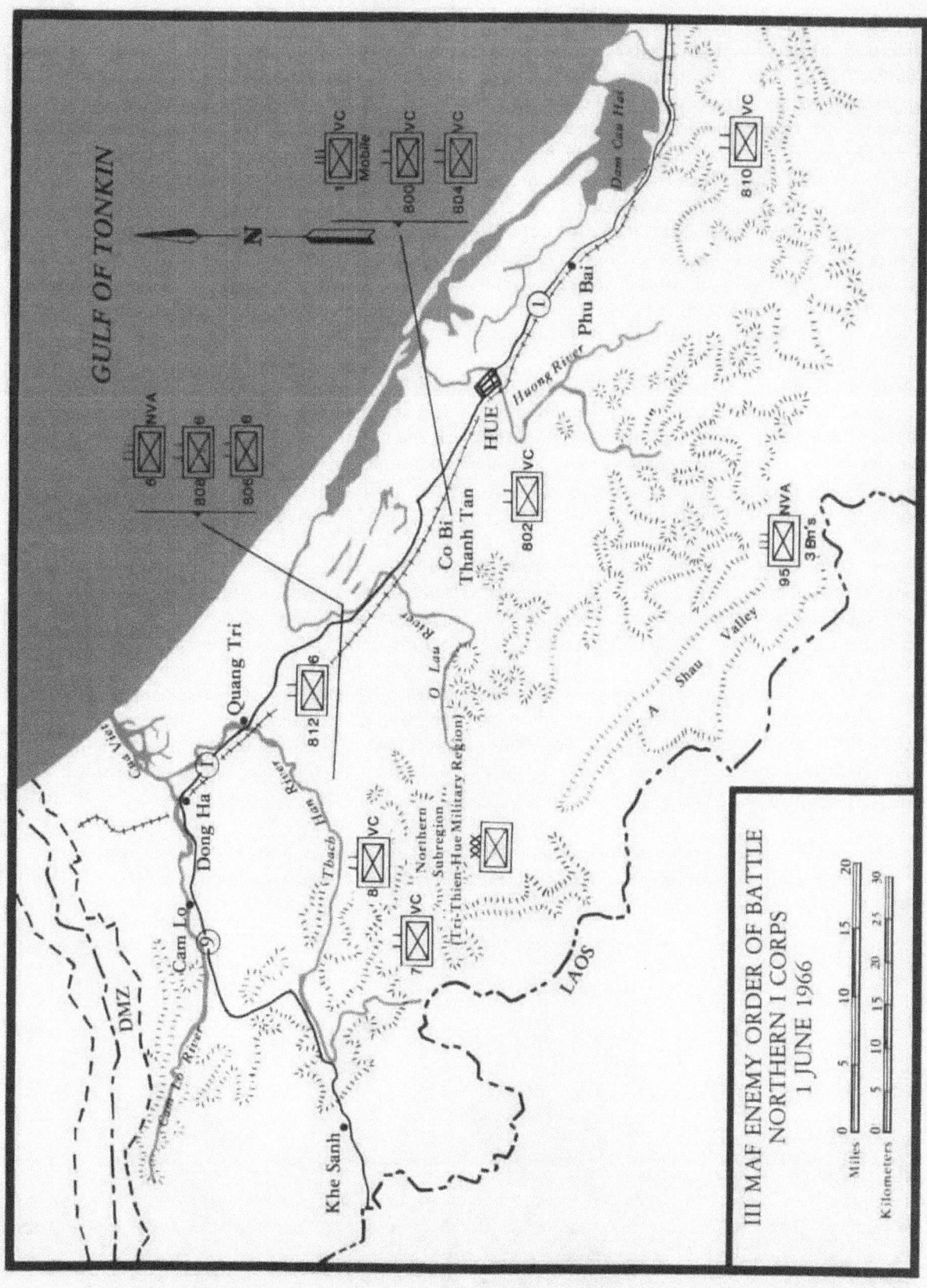

III MAF ENEMY ORDER OF BATTLE
NORTHERN I CORPS
1 JUNE 1966

Kelley's battalion, nevertheless, reached its first objective, Phase Line Bravo, some 2,000 meters southeast of LZ Raven, without encountering any opposition. As the Marines renewed their advance, however, the enemy opened up with heavy small arms fire from Ap Chinh An, the same fortified hamlet that had caused such frustration for the 1st Battalion, 4th Marines earlier in Operation Oregon. The Marine attack soon stalled. Lieutenant Colonel Kelley then ordered his Company H to swerve north in order to flank the enemy and at the same time asked for naval gunfire, artillery, and air support. Despite the employment of the supporting arms, the Marine battalion still was unable to penetrate the enemy defenses.

Lieutenant Colonel Hanifin's 2d Battalion, 1st Marines, meanwhile, had arrived at 1100 in its landing zone, LZ Shrike, approximately 9,000 meters southeast from LZ Raven. As planned, the battalion then established its blocking positions at Phase Line Delta, some 3,500 meters northwest of its LZ. At 1420, Colonel Sherman ordered Hanifin to move his battalion into new positions at Phase Line Golf, another 1,500 meters to the northwest to reinforce Kelley's battalion. As the 2d Battalion, 1st Marines advanced with Company G on the north side of Route 597 and Company H on the south, the Marines met strong enemy forces in the hamlet of My Phu. While still taking fire from its front, Company H deployed to rescue the crew of a downed Marine helicopter from HMM-161 which had crashed 1,000 meters south of the hamlet. Lieutenant Colonel Hanifin then ordered his Company F to reinforce Company G in the attack on My Phu. After accomplishing its rescue mission, Company H then maneuvered to link up with Kelley's battalion.

Through the night and early morning hours of 25-26 June, both battalions continued to encounter heavy resistance in the two hamlets. With two of his companies engaged in Ap Chinh An, Lieutenant Colonel Kelley ordered his Company E to advance southeast and attempt to reach Hanifin's battalion. Although the Marines of Company E could see the men of Company H of the 1st Marines battalion, they were unable to break through the enemy lines to make physical contact. From well dug-in positions in both hamlets, the enemy defenders, employing 60mm, 80mm, and 81mm mortars, heavy automatic and small arms weapons, fought tenaciously. At 2100, the NVA made a strong counterattack against Company H, 4th Marines, south of Ap Chinh An, but with the assistance of supporting arms the Marines repulsed the assault. Despite problems with coordination because of the proximity of the two Marine battalions to one another, Marine aircraft and artillery reinforced by the guns of the destroyer *Davis* (DD 957) repeatedly bombarded the enemy positions in the two hamlets. The *Davis* alone fired more than 530 rounds on the 25th. Believing they had the enemy force hemmed in between them, the

Marines unload supplies from a helicopter during Operation Jay in June 1966. In heavy fighting, the 4th Marines engaged three enemy battalions in northeastern Thua Thien Province.

Marine Corps Photo A187772

THE ENEMY BUILDUP IN THE NORTH

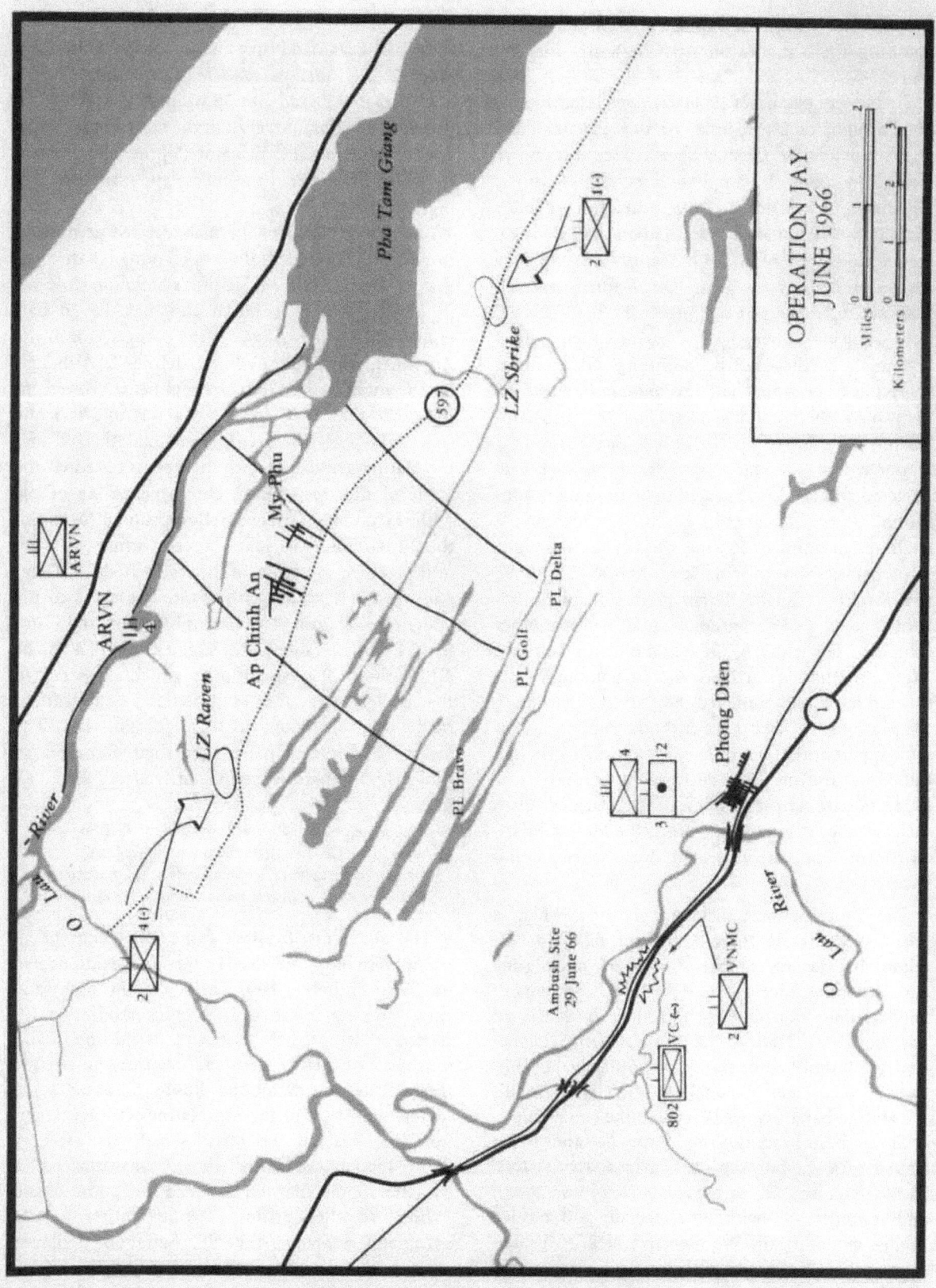

two Marine battalions waited for daylight before renewing their attacks on Ap Chinh An and My Phu.[45]

There were two other separate but related actions on the night of 25-26 June. At the request of the U.S. sector advisor, Colonel Sherman sent his reserve force, Company I, 3d Battalion, 4th Marines, together with a section of Ontos to reinforce a South Vietnamese Popular Force platoon some 5,000 meters northwest of the 4th Marines CP. As they reached the objective areas, the Marines received some scattered shots and returned the fire. The VC force quickly disengaged, leaving eight dead behind.[46] Further north, a strong NVA force, suspected to be from the *806th Battalion*, assaulted the two ARVN battalions in Lam Son-284. U.S. supporting arms broke up the attack. According to a Marine report, "two large secondary explosions were observed and the VC appeared to be running in confusion."[47]

On the morning of 26 June, the 4th Marines made its preparations for the final assault on Ap Chinh An and My Phu. Colonel Sherman reinforced Lieutenant Colonel Kelley's battalion at 0655 with another company, Company L, 3d Battalion, 4th Marines. After a preliminary artillery and air bombardment, the two battalions launched their attacks. Although the Marines met resistance in both hamlets, it was soon apparent that the bulk of the enemy forces had pulled out during the night, leaving behind a rear guard to hamper the progress of the Marines. With the assistance of supporting arms, the Marine infantry slowly but surely cleared out the remaining enemy.

The most serious incident occurred when a misdirected Marine 105mm shell fell on a 2d Battalion, 4th Marines company CP, killing one Marine and wounding three others.[48] At 1600, Company E, 2d Battalion, 4th Marines, linked up with the 2d Battalion, 1st Marines, and Lieutenant Colonel Kelley relinquished operational control of the company to Lieutenant Colonel Hanifin. By nightfall, the Marine battalions had captured the two hamlets.

Through 28 June, the two Marine battalions continued with the mop-up in their respective sectors. In My Phu, the 2d Battalion, 1st Marines, "swept and reswept . . . with only civilians and hidden bodies remaining in the objective area."[49] Lieutenant Colonel Kelley's battalion in Ap Chien An also came across "some bodies and equipment . . . in various hiding places."[50] Both the Marines and the NVA had sustained heavy losses during the fighting. From 25-28 June, the two Marine battalions took casualties of 23 dead and 58 wounded, with all but two of the deaths and seven of the injuries having occurred in the initial fighting of 25 June. The Marines recovered 82 bodies of the enemy and estimated killing 200 more.[51]

On 28 June, Colonel Sherman received permission to make Jay a one-battalion operation. He directed that Lieutenant Colonel Hanifin's battalion close out its portion of the operation and that the 2d Battalion, 4th Marines take over the entire sector in the Ap Chien An-My Phu village complex.[52] Although on the night of the 28th the regiment received intelligence that a VC force was about to attack the command post, the attack never materialized and the Marines continued with their plans to reduce the scope of the operation.[53] On the morning of the 29th, Lieutenant Colonel Kelley assumed control of the 2d Battalion, 1st Marines sector while the latter unit prepared to depart for the regimental CP. Company E, 2d Battalion, 4th Marines reverted to the operational control of its parent battalion and Company L, 3d Battalion, 4th Marines returned to the 4th Marines CP as part of the regimental reserve. In the artillery area, the 3d Battalion, 12th Marines made its preparations to leave for Phu Bai. The Marine artillerymen had staged their non-essential vehicles for departure when shortly after 0830:

> The sounds of automatic small arms and mortar firing were heard in the CP. Two large columns of smoke [rose] . . . in the air. The Battalion S-3 immediately ordered action rear on all weapons . . . in anticipation of some fire missions.[54]

The allied intelligence of the movement of an enemy battalion into the Jay area of operations had not been entirely a false alarm. On the night and early morning hours of 28-29 June, the *802d VC Battalion* departed its base area in the mountains southwest of the Marine operating area and at 0200 reached its destination on Route 1, some 2,500 meters northwest of the 4th Marines CP. Its target, however, was not the Marines' CP, but rather a South Vietnamese Marine truck convoy, due to pass by later in the morning. Armed with 75mm and 57mm recoilless rifles, 60mm mortars, and automatic weapons, the VC battalion deployed along both sides of the road and waited.[55]

The South Vietnamese convoy of 28 trucks carrying the 2d Battalion, Vietnamese Marine Corps left Hue City at 0730. Loaded on board the vehicles by company, the 1st Company was at the head of the column; the 3d Company, H&S Company, and the command group were in the center; and the 2d and 4th Companies brought up the rear. Although there had not been an ambush along this sector of Highway 1 for more than 10 months, the South Vietnamese troops faced outward and automatic weapons on the trucks were at the ready. The battalion commander provided for planned artillery coverage along the route of march and kept an artillery forward observer with him. For added insurance, a small South Vietnamese spotter plane flew overhead. In the event of an ambush, the battalion was "to dismount, form up by units, and stand and fight as . . . directed."[56]

About 0830, the Vietnamese truck convoy crossed the bridge over the O Lau River at Phong Dien and continued north. As the first echelon drove past an open 3,000-meter area, enemy gunners on the west side of the road opened up at a range of 200 meters "with a heavy volume of accurate mortar and recoilless rifle fire" at the center of the convoy. The enemy infantry then joined in with machine gun and rifle bursts directed along the entire length of the column. Ten of the trucks were hit; three were completely destroyed. The battalion commander halted the convoy and ordered his troops to dismount. Marine Captain Thomas E. Campbell, the senior U.S. advisor to the 2d Battalion, remembered that despite heavy casualties the Vietnamese Marines accomplished this in good order and deployed along the road, returning the enemy fire.[57]

The side of the road offered very little cover and the Marines continued to take casualties. Campbell recalled that they could see through the thin stand of trees to the west of the highway the "backblasts from the recoilless weapons along the crest of the low rolling hills," and enemy troops maneuvering forward. The Marine battalion commander ordered his companies to move back to the relative security of the railroad tracks which paralleled the highway, some 75 meters to the east. As the Marines, led by the H&S Company and command group, together with the 2d and 4th Companies, approached the railroad cut they were met with a "withering volume of small arms fire and hand grenades." Up to this point, all of the enemy activity had been from west of the highway and the two VC companies east of the road had allowed the Marines to come within 10 yards of their positions before opening fire. The Vietnamese Marine battalion commander was seriously wounded and "virtually the entire command group was killed outright or incapacitated by wounds." Some 15-20 Marines from the H&S Company reached the railroad cut but were mowed down by machine gun fire "directed down the railroad tracks and into their left flank." The enemy had succeeded in dividing the Marine battalion into two, one group centered around the 2d and 4th Companies together with the remnants of the H&S Company, and the second group consisting of the 1st and 3d Companies, some 500 yards away. Less than six minutes had elapsed since the ambush had been triggered.[58]

The Marines were relegated to maintaining two perimeters, separated by open ground and not mutually supporting. Fortunately for the embattled troops, a U.S. Army spotter plane arrived overhead. The U.S. Marine advisors on the ground made radio contact with the pilot and called for assistance. At this point, the 3d Battalion, 12th Marines, which had been monitoring the U.S. Marine advisor radio net, broke in and offered its services. The first artillery shells fell into the impact area at 0846. About this time a U.S. Air Force FAC(A) aircraft was on the scene and began to direct Marine F-4s, which had been circling overhead, into strikes on the enemy positions.[59]

Shortly afterward, both the 4th Marines and the ARVN 1st Division began preparations to send reinforcements to assist the beleaguered South Vietnamese Marine battalion. At 0915, Colonel Sherman, together with members of his staff and one of his company commanders, made an aerial reconnaissance of the ambush site and on his return ordered his reserve company accompanied by an Ontos platoon into the area. The ARVN division, which had been conducting a new operation, Lam Son-285, a few miles north of the ambush, sent two infantry battalions reinforced by an APC troop and tank company.[60]

At the ambush site, once the American aircraft began their strikes, the *802d Battalion* lost interest in the South Vietnamese Marines and concentrated on making good its escape. To the east of the railroad, the enemy troops had the advantage of thick cover and were able to get out relatively unscathed. To the west of Highway 1, however, the VC had to cross largely open ground before they

Marine Corps Photo 532567 (Capt Edwin W. Besch [Ret.])
An ARVN M8 armored car stands guard at 4th Marines CP during Operation Jay while Marines in background inspect weapons captured from the 802d VC Main Force Battalion. The 802d had ambushed a Vietnamese Marine battalion, but in turn was caught in the open by Marine air and ground forces together with an ARVN airborne battalion.

could reach the relative security of the hills. Marine artillery and air enjoyed a field day while the Ontos platoon, which arrived in the area shortly after 0950, "obliterated a VC squad on a ridgeline with a single 106mm salvo."[61]

Within one and one-half to three hours after the ambush, two Marine companies, I and L, 3d Battalion, 4th Marines; the Ontos platoon; and the 1st ARVN Division units, reinforced by an airborne battalion, had converged on the objective area and cut off the retreat of those enemy forces still west of the highway. Between them, the allies killed more than 185 of the enemy and captured nine prisoners. They also recovered 39 individual and eight crew-served weapons. One Marine recalled that "General Walt directed his own helicopter to land and capture a 75mm recoilless rifle abandoned by retreating VC."[62]

The victory over the *802d* had not come cheaply. The 2d Vietnamese Marine Battalion sustained casualties of 42 killed, including the battalion commander who died of his wounds, and 95 wounded. Captain Campbell, who had also been wounded in the action, later wrote that the reasons that the battalion had not suffered even more grievous losses were the:

... maintenance of unit integrity, the skillful maneuvering of these companies by their commanders, and the outright doggedness, determination, and raw courage of individual Marines.[63]

Operation Jay continued for a few more days, but the fighting was over. The two Marine companies and the Ontos platoon, which participated in the action of the 29th in support of the Vietnamese Marine battalion, returned to the 4th Marines CP the following morning. On the 30th, Lieutenant Colonel Hanifin's 2d battalion also departed for Phu Bai. The following day, Colonel Sherman closed his CP in the Jay operation and, on 2 July, the 2d Battalion, 4th Marines completed its mop up and civic action activities in the Ap Chien An and My Phu complex. During the eight-day operation, the Marines and ARVN, supported by Marine air and artillery, and naval gunfire, smashed three enemy battalions, the *802d*, *806th*, and *812th*. Marine estimates of the enemy dead in both Jay and in the reaction to the Vietnamese Marine ambush, not including those killed by the ARVN, were more than 475. Allied intelligence later learned that the *812th* literally ceased to exist, with its remaining personnel distributed among three other battalions.[64]

Following Jay, the Marines also made an attempt to finish off the *802d Battalion*, which allied intelligence believed had returned to its base area south of the old Florida area after the ambush on 29 June. Colonel Sherman assigned the operation to his 3d Battalion, which after completing Operation Athens exchanged TAORs with the 1st Battalion and had become the regimental reserve. The plan was for the Marine battalion, supported by air and artillery, to exploit a B-52 strike on the suspected enemy base camp. As planned, the 3d Battalion began the operation, codenamed Holt, on 2 July, but enjoyed meager results. For the next few days through the end of the operation on 6 July, the Marines killed seven of the enemy at the cost of one wounded Marine. The battalion had most of its difficulty with the dense foliage, which often limited its progress to a pace of 50-100 yards per hour. As one Marine officer observed, "Holt was not particularly inspiring," but it gave the Marines a taste of jungle warfare that they were soon to encounter farther north.[65]

Further Reconnaissance in the North

While the 4th Marines engaged the units of the *6th NVA Regiment* in northern Thua Thien Pro-

THE ENEMY BUILDUP IN THE NORTH

vince, the 1st ARVN Division reported that new large NVA units had infiltrated Quang Tri Province through the DMZ region. Despite the lack of contact that the 2d Battalion, 4th Marines had during Operation Reno earlier in the month, III MAF intelligence officers observed in their June report that these reports of an enemy buildup in the DMZ, "while still unconfirmed, have not been discounted."[66]

At MACV Headquarters, General Westmoreland, who believed that the enemy wanted to take advantage of the disruptions caused by the political crisis, warned his subordinate commanders that the NVA soon might mount an offensive either in the Central Highlands or through the DMZ. The MACV commander was convinced that the *NVA 324B Division* had moved into Quang Tri Province and that the "NVA had gone to great lengths to establish supply areas and structural facilities in the DMZ area and adjacent to it."[67] Yet, as Westmoreland later explained to *New Yorker* correspondent Robert Shaplen:

> I didn't want to react too quickly, and I wanted to be sure we had enough intelligence to guide us. At the time, though I had nearly two hundred and fifty thousand troops in the country, I was still operating on a shoestring, maneuvering battalions all over the place. I had to have more intelligence on what was going on up north, and there was no better way to get it than by sending in reconnaissance elements in force.[68]

The responsibility for the execution of the reconnaissance mission, of course, lay with III MAF. Since the beginning of the month, General Walt had completed contingency plans to reinforce the 1st ARVN Division and continued to work with General Lam on the possibility of combined operations with the South Vietnamese in Quang Tri Province. Following extensive sightings of enemy forces in the Cam Lo sector and, on 18 June, a mortar attack on the ARVN Cam Lo outpost, some eight miles west of Dong Ha on Route 9, the Marine command decided to begin its reconnaisance of the DMZ region.[69]

At Phu Bai, the 4th Marines had expanded their reconnaissance capability. Since March, Reconnaissance Group Bravo at Phu Bai, structured around Company B, 3d Reconnaissance Battalion, had been reinforced by a platoon from Company A and the 1st Force Reconnaissance Company. Major Dwain A. Colby, the commanding officer of the Force Reconnaissance Company, as the senior of-

Marine Corps Photo A707701 (Stephen Iannece)
The bridge spans the Ben Hai River, which divided the two Vietnams. The flag of North Vietnam can be seen on the far shore while the flag of South Vietnam is seen on the near bank.

ficer, assumed command of Recon Group Bravo. By the end of May, the 4th Marines reconnaissance zones had grown from three to six, extending from southern Thua Thien to southern Quang Tri.[70] With the decision to begin an extended reconnaissance in the DMZ sector, Colonel Sherman ordered the formation of Task Unit Charlie, with Colby in command, and consisting of: two reconnaissance platoons, one from the Force Reconnaissance Company and the other from Company A; Company E, 2d Battalion, 1st Marines; and Battery H, 3d Battalion, 12th Marines, reinforced by two 155mm howitzers.[71]

On 22 June, Task Unit Charlie moved from Phu Bai to Dong Ha and Cam Lo. The Marine artillery established firing positions at the latter base, while Company E, reinforced by an infantry platoon already at Dong Ha from the 3d Battalion, 4th Marines, provided security for both sites. Covered by the artillery, the reconnaissance Marines were to determine "the size, designation, and equipment" of enemy units in the Cam Lo area.[72]

III MAF, which still had its reservations about the existence of a large enemy force in the DMZ sector, was soon to have all of its doubts removed. On 28 June, the NVA mortared the Cam Lo base, which resulted in two dead and five wounded, and as Major Colby recollected, "a personal visit by Major General Kyle." More significant, every reconnaissance insertion, according to Colby:

> . . . encountered armed, uniformed groups and no patrol was able to stay in the field for more than a few hours, many for only a few minutes. Reports of this activity brought General Walt to the scene (probably to relieve the incompetent that couldn't keep his patrols out). But after talking to the reconnaissance teams, one of which was still in its jungle garb, having been extracted under fire minutes before General Walt's arrival, he apparently decided there was something to the rumor that the NVA was crossing the DMZ.[73]

By the end of the month, Lieutenant Colonel Hanifin opened the CP of the 2d Battalion, 1st Marines at Dong Ha and a new phase of the war was about to begin.

CHAPTER 10

Marines Turn North, Operation Hastings

*Finding the Enemy—Reactivation of Task Force Delta and Heavy Fighting Along the DMZ,
12-25 July 1966—Hastings Comes to an End, 26 July-3 August 1966*

Finding the Enemy

The reconnaissance phase of the operation in the north was to last a couple more weeks. With the arrival of Lieutenant Colonel Hanifin's 2d Battalion, 1st Marines at Dong Ha, he assumed operational control of the Dong Ha-Cam Lo sector while Major Colby retained responsibility for the reconnaissance activity. Colby recalled that the resulting command relations were delicate in that Hanifin's mission was to support the reconnaissance effort, without actual control over it. The reconnaissance commander credited both Hanifin and himself with "A great deal of tact and self-control . . . to make this relationship function."[1]

Despite reinforcement by the infantry and additional reconnaissance units as well as a change in designation from Task Unit Charlie to Detachment A, Recon Group Bravo in early July, little had changed for Colby's reconnaissance Marines. They continued to observe and encounter, in increasing numbers, uniformed regulars of the North Vietnamese Army. On 4 July, a patrol, led by First Lieutenant Theard J. Terrebone, Jr., moved into the area 16 miles west of Dong Ha where a 700 foot "sort of toothpick-type mountain stuck out in the middle of an open area," with "sheer cliff straight up and down," and known as the Rockpile, dominates the

A Marine helicopter makes a one-wheeled landing on top of the Rockpile in the DMZ sector. The Rockpile, a 700-foot mountain dominating the nearby landscape, was to become a familiar terrain feature to Marines in the "DMZ War."

Marine Corps Photo A187836

Marine Corps Photo A332831 (Maj Theard J. Terrebonne, Jr.)

Marines of 3d Platoon, Company A, 3d Reconnaissance Battalion, led by 1stLt Theard J. Terrebonne, Jr., pose at Dong Ha after a patrol extraction in early July. During this period, 14 out of 18 patrols in the DMZ sector had to be withdrawn because of enemy contact.

landscape.² During the 24-hour period the patrol remained in the vicinity of the Rockpile, the Marines observed several well-camouflaged enemy firing positions including trench lines, mortar pits, and fighting holes. After calling an artillery fire mission on some nearby enemy forces, the patrol returned to its base area. For the next 10 days, the Marines continued their reconnaissance effort, but of the 18 patrols conducted during this period, 14 had to be withdrawn because of enemy contact. The reconnaissance Marines sighted more than 300 North Vietnamese troops.³

During this period, South Vietnamese Army units operating in the same region obtained more evidence about the movement of North Vietnamese regulars across the border. On 6 July, 1st ARVN Division troops captured a NVA soldier near the Rockpile. He identified his unit as part of the *5th Battalion, 812th Regiment* of the *324B Division* and stated that the other regiments of the division, the *90th* and the *803d*, also had entered South Vietnam.

Three days later, a lieutenant from the *812th Regiment* surrendered in the same area. He provided detailed intelligence on the positions and designations of the *324B Division*, and declared that the mission of the North Vietnamese division was to "liberate" Quang Tri Province. The enemy lieutenant further explained that other NVA and VC units, both in Quang Tri and Thua Thien, were to block any ARVN reinforcements attempting to move north.⁴

This information finally convinced the senior Marine commanders that the NVA had indeed advanced into South Vietnam through the DMZ. General Kyle recommended to Walt that the Marines "move troops north to try to get them [the North Vietnamese] out of there and drive them back." Walt agreed and so advised General Westmoreland, who needed little persuasion.⁵

There followed a brief two to three days of hasty consultation and planning. On 11 July, Brigadier General Lowell E. English, the 3d Marine Division

South Vietnamese airborne troopers deploy after debarking from a Marine CH-46 helicopter to begin Operation Lam Son-289. Lam Son-289 was the South Vietnamese counterpart operation to Hastings.

ADC, conferred at Hue with General Truong, the CG, 1st ARVN Division, and Colonel Sherman of the 4th Marines about combined plans for combating the enemy threat in the north. Meeting at the 1st ARVN Division Headquarters, the three officers agreed on a general concept of operations. A Marine task force was to move into the area south of the DMZ to participate in Operation Hastings, the codename given on 7 July to the Marine reconnaissance in northern Quang Tri. ARVN forces were to engage in a counterpart operation, Lam Son-289, south of the Marines. The original plan called for a D-Day of 13 July for the new phase of Hastings.[6]

General Kyle agreed to the need for an expanded operation and authorized Colonel Sherman to establish a forward headquarters at Dong Ha. The 3d Marine Division commander, however, had reservations about the D-Day date. He believed that more detailed planning was required, especially in relation to the logistic implications, before the second phase of Hastings could begin.[7]

In Saigon, during the interim, General Westmoreland, on 11 July, met with General Cao Van Vien of the South Vietnamese Joint General Staff. According to Westmoreland, he told Vien that they knew that the *324B Division* was moving south, but not its destination. The MACV commander suggested that he and Vien meet with their respective subordinate field commanders. On 12 July, Westmoreland and Vien flew to Da Nang where they visited with Generals Lam and Walt. The four generals then went to Hue, discussed the situation with General Truong, and later attended a briefing at Dong Ha. Convinced that the enemy had moved in force across the DMZ into northern Quang Tri, Westmoreland directed Walt to move up to a division to Quang Tri. He told the III MAF commander that he would make the necessary arrangements with CinCPac to have the Seventh Fleet SLF available for the operation, while Vien promised Lam the use of five battalions of the South Vietnamese general reserve. They reassured Walt and Lam that III MAF and I Corps would have the necessary resources for the successful execution of an allied counterstroke in the north.[8]

Reactivation of Task Force Delta and Heavy Fighting Along the DMZ, 12-25 July

On the afternoon of 12 July, General Kyle ordered the reactivation of Task Force Delta at 0800 the next morning and once more selected his ADC, General English, as its commander. Colonel Sherman's 4th Marines Headquarters provided the nucleus for the staff, while Sherman himself became Chief of Staff. In addition to the 4th Marines Headquarters, Task Force Delta consisted of four infantry battalions, 2/1, 1/3, 2/4, and 3/4; one artillery battalion, 3/12; and other supporting forces. The 1st Marine Aircraft Wing was to furnish both fixed-wing and helicopter support. VMGR-152's KC-130s flew the first elements of English's command to the Dong Ha airstrip, and on 14 July, General English established his command post near Cam Lo, seven miles west of Dong Ha and south of the Cam Lo River, a tributary of the Cua Viet River which empties into the South China Sea. Dong Ha Airfield served as the command's logistic support area and provided a forward helicopter staging area.

The terrain in which the task force was to operate varied from coastal plain east of Route 1, traversable by wheeled and tracked vehicles, to dense

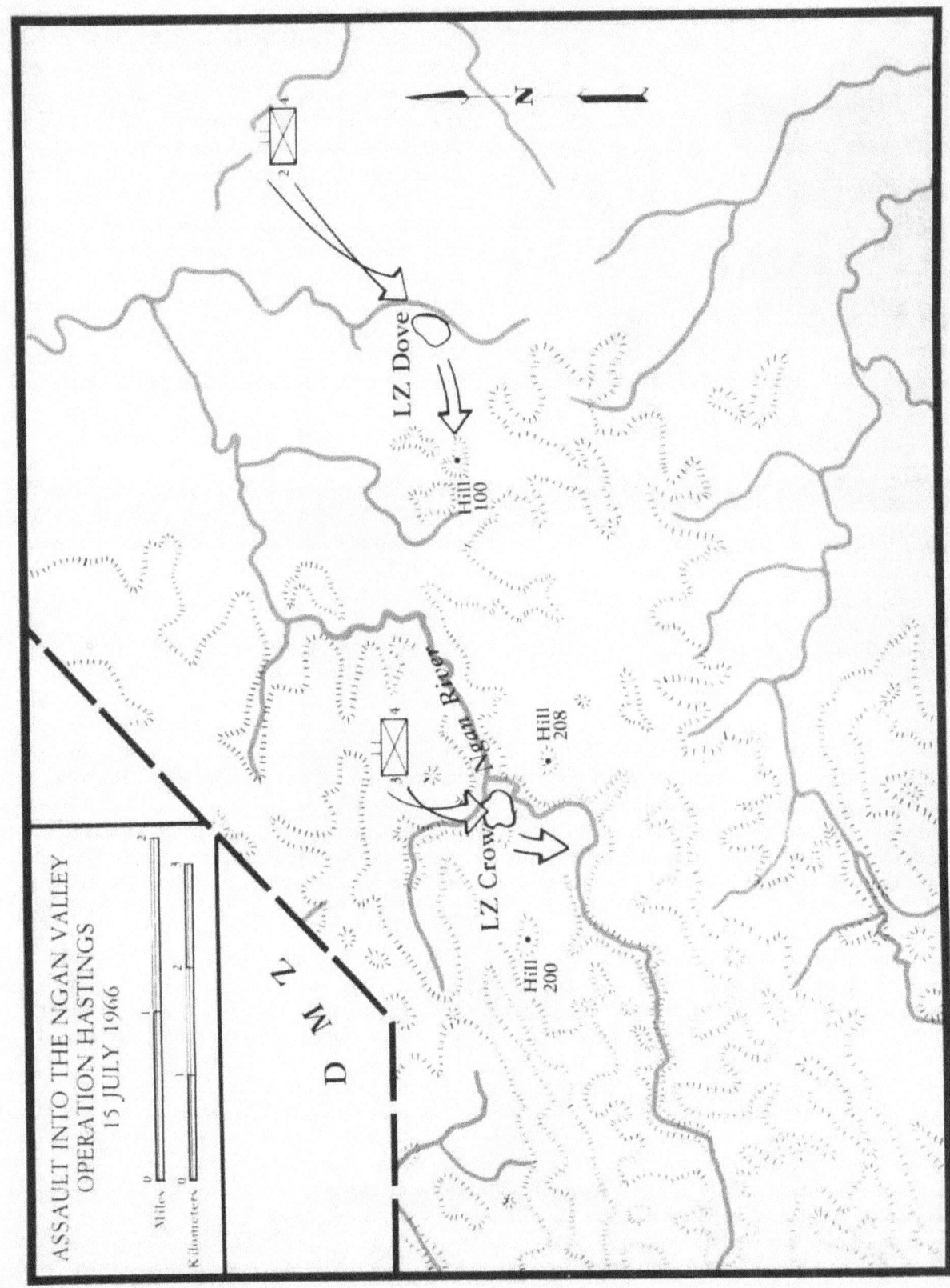

undergrowth and jungle forests inland covering the rugged mountains. Between Dong Ha and Cam Lo, the ground is fairly level and cultivated, with populated areas along the Cam Lo River. North of Cam Lo, the terrain consists of rolling hills covered with scrub growth and coarse elephant grass. West of this piedmont area, the terrain is composed of a series of ridges and steep hills rising to an elevation of 550 meters. Heavy foliage and rough terrain made all ground movement difficult and reduced the number of possible helicopter landing zones. The heaviest fighting of Hastings was to occur in the Song Ngan Valley, six miles northwest of Cam Lo and about one-to-three miles south of the DMZ.

After studying the available intelligence based on the air and ground reconnaissance, the allied commanders determined that the *90th NVA Regiment*, estimated at a strength of 1,500 men was using the Ngan Valley as one of its major infiltration routes into Quang Tri. Furthermore, they believed that the *324B Division* had established its command post on Hill 208, a strategic height overlooking the southwestern portion of the valley. Working from these premises, General English drew up his plan of action ". . . to take the enemy by surprise on his key trails and behind his own lines and to smash and destroy him before he had a chance to regain his balance and momentum."[9]

Shortly after the activation of his command and before his move to Dong Ha, General English issued his order for the expansion of Hastings. Based largely on the plan developed at the conference at Hue on the 11th, but with D-Day postponed from 13 to 14 July, and finally firmly established for 15 July, English's concept of operations called for a two-battalion helicopter assault in the Ngan Valley. Lieutenant Colonel Vale's 3d Battalion, 4th Marines was to land in the southwestern sector of the valley and establish blocking positions below the bend of the river to prevent enemy movement. Three miles further to the northeast, the 2d Battalion, 4th Marines, now commanded by Lieutenant Colonel Arnold E. Bench, was to land near the mouth of the valley and attack southwest along the high ground toward Hill 208 and the 3d Battalion's blocking positions.[10]

The plan for the Marine thrust into the Ngan Valley required an extensive buildup of allied forces in the north together with supporting operations. Two Marine battalions were to remain at the base

Marine Corps Photo A193954
Gen William C. Westmoreland, ComUSMACV (center), together with senior Marine commanders, looks at a map depicting the battle situation in Operation Hastings. Gen Walt is to the left of Gen Westmoreland; MajGen Wood B. Kyle, CG 3d Marine Division is to the left and behind Walt; and BGen Lowell E. English, the Task Force Delta commander is to the right rear of Gen Westmoreland.

areas. The 2d Battalion, 1st Marines, since 2 July commanded by Lieutenant Colonel Jack D. Spaulding, would provide security for Dong Ha, while Lieutenant Colonel Robert R. Dickey III's 1st Battalion, 3d Marines at Cam Lo protected General English's CP and the nearby artillery positions. Lieutenant Colonel Bell's 1st Battalion, 1st Marines was scheduled to join Task Force Delta at Dong Ha on 16 July to relieve the 2d Battalion, 1st Marines of its airfield security mission. On 16 July, the Seventh Fleet SLF battalion, BLT 3/5, was to conduct an amphibious assault, Operation Deckhouse II, eight miles northeast of Dong Ha. After the SLF had established a firm foothold ashore, Deckhouse II was to be terminated and BLT 3/5 was to join Task Force Delta further inland. In the meantime, the South Vietnamese 1st ARVN Division and an airborne task force were to conduct Lam Son-289. The ARVN division was to operate in the area west of Route 1, north of Dong Ha, while the airborne task force was to operate south of Route 9.* Major Colby's recon-

---

*General English observed that "General Truong [the CG 1st ARVN Division] moved his CP alongside so there was common access to all vital information of both commands." The former Task Force Delta commander remarked that this procedure had become "SOP in our battle operations." MajGen Lowell E. English, Comments on draft MS, dtd 12Jun78 (Vietnam Comment File).

Marine Corps Photo A187797

An aerial view of Landing Zone Crow which was later called "Helicopter Valley" by the Marines. Three helicopters, apparently damaged, can be seen on the ground.

naissance Marines were to screen the western approaches of the Hastings area of operations.[11]

The success of the planned extended infantry operations in northern Quang Tri depended on the close coordination of Marine supporting arms. Colonel Richard M. Hunt, the commanding officer of MAG-16, assumed the additional duty of tactical air commander for Task Force Delta and established a forward headquarters at the small airfield at Dong Ha. In his latter capacity, Hunt had control of both fixed-wing and helicopter support for Hastings. He collocated a direct air support center (DASC) with the Task Force Delta fire support coordination center at the Cam Lo CP. Major Samuel M. Morrow, commanding officer of the 3d Battalion, 12th Marines, had five artillery batteries under his operational control on 15 July. The reinforced artillery batteries consisted of 30 tubes, 18 105mm howitzers and 12 155mm howitzers. Morrow had moved one 105mm battery three miles southwest of Cam Lo to provide direct support for the ARVN task force operating south of Route 9. To support the Marine battalions, the artillery commander positioned his other batteries at the Cam Lo Combat Base.[12]

On the morning of 15 July, the Marine penetration of the Ngan Valley began. A-4 Skyhawks from MAG-12 joined F4-B Phantoms from MAG-11, bombing and napalming the two helicopter landing zones.* Once the Marine attack aircraft had completed their bombing runs, Morrow's artillery fired an opening salvo at 0725 on Landing Zone Crow, the objective of the 3d Battalion, 4th Marines. After 20 minutes of preparation fire, 20 CH-46 Sea Knight helicopters from HMM-164 and -165 brought the first wave of Marines into Crow, five miles northeast of the Rockpile.

Although the Marines met no initial resistance in the landing zone, small arms fire and the terrain took their toll of men and machines. The landing zone was small; two helicopters collided and crashed. A third CH-46 hit a tree while trying to avoid the first two. As a result of these collisions, two Marines were dead and seven were injured. All three helicopters were too badly damaged for recovery and would have to be destroyed. Later that evening, the North Vietnamese shot down another troop-laden helicopter, which fell near Lieutenant Colonel Vale's

---

*See MAG-11 Sit Rep for 15 July 66 in MAG-11 ComdC, July 66. During the rest of the day the Marine Phantoms were to fly 14 more sorties and the group's F-8 Crusaders flew several sorties in support of Hastings. The MAG-12 records do not indicate the number of sorties flown as landing zone preparation missions, but for the day of 15 July the Skyhawks flew 31 sorties, over 47 hours, and dropped more than 12 tons of bombs and two tons of napalm. See MAG-12 ComdC, July 66.

A troop-laden Marine CH-46 is in flames after being hit by North Vietnamese ground fire near LZ Crow. The resulting crash left 13 Marines dead and three injured.

CP, killing 13 men and injuring three others. Thereafter, the Marines referred to the Ngan Valley as "Helicopter Valley."[13]*

Marines from the 3d Battalion, 4th Marines are seen escaping from a crashed helicopter in Landing Zone Crow. Three helicopters were badly damaged during the landing of the battalion.

Marine Corps Photo A187270

---

*Colonel Vale recalled in 1978 that "We picked the landing site from a helicopter flying at several thousand feet (to avoid ground fire and also not to give away that we were scouting out possible landing sites)." He remembered that in the first helicopter crash that the dead Marines had been killed by the "helicopter blades as they were getting out of the helicopters." The last helicopter, carrying reinforcements from the 2d Battalion, 1st Marines, "came under ground fire from the ridge on the south side of the valley . . . The pilot tried to land in the landing zone but as he slowed down and hovered the smoke got into the flight compartment and he had to move forward to keep the smoke out. As a result, he overshot the landing zone and after moving over the CP tried to set down again. By this time the helo was rolling and barely remaining airborne. The pilot had to move forward again and then crashed on the edge of the area in which our CP and 81 mortars were set up." Col Sumner A. Vale, Comments on draft MS, dtd 12Jul78 (Vietnam Comment File).

Lieutenant Colonel Vale had arrived in LZ Crow with three of his four companies.* Company M had stayed at Phu Bai as security for the base. He established his CP in the landing zone and held Company I as battalion reserve. First Lieutenant Charles L. George's Company I formed a defensive perimeter around the landing zone. Vale's two other companies, K and L, were to establish blocking positions south and west of LZ Crow. Company L, under First Lieutenant William E. Healy, encountered occasional small arms fire as it moved to occupy Hill 200, one kilometer west of the CP.

Captain Robert J. Modrzejewski's Company K followed a trail that meandered along the southern bend of the Song Ngan. The company's objective was a ridgeline 500 meters below the river and 1,800 meters south of the landing zone.[14] As Modrzejewski's platoons advanced toward the river, NVA snipers, hidden in the dense vegetation, opened fire. The Company K commander recalled:

> Underneath the jungle canopy we found a complete 200-bed hospital in a bamboo building about 30 yards long and 20 yards wide. One man was guarding it, and we shot him. Inside we found 1,200 pounds of small-arms ammunition being guarded by three men. We shot them too.[15]

After this brief flurry, the Marine company continued to move southward toward its objective.

At 0935, while Vale's battalion was establishing its blocking positions, the Sea Knight helicopters of HMM-164 and -165 brought Lieutenant Colonel Bench's 2d Battalion, 4th Marines into Landing Zone Dove three miles to the northeast. With Companies H on the left, G on the right, and E bringing up the rear, Lieutenant Colonel Bench began advancing toward the 3d Battalion, 4th Marines. Bench's battalion, like Vale's, had left one company behind

---

*Colonel Vale remembered that there was an hour-and-a-half to two-hour delay between the first and second lifts of his battalion. As he recalled, the helicopters after making the first lift returned to Dong Ha and brought the 2d Battalion, 4th Marines into its landing zone. The former 3d Battalion commander remarked: "I never did find out why this happened. Plans for the lift had been clearly made and the rest of the 3d battalion was in the pick-up zone ready and waiting. I landed in Crow after the first lift had cleared. I had been in a command UH1E flown by Colonel Richard Hunt, the MAG C.O., and General English." Col Sumner A. Vale, Comments on draft MS, dtd 12Jul78 (Vietnam Comment File).

at the Phu Bai TAOR. Although the 2d Battalion made no contact with the enemy, oppressive heat and high elephant grass slowed progress. By midafternoon the battalion had covered less than two miles. Captain John J. W. Hilgers, the commander of Company H, in 1978 still vividly recalled:

> ... the problems we were having negotiating the terrain, particularly the vegetation. Though we knew our location, we could not see where we were going; trusting only to our compasses. The heat with no breeze and unlimited humidity was devastating.[16]

At the same time, Vale's battalion, continued to encounter heavy resistance. The North Vietnamese repulsed Company K's attempt to cross the Song Ngan, with a loss of three Marines killed and five wounded. After three more unsuccessful attempts to cross the river, Captain Modrzejewski decided to establish night positions on a hill 200 yards from the river. By this time, the NVA had begun to organize countermeasures and attacked the battalion with small arms, mortars, and machine gun fire. This fire continued unabated, even though the battalion called in air strikes and artillery on suspected enemy positions. At 1930, Lieutenant Colonel Vale reported that he was completely surrounded, but one-half hour later the enemy fire diminished. Vale believed that the opposing NVA unit had pulled back, but 45 minutes later, at 2015, a reinforced North Vietnamese company tried to overrun Company K's lines. After a nearly three-hour fire fight, the enemy finally fell back. According to Captain Modrzejewski:

> It was so dark we couldn't see our hands in front of our faces, so we threw our trip flares and called for a flare plane overhead. We could hear and smell and occasionally see the NVA after that ... but in the morning ... we found 25 bodies, some of them only five yards away, stacked on top of each other.[17]

By early evening, in the interim, Lieutenant Colonel Bench had halted his battalion about a mile short of its first objective, and directed that the battalion establish its night defenses. Earlier, about 1600, Lieutenant Colonel Vale had requested that the 2d Battalion come to the aid of the 3d Battalion, which was then under attack, but Bench had radioed back that "the terrain and time of day made immediate efforts [to reach the 3d Battalion] infeasible." With General English's permission, the 2d Battalion commander decided "to abort ... [the]

sweep mission toward Hill 208," and take advantage of the "lower, easier, terrain"along the river to close in on Vale's positions the following morning.[18] During the 15th, Task Force Delta had sustained total casualties of 18 killed and two wounded as opposed to enemy losses of 31 dead.[19]

The enemy started the next morning with a mortar attack on Lieutenant Colonel Vale's CP. The battalion commander immediately called in Marine air and artillery which silenced the enemy weapons. South of the battalion CP, Modrzejewski's company still was unable to cross the river. The advancing Marines found it difficult to flush out the camouflaged NVA. The Company K commander stopped, organized a defensive perimeter, and called for air and artillery to neutralize the enemy. During the day, Lieutenant Colonel Vale's other two companies probed north and northwest of the battalion CP. Lieutenant Healy's Company L uncovered an ammunition cache which included 35 boxes of 12.7mm ammunition, 24 antitank mines, and 1,000 rounds of small arms ammunition.[20]

To the northeast, Lieutenant Colonel Bench's 2d Battalion moved off the high ground shortly after dawn toward the Song Ngan. Advancing in a generally westerly direction, the lead company, Company G, reached the river shortly after 0800 where the Marines killed two NVA and captured their weapons. The company then followed the river southwest toward the 3d Battalion. Bench's unit had one serious clash with the NVA when Company G, about 1045, received heavy fire from enemy positions on the high ground to the west of the river. The battalion commander several years later remembered that he "called *very close* airstrikes while we took cover in the deep banks of the river."[21] Marine aircraft scored two direct hits on the enemy, but not before the Marine company sustained losses of two dead and seven wounded. Despite further occasional resistance, the lead elements of the 2d Battalion arrived at Lieutenant Colonel Vale's CP shortly after 1445.[22]

Although the link up of the two Marine battalions had not been challenged seriously, the enemy renewed attacks during the night of 16 July. Once more, Captain Modrzejewski's Company K bore the brunt of the assault. The company had remained in its defensive positions 800 meters south of the junction point of the two battalions. At 1930, the North Vietnamese attacked the entire company perimeter,

Marine Corps Photo A187778
A Marine from Company G, 2d Battalion, 4th Marines holds his rifle chest-high as he crosses a stream. The battalion is moving to link up with the 3d Battalion, 4th Marines in Helicopter Valley.

concentrating heaviest pressure on the left platoon. For the next three and a half hours, the NVA made repeated assaults against the Marine company. Modrzejewski's Marines repulsed three attacks, one of which came to within five meters of their positions. The company commander credited Marine artillery fire "and a flare ship which stayed with us all night" in helping him to stave off the enemy. In beating back the NVA, the Marines suffered one dead and five wounded. Captain Modrzejewski reported that 30 to 40 other Marines had sustained minor wounds as a result of "grenades being thrown back and forth from distances as close as 10 meters." The enemy suffered more grievous losses. According to Modrzejewski:

> . . . we could hear bodies being dragged through the jungle for four hours after the shooting stopped. A thorough search at first light revealed 79 enemy dead by body count. . . .[23]

While the two battalions had been moving toward each other in Helicopter Valley, General English repositioned his reserve. The arrival of the 1st Battalion, 1st Marines on 16 July at Dong Ha permitted the task force commander to free Lieutenant Colonel Spaulding's 2d Battalion, 1st Marines from its security mission there. Over 30 helicopters from squadrons HMM-161, -164, -265, and -163 lifted Spaulding's battalion to Landing Zone Robin, 3,000 meters east-northeast of Landing Zone Crow. From this position, the battalion could readily reinforce either Vale's or Bench's battalion.

Also on the morning of 16 July, the SLF of the Seventh Fleet began Deckhouse II on the coast east of the Hastings area of operations. With clear weather, moderate seas, and minimal surf, Companies I and K of Lieutenant Colonel Edward J. Bronars' BLT 3/5 landed with ease at 0630 across Blue Beach, 2,500 meters above the mouth of the Cua Viet River. Simultaneously Lieutenant Colonel James D. McGough's HMM-363, the SLF helicopter squadron, lifted Company L 3,500 meters inland from the landing beach. By evening, the entire BLT was ashore and had established its defensive perimeter. Although technically Bronars' BLT did not come under General English's operational control for another two days, it blocked NVA routes of advance through the DMZ into Quang Tri Province east of Route 1, and was readily available to reinforce Task Force Delta if necessary. In fact, the SLF helicopter squadron, HMM-363, immediately came ashore and was assigned to the operational control of MAG-16's forward headquarters.*

During the late afternoon of 16 July, General English achieved tactical surprise in his southwestern area of operations with the commitment of only a small force. At 1600, a platoon of Marines from Major Colby's 1st Force Reconnaissance Company rappelled from a MAG-16 helicopter onto the summit of the Rockpile. From this perch, the reconnaissance troops had a commanding view of the relatively open terrain in this sector. Three hours later, the Marines spotted a column of North Vietnamese troops below them, 2,000 meters to the east-northeast. After 155mm howitzers from the 3d Battalion, 12th Marines fired 51 rounds at the enemy column, the reconnaissance Marines reported 21 enemy dead. Later that night, the Marine platoon observed flashing lights 1,000 meters south of the Rockpile near the bend of the Cam Lo River. They called for artillery; 3d Battalion guns once more replied. The mission results could not be observed due to darkness, but the reconnaissance Marines reported "excellent effect on target."[24]

Based upon the sightings from the Rockpile, General English decided to move Spaulding's battalion from Landing Zone Robin, 10 kilometers to the northeast, into the river valley east of the Rockpile. Twelve UH-34s and eight CH-46s from MAG-16 lifted the battalion into its new area of operations during the morning of 17 July. Spaulding's battalion encountered only minor resistance.

During the 17th, the two battalions operating in Helicopter Valley also had very little contact with the enemy. In Landing Zone Crow, Lieutenant Colonel Vale abandoned any further attempts to advance to the south and ordered Captain Modrzejewski's Company K to remain in its defensive positions and not to cross the Song Ngan. Anticipating a renewed enemy night assault on his forward company, the battalion commander ordered Lieutenant Healy's Company L to reinforce Company K. By evening, Vale's and Bench's battalions had established a common perimeter.

With the enemy on the high ground south of the Ngan blocking the Marine attempts to cross the river, General English decided to change his scheme of maneuver. On the evening of the 17th, he directed the two battalions to move out of the valley the next day along a corridor to the northeast. Lieutenant Colonel Bench's 2d Battalion was to sweep and clear out any enemy as it advanced, and then establish blocking positions astride the Song Ngan, about a mile south of the DMZ. Vale's battalion, in the meantime, was to destroy the captured enemy ammunition and the three downed

---

*For reporting purposes, Operation Deckhouse II remained a separate operation from Hastings. Deckhouse II was a SLF operation under the operational control of the amphibious commander. See Chapter 19 for further discussion on the command and control of the SLF. BLT 3/5 AAR for Operation Deckhouse II and Operation Hastings, encl 6, TF Delta AAR. Colonel Noble L. Beck commented on the difference in size between the fresh SLF battalion and the understrength in-country battalions. He remembered that when General English first saw "3/5 on the move . . . in battalion column," the Marine general exclaimed, "I'd forgotten just how big a *real* battalion is. . . ." Col Noble L. Beck, Comments on draft MS, n.d. [Aug 78] (Vietnam Comment Files).

Courtesy of Wide World Photo

Marines from the 3d Battalion, 4th Marines rush for cover as the battalion's command post comes under mortar attack. The Marine radioman in the foreground carries his rifle and radio in his left hand and his armored vest in his right.

helicopters, and then move to Hill 100, a mile southeast of the 2d Battalion's blocking positions. From Hill 100, the 3d Battalion was to attack southeast across high ground on the morning of the 19th and assault Hill 208, basically the same route of attack that the 2d Battalion would have followed according to the original plan.[25]

General English also planned to insert the SLF battalion, BLT 3/5, on the 18th into a small valley, a suspected NVA marshalling area, 3,000 meters south of the Song Ngan. U.S. Air Force B-52s had bombed this area on the afternoon of 17 July and the Marine battalion was to exploit the results of this strike.* This valley, in the center of the Hastings operations area, was also an avenue of escape from the Song Ngan; the SLF battalion would be in position to support Vale's and Bench's battalions.

Deckhouse II ended on the morning of 18 July and Lieutenant Colonel Bronars SLF battalion was helilifted into its new area of operations that after-

---

*The B-52 bombers from Guam carried out five strikes during Operation Hastings. The effectiveness of the raids is difficult to determine; only the raid on the 17th was exploited on the ground.

noon. Only Captain Harold D. Pettengill's Company M encountered serious resistance after landing. After Marine jets responded to Pettengill's call for support, the Marine company overran the enemy positions, killing 21 of the enemy and capturing two machine guns and 11 rifles. During the day, BLT 3/5 Marines killed three more NVA and then established night defenses.[26].

As the SLF battalion was landing 3,000 meters to the south, the two 4th Marines battalions began to carry out General English's new orders. The 2d Battalion moved through the valley in wedge formation with Company H on the left flank. By midafternoon the battalion had completed its sweep and Company H established a blocking position on the high terrain to the north and across the river.[27]

At about 1400, the 3d Battalion started to follow the 2d Battalion out of the valley. Company K, which had remained behind to provide security for the battalion command post and the engineers, who were to blow the ammunition and destroy the helicopters, was about to depart the area of the former landing zone about one half-hour later. At this time, the enemy struck, first with mortars, then with infantry. Lieutenant Colonel Vale, who had not yet left his CP, recalled several years later:

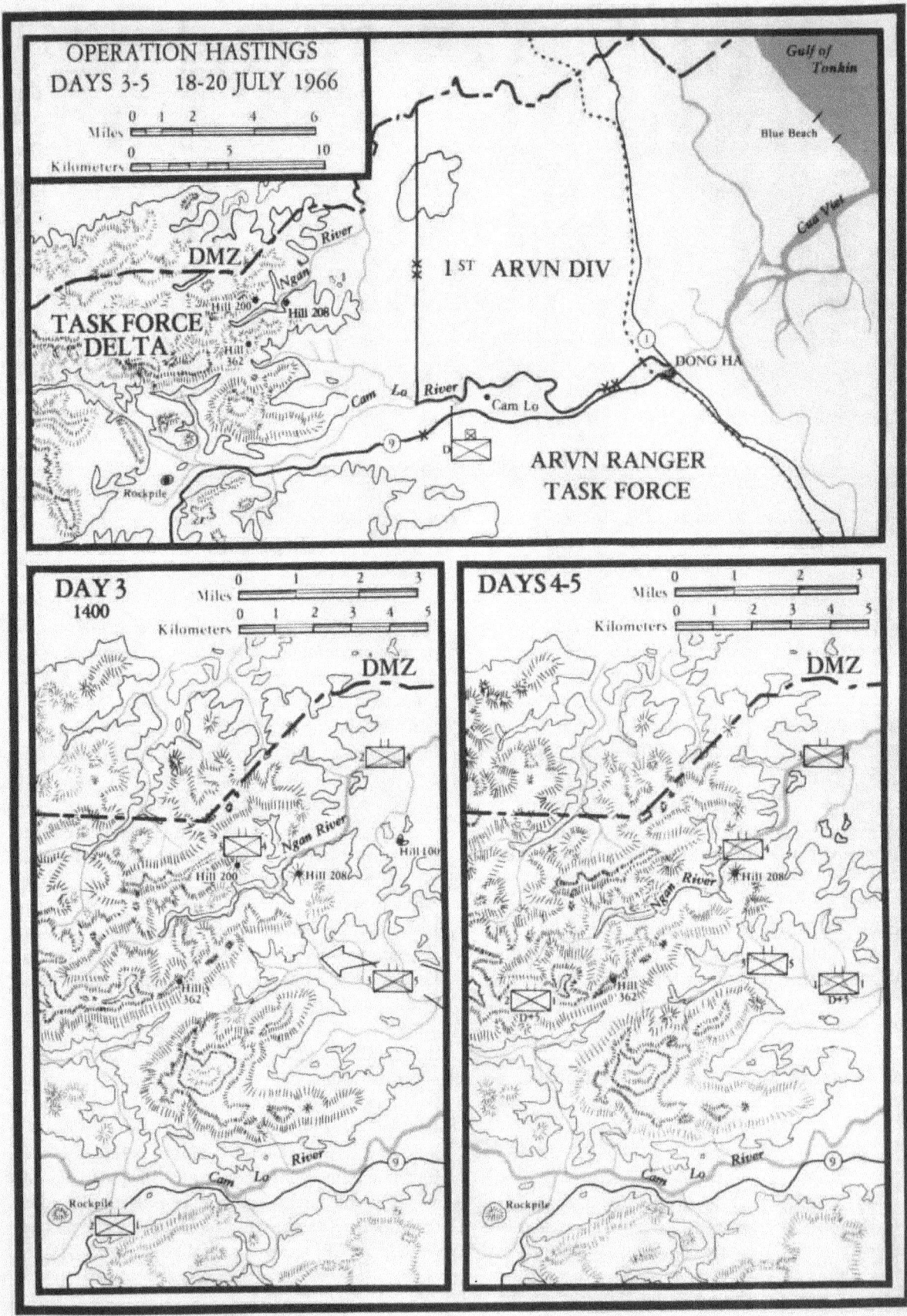

Since we had already filled in our fighting holes there was nothing to do but clear out of there on the double to the east, which we did. Unfortunately, the rear guard did not move fast enough and it was still in the area when the enemy infantry attack started.[28]

In the landing zone, Company K's 1st Platoon, under Staff Sergeant John J. McGinty, which had become separated from the rest of the company, endured the full thrust of the enemy assault. According to the platoon leader:

> . . . we started getting mortar fire, followed by automatic weapons fire from all sides . . . they were blowing bugles, and we could see them waving flags . . . "Charlie" moved in waves with small arms right behind the mortars, and we estimated we were being attacked by a thousand men. We just couldn't kill them fast enough. My squads were cut off from each other, and together we were cut off from the rest of the company. I had some of my men in the high grass, where our machine gunners had to get up on their knees to shoot, which exposed them. "Charlie" never overran us, but he got one or two of his squads between us.[29]

Captain Modrzejewski tried to maneuver his other platoons to support McGinty, but to little avail. Air and artillery support was brought in, and as Modrzejewski later recalled:

> We were getting mortars right in the landing zone and the bombs and napalm were dropping only 50 yards away from us. At one point, the NVA were trying to get the ammo out of those three wrecked helicopters that were still sitting there. Napalm got about 20 of them and then another 40, in the middle of the landing zone. I remember one kid shouting, "Here come some more Marines!" But they weren't Marines at all—they were NVA. And when they saw us, they ducked into the river on our flank. All we could see was their heads and their rifles above water—it was like shooting pumpkins.[30]

Lieutenant Colonel Vale, in the meantime, "rounded up" his command group, "particularly the radiomen, to reestablish communications and get things sorted out."[31] He directed his executive officer, Major Clark G. Henry, to bring Company L to reinforce Company K. At the same time, he radioed Lieutenant Colonel Bench to come to his assistance.

Shortly before 1700, Company L joined Company K in the landing zone while Lieutenant Colonel Bench, with a hastily formed forward headquarters and his Company G, established supporting positions on the high ground. Quickly attaining fire superiority, the Marine reinforcements relieved the pressure on McGinty's platoon. Under covering fire, McGinty and his men were able to withdraw, evacuating their wounded, but forced to leave the dead behind. Two platoons from Company I reinforced Companies K and L and according to Modrzejewski, "We formed a column of walking wounded, wounded to be carried, security, and then proceeded upstream, where the wounded were evacuated that night."[32]*

For all practical purposes, the battle was over. By 1900, the two battalions formed a common perimeter where Lieutenant Colonel Bench had left his Company E, about 1,700 meters northeast of Landing Zone Crow. The enemy's attempt to obliterate the Marine rear guard had been costly. While friendly casualties numbered 14 dead and 49 wounded, enemy losses were 138 known dead; estimates ran as high as 500.[33] Modrzejewski's Company K, especially McGinty's platoon, had been hit hard. Of the 32 men in the already understrength platoon, 8 were dead and 14 were wounded. According to Modrzejewski, "our company was down from 130 to 80, and I had kids who were hit in five or six places."[34] Both Modrzejewski and McGinty received the Medal of Honor for their actions in Helicopter Valley.

Undoubtedly, Marine supporting arms had spelled the difference between success and disaster on the 18th. Major Morrow's 3d Battalion, 12th Marines fired 120 missions, expending nearly 1,000 rounds of 105mm and 155mm ammunition in support of the Marine battalions. Aircraft from MAG-11 and -12 flew 70 close support sorties. At one time, the Marine aviators were supporting three battalions at the same time: 3d Battalion, 4th Marines in Helicopter Valley; 3d Battalion, 5th Marines to the south; and an ARVN battalion to the east, with the "action too fast to count damage."[35]

Following the heavy fighting on 18 July, the enemy attempted to avoid battle and fought only when he had no choice. The remainder of Operation Hastings, with one exception, was characterized by a series of sharp, brief clashes followed by an enemy withdrawal.

---

*Colonel Bench remembered that he and Lieutenant Colonel Vale "coordinated the evacuation of 29 *seriously* wounded." Bench praised the work of the helicopter pilots, who "on a pitch-black night . . . descended into an unlighted gorge, talked in by their exhaust glow, to have a flare popped when they were only a few feet off the landing zone." Col Arnold E. Bench, Comments on draft MS, dtd 20Jul78 (Vietnam Comment File).

Marine Corps Photo A187543
Marines from the 2d Battalion, 4th Marines move up Hill 208, the suspected CP of the 324B NVA Division. Smoke can be seen in the upper part of the picture from the airstrikes which preceded the attack.

On 19 July, the two battalions exchanged missions. The 3d Battalion, 4th Marines, with the exception of Company K which was pulled out for rehabilitation, remained in its blocking positions, while the 2d Battalion consolidated its forces for the assault on Hill 208. Captain Hilgers' Company H, which had spent a long day and night, 18-19 July, on forward positions across the Ngan under constant NVA probing, rejoined the rest of the battalion on the afternoon of the 19th, having sustained relatively light casualties. The following morning, the 2d Battalion, after heavy airstrikes, attacked over the high ground toward Hill 208, the suspected CP of the *324B Division*. According to General English, "Hill 208 was heavily fortified, but the position was only lightly defended, and the division command post still eluded us."³⁶

On the morning of 21 July, Company H, which had provided flank security for the attack on Hill 208, returned to "Helicopter Valley" to recover the Marine dead left behind during the fighting on the 18th. Moving against scattered enemy resistance, the company located six Marine bodies on a sand spit as if "they had been placed there in anticipation of evacuation." Further on, the troops found two more dead Marines, an officer and an NCO. Several NVA dead were also strewn about the former battlefield. Captain Hilgers, in 1978, remarked:

> The startling thing about the whole situation is that none of the bodies (with one exception—the first NVA encountered, had no weapon and someone had attempted to hastily cover him with dirt) had been disturbed. They all had their weapons. The Marine lieutenant still had his pistol, binoculars and wrist watch. The helicopters had not been touched.³⁷

While one platoon secured a hastily made HLZ and another platoon occupied itself with the evacuation of the Marine dead, Hilgers and his 1st Platoon continued to press forward. Later that afternoon they captured an enemy soldier, but then came under heavy enemy fire and returned to the HLZ. The following day the rest of the battalion joined Company H and continued the search of the valley.

During this time, General English began to deploy other Marine battalions farther to the south. On 20 July, Lieutenant Colonel Bell's 1st Battalion, 1st Marines joined with BLT 3/5 in the valley below the Song Ngan. The 1st Battalion had been relieved at Dong Ha by the 2d Battalion, 9th Marines which had arrived at the airfield earlier that day from Da Nang. Both Bronars' and Bell's battalions met light but persistent resistance during the next three days as they moved west. According to the BLT commander, most of the encounters were with NVA units of less than 30 men:

> The small [enemy] units appeared to be one of two types: Those who were assigned to delay and harass friendly units and those who had become separated from their present units and stumbled into contact with Battalion Landing Team 3/5.³⁸

In order to close out any avenue of retreat for the enemy, on 20 July, General English ordered Lieutenant Colonel Spaulding's 2d Battalion, 1st Marines to establish blocking positions at the western exit of the valley, 4,000 meters north of the Rockpile. By the next morning, the battalion commander had deployed two of his Companies, F and H, there. On the night of 21 July, both companies were taken under fire along their entire front. The Marines responded with small arms and mortar fire, as well as fire from the attached 4.2-inch Mortar Battery, 1st Battalion, 11th Marines. The attack was broken up.

Although the NVA made a concerted effort to eliminate the Marine blocking positions, the enemy assault became more and more disorganized as it progressed. Shortly after midnight, Lieutenant Colonel Spaulding reported that the enemy action had subsided. The Marines had suffered two killed and 13 wounded; there was no way of determining North Vietnamese casualties.[39]

For the next two days, action was sporadic, but, on the 24th, the 3d Battalion, 5th Marines found a North Vietnamese battalion 3,500 meters northeast of Spaulding's blocking positions. Lieutenant Colonel Bronars had ordered Company I, under Captain Samuel S. Glaize, to establish a radio relay station on Hill 362. Glaize's men had little difficulty reaching the top of the hill, getting there about noon, but when his 2d Platoon moved down the other side to put in forward defenses the North Vietnamese opened up. Taking full advantage of the concealment of 60- to 90-foot-high jungle growth, enemy soldiers cut down the Marines with rifle and machine gun fire.

Lance Corporal Richard A. Pittman, 1st Platoon, rushed forward with a machine gun to cover the ambushed 2d Platoon.* The platoon survivors and Pittman fought their way back to the crest of the hill, but had to leave their casualties behind. According to Lance Corporal Raymond L. Powell, one of the wounded men of the 2d Platoon, the North Vietnamese soldiers went through the American bodies, methodically shooting "anyone who moved. It was darn near like a massacre. I pretended I was dead when they got to me. They took my cigarettes and my watch, but they didn't shoot me."[40]

The North Vietnamese then turned on the Marines on the crest of Hill 362. Two enemy mortars on each flank of the Marine position began to fire with deadly accuracy. According to one of of the attached Navy corpsman, the Marines suffered most of their casualties in the first few minutes of the enemy mortar barrage.[41] The Marines quickly dug in and there were relatively few casualties from there on. They remained under constant mortar fire for the next two hours until a Marine UH-1E gunship from VMO-2 temporarily silenced the enemy weapons.[42]

As soon as Lieutenant Colonel Bronars heard about the Company I ambush, he ordered Captain Richard E. Maresco's Company K to assist Glaize. Company K moved to within 300 yards of Company I's position on Hill 362 before meeting heavy enemy resistance. Despite the cover of Marine air and artillery, Company K was unable to advance and Captain Maresco had no choice but to dig in for the night.[43]

The elements also worked against the Marines. Rain squalls of Typhoon Ora and the thick jungle canopy hindered helicopter evacuation of the wounded. Temporary landing zones had to be blasted out of the jungle. Even after engineers were lowered to the ground by hoist from helicopters to help cut landing zones, MAG-16 helicopters could only take out the 11 casualties from Company K.[44]

Captain Glaize's company spent "one long night" on Hill 362.** The North Vietnamese made repeated assaults against the Marine positions, often closing to within 15 to 30 feet of the company perimeter. Marine Corporal Mark E. Whieley exclaimed, "The Commies were so damn close we could hear them breathing heavily and hear them talking."[45] By dawn, however, the North Vietnamese had disappeared, and the Marine company remained intact.

By midmorning, under clearing skies, Company K had joined Company I on top of Hill 362. Company I had 100 casualties, 18 dead and 82 wounded, but, the enemy had been hurt too. The Marines counted 21 enemy bodies on the battlefield, recovered two NVA mortars as well as 27 rifles, a machine gun, and a recoilless rifle. Glaize's men also had captured two NVA soldiers, but one died during the night. As a

---

*Lance Corporal Pittman was later awarded the Medal of Honor.

**Captain James J. Kirschke, who at the time commanded the 3d Battalion, 5th Marines mortar platoon, recalled that about 2000, the enemy mortars once more opened up on Company I's positions. Major Robert A. Monfort, the battalion executive officer, turned to Kirschke, then a lieutenant, and asked him if he were the attacking enemy platoon commander where he would place his mortars. Kirschke "then provided the coordinates for an artillery mission which caused two secondary explosions." The mortar fire stopped. Captain James J. Kirschke, Comments on draft MS, dtd 7Jul78 (Vietnam Comment File).

Marine Corps Photo A190174
Marines evacuate the wounded from Company I, 3d Battalion, 5th Marines into a waiting helicopter. The company suffered 18 dead and 82 wounded in the fighting for Hill 362.

result of the interrogation of the surviving captive, Bronars learned that his two companies had engaged the 6th Battalion, 812th Regiment.[46]

The bloody fighting of 24-25 July marked the end of the large-scale action during Hastings. On the 25th, General Kyle met with General English at Dong Ha to discuss the battle. He ordered his task force commander to withdraw his battalions to the south and southeast because "of the difficult terrain currently being encountered, the obstacles to infantry maneuver, and the paucity of landing zones for helo assaults." Kyle suggested that the Marines "saturate those difficult terrain areas in the vicinity of the DMZ which contain clearly defined enemy military activity with maximum artillery" and air strikes.[47]*

Hastings Comes to an End, 26 July-3 August 1966

On 26 July, General English implemented his new orders. Lieutenant Colonel Bell's 1st Battalion, 1st Marines, operating in the eastern sector of the same valley as the 3d Battalion, 5th Marines, was ordered to move south toward Cam Lo. The SLF battalion, on the other hand, was to continue its advance to the southwest of the valley and operate just north of the Rockpile. Lieutenant Colonel Spaulding then moved his 2d Battalion, 1st Marines 3,000 meters east of the Rockpile into the Cam Lo River on 27 July.[48]

The Marines also began withdrawing from the Helicopter Valley region. As early as 21 July, General English had replaced Lieutenant Colonel Vale's 3d Battalion, which had been bled in the early fighting, with Lieutenant Colonel Dickey's relatively fresh 1st Battalion, 3d Marines in the blocking positions in the northern sector of the valley. Lieutenant Colonel Bench's 2d Battalion, 4th Marines had continued with its search mission in the southern portion of the valley against small but persistent enemy forces until 25 July. On one occasion, the battalion maneuvered against an enemy automatic weapon position. Bench described the event as one of the more unusual episodes of his career, declaring:

> I was on a slope of the valley . . . a fire fight was going on below me in a relatively open area. Two of my companies were engaged, and I could see both of them, as well as a

Marines from the 2d Battalion, 4th Marines move through difficult terrain in the Helicopter Valley sector. The thick elephant grass pictured above reached heights of over four feet.
Marine Corps Photo A187798

---

*Colonel Samuel M. Morrow, who as a major commanded the artillery in Hastings, recalled in 1978 that General Kyle's directive was "to hit every grid square with artillery from my position north to the DMZ and westward to Laos. My reaction to this was that we had better get the ammunition trains running throughout the Pacific because we would be out of ammunition by noon the following day." Col Samuel M. Morrow, Comments on draft MS, dtd 23May78 (Vietnam Comment File).

third one, which was behind me. I was able to control the whole operation by arm signals, and as I stood there moving my arms I could see North Vietnamese and Marines firing and falling.[49]

On the night of 24-25 July, the Marine battalion sustained casualties of one killed and 64 wounded from an NVA mortar attack.[50]* Later, on the afternoon of the 25th, the battalion CP "received a direct hit by two 250 lb bombs,"[51] dropped short of their target by U.S. aircraft, but "Miraculously, no one was killed. . . ."[52]

On 26 July, General English relieved the battle-weary 2d Battalion, 4th Marines with Lieutenant Colonel John J. Hess' 2d Battalion, 9th Marines. The following day, both Hess' and Dickey's Battalions marched south out of the valley. On the 29th, the 2d Battalion, 9th Marines arrived at the Task Force Delta CP while Dickey's battalion established a new area of operations, 3,500 meters northwest of Cam Lo.

With the withdrawal of the infantry battalions to the south, the role of the reconnaissance Marines became even more important. From the beginning of the operation, Major Colby's men had conducted deep patrols and called down supporting arms upon enemy forces. Colby had laid down four basic rules:

1. Stay together no matter what happens;
2. Upon reaching an observation post, call artillery fire upon a set of known coordinates so later fire missions can be called by shifting from a reference point;
3. Maintain constant radio communications with headquarters;
4. Never stay in one spot more than 12 hours.[53]

On 28 July, one of these patrols, led by Sergeant Orest Bishko (and accompanied by Captain Francis J. West, a Marine reservist who was on a special assignment from Headquarters Marine Corps to develop small unit combat narratives of Marines in Vietnam) reported approximately 150 to 250 North Vietnamese troops about three and one-half miles southwest of the Rockpile. The team adjusted artillery fire on the enemy force. As a result of this particular action the enemy lost 50 men.[54]

According to West, after he returned to III MAF Headquarters and described the patrol to General Walt and Colonel Chaisson, they both expressed the opinion that such missions deserved a special section in the reporting system and selected the name "Stingray" for this purpose.[55] Major Colby claimed that the marriage of the reconnaissance Marines and artillery was one of the major innovations of the war, declaring "Recon elements are a truly deadly force in hiding among enemy units with this capability in hand."[56]**

The action of 28 July was the last significant sighting of a large body of enemy troops during Hastings. The *324B Division* either had crossed into the DMZ or was hiding in the inaccessible jungle to the west. On 30 July, Lieutenant Colonel Bronars' BLT 3/5 reverted to the operational control of the Seventh Fleet and returned to the *Princeton*. Two days later, General English deactivated his headquarters and the operation came under the control of the new 4th Marines commander, Colonel Alexander D. Cereghino. Hastings officially ended on 3 August. Only Lieutenant Colonel Bench's 2d Battalion, 4th Marines, supported by an artillery battery and reconnaissance elements, remained in the Hastings area of operations.

During Hastings, Marine supporting arms played a decisive role. Marine F-4B Phantoms, A-4 Skyhawks, and F-8 Crusaders maintained a sortie rate of 100 a day, averaging 32 close air support missions, 40 interdiction missions, and 28 radar-controlled missions. During the entire operation, attack aircraft completed 1,677 tactical sorties against the enemy. At the same time, MAG-16 helicopters flew nearly 10,000 sorties and lifted a daily average

---

*Colonel Bench remarked that just before the mortar attack an attached U.S. Navy psychological warfare team began broadcasting taped appeals for the enemy to surrender. According to Bench, the NVA cleverly used "the noise shield of the broadcast" to muffle their mortar attack, thus resulting in the large number of casualties. Col Arnold E. Bench, Comments on draft MS, dtd 20Jul78 (Vietnam Comment File).

**Lieutenant Colonel Colby wrote in 1978 that in Stingray operations, the artillery, usually two guns, "was actually placed in direct support of a single recon team for the duration of its *mission*." LtCol Dwain A. Colby, Comments on draft MS, dtd 12Jun78 (Vietnam Comment File). The term "Stingray" was in use at HQMC by mid-August to describe these operations while FMFPac began reporting "Stingray" activities in its July summary, using as its starting date for statistical analysis Sergeant Howard's patrol of 13 June 1966. HQMC, G-3 Division (A03H-14), Point Paper, dtd 16Aug66 (HQMC G-3 Div, Point Papers, West Pac, Jul-Dec66), and FMFPac, *III MAF Ops*, Jul66. (See chapter 8 for the description of Sergeant Howard's patrol.)

Marines from the 3d Battalion, 5th Marines are seen in a temporary base area near Dong Ha. The "pitched tents" are actually ponchos used as tents since they were easier to carry than the shelter halves.

of 620 troops. On the ground, Major Morrow's artillery fired nearly 34,500 rounds in support of the Marine and South Vietnamese infantrymen.[57]

Logistic support during the operation had also been massive. By 18 July, the KC-130 transport planes from VMGR-152 and -352 had hauled 1.3 million pounds of supplies from Da Nang to Dong Ha. From that date to the end of the operation, the transport pilots brought in 115 tons per day to sustain the Marine task force. In addition, "Rough Rider" truck convoys, using Route 1, brought 120 tons of ammunition from Phu Bai to the task force logistic support area at Dong Ha. MAG-16 and -36 helicopters were used exclusively to move the supplies from the LSA to the battalions in the field. Despite the fact that after 21 July all CH-46A helicopters were grounded for mechanical reasons, the 42 UH-34s and four CH-37s at Dong Ha lifted an average of 75 tons per day, with a peak of 110 tons, to supply the infantry battalions.[58] General English later reminisced: "I was a battalion commander at Iwo Jima and I didn't get anywhere near the support I was able to give these Marines here."[59]

Operation Hastings/Lam Son-289, the largest and most violent operation of the war up to that point, involved 8,000 Marines and 3,000 South Vietnamese. The number of North Vietnamese regulars engaged probably equalled the total American and South Vietnamese strength. During the battle, the Marines fought elements from all three regiments of the *324B Division*: the *90th*, the *803d*, and the *812th*.

Both sides suffered heavy casualties. The Marines had lost 126 killed and 448 wounded while the ARVN had 21 killed and 40 wounded. The allies inflicted a still higher toll on the enemy; reported enemy casualties numbered over 700 killed and 17 captured. Enemy equipment losses were significant, included were over 200 weapons, 300 pounds of documents,* and over 300,000 rounds of ammunition.[60]

Summing up this major engagement along the DMZ, General Walt described the enemy in the following terms:

> We found them well equipped, well trained, and aggressive to the point of fanaticism. They attacked in mass formations and died by the hundreds. Their leaders had misjudged the fighting ability of U.S. Marines and ARVN soldiers together; our superiority in artillery and total command of the air. They had vastly underestimated . . . our mobility.[61]

---

*These 300 pounds consisted of some 6,000 individual documents and, according to General English, that for U.S. intelligence, "this was some of the most meaningful information found in South Vietnam up to this time." MajGen Lowell E. English, Comments on draft MS, dtd 12Jun78 (Vietnam Comment File).

CHAPTER 11

The DMZ War Continues, Operation Prairie

Reconnaissance in Force, 3 August-13 September 1966—Assault from the Sea, Deckhouse IV—The Continued Fighting for Nui Cay Tre (Mutter) Ridge and the Razorback—The Opening of Khe Sanh and the 3d Marine Division Moves North

---

Reconnaissance in Force, 3 Aug-13 Sep 66

Enemy intentions in the DMZ area remained a matter of conjecture during the latter stages of Operation Hastings. On 22 July, Lieutenant General Krulak stated his opinion to General Westmoreland that the North Vietnamese were attempting to avoid direct contact with the Marines. Westmoreland replied that "just the reverse was the case and that the NVA forces were not seeking to get away." The MACV commander believed that III MAF could expect to encounter large numbers of the NVA and that elements of the *324B Division*, although bloodied, were still south of the DMZ. Furthermore, he had received reports indicating that the North Vietnamese were moving two more divisions, the *304th* and *341st*, into the area immediately north of the DMZ. Marine commanders recognized a buildup of enemy forces in the DMZ, but took exception to terms such as "massive buildup," "go for broke," "significant serious threats," and similar expressions contained in messages originating from Westmoreland's Saigon headquarters. Although MACV, FMFPac, and III MAF used identical intelligence data, they continued to interpret it differently.[1]

After the closeout of Hastings on 3 August, the Marine command retained a small task force, formed around Lieutenant Colonel Bench's 2d Battalion, 4th Marines at Dong Ha, to monitor the potential threat in the north. Bench's command consisted of his four infantry companies, supported by the 1st Force Reconnaissance Company and Battery G, 3d Battalion, 12th Marines, reinforced by two 155mm howitzers. Also attached to the 2d Battalion were a platoon each from the 3d Tank Battalion, the 3d Antitank Battalion, the 3d Engineer Battalion, and a logistic unit from the Force Logistic Command. The battalion CP was established at the Dong Ha air strip, but the attached artillery and tanks were at Cam Lo; two infantry companies, F and G, provided security for the artillery positions. Two helicopter detachments, one from MAG-16 and the other from the U.S. Army 220th Aviation Company, were at Dong Ha to support the ground force.[2]

The Marine plan for the operation, codenamed Prairie, to determine the extent of NVA forces in the DMZ sector relied heavily upon the reports of Major Colby's reconnaissance Marines. UH-1Es from VMO-2 were to insert four- or five-man "Stingray" teams along suspected enemy avenues of approach. If the reconnaissance teams made contact with any NVA, they could call for artillery from Cam Lo, helicopter gunships, or Marine aircraft from Da Nang or Chu Lai. The infantry companies at Cam Lo and Dong Ha were poised to reinforce the reconnaissance patrols. Colonel Cereghino, the 4th Marines commander, held two battalions on eight-hour alert at Phu Bai to move to Dong Ha in the event of major enemy infiltration from the DMZ.

The first significant encounter during Prairie involved a Stingray patrol. On 6 August, a UH-1E inserted a five-man team in a jungle-covered hill mass 4,000 meters north of the Rockpile, approximately 1,000 meters to the southeast of the Nui Cay Tre ridgeline. The team, codenamed Groucho Marx, reported that it saw NVA troops moving along the trails and could smell smoke from enemy camp sites. The patrol twice called for the artillery at Cam Lo to fire on the suspected locations. On the morning of the 8th, the Marines saw 10 to 15 North Vietnamese troops moving in skirmish line 100 meters away, apparently looking for the American patrol. The team leader, Staff Sergeant Billy M. Donaldson, radioed Major Colby and reported the situation. Colby sent a pair of gunships to cover the patrol and then asked "if they thought we could get some prisoners out of there if I sent in a reaction force. They said affirmative and that there was a landing zone within 150 meters of them."[3]

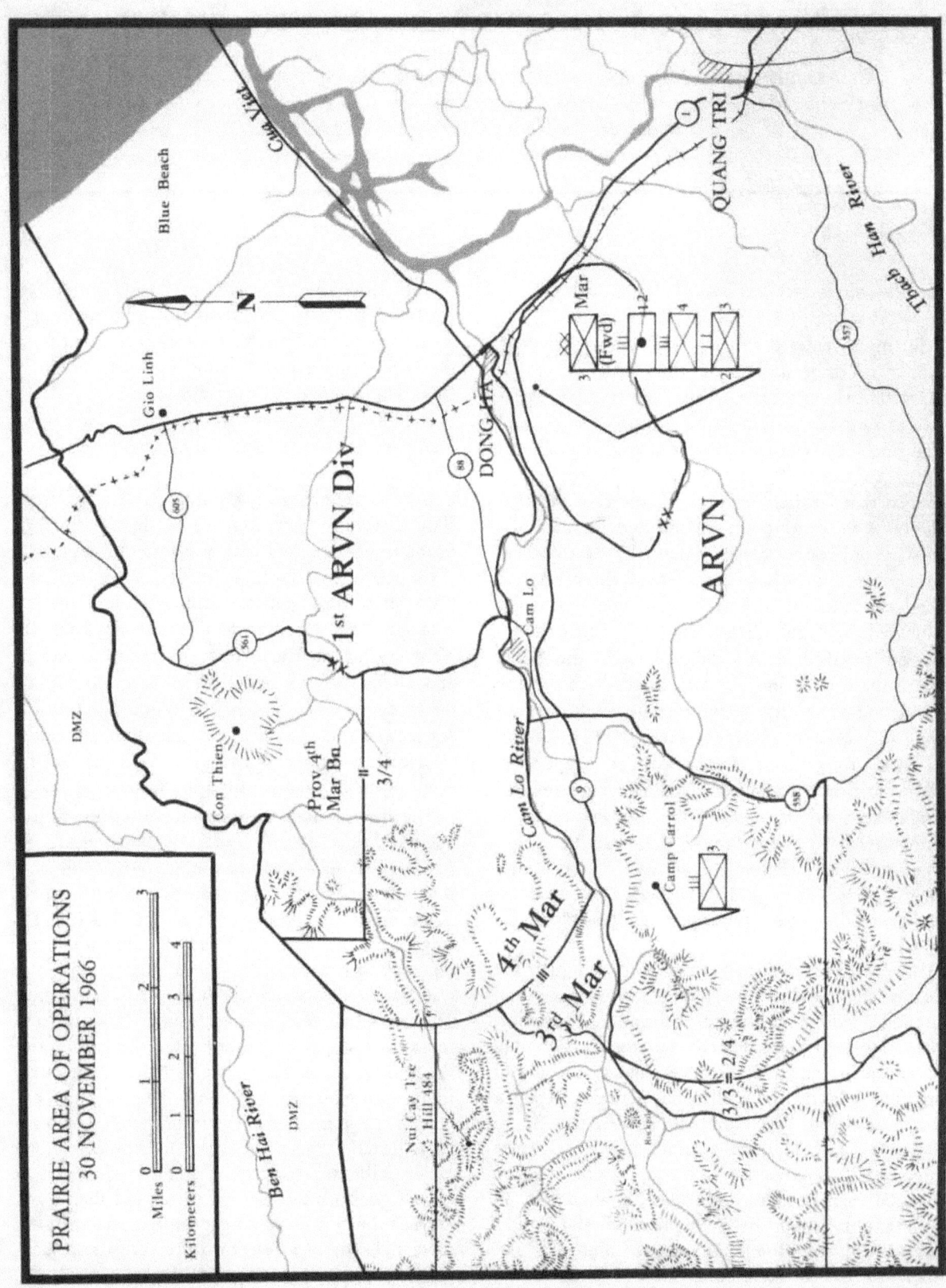

Shortly afterward, six HMM-265 CH-46s landed in the zone, debarking a 40-man Marine platoon from Company E led by Second Lieutenant Andrew W. Sherman. By the time Sherman's platoon reached the reconnaissance team's perimeter, the enemy had disappeared. After a short, futile search for the North Vietnamese, Sherman asked for helicopters to lift the Marines out of the area.

In midafternoon, eight UH-34s from HMM-161 arrived overhead to extract the Marines. The first helicopter landed in the improvised landing zone without incident, but when it took off, North Vietnamese troops opened fire from a ridgeline to the north. Five UH-34s landed, but were able to evacuate only 20 of the 45 Marines because of the heavy fire. Lieutenant Sherman waved off the rest of the helicopters and set up a defensive perimeter.

At this point, the enemy, in company strength, tried to assault the Marine position. The American defenders turned them back with hand grenades and small arms fire, but Sherman was killed. His platoon sergeant, Sergeant Robert L. Pace, took command, but was wounded during the next NVA assault and command passed to Staff Sergeant Donaldson.

Surrounded, the small Marine force called for supporting arms. The 155s at Cam Lo responded immediately and at 1830, F-4B Phantoms from MAG-11 arrived overhead and stopped one NVA assault. Sergeant Donaldson was severely wounded during the last attack.[4]

At Dong Ha, the Company E commander, Captain Howard V. Lee, asked Lieutenant Colonel Bench for permission to take a relief force into the battle area to evacuate the Marines. The battalion commander finally acceded to Lee's entreaties and the captain gathered together seven volunteers besides himself. Three HMM-161 UH-34s flew the relief force to the battle site, but enemy fire forced the helicopters to land outside the Marine perimeter. Only three of the volunteers, including Lee, were able to reach the defenders. A VMO-2 UH-1E, piloted by Major Vincil W. Hazelbaker, evacuated the remaining Marines from the aborted relief expedition and flew them back to Dong Ha. Upon arriving in the shrinking Marine perimeter, Captain Lee immediately took command, reorganized the defenses, and supervised the distribution of ammunition which the helicopters had dropped inside the position.[5]

The enemy continued to close in on the Marines, and, at the same time, prevented any more helicopters from landing. NVA ground fire drove off two HMM-265 CH-46s carrying additional Company E troops and hit one UH-1E gunship killing a crew member and wounding another. The Marine defenders repulsed repeated assaults on their positions, but their situation deteriorated. At 2030, Lee radioed Bench that he had only 16 men still able to fight. The company commander, himself, had been wounded twice, a slight nick on the ear when he first debarked from the helicopter and later severely, when an "NVA grenade . . . exploded no more than two feet" from him, "sending fragments into . . . [the] right eye and the right side of [his] body."[6]

Lieutenant Colonel Bench provided what support he could. He ordered all available artillery, firing at maximum range, including a section of 81mm mortars from the Marine outpost on the Rockpile, to hit the enemy-held hill mass north of Lee's perimeter. The 105 battery was out of range and Bench ordered it and a section of M-48 tanks to displace so that at first light they would be able to support the surrounded Marines.

Although Marine high performance close air support was called off because of darkness and low ceiling, VMO-2 UH-1E gunships made numerous rocket and strafing runs on enemy positions. A Marine C-117 flare ship arrived to provide illumination, but each lull between flare drops allowed the enemy to move closer. Later that night, two Air Force AC-47s arrived and strafed the hill slopes outside the Marine perimeter.

Several helicopters from MAG-16 made repeated resupply attempts. Major Hazelbaker, when he evacuated the stranded Marines outside the perimeter, was able to get in close enough to the defenders' positions for his crew to push out several boxes of 7.62mm linked ammunition. Enemy fire, however, aborted all other such attempts. Shortly before midnight, Lee reported that his troops were almost out of ammunition. Hazelbaker volunteered to fly another resupply mission and successfully landed his aircraft inside the Marine defenses.

While the UH-1E was on the ground and the troops and crew were unloading the ammunition, an enemy rocket "impacted on the rotor mast," crippling the helicopter. After helping two wounded crewmen out of the damaged craft, Major Hazelbaker and his copilot joined the fight on the ground.[7]

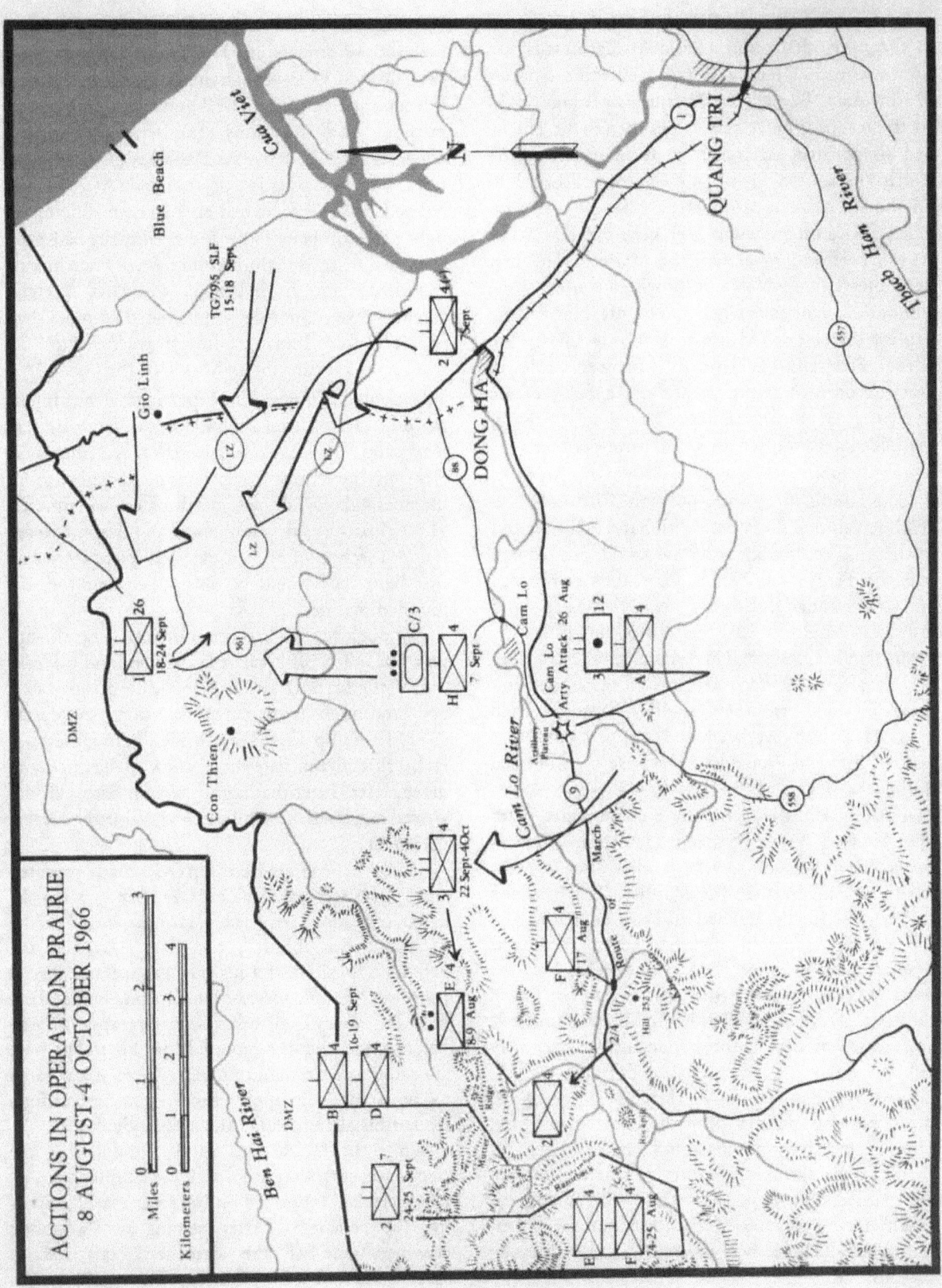

The enemy attack which damaged the Huey was the last major effort against the Marine position. The helicopter crew distributed ammunition and incorporated the helicopter's M-60 machine guns in the defense. Major Hazelbaker and Captain Lee waited for the NVA to make their next move. According to a Navy corpsman in the perimeter:

> The rest of the night was quiet . . . You could hear them [the NVA] drag off the bodies. Some would come right up to the brush line and just start talking. Every time we shot at them another grenade would come in. They were trying to feel out our position.[8]

In the early morning hours, Captain Lee, weak from loss of blood, relinquished command to Major Hazelbaker. At dawn, the major directed a Marine napalm strike on the enemy positions; NVA fire completely stopped. Two hours later, Company F and the battalion command group arrived at the Marine-held hill, followed shortly by the rest of Company E. The two units fanned out, but the enemy had left the immediate area.

The Groucho Marx fight was over and the last Marines were lifted out that afternoon. The Marines had lost five killed and 27 wounded. Four of the dead Marines were from Company E, while one was a UH-34 gunner from HMM-161, killed by enemy ground fire. Of the wounded, 15 were from Company E, one from the 1st Force Reconnaissance Company, and the remainder from the MAG-16 helicopter crews including three pilots. The Marines counted 37 enemy bodies on the slopes of the hill, but bloodstains and drag marks indicated that the enemy had suffered much heavier casualties. The Marines recovered a document from one of the NVA bodies, which indicated that the dead man had been a company commander. For the Groucho Marx action, Captain Lee received the Medal of Honor, while Major Hazelbaker was awarded the Navy Cross.[9]

Prairie was just beginning. The action of 8-9 August convinced Colonel Cereghino, an experienced infantry officer who had served in both World War II and Korea, that the enemy had returned in strength.[10] On 13 August, he established a forward command post at Dong Ha and moved Lieutenant Colonel Jack Westerman's 1st Battalion, 4th Marines north from Phu Bai. In addition, the infantry was reinforced by Major Morrow's 3d Battalion, 12th Marines and Captain John H. Gary's Company C, 3d Tank Battalion. Westerman's battalion was to relieve

Marine Corps Photo A187655
MajGen Wood B. Kyle, Commanding General, 3d Marine Division (back to camera), greets two members of Company E upon their return to Dong Ha. Elements of the company reinforced a reconnaissance team near the DMZ and stood off an attack by a North Vietnamese battalion.

Bench's battalion at Dong Ha and Cam Lo. Colonel Cereghino then ordered Bench to conduct a reconnaissance in force along Route 9 between Cam Lo and the Rockpile, followed by a search and destroy mission north of that site. Bench's 2d Battalion, 4th Marines left Cam Lo on 17 August after being relieved by Westerman's unit.

The 2d battalion with three companies, Company H remaining at Cam Lo, departed the base area about 0730 on foot. Marine air and artillery pounded suspected enemy strong points along the battalion's route of march. At 1215, Marine fixed-wing attack aircraft bombed Hill 252, whose steep cliffs overhung a bridge on Route 9, spanning the Song Khe Gio, a small north-south tributary of the Cam Lo River. After the airstrike, Company F, the lead company, pressed forward, but "was stopped dead at the bridge held by a bunker complex carved out of the sides of Hill 252."[11]

With his lead company unable to move, and his other two companies unable to maneuver to support Company F because of heavy enemy automatic weapons fire and NVA snipers well-hidden in

Marine Corps Photo A188143

A Marine tank column is shown advancing along Route 9. M48 tanks, like those pictured here, provided much needed support to the infantry road reconnaissance during Operation Prairie.

camouflaged "spider traps," Lieutenant Colonel Bench called for artillery and air support. The resulting airstrikes and artillery missions, however, had little effect on the enemy concrete and metal-plated bunkers dug into the solid rock of Hill 252. Bench then requested Colonel Cereghino to reinforce his battalion with a section of tanks from the tank company at Cam Lo. The two M-48 tanks from Company C arrived at the Company F forward positions about 1600. After another airstrike, the M-48s with their 90mm guns laid direct fire into the enemy bunker complex. With the assistance of the tanks, the Marine infantry company withdrew to the night defensive positions of the rest of the battalion. Another tank from Company C reinforced the infantry and during the evening of 17 August, Marine air and artillery, as well as the tanks, continued to hit the enemy fortifications. About 1940 an air observer spotted about 40 enemy troops moving off Hill 252 in a southwesterly direction and called an air strike "with good coverage on target." For the day, the Marines sustained casualties of two dead and five wounded, all from Company F, while killing about 20 of the enemy.[12]

On the morning of 18 August, following a further bombardment of the enemy bunkers, Company G forded the Khe Gio south of the bridge and took Hill 252 from the rear, while the rest of the battalion continued its advance along Route 9. The Marines of Company G found in the former enemy fortifications three dead NVA soldiers, a light machine gun, and an inscribed sword. Reinforced by yet another tank section, the 2d Battalion completed its reconnaissance of Route 9 that evening, encountering only minor resistance, and established its night defensive positions north of the Rockpile. The tank platoon returned to Cam Lo the following day while the 2d Battalion began its search and destroy mission in the high rugged terrain between the Rockpile and the Nui Cay Tre ridgeline. Although employed in relatively poor tank country, the M-48s had proved effective against an enemy strongpoint which Marine infantry and other supporting units had not been able to neutralize.[13]

For the next six days, the battalion found itself heavily engaged with elements of the *803d NVA Regiment*. Lieutenant Colonel Bench had established his command post on a mountain some 2,000 meters northeast of the Rockpile and ordered his three companies "to fan out" and search the prominent terrain features 500 to 1,000 meters to the north, northwest, and northeast. On the 19th, Company E in a reconnaissance of a wooded ridge came across two concrete enemy bunkers. As the Marines maneuvered to reduce the enemy defenses, NVA 12.7mm machine guns on each flank and from the bunkers caught one Marine platoon in a crossfire. At the same time, enemy gunners mortared the company rear which had laid down a base of fire. Despite sustaining casualties of two dead and 14 wounded, the Marine company, supported by the 155mm howitzers at Cam Lo, Marine fixed-wing airstrikes, UH-1E gunships, 81mm mortars, and 106mm recoilless rifles, destroyed the enemy defenses and gun positions and killed a possible 30 of the enemy. From the 20th to the 22d, and after a B-52 strike in the valley behind the former enemy positions, the companies of the battalion continued to catch glimpses of enemy troops and occasionally were the targets of enemy mortars and heavy machine guns.[14]

At this time, Lieutenant Colonel Bench became concerned with a new turn of events that threatened the 11-man outpost on the Rockpile. The sheer cliffs of the 700-foot outcropping prevented resupply of the Marines there except by helicopter. Indeed, the Marine pilots had to perform the demanding maneuver of landing one wheel of their helicopter on the edge of the Rockpile while the aircraft hovered until the cargo could be unloaded. On 21-22 August, an enemy 12.7mm machine gun, positioned strategically midway between the Rockpile and another hill mass, nicknamed the

Marine Corps Photo A332463 (LtCol Curtis G. Arnold)
A Marine helicopter provides resupply for the Rockpile. One wheel rests on the wooden ramp while the aircraft hovers until it can be unloaded.

Razorback because of its sharp contours, 1,000 meters to the northwest, opened fire on the resupply aircraft. Repeated attempts by Marine air and artillery failed to silence the gun, which imperiled the helicopter lifeline to the Rockpile. Moreover, on the morning of the 22d, Bench and his command group observed enemy troops at the base of the Rockpile and took them under fire with 106mm recoilless rifles and called an airstrike. Captain John J. W. Hilgers, who had become the 2d Battalion S-3 earlier that month, recalled in 1978, that he and Bench "went on an air recon and came close to being shot out of the sky by the 12.7 whose position we inadvertently flew over and located."[15]

At this point, the morning of the 23d, Bench decided that he had to eliminate the enemy machine gun. He ordered Captain Edward W. Besch, who had relieved Captain Lee as commander of Company E after the action of 9 August, to "conduct a reconnaissance in force to locate and neutralize the 12.7 and supporting forces." Captain Hilgers recalled several years later that he briefed Besch and recommended that the company commander establish a base of operations near two "knobs" in the vicinity of the gun where helicopters could get in, but not to "count on [their] availability. . . ."[16]

Shortly after 1000, Besch departed the battalion CP with his company, which he later remembered consisted of less than 60 personnel, divided into two platoons of two squads each. About two hours later the Marine company arrived in the general objective area, some two miles to the southwest of its starting point. Besch established his base camp in the valley between the two "knobs," some 300 meters to the east of the southern portion of the Razorback. Finding little sign of any enemy in the immediate vicinity, he took three squads of the company to ex-

A view of the Rockpile (in the foreground) looking northwest to the Razorback (in the immediate background). Enemy gunners positioned strategically near the Razorback threatened the helicopter lifeline to the Rockpile.

Marine Corps Photo A332474 (LtCol Curtis G. Arnold)

plore the "rock face" of the hill mass. To cover his movements, Besch left in the camp site, under his executive officer, the remaining squad, reinforced by 60mm mortars and a 106mm recoilless rifle which had been brought in by helicopter earlier in the day.[17]

About 1400, Captain Besch with the forward elements of his company came upon a bowl-shaped ravine in the southeastern sector of the Razorback, honeycombed with caves. Besch several years later remembered that some of the "cave passageways were large enough to drive two trucks through, side by side. . . ." The Marines than began a systematic search of the caves. While encountering no enemy, the Marines found evidence, such as spent 12.7mm machine gun rounds, of recent occupation. With the exploration of the caverns taking him longer than he expected, Besch sent one of the squads back to look for the enemy machine gun on the low ground below the Razorback. The squad found no gun and returned to the company rear position held by the executive officer. Besch, in the meantime, with the remaining two squads continued to investigate the caves.[18]

Shortly after 1630, Besch made preparations to return to his base camp and close out the operation. A Marine helicopter already had lifted out the 106mm recoilless rifle and flew it back to its former positions with the battalion. About 10 minutes later, the Marines heard voices inside one of the caves. Hoping to take a prisoner, Besch attempted to coax out the NVA soldiers. Besch recalled that three shots rang out from inside the cave and:

> Within seconds, squads of NVA soldiers . . . simultaneously erupted from five or six concealed caves in the craggy rock wall and immediately shot down the surprised Marine squad near the cave.[19]

The surviving Marines on the Razorback took what cover they could. Besch remembered that he and one of his two radiomen jumped into a bomb crater. Realizing that the other man was dying from a wound in the chest, Besch took the radioset and asked for supporting fires from the two squads still in the rear camp site. According to Besch, he and the small group with him survived only by feigning death.[20] Other remnants of his small force were scattered all along the ravine. The second radio operator, separated from Besch, radioed Lieutenant Colonel Bench that the North Vietnamese soldiers were, "real close and closing on their flank, still throwing grenades and firing weapons."[21]

At this point, Lieutenant Colonel Bench, already concerned by the lapse of time that Besch had been on the Razorback, hastily prepared his plans for the relief of the embattled company. With Company E's forward positions on the outside fringes of the 155mm fan from Cam Lo, thus making the employment of artillery impractical, the battalion commander immediately requested both fixed-wing and helicopter gunships on station. At the same time, he formed a composite company by taking a platoon each from Companies F and G and his Headquarters and Service Company. His operations officer, Captain Hilgers, volunteered to take charge of the relief force and Bench reluctantly assented since he had no one else to send.[22]

By late evening, Marine helicopters had landed Hilgers' makeshift company, reinforced by two 106mm recoilless rifles, flamethrowers, and .50 caliber machine guns, near the Company E base camp. After joining the rear elements of Company E, Hilgers later commented that he had "little choice under the circumstances," but to send the platoon from Company F to the immediate relief of the trapped men and to deploy the Company G platoon "around to the south to protect our highly vulnerable southern flank where known NVA units were located, including the 12.7." He stated that he "took a calculated risk that no enemy units were located on our northern flank as Besch had been in

A view from the 2d Battalion, 4th Marines command post looking toward the Rockpile (extreme left of picture) and the Razorback ridgeline. Two bombs have just exploded behind the forward elements of Company E trapped on the Razorback by enemy troops.

Marine Corps Photo 532579 (Capt Edwin W. Besch)

that area."²³ By this time the Marine jets had arrived overhead and bombed a valley to the west that the North Vietnamese were using in an attempt to flank the Marines. Two Marine VMO-2 gunships about 25 minutes later also strafed the enemy.

During the night, the Marines brought their entire arsenal into the battle. Marine artillery and flareships provided illumination and a U.S. Air Force AC-47 opened up with 7.62mm mini-guns on enemy bunkers. After the first flare dropped, the surviving radio operator of Company E, although wounded, contacted Hilgers and attempted to direct 106mm recoilless rifle fire against the North Vietnamese troops. He died of his wounds while still trying to adjust the missions.²⁴

With the assistance of the illumination provided by the flares, the Company F platoon, under 2d Lieutenant Stephen F. Snyder, made its way through the difficult jungle terrain to the face of the Razorback. Shortly after 0030 on the 24th, the platoon reached the eastern lip of the natural bowl where the trapped men were, only to find Besch's Marines scattered below, and the North Vietnamese in control of the remaining three ledges of the ravine. Snyder hastily set up his defenses and then led a four-man patrol toward the western rim of the bowl where Besch had gathered together a few of his men to the side of a North Vietnamese-held cave. A North Vietnamese grenade barrage forced the patrol to turn back, but not before it had come within 15 meters of the remnants of Company E and rescued two of the wounded. Returning to its defensive positions, the Company F platoon laid down a base of suppressive fire and directed 106mm recoilless rifle missions upon the enemy positions.²⁵

At about 0600, it became apparent that the North Vietnamese were about to launch a final attack upon the Marines. Snyder, instead of waiting for the assault, ordered a counterattack. Captain Besch several years later recalled that as the North Vietnamese troops came out of the caves and formed in the open, Snyder's men took them under fire. According to Besch, the enemy troops "were very quickly (within seconds, like turning down a radio volume button . . .) annihilated by the Marines, one of whom shouted, 'One of 'em is still moving, shoot the son-of-a-bitch,' and nearly every Marine reopened fire."²⁶ In the exchange of fire, Snyder was killed, his platoon sergeant badly wounded, and finally the platoon guide, Sergeant Patrick J. Noon, Jr., took over the relief platoon.

With daybreak, Lieutenant Colonel Bench was able to bring additional units into the battle. He sent the rest of Company G to reinforce Hilgers' composite force. Later that morning, Marine helicopters lifted two platoons of his reserve company, Company H, from Cam Lo to the battalion sector, thus allowing the remaining elements of Company F to go forward. One platoon of Company H accompanied a platoon of M-48 tanks from Cam Lo along Route 9 to the objective area. With the reinforcements, the 2d battalion went into the attack, but at a painfully slow pace. Firing from behind rocks and from caves, the North Vietnamese had the advantage of terrain. With the employment of recoilless rifles and the tanks at point-blank ranges, the battalion eventually gained the upper hand. Under cover of artillery, which also had moved forward, and air, the Marines blasted the NVA out of their caves. By midmorning, the forward

The face of the Razorback as seen by the relief force of the 2d Battalion, 4th Marines, commanded by the battalion's operations officer, Capt John J. W. Hilgers. The barrel of a Marine 106mm recoilless rifle can be seen in the foreground.

Marine Corps Photo A332794 (LtCol John J. W. Hilgers)

elements of the relief force reached the battered Company F platoon and remnants of Company E. Bench's unit continued to scour the ridges for the next two days, searching caves and bunkers for the enemy, but the fight for the Razorback was over.

Losses on both sides were heavy, but the NVA had suffered a serious reverse. They had lost their outpost and no longer were in a position to threaten the Marines on the Rockpile. During the engagement, the 2d Battalion, 4th Marines sustained more than 120 casualties, including 21 dead. Eleven of the dead and 13 of the wounded, including Captain Besch whose arm was shattered, were from Company E. Estimates of enemy dead ranged from 120 to 170.*

The Marines took one prisoner who identified himself as a sergeant and a member of the *803d Regiment, 324B Division*. The enemy soldier told his captors that his battalion's mission was to neutralize the Rockpile and then sweep eastward to join in an attack on the 3d Battalion, 12th Marines positions at Cam Lo.[27]

The NVA sergeant's information proved timely. During the early morning hours of 26 August, the enemy launched a two-company attack against the Marine artillery near Cam Lo. At 0300, 1st Lieutenant Gerald T. Galvin, the commander of Company A, 1st Battalion, 4th Marines, whose unit was responsible for the security of the perimeter, reported to his battalion commander, Lieutenant Colonel Westerman, that three of his outposts had seen movement to their front. Westerman ordered the company to "just sit tight and keep observing"

and to report any new development.[28] About fifteen minutes later, Lieutenant Galvin called back and declared that five outposts had spotted enemy troops moving toward their positions. According to Colonel Cereghino, who was with the battalion commander at Dong Ha, Westerman was about to send reinforcements to the company. Cereghino decided, however, that it would be too complicated an operation to move the Marines out in the dark. He believed that Galvin and his men "were in good shape, confident and gung ho" and that they could hold their own against any attacking force.[29] The regimental commander told Westerman "to hold up but to be prepared to move troops in a matter of minutes."[30] Lieutenant Colonel Westerman then directed Galvin to withdraw the outposts to the main perimeter and wait for the enemy to come through the wire, about 90 meters to the front.

The idea was to allow the NVA troops to crawl through the wire and then illuminate the area, making the North Vietnamese easy targets. The plan worked, in part. The wire channelized the infiltrators, the artillery fired illumination rounds, and an AC-47 dropped flares. On a prearranged signal, the Marines on the perimeter opened up on the attacking force, by then 40 to 50 meters in front of the Marine positions.

The enemy, however, was not entirely unsuccessful. Somehow the first wave passed through the Company A positions unnoticed and did do some damage. According to Lieutenant Colonel Westerman:

> They [the NVA] snuck on through before we ever illuminated the area. . . . as you know, they're real proficient at moving at night . . . very silently, very slowly, and very patiently. . . . [the NVA] did get through even though our people were waiting for them. They crawled in between the holes, and our people never even realized that they passed through their positions.[31]

Those enemy troops that did get through placed explosive charges all over the positions, blowing up tents, trailers, and one tank retriever.

The destruction could have been much more extensive. Just the previous day, the 155mm howitzers had moved to new revetments further west to provide for better coverage of the Razorback-Rockpile complex. At the same time, the 3d Battalion, 12th Marines had also changed the location of its fire direction center. The NVA attacking force had excellent intelligence on the location of the old posi-

---

*Both the III MAF and 4th Marines ComdCs for this period show 26 NVA confirmed dead, but these figures were apparently from preliminary reports. The 2/4 AAR does not furnish a total casualty count, but Shaplen, in his account, lists 170 KIA. Shaplen, "Hastings and Prairie," p. 180. Lieutenant Colonel Bench's comments to the Historical Division state 137 enemy were killed. LtCol Arnold E. Bench, Comments on draft MS, dtd 12Sep69 (*Vietnam Comment File*). Figures do not agree on Marine casualties. The 4th Marines shows 11 Marines KIA in its AAR, but this reflects only the casualties of Company E. Lieutenant Colonel Bench's comments list 21 Marines KIA, while Shaplen speaks of a "score" of Marine dead. Indicative of the heavy fighting was the number of medals awarded. Captain Hilgers, Lieutenant Snyder, and Sergeant Noon received the Navy Cross, while Corporal Paul M. Reed, one of the radio operators of Company E, and Corporal William F. Wright, a radio operator with the platoon from Company F, both received the Silver Star.

tions and these moves helped to diffuse the effects of the raid. Yet, the largest factor in keeping the damage to a minimum was the rapid response of the Marine defenders. Within two hours, Company A and a security force from the 3d Battalion, 12th Marines had control of the situation. The Marines captured one NVA soldier. He identified himself as a member of the *812th Infantry Regiment, 324B NVA Division*, which in coordination with a local VC unit, had made the attack. Had this unit been able to join with the battalion from the *803d NVA Regiment* as originally planned, the attack on the Marine artillery position might well have been much more serious.* As it was, nine Marines were killed and 20 wounded. None of Major Morrow's artillery pieces were damaged.

This action at Cam Lo was the last significant contact in Operation Prairie during August. Lieutenant Colonel Bench's battalion returned to Dong Ha on 29 August to relieve the 1st Battalion, 4th Marines. The latter battalion moved from Cam Lo and Dong Ha and conducted a reconnaissance in force along Route 9, but met little resistance.

The month was a bloody one for both the Marines and NVA. According to Marine reports, Prairie accounted for over 200 enemy dead, while the Americans suffered 37 killed and 130 wounded during this phase of the operation.

Colonel Cereghino realigned his forces. On 27 August he assigned Lieutenant Colonel John J. Roothoff's 2d Battalion, 7th Marines, which had just arrived from Chu Lai, the area of responsibility formerly held by the 2d Battalion, 4th Marines, including the Rockpile. When Westerman's battalion completed sweeping Route 9 into the Thon Son Lam area, 1,500 meters west of the Rockpile, it returned to Dong Ha, arriving on 7 September. It relieved Bench's 2d Battalion of the defense missions at both Dong Ha and Cam Lo.

At this point, Colonel Cereghino decided to extend his area of operations to the Con Thien region, due north of Cam Lo and adjacent to the DMZ. Bas-

---

*Colonel Cereghino commented that even if the battalion from the *803d* had been on the scene, the attack had no chance of success, "because we were loaded and locked [at Dong Ha] and but a few minutes away, had Lieutenant Galvin or Major Morrow needed us." Col Alexander D. Cereghino, Comments on draft MS, dtd 17Aug78 (Vietnam Comment File).

Marine Corps Photo A187790

Enemy dead lie inside the Cam Lo perimeter after their mostly aborted attack on the Marine artillery. Smoke from a destroyed tank retriever can be seen in the background.

LtGen Victor H. Krulak, CGFMFPac (center), discusses the battle situation with LtCol John J. Roothoff, Commanding Officer, 2d Battalion, 7th Marines, whose battalion had just relieved the 2d Battalion, 4th Marines in the Rockpile sector, and Col Alexander D. Cereghino, Commanding Officer, 4th Marines. MajGen Wood B. Kyle, CG 3dMarDiv, is standing behind Gen Krulak.

Marine Corps Photo A187832

ed on new intelligence that a battalion of the *324B Division* was moving into the area, the 4th Marines commander ordered Lieutenant Colonel Bench to conduct a reconnaissance in force to determine the extent of enemy activity. Company H, accompanied by a platoon of tanks from Company C, 3d Tank Battalion, left Cam Lo on the morning of 7 September. MAG-16 helicopters ferried the rest of the battalion into landing zones around Con Thien. The first significant contact occurred the next morning when Company G ran into an enemy platoon 1,000 meters northeast of the ARVN Con Thien outpost. The firefight lasted for three hours before the enemy disappeared. Five Marines were killed.

The next day, Bench's Companies E and F, reinforced by tanks, engaged a NVA company two miles south of the DMZ. The enemy had expected the Marines. Numerous firing positions and trenches had been dug, extending into the demilitarized area itself. Lieutenant Colonel Bench ordered the tanks to fire point-blank into the enemy positions; after stiff resistance the NVA disengaged. The Marines counted 20 bodies and estimated that they had killed at least another 14. Bench's unit sustained three killed and 17 wounded. The battalion continued its reconnaissance in the area until the 13th, but met only scattered resistance and then returned to Cam Lo.

Assault From The Sea: Deckhouse IV

The reconnaissance by the 2d Battalion, 4th Marines confirmed that elements of the *90th NVA Regiment*, a subordinate unit of the *324B Division*, were now operating south of the DMZ. General Walt had already planned an operation to determine the extent of enemy infiltration in the eastern portion of the Prairie area of operations. On 3 September, he requested that General Westmoreland obtain permission from the Seventh Fleet to use the Special Landing Force in the Con Thien-Gio Linh area.[32] After General Westmoreland acceded to the III MAF request, General Walt held a planning conference on 7 September at Da Nang, attended by representatives of the amphibious ready group and the SLF to work out the details. At that time, they changed D-day from 12 September to the 15th. In effect, the SLF operation, Deckhouse IV, was to continue the reconnaissance in force that Bench's unit had just carried out in this area.*

The operational concept provided for one company of BLT 1/26 (Lieutenant Colonel Anthony A. Monti) to land across Blue Beach, two miles south of the DMZ, north of the Cua Viet River. Lieutenant Colonel James D. McGough's HMM-363 was to bring the other companies into landing zones further inland, west of Highway 1. After the beachhead was secured and the artillery unloaded, Company A was to join the rest of the battalion west of the highway, six miles inland.

The assault phase went almost without incident. At 0700 15 September, the first wave of Company A in 11 LVTs from the USS *Vancouver* (LPD 2) secured Blue Beach without resistance. Forty minutes later, the first heliborne elements landed from the *Iwo Jima* (LPH 2); again no opposition. Later that day, HMM-363 lifted Company A and the artillery battery from the beach area to positions west of Route 1, where they joined the rest of the battalion.

Early that afternoon, the Marines experienced the first serious contact with the NVA. At 1330, a platoon from the 3d Reconnaissance Battalion, attached to the BLT for the operation, encountered a NVA company five miles northeast of Dong Ha while reconnoitering the southwestern portion of the objective area. The well-camouflaged NVA soldiers were moving down a trail in single file, and almost bumped into the Marines. Both units opened fire simultaneously. The reconnaissance Marines, vastly outnumbered, called for help. Marine helicopters arrived to attempt an evacuation, but heavy ground fire prevented them from landing. Five helicopters were hit and two crewmen were wounded in the abortive attempt.

At this point, the Marines on the ground called for supporting arms. The 107mm howtar battery attached to BLT 1/26 pounded the area with continuous fire and four F4Bs from MAG-11 bombed,

---

*There had been some changes within the SLF since Operation Hastings in July. Colonel Harry D. Wortman relieved Colonel Richard A. Brenneman as SLF commander on 31 August. On 5 August, BLT 1/26, which had sailed in new shipping from San Diego, was designated the SLF battalion. After a landing exercise in the Philippines, the battalion participated in Operation Deckhouse III with the 173d Airborne Brigade in III Corps until 29 August.

strafed, and rocketed the enemy positions, allowing the helicopters to make a second attempt to extract the patrol. This time the extraction proceeded smoothly.

During the two-hour engagement, the Marine patrol suffered one killed, six wounded, and one Marine unaccounted for. The troops tried to find the missing man, but enemy fire forced them to give up the search. The patrol claimed that it had killed at least nine NVA and estimated that at least 30 North Vietnamese were killed by supporting arms.

After the extraction of the Marine reconnaissance element, Lieutenant Colonel Monti, the BLT commander, ordered Company A to move from its positions on Route 1 at daybreak and work its way over to the area where the action had occurred. By the evening of the 16th, the Marine company had arrived at its objective and dug in for the night. At 0330 the next morning, the NVA attacked under cover of mortar fire. Company A, supported by naval gunfire and artillery, repulsed the attackers. At first light, patrols were sent out; the Marines found 12 bodies and captured a wounded NVA soldier. The Americans found a cigarette lighter on the wounded man which belonged to the missing reconnaissance Marine. The prisoner claimed that the Marine had died and that he had helped to bury him. The prisoner was evacuated to the *Iwo Jima* for treatment; he died on the operating table. Later that day, a Marine patrol found the grave of the dead American.

The battalion encountered much more opposition in the northwestern area near the DMZ. On the 16th, Company D came under heavy mortar fire, less than a mile from the DMZ. The mortar positions were so close that the Marines could hear the rounds drop into the enemy tubes. The Marines called for naval gunfire and the heavy cruiser *Saint Paul* (CA 73) responded with eight-inch guns. During the follow-up search, the Marine company found three destroyed mortars and 14 bodies.

South of Company D, Company B was also hit. One of its platoons walked into an enemy ambush on the outskirts of a hamlet. The Marines, outnumbered, took cover in the rice paddies. Once more air and artillery were called. After a 75-minute engagement, the enemy broke contact. The Marines were unable to determine enemy casualties; Company B suffered two dead and nine wounded.

The Marines soon discovered that the North Vietnamese had constructed a large tunnel and bunker complex in the Con Thien and Gio Linh areas. Each time the battalion probed the northwestern portion of its area of operations, the enemy responded with heavy fire from well-concealed positions. Although Deckhouse IV officially ended on 18 September, the battalion remained ashore and came under the operational control of the 4th Marines until 24 September. The next day, the 25th, the battalion reverted to its SLF role and left the DMZ sector. During the period the battalion was committed to operations ashore, it killed at least 200 of the enemy at a cost of 203 casualties including 36 killed.[33]

The Continued Fighting for Nui Cay Tre (Mutter) Ridge and the Razorback

While the SLF explored the swamps and rice paddies of the northern coastal plain of Quang Tri Province, action intensified in the western sector of the Prairie operation area. In contrast to the relatively flat eastern terrain, this fighting took place in the mountains and gullies north of the Rockpile, centering on the Nui Cay Tre ridgeline. According to American intelligence agencies, the North Vietnamese *324B Division* had established extensive defenses there to protect its infiltration routes. On 8 September, the 1st Battalion, 4th Marines returned to the Rockpile from Dong Ha and relieved the 2d Battalion, 7th Marines. Colonel Cereghino ordered Lieutenant Colonel Westerman to conduct a deep reconnaissance toward Nui Cay Tre to determine the extent of enemy operations in the area. On 15 September, Companies B and D left the battalion perimeter near the Rockpile and advanced toward the southern approaches of the ridge.

The enemy struck at noon the next day. At that time, both companies were moving in column, with Company D in the lead. The NVA allowed the first two platoons to enter their ambush position before opening fire. Captain Daniel K. McMahon, Jr., the Company D commander, then pushed his third platoon forward into the fight. Lieutenant Colonel Westerman ordered Company B to move up to the forward company's positions. The two companies established a perimeter and Captain McMahon reported to Westerman: "We have 'em just where we want them, they're all the way around us."[34] The two Marine companies were surrounded by a North Vietnamese battalion and the fight would last two and one-half days.

The Marines dug in. Marine air and artillery provided constant supporting fire. Helicopters from MAG-16 also played a vital role in sustaining the surrounded troops. The Marines on the ground hacked out a crude landing zone, for resupply helicopters. Colonel Cereghino ordered Lieutenant Colonel Roothoff to move his battalion to assist Westerman's two companies. After a two-day march from Cam Lo, the lead elements of the 2d Battalion, 7th Marines reached the surrounded units the evening of 18 September, later joined by the rest of the battalion, and the relief was completed.

The enemy was gone, but Marine air, artillery, and the two infantry companies were credited with killing at least 170 of the North Vietnamese. Nine Marines from Westerman's battalion were killed in the battle.

An 81mm mortar team from the 2d Battalion, 7th Marines exchanges fire with the enemy near the Rockpile-Razorback complex. According to the original caption, the NVA, firing an 82mm mortar, returned round for round.

Marine Corps Photo A187852

The 1st Battalion, 4th Marines units returned to the battalion command post near the Rockpile on 19 September, while the 2d Battalion, 7th Marines continued to patrol in the Nui Cay Tre area. Lieutenant Colonel Roothoff's companies operated south of the Nui Cay Tre ridge for the next two days, coming under increasing enemy pressure, but then the battalion was ordered to withdraw to positions near the Rockpile.

Colonel Cereghino had two reasons for moving Roothoff back to the Rockpile. To attack the ridge from the south was futile; it was apparent that the North Vietnamese were strongly entrenched there, waiting for the Marines. Secondly, the North Vietnamese had returned to the Razorback and were mortaring the Rockpile. The regimental commander decided first to clean out the Razorback.

Lieutenant Colonel Roothoff established a combat base west of the Rockpile on 22 September, and ordered Companies F and G to sweep to the Razorback. On the 24th, a Company G patrol spotted five North Vietnamese soldiers on the western slopes of the hill mass and killed them, but 10 minutes later the company reported that it was under fire and "unable to advance or withdraw." The battalion commander ordered Company F to go to the assistance of Company G, but heavy enemy fire prevented the two companies from joining. Lieutenant Colonel Roothoff then directed both companies to back off so that air and artillery could hit the area.[35]

A platoon of Company F commanded by First Lieutenant Robert T. Willis was moving to the relief of Company G when it came upon a trail which led the Marines into the enemy base camp. As the platoon entered the camp, the point man suddenly stopped because he heard a noise. Lieutenant Willis went forward to see what was happening. An enemy soldier, probably a sentry, fired, killing a machine gun team leader and slipped away. The Marines entered the camp from the rear, destroyed an enemy mortar, and then waited. According to Lieutenant Willis:

> We sat in their own positions practically and waited for them [the NVA] to come back to their base camp from their attack on Golf Company. Two of my people who had reported to my unit at Cam Lo eight days earlier killed seven of the [NVA] coming up the trail where they were hitting Golf Company. They tried to mortar us—mortar their own base camp . . . We kept moving toward them and finally got them pinned in a gulch . . . We couldn't

get into it and they couldn't get out of it. We called for air and artillery and pretty well destroyed it.[36]

The platoon was credited with killing 58 NVA. Company F reported three dead and 17 wounded while Company G suffered 3 Marines killed, 26 wounded, and 7 missing.[37]

The 2d Battalion, 7th Marines participation in Prairie was over. On 28 September, the battalion began moving to the rear. Two days later, Company G recovered the bodies of the seven Marines missing since the 22d, and then left for Dong Ha. At Dong Ha, Lieutenant Colonel John J. Hess' newly arrived 2d Battalion, 9th Marines relieved Roothoff's battalion, which rejoined its parent regiment at Chu Lai.

Earlier in the month, Colonel Cereghino had developed another plan to drive the North Vietnamese off the Nui Cay Tre ridgeline to protect the Rockpile—Razorback—Thon Son Lam area. He intended to have Lieutenant Colonel William J. Masterpool's 3d Battalion, 4th Marines, which had arrived at Dong Ha from Phu Bai on 17 September, attack the Nui Cay Tre heights. The attack was to come in from the east to cut into the enemy's flank. This attack was to result in the longest action of Prairie, from 22 September until 5 October.

On the morning of 22 September, Marine air and artillery, in an attempt not to give away the actual landing zone of Masterpool's battalion, bombarded a false target area. Three minutes after the artillery, commanded since the end of August by Lieutenant Colonel Charles S. Kirchmann, stopped firing, eight MAG-16 CH-46s brought the first elements of the 3d Battalion into the actual landing zone, 4,500 meters to the east of the Nui Cay Tre ridgeline. The battalion secured its two objectives, roughly 1,500 meters northwest of the LZ on the first day and dug in for the night. During the first few days, the Marines had as much trouble with the terrain as they did with the enemy. According to some veteran troops, the ground was covered with the densest vegetation they had encountered. At the foot of the ridgeline, there was a six-foot layer of brush which rose straight up to a canopy of bamboo and deciduous trees. Some of these trees were eight feet in diameter and the canopy was so thick that almost no light penetrated the jungle below.

The lead units of the battalion, Companies K and L, began their ascent, each Marine carrying only his

Marine Corps Photo A187871
A wounded Marine is being carried by four of his comrades to an evacuation site. The battalion encountered strong enemy resistance near the Razorback.

weapon, ammunition, two canteens, a poncho, and two socks stuffed with C-rations in his pockets. The only method of resupply was by helicopter and the Marines had to hack out the landing zones with what little equipment they had. Engineers used chain saws and axes to clear an LZ, but only the smaller UH-34s could land in these restricted sites, thus limiting the amount of supplies that could be brought in at one time. The only way the lead elements could move through the jungle was in column, slashing at the dense growth with their machetes. Occasionally they had to wait for bombs and napalm to blast or burn the jungle so the column could move again.[38]

Lieutenant Colonel Masterpool compared his tactics with the action of a ballpoint pen. According to the battalion commander:

The idea was to probe slowly with the tip of the pen and then, when contact was made, retract the point into the pen's larger sleeve; that is, as soon as contact was made, supporting fire including napalm was directed onto the enemy positions.[39]

Two hills dominated the ridgeline, Hill 484, the Marines' final objective, and Hill 400, 3,000 meters east of 484. As the lead element, Company L, approached Hill 400, the closer of the two heights, it became obvious that the Marines were entering the enemy's main line of resistance. According to the company commander, Captain Roger K. Ryman:

> As we got closer to 400, moving along some of the lower hills in front of it, we saw more and more enemy positions, including enough huts in the ravines to harbor a regiment, and piles and piles of ammunition. NVA bodies lying about and hastily dug graves were signs that we were moving right behind them.[40]

The North Vietnamese resistance was skillful. Ryman recalled:

> Their fire discipline remained excellent. Invariably they'd pick just the right piece of terrain, where it was so narrow that we couldn't maneuver on the flanks, and they'd dig in and wait for us in the bottleneck. Sometimes they'd let the point man go by and then let us have it. On other parts of the ridgeline trail, where it dipped down through the thickest sections of the jungle, we would suddenly see a patch of vegetation moving towards us, and that was the only way we could detect an enemy soldier. Once, I heard a sudden snicker when one of our men slipped. The sound gave away a concealed enemy position a few feet away, and started a fire fight. The NVA was damn clever. We'd walk the artillery in—that is, direct fifty yards at a time towards us, sensing by sound where it was dropping. Then we'd pull back, opening the artillery sheath, and call for saturated firing in the area. But the NVA would guess what we were doing, and when we pulled back they'd quickly follow us into the safety zone between us and where the shells were dropping. And when the shelling stopped, they'd start shooting again.[41]

In spite of the slow going, by dusk on the 26th, Company L, reinforced by Company K, had secured a portion of Hill 400 and was dug in for the night.

The heaviest fighting occurred during the next two days. At 0730 on 27 September, Company K, commanded by Captain James J. Carroll, moved toward its next objective, 1,000 meters to the southwest, when it ran into the enemy. At noon, the company reported NVA all around its flanks on the lower leg of L-shaped Hill 400. After an hour and half, the North Vietnamese broke contact. Carroll's company already had 7 dead, 25 wounded, and 1 missing. Lieutenant Colonel Masterpool ordered the rest of the battalion to join Company K and set up defensive positions.

The next morning Company K pushed forward once more but immediately encountered enemy troops in heavily reinforced bunkers. The Marines pulled back and called in artillery. Captain Carroll sent a patrol out to search for the Marine reported missing during the previous day's fighting. At this point, the NVA counterattacked. Elements of Companies I and M reinforced Carroll's company and helped to throw back the enemy. One of Captain Carroll's platoon leaders, Sergeant Anthony Downey, described the action: "The stuff was so thick you couldn't tell who was firing, Charlie or us. They had everything—mortars, mines, and heavy weapons—and they had ladders in the trees for spotters to climb up and direct fire."[42] The Marine companies killed 50 of the enemy while six Marines died and nine were wounded. They also found the body of the Marine missing from the previous day's fighting. By the end of the 28th, the Marines con-

During the fighting for Nui Cay Tre, a Marine from Company M, 3d Battalion, 4th Marines rushes forward carrying a 3.5-inch rocket round in his hand. One of the remaining Marines is seen talking on the radio while the other uses his compass to get a position fix.

Marine Corps Photo A187904

trolled Hill 400 and prepared to advance to Hill 484.[43]

Lieutenant Colonel Masterpool continued his step-by-step approach, alternating companies as the advance units. On 2 October, Captain Robert G. Handrahan's Company M secured a third hill between Hills 400 and 484, 500 meters east of Hill 484. The rest of the battalion joined the lead company later that day and prepared defensive positions for the night. The next day Company I found 25 enemy bunkers on "the Fake," the name the Marines gave the hill since it was not specifically marked on their maps. The bunkers contained ammunition, equipment, and documents, but no NVA. The Marines were ready to take the final objective, Hill 484.

At 0930 on 4 October, Captain Handrahan's 1st Platoon led the assault against heavy resistance from well-concealed bunkers. The Marines tried a frontal assault but were thrown back. Then, while the 1st Platoon put down a base of fire, the 2d Platoon tried to envelop the enemy's left, but this action also failed when the North Vietnamese countered with grenades from the upper slope. Because of the steepness of the terrain and the inability of Handrahan to call in supporting arms "without significant damage to . . . [his] company," Lieutenant Colonel Masterpool ordered the company to pull back to "the Fake."[44] Marine air and artillery then attempted to soften the North Vietnamese positions.

Marine Corps Photo A188472

Capt James J. Carroll, Commanding Officer, Company K, 3d Battalion, 4th Marines, throws a grenade at the enemy during the struggle for Nui Cay Tre. Carroll was posthumously awarded the Navy Cross and the artillery plateau was renamed Camp Carroll in his honor.

An M60 machine gun crew provides covering fire for the advance up Nui Cay Tre. This fighting was some of the heaviest of the war.

Marine Corps Photo A187837

At 1000 the next morning, and after another airstrike on the enemy, Company M advanced once more against Hill 484. Believing that artillery would be useless because of the slope, Handrahan the previous night had arranged for direct fire from the tank company at two concentration points. The company commander recalled that:

> As we approached the crest, I requested fire on concentration point one, intending to shift as we neared the top . . . We had agreed on five rounds but only two came at the target and they were well over.[45]

Handrahan remembered that he then heard "explosions to my rear. I again requested support over the TAC net but was informed that they were receiving incoming. I continued without support." Company M's 2d platoon gained the crest of Hill 484 at 1200, followed by the 1st Platoon. The NVA held on until 1330 and then broke contact and fled into the

Marines from Company K, 3d Battalion, 4th Marines examine a captured enemy machine gun position on Nui Cay Tre. The broken and stripped trees are a result of a pre-attack airstrike.

Marine Corps Photo A187841

Marine Corps Photo A187838

1stLt Edward J. Crowell of Company M, 3d Battalion, 4th Marines reports that the company had secured Hill 484. The taking of Hill 484 on 5 October ended the fight for Nui Cay Tre.

jungle, leaving behind 10 bodies. Captain Handrahan later wrote that his men saw numerous blood trails and recovered some 16-20 weapons.[46]

Handrahan's company sustained only six wounded in the attack, but further to the rear, Marine tank shells accidentally fell upon Hill 400, killing three Marines and wounding 10 others. Among the dead was Captain James J. Carroll who had been directing fire against Hill 484. The young captain, who had arrived in Vietnam only the month before, had described the fight for Hill 400, as "the high point of my career," and ironically, was to die there as a result of American fire.[47]* Carroll was awarded the Navy

---

*Major Handrahan commented that he and Captain Carroll had laid in the tank fire the previous evening, but later learned "that the tanks we adjusted had been replaced and guns were relaid." Maj Robert G. Handrahan, Comments on draft MS, dtd 12Jun78 (Vietnam Comment File).

The 3d Battalion, 4th Marines holds a special ceremony at Dong Ha in honor of its fallen members in the struggle for Nui Cay Tre. The ridgeline was renamed "Mutter" Ridge, after the radio call sign of the 3d Battalion.

Cross for his actions during Prairie and the artillery base west of Cam Lo was renamed Camp Carroll in his honor.

The battle for Nui Cay Tre was over, but the price had been high, both for the Marines and the North Vietnamese. From 22 September through 4 October, the 3d Battalion, 4th Marines suffered 20 dead while killing 100 enemy. Nui Cay Tre thereafter was known as "Mutter" Ridge, after the call sign of Masterpool's 3d Battalion.

*The Opening of Khe Sanh
and the 3d Marine Division Moves North*

Generals Walt and Kyle watched the intensifying action in northern Quang Tri Province with growing concern. In Saigon, General Westmoreland took an even more alarmed view of the situation. He foresaw the likelihood of large numbers of North Vietnamese troops moving south through the DMZ and was apprehensive of what "might occur if the two NVA divisions did, in fact, elect to move into the Quang Tri area." He especially feared that the North Vietnamese might skip around the main Marine defenses keyed on the Rockpile and Dong Ha and attempt to open a corridor in the northwest corner of Quang Tri Province in the mountains bordering both Laos and North Vietnam. General Westmoreland suggested that General Walt reinforce Khe Sanh, 17 kilometers southwest of the Rockpile and 22 kilometers south of the DMZ, with a Marine battalion.[48]

The Marine command resisted Westmoreland's suggestion until the matter came to a head. More than one Marine general expressed the belief that Khe Sanh had no basic military value. General English, the 3d Marine Division ADC, declared

"When you're at Khe Sanh, you're not really anywhere. It's far away from everything. You could lose it and you really haven't lost a damn thing."⁴⁹ Despite Marine protests, it was soon obvious that III MAF would have to move into the area. The catalyst was a 26 September intelligence report that pinpointed a North Vietnamese troop concentration and base camp only 14 kilometers northeast of Khe Sanh.⁵⁰* General Walt bowed to the inevitable and ordered Lieutenant Colonel Peter A. Wickwire's 1st Battalion, 3d Marines, already on the alert to move to Dong Ha from Da Nang, to move to Khe Sanh instead. This was done reluctantly; the III MAF G-3, Colonel Chaisson, aptly declared:

> We were not interested in putting a battalion at Khe Sanh . . . [but] had we not done it, we would have been directed to put it out there . . . we put it out just to retain that little prestige of doing it on your own volition rather than doing it with a shoe in your tail.⁵¹

In any event, Lieutenant Colonel Wickwire received only 12 hours' notice that the battalion's next location was to be in Khe Sanh.**

---

*Lieutenant Colonel Fredric A. Green, who at the time was on the III MAF staff, observed that the 26 September report that pinpointed the North Vietnamese concentrations near Khe Sanh was a MACV intelligence report and not one from III MAF. Green remarked: "III MAF had been monitoring the base camp and infiltration for several months. This was neither new, threatening, nor alarming." LtCol Fredric A. Green, Comments on draft MS, n.d. [Jun 78] (Vietnam Comment File).

**General Westmoreland commented that he understood why the Marine command from its local perspective was reluctant to go into Khe Sanh. From the MACV point of view, however, Westmoreland stated that he had to consider the following main points:
"/1/ A need for the base to launch intelligence operations into Laos such as cross border covert patrols, and responsive intelligence flights by small observation aircraft.
/2/ A northern anchor to defenses south of the DMZ. A base from which major movement from Laos along Route 9, could be blocked. An area near the border from which operations could be launched to cut the Ho Chi Minh trail in Laos when, and if, authorized by political authority.
/3/ To position ourselves to fight large North Vietnamese Army units without delivery of our fires (artillery and tactical air) being complicated by the proximity of civilian population.
/4/ Finally, I wanted the Marines to get to know the area and to gain confidence in fighting there if required."
Gen William C. Westmoreland, Comments on draft MS, dtd 27May78 (Vietnam Comment File). See also Westmoreland, *A Soldier Reports*, p. 109, and Chapter 9 of this volume.

Marine Corps Photo A187956
The 1st Battalion, 3d Marines conducts a patrol near Khe Sanh. Montagnard tribesmen and their elephants were a common sight at this new Marine base.

On 29 September, Marine KC-130 transports ferried Wickwire's battalion, reinforced with an artillery battery, to Khe Sanh. Its new mission was to determine the extent of the enemy buildup in the area. Lieutenant Colonel Wickwire established liaison with the U.S. Army Special Forces advisor at Khe Sanh who believed that the area was in imminent danger of being overrun.⁵² The Marines established their area of operations, coordinated their activities with the ARVN in the area, and manned defensive positions around the Khe Sanh airstrip. The 1st Battalion conducted extensive patrolling out to maximum artillery range, but made little contact with any North Vietnamese troops. The original 30-day stay of the 1st Battalion, 3d Marines was extended into 1967. During this period, the Marines killed 15 North Vietnamese troops, but North Vietnamese intentions remained obscure.

According to Colonel Chaisson:

> Since we put it [1/3] out there, there has been no increase in the threat that existed at the time, nor may I add was there any substantial decrease in the threat that was in that particular area. They're still picking up about the same type of sightings. Nothing that alarms you, but enough to convince the people who want to read the mail that way that there could be one or more battalions in the northwest corner [of South Vietnam].⁵³

THE DMZ WAR CONTINUES, OPERATION PRAIRIE

At the time of the move to Khe Sanh, MACV received reports of an "unprecedented rapid buildup of enemy forces . . . along the entire length of the DMZ." Westmoreland was convinced that the North Vietnamese were preparing a massive advance into Quang Tri Province.[54]*

Reacting to this intelligence, III MAF reestablished Task Force Delta and reinforced the northern border area. On 1 October, General English, the 3d Marine Division ADC, opened the Task Force Delta command post at Dong Ha and assumed responsibility for the Prairie Operation from Colonel Cereghino. With the positioning of Wickwire's battalion at Khe Sanh and the arrival of Lieutenant Colonel William C. Airheart's 2d Battalion, 5th Marines at Dong Ha from Chu Lai on 30 September and 1 October, English had six infantry battalions under his command, reinforced by Kirchmann's artillery and other supporting units.**

Reshuffling of III MAF units throughout northern I Corps continued during the first weeks of October. On 6 October, General Walt ordered the 3d Marine Division to displace from Da Nang into Thua Thien and Quang Tri Provinces. With this move the 1st Marine Division assumed the responsibility for the Da Nang TAOR in addition to the Chu Lai area of operations. Four days later, General Kyle opened the new 3d Marine Division CP at Phu Bai, but left one regiment, the 9th Marines, at Da Nang, under the operational control of the 1st Marine Division. At the same time, General Westmoreland moved one U.S. Army battalion, the 4th Battalion, 503d Infantry, 173d Airborne Brigade, to Da Nang to reinforce

Marine Corps Photo A187940
Headquarters personnel from the 3d Marine Division load trucks at Da Nang for the move to Phu Bai. The 1st Marine Division assumed control of the Da Nang TAOR while the 3d Division retained responsibility for operations in Quang Tri and Thua Thien Provinces.

Three Marines from the 3d Marines relax for a moment in November 1966 during Operation Prairie and attempt to keep dry. During the northeast monsoon season, both the allies and the NVA curtailed their activities in the DMZ sector.

Marine Corps Photo A188069

---

*General English recalled that a CinCPac intelligence analysis predicted that the NVA were to launch a "three-division attack in 72 hours." BGen Lowell E. English intvw by FMFPac, 9Jan67 (No. 402, Oral Hist Col, Hist&MusDiv, HQMC). Lieutenant Colonel Green remarked that ". . . this hypothesis was intensely war-gamed at III MAF Headquarters by a Special War Games Group appointed by General Walt. Results were used to brief Walt, Westmoreland, and were the basis of III MAF and MACV contingency planning." LtCol Fredric A. Green, Comments on draft MS, n.d.[Jun78] (Vietnam Comment File). See Chapter 21 for the discussion of U.S. contingency plans.

**The six were 1st Battalion, 4th Marines; 3d Battalion, 4th Marines; 2d Battalion, 5th Marines; 1st Battalion, 3d Marines; 2d Battalion, 9th Marines, and 3d Battalion, 7th Marines. The latter two battalions had just relieved 2d Battalion, 4th Marines and 2d Battalion, 7th Marines in the Prairie area of operations.

the TAOR there. Two Army artillery battalions, the 2d Battalion, 94th Artillery and the 1st Battalion, 40th Artillery, arrived in the Prairie area. Colonel Benjamin S. Read, the commanding officer of the 12th Marines, who had moved his CP from Da Nang to Dong Ha, had command of both the Marine and Army artillery in Prairie. General Kyle deactivated Task Force Delta and established a 3d Marine Division (Forward) Headquarters at Dong Ha to control the operation. General English still retained command, but received additional staff personnel for his headquarters.

During this same period, the 3d Marines, under Colonel Edward E. Hammerbeck, took over the western half of the Prairie TAOR while the 4th Marines assumed the responsibility for the eastern half. Colonel Cereghino's headquarters was located at Dong Ha and his area of operations extended for roughly 5,000 meters eastward of Con Thien. One battalion, the 2d Battalion, 5th Marines, took over Con Thien from the ARVN while the other two battalions of the regiment, the 3d Battalion, 7th Marines and 1st Battalion, 4th Marines, operated closer to Dong Ha and Cam Lo. The 3d Marines was responsible for the defense of the Camp Carroll*- Rockpile area while Wickwire's unit at Khe Sanh reported directly to General English.

Despite the massive III MAF preparations, or perhaps because of them, the expected enemy offensive never materialized. There had been no major action in the region since the capture of "Mutter" Ridge, although Airheart's battalion experienced some probes in mid-October. During November, intelligence sources indicated that the *324B Division* had retired north of the DMZ, although elements of the *341st Division* had infiltrated into the Cua Valley in the southern portion of the Prairie TAOR. Apparently, the mission of the *341st Division* had been to strengthen and train guerrilla units in the area. Although the enemy chose to remain inactive in the northern area during the northeast monsoon season, there was every indication that fighting would start again once the rains stopped.**

By the end of the year with the diminishing activity on the northern front, the Marine command reduced the infantry strength of the 3d Marine Division in Prairie to one regiment, the 3d Marines, and four battalions. The 4th Marines just before Christmas moved back into the Co Bi-Thanh Tan sector to conduct Operation Chinook.

For all intents and purposes, Prairie was no longer an operation, but rather an area of operations. The Marines had established another base area similar to those at Chu Lai, Da Nang, and Phu Bai. At the height of the Marine buildup in mid-November, General English commanded a force of approximately 8,000 Marines, including eight infantry battalions, supported by the 12th Marines. Marine artillery, reinforced by the two Army 175mm battalions, Navy gunfire ships, and Marine air, covered the entire DMZ area from the western border with Laos to the South China Sea.

Dong Ha had become a forward Marine base and the center of operations in the northern area. Its airfield and that at Khe Sanh had been lengthened so that both easily could handle KC-130 transports. The Marines and Navy also developed a sizeable port facility at Dong Ha to accommodate craft bringing supplies up the Cua Viet River. Within the Prairie TAOR, Marine helicopters resupplied individual units from Dong Ha.

During Prairie in 1966, the Marines had prevented the NVA from establishing a major operating base in northern Quang Tri Province and had killed over 1,000 of the enemy. Colonel Cereghino remembered, "At the beginning of Prairie we were fighting well trained and well equipped soldiers. At the end we were running into poorly equipped young soldiers and frustrated commanders."[55]

Yet the cost had been high in both men and Marine objectives. The Marines sustained casualties of 200 dead and well over 1,000 wounded. A sizeable Marine force still remained in the DMZ sector and the resulting dislocation of Marine units in the southern TAOR's seriously hampered the Marine pacification campaign.

---

*Colonel Edward E. Hammerbeck, who had assumed command of the 3d Marines in August, commented that in October 1966 when he established his CP in the north, the artillery plateau had not yet been designated Camp Carroll. He recalled that the official dedication of the base camp of the 3d Marines and the artillery plateau to Camp Carroll occurred on 10 November 1966, the Marine Corps Birthday. Col Edward E. Hammerbeck, Comments on draft MS, dtd 9Jun78 (Vietnam Comment File).

*The monsoon rainy season in most of I Corps begins in the latter part of October and ends in February.

PART V
THE UNRELENTING WAR IN CENTRAL AND SOUTHERN I CORPS, JULY-DECEMBER 1966

CHAPTER 12
The Struggle for An Hoa, Operation Macon
The First Clash—The Operation Expands—Macon Continues—Macon Ends but Little Changes

The First Clash

Before Operations Hastings and Prairie diverted Marine forces from the southern TAORs, the three regiments at Da Nang, the 1st, 3d, and 9th Marines, in Operation Liberty,* had reached the line of the Ky Lam and Thu Bon Rivers, 20 miles south of the airbase. Behind the advance of the infantry, the engineers followed and opened up new lines of communication. On 4 July, the 3d Engineer Battalion completed the first leg of a road, appropriately named "Liberty Road," which ran from the 9th Marines CP on Hill 55 south to Route 4, a distance of roughly 3,500 meters. During their southward push, the Marines forced the enemy *R-20 Doc Lap Battalion*, which had reinfiltrated north of the Thu Bon and Ky Lam during the spring political crisis, to withdraw again south of the two rivers.[1]

Unexpectedly, the Marines received excellent intelligence which accurately stated the *R-20*'s location and intentions. On 1 July, a 28-year-old squad leader from the *1st Company, R-20 Battalion* surrended in the 9th Marines sector. During interrogation, the prisoner revealed that his unit had retreated south of the Thu Bon when the Marines approached the river. He indicated that the mission of the enemy battalion was to prepare defensive positions and counter any Marine attempt to cross the Ky Lam-Thu Bon line. To secure their defenses, the enemy troops removed the civilian population and built fortifications. The prisoner told his interrogators that the *R-20* contained 300 main force troops and guerrillas, armed with rifles and 60mm and 81mm mortars. The prisoner implied that the morale of the battalion had suffered and that the troops were short of both food and ammunition.[2]

The 9th Marines confirmed some of this information from other sources. On 2 July, Captain George R. Griggs, the S-2 of the 9th Marines, received a report from I Corps, stating that a Viet Cong battalion was operating south of the Thu Bon reinforced by two local guerrilla companies. The I Corps report placed the strength of the battalion at 500 men, armed with five 12.7mm antiaircraft machine guns, three 81mm mortars, and an unspecified number of 57mm recoilless rifles, as well as individual weapons. This report also reinforced the impression that the enemy planned to contest any Marine advance south of the rivers. Marine tactical air observers from VMO-2 reported freshly dug trenches and fortifications in the area, more evidence that the Viet Cong were attempting to establish a stout defense of the An Hoa region.[3]

Despite the intelligence that the Marines had obtained of enemy plans, the Viet Cong initiated the action. On 4 July, the same day the Marines opened Liberty Road, two companies of the *R-20 Battalion*

This picture presents an overview of the An Hoa industrial area, looking south toward the Que Son Mountains. The 3d Battalion, 9th Marines base camp can be seen to the right of the buildings of the complex.

Marine Corps Photo A187411

---
*See Chapter 6 for a description of Operation Liberty.

moved west toward the Thu Bon River. The Viet Cong commander probably was aware that Marine units were operating in the area and took appropriate precautions. That afternoon, he established a three-sided ambush between the hamlets of My Loc (3) and My Loc (4), approximately 2,500 meters south of the river and three miles northeast of the An Hoa airstrip.

At this time, the 3d Battalion, 9th Marines, which continued to make An Hoa its base of operations since Operation Georgia in May,* was involved in a routine search and clear mission in its sector. On 4 July, Company I had established a blocking position along the northwest fringe of the battalion's TAOR, the southern bank of the Thu Bon, while Company K advanced from the southeast. Company L was held at An Hoa as security for the airstrip and the battalion CP. Company M had been detached and was operating north of the Thu Bon during this period. Through the morning and early afternoon, the most unpleasant aspect of the operation was the oppressive heat.

The transition to battle was sudden and violent. Company K, pushing to the Thu Bon, entered the VC ambush position. At 1520, VC grenade launcher teams fired into the Marine column, knocking out one of the amphibian tractors supporting the company. Simultaneously, the rest of the ambush party opened up with mortars, machine guns, and small arms. The initial burst killed the crew chief of one of the LVTPs and two other Marines were wounded. Captain Valdis V. Pavlovskis, the company commander, reorganized his troops and ordered his men to close on the VC positions, at the same time reporting his situation to the battalion CP.

When he learned about the ambush of his company, Major George H. Grimes, who had assumed command of the battalion at the end of June, ordered Company I to protect the left flank of the engaged unit. Then he asked the regimental commander, Colonel Edwin H. Simmons, to provide helicopters to carry Company L from the airstrip to Hill 42, two kilometers south of My Loc (4). Grimes also asked for the return of Company M to battalion control. Upon the approval of both requests, MAG-16 received the mission to provide the helicopter support.

---

*See Chapter 5 for a description of Operation Georgia.

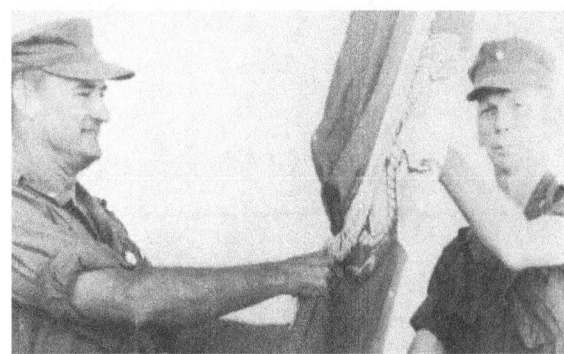

Marine Corps Photo A187566

LtCol Paul C. Trammell (left), the former commander of the 3d Battalion, 9th Marines, presents the battalion colors to the new battalion commander, Maj George H. Grimes, in a change of command ceremony at An Hoa during June 1966. Maj Grimes commanded the battalion during the first phase of Operation Macon in An Hoa.

Company K's situation remained tenuous for the next two hours. Company I tried to move to support Company K, but also ran into heavy Viet Cong opposition. Captain Pavlovskis' company held on, taking every advantage of the cover afforded by the hedgerows and bamboo groves that separated the rice paddies. Seven more Marines were dead, another 14 were wounded, and another tractor was out of commission. Heavy enemy machine gun fire drove off evacuation helicopters. Although the Marines called for artillery fire, Battery F, 2d Battalion, 12th Marines, in support of Grimes' battalion, could not fire. The enemy was too close.

When Company I finally reached Company K at 1730, the tide turned. The Viet Cong commander, realizing that he would be hemmed in by superior Marine forces, decided to abandon his ambush site. An aerial observer in a VMO-2 UH-1E spotted 200-250 VC moving northwest and called in airstrikes and artillery. Between 1800 and 1900, MAG-12 A-4s and MAG-11 F-4Bs struck the exposed enemy. In addition, Battery F fired 516 105mm rounds at the Viet Cong troops. Although the wing reported "50 VC KBA, confirmed, and 25 KBA probable," ground estimates of the strikes' effectiveness varied between 12 and 62 VC dead.[4]

As enemy resistance diminished, HMM-265's CH-46As were able to land to take out casualties. Two of the helicopters were hit by enemy antiaircraft fire and one crewman suffered minor injuries. The major

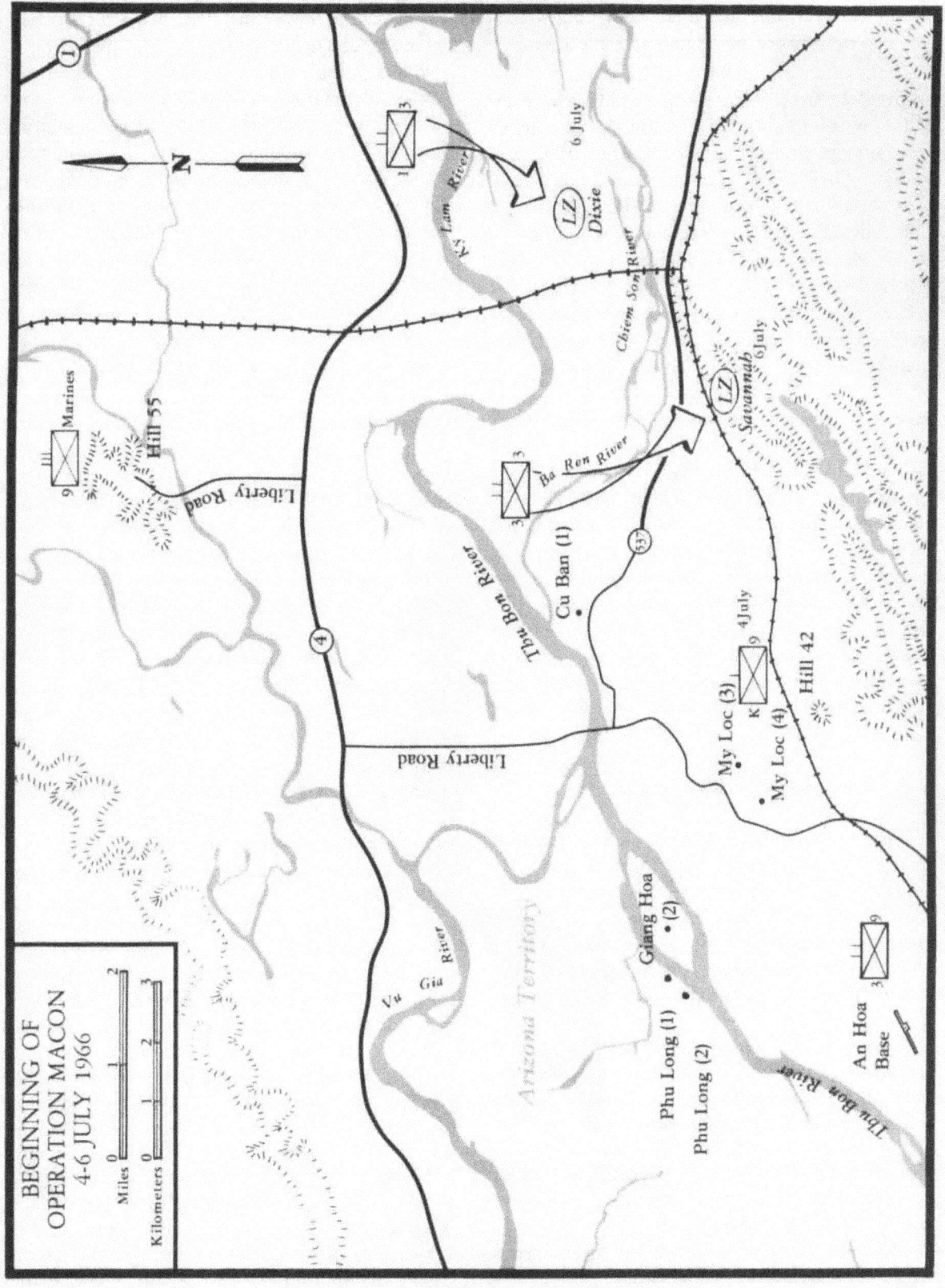

action was over, but that night both Companies I and K were harassed by mortars and minor probes.

The Marines continued preparations to trap the elusive *R-20*. In accordance with Major Grimes' plan, MAG-16 helicopters lifted Company L from the An Hoa airstrip to Hill 42 shortly after 1800 and brought Company M back to An Hoa where it became the battalion reserve. At first light 5 July, Companies K and I resumed the offensive against the *R-20 Battalion*. Throughout the day, both Marine companies encountered light resistance.

Even though the intensity of the fire fights never reached that of the previous day, there were several sharp encounters. At 0840, Company K was fired on by a VC squad; one Marine was killed. Captain Pavlovskis requested artillery fire; 150 rounds from Battery F fell on the enemy positions. Marines counted 12 VC bodies. Shortly afterward, Company I, operating just to the west of Company K, observed an enemy platoon 1,500 meters to the northeast. Once again the Marines called in artillery. By midafternoon, Company L had joined the other two companies in the northwest sector of the An Hoa Basin and the search for the *Doc Lap Battalion* continued. By the end of the day, the Marine battalion reported that it had killed 17 more enemy and estimated another 20 to 30 "possibles."[5]

The Operation Expands

During the afternoon of the 5th, General Walt changed the entire dimension of the operation. He believed that the Marines had the opportunity to eliminate the *R-20 Battalion*. The III MAF commander ordered the initiation of Operation Macon, which would involve five Marine battalions in addition to the South Vietnamese forces normally assigned to this sector.[6]

The writing of the Macon operation plan, like so many operations in Vietnam, was completed 24 hours after initial contact had been made. The 3d Marine Division did not publish its "frag" order until 1545 on the 5th, but its mission statement read: "Commencing 4 July 1966 3d MarDiv conducts multi-bn S&D opn in An Hoa area . . . ."[7] It was not until the early hours of 6 July, that the 9th Marines, the regiment responsible for the operation, issued orders to its subordinate battalions.[8]

There were several reasons for the time lag between the issuance of the division and the regimental order. The major one was that the division directive was purposely vague, allowing the regimental commander to fill in the details. The regiment's mission was to destroy "enemy forces, facilities and influence."[9] Colonel Drew J. Barrett, Jr., newly arrived in Vietnam after graduating from the Army War College, became responsible for the operation when he assumed command of the 9th Marines from Colonel Simmons on 5 July. Barrett, a former battalion commander in Korea and veteran of Guadalcanal, immediately told his staff to determine the area of operations for each unit, and the helicopter landing zones within these areas, as well as landing times.

The concept of operations for Macon called for a three-phased operation. In the first phase, which had already begun with the ambush of Company K, Major Grimes' 3d Battalion would continue operations in the An Hoa northern sector, while the other two battalions of the 9th Marines established blocking positions north of the Thu Bon and Ky Lam Rivers. The second phase would consist of the helicopter lift of two battalions from the 3d Marines into two landing zones, one just east of the main north-south railroad and the other 4,000 meters to the southwest of the first. Grimes' battalion would then attack in a northeasterly direction toward the battalion positioned along the railroad. The third phase, if necessary, would be a one-battalion sweep in the area between the Ky Lam and Chiem Son Rivers, east of the main railroad line. General Walt expected the entire operation to end in 14 days, but the course of events extended Macon into the latter part of October.[10]

For all practical purposes, both the division and regimental orders changed very little for the battalions of the 9th Marines. Major Grimes' battalion continued Phase I operations in the An Hoa region, while Lieutenant Colonel Richard E. Jones' 1st Battalion, 9th Marines and Lieutenant Colonel John J. Hess' 2d Battalion, 9th Marines conducted operations in their sector of the TAOR and assumed blocking positions north of the Thu Bon and Ky Lam Rivers.

The second phase of Macon began on the morning of 6 July as the 12th Marines fired over 500 rounds of landing zone preparation fire and MAG-12 A-4s strafed the LZs for 20 minutes. At 1000 that morning, 20 CH-46s from HMMs-164 and -265 began the lift of two companies from Lieutenant Colonel

Marine tanks and infantry deploy in Operation Macon. The tread marks of the tanks provide a foot path for the troops in the tall grass.

Robert R. Dickey III's 1st Battalion, 3d Marines to Landing Zone Dixie, 1,500 meters south of the Ky Lam River and east of the railroad track. An hour later, the Marine helicopters completed the lift of two companies of the other battalion, the 3d Battalion, 3d Marines, into Landing Zone Savannah, southwest of Dixie. In that one hour, Lieutenant Colonel Herbert E. Mendenhall's HMM-265 and Lieutenant Colonel Warren C. Watson's HMM-164 had ferried over 650 troops into the battle area without incident.[11]

The only complication was a mixup in the flight schedule which resulted in a 30-minute delay in the arrival of Lieutenant Colonel Earl "Pappy" R. Delong, the commanding officer of the 3d Battalion, 3d Marines, and the rest of his command group. Two of his infantry companies were already in the objective area.[12] By noon, both battalions had reached their assigned blocking positions. Dickey's 1st Battalion established defenses along the north-south railroad track, while Delong's 3d Battalion protected the approaches to the southern foothills.

As the two 3d Marines battalions sealed off the eastern and southern exits of the battlefield on the morning of the 6th, the 3d Battalion, 9th Marines attacked from Route 537, its line of departure, toward the northeast. The battalion was reinforced by tanks and amphibian tractors. On 7 July, six tanks and two LVTs crossed the Thu Bon and entered the operation, later joined by eight tanks, one tank retriever, five LVTP-5s and two LVTP-6s.[13] By 10 July, the infantry and mechanized units reached the lines of the 1st Battalion, 3d Marines at the railroad. The second phase of Macon came to an end.

The VC had offered little resistance. The Marines encountered snipers, but no large VC force. Occasionally enemy gunners lobbed mortar rounds into Marine formations, but the anticipated large contact did not materialize. By the end of Phase II, the 9th Marines claimed to have killed 87 enemy, at the cost of eight Marines dead and 33 wounded.[14]

After consulting with General Kyle, on the afternoon of 10 July, Colonel Barrett issued orders to begin Phase III. The next morning, the 9th Marines commander ordered Dickey's battalion to attack east of the railroad together with the 51st ARVN Regiment, while Major Grimes' 3d Battalion, 9th Marines retraced its steps to the west from the railroad. At the same time, Colonel Barrett made some adjustment in his forces. One company and the command group from the 3d Battalion, 3d Marines were released from Macon and the other

Marine Corps Photo A193947

SSgt Charles W. Pierce, a tank section leader, scans the landscape in the An Hoa sector during Operation Macon. The M48 tank is armed with .50 caliber (pictured above) and .30 caliber machine guns and a 90mm gun.

Marine Corps Photo A187262

During the sweep in Operation Macon, a Marine checks the identity card of a Vietnamese civilian. The women are using the traditional Vietnamese carrying poles with ropes attached at each end to balance their burdens.

company was attached to Dickey's 1st Battalion, 3d Marines. Company K, 3d Battalion, 9th Marines and the mechanized units also reinforced Lieutenant Colonel Dickey's unit.[15]

Phase III of Macon began shortly after 0600 on the 11th, when two companies of the 1st Battalion, 3d Marines crossed the line of departure. From 11 to 14 July, the only significant encounter occurred in the 3d Battalion, 9th Marines area of operations west of the railroad tracks. A VC platoon mortared the battalion command post early on 12 July. At 0250 that morning, 40 to 60 mortar rounds and small arms fire hit in the CP area. Major Grimes called for an artillery mission on the suspected VC mortar site; no results could be observed. Three Marines were slightly wounded by the VC attack.

In the eastern sector of Macon, Lieutenant Colonel Dickey's 1st Battalion, 3d Marines, supported by the tanks and LVTs, reached its objective, 7,000 meters east of the railroad on the afternoon of 13 July. The battalion commander summed up his unit's participation succinctly: "The results of this operation were negligible. . . . During a three-day sweep of the area no VC were encountered."[16]

At this point, it appeared to General Kyle that no large VC units were operating in the An Hoa area. On the afternoon of the 13th, he ordered Colonel Barrett to terminate Macon the next day and return the 1st Battalion, 3d Marines to its parent organization.[17] Company K, 3d Battalion, 9th Marines was to return to its own battalion and accompany the armored column to the Thu Bon River. At 0800 14 July, Colonel Barrett reported that Operation Macon was over.

Suddenly, the situation changed. A Marine reconnaissance patrol, operating in the southern foothills, spotted 300-400 Viet Cong moving through a pass into an assembly area seven miles east of the An Hoa airstrip. The patrol called for both artillery and air support. Marine aircraft hit the enemy with napalm, rockets, and bombs, while four supporting artillery batteries fired 105mm, 8-inch, and 155mm shells into the area.* This air and ground bombardment kill-

---

*Over 30 artillery pieces supported Operation Macon during Phases II and III. Battery A, 1st Battalion, 12th Marines; Battery D, 2d Battalion, 12th Marines; and Battery E, 2d Battalion, 12th Marines maintained firing positions north of the Thu Bon and were controlled by the 2d Battalion, 12th Marines Headquarters. These batteries were reinforced by a platoon of 155mm howitzers from Battery L, 4th Battalion, 12th Marines and a composite battery consisting of two self-propelled 155mm guns and two self-propelled 8-inch howitzers. Only Battery F, 2d Battalion, 12th Marines was located south of the Thu Bon and Ky Lam Rivers. The battery was positioned on the An Hoa airstrip itself. Through 1430 on 14 July, the 2d Battalion, 12th Marines had fired more than 8,500 rounds in support of Macon. 2d Battalion, 12th Marines ComdC, Jul66, p. 3.

ed at least 30 *R-20 Battalion* soldiers, once more frustrating that unit's attempt to move into the An Hoa region.[18]

Macon Continues

Faced with the evident enemy presence in the southern foothills near An Hoa, Generals Walt and Kyle decided not to close out Operation Macon. The III MAF commander reported to General Westmoreland on 14 July that Macon would continue and later that evening General Kyle told the 9th Marines to disregard his previous order to terminate the operation.[19] He advised Colonel Barrett: "Operation in the An Hoa operating area outside presently established 3d MarDiv TAOR will continue to be named Operation Macon on an indefinite basis."[20] The next morning, Colonel Barrett ordered his 3d Battalion to continue operations in the An Hoa area.

The continuation of Macon did not disrupt the plans of the 3d Battalion, 9th Marines. The battalion

A member of the South Vietnamese Regional Forces, right, identifies a prisoner captured during Macon as a Viet Cong. The Marines are from the 1st Battalion, 3d Marines.

Marine Corps Photo A187257

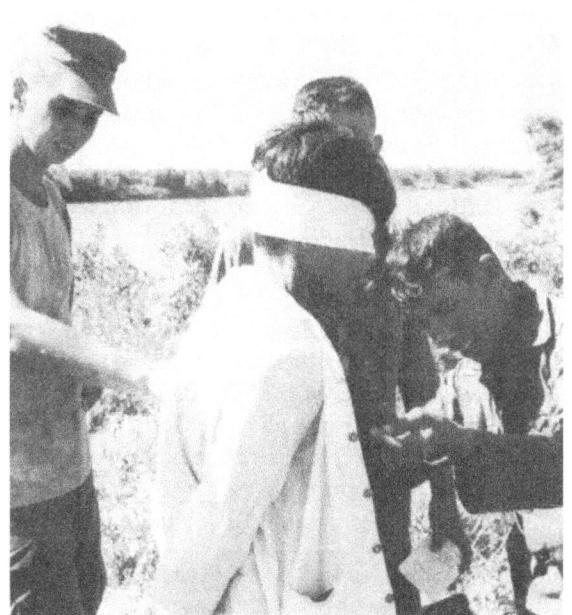

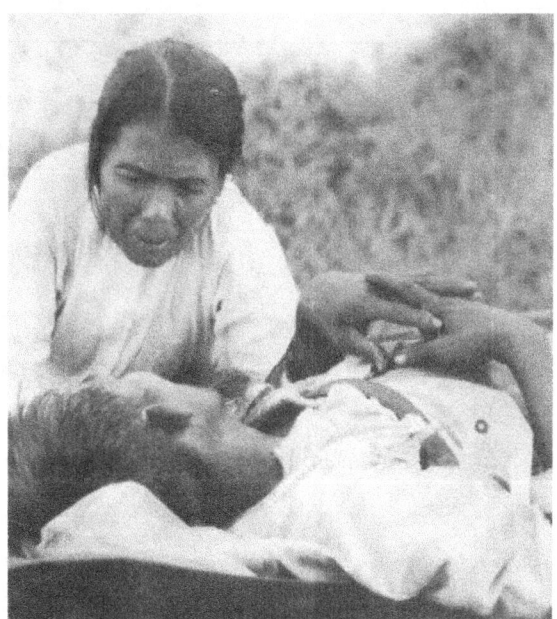

Marine Corps Photo A187258

A Vietnamese woman tries to comfort her seriously wounded husband as he waits evacuation to a hospital. The Viet Cong had mortared their village.

had intended to keep its command post at the An Hoa airstrip and conduct clearing operations to support the engineers who had started the extension of Liberty Road beyond the Thu Bon. In fact, at this time, the engineers were working on two extensions of the road, one leading south from Route 4 to the Thu Bon, while the other led north from An Hoa to the river. Macon was reduced to a one-battalion search and clear operation with the missions of keeping the lines of communication open in the An Hoa region and providing security for both the Marine engineers and civilian construction workers.[21]

Interest in the An Hoa region and the extension of the road was not confined to the Marine command. During one of his periodic visits to III MAF, General Westmoreland toured An Hoa in the latter part of July and specifically asked Colonel Barrett what forces were necessary to secure Liberty Road. The Marine colonel replied "We intend to secure it by using the forces we are now using, elements of two Marine companies and part of the 2d Battalion, 51st ARVN Regiment on the south side . . . of the river."[22]

Although the 3d Battalion, 9th Marines was operating primarily against the guerrilla forces remaining in the An Hoa region during this phase of

Marine engineers work on the extension of Liberty Road to An Hoa. The troops are laying down abutments for a pontoon ferry which will link An Hoa to Da Nang.

The Viet Cong had skillfully hidden grenades in the rice vat pictured below. The opening of the vat had been covered by the simple "trap door" held above.

Macon, it continued to be alert to the possibility of enemy main force unit infiltration. Local South Vietnamese authorities indicated that two enemy battalions, neither identified as the *R-20 Battalion*, were in the rugged hills south of An Hoa. One of the battalions was reputed to be North Vietnamese.[23] Throughout the remainder of July and August, Marine reconnaissance patrols spotted small groups of enemy soldiers in the mountainous terrain.

Nevertheless, through August, contact with the enemy in Operation Macon was only sporadic and few enemy units of any size were engaged. Indeed the major action for the 3d Battalion occurred outside of the Macon area of operations in support of a Navy detachment conducting a hydrographic survey of the Thu Bon River. On the morning of 20 August, the battalion with two of its own companies and a company from the 1st Battalion, 9th Marines reinforced by tanks and amphibian tractors crossed the river onto the peninsula formed by the Vu Gia and Thu Bon Rivers—the so-called "Arizona Territory" where Operation Mallard had taken place earlier.*

Shortly after noon, the battalion encountered about 100 VC from the *R-20 Battalion* in the hamlets of Giang Hoa (2) and Phu Long (1) and (2) on the western banks of the Thu Bon. Unwilling to stand up to the Marines who were supported by air and artillery, the VC fought a series of delaying actions and made good their escape to the west and north. The Marines sustained casualties of five dead

---

*See Chapter 3.

and 16 wounded while killing at least 10 of the enemy. Most of the Marine casualties were a result of enemy mines. With the completion of the survey, the 3d Battalion returned to its An Hoa base that evening.[24]

In Operation Macon during the month, the battalion confined its activities to ambushes, patrols, and outpost operations along Liberty Road while the VC attempted to disrupt its construction. On three occasions, the Marines caught enemy troops in the open. Enemy mining incidents and ambushes increased markedly during this period, but progress on the road continued. Major Fred D. MacLean, Jr., who relieved Major Grimes at the beginning of the month, later remembered that on 27 August, "the first convoy from Da Nang rolled into An Hoa using the completed Liberty Road."[25]

Macon remained at a low level of activity until 3 September when the 3d Battalion once more met its old adversary, the *R-20 Battalion*. Shortly after 1200, a platoon from Company I encountered a VC company near Cu Ban (1) on the Thu Bon River. In a fire fight that lasted nearly two hours, the Marine platoon sustained 15 casualties including five dead. Although the Viet Cong unit escaped to the east, it left behind 32 bodies.

This action was not to be an isolated incident. On 5 September, the 3d Company, 2d Battalion, 51st ARVN Regiment and Company K, 3d Battalion, 9th Marines engaged the rest of the *R-20 Battalion* along Route 537, two kilometers southeast of the site of the fighting on the 3d. Both the American and South Vietnamese companies had just left blocking positions from which they supported a clearing operation by other elements of the Vietnamese battalion. Both Company K and the Vietnamese 3d Company were moving west along the road when enemy troops in sites paralleling the highway opened fire on the ARVN company. The Marines tried to assist the South Vietnamese, but soon were unable to maneuver. Battery D, 2d Battalion, 12th Marines, north of the Thu Bon, fired at the enemy positions. Major MacLean ordered Company I to attack southeast from its outpost at Phu Lac (6) to pinch the VC between it and the two engaged companies. Apparently the VC expected the American reaction. No

The first convoy using the completed Liberty Road rolls into An Hoa on 27 August 1966. The 6x6 Marine truck, carrying C-Rations, passes an honor guard and a reviewing stand during a ceremony marking the occasion.

Marine Corps Photo A187862

sooner had Company I advanced when enemy gunners, firing a 57mm recoilless rifle, disabled an Ontos supporting the company. By 1130, both Marine companies and the ARVN unit were heavily engaged.

Major MacLean requested more support, both artillery and air. Battery D responded with 158 rounds and was rewarded with "excellent effect on target."[26] At 1330, Marine planes appeared and repeatedly struck the enemy forces, but the VC fought back stubbornly. Marine 8-inch howitzers and 155mm guns reinforced the fires of Battery D and Marine air again bombed and strafed the enemy.

Slowly the Marine and ARVN companies gripped the VC between them in a pincer movement, but Companies I and K were not able to link up and surround the enemy before nightfall. At dawn the next morning, the three allied companies moved forward once more. To no one's surprise, the VC were gone. The Marines did find 29 enemy dead, and surmised that the VC had suffered so many casualties that they had been forced to abandon the bodies.[27] The allied forces were also hit hard: the Marine companies suffered three dead and 83 wounded, and the ARVN unit reported 25 wounded.[28] The 9th Marines intelligence section concluded that the heavy contacts of 3 and 5 September lent "substance to the belief that the area south of the Song Thu Bon is considered by the Viet Cong to be one in which they may still operate in major unit strength, though with increasingly less impunity."[29]

This flareup of action in the first part of September was the last significant engagement during Macon. During the rest of the month, the Marines continued to encounter Viet Cong units of squad size or less, but always at a distance. After an initial exchange of fire, the enemy troops would break contact and elude Marine pursuit. The Marine battalion reported that the total number of incidents and friendly casualties for September decreased, although enemy mining and boobytrap activity remained the same.[30]

Macon Ends but Little Changes

In October, Operation Macon finally came to an end. During the month, the Viet Cong guerrillas continued to probe Popular Force and Regional Force outposts near the Marine positions, but Marine contact with enemy forces declined significantly. The 3d Battalion, 9th Marines encountered no major Viet Cong main force unit. On 27 October, General Walt authorized the termination of the operation and at noon the next day, Macon came to a close, 117 days after it had started. During this period, the Marines had killed about 380 of the enemy, while suffering 196 casualties, 24 of whom were killed.[31]

The ending of the operation had very little meaning for the 3d Battalion, 9th Marines. Although the 3d Marine Division moved north on 10 October, the 9th Marines remained behind and the 3d Battalion continued to operate in the An Hoa region, even after Macon had officially ended. Major MacLean's battalion provided security for Liberty Road, protected the river crossing, and assisted the South Vietnamese. Behind the Marine infantry, engineers and Seabees entered An Hoa and joined with the Vietnamese to finish construction of the industrial complex.

CHAPTER 13
The Continuing War

Operations Washington and Colorado — The September Election — The Marine TAORs, July-December 1966

Operations Washington and Colorado

In the less densely populated sector of the 1st Marine Division at Chu Lai, the Marine command continued to concentrate its efforts on the elimination of the Viet Cong-North Vietnamese main force military structure in southern I Corps. During the early summer, General Fields and his staff completed their preparations for the much postponed campaign in the Do Xa region, the suspected location of the enemy *Military Region V Headquarters*.* With the close out of Operation Kansas at the end of June, on 4 July Fields informed III MAF that he was prepared to carry out the operation, codenamed Washington, in the Do Xa. According to the 1st Division plan, the 1st Reconnaissance Battalion was to make an extensive reconnaissance of the Do Xa, with the capability of calling in air and artillery on appropriate targets of opportunity. If the reconnaissance Marines determined a large enemy presence in the Do Xa, a two-battalion Marine strike force at Chu Lai stood ready to exploit the intelligence. Thus, Fields planned to use the same tactics that had worked so well earlier in Operation Kansas — first, reconnaissance and then, exploitation.[1]

General Walt agreed to the operation and obtained the necessary concurrences from MACV and the South Vietnamese I Corps command. Westmoreland readily approved the concept and later exclaimed to Admiral Sharp that the enemy could not feel safe in any of his base areas.[2] The South Vietnamese were less exhuberant. In his concurring letter, which was dated 6 July and arrived after the operation already had begun, the I Corps Chief of Staff saw no difficulty with the operation, but requested that the Marines coordinate their activities very closely with the 2d ARVN Division "in order to avoid mistakes."[3]

On the morning of 6 July, Marine helicopters transported Lieutenant Colonel Arthur J. Sullivan, commander of the 1st Reconnaissance Battalion, together with his command group and Company A, to the district town of Hau Duc in the northern fringes of the Do Xa sector, some 30 miles west of Chu Lai. With the establishment of the base camp for the operation, Marine CH-46s brought into Hau Duc the following morning two 105mm howitzers from Battery E, 2d Battalion, 11th Marines to provide artillery support. Another 105mm platoon from

A Marine reconnaissance team scrambles out of a CH-46 helicopter on a mission. The reconnaissance teams usually remained within artillery range and called in artillery and air on unsuspecting enemy. These "Stingray" tactics were used successively in Operations Kansas, Hastings, and in early July during Operation Washington in the enemy Do Xa base area, west of Chu Lai.

Marine Corps Photo A421476

---

*See Chapter 8 for the discussion of the planning relative to an operation in the Do Xa and for a description of Operation Kansas, which caused the last postponement of a Do Xa operation.

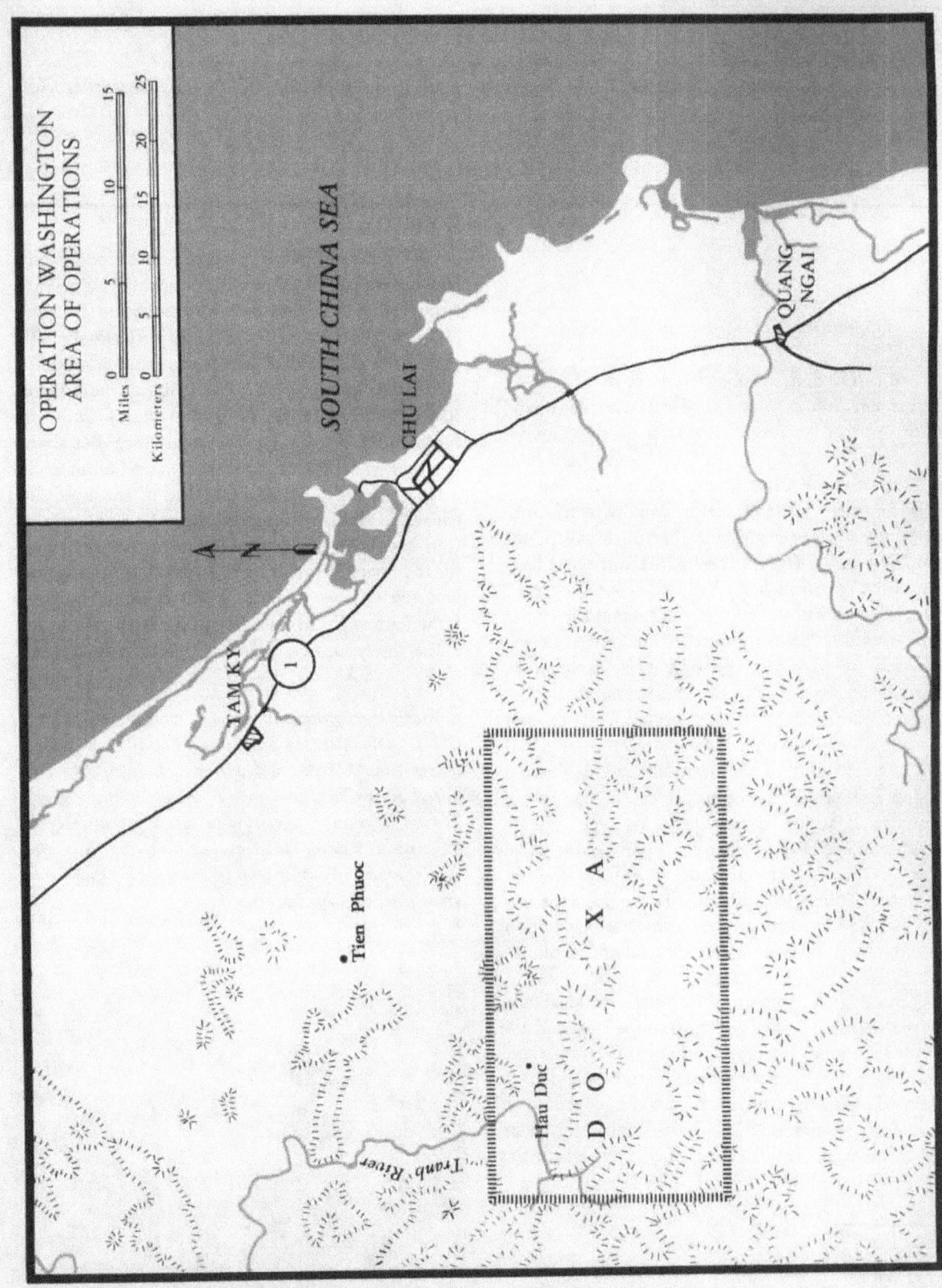

Battery D, 1st Battalion, 11th Marines, located since Operation Kansas at the Tien Phuoc Special Forces Camp 17 miles to the north, was in position to reinforce the fires from Hau Doc.[4]

For the next eight days, the 1st Reconnaissance Battalion with three of its companies and reinforced by a platoon from the 1st Force Reconnaissance Company ranged over a 280-square-mile area of the Do Xa. Despite the rugged mountainous terrain and the paucity of landing zones, all of the patrol insertions with one exception were by helicopter, with the pilots faking two insertions for every one made. When beyond the range of the supporting artillery, the reconnaissance Marines were able to call in close air support through the use of an airborne radio relay in a C-117 dedicated to the operation. All told, in 46 sightings, the reconnaissance patrols observed 201 VC. As a result of ground combat and supporting arms fire, the 1st Reconnaissance Battalion accounted for 13 VC KIA and four prisoners. The most significant encounter occurred on 10 July when a patrol from the 1st Force Recon Company platoon ambushed a group of VC below the Song Tranh, about 10,000 meters west of Hau Duc. Of the nine VC caught in the ambush, the Marines killed two, captured four (two men and two women) while the remaining three escaped. The prisoners, apparently couriers, had documents on them relating to the Communist organization in Quang Tin Province.[5]

With relatively few sightings of organized enemy forces, the 1st Division ended Operation Washington on 14 July without inserting any infantry units into the operations area. Lieutenant Colonel Sullivan, the reconnaissance battalion commander, believed that his unit had disrupted the enemy lines of communication.[6] General Fields, however, was dubious about the importance of the Do Xa region. He stated at a commander's conference that as a result of Operation Washington, "We found that there is nothing big in there [the Do Xa]."[7]

At this point, the 1st Marine Division again became concerned about the *2d (620th) NVA Division* which had once more penetrated the strategic Que Son Valley along the Quang Nam and Quang Tin border. Intelligence sources in mid-July reported that the enemy division, which during Operation Kansas had retreated into the mountains north and southwest of Hiep Duc, was once more on the move. Its *3d NVA Regiment*, part of which had engaged

Marine Corps Photo A369470

A Marine from Company H, 2d Battalion, 5th Marines finishes a cigarette while he waits in an assembly point for the beginning of Operation Colorado. Colorado, in August 1966, was a combined operation in the Que Son Valley, the scene of previous Marine large operations in 1966, Operations Double Eagle II and Kansas, and Operation Harvest Moon in December 1965.

Sergeant Howard's platoon in the fight for Nui Vu,* had departed its mountain bastion south of An Hoa and advanced southeast toward the coastal plain. The *21st NVA* was believed to be near the district town of Que Son, while the division's remaining regiment, the *1st VC*, was positioned somewhere between Que Son and Thang Binh, a village 20 kilometers north of Tam Ky on Route 1.[8]

As early as 18 July, General Fields informed III MAF that he wanted to exploit this intelligence with a multibattalion operation in the Que Son region. On 30 July, the 1st Division commander issued his planning directive to Colonel Charles F. Widdecke,

---

*See Chapter 8 for a description of the Nui Vu battle and for a general description of the Que Son area.

LtCol McDonald D. Tweed, Commanding Officer, HMM-361, briefs his pilots prior to the helicopter lift of the 5th Marines into Operation Colorado. Marine helicopters ferried some 3,000 allied troops into the objective area on D-Day for the operation, 6 August 1966.

the 5th Marines commanding officer, for a search and destroy operation in the Hiep Duc-Song Ly Ly Valleys coordinated with the South Vietnamese 2d ARVN Division.[9] The date for the beginning of the operation was contingent upon the end of Operation Hastings in the DMZ sector.[10] While Colonel Widdecke and his staff worked on the plans, General Fields met on 2 August with General Walt, who decided that the reduction of Marine forces in the DMZ would allow the operation to begin in three or four days. By 4 August, the Marine and ARVN commands had completed their arrangements and issued their implementing orders.[11]

Colorado/Lien Ket-52 was to be a combined operation in which Colonel Widdecke's 5th Marines and the 2d ARVN Division were to locate and destroy the *2d NVA Division*. The command posts of the Marines and ARVN were to be collocated at Tam Ky.* An ARVN task force, consisting of the 6th ARVN Regimental Headquarters with its 2d and 4th Battalions, reinforced by the 2d and 3d Armored Personnel Carrier (APC) Troops of the 4th ARVN Armored Cavalry, was to cross the line of departure near Thang Binh on the morning of 6 August and attack in a southwesterly direction toward Que Son. Southwest of Que Son, a task force of three South Vietnamese Marine battalions was to establish blocking positions to support the western thrust of the 2d ARVN Division task force.

While the Vietnamese mounted their operations north of the road, MAG-36 helicopters were to lift a company from Lieutenant Colonel Walter Moore's 2d Battalion, 5th Marines into a landing zone southwest of Hiep Duc. If Moore's troops made contact, the rest of the battalion was to reinforce the initial landing party and exploit the opportunity. If there was no contact, the helicopters were to shuttle the 2d Battalion into new positions, 1,000 meters east of Hiep Duc and repeat the process. The plan required Lieutenant Colonel Harold L. Coffman's 1st Battalion, 5th Marines to reinforce Moore's battalion if necessary, and, if not, to enter the operation on the next day in an area eight miles due south of Que Son. Both Marine battalions were to use the same tactics — search an area, engage the enemy if possible, and if not move on to another objective, either on foot or by helicopter. Colonel Widdecke's 3d Battalion, commanded by Lieutenant Colonel Edward J. Bronars, was to remain in reserve, providing security for the proposed artillery positions, just below the Thang Binh-Hiep Duc Road and 2,000 meters west of the railroad. As the operation developed, the battalion was to move southwest to form blocking positions for the southern portion of the Colorado area.[12] Each of the 5th Marines' battalions left one infantry company behind in the Chu Lai TAOR as part of the defense force there.

A large array of allied supporting arms was prepared to back up this offensive by the 5th Marines and 2d ARVN Division. Three destroyers and a cruiser were offshore ready to engage. The U.S. Air Force provided two B-52 Arc Light strikes on 6 and 7 August against targets in the mountains south of the Colorado area where intelligence agencies believed there was a large enemy base and assembly area. Both the South Vietnamese and the Marines furnished artillery. Lieutenant Colonel Joe B. Stribling's 2d Battalion, 11th Marines was in direct support of the 5th Marines with 30 tubes, ranging from 4.2-inch mortars to 8-inch howitzers. At the same time, the wing commander, Major

---

*Brigadier General William A. Stiles recalled that although the 5th Marines in fact controlled the operation, his Task Force X-Ray Headquarters deployed to the field during Colorado and was collocated at Tam Ky. BGen William A. Stiles, Comments on draft MS, dtd 15May78 (Vietnam Comment File).

THE CONTINUING WAR

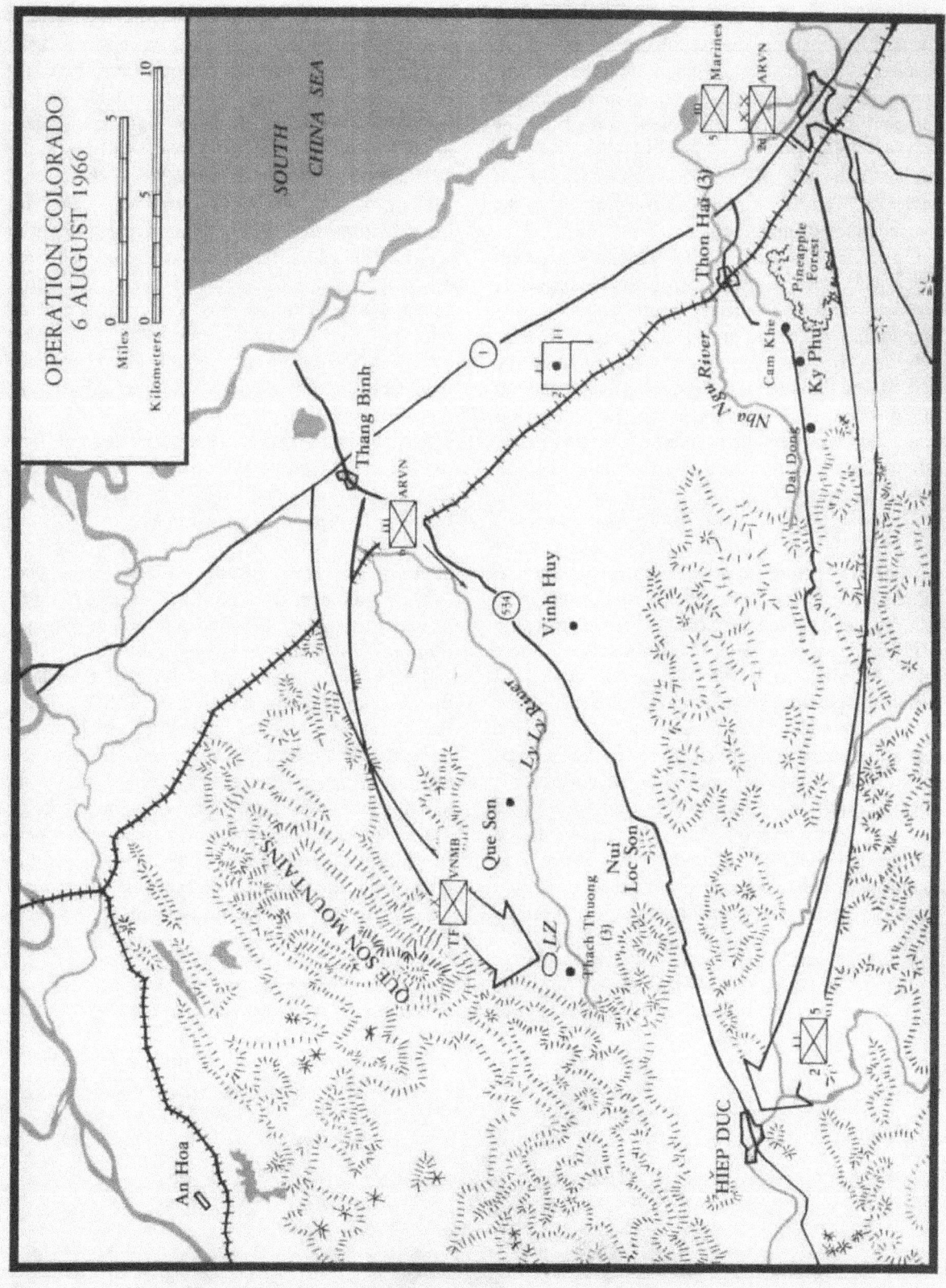

General Louis B. Robertshaw, ordered both Colonel Richard M. Hunt, the commanding officer of MAG-16, and Colonel William G. Johnson, the commanding officer of MAG-36, to make available for the operation all helicopters that could be spared. Lieutenant Colonel Robert J. Zitnik, the S-3 of MAG-36, was in the 5th Marines' operations center at Tam Ky to assist in coordinating the helicopters and the infantry.

On D-Day, 6 August, both helicopter groups ferried 3,000 allied troops into the battle area while MAG-11 and -12 aircraft made landing zone preparatory strikes and provided air support. Marine F-4s, F-8s, and A-4s flew more than 80 sorties on the first day of the operation expending more than 30 tons of bombs, 8.5 tons of napalm, 924 rockets, and 4,500 20mm rounds. In addition to bringing in the infantry, III MAF helicopters carried more than 50 tons of cargo to supply the ground troops.[13]

The only significant action on the first day occurred in the South Vietnamese Marine sector of the battlefield. All three of the Vietnamese Marine battalions encountered heavy rifle fire when they arrived in the landing zones west of Que Son. During the first few hours of 6 August, the South Vietnamese killed 50 enemy and took 20 prisoners. All of the prisoners were from a signal company attached to the *1st Battalion, 3d NVA Regiment*, apparently the rear guard covering the retreat of the rest of the regiment. The South Vietnamese Marines pursued the enemy unit in a northwesterly direction, but contact was lost toward evening. The Vietnamese Marine commander believed that the NVA force had established defenses near the hamlet of Thach Thu'ong (3), close to a small ridgeline 1,000 meters north of the Ly Ly River. The Vietnamese Marines planned to press the attack the next morning. During the first day's action, the South Vietnamese killed 71 enemy troops at a cost of three killed and 23 wounded. One of the wounded was Captain Cornelius H. Ram, the senior U.S. Marine advisor to the 1st Vietnamese Marine Battalion.[14]

On 7 August, the South Vietnamese waited for U.S. Marine aircraft to pound the enemy positions in Thach Thu'ong (3), before attacking, but the weather favored the entrenched NVA. The entire battle during that day was fought in a driving rainstorm, and because of poor visibility, airstrikes could not take place until 1330 that afternoon. Even then they had only a limited effect on the enemy's defenses. Following the air attack, the Marines tried a frontal assault against Thach Thu'ong (3). The troops had to cross 400-500 meters of flooded paddy land against heavy fire. After two unsuccessful attempts, the South Vietnamese Marine battalions pulled back to their former positions and called for more air and artillery support. Despite the poor visibility, although the rain had stopped, Marine planes, directed by U.S. advisors on the ground, continued to bomb the enemy positions. Artillery and air blasted the enemy-held hamlet throughout the night and into the morning. At 0930 8 August, the Vietnamese Marines once more attacked, still under the canopy of supporting arms. This time, the South Vietnamese met no opposition; the enemy had retreated. When the South Vietnamese entered Thach Thu'ong (3), they found a trench containing the bodies of seven enemy soldiers, while another ditch held the jumbled remains of 30 more.[15] Throughout 8 and 9 August, the South Vietnamese

A Marine UH-34 lifts off while troops from the 2d Battalion, 5th Marines deploy under cover of smoke during Colorado. The battalion encountered little opposition during the first days of the operation.

Marine Corps Photo A369410

THE CONTINUING WAR

Marine Corps Photo A371290

The 5th Marines have established their command post for Operation Colorado on the well-manicured lawn of the Tam Ky District Headquarters. At the request of the South Vietnamese authorities, the Marines had not dug individual holes, but the orders were changed after enemy gunners attacked the CP with recoilless rifle fire and mortars.

continued to search for the NVA, but without success.

During the first three days of Operation Colorado, the 5th Marines encountered little resistance. Lieutenant Colonel Moore's 2d Battalion, 5th Marines explored the southwestern portion of the Colorado TAOR near Hiep Duc during 6 and 7 August and made no contact. On 8 August, the battalion returned to Tam Ky to provide security for the regimental CP,* still without meeting any sizeable Viet Cong or NVA force. The next day, the battalion was helilifted into landing zones in the western portion of the Ly Ly River Valley with the mission of cutting off the retreat of the enemy unit which had engaged the Vietnamese Marines. This effort proved futile; on 10 August the battalion returned to Tam Ky.

---

*Colonel Zitnik, who was the air coordinator for the operation, recalled that after the battalion returned to Tam Ky, enemy gunners attacked the CP with recoilless rifle fire and mortars and then made good their escape. Zitnik remembered that the local government headquarters at Tam Ky was "considered safe" and that the Marines at the request of the South Vietnamese had not dug individual bunkers "in the relatively nice lawns." According to Zitnik, "the headquarters grounds took on a new appearance" the following morning. The Marines suffered only a few minor casualties and none of the helicopters were damaged since they had returned to Ky Ha for the night. Col Robert J. Zitnik, Comments on draft MS, dtd 6Jun78 (Vietnam Comment File).

Lieutenant Colonel Coffman's 1st Battalion, 5th Marines had operated with the same lack of success in its portion of the TAOR east of Que Son and west of Route 1. Coffman's companies had conducted search and destroy missions throughout the area. On the morning of 10 August, he consolidated his battalion near Dai Dong, just south of the Nha Ngu River, approximately six miles west of the railroad. Coffman's objective for the day was the large hamlet of Thon Hai (3), astride the railroad.

As the battalion's three companies moved out in column at 0830, they began to encounter opposition. At first, the enemy used only long-range rifle fire. The Marines answered with their own small arms. At 1100, the battalion arrived at Ky Phu hamlet, the scene of a heavy battle the previous year during Operation Harvest Moon. Lieutenant Colonel Coffman halted the battalion. He discussed the situation with his company commanders and

Col Charles F. Widdecke, Commanding Officer, 5th Marines (center), discusses the situation with LtCol Harold L. Coffman, Commanding Officer, 1st Battalion, 5th Marines (left), and an unidentified officer in the hamlet of Ky Phu, the scene of heavy fighting in previous operations. The Viet Cong influence is obvious as indicated by the scrawled warning on the wall to U.S. troops.

Marine Corps Photo A369451

Marine Corps Photo A372957

Marines of Company C, 1st Battalion, 5th Marines take cover near the hamlet of Cam Khe as they come under enemy automatic fire. The company finally cleared a North Vietnamese trenchline and organized resistance ended.

A Marine from the 2d Battalion, 5th Marines leaps across a break in a dike in the flooded rice paddies during Colorado. Some of the heaviest fighting in the operation occurred during a driving rainstorm.

Marine Corps Photo A369409

ordered them to respond more selectively to enemy harassment. Colonel Widdecke arrived for a short conference and directed Coffman to continue his advance. At 1400, the battalion resumed its march to the east.[16]

Dark clouds massed overhead as the afternoon wore on and soon the Marines were plodding through a heavy rainstorm. Shortly after 1500 the Marines reached the small hamlet of Cam Khe, 1,000 meters northeast of Ky Phu. As Company A pushed through the outskirts of the hamlet, the Marines spotted 30 NVA running across a paddy. In a quick burst of fire, the Marines cut down the enemy force in the open field. Another body of NVA troops took the Marines under fire. All three Marine companies found themselves heavily engaged at close quarters. Armed Hueys from VMO-6 were overhead, but were unable to see, much less provide covering fire for fear of hitting friendly troops. The rain finally stopped at 1730 and the sky cleared, allowing the Hueys and jets to strike. While the armed helicopters provided suppressive fire, two MAG-12 A-4s eliminated two NVA heavy machine guns. Shortly afterward, Company C cleared a trench line of NVA and organized resistance ceased. By nightfall, the enemy had broken contact and the Marines had organized their defenses. Taking no chances, artillery, naval gunfire, and aircraft provided a curtain of fire around the battalion's positions throughout the night.

The next morning, 11 August, the Marines

surveyed the results of the previous day's battle. Although suffering 14 dead and 65 wounded, the 1st Battalion, 5th Marines had killed more than 100 North Vietnamese. Among the enemy dead was a company commander whose body yielded several documents. The Marines learned that they had engaged two battalions of the *3d NVA Regiment*. The Marine battalion continued to patrol the previous day's battlefield, but was met by only occasional snipers. The only surprise occurred that afternoon when General Wallace M. Greene, Jr., the Commandant of the Marine Corps, in Vietnam on an inspection tour, visited the 1st Battalion, 5th Marines' sector. He spoke to 1st Lieutenant Marshall B. (Buck) Darling, the commanding officer of Company C, and asked him about the action of 10 August: "Well, General," Darling replied, "we got into a fight with the enemy." The Commandant then asked what he did. "General," he said "we killed them."[17]

But the Marines had not killed all of the enemy. After the heavy fighting on the 10th, the North Vietnamese battalions retreated to the north where they engaged the South Vietnamese Marines three days later. The Vietnamese Marine task force, supported by ARVN APC units, was attacking to the east toward Thang Binh when the North Vietnamese struck just north of the village of Vinh Huy, four miles west of the railroad and nine miles northwest of Cam Khe where Coffman's battalion had met the enemy. At least two NVA battalions contested the Vietnamese Marine advance. The action, which began at 1030 on 13 August, continued through the afternoon. During that time, 1st MAW aircraft flew more than 50 sorties in support of the South Vietnamese units. After the air strikes, Lieutenant Colonel Douglas T. Kane, senior advisor to the Marine task force, noted a marked decrease in enemy fire.[18] Still, the issue was in doubt.

At 1600, the 6th ARVN regimental commander ordered one of his APC troops, reinforced by infantry, to attack the flank of the enemy to relieve the pressure on the Vietnamese Marine battalions. The armored personnel carrier attack had mixed results. Opening up with a furious fusillade from their .50 caliber machine guns, the personnel carriers not only took the enemy under fire but also the Marine battalions. Lieutenant Colonel Kane radioed the U.S. Army advisor with the ARVN regiment and told him about the problem, asking him to try to redirect the

Marine Corps Photo A801848
Gen Wallace M. Greene, Jr., Commandant of the Marine Corps, discusses the fighting in Cam Khe with LtCol Coffman, Commanding Officer, 1st Battalion, 5th Marines (right), and 1stLt Marshall B. "Buck" Darling, Commanding Officer, Company C, 1st Battalion, 5th Marines (center). Lt Darling told the Commandant, "General, we killed them."

attack of the APCs. The Army advisor replied that the APCs could not be controlled. Kane then asked the advisor to tell the APCs to cease fire, but received the reply "that they . . . only ceased fire . . . when they were out of ammunition."[19] One hour and 50,000 rounds later, the armored personnel carrier assault ended, but not before a number of Marines were casualties. At dusk, the Vietnamese Marine task force commander ordered his battalions to dig in for the night and evacuate the dead and wounded. The Vietnamese Marines lost 26 killed and 54 wounded as a result of this day's action.

On the morning of 14 August, one Vietnamese Marine battalion and the APC troop swept the battle area; the enemy was no longer there, but had left behind 140 of its dead. For the South Vietnamese, this was the last major engagement in Colorado/Lien Ket-52. The Vietnamese Marines ended the Vietnamese portion of the operation when they arrived at Thang Binh that evening.

The U.S. Marines finished Colorado/Lien Ket-52 seven days later. After the heavy action of 10 August, the 5th Marines encountered little opposition. On 12 August, the 1st Battalion, 5th Marines moved to the eastern portion of the Colorado area and conducted a search and destroy mission in the

Marines move through typical Vietnamese village during Operation Colorado. The villagers are nowhere to be seen, either having taken refuge in their shelters, or having fled the hamlet altogether.

"Pineapple Forest," so named because of its shape on tactical maps. "The Pineapple Forest," southeast of Ky Phu and Cam Khe, is studded with low lying hills, interspersed by rice paddies and hamlets. The battalion found a large rice cache, but encountered only fleeting resistance from local guerrillas. Before ending their mission in the "forest," the Marines moved most of the civilian population to more secure areas. In the meantime, on the 13th, Lieutenant Colonel Moore's 2d Battalion established blocking positions southwest of the Vietnamese Marines when they made contact with the enemy. The North Vietnamese remained far afield from the 2d Battalion and the situation was, "perimeter alert and secure; night ambushes being sent in; no enemy contact."[20] Moore's battalion returned to Tam Ky on 15 August and all battalions of the 5th Marines began displacing to the Chu Lai TAOR three days later. Colorado officially ended on 22 August.

Although Colorado/Lien Ket-52 had succeeded in driving the *NVA 2d Division* out of the Que Son Valley temporarily, the allies only accomplished half of their task. Colorado was supposed to be the first of a series of operations to bring the entire Hiep Duc-Que Son area under the blanket of III MAF security. Because of the increasing commitment of Marine forces near the DMZ after August, General Walt's plans for pacifying the valley at this time were preempted. In fact, it was not to be until April 1967 that the Marines once more entered the region in force.

The September Election

Despite the North Vietnamese incursion into the DMZ during the fall of 1966, the South Vietnamese were still able to take the first steps toward representative government and attempt to redeem the promises of the Honolulu Conference. On 11 September, a nationwide election selected delegates to form a Constituent Assembly and draw up a new constitution for the nation.

The decision to hold an election in Vietnam during this period was a precarious undertaking, especially in I Corps. Memories of the spring "Struggle Movement" which had so disrupted the cities of Da Nang and Hue only a few months before were still fresh. Certain Buddhist leaders who had been in the forefront of the opposition asked the people to boycott the election. There was no doubt that the VC also would try to disrupt the electoral process. The fact that the North Vietnamese had drawn several Marine units away from the populated regions into the DMZ area complicated the situation. It was expected that the VC would attempt to exploit any void in local security caused by the departure of Marine units. Considering all of these handicaps, the electoral turnout in I Corps was surprising. Approximately 87 percent of the 900,000 eligible voters, who lived in relatively secure areas where government control existed at least during daylight, voted, compared to 81 percent eligible voter participation in the country at large. In the cities of Hue and Da Nang, voter participation percentages were 81 and 85 respectively.

The success of the electoral process in I Corps was partially attributable to the close cooperation and careful preparation on the part of the Marines, the U.S. civilian advisory organization, and the Vietnamese authorities. As early as July, the Marines noted an increasing awareness of the election among the people. Even in remote areas of Quang Nam Province, the government had distributed posters and banners announcing the election.[21] While the Vietnamese were responsible for conducting the elections and providing security for the polling places, American troops were to see that the enemy was unable to take advantage of the situation.

On 26 August, General Walt established the policy that his forces were to follow during the election. He told his subordinate commanders that they should avoid any semblance of interference in the electoral process. American troops were to stay away from the immediate vicinity of polling places and populated areas. The general observed that the South Vietnamese Army was to stand down from major operations during the electoral period and assume responsibility for protecting the election. Each Marine regiment was to maintain one battalion command group and three rifle companies on an

Marine Corps Historical Collection
Vietnamese citizens obtain voting identification cards for the 11 September 1966 election in a voter registration office. Approximately 87 percent of the 900,000 eligible voters in I Corps went to the polls on election day.

alert status to assist the Vietnamese in the event the VC attacked. Although no large Marine units were to remain in the populated areas, Marine helicopters were to provide aerial surveillance of the III MAF TAOR. In addition, Marine artillery was to increase its harassment and interdiction of suspected enemy lines of communications and at the same time be prepared to support the Vietnamese Army. Most importantly, the Marine infantry battalions were to conduct large screening operations to prevent VC or NVA main force units from entering the populated areas. It was expected that the widely dispersed ARVN forces would be able to handle the local guerrillas.[22]

General Walt was seriously concerned about the VC threats to dismantle the electoral process. In its August report, the Marine command noted that the VC had initiated an all-out propaganda and extortion campaign to prevent the election.[23] The 9th Marines reported that the VC had tasked local cadre and guerrilla forces with most of the operations to counter the government election. Colonel Barrett, the regimental commander, was unable to determine any specific mission for larger enemy formations, but was sure "they will be employed to exploit any opportunity where a larger force is required to disrupt the election."[24] The Marines were determined that this opportunity would not arise.

During the period 1-11 September, General Walt put nine battalions in the field to conduct search and destroy operations away from the populated areas. The purpose of these operations was to keep the large enemy units off balance and away from the people. They were successful. Although there were 34 Viet Cong incidents on the day of the election in I Corps, no large enemy unit broke through the Marine screen. Most of the enemy incidents were isolated attacks. For example, the 1st Marines reported that two polling areas in its TAOR were hit by mortar fire, three rounds falling on each of the sites, but causing only minor disruption.[25]

Perhaps Colonel Barrett offered the best explanation for the Communist failure to stop the election when he declared:

> It is felt that the Viet Cong had never intended to conduct an extensive antielection campaign of a military nature since he did not possess sufficient resources to overcome the preventive measures initiated by the GVN, but rather he hoped that through propaganda against the election and threat of violence against those who participated he would successfully intimidate large numbers of voters and discourage them from going to the polls. His bluff was called as the results show.[26]

The Marine TAORs, Jul-Dec 1966

Despite the success of the election, there were few victories for the Marine Corps pacification campaign in central and southern I Corps in late 1966. Pacification progress depended upon the individual Marine battalion. The Marine pacification concept dictated that the Marine battalions provide security for local villages and hamlets by constant small unit patrolling. From March through August 1966, III MAF units conducted more than 68,000 patrols, ranging in size from four to 40 men. Only 10 percent of these patrols made contact with the enemy, but the Marines maintained that the remaining 90 percent were equally beneficial. As Colonel Chaisson, the III MAF G-3, explained, "all of these small unit operations are conducted in the guerrilla environment. They are trying not only to kill the guerrillas but to curtail his freedom of movement."[27]

There were other reasons for the extensive patrolling of the Marine TAORs, not the least of which related to base defense. On the night of 23 July, Viet Cong gunners, from positions behind a Buddhist temple 2,600 meters southwest of the Marble Mountain Facility, lobbed 40-50 81mm mortar shells in a seven-minute barrage onto the airfield parking apron. Although little damage occurred, the attack exposed the vulnerability of the base to such hit and run tactics. Lieutenant Colonel Emerson A. Walker, whose 3d Battalion, 1st Marines was responsible for the southeastern sector of the Da Nang TAOR, recalled that "General Walt let all echelons know that he did not expect this to happen again." Walker remembered that the engineers constructed two 50-foot wood towers in his sector. According to the battalion commander, his Marines mounted a rocket launcher and machine gun on the towers and manned both weapons around the clock. Walker claimed that: "The towers proved to be such a formidable threat that all Viet Cong mortar activity ceased in that area."[28]

The opening of the new front along the DMZ together with the heavy emphasis on base defense

The 2d Korean Marine Brigade on 20 September 1966 marks the first anniversary of its arrival in South Vietnam in a formal ceremony. The honor guard carries the Korean National flag (left) and the colors of the brigade (right). The Korean Marines reinforced III MAF in August 1966.

Marine Corps Photo A369489

and pacification in the southern TAORs placed a heavy strain on Marine manpower resources. This was somewhat alleviated with the long-planned deployment of the 2d Korean Marine Brigade to I Corps. The first echelons of the Korean Brigade arrived on 18 August and were assigned a TAOR in northern Quang Ngai Province on the Batangan Peninsula, 17 miles southeast of the Chu Lai Airfield. By the end of the month, the full brigade was established on the peninsula which was incorporated into the Chu Lai TAOR. The command relationship between the Koreans and the American Marines was delicate. General Walt did not have operational control of the Korean Brigade, but he did have coordinating authority. Although the III MAF commander could not order the Koreans to do anything, he and Brigadier General Lee Bong Chool, the Korean Brigade commander, who had attended the Marine Corps Schools at Quantico, formed a working arrangement that satisfied both sides.[29]*

Even with the reinforcement of the Koreans, the increasing demands of the war in the north caused a serious setback to Marine pacification plans. The move of the 3d Marine Division to Phu Bai and the shift of the 1st Marine Division Headquarters to Da Nang not only disrupted the pacification campaign, but ended any chance to join the Da Nang and Chu Lai TAORs by the end of the year.

At Chu Lai, the 1st Division established an entirely new command structure. On 10 October, the new division commander, Major General Herman Nickerson, Jr., a holder of the Silver Star and veteran of World War II and Korea, who had just relieved General Fields, moved his headquarters to Da Nang. He spoke with some regret about leaving Chu Lai, "Very pleasant CP, beautiful, but I didn't get to stay there very long."[30]

---

*Victor K. Fleming, Jr., a former Marine captain who served in the 7th Marines S-3 section during this period, recalled that there were some misunderstandings between the Koreans and the Chu Lai Marines before the rough edges in the command relations were smoothed out. On one particular occasion, the Koreans launched an operation near the Marine TAOR without informing the Marine units responsible for that sector. According to Fleming when the American command asked why it had not been notified, General Lee replied, 'Why should I? You don't tell me what you are doing.' This incident led to an immediate overhaul and improvement of liaison between the two commands." Victor K. Fleming, Jr., Comments on draft MS, dtd 17Jun80 (Vietnam Comment File).

Marine Corps Photo A369613

MajGen Herman Nickerson, Jr., (front passenger seat of the jeep) has just arrived at the Chu Lai Airfield to relieve MajGen Lewis J. Fields, Commanding General, 1st Marine Division (rear seat). General Nickerson assumed command of the division the following day, 1 October 1966, and a few days later moved the division headquarters to Da Nang.

Brigadier General Stiles, the assistant division commander, then assumed command of the Chu Lai TAOR. Stiles reformed his Task Force X-Ray command which now consisted of four Marine infantry battalions and supporting forces. The 7th Marines had operational control of the four infantry battalions at Chu Lai while the 5th Marines Headquarters served as a coordinating headquarters for the task force.

At best this was an ad hoc arrangement. The strain on the overly extended units at Chu Lai remained great. Battalions still operated miles from Chu Lai and yet remained responsible for their sector of the TAOR. Lieutenant Colonel Warren P. Kitterman, who commanded the 2d Battalion, 7th Marines, remembered that during an operation in southern Quang Ngai Province during late 1966, he, in effect, maintained three separate command posts. His executive officer "ran the TAOR [at Chu Lai] with four platoons from four different battalions," while his operations officer had "tactical control" of the battalion in the operation. Kitterman, himself, "was coordinating 2/7 with an ARVN Bn, an ARVN

Parachute Company, an ARVN arty battery, and H/3/11."³¹

Much the same situation existed in the Phu Bai TAOR. Although General Kyle had established the 3d Division Headquarters at the Phu Bai base in October, only one or two battalions actually operated in or near the TAOR. The 3d Division Headquarters took over from the 4th Marines, which regiment up to that point had maintained a rear headquarters at Phu Bai and direct control of the TAOR and the units there. This included the 2d Battalion, 4th Marines, a provisional artillery battery, and support elements. On 11 October, the newly arrived 2d Battalion, 26th Marines moved from Da Nang to Phu Bai. After operating for a short period just south of the Phu Bai TAOR, the latter battalion began on 29 October Operation Pawnee III in Phu Loc District, north of the strategic Hai Van Pass, with the mission to keep Route 1 open between Da Nang and Phu Bai. In November, the 1st Battalion, 4th Marines relieved at Phu Bai the 2d Battalion, 4th Marines which returned to Okinawa under the recently resumed intratheater battalion rotation policy.* Finally in early December, the 2d Battalion, 9th Marines replaced the 1st Battalion, 4th Marines, which in turn rotated to Okinawa.³²

With a lull in Operation Prairie in the north, General Kyle, in mid-December, decided to move a battalion back into the Co Bi-Thanh Tan sector, the old Cherokee and Florida operating area, 13 miles northwest of Hue, and where the enemy was once more active. On 10 December, VC units in well-coordinated attacks struck three South Vietnamese strongpoints, including the Phong Dien District Headquarters and the An Lao Bridge across the Bo River. Suspecting that elements of the *6th NVA* again were attempting to infiltrate from their mountain base areas into the coastal populated region, General Kyle, on 17 December, ordered the just-arrived 3d Battalion, 26th Marines from Dong Ha into the Co Bi-Thanh Tan corridor. Travelling by truck from Dong Ha and with an attached artillery

---

*The arrival of the 26th Marines and its battalions in WestPac in August and September allowed the Marines to reinstitute the intratheater rotation of battalions between Okinawa, Vietnam, and the SLF which had been suspended since March. (See Chapter 4). See Chapter 18 for further discussion of the 26th Marines and the battalion rotation policy.

Marine Corps Photo A188089
Marines of Company I, 3d Battalion, 26th Marines check the identity cards of suspected Viet Cong. The battalion is participating in Operation Chinook during December 1966 in the old "Florida" area, the Co Bi-Thanh Tan sector in Thua Thien Province.

battery, the 3d Battalion established, on 19 December, its CP west of Route 1, some 3,000 meters south of Phong Dien. After minor skirmishes with the Marines during the first two days, the enemy *802d VC Battalion* launched two sizeable attacks against the Marine positions in the early morning hours of 22 and 23 December. In both cases, the enemy employed the same tactics; a mortar barrage, followed by a ground probe of the Marine perimeter. The VC then would withdraw, taking most of their casualties with them.³³

At this stage, 23 December, General Kyle elected to expand the operation, now codenamed Chinook, in the Co Bi-Thanh Tan, even further. He reinforced the 3d Battalion with the 2d Battalion, 26th Marines, which moved from the Pawnee area into the Chinook sector, north of the O Lau River. At the same time, he ordered the 4th Marines Headquarters to deploy from Prairie and take control of the units in Chinook. These now included, in addition to the two infantry battalions, the 3d Battalion, 12th Marines, reconnaissance troops from Phu Bai, and support units. Colonel Cereghino, the 4th Marines commander, opened his CP in the Chinook area on Christmas day. Hampered by the northeast mon-

THE CONTINUING WAR

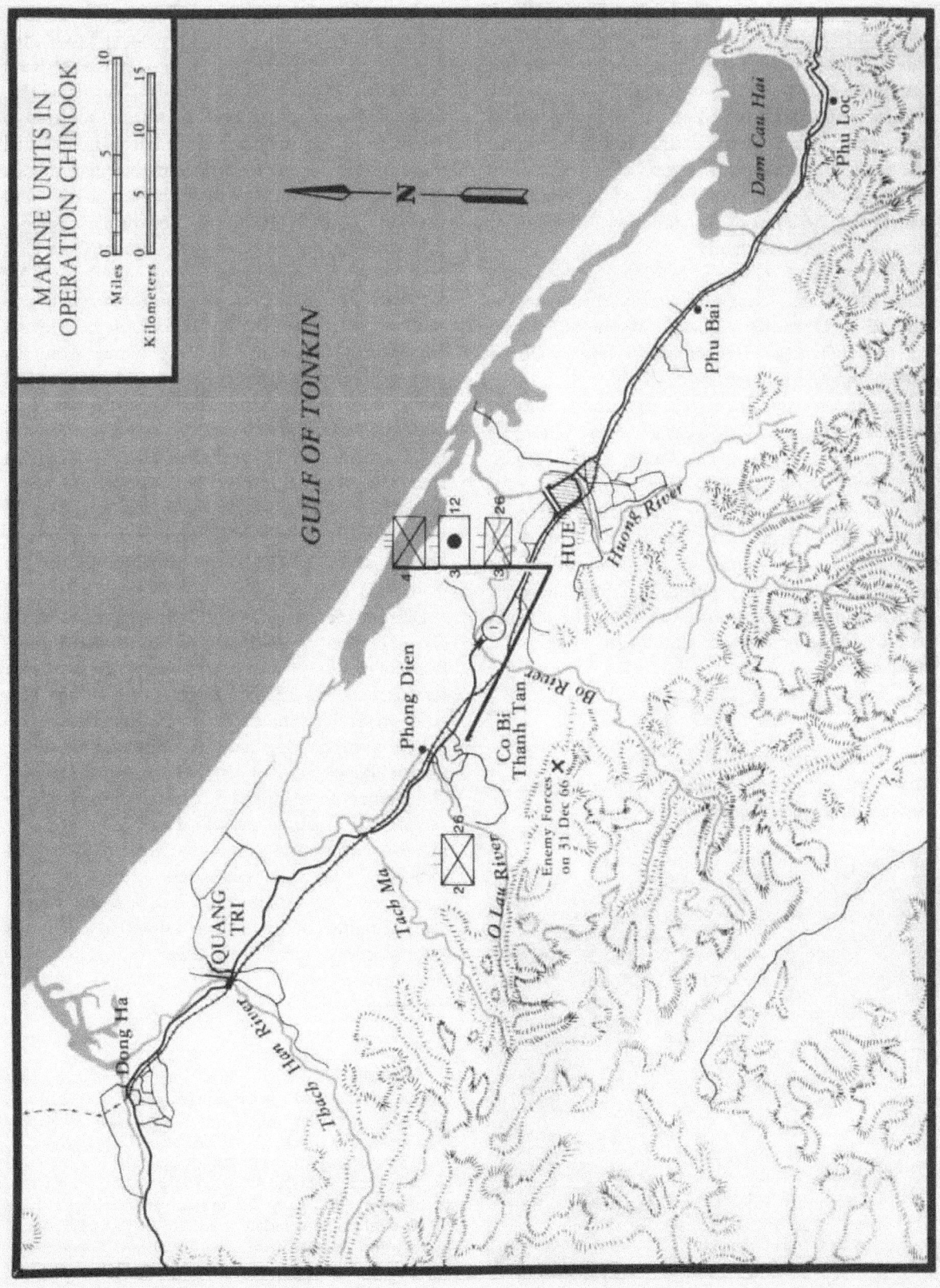

soon, which limited the availability of both fixed-wing and helicopter support, the two infantry battalions encountered few enemy troops during the rest of the month. The most dramatic event occurred during the supposed New Year's truce period. On 31 December, Marine reconnaissance patrols, screening the foothills to the south of the Co Bi-Thanh Tan, observed more than 1,000 enemy troops, taking advantage of the terms of the standdown and moving north toward the lowlands.

After III MAF convinced MACV that the enemy force presented a clear and present danger to the Marines in Operation Chinook, Marine air and artillery bombarded the Communist troops. Operation Chinook continued into 1967.³⁴

In the heavily populated Da Nang TAOR, pacification continued to be the prime concern of the Marine forces there. The TAOR contained both the I Corps National Priority Area and fledgling An Hoa industrial site. During the spring and early summer, the Marine battalions had challenged the long-standing Communist domination south of the air base. This entire pacification effort, however, depended in great part on the ability of the Marines to provide the necessary security in the villages and hamlets.

The pacification effort south of Da Nang can be an "odorous" job. Troops from the 1st Marines probe a manure pile for hidden weapons.

Marine Corps Photo A369663

When General Nickerson's 1st Marine Division assumed responsibility for the Da Nang TAOR, the 3d Marines was the only infantry regiment to leave Da Nang; both the 1st and 9th Marines remained. Colonel Donald L. Mallory's 1st Marines reverted to 1st Marine Division operational control and retained responsibility for the southeastern portion of the Da Nang TAOR. Colonel Mallory, holder of the Navy Cross and former Assistant G-3 of the 1st Division, had assumed command of the regiment from Colonel Mitchell in August. Colonel Robert M. Richards' 9th Marines took over the western and southern portions of the TAOR formerly held by the 3d Marines. Richards, a 1942 Naval Academy graduate, relieved Colonel Barrett as the regimental commander on 8 October. The U.S. Army's 4th Battalion, 503d Infantry occupied the northern sector of the Da Nang TAOR, including the Hai Van Pass area.* The Army battalion was not under the operational control of a Marine regiment, but operated directly under General Nickerson. It was planned to hold at least eight infantry battalions in the Da Nang TAOR.³⁵

Despite the demands on Marine resources at Da Nang, General Walt continued his unstinted effort to make the An Hoa industrial complex a show case for pacification. He held at least one Marine battalion in An Hoa and pressured the government and MACV to support the industrial development there. Colonel Edward L. Bale, Jr., the 1st Marine Division G-4, remembered that the "extensive efforts of the 1st Marine Division and the Force Logistic Command to supply and support the An Hoa industrial complex . . . at times reduced our own forces . . . as to approach the danger point. Yet, it demonstrated the willingness of III MAF to support the only industrial development in the area."³⁶

---

*Col Walter S. Pullar, Jr., who as a major was executive officer and for a short period commanding officer of the 2d Battalion, 26th Marines, recalled that when the 1st Battalion, 3d Marines departed for Khe Sanh at the end of September (See Chapter 11), he commanded a provisional battalion consisting of a reinforced company from the 2d Battalion, 26th Marines, and one from the 2d Battalion, 3d Marines. This battalion assumed responsibility for the northern sector including the Hai Van Pass until relieved by the Army battalion from the 503d Infantry. Col Walter S. Pullar, Jr., Comments on draft MS, dtd 22May78 (Vietnam Comment File).

The An Hoa project had as much difficulty, if not more, with the South Vietnamese Government than with the Viet Cong. Some members of the government believed that the industrial complex was doomed to failure. General Westmoreland had proposed that the U.S. Embassy use its influence with the Vietnamese authorities to support the project. In the meantime, USAID officials began studies to determine the economic feasibility for the industrial exploitation of An Hoa.

One of the greatest threats to the entire An Hoa program was the fact that some of the key officials, including Mr. Can, the project director, were being drafted into the South Vietnamese Army. General Walt believed that if Can departed, progress at An Hoa would cease. The III MAF commander personally asked General Westmoreland to intercede with the South Vietnamese authorities to have Can deferred.[37] By the end of October, a compromise had been reached. The An Hoa employees were to be drafted, but required to serve for only one month in the army. After their month's service, they were to be transferred into the Popular Forces and returned to An Hoa.[38]

The future of An Hoa was still unclear at the end of 1966. The industrial complex depended on coal from the Nong Son mine, 12 miles southwest of the factory site. Viet Cong guerrillas operated in some strength near the mine. Transporting the coal to An Hoa was also a problem. Activities at the industrial complex during this period were largely confined to renovating the plant and obtaining spare parts so the fertilizer factory could start production. According to Lieutenant Colonel Donald L. Evans, Jr., the recorder for the I Corps Joint Coordinating Council during much of 1966 and later head of the Civil Affairs Branch at Headquarters Marine Corps: "At this point [December 1966] very little had been accomplished except to focus attention on An Hoa as a potential industrial site."[39]

The main pacification concern of the South Vietnamese officials in I Corps during this period was progress in the National Priority Area, encompassing portions of Hoa Vang, Hieu Duc, and Dien Ban Districts south of Da Nang. Although Marines did not participate directly in the campaign, the entire priority area was in the Da Nang TAOR. Battalions from the 1st and 9th Marines were prepared to assist the South Vietnamese units in the area, and in Oc-

Marine Corps Photo A187438
Mr. Le Thuc Can, project director, briefs a visiting team of USAID officials on the An Hoa Industrial Project. Can and other project officials faced induction into the Vietnamese Army, but upon the personal intervention of Generals Walt and Westmoreland, an accommodation was reached with the Vietnamese authorities and the project was continued.

tober, General Lam, the I Corps commander, assigned the entire 51st ARVN Regiment to the pacification campaign with two battalions operating in the National Priority Area. In addition, four Revolutionary Development teams were working in the priority area and six other teams which were to be assigned were in training at the Vung Tau Training Center. Despite this intensive effort, government forces succeeded in securing only 18 of the 38 hamlets in the National Priority Area that were scheduled to be pacified in 1966.[40]

According to allied plans, the Vietnamese were to take over more of the pacification program in 1967. In I Corps, the ARVN forces were to have the primary mission of supporting Revolutionary Development, while Marine forces were to be deployed more and more against the enemy main force units. Yet, the Marines were still to secure their TAORs and clear the areas in the vicinity of the established bases. In a sense this could be called the beginning of Vietnamization, but several senior Marine officers doubted that the Vietnamese Army was prepared to take over the pacification program. In any event, pacification ended on a sour note in 1966; III MAF reported that no hamlets were added to the secure category in I Corps during December.[41] General English summed up the Marine frustrations for the year: ". . . too much real estate—do not have enough troops."[42]

PART VI
PACIFICATION: THE ELUSIVE GOAL

CHAPTER 14
Marine Corps Pacification

County Fair and Golden Fleece — Combined Action — Personal Response — Kit Carson — Psychological Warfare — Civic Action — The I Corps Joint Coordinating Council

County Fair and Golden Fleece

In developing their pacification concepts, the Marines drew upon a wealth of experience and history. General Walt recalled his early training as a young officer when he learned the fundamentals of his profession from Marines who had fought Sandino in Nicaragua and Charlemagne in Haiti. These veterans had stressed tempering the struggle against insurgents with an understanding and compassion for the people.[1] As early as 1935, the Marine Corps published its *Small Wars Manual* which emphasized the lessons learned by Marines who fought the campaigns against the guerrillas of their day.[2]

According to the 1940 edition of the *Small Wars Manual*, "small wars" involved diplomacy, contact with the lowest levels of the civilian population, and the uncertainties of political disruption. The goal of "small wars" was to gain decisive results with the least application of force and the minimum loss of life. Caution was to be exercised, and the population was to be treated with "tolerance, sympathy, and kindness."[3]

Although this philosophy formed the basic structure of Marine Corps "small wars" theory, III MAF found it necessary to develop pacification tactics to meet the conditions unique to South Vietnam.*

Two innovations which showed promising potential were the County Fair and Golden Fleece programs. Both had their origins in late 1965 and were refined during the course of 1966.

The 9th Marines initiated prototype County Fair operations in late 1965 and in early 1966 in response to the need for new techniques to secure its area of operations south of the Da Nang Airbase. Containing an extended area dotted with hamlets and villages, the 9th Marines TAOR was one of the most densely populated areas of South Vietnam with over 1,000 inhabitants per square mile. The Marine regiment realized that it had to eradicate the VC guerrillas and political cadre in order to pacify the hamlets. Employing traditional cordon and search tactics, the Marines began a continuing effort in the villages to clear out the VC. The County Fair technique was an outgrowth and elaboration of these tactics.[4]

Begun on an experimental basis in February 1966, this technique emphasized coordination and cooperation with South Vietnamese military and civilian authorities to reestablish government control of a community without alienating the people. While Marines cordoned a village, ARVN troops and police gathered the inhabitants at a designated collection point. The South Vietnamese troops then searched the hamlet for any VC who might still be hiding. During this time, South Vietnamese ad-

---

*Two former III MAF staff officers emphasized that from the very beginning the Marine command had focused on pacification. Colonel Robert B. Watson, as an operations analyst, had earlier served on the staff of the Development Center at Quantico, Virginia. He recalled that in 1962 when General Walt became Director of the Center that the War Games Group had been directed to war game the landing of a reinforced Marine amphibious force at Da Nang. Watson claims that the results of this game, "Operation Cormorant," proved very predictive of later operations by the Marines against the VC guerrilla forces. General Walt had been alerted to the problems of operations against enemy forces where no FEBA [forward edge of the battle area] was established, where the enemy was so elusive and where significant portions of the offensive force had to be committed to the security of the support areas." Col Robert B. Watson, Jr., Comments on draft MS, n.d. [Jun 78], (Vietnam Comment File). Colonel Donald L. Evans, who served as the recorder of the I Corps Joint Coordinating Council, observed that although "some of our [pacification] techniques where still a little ragged and sporadically applied in 1966 . . . I believe that our approach was sound and quite well developed by this . . . time. Many Army folks who believed in pacification or were involved in it in those days readily admitted to me that the Marine approach was sound. . . . "Col Donald L. Evans, Comments on draft MS, dtd 17Jun78 (Vietnam Comment File).

Marine Corps Photo A186992

The 3d Marine Division Drum and Bugle Corps plays for the entertainment of assembled villagers during a "County Fair" in April 1966. County Fair operations were sophisticated cordons and searches, involving U.S. Marines and South Vietnamese troops while local government officials and police checked identity cards and conducted a census. Band concerts helped to provide a festive atmosphere while the other aspects of the operation were completed.

ministrative officials and police processed the villagers at the collection center, taking a census, issuing ID cards, and interrogating the population about their background and the location of members of their families. In addition, the people were fed, provided medical assistance, and entertained. A significant feature of the entertainment was that it permitted the government to present its case to the villagers in the form of movies, speeches, folk music, and drama.

Throughout these activities, the Marines remained as unobtrusive as possible, except to furnish medical and limited logistical assistance. The idea was not to overwhelm the local populace with the American military presence, but to provide a climate in which the local Vietnamese military, police, and civilian administrators could operate.[5]

One of the more successful of these combined operations was the 9th Marines' County Fair-11 in the hamlet of Thanh Quit (3) during April 1966. The hamlet, located in a small triangle between the Thanh Quit and Vinh Dien Rivers and 1,500 meters east of Route 1 below Da Nang, often served as a haven for local guerrillas. On the morning of 26 April at 0500, Lieutenant Colonel William F. Donahue's 2d Battalion, 9th Marines established blocking positions east of the hamlet while an ARVN company blocked to the west. One hour later, two companies of the 3d Battalion, 51st ARVN Regiment advanced north from the Thanh Quit River into the hamlet. The South Vietnamese soldiers surprised a guerrilla unit in Thanh Quit (3). Realizing they were trapped, the VC fought stubbornly. The ARVN killed 45 of the guerrillas, captured 17 prisoners, and confiscated 14 weapons. The Marines in the blocking position suffered no casualties while the ARVN battalion sustained one dead and 14 wounded during the action.[6]

The success of this operation and another in April, during which the Marines and South Vietnamese captured a VC district official, caused General Walt to order the expansion of the program throughout the Marine TAORs during the following months. Many of the regiments prepared standing operating orders for the conduct of these operations and developed fairly elaborate procedures to create a festive atmosphere. At the collection points, the tents were decorated with bunting and flags. A Marine division band or drum and bugle corps often played martial airs, followed by South Vietnamese

In County Fairs, the allies take elaborate measures to ensure that they get their message across to the assembled villagers. In the picture, members of the Quang Ngai Drama Team perform in a skit which condemns Viet Cong terrorism and praises U.S. assistance.

Marine Corps Photo A369174

The County Fair had two faces. While the villagers listen to music, troops from the 51st ARVN Regiment search out suspected VC tunnels and hiding places.

troubadors who continued to entertain the villagers. Although creating a "county fair" atmosphere, the purpose remained to ferret out the VC. By the end of June, the Marines and the South Vietnamese had conducted 25 of these operations with a fair measure of success. In other corps areas, U.S. Army units adopted the County Fair concept, but changed the name from County Fair to "Hamlet Festival."[7]

In a letter to General Walt on 4 July, General Westmoreland specifically mentioned County Fair as a desirable technique to enhance village and hamlet security. Although he observed that such operations tied down U.S. units and required the retention of a reserve, Westmoreland declared:

> The Hamlet Search [County Fair] concept offers a realistic prospect for developing meaningful and lasting security in areas where it is conducted; and to the extent that this is the real objective of all our military operations, every opportunity for successful achievement of this goal should be pursued.[8]

He reminded Walt that County Fair operations were not necessarily appropriate for universal employment throughout Vietnam and that he did not want any dissipation of U.S. strength "to the detriment of our primary responsibility for destroying main force enemy units."[9]

The MACV commander continued to demonstrate interest in the County Fair program and on 10 July, he requested III MAF to report on its County Fair activities for the preceding four-month period. The Marines were not only to furnish the total number of operations for each month from March through June, but were to provide the following data as well: names and coordinates of hamlets searched; number of suspects detained; number of enemy killed and captured; number and type of weapons seized; and number of hamlets in which the enemy "infrastructure" was considered destroyed.[10]

The month of July was to be the highwater mark for the number of III MAF 1966 County Fair operations. During the month, Marine units conducted 21 such operations near Da Nang: nine by the 3d Marines, eight by the 1st Marines, and four by the 9th Marines. Colonel Bryan B. Mitchell, the 1st Marines commander, observed that his units, cooperating with the South Vietnamese, provided "the first real GVN influence in many of the hamlets during the past three years."[11]

Lieutenant Colonel Robert R. Dickey, III, whose 1st Battalion, 3d Marines had just completed County Fair 4-11 on 28 July in Kim Lien hamlet six miles northwest of the airbase in the 3d Marines TAOR, was less sanguine. He wrote:

> Increased search skills and techniques of both Vietnamese and Marines are needed. The villagers aid the VC due to friendship and personal relations, not politics. District officials should get to know needs of people and offer tangible evidence of GVN presence.[12]

Lieutenant Colonel Dickey had touched upon only one of the problems that the County Fair concept was to encounter during the remainder of 1966. By the end of July, General Walt wanted to increase the number of County Fair operations to an average of at least 10 a week, but III MAF never attained this goal in 1966. With the diversion of battalions to the northern battlefront, the Marine regiments did not have the troops in the southern TAORs that would make an expanded County Fair program feasible. Furthermore, South Vietnamese officials on the district level were not fully cooperative. At the close of a visit to Vietnam in early September, General Krulak remarked that Marine commanders had complained to him that the "absence of Vietnamese participants had slowed down our County Fair program far below that of which we are capable and below that which we had planned."[13] Krulak agreed with General Walt's contention that the Marines should not go into a pacification endeavor unless there was adequate South Vietnamese military and civilian representation. Although General Lam had assigned the entire 51st ARVN Regiment to the pacification program in the I Corps national priority area south of Da Nang, the decline in the frequency of County Fair operations continued. By the end of the year, III MAF was conducting an average of four per month.

During the 88 County Fair operations conducted during 1966, over 46,000 South Vietnamese villagers were screened and more than 20,000 of them were provided medical treatment. These same operations accounted for 192 enemy killed and 262 captured. Although this represented an average of only slightly more than five VC per operation, the enemy casualties were local guerrillas and political cadre, the basis of VC control in the countryside. The loss of these men in sufficient numbers could destroy the Communist influence among the people. The County Fair program was a useful technique of gaining control and extending influence.[14]

In contrast to the frustrations experienced by the Marines in conducting County Fairs, their rice-protection campaign was more successful. Begun during the fall harvest season of 1965 and named Golden Fleece, the concept called for a Marine battalion to maintain security around the rice paddies while the peasants harvested the grain. These operations allowed the Vietnamese farmer to keep his produce, while preventing the Viet Cong from collecting their usual percentage of the crop. The Golden Fleece campaign deprived the VC of badly needed supplies, and furnished the uncommitted South Vietnamese peasant an incentive to support the government cause. Marine staff officers estimated that the III MAF rice protection program kept over 500,000 pounds of rice from the grasp of the enemy during the 1965 harvest season.[15] III MAF expanded these operations during the 1966 harvest seasons. At the end of September, General Walt observed that more rice was withheld from the Viet Cong during the month than during any previous season in years.[16]

One of the most productive of all such operations was Golden Fleece 7-1 carried out by Major Littleton W. T. Waller II's 1st Battalion, 7th Marines in Mo Duc District south of the city of Quang Ngai.* The Marine battalion entered the district, 25 miles from its Chu Lai area of operations on 8 September to conduct a search and destroy operation. The operation, labeled Fresno, was designed to prevent enemy main force units from disrupting the constitutional election. Although Fresno did end after the election, there was a sudden change of plans. In a conversation with General Walt, General Lam, the I Corps commander, observed that for years the Viet Cong had collected nearly 90 percent of the rice harvested in the Mo Duc region. General Walt suggested that the Marine battalion remain in the area to help pro-

---

*Major Waller is the grandson of Major General Littleton W. T. Waller, USMC, of Boxer Rebellion and Philippine Insurrection fame.

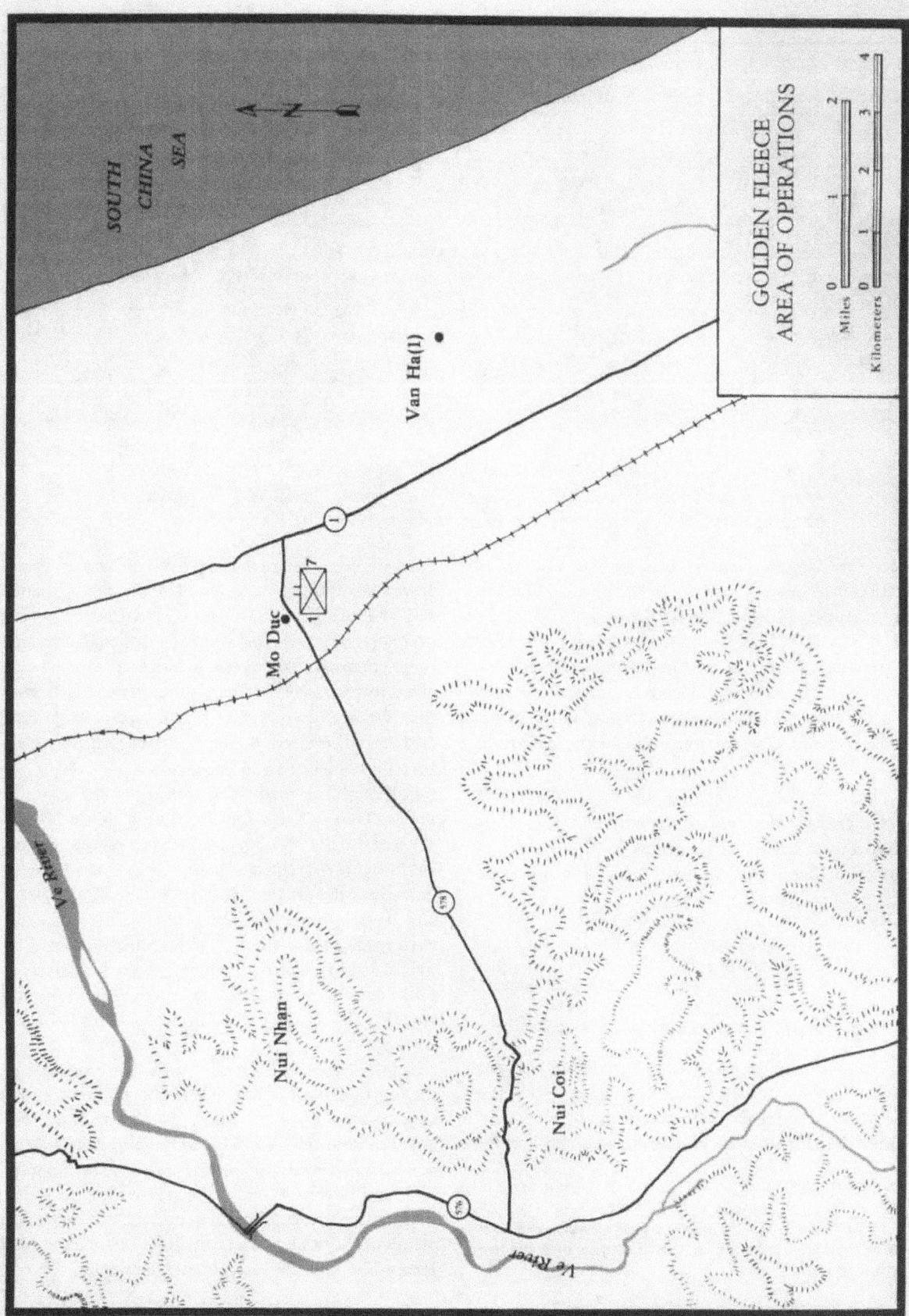

Marines of the 1st Battalion, 7th Marines conduct Golden Fleece 7-1, a rice protection operation, in the Mo Duc sector of Quang Ngai Province. The Marine on the right is checking identity cards while the Marine on the left stands guard.

tect the harvest. General Lam agreed and on 16 September, Major General Fields, the 1st Division commander, ordered Colonel Lawrence F. Snoddy, Jr.,* the 7th Marines commander, to terminate Operation Fresno at midnight and immediately begin Operation Golden Fleece 7-1. Colonel Snoddy visited Major Waller's command post south of the village of Mo Duc and told him of the change in plans.[17]

The informality of the planning for Golden Fleece 7-1 may have deceived the enemy and apparently contributed to the effectiveness of the operation. Major Waller later commented that the operation was approached on a low key:

> There was a minimum of fuss and coordination with the ARVN Division in Quang Ngai [the 2d ARVN Division]. Perhaps this low level approach accounted for the enemy not getting the word. At any rate, if he did get the word, he did not seem to think we would affect his plans.[18]

Allied intelligence sources had indicated that two VC battalions, the *38th* and *44th* were in the area with two local force companies. These forces totaled approximately 900 men and agents reported that the

---
*Colonel Snoddy in 1972 legally changed his name from Snoddy to Snowden. He retired from active duty in 1979 as a lieutenant general.

enemy units were operating freely in the area, the *38th* west of Route 1 and the *44th* in the paddy lands east of the highway. During Fresno and the period immediately preceding the constitutional election, these enemy battalions had avoided all contact with allied forces in the Mo Duc region. Perhaps believing that the Marine battalion would return to its base area after the election, the Viet Cong commanders become bolder after 16 September.

Although the enemy had at least two battalions in the Mo Duc area, the fighting during Golden Fleece 7-1 was usually on a small-unit level. Marine patrols either sighted or engaged enemy units attempting to move into the fertile lowlands. Marine air, artillery, and naval gunfire was called on to finish the job. Battery G, 3d Battalion, 11th Marines reinforced by five U.S. Navy destroyers offshore provided direct artillery support to the infantry battalion, and Marine aircraft from Chu Lai and Da Nang furnished close air support.

While 2d ARVN Division units were protecting the rice fields east of Route 1, Major Waller sent platoon and squad patrols along the access routes into Mo Duc from the west. The Song Ve constituted the northern and western boundary of the area of operations and Highway 578, the southern. Special South Vietnamese observation units, called *Dac Cong*, supplemented the Marine patrols. By entering the Nui Nham-Nui Coi hill mass, which dominated the en-

quickly checked with the battalion command post and learned that the troops he had spotted were not ARVN, but VC. The Marines opened fire on the enemy and also called in artillery and air as the VC fled. A Marine tactical aerial observer in a UH-1E helicopter, controlling the airstrike, reported at least four enemy killed. When the Marine patrol swept the area, they found a base camp that the enemy had established, apparently for rice collection.[20]

Through 21 September, Major Waller continued the same tactics, deploying small patrols into the hinterlands and conducting company sweeps in the lowlands west of Route 1. On the 21st, the Marines readjusted their boundary with the 2d ARVN Division in order to attack the hamlet of Van Ha (1), 2,000 meters east of Highway 1, long a Viet Cong strongpoint. The hamlet was honeycombed with bunkers and interlocking tunnels. The district chief stated that no South Vietnamese Government force had dared to enter this complex for over four years.

Expecting heavy enemy resistance, Major Waller stationed Company A in blocking positions that night and called for an intensive air, artillery, and naval bombardment the next morning. After the bombardment, he launched a three-company attack

Marine Corps Photo A369479
The 1st Battalion, 7th Marines advance on the hamlet of Van Ha (1) in Operation Golden Fleece 7-1. The hamlet was a known Viet Cong stronghold.

After taking Van Ha (1), the Marines found a granary holding 727 tons of rice. Here a Marine holds a burlap bag open for one of the 8,000 workers that were brought in to take the rice to Mo Duc.

Marine Corps Photo A369606

tire region, the Marines and their South Vietnamese allies probed much further to the west than the VC expected. The roving patrols provided excellent information which resulted in most of the Viet Cong casualties. For example, a *Dac Cong* outpost in the northern area of operations sighted three enemy platoons approaching the Song Ve on the night of 19 September and called for artillery and naval gunfire. A nearby Marine reconnaissance patrol observed and adjusted the fires. This particular action resulted in the death of 47 Viet Cong.[19]

On another occasion, a Marine patrol saw what appeared to be 75 ARVN troops in a position where no friendly units were supposed to be. The patrol leader

Marine Corps Photo A369612

Marines from the 1st Battalion, 7th Marines assist in the evacuation of villagers from Van Ha (1) to resettlement in Mo Duc. Many of the 700 refugees claimed that they had wanted to leave Van Ha, but had been prevented by the VC.

on the hamlets. Although a few VC had probed Company A's positions during the night, the Marine advance encountered only token opposition. Once they secured the hamlet, the Marines found Van Ha (1) to be a well-established logistic base. A granary within the hamlet held over 727 tons of rice.

Major Waller contacted the district chief and assured him that the Marines would remain in the village, if the South Vietnamese could haul the rice away. The chief agreed and provided a force of more than 8,000 workers to move the rice from Van Ha to Mo Duc, the district capital. In less than 50 hours, the South Vietnamese had removed the rice, as well as the household effects of approximately 150 families living in the village. In addition to the villagers' furniture, they gathered up the cattle, hogs, ducks, and chickens and transferred everything to the district town. Over 700 civilian refugees from Van Ha were relocated to Mo Duc where they were processed. Many of the villagers claimed that they had wanted to leave Van Ha for some time but were prevented by the VC.[21]

At this point the South Vietnamese Government decided to settle the problem of Van Ha (1), once and for all, so that it could no longer serve Communist purposes. The district chief, a Mr. Lieu, asked Major Waller to destroy the entire village. Waller's men used 13,500 pounds of explosives "to destroy a total of 554 bunkers, 123 houses, 50 caves, 130 sheds, and 125 wells, [in the process] producing 24 secondary explosions."[22]

The battalion left Van Ha (1) on the 26th and closed out Operation Golden Fleece 7-1 the next day. On the 27th, Mr. Lieu hosted a traditional Vietnamese banquet for the Marines in Mo Duc. The Vietnamese officials expressed their appreciation for what the Marines had accomplished and presented gifts to Major Waller. According to the battalion's report, more than 5,000 South Vietnamese lined the streets of Mo Duc to bid the unit farewell as the Marines boarded trucks for the return to Chu Lai.[23]*

The results of the operation were impressive both in number of enemy casualties and the amount of rice salvaged from the Communists. Marines claimed 240 enemy dead at the cost of one Marine killed and 19 wounded. The district chief estimated that over 7,000 tons of rice were harvested and kept out of the hands of the enemy. Major Waller doubted that the VC had been able to obtain more than 15 percent of the total crop before the Marines had arrived.[24] Most significantly, none of the harvesters working in rice paddies protected by the Marines had been bothered by enemy troops or tax collectors. Major Waller had nothing but praise for Mr. Lieu and his U.S. Army advisor, Major Richard A. Weaver, both of whom had cooperated fully with the Marine battalion.[25]

Lieutenant General Krulak summed up the accomplishment of the Golden Fleece operations in the following manner:

> The Golden Fleece effort by III MAF organizations is keyed to the various times when rice crops become ripe. As such it is nearly a continuous project. Golden Fleece 7-1 was a particularly good example. . . . The VC were determined to get their hands on the rice this time, and came out in the open to fight for it. . . .I believe that Golden Fleece, along with County Fair, Combined Action units and the other Revolutionary Development efforts—halting though they are—are giving the Viet Cong basic structure a hard time.[26]

---

*A few months after the Golden Fleece operation, Marines in Operation Sierra returned to Mo Duc where they again enjoyed excellent relations with the local authorities and population. Lieutenant Colonel Warren P. Kitterman, whose 2d Battalion, 7th Marines participated in the latter operation, recalled several instances of friendliness on the part of both officials and villagers. He particularly remembered the "fine food and entertainment" provided by the ARVN battalion at Mo Duc and the villagers on Christmas Eve. Kitterman related: "About midnight, after making prior arrangements with my direct support battery commander, I gave a short 'thank you' speech. I concluded by saying, 'All we need to make it a perfect Christmas Eve is for a star to appear in the east.' At that instant, five illuminating rounds popped in the east in the shape of a star. Everyone was surprised and delighted, including the battalion chaplain." LtCol Warren P. Kitterman, Comments on draft MS, dtd 16Jun78 (Vietnam Comment File).

Combined Action

The combined action program had its inception in the summer of 1965 at Phu Bai as an expedient to improve base security. The concept involved the assigning of a Marine squad to a South Vietnamese Popular Force (PF) platoon. In the early stages of the program, III MAF accepted only handpicked volunteers for combined action units. These Marines received rudimentary training in Vietnamese language, history, customs, and military and governmental organization. Initially, five combined action platoons were formed at Phu Bai. These Marines entered into the life of their assigned village and were integrated into its defense. They offered military training to the local PF platoons, while at the same time participating in civic action.[27]

In January 1966, General Walt authorized the expansion of the program. A second combined action effort was started at Da Nang, where Marine squads were paired off with the seven PF platoons stationed around the airbase. By July, III MAF had 38 combined action platoons, scattered throughout the three Marine enclaves. The number of platoons grew to 57 by the end of the year: 31 at Da Nang and 13 each at Phu Bai and Chu Lai.[28]

The combined action program, like the County Fair and the Golden Fleece operations, developed into an integral component of the Marine pacification strategy. Both Generals Walt and Krulak gave

LtGen Krulak, CGFMFPac, inspects a combined action unit on 31 December 1966. Gen Krulak was an avid supporter of the combined action concept which integrated a South Vietnamese Popular Force platoon with a Marine squad.

Marine Corps Photo A801024

the concept their unstinted support and were avid crusaders, attempting to convince MACV to expand a similar program to all of Vietnam. The Marines assembled very convincing statistics to back up their strong beliefs. A FMFPac report prepared in January 1967 observed that the 22 Vietnamese villages in the Marine TAORs that had an active combined action program for six months or longer averaged a grade of 60 percent on the III MAF pacification scale. This was a rise of nearly 20 percentage points since the combined action platoons were stationed in these villages. The report pointed out one other significant trend. It noted that the South Vietnamese PF, a home guard directly responsible to the district chief for the defense of their particular villages, was generally regarded as the poorest of all the South Vietnamese forces. According to the FMFPac study, the desertion rate from the PF was almost four times that of the ARVN. For the period August through December 1966, the report cited statistics which revealed over 39,000 PF troops had deserted, representing nearly 25 percent of the total nation-wide PF strength. During this same period there were no recorded desertions of PFs assigned to the Marine combined action units. Other figures included in the report indicated that the kill ratio of the Marine combined action platoons was 14 VC to 1 Marine or PF soldier, as contrasted with a 3 to 1 ratio for regular PF units. The report concluded:

> This tends to underscore the improved military performance that *is* possible through the melding of highly motivated professional Marines with heretofore poorly led, inadequately trained, and uninspired Vietnamese—who now are finding leaders who are qualified and who take a personal interest in them.[29]*

The rapid expansion of the combined action program did cause some problems. Although no specific billets had been allotted to the program, there were approximately 2,000 Marines assigned to combined action units. These men came directly out of the manning level of the individual infantry battalions.

As could be expected, Marine battalion commanders were often reluctant to send their best and seasoned NCOs and riflemen into the program while receiving no direct recompense in return.[30]

The necessary complexity of command and control of the combined action units was also troublesome. There were two chains of command, one Vietnamese and one American. Coordination and cooperation were the core of the entire program. Two or more combined action platoons were coordinated by a combined action company headquarters, commanded by a Marine captain, with a PF lieutenant as his deputy. The Marine battalion commander was responsible for coordinating patrol activity and combat support of combined units in his TAOR, so for practical purposes, the Marine battalion commander actually exercised operational control of these combined action units.**

Although the district chief, in effect, relinquished command of his PF units assigned to the combined action platoons, he still retained administrative responsibility. In addition, the district chief usually suggested which villages were to be assigned combined action units and made the necessary arrangements with the hamlet and village chiefs. Moreover, the district chief was in a position to undercut the program by simply transferring his PF troops out of the combined action unit.

At the platoon level, cooperation and trust were most important. A typical South Vietnamese PF platoon consisted of one officer and 37 enlisted men, organized into three 11-man infantry squads and a five-man headquarters group. A platoon was usually responsible for an entire village complex, deploying individual squads into the most important hamlets making up the village. The combined action platoon was the unit that resulted from combining a 14-man

---

*One of the most important assets of the combined action platoons was their knowledge of the local situation. Colonel Clyde D. Dean recalled that as S-3 of the 3d Battalion, 3d Marines at Da Nang in May 1966 during the political crisis the combined action platoons provided "our best on-site intelligence of who was who and where. . . . I personally felt our CAPs were our best eyes and ears around the base." Col Clyde D. Dean, Comments on draft MS, dtd 27Aug78 (Vietnam Comment File).

**Colonel Noble L. Beck, the 3d Marine Division G-3, observed that although in theory the battalion commander was to exercise operational control, "it didn't work as smoothly as stated except in those instances where the battalion was in a static situation. Most often, the infantry battalions were on the move from one area to another while the combined action units normally remained in the same location. It was not infrequent that the infantry command was called upon to come to the aid of a combined action unit with its 'tail in a crack' in a situation unknown to the infantry commander in advance, and often this found him in an awkward tactical posture for response." Col Noble L. Beck, Comments on draft MS, n.d. [Aug 78] (Vietnam Comment File).

A South Vietnamese village chief goes over patrol routes with Cpl John J. Shylo, an assistant combined action unit squad leader. The term combined action company, or CAC as seen on the oil drums, was later redesignated combined action platoon or CAP because of unpleasant connotations in the Vietnamese language.

Marine rifle squad plus a Navy corpsman, with a PF platoon. The Marine NCO squad leader became the advisor to the Vietnamese platoon leader, while each of the three Marine fire teams was assigned to an individual PF squad. Both the Vietnamese militiamen and the individual Marines soon discovered they each had something to learn from the other. While the Marines taught the PFs basic small-unit tactics and discipline, they themselves obtained knowledge of the terrain, local customs, and valuable intelligence about the enemy. When the combined action platoon functioned properly, there was a mutual exchange that was helpful to both the Americans and South Vietnamese.

The combined action platoon in the village of Binh Nghia in the Chu Lai TAOR provided an excellent example of this process at its best. Located in Binh Son District four miles south of the Chu Lai Marine base in the 1st Battalion, 7th Marines TAOR, Binh Nghia consisted of seven hamlets, three named My Hue and four called Binh Yen Noi. The entire village complex was only two miles long, enclosed on the north by an expanse of sand dunes and on the south by the Song Tra Bong. According to allied intelligence sources, two independent VC companies and one main force battalion were operating in Binh Son District. The district chief estimated that more than 750 men from Binh Nghia, alone, had left their homes to join the Viet Cong. Despite this apparent loyalty to the enemy, in June 1966 the Marines and South Vietnamese decided to establish a combined action platoon in the village.

The recommendation to establish the combined action platoon in Binh Nghia was made by the district chief. His U.S. Army advisor, Major Richard Braun, convinced General Walt that he should place a Marine squad with the PF in this sector. According to one Marine observer, the conversation between Braun and Walt went as follows:

> "If you had them [a combined action platoon] where would you put them?" Walt asked.
>
> "There's a big village not far from here. It sits along a river which the Cong use to move supplies back up into the mountains. As a matter of fact, it's just south of Chu Lai airfield. The government forces were chased out of the village a couple of years ago. A platoon of Cong live there regularly now, and sometimes a company or more come in to resupply or rest."
>
> "Why pick there to start?" Walt asked.
>
> "I didn't, sir. The district chief did. He has this outstanding police chief who's being badmouthed by some of the local politicians. These pols make the mafia look like a bunch of Trappist monks. The district chief's afraid this police chief will say the hell with it and transfer to another district. But his family's from this village and his mother still lives there. The district chief says he'll stick around if we make a play for that village. The police want some Americans along if they're going in there. They don't think too much of the local troops in this district. . . ."
>
> "I'll see that he [the police chief] gets them," Walt replied. "By the way, what's the name of that village?"
>
> "We call it Been Knee-ah, sir."[31]

On 12 June, a Marine squad led by Corporal Robert A. Beebe entered the village. They were met there by Ap Thanh Lam, the police chief mentioned by Braun in his discussion with General Walt. The local force in Binh Nghia consisted of 15 policemen and 18 PF troops, somewhat of a variance from the normal makeup of a combined action platoon. Lam and Beebe set up their headquarters in a villa that had been abandoned by a rich landowner in 1950 when the Viet Minh first entered the district. The old house was on the outskirts of Binh Yen Noi (3), the largest and southernmost hamlet of the village complex. Lam persuaded Beebe that it was too dangerous to live in the hamlets at night and that the Marines and the PFs should transform the villa into a fortified position. Corporal Beebe set the example for the South Vietnamese the first night they

Marine Corps Photo A369600
A combined action unit in a hamlet in the Chu Lai TAOR presents arms at morning colors as the South Vietnamese flag is raised. By early 1967, the Marines had established 57 combined action platoons.

were in the hamlet. After working all day erecting the fortifications, he personally led a night patrol. Although Beebe left Vietnam after only a few weeks in the village, he believed that his combined action platoon was accomplishing its mission. In his final report, he wrote:

> On June 10th, 1966 one squad of Marines from Company C, 1st Battalion, 7th Marines were picked to join the Popular Force unit at Binh Yen Noi. It is obvious to those who have initiated and followed the PF program that it has been a success. Since the Marines have begun their instructions, the confidence and skill of the PFs have risen considerably. The PFs are now a well-organized efficient combat unit. This program has also strengthened the relationship between the Marines and the PFs and civilians in the area. The effect of this had been the strengthening of the defensive posture of the area.[32]

Beebe had painted too rosy a picture. The Viet Cong were completely aware of the fact that if they allowed a Marine squad and some local militiamen to push them out of the village, their hold over the population would crumble. The morning that Beebe left the village, a VC assassination squad entered the home of Chief Lam's mother and killed Lam who had spent the night there. At the end of June, the Marines suffered their first casualty. Private First Class Lawrence L. Page, the youngest man in the squad, was killed in a Viet Cong ambush while on a night patrol.

Saddened by the deaths, the Marines were determined to stay put. Beebe's successor, Sergeant Joseph Sullivan, adopted an aggressive program. Marines and PFs conducted night patrols and established ambushes even in the My Hue hamlets north of Fort Page, as the villa was renamed after Page's death. Later in the month, five Marines and three PF troops set up an ambush on the northern bank of the Tra Bong. Apparently the Viet Cong had watched the patrol establish its position and attempted to maneuver around them to hit the ambushers from the rear. The Marine patrol leader had taken no chances and had stationed a PF soldier as a rear lookout. He saw the enemy crawling along the rice paddy dikes and quietly gave the alarm. The patrol leader turned his men around and allowed the VC to approach within 50 yards before giving the order to fire. In eight minutes, it was all over. The patrol counted 21 enemy dead, including a VC company commander and a platoon leader. There were no casualties in the combined action platoon.[33]

Throughout July and much of August, the combined action unit at Fort Page engaged in over 70 firefights and averaged almost 11 contacts a week. The Marines and their PF allies proved themselves superior to the Viet Cong in both night patrolling and fighting. By the end of August, the combined action platoon thought it had wrested control of Binh Nghia from the Viet Cong. There had been no significant contact with an enemy unit for over two weeks. According to Marine estimates, the village's pacification category had risen from the contested stage to a figure of 75 percent pacified.

Once more, however, the Viet Cong forced the Marines to reassess the situation. On the night of 14 September several Marines and PFs were out on patrol, while six of the Americans, including Sergeant Sullivan, remained at the fort with 12 PFs. Although the combined action unit had not engaged the VC for over two weeks, there were disturbing rumors that VC forces across the river had been reinforced by North Vietnamese regulars. To insure the security of the fort, Sergeant Sullivan had asked the South Vietnamese PF leader to place a seven-man detachment in the hamlet of Binh Yen Noi to protect his rear. This detachment discovered nothing unusual in the hamlet and decided to go home to bed, rather than spend the night in the cold drizzle that began to fall. Apparently the enemy had maintained close observation of the fort. A company of North Vietnamese regulars from the *409th NVA Battalion*, approximately 60 men, joined 80 Viet

Cong and crossed the Tra Bong River. Probably guided by villagers, the enemy infiltrators slipped through the hamlet of Binh Yen Noi undetected and attacked the fort from two directions. In the ensuing battle, five Americans, including Sergeant Sullivan and the Navy corpsman, were killed. The other Marine in the fort was wounded as were five of the PFs; the remaining seven PF troops held out. A reaction force from Company C, 1st Battalion, 7th Marines and the rest of the combined action force came to their rescue and the VC broke contact.*

Instead of breaking the morale of the combined action platoon, this attack strengthened the bond between the remaining Marines and the PFs. On 15 September, Colonel Snoddy offered the combined action Marines the opportunity to abandon Fort Page and to a man they elected to stay. They had gained a strong affection for Binh Nghia; it was their village and they were determined to protect it. That day the villagers held a funeral service honoring the Marines and PF troops who had died in the defense of Fort Page.

On the night of the 16th, the Viet Cong came back to Binh Nghia; this time they received an entirely unexpected reception. Apparently believing they no longer had anything to fear, they walked boldly down the hamlet's main street toward the market place. They literally bumped into a Marine PF patrol coming from the other direction. Recovering from their surprise first, the Marines and PFs opened fire and gave the alarm. In less than 10 minutes, other members of the combined action unit reinforced the patrol led by Sergeant James White, Sullivan's replacement. The enemy tried to get back to the river bank and cross, leaving a rear guard to provide covering fire. An old woman pointed out to the Marines and PFs the positions of the VC. The unit blasted the enemy rear guard trying to escape in small wicker boats. While the shooting continued, the villagers gathered on the river banks to watch the show. According to one Marine, "You would have thought it was daytime out there . . . it was incredible."[34] The combined units accounted for 10 known dead VC and un-doubtedly killed others in the water. There were no Marine or PF casualties.

The Marines in this particular combined action unit had gained a new perspective on the war. They realized there was to be no easy victory over the Viet Cong. The PFs were becoming better soldiers, but the Marines had attained something as well. They now understood the villagers and looked upon them as people to be protected and helped. One corporal put it in these words: "Hell, this is our village, it's why we're here."[35] An indication of the acceptance that the Marines had achived occurred during the last week of December. The villagers held a fair and the Marines were invited, not as guests, but as participants.

Although the Marines in Binh Nghia had achieved a modicum of success in their efforts, the Marine command was not satisfied with the overall progress of the combined action program. General Walt had hoped to establish 74 units by the end of the year, but the government had not provided enough PFs to achieve this aim. Nonetheless, the Marines believed that the combined action concept held promise for the future. General Krulak stated this belief in the following words:

> This idea has the greatest leverage of any concept yet to emerge from this war. Here is a case where the whole is greater than the sum of its parts. The Marines learn from the PF and the PF, mediocre soldiers to say the least—learn volumes from the Marines. They become skillful and dedicated units, and no hamlets protected by a combined action platoon has ever been repossessed by the Communists. . . . It [combined action] set the tone for what I honestly believe may be the key to the whole Vietnam war.[36]

Personal Response

The combined action program was important because it achieved one of the basic goals of the pacification effort, the unity of interest between the South Vietnamese villager and the individual Marine. For pacification to work in the TAORs, this same unity of interest had to be established between the regular Marine battalions and the local populace. The Marines in the regular, organized units had to realize that their mission was the protection of the people, while the Vietnamese peasant had to learn to overcome his fear of the Americans.

Generals Krulak and Walt were both aware how important attitudes were and both were interested in

---

*The VC had chosen a propitious time for their attack. Most of 1/7 was conducting Operation Fresco/Golden Fleece 7/1, while the remaining elements of the battalion were stretched thin in the Chu Lai TAOR.

means of determining the extent of the problem and developing a program that would avoid unfortunate incidents. The interest reflected by these two Marine generals created the Marine Personal Response Program during the summer of 1966. General Krulak discussed the question with the FMFPac chaplain, Captain John H. Craven, USN. In July 1966, Captain Craven assigned one of his new chaplains to be the Fleet Marine Force Personal Response Officer. His choice was Lieutenant Commander Richard McGonigal, who was not only a chaplain but also held a master's degree in sociology.*

Chaplain McGonigal arrived in Vietnam on 5 July for a brief indoctrination visit. General Walt expressed his interest in the project and offered the chaplain the full cooperation of his staff. Lieutenant Commander McGonigal decided to take a sample survey of approximately two percent of the total III MAF force and a smaller sample of the South Vietnamese who had a close association with Americans. After refining his questionnaires and interviewing techniques, McGonigal conducted the attitude survey during the first two weeks of September.

The initial sampling revealed that a large percentage of the Marines tested held negative feelings for the South Vietnamese. Only 43 percent of the Marines indicated that they liked the local population. The South Vietnamese, on the other hand, showed a more positive feeling toward the Americans. Over 70 percent of them stated that they generally liked Americans, but 46 percent declared that Americans did not like them.

Other aspects of the survey showed that individual Marines indicated a certain ambivalence toward the population, rather than an intense dislike. Most importantly, the sampling of combined action platoon Marines and their PF partners revealed an overwhelming feeling of trust and confidence in one another.

Chaplain McGonigal had accomplished a portion of his aims with the September survey. These were to determine the existing attitudes toward the Vietnamese, where the greatest problems were, and how these attitudes were acquired. He believed that he needed a much larger and more refined testing procedure before he could begin to develop a program to overcome frictions between Marines and the Vietnamese. From December 1966-January 1967, he conducted another survey, followed by a third in June 1967. Based on his intensive study of over 10 percent of the Marines assigned to III MAF, Chaplain McGonigal reached the conclusion:

> The name of the game in Vietnam is relationship. When a Marine sees the ancient Vietnamese grandmother who smiles at him with her betel nut stained ebony teeth as a *full-fledged human being*, he is ready to operate more effectively than we hoped. He becomes more careful in his use of firepower, more sensitive in dealing with refugees and a better trainer of host counterparts.[37]**

The need for Marines to remember that the Vietnamese civilians were more often victims of the war, rather than the enemy, was dramatized during the latter half of 1966 by three shocking and tragic incidents. In one, a Marine on a combat patrol during August told other members of the patrol that he intended to shoot a Vietnamese villager in order to flush out the VC. No one took the Marine seriously until he suddenly shot a farmer as he was showing

---

*Chaplain Craven observed that Personal Response had "its genesis in Exercise Silverlance in March 1965 when I succeeded in getting Chaplain Robert L. Mole assigned to the staff of the Troops Exercise Coordinator and we were able to crank some realistic problems involving local religions and customs into the Exercise . . . It was on the plane to observe this Exercise that I asked General Krulak about requesting a chaplain for FMF Pacific to work full time in this field, and so the Southeast Asia Religious Research Project was born. This young project grew . . . into the Personal Response Project." Stating that although Chaplain McGonigal was the first specific Personal Response Officer, Captain Craven noted that Chaplain Mole in the summer of 1965 started the project by beginning "first hand research in the religions, customs, and value systems of Southeast Asia." Capt John H. Craven, CHC, USN, Comments on draft MS, dtd 2Jul78 (Vietnam Comment File), hereafter Craven Comments.

**Colonel Drew J. Barrett, who assumed command of the 9th Marines in July 66 commented on the requirement for such a program: "I felt helpless and inadequate because I had little knowledge of Vietnam, its people, and its culture. As the war progressed we recognized this, and within capability tried to include treatment of these matters in training syllabi and in all orientation materials. However, especially in this kind of conflict, it was impossible to fill this big void with short-cut measures." Col Drew J. Barrett, Comments on draft MS, dtd 5May78 (Vietnam Comment File). Despite such recognition of the value of the Personal Response Project, Chaplain Craven remembered that during his three years as FMFPac Chaplain and five years as the Chaplain of the Marine Corps, "I was always walking a fine line between Marine officers on one hand who questioned the need for any such project, and chaplains on the other hand who felt that chaplains should have nothing to do with the project." Craven Comments.

his ID card. The other Marines reported the outrage when the patrol returned to base. A general court-martial found the Marine guilty of murder and sentenced him to life imprisonment and a dishonorable discharge.

One month later, another patrol, composed of eight Marines, raided a South Vietnamese hamlet. They killed five villagers and raped an 18-year-old girl. The same month, three other Marines killed an old woman and placed her body in a hay stack which they set afire. As they left the burning pyre, they discovered an elderly man who had observed their actions. They shot him and one of the Marines cut off the man's ear. All the Marines involved in these incidents were charged and faced court-martial by the end of the year.*

The response of the Marine command to these tragedies reflected General Walt's determination that they would not reoccur. On 17 November, he sent a personal message to General Westmoreland giving the full details of each incident and the actions that he had taken.

More significantly, General Walt reiterated basic guidelines to his senior commanders to prevent future outrages. He made no recriminations, but also allowed no excuses. He stated simply:

> I know that all of you are deeply concerned and are taking the actions you consider appropriate. . . . The following observations and suggestions appear to me to be worthy of your consideration. It is an oversimplification to lay the blame on the quality of leadership, at least not as a blanket indictment as it is usually employed. I believe, however, that perhaps the focus of our leadership has been too sharply concentrated on our operational problems and we may need to reorient and broaden this focus to devote more time and attention to the training of our younger, less mature leaders and to more eyeball-to-eyeball talks with all our troops. . . . We have had to rely frequently upon inexperienced noncommissioned officers in positions of great responsibility. To overcome the effects of this we need a period of intensive personal effort by our mature experienced officers and noncommissioned officers to counsel and train their juniors. Formal schools are not practical in our present tactical dispositions, but frequent informal sessions are possible and offer potentially rich

---

*In his best selling memoir, Philip Caputo, a former Marine lieutenant, described an earlier incident in 1966 when a patrol led by him killed two Vietnamese villagers. Caputo and five of his men were charged with murder. A court-martial found one of the men innocent and the charges against Caputo and the rest of the men were dropped. Philip Caputo, *A Rumor of War* (New York: Holt, Rinehart, and Winston, 1977), pp. 314-336.

> rewards. We need discussions of such fundamental subjects as are illustrated in the material published in connection with the personal response study. Recent events offer convincing evidence that the general attitude toward the Vietnamese people is manifestly poor and must be changed. There are also strong indications that we need personal attention to the responsibilities of leadership and vigorous efforts to weed out those who are ineffective. . . . In coordination with these efforts, I believe we can eliminate some of our future problems by screening out commands to separate those men whose records demonstrate their unfitness or unsuitability for retention, particularly at a time when the demands of our service call for self-discipline in a greater measure than ever before. . . .

The general continued:

> A more careful examination of our disciplinary reports and increased efforts to make our trials and punishments as prompt as we can make them, within the law, offers another area for attack against a situation that we all recognize is not going to be resolved by any one magic formula. . . .
>
> I cannot believe that our men fully understand and appreciate how disastrous their sometimes thoughtless actions can be to our efforts here. One man, through crime, or just plain wanton disregard of human dignity can undo in a few minutes the prolonged efforts of a reinforced battalion. We make propaganda for the enemy with every heedless act toward the Vietnamese as a people and as individuals. At the same time, we undo all the good that had been done. We must get this message across.[38]

Kit Carson

Although Chaplain McGonigal's 1966 survey and General Walt's message reflected some of the negative features resulting from Marine infantry units operating in populated areas, Marines more often than not demonstrated that they could work with individual South Vietnamese to bring stability to the countryside. One of the most unusual and yet successful of these attempts was the formation of special cadre made up of former VC. These men, former enemy troops, had taken advantage of the government "open arms" (Chieu Hoi) policy and rallied to the government cause.

The Marines began to use a selected few of these "ralliers" or Hoi Chanhs during the spring of 1966. In May, a group of VC surrendered to units of the 9th Marines, asking for asylum. The enemy immediately started a rumor among the people that the Marines had tortured and killed one of the ralliers by the name of Ngo Van Bay. Colonel Simmons, the regimental commander, asked Bay and two of his

Former Viet Cong who defected to the government attend an indoctrination class. The Marines recruited several of these "ralliers" or Hoi Chanhs as "Kit Carson scouts" to accompany Marine units in the field.

A former VC (right), now a Kit Carson scout assigned to the 1st Battalion, 26th Marines in the An Hoa sector, points out a possible enemy hiding place. These former VC were not only a valuable tactical asset, but served to further allied propoganda.

Marine Corps Photo A370000

compatriots to return to the village and put the rumor to rest for once and for all. The three former Viet Cong agreed and, according to Simmons, this, in a small way, was the beginning of the program.[39]

Other Marine units at Da Nang, and eventually in all of the TAORs, started using former VC as scouts, interpreters, and intelligence agents. By October 1966, the program was established on a permanent, official basis. General Nickerson, the commanding general of the 1st Marine Division, who was part-Indian and a Western history buff, designated the former VC working with the Marines as "Kit Carson scouts." He selected the name because the Hoi Chanhs working with the Marines were good scouts, in the tradition of Kit Carson, the famed frontiersman, Indian agent, and soldier.*[40]

---

*The name of Kit Carson was doubly appropriate since Carson had served with Lieutenant Archibald Gillespie, USMC, during his secret mission to California for President Polk in 1846. According to General Nickerson, another reason for the designation Kit Carson was to "provide the initials KC as counter to VC." LtGen Herman Nickerson, Jr., Comments on draft MS, dtd 1May78 (Vietnam Comment File).

From October to December 1966, III MAF credited the Kit Carson scouts with the killing of 47 VC, the capture of 16 weapons, and the discovery of 18 mines and tunnels.[41] The scouts repeatedly proved themselves a valuable tactical asset. For example, in November, one scout attached to the 1st Marines at Da Nang led a Marine company at night over unfamiliar terrain to an objective area, resulting in the surprise and capture of 15 Viet Cong.

The scouts provided more than just tactical capability. They were also a valuable propaganda tool. Villagers were much more ready to listen to them than to representatives of the government. During a December County Fair one scout gave a speech to the gathered villagers and evoked applause from his audience several times. According to the Marine report, the scout then:

> ... ventured into the VCC/VCS compound and spoke to them.... A definite response was observed by the facial expressions of some of the individuals. Attention seemed to follow the Kit Carson Scout wherever he went, including an apparent interest generated among the ARVN troops who participated in the operation.[42]

Psychological Warfare

The Kit Carson program was only part of an intensive psychological warfare campaign that III MAF had begun in the latter half of 1966. In fact, it was an officer in the III MAF Psychological Warfare Section, Captain Stephen A. Luckey, who recommended the formal implementation of the Kit Carson project and it was the Psychological Warfare Section that developed the Kit Carson SOP. The section had consisted of only Luckey and a senior staff NCO until 4 August, when General Walt assigned Colonel Robert R. Read as the psychological warfare officer. In September the section became a special staff section, directly responsible to the III MAF Chief of Staff. According to the force order establishing the section, Colonel Read had four basic missions:

1. to reduce the combat efficiency of the VC;
2. to further the effort of the South Vietnamese Government in establishing control by attempting to modify attitudes and behavior of special audiences;
3. to coordinate psychological operations with civic action programs;
4. and finally to obtain the assistance and cooperation of the South Vietnamese villagers.[43]

General Walt did not expect Colonel Read to accomplish miracles, but he wanted "an increased emphasis on psychological operations by all III MAF commands." Colonel Read was to coordinate the III MAF efforts within the command and with the ARVN, MACV, and U.S. Information Agency and its South Vietnamese counterpart. Read remembered that his two initial problems were that "There were no T/O billets for PsyWar personnel and there were no Marines trained in PsyWar operation." He and his small staff took several steps to overcome these difficulties. They persuaded III MAF to direct its subordinate organizations to establish psychological warfare sections and instituted monthly meetings of PsyWar personnel. Moreover, III MAF requested Headquarters, Marine Corps "to provide school trained PsyWar personnel in replacement drafts, which they did." On 18 September, Read obtained operational control of the U.S. Army's 24th Psychological Operations Company's two detachments in I Corps, one at Da Nang and the other in Quang Ngai. Believing that the physical separation seriously hampered the company, Read consolidated both detachments at Da Nang and established there in October a Psychological Warfare Operations Center. By the end of the year, III MAF had a coordinated program that included the preparation of leaflets and broadcasts aimed at the enemy forces, as well as the screening of Hoi Chanh's for employment as Kit Carson scouts. According to Read, the increase in former VC rallying to the Vietnamese Government through the Chieu Hoi program was in part due to the new emphasis on psychological warfare operations.[44]

Civic Action

The people needed more than just words to persuade them to join in the national effort against the Communists. An integral part of the Marine pacification campaign was its civic action program, aimed at improving the lot of the Vietnamese peasant as well as giving him a reason to support the government. According to Brigadier General Jonas M. Platt, General Walt's Chief of Staff during most of 1966, an effective civic action program had to fulfill certain requirements: it had to meet not only the needs of the people but involve them; the Marines should listen to what the people wanted and then offer them material and advice; work had to be done by the populace themselves.[45]

SSgt Gerald E. Anderson from the 3d Tank Battalion assists a Vietnamese farmer to put up a windmill to pump water from the Song Cau Do. Another Marine, Sgt Enos S. Lambert, Jr. (hidden by the windmill except for his arm), helped with the project. The 3d Tank Battalion had a well-coordinated civic action program in the Hoa Tho Village complex south of Da Nang.

Marines were to ensure that the Vietnamese Government received the credit for the various projects. Provincial, district, and village officials had to be involved from the beginning in both the planning and execution of any project. The entire effort was dependent upon coordination with the Vietnamese Government and U.S. civilian agencies so that the projects had the desired impact upon the local populace.⁴⁶*

---

*General Wallace M. Greene, Jr., the Commandant of the Marine Corps during this period, observed that the civic action program in Vietnam "was made possible by a *tremendous* effort mounted in the U.S. to collect medicine, clothing, soap and food. The National Junior Chamber of Congress was largely responsible in the success of the program which resulted in *trainloads* of contributions from manufacturers and the public proceeding to West Coast ports to be loaded on government transports and ships, e.g. aircraft carriers and civilian freighters, for movement to South Vietnam." Gen Wallace M. Greene, Jr., Comments on draft MS, dtd 5May78 (Vietnam Comment File).

The activities of Lieutenant Colonel William R. Corson's 3d Tank Battalion in the Hoa Tho village complex, on the northern bank of the Cau Do River, provided an excellent example of a coordinated civic action program. In December, the battalion's civic action team sponsored a farmers' meeting in the hamlet of Phong Bac. The village chief of Hoa Tho and the hamlet chiefs participated in the event; over 80 farmers attended. They discussed raising live stock and a representative from the U.S. Army 29th Civil Affairs Company distributed seed to the farmers. After the meeting, the village chief took the occasion to tell the people of the hamlet about the Marines. He stressed that the Marines were guests of the Government of Vietnam and that they were only trying "to help the Vietnamese people in the struggle for freedom and fight against Communism."⁴⁷

By the end of 1966, the Marines had accumulated impressive statistics reflecting the assistance they had furnished to the South Vietnamese. Marine units entered hamlets and villages 25,000 times during

A Navy corpsman with the 1st Battalion, 11th Marines at Chu Lai treats an old man's infected foot. Medical assistance was one of the most popular and effective of the Marine Corps civic action efforts.

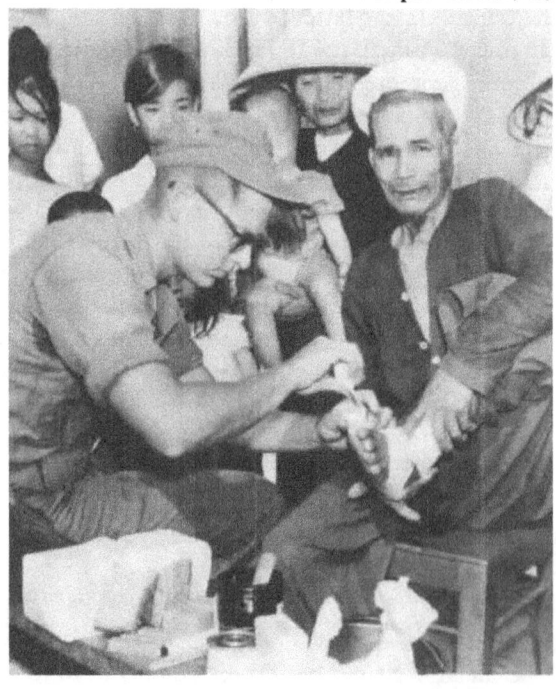

the year for the express purpose of conducting civic action. Navy corpsman and doctors attached to the Marines provided medical treatment for over a million South Vietnamese and trained more than 500 Vietnamese to assist in meeting the health needs of the population. Even more significantly, South Vietnamese villagers and Marines working together, completed 1,100 construction projects. The Marines had supported schools, assisted in the resettlement of victims of the war, provided basic items such as soap and food, and generally attempted to make life somewhat easier for the civilian population, caught in the webs of war. To the Marines, civic action was more than just a giveaway, but a weapon designed specifically to win the people to the government cause.[48] One young Marine officer, First Lieutenant Marion (Sandy) L. Kempner, described the intermingling of the anti-guerrilla war and the civic action program in the following terms:

> We have been doing a lot of work in the villages lately, of the community development type, so it looks as though I will never get away from the Peace Corps days. We must be really messing up these people's minds: by day we treat their ills and fix up their children and deliver their babies and by night, if we receive fire from the general direction of their hamlet, fire generally will reach them albeit not intentionally; they must really be going around in circles. But I guess that just points up the strangeness of this war. We have two hands, both of which know what the other is doing, but does the opposite anyway, and in the same obscure and not too reasonable manner—it all makes sense, I hope.[49]

The I Corps Joint Coordinating Council

The Marines never presumed that they had the sole solution for "winning the hearts and minds" of the people. They were among the first to recognize that they needed assistance from the other U.S. agencies in Vietnam, civilian as well as military, and from the Vietnamese themselves. The U.S. Army 29th Civil Affairs Company had arrived in June 1966 to furnish expert assistance to the Marines in their relations with the South Vietnamese civilians. Long before that, General Walt had recognized the need for coordination. In August 1965, he had contacted Marcus Gordon, the chief of the U.S. Operations Mission for I Corps at that time, and suggested the formation of an interagency clearing committee. The result of his efforts was the creation of the I Corps Joint Coordinating Council (JCC). Eventually, representatives from American civilian agencies, Marines, and the South Vietnamese I Corps command met weekly to try to give unified direction to the allied civic action effort.

Although the spring political crisis temporarily halted the functions of the council, it began to meet on a regular basis once again in July 1966. By this time the JCC had sponsored several subordinate committees designed to meet specific problems: public health, psychological warfare, roads, commodities distribution, port affairs, and education, and by the end of the month, the council was prepared to expand its activities even further.

The I Corps Joint Coordinating Committee which was established to provide liaison and direction to the various U.S. and South Vietnamese military and civilian agencies' assistance programs, poses for a group picture in August 1966. LtCol Donald L. Evans, the recorder of the committee, is third from the left in the back row, and MajGen Lewis B. Robertshaw, Commanding General, 1st Marine Aircraft Wing, the chairman of the committee, is fourth from right in the front row.

Marine Corps Photo A801957 (LtCol R.J. O'Leary)

On 3 August, Mr. Gordon suggested that the JCC should concern itself with all of I Corps. He observed that, until now, the cities of Da Nang and Hue, and the Marines TAORs had received most of the council's attention. He stated that the JCC, as the overseeing body, could function more significantly if it considered all projects in the context of all of I Corps. Major General Robertshaw, Commanding General of the 1st MAW and permanent chairman of the JCC, agreed with Gordon's remarks and suggested that the group should hold one meeting a month in a different provincial capital to give the South Vietnamese provincial officials and their American advisors the opportunity to discuss their particular problems with the JCC.[50] The JCC concurred with General Robertshaw's suggestion. For the rest of the year, it held its monthly meeting in a different provincial capital, on a rotating basis.

In addition, the JCC encouraged the provinces to establish their own committees to coordinate Revolutionary Development efforts at the provincial level. By the end of December, three provincial committees had been formed. Although the provincial committees mirrored the organization, mission, and functions of the I Corps JCC, they were not subordinate to the larger council, but operated independently. The important aspect of both the I Corps JCC and the provincial committees was that they provided a vehicle for the coordination of the military and civilian aspects of pacification, and at the time the only such organizations at the corps and province levels in South Vietnam.

CHAPTER 15
Pacification, the Larger Perspective

Pacification Receives Priority — Reorganization and Support of Revolutionary Development — Measurements of Progress

---

Pacification Receives Priority

The actual pacification gains in 1966 were relatively modest. Although the government had hoped to have placed Revolutionary Development teams in over 300 villages by the end of the year, the Vietnamese were only to fulfill approximately one-third of this goal. General Westmoreland estimated that the percentage of the South Vietnamese population that lived in relative security had risen from 50 percent to approximately 60 percent, due largely to the presence of American troops, rather than to any effort on the part of the Vietnamese themselves.[1] The major element of change in pacification during 1966 was the redirection and new emphasis given to the entire concept by MACV and the South Vietnamese.

The February Honolulu Conference established six primary aims to be accomplished by the end of 1966. Four of these pertained to defeating the enemy's main force units and to opening up lines of communication in the country. The other two applied to the "other war" being waged in the countryside. The allies were to expand secured areas and the government was to complete the pacification of high priority areas.[2]

In April 1966, Deputy Ambassador William Porter established a special task force to determine American interagency priorities to support the South Vietnamese Revolutionary Development Program.

President Johnson (center of picture with back to camera) meets informally with South Vietnamese leaders and Adm Ulysses S. Grant Sharp, Commander-in-Chief, Pacific Command, in Honolulu during February 1966. Seated to the left of the President is the South Vietnamese Chief of State, Nguyen Van Thieu, and on the right is Prime Minister Nguyen Cao Ky. Adm Sharp is on the sofa facing the President. MACV was a subordinate unified command under Adm Sharp.

Marine Corps Historical Center

This group made its report in July and in its introduction declared:

> After some 15 months of rapidly growing U.S. military and political commitment to offset a major enemy military effort, the RVN has been made secure against the danger of military conquest, but at the same time it has been subjected to a series of stresses which threaten to thwart U.S. policy objectives. . . .[3]

The task force stated that the lack of success was due to a variety of reasons, but in essence, should be attributed to the fact that the South Vietnamese had provided relatively little protection for the hamlets. In its report, the committee made 35 recommendations, which it divided into 16 "highest priority" tasks, followed by 10 "high priority" tasks, and finally a nine-point list of lesser priority programs. One Defense Department historian noted that in at least one of the 35 different priorities one could fit nearly every program and policy then pursued in Vietnam.[4] Although the committee's report lacked a degree of focus, many of its recommendations were accepted. One of these was the formation of still another study group to examine the roles and missions of each of the military and paramilitary organizations in Vietnam.

In July, the U.S. Mission Council directed a staff member, Army Colonel George D. Jacobson, to head an interagency committee which was to study the entire problem of Revolutionary Development. The committee submitted its findings and recommendations to Deputy Ambassador Porter on 24 August. The study group warned that the Revolutionary Development cadres were not a panacea in themselves. According to the study, Revolutionary Development demanded a radical reform within both the Government of Vietnam and its armed forces for success. The committee noted that such a radical change in the government and armed forces was very unlikely, unless the U.S. military and civilian officials exerted strong pressure on the Vietnamese at a very high level. Jacobson's group emphasized that the goal of the Americans in Vietnam was the establishment of a South Vietnamese Government which was capable of gaining popular support and winning the war. The committee commented that although American forces should have the destruction of the enemy's main forces as their primary mission, U.S. troops could join with local ARVN and paramilitary forces in clearing operations to support Revolutionary Development. The study group specifically cited the Marine combined action and County Fair programs as activities to be encouraged.

The roles and mission group placed major emphasis upon changing the role of the Vietnamese Army. Analyzing the course of the war, the study panel noted that the ARVN had played only a minor part in brunting the challenge of the North Vietnamese and Viet Cong regular forces. On the other hand, most of the war against the local guerrillas in the countryside had fallen upon the shoulders of the regional and popular force militiamen, who, by themselves, were unable to meet the challenge. The committee strongly urged that the entire orientation of the regular South Vietnamese Army be directed toward providing security for revolutionary development. Through coordination with the local government forces, the Army could conduct aggressive small-unit operations, night and day, in and around government-controlled hamlets and villages, as well as in areas to be pacified. The report called for an overhaul of the South Vietnamese Army command system in relation to pacification. According to the group's recommendations, most of the ARVN combat battalions should be assigned to area commanders for extended periods of time and Army division commanders should not be permitted to withdraw those battalions during that specified assignment. The aim was to remove the division commanders from the Revolutionary Development chain of command. It was the belief of the study group members that ARVN division commanders and staffs were preoccupied with the large-unit war and would not or could not give revolutionary development the attention it required.[5]

Although General Westmoreland disagreed with the recommendation to take away the division commanders' responsibility for pacification, he, too, was arriving at the opinion that the South Vietnamese Army should be reoriented toward support of Revolutionary Development. In fact, this was to be the main thrust of the U.S.-South Vietnamese Combined Campaign Plan for 1967. The MACV staff had started its planning for 1967 during the spring of 1966 and by midsummer most of the concepts had been worked out. On 7 July, the Mission Council authorized General Westmoreland to establish a planning group to coordinate U.S. planning for Revolutionary Development and to participate with

U.S. Secretary of State Dean Rusk (center of picture) confers in Saigon with South Vietnamese Prime Minister Ky and U.S. Ambassador to South Vietnam, Henry Cabot Lodge, Jr. Ambassabor Lodge was a strong proponent of an active pacification program.

the Vietnamese in forming the 1967 Revolutionary Development plan.

On 10 August, U. S. Army Major General John C. Tillson III, the MACV J-3, reported to the Mission Council on the progress of the planning effort for 1967. He noted that the MACV concept was coordinated closely with the Jacobson Task Force on Roles and Missions. General Tillson told the Council members that the American staff proposed to the Vietnamese that the ARVN assume the primary mission of direct support for Revolutionary Development, while U.S. military forces met the threat of the VC/NVA main forces and carried offensive operations into the enemy's base areas. According to Tillson, General Westmoreland had already reached an agreement with General Vien of the Vietnamese General Staff that the ARVN would devote at least half of its effort in the I, II, and III Corps areas to direct support of Revolutionary Development. In the Mekong Delta, or IV Corps, where there were no U.S. troops at the time, the South Vietnamese Army was to allocate at least 25 percent of its force to pacification. General Tillson indicated that greater emphasis on the pacification program on the part of the Vietnamese Army would require some changes of South Vietnamese attitudes.[6]

General Westmoreland summed up the entire concept of the strategy that the allied forces were to follow in a message to Admiral Sharp on 26 August. He stated that American forces would provide the shield behind which the South Vietnamese could shift their troops in direct support of Revolutionary Development. The MACV commander declared, "Our strategy will be one of a general offensive with maximum practical support to area and population security in further support of Revolutionary Development."[7] Although emphasizing Revolutionary Development, General Westmoreland continued to stress that American forces, in coordination with the Vietnamese, had to take the fight to the enemy "by attacking his main forces and invading his base areas."[8]* He declared that there could be no Revolutionary Development unless the

---

*General Greene, the Marine Corps Commandant during this period, observed in his comments that Westmoreland's strategy as outlined in the message to Admiral Sharp was "*Still* the search and destroy concept." Greene believed that the South Vietnamese Armed Forces at the time were unable on their own to support Revolutionary Development and that "Westmoreland's 'shield' should have been established on the perimeter of secured areas and great effort devoted to bringing the people into the national fold. . . .The goal should have been positive local security for the population in the villages and hamlets," and that not enough U.S. forces were providing area security. Gen Wallace M. Greene, Jr., Comments on draft MS, dtd 5May78 (Vietnam Comment File).

enemy's main force units were prevented from gaining access to the populated areas. In an appendage to the message, Ambassador Lodge indicated his concurrence with the overall MACV strategy, although stressing more than Westmoreland the importance of pacification. The Ambassador wrote:

> After all, the main purpose of defeating the enemy through offensive operations against his main forces and bases must be to provide the opportunity through Revolutionary Development to get at the heart of the matter, which is the population of RVN.[9]

By this time, the combined planning for 1967 was well under way. On 17 September, the MACV and the South Vietnamese staffs published the first draft of the Combined Campaign Plan and submitted it for staffing and coordination. During the following week, representatives from both Vietnamese and American commands visited each of the corps areas and presented copies of the draft plan to the Vietnamese Corps commanders and the American component commands. By the first week in October, all echelons of the Vietnamese and MACV chain of command had commented on the overall plan. In the interim, the Joint U.S. Agency Planning Group, in coordination with General Thang's ministry, had designated the four national priority areas and developed the general guidelines for Revolutionary Development in 1967.[10]* After incorporating these concepts, as well as the comments from the Vietnamese and American field commanders, the final version of the plan was prepared and on 7 November, General Westmoreland and General Vien, as Chief of the Vietnamese Joint General Staff, signed the document in a formal ceremony.

The signing of the combined plan was only the beginning of the real work in forming the strategy for the next year. Much of this burden fell upon the major subordinate American and South Vietnamese commanders who had to prepare their own plans in accordance with the new guidelines. The combined plan's reemphasis on pacification, redirecting the Vietnamese Army from search and destroy operations to the support of Revolutionary Development, caused further complications. As a result, the military planners had to take into consideration the provincial Revolutionary Development programs which had yet to be completed. On 14 November, General Thang, accompanied by members of his staff and both American civilian and military advisors, began to visit each of the 44 provinces to review and approve provincial Revolutionary Development plans.

One week later, General Westmoreland briefed the Mission Council on the allied objectives as outlined in the new plans. He explained that the primary mission of the Vietnamese Armed Forces was to support the Revolutionary Development activities, with particular emphasis upon the national priority areas. American forces were to reinforce the Vietnamese Army, but destruction of the Viet Cong and NVA main force and base areas was their primary mission. According to the plan, there was to be no clear-cut division of responsibility. ARVN forces would still conduct search and destroy missions while the American forces would continue to provide direct support and assistance to Revolutionary Development activities.

The plan contained two significant innovations. It required the Vietnamese and American subordinate commands to prepare supporting plans designed specifically to accomplish the objectives of the various provincial Revolutionary Development plans. The combined plan also required quarterly reports which would indicate progress in achieving these goals.[11]

On 20 December, General Thang had completed the review of most of the provincial plans. With the reception of the various subordinate campaign plans, on 29 December, General Westmoreland signed a combined MACV/JGS directive which required the preparation of sector security plans to coordinate military support of Revolutionary Development in each province. This directive was published the next month. By the end of the year, the Vietnamese general staff announced that 40 to 50 ARVN battalions were to provide security for the pacification effort in the selected priority areas.

South Vietnamese mobile training teams had already been established to instruct ARVN battalions in Revolutionary Development. These teams

---

*The national priority areas remained much the same as they had been during 1966, although there was some expansion in all of the corps areas with the exception of ICTZ. There was to be no overall Revolutionary Development GVN Plan for 1967. Instead the Ministry of Revolutionary Development, assisted by the Joint U.S. Agency Planning Group, was to develop detailed guidelines for provincial RD plans. Each province then was to develop its individual plan for Revolutionary Development. The aggregate of the 44 provincial plans was to constitute the Vietnamese Government's RD plan.

were to indoctrinate the South Vietnamese troops with a positive attitude toward the population as well as understanding of the pacification mission. All Vietnamese maneuver battalions, with the exception of the general reserve, were slated to receive this training.

Reorganization and Support of Revolutionary Development

Throughout the latter half of 1966, the Americans and South Vietnamese continued to adjust and examine their pacification organizations and concepts, while still planning for 1967. General Westmoreland, in a message to Admiral Sharp, explained that Revolutionary Development goals and supporting plans were nonexistent when the 1966 combined plan was developed. He noted that in the period from March to December 1966 goals were changed three times. He declared that the 1966 military buildup provided the necessary security which permitted American and South Vietnamese commands to turn their attention toward Revolutionary Development.[12] The general observed that very often Revolutionary Development had not functioned properly because of a lack of command interest, but he believed that with the renewed emphasis upon pacification since July, "the overall organization appears to be functioning more effectively."[13]

One of the basic changes that the South Vietnamese made during the year was to expand General Thang's authority. On 12 July, his title was changed from Minister for Revolutionary Development to Commissioner-General for Revolutionary Development. The new title included responsibility for the Ministries of Public Works, Agriculture, and Administration in addition to his own ministry. Two months later, his authority was expanded again; on 23 September he became Assistant to the Chief, Joint General Staff for Territorial Affairs and Pacification. General Thang still retained control of Revolutionary Development, but had gained the additional responsibility for the development of military policy in support of Revolutionary Development. His new powers also made him responsible for the training, disposition, and employment of the South Vietnamese Regional and Popular Forces.

The purpose of the reorganizations was to provide the South Vietnamese with a centrally directed pacification program which could respond to local needs. General Thang organized Revolutionary Development councils on district, province, and corps levels. The chairman of each district council automatically became a member of his provincial council. In like fashion, the chairman of each succeeding council became a member of the next higher level council. General Thang served as Secretary General of the National Central Council and the Revolutionary Development Ministry was the executive agency of the National Council. On each level, the military commander who was responsible for overall security was also a council member, thus integrating the military and civilian aspects of pacification.

During this period, General Westmoreland also modified his 1966 plans to include stronger support for Revolutionary Development. On 20 July, the MACV commander issued a directive outlining the planning programs for his staff. The order, in no uncertain terms, stated that all MACV concepts and plans ". . . must be closely integrated with and support the National Revolutionary Development Program."[14] General Westmoreland noted in his 26 August message to Admiral Sharp that his Southwest Monsoon Planning Directive for the period 1 May through 31 October 1966, which supplemented the 1966 combined plan, required general security and support of Revolutionary Development. Although the overall strategy was to contain the enemy through spoiling attacks against his main force units, the American command was to use all available remaining units for area and population security in support of pacification. The MACV commander declared that all had not gone as planned:

> The threat of the enemy forces (VC and NVA) has been of such magnitude that fewer friendly troops could be devoted to general area security and support of Revolutionary Development than visualized at the times our plans were prepared for the period.[15]

In the other supplemental plan for 1966, the Northeast Monsoon Campaign Plan covering the period 1 November 1966 to 1 May 1967, General Westmoreland intended to continue a general offensive "with maximum practical support of . . . Revolutionary Development."[16] He visualized that a large number of American maneuver battalions would be committed to TAOR operations. Their missions were to encompass base security as well as support of Revolutionary Development. The American forces were to conduct numerous patrols throughout their TAORs, while at the same time maintaining an active civic action program. U.S. troops were to work in close association with ARVN and the local militia, bolstering the South Vietnamese combat effectiveness. Westmoreland believed that American division commanders, working in close association with their ARVN counterparts, would be able to influence the South Vietnamese to pay more attention to pacification.[17]

Throughout the remainder of the year, General Westmoreland periodically reported on the continuing participation of American troops in support of the pacification program. On 16 September, he informed Admiral Sharp that during the period 28 August-3 September, 73 U.S. battalion days were devoted to pacification. He indicated that he planned to employ as many as half of the American infantry battalions to support pacification in their respective TAORs.[18] On 19 September, he told Ambassador Lodge that approximately 40 percent of the U.S. forces were engaged in providing area security, while the other 60 percent were involved in offensive operations against main force units.[19] A few weeks later, Westmoreland indicated to Admiral Sharp that although units with the priority mission of security would be employed against enemy main force troops, they would not be committed out of their TAORs for extended periods of time.[20] General Westmoreland believed the basic contribution of the American forces was their success against regular enemy units, and he contended that this success permitted the development of plans to assign the South Vietnamese Army to Revolutionary Development protection in 1967.[21]

The most important changes in the U.S. pacification organization were to be made in the civilian organization in South Vietnam. For some time, senior American officials had believed that the American civilian apparatus in support of South Vietnamese Revolutionary Development needed better coordination and direction. In mid-August, Presidential advisor Robert W. Komer prepared a memorandum entitled "Giving a New Thrust to Pacification," in which he proposed three alternative means of providing central direction to the pacification effort. These were:

> Alternative one—Put Porter in charge of all advisory and pacification activities, including the military.

> Alternative two—Unifying the civilian agencies into a single civilian chain of command, and strengthen the military internally—but leave civilian and military separate;

> Alternative three—Assign responsibility for pacification to Westmoreland and MACV, and put the civilians in the field under his command.[22]*

The significance of these proposals was that alternatives two and three foreshadowed the actual changes that were to occur. At the Manila Conference, the South Vietnamese leaders vowed their intent to commit ARVN forces to clear and hold operations in support of Revolutionary Development. Shortly afterwards, Secretaries McNamara and Rusk sent a joint message to Ambassador Lodge directing him to consolidate U.S. civilian support of Revolutionary Development under one office.

According to the authors of the *Pentagon Papers*, "this cable was not repeated to Saigon until after the Manila Conference; presumably in the intervening period, the President had a chance to talk to Lodge and Westmoreland about the matter, since they were both at Manila. . . ."[23] The President arrived in the Philippines on 23 October. The seven-nation conference (the United States, New Zealand, Australia, Thailand, Republic of Vietnam, Republic of the Philippines, and Republic of Korea) took place on 24-25 October.[24]

One month later, Ambassador Lodge announced the formation of the Office of Civil Operations (OCO). This office, as an Embassy activity, was to direct all American civilian support of Revolutionary Development. The deputy director of USAID in South Vietnam, L. Wade Lathram, became the first director of the new organization. One of the new

---

*In its comments, the Center of Military History observed that Presidential advisor Komer had agitated for increased support of pacification long before his August memorandum. Several U.S. civilian agencies, specifically the Agency for International Development, the U.S. Information Agency, and the Central Intelligence Agency, "had a stake in some aspect of the pacification process [in Vietnam], and it was the lack of focus of their efforts as well as those of the U.S. military that eventually prompted the President to integrate civil and military support of pacification under Westmoreland and to appoint Komer as Westmoreland's deputy for Pacification." CMH, Comments on draft MS, dtd 17May78 (Vietnam Comment File). For a detailed study of the reorganization of the pacification program, see: Thomas W. Scoville, "Reorganizing for Pacification Support," MS (to be published by CMH).

features of the reorganization was the appointment of a regional director to each of the four corps areas, with full authority over all American civilians in his respective region and responsible directly to Lathram.

Lathram's organization was to last only a few months. In May 1967, Presidential advisor Komer's third alternative was adopted. General Westmoreland assumed full control of both the American civilian and military pacification effort. Komer became General Westmoreland's Deputy for Civil Operations and Revolutionary Development Support (CORDS), with the rank of ambassador, and assumed full responsibility for the entire program.

Measurements of Progress

Since 1964, MACV had issued a monthly report, which attempted to depict in map form the status of pacification in South Vietnam. The map showed areas under five categories: 1. pacified; 2. undergoing pacification; 3. cleared of significant VC military units; 4. controlled by neither GVN nor the VC; and, 5. controlled by the VC. Although the American command together with the Embassy made minor modifications in format during 1965 and early 1966, Washington authorities had serious reservations about the objectivity and accuracy of the pacification reporting system.[25]

Independently, the Marine Corps developed its own criteria for pacification in the I Corps TAORs. In February 1966, General Walt inaugurated a reporting system which required subordinate commands to submit a monthly analysis of the degree of pacification in each village in its area of operations. The analysis was made on the basis of five general progress indicators:

1. Destruction of enemy units
2. Destruction of enemy infrastructure
3. GVN establishment of security
4. GVN establishment of local government
5. Degree of development of New Life Program

Each indicator was given a value of 20 points, with 100 points for the entire system. Each general criteria included a further breakdown. Under the heading of "Establishment of Local Government," there were the following subdivisions:

    a. Village chief and council in office . . . . 4 points
    b. Village chief residing in village . . . . 3 points
    c. Hamlet chiefs and councils in office . . . . . . 4 points
    d. Hamlet chiefs residing in hamlet . . . . 4 points
    e. Psychological operations and information program established . . . . 3 points
    f. Minimum social and administrative organization . . . . 2 points
    TOTAL . . . . 20 points[26]

Each component of the system was dependent on the other, providing a balance to the total picture. No great achievement in the category "Establishment of Local Government" could be expected unless advances had also been made in the first category, "Destruction of Enemy Units." A high score in "Establishment of New Life Program Development" would only be possible if it were accompanied by gains in security and the establishment of local government apparatus in the villages. A score of 60 points for a village indicated that a "firm GVN/US influence" had been established, and if a village attained the mark of 80 points, it could be considered pacified.

The formulation of the Marine Corps indices of progress was to have an impact that extended beyond the confines of I Corps. In Washington, the Administration had established an interdepartmental committee, headed by George Allen of the Central Intelligence Agency, to come up with a common denominator to measure progress. The Allen study group visited III MAF in May and borrowed freely from the Marine system in preparing its own measurement indices. The result was the Hamlet Evaluation System (HES). After a field test in South Vietnam, the U.S. Mission Council, on 13 December, approved the implementation of HES throughout the country as soon as practical.[27]

Although the Allen concept had some very striking similarities to the Marine evaluation system, there were also some basic differences. The most important of these were the assigned report originators and the primary units to be measured. In the Marine report, the Marine field commander attempted to grade the pacification progress of each village in his TAOR. On the other hand, the HES report was made by the U.S. district advisor in conjunction with the South Vietnamese authorities; the American advisor and his Vietnamese counterpart attempted to evaluate each individual hamlet within their district.

There were other differences between the two reporting systems. HES utilized a letter grading procedure to measure the rate of pacification progress, as compared to the Marine numerical designation.

The HES grades ran from A to E with an A-rated hamlet indicating the highest degree of pacification. Yet, according to one Marine Corps source, both evaluation reports eventually complemented one another and told much the same story.[28]

Both reports were attempting to measure what to many was unmeasurable: how to quantify security, or how to give a numerical rating or letter grade to a man's devotion to a cause. Marine staff officers raised these same questions. At a 3d Marine Division briefing in April 1967, Lieutenant Colonel Edward R. McCarthy, the division civil affairs officer, observed:

> We are required to furnish monthly, a report on the pacification progress of villages located in areas in which we operate.... As you can see, it requires a good deal of detailed information about each village and assigns a weight to each item. The total apparently gives a rating of pacification progress. This bothers us a good deal because it is difficult for us to obtain accurate data and the report is only a best estimate on our part. In many cases the score does not represent the real situation. Additionally, there is at least an inference that we are engaged in pacification operations in those villages upon which we report. In most cases this is not true; we are merely providing a modicum of security and conducting some military civic action. We are not equipped, for example, to remove the VC infrastructure, the key element of any pacification operation. We understand that a great deal of credence is placed in this report and that it was the forerunner of the even more detailed hamlet evaluation report which must now be completed every month by subsector and sector advisors. We recognize the pressures for quantifying this information but we hope that those at higher echelons are fully aware of the problems that are inherent in such an approach.[29]

The briefer's remarks placed the measurement reports in perspective. Both evaluation systems were useful tools; they provided American and South Vietnamese commanders and officials with an educated guess about where problems existed and where progress had been made; but the emphasis is on the word "guess." Both reports attempted to establish rational criteria to indicate the status of each village or hamlet. What could not be assessed was the fact that an individual's sense of security and loyalty was not necessarily dependent upon appeals to reason, but also depended upon emotional and psychological factors. The reports were able to furnish general trends in a given area, but could not be an absolute replica of reality, and indeed in most cases were inflated.[30] One Marine general noted, "There are various indices by which a hamlet is judged 'secured' or 'pacified': one of the most pragmatic

Marine Corps Photo A188021

LtCol Warren P. Kitterman, Commanding Officer, 2d Battalion, 7th Marines, presents a gift to an elder of a Vietnamese hamlet in the Chu Lai sector. Progress in pacification depended very heavily on the presence of the Marine battalions.

and useful is whether or not the chief sleeps in his hamlet at night."[31]

Much of the pacification program depended on whether the hamlet or village chief backed it and whether he felt secure in his position. Lieutenant Colonel Warren P. Kitterman, the commander of the 2d Battalion, 7th Marines, remembered that one hamlet chief told him: "I believe in what you are doing and will cooperate in every way; however, if I openly endorse your presence, what happens to me when you are gone?" The Marine battalion departed Chu Lai for Da Nang in early 1967 and Kitterman recalled: "The chief reminded me of what he had said, with a smile on his face. I understood."[32] This incident in microcosm illustrated the mecurial quality of pacification progress.

PART VII
SUPPORTING THE TROOPS

CHAPTER 16

Marine Aviation in 1966

Wing Organization and Expansion—The Pilot Shortage—Marine Aircraft: The New and the Old—Relations with the Seventh Air Force—Marine Air Control Systems—Air Defense—Air Operations

---

Wing Organization and Expansion

The 1st Marine Aircraft Wing was a widely dispersed organization in January 1966. Its headquarters, two fixed-wing tactical groups, MAGs-11 and -12, and two helicopter groups, MAGs-16 and -36, were all operating in I Corps in support of III MAF ground units. One helicopter squadron, HMM-363, was at Qui Nhon in II Corps under the operational control of the Commanding General, U.S. Field Forces, Vietnam. In addition, several other wing organizations, including the helicopter squadron serving with the Special Landing Force of the Seventh Fleet, were located outside Vietnam. Most of the out-of-country wing elements operated under the 1st Marine Aircraft Wing (Rear), commanded by Colonel Harry W. Taylor, at Iwakuni, Japan. At this time, 1st MAW (Rear) consisted of Marine Wing Service Group-17 and one fixed-wing group, MAG-13, at the Marine Air Station, Iwakuni, and a Marine transport refueling squadron, VMGR-152, a Marine air control squadron, MACS-6, and the helicopter squadrons at Futema, Okinawa. According to Colonel Taylor, General McCutcheon, the wing commander, in actual practice still retained direct control of the units of the 1st MAW (Rear):

> He directed the rotation of fixed-wing squadrons. He delegated and relieved the SLF helo squadrons. He transferred people back and forth. He directed the utilization of the KC-130s on Okinawa.¹

The III MAF staff noted with concern that the wide dispersal of the wing had caused some fragmentation of the Marine air-ground team. Colonel Edwin H. Simmons, the III MAF G-3, observed in January 1966 that the dispersal and varied responsibilities of the wing, "although not precluding adequate support for III MAF, still had a detrimental effect on the Marine command's capability to pursue its primary mission."² General McCutcheon later observed that the wing's size had increased to such an extent that his staff could not be expected to manage men and equipment spread all over the Pacific.³

To ease General McCutcheon's burden, General Krulak ordered the dissolution of the 1st MAW (Rear) on 15 April. Colonel Taylor became the 1st MAW Chief of Staff while the commanding officer of MAG-13, Colonel Edwin A. Harper, became the senior Marine aviation officer in the Western Pacific outside Vietnam. He was responsible for the Marine aviation units not "in-country" and he reported directly to the newly reactivated 9th MAB.* Colonel Harper and his successor, Colonel Douglas D. Petty, Jr., were charged with the administrative tasks pertaining to wing aviation not in Vietnam. In addition, MAG-13 served as a home base for squadrons as they rotated to and from Vietnam.**

The 1st MAW still continued to grow during 1966. In January, the wing had eight helicopter squadrons and eight fixed-wing squadrons in Vietnam. By the end of the year, the number had grown to 21, 10 helicopter squadrons and 11 fixed-wing squadrons. An additional group headquarters also was added. Colonel Petty brought MAG-13 to Chu

---

*The 9th MAB was reactivated on 1 March 1966 and eventually assumed command of those major Marine ground and air components in the Western Pacific that were not deployed to Vietnam, with the exception of the 3d Force Service Regiment on Okinawa. For further discussion of the 9th MAB see Chapter 17. Another exception was MWSG-17. Although at Iwakuni until September, it remained under the direct operational control of the 1st MAW throughout this period.

**The intratheater squadron rotation program was similar to that later inaugurated by the infantry units. Helicopter squadrons rotated from Futema, Okinawa, to either Vietnam or the Special Landing Force of the Seventh Fleet and vice versa. The fixed-wing squadrons rotated from Iwakuni, Japan, to Vietnam and back again.

Col Douglas D. Petty, Jr. (left), Commanding Officer, MAG-13, poses upon his arrival at Chu Lai Airfield with the 1st Wing commander, MajGen Louis B. Robertshaw. The completion of the 10,000-foot main runway at Chu Lai in September permitted the stationing of another fixed-wing aircraft group at the base.

Lai in September 1966.* The wing's personnel strength was over 15,000 in December, an increase of nearly 6,000 over the January figure.

The Pilot Shortage

The rapid deployment of Marine aviation units to Vietnam caused serious personnel problems. During his October visit to Vietnam, General Krulak noted that the two helicopter groups, MAGs-16 and -36, faced shortages in both pilots and certain critical ground personnel. The wing commander, Major General Louis B. Robertshaw, who had relieved General McCutcheon on 16 May, expressed his concern to Krulak about the adequacy of the pilot replacement program. While visiting one of the Marine attack squadrons, General Krulak took the opportunity to have an informal discussion with the officers. He later remarked:

> It was a fine group, and I gained many impressions from them; none particularly new. Their morale is high. None of them feel that they are working too hard, and all of them feel that their equipment is adequate. They are convinced of the wisdom of our actions in Vietnam and proud of their unit and loyal to the Marine Corps. However, several things trouble them, and it is these things which are causing much of our personnel attrition. Specifically they are apprehensive of the frequency with which they are going to have to return to Vietnam for another tour. They certainly do not like the thought of coming back twice before everyone else has gone once.[4]

By October, the pilot shortage had become so acute that the Department of Defense announced on the 17th that it would keep approximately 500 pilots and aviation maintenance officers in service for as long as an extra year.[5] In addition to deferring releases and retirements of Marine aviation officers, the Corps took other short-range actions to ease the situation. Certain aviation billets were filled by ground officers when feasible, and the number of pilots slated to enter professional schools was sharply reduced. Long-term measures included the shortening of the helicopter pilot training program, increasing the number of Marine pilot trainees at the Pensacola Naval Air Station, and turning over some of the training of jet pilots to the Air Force.[6]

Reviewing the major personnel events of the previous year at the July 1967 General Officers Symposium, Major General Jonas M. Platt, the Marine Corps Deputy Chief of Staff, G-1, stated that the pilot shortage occurred almost overnight. He believed that the rapid buildup of new aviation units, additional overseas deployments, and the active recruitment of pilots by commercial aviation companies placed an unexpected strain on Marine pilot resources.[7] At the same conference, General McCutcheon, now Deputy Chief of Staff (Air), sardonically remarked: "Surely everyone knows there is no pilot shortage; it is merely that requirements exceed resources." McCutcheon then declared:

> Requirements increased due to increased deployments, need for a pipeline, and approval for activation of new units both permanent and temporary. Resources have not kept pace. A requested increase in the pilot training rate was refused. Retention of aviators on active duty fell far below our earlier projections. This triple squeeze left us in a real bind.[8]

---

*The completion of the permanent 10,000-foot airfield at Chu Lai, in addition to the SATs field, provided the additional space to accommodate MAG-13. MAG-15's Headquarters arrived at Iwakuni from the U.S. and relieved MAG-13 as the control headquarters for 1st Marine Aircraft Wing aviation outside Vietnam.

A Marine Douglas A-4 Skyhawk makes a Morrest landing at the Chu Lai SATS Airfield, similar to a landing on a carrier deck. SATS translates into short airfield for tactical support and is an expeditionary airfield characterized by a portable aluminum runway and aircraft landing and recovery devices.

Marine Aircraft: The New and the Old

Accompanying the growth in personnel and squadrons in Vietnam was the introduction of several new types of aircraft during the year. As General McCutcheon later explained:

> Aviation is a dynamic profession. The rate of obsolecence of equipment is high and new aircraft have to be placed in the inventory periodically in order to stay abreast of the requirements of modern war. In 1965, the Corps was entering a period that would see the majority of its aircraft replaced within four years.[9]

The first of the new aircraft to arrive in 1966 was the Boeing Vertol CH-46 Sea Knight. On 8 March, Lieutenant Colonel Warren C. Watson's HMM-164 flew off the USS *Valley Forge* (LPH 8) with 24 Sea Knight helicopters and moved to the Marble Mountain Air Facility near Da Nang.* On 22 May, a second CH-46 squadron, HMM-265, arrived at Marble

---

*The CH-46 aircraft was designed to carry a four-man crew and 17 combat-loaded troops, approximately double the load of the older UH-34 helicopter transports. The CH-46 was a twin-turbine, tandem-rotor transport with a combat radius of 115 miles, and a cruising speed of 115 knots, approximately 25 knots faster than that of the UH-34.

A Marine Boeing Vertol CH-46 twin-turbine, tandem-rotor transport helicopter from HMM-164, the first CH-46 squadron to arrive in Vietnam, refuels at Dong Ha Airfield during Operation Reno in May 1966. The propeller-driven aircraft facing the helicopter is a Douglas A-1 Skyraider still being flown by the South Vietnamese Air Force and U.S. Air Force air commando squadrons in 1966.

Marine Corps Photo A421467

A Marine mechanic makes adjustments on the rotor blades of a CH-46 helicopter at Marble Mountain Air Facility. During 1966, the Marines equipped these aircraft with newly designed air and fuel filters because of sand and dust getting into the engines and fuel systems. In 1967, rear tail sections on the aircraft began falling off, which required the Marine Corps to ground all CH-46s in Vietnam and return them to Okinawa for structural modification.

Mountain. By the end of the year, there were four Marine Sea Knight squadrons in Vietnam, the two at Da Nang and HMMs-165 and -262 assigned to MAG-36 at Ky Ha.

After arriving in Vietnam, unforeseen technical difficulties developed with the CH-46. When operating close to the ground, the helicopter's rotors stirred up large quantities of sand and dirt which were sucked into the craft's compressor, burning out the engines. In May, a team of technical experts from the Boeing Vertol Corporation and the General Electric Corporation, the manufacturer of the turbine engine, arrived at Marble Mountain to investigate the situation. They devised an air filter to be installed on the front of the engines. The first filter kits arrived in July. By this time, the Marines discovered that fine powdered sand and dust were also getting into the fuel system, causing erratic operation of the engines. By 21 July, the wing grounded all of the CH-46s, except for emergency flights. With the assistance of the Boeing Vertol Corporation and the Naval Air Systems Command, the Marines equipped all of the Sea Knight aircraft with both air and fuel filters by the end of September and solved these particular problems.[10]*

Several new jet aircraft arrived in Vietnam during the latter part of 1966. These were the A6A Grumman Intruder attack aircraft;** the EA6A, the electronic countermeasures version of the Intruder; and the RF-4B, the photo-reconnaissance model of the F4B Phantom II. The EA6A and RF-4Bs were assigned to VMCJ-1, providing the Marine Corps reconnaissance squadron with the most sophisticated aircraft in the U.S. inventory to carry out intelligence missions over both North and South Vietnam.

The arrival of VMF(AW)-242, the A6A Squadron, brought a much needed all-weather capability to the

---

*Colonel Robert J. Zitnik, who commanded VMO-6 and served on the MAG-36 staff in 1966, observed that "Sand and dirt damage was not new to helicopters.... Yet the H46 engines were the first engines to be damaged." Col Robert J. Zitnik, Comments on draft MS, dtd 6Jun78 (Vietnam Comment File). The problem with the sand and dirt was not to be the last of the troubles for the CH-46. Both the CH-46A introduced in 1966 and the CH-46D, a newer and more powerful version, which entered Vietnam in 1967, were grounded during 1967 when tail sections on both models started falling off in flight. During the time the aircraft were down, the entire "fleet" of CH-46 helicopters in Vietnam was rotated to Okinawa for structural modification. For further discussion of the problems with the CH-46, see LtCol William R. Fails, *Marines and Helicopters, 1962-1973* (Washington: Hist&MusDiv, HQMC, 1978), pp. 101-2, 121-24; LtCol Lane Rogers and Major Gary L. Telfer, draft MS, "U.S. Marines in Vietnam, 1967," Chapter 11. See also Col Thomas J. O'Connor, Comments on draft MS, dtd 10Jun78 (Vietnam Comment File).

**The A6A Grumman Intruder was a twin-jet, low-level attack bomber specifically designed to deliver weapons on targets completely obscured by weather or darkness. It was manned by a crew of two and could carry an 18,000-pound payload. It was equipped with a digital-integrated attack navigation system and a Kaiser electronic-integrated display system enabling the pilot to "see" targets and geographical features at night or in bad weather by means of two viewing screens in the cockpit which provided a visual representation of the ground and air below and in front of the aircraft.

wing. During the worst monsoon rains in December, the squadron's 12 A6As dropped nearly 38 percent of the total ordnance dumped over enemy targets by III MAF aircraft.[11] Major General Robertshaw, who just prior to assuming command of the wing had served a tour as Deputy Chief of Staff (Air) at Headquarters Marine Corps, in 1978 remembered that the A6As were introduced into Vietnam so as not to:

> . . . deny support to Marines, yet subtle enough to protect them from Seventh Air Force's eager appetite to commit them primarily to the Northern Route Package Areas [selected bombing target areas in North Vietnam] prematurely. By installation of radar reflectors at various outposts and Special Forces forward bases and limiting their introduction north to the lower Route Package areas [targets in southern North Vietnam], an orderly progression to the most demanding capabilities of A6 [aircraft] was effected to final full exploitation.[12]

The arrival of the new aircraft did not mean the immediate retirement of the older craft. During 1966, the UH-34 transport helicopters continued to be the mainstay "in the troop lift department." One experienced helicopter commander commented that:

> The H34s had been stripped of every possible item such as seat pads, windows, doors and whatever else could be spared in order to improve the troop lift capability. . . . These aircraft, with many times overhauled engines, were surprisingly effective under the extreme operating conditions—almost always at their maximum gross weight and frequently over the recommended hovering limits.[13]

Two Sikorsky UH-34D Sea Horse transport helicopters are seen lifting off after bringing Marine riflemen into a landing zone. The older UH-34s continued to be the mainstay of helicopter trooplift during 1966.

Marine Corps Photo A421623

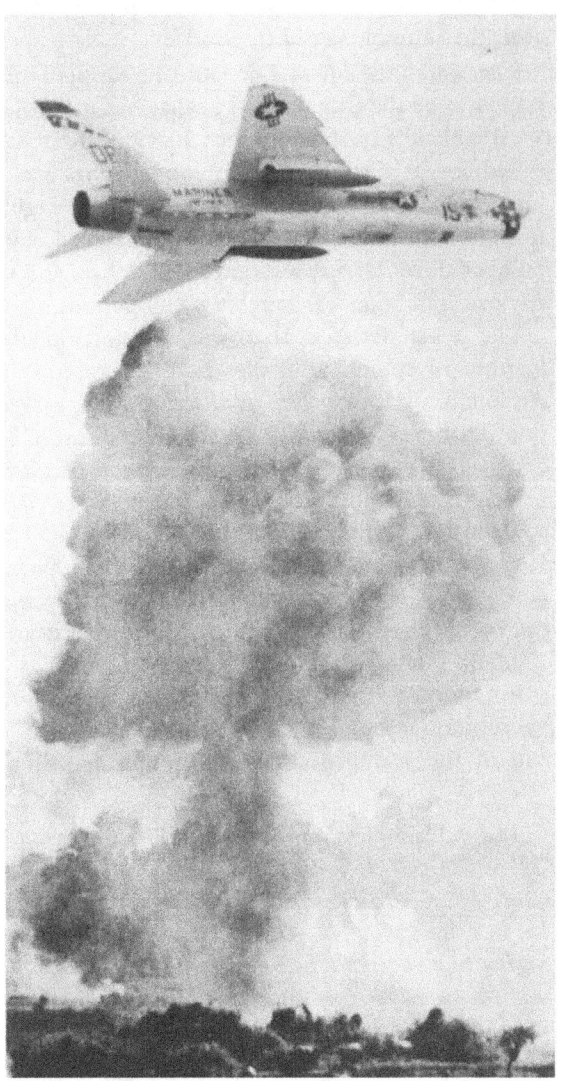

Marine Corps Photo A421419

A Marine F8-E Chance-Vought Crusader from VMF (AW)-232 prepares to attack a Viet Cong position in January 1966. Another Crusader, barely visible in the upper right of the picture, dropped the bomb which caused the explosion pictured here.

One fixed-wing squadron, VMF(AW)-232, continued to fly the F-8E Chance-Vought Crusader.* This swept-wing fighter, originally designed for high-speed aerial combat, nevertheless was a respectable close air support aircraft. It was equipped with 20mm cannon and was the only Marine aircraft in

---

*The Crusader was eventually to be replaced by the F4B Phantom II.

Vietnam configured to carry a 2,000-pound bomb until the introduction of the A6A.

The workhorse for Marine close air support continued to be the Douglas A-4 Skyhawk. Colonel Jay W. Hubbard's MAG-12, which included four A-4 squadrons at Chu Lai, consistently maintained a high sortie rate. The A-4 was a small, highly maneuverable attack jet and extremely accurate bomber. It could carry a variety of ordnance, and its payload limitation was roughly 8,000 pounds.

The most versatile fixed-wing aircraft in the Marine inventory was the F-4B Phantom II. Although a relatively new addition to Marine aviation, Phantom squadrons were among the first to be deployed to Vietnam in 1965. By the end of 1966, new F-4B squadrons had arrived, one with MAG-11 at Da Nang and three with MAG-13 at Chu Lai. The F-4B was designed for both an air-to-air and air-to-ground role. It was one of the fastest interceptors in the world, but it could also carry a payload of nearly 16,000 pounds, second only to the A6A.

In addition to the 11 fixed-wing and seven helicopter transport squadrons, the 1st MAW by the end of the year had three observation squadrons

Col Leslie E. Brown (right of picture), Commanding Officer, MAG-12, later relieved by Col Jay W. Hubbard, poses with his squadron commanders at Chu Lai in early 1966. The MAG-12 squadrons flew the highly maneuverable Douglas A-4 Skyhawk, which was the workhorse of Marine close air support in 1966.

Marine Corps Photo A701486

Marine Corps Photo A189384
An unarmed Bell UH-1E helicopter approaches an LZ in Operation Prairie. The unarmed "Hueys" were commonly called "Slicks," and used for a variety of missions, not the least of which was medical evacuation. Armed Hueys carried four fuselage-mounted M-60 machine guns and two to four 2.75-inch rocket pods to be used in LZ preparation and in a ground support role.

(VMO) equipped with UH-1E helicopters.* The Bell UH-1E or "Huey," as it was popularly known, was the only aircraft assigned to the observation squadrons. The VMO squadrons' mission had been extended beyond observation. Unarmed Hueys, commonly called "slicks," were used for a variety of purposes, not the least of which was medical evacuation. One former MAG-16 commander, Colonel Thomas J. O'Connor, remembered: "I recall having no "Hueys" at times for battalions, colonels, and generals. But the medevac helicopter was a sacred high-priority requirement."[14] Other Hueys were armed and assigned to provide helicopter escort, landing zone preparation, aircraft control for fixed-wing strikes, and close support of ground troops. The gunships were armed with four fuselage-mounted M-60 machine guns, two to four 2.75-inch

---

*VMO-2 and -6 were located at Marble Mountain Air Facility at Da Nang and Ky Ha Air Facility at Chu Lai, respectively, during 1966. VMO-3 arrived at Chu Lai on 29 December 1966.

Marine Corps Photo A189763

A Marine McDonnell F-4B Phantom II is shown in flight in April 1966. The Phantom was the most versatile of the Marine fixed-wing aircraft in 1966, designed as one of the fastest interceptors in the world and also capable of carrying a payload of 16,000 pounds.

rocket pods, and two door M-60 machine guns—sufficient to provide an impressive volume of fire.

There was much debate within the Marine Corps about the use of the Huey as a close support weapon. Some commanders argued that there was a tendency on the part of some ground officers to call for Huey close air support when fixed-wing aircraft were available and more appropriate for the occasion.*

In any event, the increased use of the Huey in a close air support and escort roles reduced its availability for observation and coordination missions. One 3d Marine Division staff officer, Colonel George E. Carrington, Jr., later commented that in early 1966 the Marines were "short of AOs [air observers] and artillery observation spotter planes. The helicopters were too expensive, rare, and needed for other purposes and we suffered. . . ."[15] This situation was somewhat alleviated with the arrival in August of a detachment of 10 Cessna O-1C Birddog light fixed-wing observation aircraft which were assigned to Headquarters and Maintenance Squadron (H&MS) 16 at Marble Mountain. By October, the detachment supported all three Marine enclaves as well as the 3d Marine Division (Forward) at Dong Ha.[16]

Several other independent detachments of specialized aircraft also operated with the wing and most were assigned to the H&MS of the various groups. A detachment of eight Sikorsky CH-37 helicopters was attached to H&MS-16. The CH-37s were being phased out of the Marine inventory and being replaced by the newer Sikorsky CH-53 Sea Stallions. The wing also had seven C-117 twin-engine Douglas Skytrain transports which were attached to each of the groups, one each to H&MS-11, -12, -13, -16, and -36, and two to H&MS-17. These transports made the routine administrative and logistic flights between the Marine bases and were also employed as flare planes for night operations. One Marine aviator remembered that the crews at

---

*General Wallace M. Greene, Jr., the Commandant of the Marine Corps during this period, observed in his comments that some of the opposition to arming the UH-1Es, "was due to the availability of Army armed Hueys to support USMC requirements—'if the Army can provide, why should we?'" In October 1964, General Greene had directed the development of a high priority project to develop a weapons kit for Marine Corps UH-1Es. Gen Wallace M. Greene, Jr., Comments on draft MS, dtd 5May78 (Vietnam Comment File) and LtCol William R. Fails, *Marines and Helicopters, 1962-1973* (Washington: Hist&MusDiv, HQMC, 1978) p. 89. For a further discussion of this subject see, "Armed Helicopters," Issues Section, *Marine Corps Gazette*, May 1966, v. 50, no. 5, pp. 45-51 and Fails, *Marines and Helicopters*, pp. 85-91.

Marine Corps Photo A186825

A heavy Sikorsky CH-37 twin-engine helicopter is seen recovering a damaged UH-34. The CH-37s were being phased out of the Marine inventory and being replaced by the newer Sikorsky CH-53 Sea Stallion heavy helicopter.

first threw the "flares out by hand until a more sophisticated chute device was made."[17]

The KC-130 Hercules aircraft of VMGR-152 provided an even greater logistic lift capability for III MAF. With their 15-17-ton capacity, these transport planes shuttled men and material between bases in Vietnam, Japan, Okinawa, and the Philippines. Although permanently based on Okinawa, a detachment of four planes was always maintained at Da Nang. The KC-130 was primarily configured for in-flight refueling missions. In fact, it was this refueling capability of the Marine transports which originally allowed the Marine Corps to have the "Hercules" aircraft in its inventory. When the Marine Corps had initially obtained the aircraft there had been a debate between Air Force and Marine aviation circles whether the KC-130 was basically a tanker or a transport. The Marines used it as both.

Relations with the Seventh Air Force

A more significant debate between Marine and Air Force officers was over the control of Marine aviation in Vietnam. Much of this problem had been settled by the time the 9th MEB arrived at Da Nang in the spring of 1965. Admiral Sharp and General Westmoreland, after some initial disagreement, worked out the basic guidelines in May 1965. Major General Joseph H. Moore, the Commanding General, 2d Air Division, later to become the Seventh Air Force, was assigned as the Deputy Commander USMACV (Air). In this capacity, he had "coordinating authority" for tactical air support in South Vietnam, but not operational control of Marine air.* General McCutcheon, as Commanding General, 1st Marine Aircraft Wing, was the III MAF air commander under General Walt and controlled all aircraft operating in support of III MAF forces. Marine ground units had first priority on 1st MAW aircraft. General McCutcheon furnished General Moore with a copy of all 1st MAW mission orders in order to assist the latter with his coordinating responsibilities. Once the wing had determined the number of missions to be flown in support of III MAF, the Marines notified MACV of any excess sorties which were available. The 2d Air Division was then able to task these aircraft to support other U.S. or allied forces. On 13 July 1965, General Westmoreland promulgated these concepts in his MACV Aviation Directive 95-4.[18]**

During 1965, Generals McCutcheon and Moore made one other major agreement pertaining to American aviation in Vietnam. This understanding applied to air defense operations in the event of North Vietnamese air attack against the south. The Marines recognized General Moore's overall air defense responsibility in his capacity as Mainland Southeast Asia Air Defense Regional Commander. Questions, nevertheless, remained about how control was to be exercised. These were settled on 6 August 1965. The Air Force was to have overall air defense responsibility, while the Marine wing commander was to designate which forces under his com-

---

*JCS Publication 2, *Unified Action Armed Forces* defines coordinating authority as: "A commander or individual assigned responsibility for coordinating specific functions or activities involving forces of two or more Services or two or more forces of the same Service. He has the authority to require consultation between the agenices involved, but does not have the authority to compel agreement."

**Although a new MACV directive 95-4 was promulgated on 25 June 1966, there was no change in the provisions relating to control of Marine air. The new order reflected the transformation of the 2d Air Division to the Seventh Air Force.

mand would participate in air defense. He agreed that the Air Force "would exercise certain authority over those designated resources to include scramble of alert aircraft, designation of targets, declaration of HAWK missile control status, and firing orders."[19] General McCutcheon observed that this understanding, combined with the MACV July directive, was to provide the basic policy for "command, control, and coordination of Marine aviation in Vietnam until early 1968 and they were entirely adequate as far as III MAF was concerned."[20]

The subject of air control was never a dead issue and the relationship between the Seventh Air Force and the Marines remained extremely sensitive throughout 1966. General Greene, the Marine Corps Commandant, remembered that on visits during the year to Saigon, he:

> . . . contested this issue directly with General Westmoreland and General Moore. General Westmoreland always shifted the argument to General Moore—never making a decision about specifics himself. I became firmly convinced that General Moore was attempting to establish a precedent in Vietnam for taking complete control of Marine Corps aviation. . . .[21]

Major General Robertshaw, the wing commander, later wrote:

> They [the Seventh Air Force] issued several directive messages limiting our freedom to bomb in and around the DMZ for instance. In each case we referred to 95-4, sent our reply to MACV vice Seventh Air Force who for some strange reason never used the MACV title in issuing such directives. Had he done so [limited the bombing] we would have been severely handicapped and might have had more trouble in conducting air operations as we desired within I Corps anywhere, anytime, and [against] any target. III MAF not only had the right to do so but the responsibility.[22]

Despite differences of opinion pertaining to the interpretation of the MACV directive, the fact remained that III MAF controlled Marine air until "single management" was introduced in the spring of 1968.

Marine Air Control Systems

III MAF exercised control of its aviation assets in Vietnam through its tactical air direction center (TADC) at wing headquarters in Da Nang. The TADC monitored the employment of all Marine aircraft and determined what planes would be assigned to non-preplanned missions. The TADC carried out its mission through two subordinate agencies, the tactical air operations center (TAOC) and the direct air support centers (DASCs).

While the TAOC, maintained by Marine Air Control Squadron 7 (MACS-7), was the wing's main control center for antiair warfare and air traffic control, the DASCs were the centers for control of direct air support of ground forces. Two Marine air support squadrons (MASS-2 and -3) provided the personnel and equipment to operate and maintain the DASCs. Originally, a DASC was established with each of the two Marine divisions' organic fire support coordination centers at Da Nang and Chu Lai. When the 3d Marine Division moved to Phu Bai in October and assumed responsibility for the entire northern area, DASCs were established at the division's command posts at Phu Bai and at Dong Ha.

Sometimes smaller "modified" DASCs were created for special operations. For example, during Operation Double Eagle in January and February, General Platt's Task Force Delta established a "mini" DASC in the Johnson City logistic support area (LSA) so the task force could control aircraft assigned to it. During many other operations, airborne DASCs on board KC-130s were employed, when the distance from ground DASCs was such that normal ground-to-air communication was unreliable.

The Marine air support squadrons also provided air support radar teams (ASRTs) equipped with the TPQ-10 radar. The TPQ-10 equipment provided the Marine Corps with the capability to control air support regardless of weather conditions. With their radar the ASRTs could track and control an aircraft equipped with a receiver within a radius of 50 miles, and tell the pilot when to drop his ordnance. The A-4, A-6, and F-4B all carried these receivers. The Marines also used the TPQ-10 radar to guide helicopters to forward bases. By December 1966, the wing had five ASRTs in operation to provide an all-weather air support system to cover the entire ICTZ coastal region and much of the mountainous area to the west. A FMFPac report observed that during the worst of the monsoon season in I Corps, from October-December 1966, the teams controlled 4,993 sorties, 31 percent of the combat sorties flown by Marine aircraft.[23]

Air Defense

In the unlikely event that the North Vietnamese decided to launch air strikes against vulnerable allied targets in South Vietnam, the American command had made the necessary defensive arrangements and preparations to thwart any such attack. As the Mainland Southeast Asia Air Defense Regional Commander, the Commanding General, Seventh Air Force had the responsibility for air defense in South Vietnam. In I Corps, the Seventh Air Force exercised this jurisdiction through its control and reporting center (CRC) located on Monkey Mountain, east of the city of Da Nang on the Tiensha Peninsula. The air defense battle commander at the CRC reported directly to the Seventh Air Force Tactical Air Command Center at Tan Son Nhut Airfield near Saigon. He had the authority to designate aircraft as hostile, to scramble alert aircraft, to establish weapons control status for the Marine Light Antiaircraft Missile Battalions (LAAMs), and to coordinate both fighter interceptors and surface-to-air missiles against enemy aircraft. At the end of 1966, the Seventh Air Force air defense commander in I Corps could call on 69 Marine fighters, 55 U.S. Air Force fighters, 88 U.S. Army multiple .50 caliber or 40mm antiaircraft weapons, and two U.S. Marine LAAM battalions armed with HAWK missiles.²⁴*

In I Corps, the major ground antiair defense was centered around the Marine 1st and 2nd LAAM Battalions, located at Da Nang and Chu Lai respectively. Both battalions had deployed to Vietnam in 1965. Indeed, the 1st Battalion was one of the first contingents to enter Vietnam, arriving at Da Nang in February 1965. In September 1965, the 2d Battalion established its base of operations at Chu Lai. Each battalion had three firing batteries and had as its basic load 108 HAWK missiles (36 per battery) and another 70 in reserve. Both battalions came under the Marine Wing Headquarters Group-1 for administrative control. Each battalion also established its own Antiaircraft Operations Center which was responsive to the Air Force CRC on Monkey Mountain for air defense control and coordination. Both battalions maintained liaison officers with the CRC to enhance this coordination.²⁵

At the beginning of 1966, the 1st LAAM Battalion at Da Nang under Lieutenant Colonel Clyde

---

*The acronym HAWK stands for Homing-All-the-Way-Killer. The HAWK air defense is a mobile, surface-to-air guided missile system designed to defend against enemy low-flying aircraft and short-range rocket missiles.

Marine Corps Photo A421300
Marines of the 2d Light Antiaircraft Missile Battalion at Chu Lai make adjustments to three HAWK missiles mounted on their pod. These mobile, surface-to-air guided missiles were designed to defend against enemy aircraft flying at low altitudes.

L. Eyer** had a total strength of 479 officers and men. Its Headquarters Battery and Battery A were located on the airfield itself while Battery B was on Hill 327 to the west of the airbase. Battery C was in the northern part of the Tiensha Peninsula to the east of the Air Force CRC. To increase the effectiveness of its defensive coverage, the battalion moved Battery A to new firing positions on Hill 724, north of the Hai Van Pass, in August, after the Seabees had hacked out a base camp for the battery in the rugged terrain. At the same time, the battalion created an Assault Fire Unit with 15 missiles, which in September deployed to Hill 55, south of Da Nang, where it provided coverage for the Vu Gia River Valley.²⁶

At Chu Lai, the 2d Battalion, totaling about 460 officers and men under Major Edward F. Penico,*** remained in basically the same positions throughout the year. Battery A was in position on Ky Hoa Island

---

**LtCol Eyer later in the year was relieved by Major Thomas G. Davis, who in turn was relieved by Lieutenant Colonel Merton R. Ives.

***Major Penico was relieved by Lieutenant Colonel Thomas I. Gunning at the end of July 1966.

north of Chu Lai while Batteries B and C were located respectively immediately north and south of the airfield. At the end of the year, the battalion planned to move Battery C to Hill 141, further southeast of the airfield to provide better antiair cover for the Song Tra Bong Valley.[27]

During the course of the year neither battalion had occasion to fire any of its missiles with the exception of the accidental discharge of two HAWKs in June at Da Nang. Both missiles "were command destructed after lift-off," with no damage done.[28] Each battalion, nevertheless, kept busy with antiair exercises and practice raids using Marine fixed-wing aircraft as "targets" to test the battalion control and communications system. For example, the 1st Battalion reported in December 1966 that since 1965 it had "engaged" 1,632 of the 1,751 "raids" conducted by friendly aircraft, a successful engagement percentage of 93.3 for that extended period.[29] The 2d Battalion at Chu Lai could boast of similar success.

By the end of 1966, the American command believed that its air defense capabilities were more than adequate to overcome any potential air threat. Specifically, in relation to the LAAM battalions, Admiral Sharp, on 27 August, in a reevaluation of Southeast Asia air defenses decided against a planned deployment of a fourth HAWK battery to each of the missile battalions.[30] Earlier, the battalions had received a new stock of missiles to replace their old, which were suspected of having cracked motor casings.[31] Major General Robertshaw, the 1st Wing commander, later observed that the LAAM battalions were "no small deterrent to the enemy. They had their moments, took their knocks, and prided themselves in being always ready."[32]

Air Operations

While prepared defensively, the 1st MAW made a considerable offensive contribution to the overall U.S. military campaign in Vietnam during 1966. Marine helicopters transported both U.S. and allied forces into battle and sustained them logistically. Huey gunships provided close-in air cover while fixed-wing attack aircraft flew close air support, direct air support, and interdiction missions. Although its primary mission was the support of III MAF ground forces, the Marine wing in accordance with the MACV air directive played a significant role in Seventh Air Force air operations, both in South Vietnam and out-of-country.

The statistics of Marine flight operations in 1966 present an almost herculean effort. Marine helicopters flew well over 400,000 sorties during the year, averaging more than 30,000 sorties a month. The number of Marine helicopter sorties reached over 40,000 in July when the ground war extended to the DMZ. In December, a fairly representative month, the wing's helicopters, in over 32,000 sorties of which 75 percent were in support of III MAF, transported over 47,000 passengers and lifted 3,549.9 tons of cargo. The Marines lost a total of 52 helicopters, 39 in combat, and had a total helicopter inventory in Vietnam at the end of the year of 234 aircraft.[33]

Fixed-wing jet operational statistics for 1966 also provide an impressive overview of that aspect of the Marine air war. Marine jets flew over 60,000 sorties during the year at a cost of 51 aircraft, 24 of which were shot down by enemy ground fire. Of this total number of sorties, approximately 43,000 supported III MAF and allied operations in I Corps while another 17,000 supported the Seventh Air Force air campaign over South Vietnam, Laos, and North Vietnam.[34]

During the first half of 1966, Marine senior commanders had become concerned about the number of missions that the 1st MAW contributed to the Seventh Air Force, especially to the bombing in the panhandle of southern Laos. In December 1965, as part of the overall "Steel Tiger" air interdiction campaign in Laos, General Westmoreland had inaugurated, with the implicit consent of the Laotian Government, a new bombing effort labeled "Tiger Hound." The concept called for Air Force small fixed-wing observation aircraft, flying up to 12 miles into southeastern Laos, to direct U.S. airstrikes on targets of opportunity.[35] Marine attack aircraft flew 3,629 Steel Tiger/Tiger Hound sorties in support of the Seventh Air Force during the first three months of 1966, over 25 percent of the total wing jet sorties for that period.[36]

Believing that the air campaign in Laos was having an impact on enemy infiltration, General Westmoreland in March presented a plan to Admiral Sharp and the Joint Chiefs of Staff to expand "Tiger Hound" operations to include the southern panhandle of North Vietnam, the so-called Route Package 1 (RP-1), extending 50 kilometers above the DMZ. Up

1st MAW Fixed-Wing Jet Sorties, 1966*

Month	Total**	Support of III MAF and I Corps ARVN Units	Support of 2d AD/7th AF			
			Total	Steel Tiger/ Tiger Hound	Tally Ho/ Rolling Thunder	In-Country
Jan	4171	2304	1867	1010		857
Feb	4164	2732	1432	960		472
Mar	5550	2546	3004	1659		1345
Apr	4957	2444	2513	1380		1133
May	4428	2518	1910	1134		776
Jun	4538	3028	1510	926		584
Jul	5570	4613	957	284	404	269
Aug	5761	4699	1062	9	793	260
Sep	5696	4796	900	16	825	59
Oct	4766	4154	612	72	535	5
Nov	5097	4452	645	56	576	13
Dec	5422	4648	774	233	518	23
Total	60120	42934	17186	7739	3651	5796

*Does not include ECM/ElInt or photographic sorties
**Figures derived from 1st MAW ComdCs, Jan-Dec 1966

to this point, the air war over North Vietnam had been directly under the command of Admiral Sharp. Westmoreland, in effect, was asking to assume direct control of the air space over what he called the extended battlefield, the Laotian panhandle and southern North Vietnam. On 1 April, Admiral Sharp assigned to General Westmoreland the "primary responsibility for armed [air] reconnaissance and intelligence in the southernmost portion of Northern Vietnam." The other aspect of the Westmoreland plan continued to be discussed at the JCS and Department of Defense level.[37]

Just prior to Sharp's decision, Lieutenant General Krulak at FMFPac alerted the Commandant, General Greene, to the possibility of a new role for MACV in the air war over the north and the implications of such a role for Marine air. Krulak observed that although the 1st MAW was heavily committed to the "Steel Tiger" campaign over Laos, its activity in the "Rolling Thunder" strikes in the north had been limited to electronic intelligence and countermeasures and combat air patrols. While not voicing disagreement with an expanded MACV/Seventh Air Force air authority, Krulak was uneasy about Marine participation in a Seventh Air Force Rolling Thunder campaign. He stated: "There will be the requirement for operating under two distinct sets of rules in two different geographical areas."[38]

At III MAF Headquarters, both General McCutcheon, the 1st Wing commander, and General Walt expressed reservations about the number of sorties that the wing supplied to the Seventh Air Force. On 7 April, McCutcheon radioed Krulak that he still had not heard from the Seventh Air Force about the way MACV would implement its air campaign in the north when it received the authority. The wing commander remarked, "I am sitting back on this one and waiting to see what they come up with." General McCutcheon then reported to Krulak the extent of Marine jet operations through March and declared that he was cutting down on the sortie rate, observing that he did not want to "push ops any higher and [did not] want to get in a bind on ordnance."[39]

Three days later, 10 April, the commander of the Seventh Air Force, General Moore, visited General Walt at Da Nang, and asked that the Marine command increase its monthly jet sorties for Seventh Air Force missions by 30 percent. Walt denied the request and took his case directly to General Westmoreland. The III MAF commander observed that during March, a record month for Marine fixed-

VMCJ-1 Electronic Countermeasures, Electronic Intelligence, and Photo Sorties, 1966*

Month and Aircraft Type	ECM in NVN		EIInt in NVN		EIInt in III MAF or In-Country		Photo support of III MAF	
	7th AF	7th Flt	7th AF	7th Flt	III MAF	In-Country	In-Country	Out-of-Country
Jan66								
EF10B	57	2	73					
RF8A							104	
Feb66								
EF10B	58	20	13	2	6			
RF8A							115	
Mar66								
EF10B	54	37	2			14		
RF8A							160	
Apr66								
EF10B	56	63	2	2				
RF8A							152	
May66								
EF10B	58	70	9			1		
RF8A							148	
Jun66								
EF10B	77	106	1					
RF8A							167	
Jul66								
EF10B	22	142	2		12			
RF8A							168	2
Aug66								
EF10B	15	219	2		1			
RF8A							175	3
Sep66								
EF10B	18	151	8		1			
RF8A							146	10
Oct66								
EF10B	9	94	6	4	8			
RF4B							2	
RF8A							141	2
Nov66								
EF10B	6	70		2	17			
EA6A	4	42	3		9			
RF4B							154	
RF8A							55	
Dec66								
EF10B	31	112			26			
EA6A	16	44			10			
RF4B								
RF8A							115	21
Totals	481	1172	121	10	90	15	1802	38

*Figures from VMCJ-1 ComdCs, Jan-Dec66.

wing operations, the 1st MAW had given over half of its total sorties to the Seventh Air Force, of which over half supported the bombing campaign over Laos. General Walt frankly stated that he could not sustain that tempo of air operations. Walt estimated, given his resources in spare parts and ordnance, that he could only support a monthly rate of 4,700 sorties per month as compared to the 5,500 figure reached in March. Of these 4,700 sorties, the Marine command required about 2,500 for its own purposes. The remaining 2,000 sorties, Walt declared, would be given to MACV/Seventh Air Force: "You can frag us for whatever are deemed the priority targets, in or out of country. We will fly south, west, or north."[40]

True to Walt's word, 1st MAW fixed-wing attack aircraft during the next two months averaged a monthly sortie rate of 4,700, flying slightly above the mark in April and slightly below in May. Nearly half of these sorties were in support of the Seventh Air Force with close to 60 percent of those missions over Laos. General Krulak continued to worry about the implications of these statistics. In a message to General Walt on 10 June, he declared that he recognized the desire of III MAF to demonstrate Marine flexibility but wondered about the wisdom of providing such a large percentage of Marine fixed-wing operations to the Seventh Air Force. He observed that the CinCPac rationale for the number of Marine fixed-wing squadrons in Vietnam rested on the support required by III MAF ground forces. Krulak feared that the sortie figures could be used against the Marines in interservice differences over the employment of Marine air.[41]

The concerns voiced by Krulak soon became moot since the enemy buildup in northern I Corps absorbed more and more of the resources of both Marine air and ground units. In June, the wing flew over 4,500 jet sorties with over 65 percent of them in support of III MAF. During July, when the Marines began Operation Hastings in northern Quang Tri Province, the wing's attack sorties reached a peak of 5,570 with over 80 percent flown in support of Marine ground units. In Hastings alone, Marine jets flew 1,600 sorties, a record number up to that time for any one operation. At the same time, Marine jets began to fly strikes north of the DMZ. With the beginning of what could be called the "DMZ War," General Westmoreland received the authority to start under his control the bombing campaign of Route Package 1, code named "Tally Ho." Patterned after the "Tiger Hound" operations over Laos, the Seventh Air Force began to fly its first Tally Ho missions over North Vietnam on 20 July. Of the 950 sorties that the 1st MAW provided the Seventh Air Force during July, over 400 were in support of the Tally Ho campaign.[42]

The pattern of wing jet operations established in July continued through the end of the year. During this five-month period, even with the arrival of additional fixed-wing Marine squadrons, the wing still flew 80 percent of its sorties in support of Marine forces. Of the 4,000 sorties provided to the Seventh Air Force, 80 percent of them were Tally Ho missions, thus in effect, supporting the Marine DMZ campaign in Operation Prairie.[43]

One Marine Corps fixed-wing squadron, Marine Composite Reconnaissance Squadron (VMCJ)-1 played a unique role in the air war. Tasked with the missions of providing aerial photographic reconnaissance and locating and jamming enemy radars and communication networks, the squadron flew over 3,720 sorties during the year. About half of these sorties were photographic reconnaissance missions in support of III MAF flown by both the older Chance-Vought RF-8As, the photoplane version of the Crusader fighter, and the new RF-4Bs, which arrived in October. In contrast to the photographic missions, the vast number of the electronic countermeasure (ECM) and electronic intelligence (ElInt) sorties supported the Seventh Air Force and Seventh Fleet Rolling Thunder campaign over North Vietnam. VMCJ pilots, in both the older Douglas EF-10B, a modified version of the Navy F3D night jet fighter, and the new EA6A aircraft, which arrived in October, flew over 60 percent of these missions in support of the Seventh Fleet. Indeed, one senior Marine aviator, Brigadier General Hugh M. Elwood, who relieved Brigadier General Carl as assistant wing commander in April 1966, later commented, "it was a fact that Seventh Fleet did not launch against Hanoi until a VMCJ ECM plane from Da Nang was on station and doing its thing west of Hanoi."[44]

The Okinawa-based Marine Aerial Refueler Transport Squadron (VMGR)-152, reinforced with a detachment from VMGR-353, also performed extensive but often unheralded services. In addition to over 130 refuelling missions, both north and south of the 17th Parallel, the Marine KC-130 transports made over 13,880 flights during the year, over 10,550 of them in South Vietnam. In this period, the transports carried over 124 million pounds of cargo and ferried more than 115,400 passengers.[45] The high water mark for the squadron was the support that it provided for Operation Hastings. From 15 July to 4 August, the Marine KC-130s flew 1,229 missions into Dong Ha, carrying 14,190 passengers and 6,764.1 tons of cargo. During the first five days of the operation, 12 of the squadron's transports made 500 sorties, including 84 night landings at the dirt airstrip at Dong Ha.[46] General Elwood observed that Hastings for the Marine transports "became a crash, all-out effort . . . in the course of which some 20 odd engines were completely chewed up by the laterite at Dong Ha. . . . Hastings simply could not have been without the Marines' own organic air transports."[47]

This statistical review of Marine air operations in 1966 tells only part of the story; it reveals the magnitude of the wing's task, but little of the underlying human drama concealed by mere numbers. For this, we must look to the personal experience of the men themselves, such as that of Lieutenant Colonel House, the commanding officer of HMM-163, who was both awarded the Navy Cross and given a letter of reprimand for his exploits during the evacuation of the A Shau Special Forces Camp.* Major Luther A. Lono, the VMGR-152 operations officer, in his casual description of KC-130 landings at the Dong Ha airstrip, captured the dangers and difficulties of his squadron's airlift of troops and materiel in Operation Hastings: "When we made our first night landing . . . the only lighting the field had was the lights of a jeep or truck at the approach to the runway. It was a little hairy." The Marines then used flare pots to light up the runway, "but the backwash from the engines kept blowing them out."[48]

In much the same manner, Major Billy D. Fritsch, an F-4 pilot from VMFA-323, told of his adventures during Hastings. On the afternoon of 15 July, Fritsch had just dropped his napalm canisters on three huts approximately 5,000 meters west of the Rockpile when a nearby Air Force forward air controller notified him that he was trailing smoke. The Marine pilot applied full power and pulled back on

*See Chapter 4.

Marine Corps Photo A421532
A Marine Lockheed KC-130 Hercules refueler transport passes a Marine air traffic control radar after making a ground-control approach landing at Phu Bai. During 1966, these large transports flew over 130 refueling missions both north and south of the 17th Parallel and carried over 124 million pounds of cargo and 115,400 passengers.

the control stick, but the jet did not respond. When the Phantom failed to clear some tall trees, Major Fritsch and his backseat flight officer, First Lieutenant Charles D. Smith, Jr., ejected and parachuted to the ground. Thirty minutes later, the Marines were rescued by an Air Force evacuation helicopter. When asked to sum up his experience, Major Fritsch lightly remarked: "I highly recommend those ejection seats, they definitely work as advertised."[49] Incidents such as these gave an added dimension to the bare statistics of number of sorties during any given month.

CHAPTER 17
Artillery Support in 1966

Organization and Employment, January-June 1966 — The Guns Move North and Restructuring the Command, July-December 1966

Organization and Employment, January - June 1966

At the beginning of the year, only the 3d Marine Division's artillery regiment, the 12th Marines, was in Vietnam. Colonel James M. Callender, the regimental commanding officer, maintained his headquarters west of the Da Nang Airfield and operated directly under the division. There, the regiment ran the division fire support coordination center (FSCC) and had direct operational control of the two artillery battalions in the Da Nang TAOR, the 1st and 2d Battalions, 12th Marines. Two independent units were also under Callender's direct control: the 1st 8-inch Howitzer Battery (Self-Propelled) (-) and the 3d Platoon of the 3d 155mm Gun Battery (Self-Propelled).

The regiment's 3d Battalion, under Lieutenant Colonel Leslie L. Page, formed the nucleus of the Chu Lai Artillery Group. Lieutenant Colonel Page commanded the group which consisted of his own unit and the 3d Battalion, 11th Marines. The Chu Lai Artillery Group was under the operational control of General Platt's command group. The two artillery battalions provided direct support for the infantry regiments at Chu Lai; the 3d Battalion, 11th Marines for the 7th Marines and the 3d Battalion, 12th Marines for the 4th Marines. The 3d 155mm Gun Battery (SP) (-) and the 1st Platoon, 1st 8-inch Howitzer Battery, both attached to the 3d Battalion, 12th Marines, were responsible for general support artillery missions at the Chu Lai base. Lieutenant Colonel Page also had the added duty of directing FSCC operations for General Platt.

At Phu Bai, the 4th Battalion, 12th Marines provided the artillery support. The battalion, like the infantry battalion, the 2d Battalion, 1st Marines, in the enclave, was under the operational control of the 3d Marines at Da Nang. Lieutenant Colonel Edwin M. Rudzis, the 4th Battalion commander, had under him a total of 24 artillery pieces, including 105mm howitzers, 107mm howtars, and both towed and self-propelled 155mm howitzers.* Another 105mm howitzer battery arrived at Phu Bai in early March and raised the total of guns to 30. Lieutenant Col-

---
*See Chapter 4.

A 155mm M109 self-propelled howitzer prepares to fire from a position near Phu Bai in 1966. Empty shell casings can be seen in the right foreground. The 155mm howitzers had an approximate range of 15,000 meters.

Marine Corps Photo A188624

Sgt Leroy Lavoie from the 1st Battalion, 12th Marines fires a 105mm howitzer in support of Marine infantry in the An Hoa sector south of Da Nang. The 105mm M101A1 is a general purpose light artillery piece with a maximum range of 11,000 meters.

onel Rudzis later remarked, "that if the Infantry is the Queen of Battle, then at this time, the artillery [at Phu Bai] was a Duke's mixture."[1]

This ad hoc arrangement of III MAF artillery remained in effect for only a brief period. With the incremental arrival of the 1st Marine Division units at Chu Lai, there began a reshuffling of both infantry and artillery battalions between the three enclaves. The 1st Division artillery regiment, the 11th Marines, assumed command of the artillery at Chu Lai and, at the end of March, Lieutenant Colonel Page moved his 3d Battalion Headquarters to Phu Bai. Lieutenant Colonel Rudzis and his 4th Battalion command group then departed for Da Nang where he took over control of two of his own batteries, K and L, and the 1st 155mm Gun Battery (SP). By June, the Marines had achieved a semblance of unit integrity, with 3d Marine Division artillery in most cases supporting 3d Division infantry units and 1st Division artillery its own infantry battalions.

Lieutenant Colonel John B. Sullivan's* 11th Marines was responsible for artillery support in the Chu Lai TAOR while Colonel Callender's 12th Marines supported the Da Nang and Phu Bai TAORs. At Chu Lai, Lieutenant Colonel Sullivan had three of his organic battalions under his command: the 2d Battalion, 11th Marines in direct support of the 5th Marines; the 3d Battalion, 11th Marines in direct support of the 7th Marines; and the 4th Battalion, 11th Marines in general support of the Chu Lai TAOR. Colonel Callender, on the other hand, had all of his organic artillery battalions under his command, as well as the 1st Battalion, 11th Marines in direct support of the 1st Marines at Da Nang. The other artillery units at Da Nang had the following missions: 1st Battalion, 12th Marines in direct support of the 3d Marines; the 2d Battalion, 12th Marines in direct support of the 9th Marines; the 4th Battalion, 12th Marines in general support. At Phu Bai, the 3d Battalion, 12th Marines was in direct support of the 4th Marines.**

Although the organization of the III MAF artillery arm was conventional, the nature of the war added a new dimension to its employment. Since there were no frontlines in the sense of a conventional war, artillery had to be able to fire in all directions within the TAOR. The proximity of large airbases and populated areas added restrictions; flight patterns and the possibility of killing innocent civilians were major considerations in the use of artillery.

By mid-1966, both the 11th and 12th Marines had developed several techniques for dealing with these realities. Both the 1st and 3d Division FSCCs put a premium on cooperation and coordination with the wing's DASCs and the ARVN FSCCs in their vicinity. After determining that restrictive fire plans and fire zones were too cumbersome for both Marine air and artillery, the artillery units initiated a procedure called Save-A-Plane to avoid hitting friendly aircraft. The battalion or regimental FSCC involved would radio when and where artillery was going to fire. After receiving this message, it was the pilot's responsibility to avoid the restricted firing areas.

Similarly, procedures were worked out with the South Vietnamese so that Marine artillery could res-

---

*Colonel Peter H. Hahn brought the 11th Marines Headquarters to Vietnam on 16 February and assumed command of the artillery units at Chu Lai on 1 March. Lieutenant Colonel Sullivan assumed command of the 11th Marines on 17 June, relieving Colonel Hahn.

**The 5th Marines had arrived in Vietnam in May and assumed control of the TAOR formerly held by the 1st Marines. The latter regiment, which had relieved the 4th Marines at Chu Lai at the end of January, moved to Da Nang in June. The 4th Marines assumed command of the Phu Bai TAOR on 26 March. See Chapters 4 and 8.

Marine Corps Photo A187767

A Marine forward artillery observer directs fire in support of the 1st Battalion, 1st Marines during Operation Virginia near Khe Sanh. His radioman can be seen sitting in the background relaying target information to the artillery battery.

pond effectively in support of their infantry units. By February 1966, the 3d Marine Division reported that much of the red tape involved in supporting ARVN troops had been eliminated. Colonel Callender's 12th Marines was able to respond quickly to fire support requests from the ARVN 51st Regiment operating south of the Da Nang base. Prior to that time, it had been necessary for the Marines to obtain clearance from the Da Nang Special Sector Headquarters.² By midyear, both the 11th and 12th Marines were supporting ARVN infantry units as a matter of course.

Artillery batteries not only remained in support of infantry units within the TAORs, but often deployed outside of the TAORs either to support specific operations or outposts. Double Eagle provided an excellent example of Marine artillery's mobility. During the operation, more than 45 artillery displacements were made. According to General Platt, who commanded Task Force Delta in that operation, the batteries were "rapidly displaced inland by helicopter or laterally, in small boats and craft . . . in order to keep the deep-ranging infantry within artillery firing fans."³ By June, far-flung Marine offensive operations had become routine. Infantry battalions and artillery batteries were married into large task forces, operating far from the Marine bases.

The Guns Move North and Restructuring the Command, July-December 1966

With the movement of the 3d Marine Division north of the Hai Van Pass and the assumption of both the Da Nang and Chu Lai TAORs by the 1st Marine Division, the artillery regiments, like all the other components of the two divisions, underwent a major realignment. The 12th Marines moved to the DMZ area, but retained a provisional artillery battalion consisting of two 105mm howitzer batteries, a 107mm mortar battery and the 1st 155mm Gun Battery at Phu Bai. Colonel Benjamin S. Read,* the 12th Marines commanding officer, established his headquarters at Dong Ha where his 4th Battalion provided general support. His 1st Battalion at the "artillery plateau," which later became Camp Carroll, furnished direct support to the 3d Marines, and the 3d Battalion, divided between Cam Lo and Con Thien, directly supported the two infantry battalions in the eastern DMZ area. Two U.S. Army artillery battalions, the 2d Battalion, 94th Artillery, and the 1st Battalion, 40th Artillery, armed with 175mm guns (SP) and 105mm howitzers (SP), respectively, reinforced the general support fires of the 4th Battalion, 12th Marines.**

---

*Colonel Read assumed command of the regiment from Colonel Callender in July 1966. The new regimental commander had commanded a battery of the 15th Marines in WW II on Guam and Okinawa. In Korea, in 1950, he commanded an 11th Marines battery.

**One battery, Battery B, 1st Battalion, 13th Marines, was stationed at Khe Sanh in direct support of the 1st Battalion, 3d Marines. Individual batteries of the 13th Marines, the artillery regiment of the 5th Division, arrived in-country with battalions of the 26th Marines. These batteries, like the battalions of the 26th Marines, represented no basic reinforcement of Marine units in Vietnam. They replaced individual batteries of the 11th or 12th Marines, which rotated either to Okinawa or the SLF as part of the intratheater transplacement system. See Chapter 18.

ARTILLERY SUPPORT IN 1966

Marines from Company K, 3d Battalion, 4th Marines pose on 10 November 1966 (the Marine Corps Birthday) in front of a new sign, carrying the new designation of the former "artillery plateau," renamed Camp J. J. Carroll in memory of the former Company K commander. Capt Carroll died in the assault on "Mutter" Ridge in October.

Assuming the responsibility for both the Da Nang and Chu Lai TAORs severely strained the 11th Marines. The regiment assumed command of its 1st Battalion at Da Nang, as well as the 2d Battalion, 12th Marines at the same base. In addition, the 1st 8-inch Howitzer Battery at the air base came under the regiment's command. Colonel Glenn E. Norris, an experienced artilleryman fresh from service with the U.S. Military Assistance Advisory Group on Taiwan, described the problems at his new command post at Da Nang in this manner:

> When we moved to the Da Nang TAOR I felt there was a deficiency, especially in heavy artillery . . . we operated with only three 8-inch howitzers and three 155mm guns. As you know, these weapons were old and it was quite a job to keep them up. Six weapons, considering their age and maintenance, were not satisfactory.[4]

At Chu Lai, Colonel Norris had little worry about long-range artillery support. The October arrival of Battery A, 2d Battalion, 94th Artillery (USA), with its four 175mm guns, reinforced the 4th Battalion,

Men from Battery H, 3d Battalion, 12th Marines fill sand bags to place around their 105mm howitzer positions at Dong Ha in May 1966. The artillery battery had accompanied the 2d Battalion, 4th Marines to northern I Corps during Operation Reno, a prelude to the larger deployment north in July.

Marine Corps Photo A187147

Marines from Battery D, 1st Battalion, 13th Marines fire in support of the 1st Battalion, 26th Marines during Operation Prairie in September 1966. Individual batteries of the 13th Marines accompanied the battalions of the 26th Marines into Vietnam.

11th Marines, which was providing general support for the Chu Lai base and the Korean Marines further south.* One Marine provisional battery of four towed 155mm howitzers was at the Quang Ngai Air Base near Quang Ngai City providing general support for the 2d ARVN Division operating in that area.**

Although the 2d and 3d Battalions of the 11th Marines continued to support the 5th Marines and 7th Marines, respectively, at Chu Lai, individual batteries or platoons operated outside the TAOR. For example, Battery F, 2d Battalion, 11th Marines, stationed four 105mm howitzers at the Tien Phouc Special Forces Camp to furnish direct support to the 1st Reconnaissance Battalion's operations. During November, two 105mm howitzers from Battery H, 3d Battalion, 11th Marines, moved out of the Chu Lai TAOR to Ha Thanh Special Forces Camp in the mountains 15 miles west of Quang Ngai City.

The move of the 11th Marines Headquarters to Da Nang left only a headquarters detachment with Task Force X-Ray, causing a void in the command and control of the widely dispersed Chu Lai artillery.

General Krulak had recognized this from the very beginning and notified General Walt that he was asking for authority to move the 1st Field Artillery Group (FAG) from Okinawa to Chu Lai. He explained, "This is a pretty able outfit. It has 22 officers and 127 enlisted; communications, motor transport and an operations platoon that includes a fire direction, survey, and meteorological capability."⁵ The FAG arrived at Chu Lai on 30 November and the next day, took control of all of the Chu Lai artillery from the 11th Marines (Rear). Lieutenant Colonel Joe B. Stribling, Norris' executive officer, assumed command of the new organization from Lieutenant Colonel Joseph M. Laney, Jr.*

The new command functioned smoothly. Lieutenant Colonel Stribling observed in his December report that the FAG was directing supporting fires for the defense of the Chu Lai base as well as for operations outside of the TAOR, including support for the ARVN, Koreans, Stingray operations, and search and destroy operations.⁶

These adjustments did not alter the fact that a significant proportion of Marine artillery was in northern Quang Tri Province at the end of the year. Of more than 250 artillery tubes assigned to the two artillery regiments, over 80 pieces, ranging from 4.2-inch mortars to the U.S. Army's 175mm guns,

---

*In addition to its organic 155mm howitzers (SP), the 4th Battalion had the 3d 8-inch Howitzer Battery (SP) of six 8-inch SP howitzers and the 3d 155 Gun Battery (SP) with six 155mm guns under its operational control.

**This battery was also under the operational control of the 4th Battalion, 11th Marines.

*Lieutenant Colonel Laney, who was junior to Stribling, became the FAG's executive officer.

Marines from Battery M, 3d Battalion, 12th Marines fire their 155mm M114A towed howitzers in October 1966 from positions at the Marine "artillery plateau" (redesignated the following month to Camp J. J. Carroll). Marine artillery fired over 28,600 rounds during the month in support of the infantry in the DMZ sector. This expenditure was exceeded in December by 6,000 rounds.

were strung along the DMZ. Although Marine infantry contact with enemy troops in the area dropped sharply from September and October, the artillery effort did not diminish. In fact, the 12th Marines fired approximately 8,000 more rounds in Quang Tri Province during December than in October.*

In Thua Thien Province, two changes in the artillery organization occurred in December. First, the 4th Battalion, 12th Marines assumed control of the artillery at Phu Bai. Lieutenant Colonel David G. Jones, the battalion commander, later recalled that General Kyle wanted "a 'numbered battalion' headquarters" there and, on 17 December, Jones established his new command post at the base.[7] One week later, another battalion headquarters, the 3d Battalion, 12th Marines, took command of the artillery committed to Operation Chinook in northern Thua Thien.

The continued depletion of the artillery at Da Nang and Chu Lai to counter the enemy in the north caused some difference of opinion within the Marine command. General Nickerson, the commanding general of the 1st Marine Division, in a message to General Walt on 30 November, observed that the artillery at both Da Nang and Chu Lai was insufficient and that the situation at Da Nang would become even worse. He pointed out that the Army artillery battery which supported the battalion from the 503d Airborne Battalion was leaving with that unit and he was receiving no replacements or reinforcements.**

---

*The regiment fired 10,388 missions, expending 36,869 rounds during December, as opposed to 6,643 missions and 28,430 rounds during October. See 12th Marines, Table of Ammunition Expenditures and Types of Missions Fired, encl 2, 12th Marines AAR, Operation Prairie I, dtd Feb67.

**Although the 1st Armored Amphibian Company had arrived from the U.S. with 12 LVTH-6s, an armored amphibian assault vehicle mounting a 105mm howitzer, the company represented no true reinforcement for the Da Nang TAOR. Upon the arrival of the company, a platoon of six LVTH's that had been at Da Nang since 1965 moved to the DMZ. Of the remaining two platoons of the company, one stayed at Da Nang while the other joined the SLF.

General Nickerson stated that he needed at least seven direct support batteries at Da Nang instead of six and declared that the "shortage of general support artillery in Da Nang continues to be critical." The 1st Division commander considered it inadvisable to move a general support battery from Chu Lai to Da Nang and requested reinforcement from "external resources."[8] Although sympathetic to General Nickerson's predicament, General Walt was forced to deny the request. The III MAF commander declared that the artillery allocation was "appropriate in light of assets available." He further stated that there was little likelihood of III MAF receiving any additional artillery in the foreseeable future.[9]

Despite General Nickerson's reservations, the tactical deployment of his artillery was such that it could counter any likely attempt by the North Vietnamese and Viet Cong to overrun Marine positions. The most lucrative targets for Marine supporting arms were provided by the more conventional war in the DMZ where division faced division, rather than the counterguerrilla campaign in the heavily populated area south of Da Nang. In any event, Marine artillery spanned the length of I Corps from the DMZ to Quang Ngai and in the words of Shakespeare: "The cannon have their bowels full of wrath, and ready mounted are they to spit forth their iron indignation."[10]

CHAPTER 18

Men and Material

Manpower—Logistics, Medical Support, and Construction

Manpower

By the beginning of 1966, all of the Armed Forces were feeling the drain on manpower resources. Hanson Baldwin, the military analyst for the *New York Times*, wrote in February 1966, "The Nation's armed services have almost exhausted their trained and ready military units, with all available troops spread dangerously thin in Vietnam and elsewhere."[1]

Baldwin's article touched on the sensitive issue of raising enough troops to fulfill General Westmoreland's increasing Vietnam requirements. In December 1965, Secretary McNamara had approved the deployment of 184,000 troops to Vietnam during 1966, nearly twice the number of American troops already there. Throughout 1966, various echelons of the American command, from the President to MACV, studied and restudied alternative deployment plans. Considerable debate existed within the U.S. Government about the eventual size of the American commitment, but, by June 1966, President Johnson and Secretary McNamara had made two important decisions. They rejected any callup of the Reserves and established the projected strength of American forces in Vietnam for the end of the year to be 390,000 men. According to these projections, by December 1966 General Westmoreland would have 79 maneuver battalions and supporting air and ground units under his command.*

The Marine Corps found itself in the same manpower dilemma as its sister Services. The Corps was committed to a 70,000-man force in Vietnam, which meant that by the end of the year, the entire 1st and 3d Marine Divisions and most of the 1st Marine Aircraft Wing would be in Vietnam. Compounding the difficulty for the Marine Corps was the fact that the tour of the individual Marine was 13 months. Not only were new units being deployed to Vietnam, but replacements for Marines whose overseas tours were almost over also had to be sent to Vietnam.** Thus the actual number of Marines that served in Vietnam

---

*This represented an increase of approximately 22,000 troops, including four maneuver battalions over previous projections. During 1966, several deployment plans were approved and then modified. These had several designations, i.e., Phase II, Phase IIA, and Program 3. Other plans were still being studied. For a detailed account of the overall U.S. planning efforts, see "U.S. Ground Strategy and Force Deployments 1965-67," *Pentagon Papers*, bk 5, sec. IV-C-6, v. I, pp. 25-51. Maneuver battalions referred to both tank and infantry battalions. On 21 December 1966, MACV had 69 infantry and 10 tank battalions. At least one of the Service chiefs, General Wallace M. Greene, Jr., the Commandant of the Marine Corps, disagreed with the decision not to call up the Reserves. In his comments, General Greene refers to this decision as "a fatal mistake. . . ." Gen Wallace M. Greene, Jr., Comments on draft MS, dtd 5May78 (Vietnam Comment File).

**In September 1965, the Marine Corps ended its peacetime intertheater battalion rotation between the Eastern Pacific and Western Pacific and went to an individual replacement system, although a modified intratheater battalion rotation among battalions assigned to the SLF, Vietnam, and Okinawa was established. Colonel John P. Lanigan, who served as the 3d Marine Division G-1 in 1966, observed that the establishment of the individual replacement system "required a complete reshuffling of personnel between battalions in WestPac [code named Operation Mixmaster]. . . . This had a rather drastic and undesirable effect on the integrity and morale of the battalions concerned." Commenting on this problem from the FMFPac perspective, Colonel John E. Greenwood, who served on both the III MAF and FMFPac staffs, remembered that General Krulak, CGFMFPac at the time, "maintained that the Marine Corps should never again stabilize units or adopt a policy of unit rotation. . . . His [Krulak's] conclusion—organize in peacetime, the way you must organize and operate in war." Col John P. Lanigan, Comments on draft MS, dtd 8Jun78 and Col John E. Greenwood, Note on Lanigan Comments, dtd 12Jun78 (Vietnam Comment File). See Shulimson and Johnson, *U.S. Marines in Vietnam, 1965*, p. 117 for discussion of the old transplacement system and Operation Mixmaster.

became the Commanding General, 5th Marine Division, in addition to his other duties.

On 28 July, BLT 1/26, the first unit of the division to be deployed, arrived at Okinawa and became the SLF battalion, relieving BLT 3/5. The 3d Battalion was sent to Chu Lai, bringing III MAF to a strength of 18 battalions, the total authorized for the Marine command in 1966. In August, RLT 26 Headquarters arrived at Okinawa and BLT 2/26 relieved the 3d Battalion, 3d Marines at Da Nang. The latter battalion departed Vietnam for Okinawa. These forces represented no reinforcements for III MAF, but reestablished the Pacific command's capability to meet contingency situations.

Even the earlier deployment of the 1st Marine Division in 1966 had not eased the III MAF manpower situation. Because of the intricacies of the individual replacement system, both the 1st and 3d Divisions were understrength by midyear. In June the 1st Marine Division reported that the average strength of an infantry company was 2.8 officers and 151 enlisted.* The 3d Division furnished generally the same figures for the month, stating that its average company strength was 2.9 officers and 148 enlisted men. During July, these averages remained at the same level. By August, both Marine divisions indicated that the average infantry company strength had risen to 4.3 officers and 155 men for the 3d Division and 3.8 officers and 160 men for the 1st.[3] By the end of the month, the 1st Marine Divi-

Marine Corps Photo A187876

While their gear is being lowered from a troop transport, men of the 1st Battalion, 26th Marines wait on board a landing craft before going ashore at Da Nang. The 26th Marines, part of the newly formed 5th Marine Division, arrived in the Pacific in August and during the remaining months of the year, its battalions replaced other battalions in Vietnam as part of the intratheater battalion transplacement system.

during 1966 was much larger than 70,000. Since there was no Reserve mobilization, the Marines were authorized to accept some draftees and also expand their authorized strength from 231,000 to 286,000.[2]

In December 1965, Secretary McNamara had approved the reactivation of the 5th Marine Division; personnel were to come, partially, from the new augmentation allowed the Marine Corps. On 1 March 1966, the Defense Department officially announced the formation of the division. The base commander of the Marine Base at Camp Pendleton, California, Major General Robert E. Cushman, Jr.,

---

*The authorized strength of a Marine infantry company was six officers and 210 enlisted men. Several former battalion commanders commented on the manpower shortages in their respective units. Lieutenant Colonel Emerson A. Walker, who commanded the 3d Battalion, 1st Marines at Da Nang, remembered that he lost 85 percent of his officers and 75 percent of his senior noncommissioned officers within a 60-day period. Another officer, Colonel Birchard B. Dewitt, who commanded the 3d Battalion, 7th Marines, recalled that in June 1966, he had only 14 officers in his battalion, including the battalion surgeon and chaplain: "Each infantry company had *one* officer except India which had the luxury of having two." Lieutenant Colonel Ralph E. Sullivan, who commanded the 1st Battalion, 4th Marines, observed, "Rifle company strengths . . . do not begin to tell the story. You might have 148 enlisted on the rolls of a rifle company, but by the time you subtracted those sick, lame, and lazy, R&R, etc., etc., and etc., you were lucky to put 110 men in the field." LtCol Emerson A. Walker, Comments on draft MS, n.d. [Jun78], Col Birchard B. Dewitt, Comments on draft MS, dtd 6Jul78, and LtCol Ralph E. Sullivan, Comments on draft MS, dtd 9May78 (Vietnam Comment File).

sion was almost at authorized strength, but the 3d was still short 2,000 men.[4]

By October 1966, General Walt was faced with an expanded war. The Marines were moving toward the DMZ, while still conducting major operations and maintaining the southern TAORs. In addition, programs such as combined action were draining men from infantry units. Colonel Chaisson, the former III MAF G-3, stated that although the personnel shortage did not inhibit assigning battalions to a specific mission, "It was a matter of how far people can be pushed."[5]

The presence of the 26th Marines units in the Western Pacific provided some help. It allowed FMFPac to reinstitute the intratheater rotation program which had ended the previous March.* Under the system, the SLF battalion would relieve a battalion in Vietnam; the latter battalion would displace to Okinawa; a fresh battalion on Okinawa would then become the new SLF battalion with the Seventh Fleet. From August to December 1966, six battalions participated in the program. By the end of the year, all three battalions of the 26th Marines were in South Vietnam.** Although not providing General Walt with additional troops, this intratheater transplacement of battalions allowed him, at least periodically, to refurbish his forces.

During this period, Generals Greene and Krulak also took measures to expedite the movement of personnel to Vietnam. After a visit to III MAF in October, General Krulak reported that the Commandant had inaugurated an increase in programmed replacements which would ease the situation by the end of the year.[6] One of the first steps that Headquarters Marine Corps took was to defer the activation dates of the 5th Marine Division units, with the exception of the 26th Marines, from 1966 to 1967.[7] This allowed the Marine Corps to divert individual Marines who would have been assigned to these units to the Southeast Asia manpower pool. In January 1967, the manpower situation had improved to the extent that most battalions had 1,200 to 1,300 Marines, in comparison to a strength of about 800 men a few weeks before.[8] By July 1967, the Marine Corps could boast that it had completed both the scheduled buildup to a total strength of 286,000, as well as programmed deployments to the war zone, without missing any target dates.[9]

Logistics, Medical Support, and Construction

By the beginning of 1966, the rapid buildup of Marine forces had created a grim logistic situation. Shortages occurred in spare parts, fuel, and certain types of ammunition. The wear and tear on equipment caused by heavy usage, heat, sand, and humidity, compounded by the monsoons, created additional frustrations.[10] Complicating the situation even more was the slow unloading of vessels in the undeveloped I Corps ports. For example, cargo unloaded at Da Nang had to be reloaded on LSTs in order to be landed at the shallow draft ramp at Chu Lai. At the beginning of December 1965, 17 ships were in Da Nang Harbor unloading or waiting to be unloaded. The figure had been reduced to 12 by the end of 1965, but seven of these ships had been in port longer than two weeks and four had been there for over a month. General Walt described the III MAF logistic status as follows: "We were operating on a 'shoe string'—a critical period—when only exceptional ingenuity, initiative and extremely hard and dedicated labor kept the supplies flowing to the fighting troops."[11]

Many of the difficulties had been anticipated by the Marine and Navy commanders. Vice Admiral Edwin B. Hooper, at that time Commander, Service Force, U.S. Pacific Fleet, commented that he had initiated a number of actions in November 1965 to ease the unloading problem. These included a program for all-weather packaging and pallet loading of cargoes for ships destined for Da Nang or Chu Lai. In December he requested that the Military Transport Management Terminal Service (MTMTS) in San Francisco "assemble full ship loads for direct sail to Da Nang," and that MTMTS segregate Chu Lai cargo so that it could be handled expeditiously at Da Nang. He also instituted a program at Subic Bay for unloading cargo from deep-draft ships onto LSTs. The admiral assigned four LSTs to shuttle supplies between Subic, Da Nang, and Chu Lai. The unloading situation was resolved by close cooperation between the Navy and Marines. Admiral Hooper visited General Walt in December 1965,

---

*See Chapter 4.

**The 3d Battalion, 26th Marines arrived in the Western Pacific during October.

An aerial view of the Da Nang River, going past Museum Landing Ramp to the Bridge Cargo Facility at Da Nang. Da Nang was second only to Saigon as a port in Vietnam.

A Navy petty officer stands on a "city block" of C-Rations at a Da Nang pier. The Naval Support Activity, Da Nang was responsible for common item support for U.S. forces in I Corps.

afterward noting that General Walt was particularly cooperative—as always:

> I briefed him and key staff officers after dinner at his quarters then on a hill west of Da Nang. He offered the help of his troops whenever needed, and then took steps to improve the flow of trucks during peak periods. The Marine shore party did its part until the last remnant at Da Nang was relieved. . . .[12]*

As a result of these steps, by the end of January 1966, General Walt could report that the Chu Lai backlog had been reduced to the lowest figure in over five months.** In late February, the III MAF

---

*The Marine shore party was attached to the Naval Support Activity, Da Nang, which was responsible for common item support to U.S. forces in I Corps as well as the operation of the unloading activities of all beaches and ports in I Corps. Until the Support Activity reached full strength on 11 March, elements of the 3d Shore Party Battalion assisted the Navy in the unloading of ships at Da Nang. Until 1 April, the Naval Support Activity, Da Nang reported directly to General Walt in his capacity as Naval Component Commander. See Chapter 1 and Shulimson and Johnson, *Marines in Vietnam, 1965.*

**In relation to the situation at Chu Lai, Admiral Hooper observed, "I don't believe that anyone who was not there at the time can appreciate the difficulties of getting supplies in by sea and over the beach, especially during the Northeast Monsoon Season . . . . The shuttling of supplies by sea by NavSupAct [Naval Support Activity], Da Nang and beach operations were touch and go for a long time, especially since the dredge we requested from Saigon, and expected momentarily, kept being delayed. . . . It was not until mid-January 1966 that a 11-foot deep pass had been made through the shoal water at the mouth of the Troung River, and not until 20 March that a 14-foot channel was available." VAdm Edwin B. Hooper, Comments on draft MS, n.d. [May78] (Vietnam Comment File).

An aerial view of Force Logistic Support Group Bravo at Chu Lai. The group was a component part of the III MAF Force Logistic Command and provided centralized control of supplies, construction, and administrative support at Chu Lai.

commander was able to declare that for the first time there were no ships in the Da Nang Harbor waiting to be unloaded.[13] Admiral Hooper commented, "From there on in [late February 1966], no other port ever matched the performance of Da Nang."[14]

The Marine Corps had initiated several of its own measures to ease the logistic strain. Late in 1965, General Krulak introduced the Red Ball and Critipac programs. The Red Ball system, started 22 September 1965, had as its basic purpose the identification of the critical logistical problems in the Western Pacific. When an important item was found to be in short supply it was given a Red Ball, or high priority, designation. All FMFPac supply echelons were then alerted and individual action officers were assigned to monitor the status of these items. These officers had the responsibility of insuring that the Red Ball item was shipped to Vietnam as quickly as possible. FMFPac inaugurated the Critipac system in November 1965. Under this concept, the Marine Corps Supply Center at Barstow, California sent each major Marine unit in Vietnam, usually battalion-size, one 400-pound box of critical supplies normally required on a routine basis, but rapidly expended by the deployed units.[15]

Both of these systems continued to be refined after their inception. At the beginning of 1966, General Walt had declared that only those repair parts for equipment, the loss of which would substantially reduce unit combat effectiveness, could be placed in Red Ball status. The III MAF commander also made similar recommendations for the Critipac program. The Red Ball system had improved the stock level of critical supplies to the extent that the criteria for Red Ball now included such items as "blank forms and typewriters."[16] During March, General Walt ordered III MAF to computerize Red Ball records to reduce his headquarter's administrative workload.[17] At the end of the month, General Greene formally recognized the FMFPac Red Ball program and ordered all Marine supply activities to support the system.[18]

The most important logistic development during this period was the establishment of the Force Logistic Command on 15 March. Until that time, Colonel Mauro J. Padalino's Force Logistic Support Group (FLSG) had been the central supply agency for III MAF. During 1965, the FLSG had grown from slightly less than 700 personnel to more than 3,000 officers and men by the end of the year. Based

An aerial view of Force Logistic Support Group Alpha at Da Nang. The group performed the same services at Da Nang as Bravo did at Chu Lai.

on the nucleus of the 3d Service Battalion, the FLSG had been reinforced by 1st Service Battalion units and elements of the 3d Force Service Regiment.* The FLSG Headquarters was at Da Nang while two Force Logistic Support Units (FLSU) were established at Chu Lai and Phu Bai. As early as September 1965, General Krulak was of the opinion that it was necessary to transform the FLSG into a Force Logistic Command, but the first steps toward the transformation were not taken until early 1966. In mid-January, Colonel Padalino chaired a three-week conference at FMFPac Headquarters in Honolulu at which a mission, and provisional Tables of Organization (T/O) and Equipment (T/E), for the new command were determined.[19] On 19 February, General Krulak provided General Walt the basic guidance for the establishment of the logistic command. General Walt's headquarters published its standing operating procedures on 13 March and the Force Logistic Command (FLC) came into existence two days later.[20]

The establishment of the FLC was more of a change in name than function. At Da Nang, the FLSG became FLSG Alpha and remained under the command of Colonel Padalino. He also retained control of the FLSU at Phu Bai. The FLSU at Chu Lai became FLSG Bravo which reported directly to the FLC. Colonel George C. Axtell, Jr., formerly General Walt's III MAF Chief of Staff, assumed command of the FLC.[21]

One of the basic problems facing the new command was the lack of covered storage space. To alleviate the situation, III MAF allocated nine of the first 12 Butler buildings to arrive in Vietnam to the logistic command.[22] By the end of April, FLC had funded over 40 million dollars for facilities construction. The funding included the development of an entirely new cantonment for FLSG Alpha at Da Nang. Seabees of the 30th Naval Construction Regiment (NCR) had already erected 16 Butler buildings in the logistic group's new location on Red Beach, seven miles northwest of the old FLSG site. At Chu Lai, Naval Mobile Construction Battalion (NMCB) 4

---

*The 3d Force Service Regiment was responsible for logistic activities on Okinawa. Although separate units of the regiment were stationed in Vietnam, the regimental flag never left Okinawa. The 1st Service Battalion was the logistic support battalion of the 1st Marine Division, just as the 3d Service Battalion supported the 3d Marine Division. As indicated in the text, the service battalions became part of the Force Logistic Support Group which operated directly under III MAF rather than the divisions.

from the 30th NCR was working on semipermanent construction for FLSG Bravo. In addition, the FLC had contracted with civilian firms for construction of a second ammunition supply point at Chu Lai and for the improvement of the existing ammunition supply point at Da Nang, as well as the construction of a second Da Nang ammunition supply point.[23]

By midyear, the FLC was in full operation. Despite the disruptions of the spring political crisis, the construction program was generally on schedule. More significantly, the command had grown to a strength of over 5,300 officers and men; nearly 2,000 personnel had joined since March. During this period, the III MAF logistic organization processed more than 127,000 requisitions. In addition, the FLC began to perform limited 4th echelon maintenance of deadlined equipment which previously had to be evacuated to Okinawa for repair.[24]

The true test of the Marine logistic organization came when Marine operations moved into northern Quang Tri Province. During Operation Hastings, for example, more than 4,000 tons of supplies were flown from Da Nang to the makeshift airfield at Dong Ha. Furthermore, two Navy barges ferried over 240 tons of ammunition to Dong Ha from Marine stockpiles at Da Nang.[25] General Westmoreland expressed his surprise at the Marine logistic flexibility to General Krulak. According to General Krulak:

> In connection with deep operations of the Hastings variety, General Westmoreland commented that he had been concerned earlier with the possibility that the Marines might be incapable of sustaining such large endeavors logistically. He observed that their excellent logistic performance throughout Hastings had gratified and reassured him. I replied that basically, the Marines have a balanced logistical system, capable of sustaining operations such as Hastings.*[26]

With the continuation of the DMZ war and the movement of the 3d Marine Division north, the Dong Ha logistic base expanded. In early October, the Dong Ha Logistic Support Area (LSA) contained a sizeable ammunition dump as well as a rations dump, operated by a 150-man team. The Marine logisticians had prepared plans for the buildup of the Dong Ha LSA to provide a 30-to-45-day level of supply to support division units operating in the DMZ area. Colonel Axtell noted that the Marine command was examining the feasibility of removing a sand bar blocking the Cua Viet River so that LCUs could enter and leave the stream and resupply Dong Ha on a 24-hour basis.[27] Admiral Hooper commented that when the water was low, shifting sand bars blocked the way upstream, but Naval Support Activity, Da Nang mounted a crawler crane with a "clam shell" on a LCU for dredging and was able to keep the river route open. The Naval Support Activity and the FLC provided the Marines with over 35,000 tons of supplies via the water passage to Dong Ha.[28]

By the end of the year, the logistic organization in the northern two provinces had been revamped. The FLSU at Phu Bai had become FLSU-2, responsible for logistic support at Phu Bai and Dong Ha, as well as the Marine battalion at Khe Sanh. FLSU-2 was now a major subunit of the FLC. Its new status was

A view of the III MAF ammunition dump at Dong Ha. With the movement of the 3d Marine Division to the DMZ sector, the Marines established another logistic support area.

Marine Corps Photo A188161

---

*For a detailed account of Operation Hastings, see Chapter 10.

officially recognized on 1 December when the unit became independent of FLSG Alpha reporting directly to the FLC. By the end of December, the unit had reached a strength of nearly 900 men, over a third of whom were engaged in support of the Prairie Operation.[29]

By the end of 1966, the Marine Corps had completed major modifications of its logistic system to support Marine combat operations in the five northern provinces. Its world-wide logistic network extended from Albany, Georgia, and Barstow, California, through the 3d Force Service Regiment, Okinawa, and then to the I Corps Tactical Zone. The III MAF FLC monitored all logistic activities under its control with electronic data processing systems.

Despite the refinements in the logistic system, shortages still existed in certain areas. Colonel Franklin C. Thomas, Jr., commanding officer of MAG-11, observed that high-level statistical analysis did not always reflect the needs of the units in the field. He recalled:

> It took me a long time to find out why we could only obtain 250-pound bombs when we consistently requisitioned 500-, 750-, and 1,000- pound bombs. All we had in any numbers were 250's and so that is what we were using, although for most of our targets they were almost ineffective. Finally, it became apparent that our resupply was being done on the basis of our usage reports rather than from our requisitions. To my shame I began falsifying my usage data, and within two months we began to receive the heavier weapons which increased our effectiveness (not to mention our morale).[30]

In a somewhat lighter vein, Colonel James M. Callender, the commander of the 12th Marines, remembered that during an inspection trip, General Krulak asked one of the artillery section chiefs if he had any problems:

> The sergeant's reply was "only one, General; I'm trying to clean this 105mm howitzer with a 90mm bore brush!" . . . within three days, the 12th Marines had a corner on most of the bore brushes in the western world.[31]

Even with shortages, III MAF was able to support all tactical operations and Marine logisticians by the end of the year had initiated remedial actions. At the end of 1966, the FLC and the 3d Force Service Regiment were filling 85 percent of all requisitions. Maintenance also improved; the deadline rate for combat-essential material was reduced from over 12 percent to eight percent by the end of December, although the deadline rate of Marine engineer equipment and generators still remained high. One Marine logistician, Colonel Edward L. Bale, Jr., the 1st Marine Division G-4, summed up the logistic situation as follows: "III MAF was faced with supply, maintenance, construction tasks not previously confronting Marine Corps forces. The ability to support the combat elements from CONUS via Okinawa with the limited stock fund assets, maintenance, and construction was, in many ways, remarkable."[32]

Colonel Axtell, who was relieved as commanding officer of the FLC by Brigadier General James E. Herbold, Jr., described the role of the FLC in the following words:*

> The FLC has a role to provide an organization by relieving the operational commander of many of the day to day details in services. We think of it as a maintenance and supply function, but there are also other attendant services that can be provided to relieve divisions and wings . . . such as a transient center . . . handling reports, and an administrative headquarters to administer force units. I would like to suggest the FLC in its role reflects the capability of the Marine Corps to organize and adjust its forces to use the minimum of resources to accomplish a task.[33]

No logistic discussion would be complete without an account of the medical support provided by the Navy. Responsible for all medical assistance to the Marines, naval medical personnel managed all of the III MAF medical facilities down to the individual battalion and squadron aid stations. At the lowest level, a Navy corpsman accompanied each Marine rifle platoon into action. Part of the Marine division organization, two medical battalions, the 1st and 3d, reinforced at the end of 1966 by the 1st Hospital Company, were responsible for the Marine intermediate medical facilities at Chu Lai, Da Nang, Phu Bai, and later in the year at Dong Ha, as well as direct support for individual operations. Commanded by a Navy doctor, each battalion consisted largely of naval personnel reinforced by a few Marines for administrative and support purposes. For the most serious and more complex cases, the Naval Support Activity, Da Nang ran its own hospital. Opening in

---

*General Herbold, an experienced logistician, was Chief of Staff of the Marine Corps Supply Activity, Philadelphia prior to his promotion on 8 September 1966 to brigadier general. He assumed command of the FLC on 3 October 1966.

January with only 50 beds, this hospital had room for over 400 beds at the end of the year. Besides X-ray and modern laboratory facilities, the hospital had departments and clinics in neurosurgery; urology; eye, ear, nose, and throat ailments; and preventive medicine. In March 1966, the newly refitted hospital ship *Repose* (AH 16) arrived off I Corps to provide additional medical support for the Marines. With 560 beds, the *Repose* had medical facilities and equipment to rival a modern hospital in the United States. During Operations Hastings and Prairie, Marine helicopters often evacuated casualties directly from the battlefield to the *Repose* with as many as 98 brought on board the ship in one day.[34]

The operating room, like the battlefield, had its dramatic moments. One of the more spectacular involved the removal of a live grenade from the throat of a wounded Marine private on 20 December 1966 at the 3d Medical Battalion facility at Da Nang. Apparently the grenade entered the Marine's mouth in a downward trajectory, broke the jaw, and lodged into the heavily-muscled part of the tongue, pushing aside the voice box. Since the X-ray only showed a gray opaque object in the throat, the naval surgeon, Lieutenant Commander James G. Chandler, was unaware of the presence of the grenade until he made his incision. At first, Chandler thought the object to be some sort of detonator and consulted with another surgeon. The two doctors then decided that "it would be pretty safe to remove anything which had cracked the jaw." With his forceps unable to secure the object, Chandler used his fingers and "popped it into his hand." The Navy surgeon recalled that he then asked what the thing was and "someone said a M-79 grenade." Carrying the grenade gingerly in his left hand, Chandler then walked out of the operating room to a ditch some distance from the medical facility. He gently placed the grenade inside the ditch, "took about four steps calmly and then ran like hell." A Marine demolition team later safely exploded the live grenade. The patient also recovered.[35]

Although the Navy doctors and corpsmen played a large role in the Marine Corps civic action program, treating well over a million South Vietnamese civilians in 1966, their greatest and most important contribution was the saving of the lives of the wounded. With the use of the helicopter, a wounded Marine, on the average, could expect to be at a medical facility within a half hour after the evacuation aircraft was requested.[36] Of the nearly 6,400 Marines and sailors of III MAF wounded during 1966, 214 died of their wounds, a mortality rate of less than four percent.[37] The following excerpt from the Navy Unit Commendation awarded to the 3d Medical Battalion applied as well to the entire Navy medical support in I Corps:

> The officers and men . . . despite shortages of personnel and medical supplies—and adverse conditions of heat, humidity and monsoon rains—succeeded in reducing the mortality rate of wounded U.S. Marines to the lowest figure in wartime history.[38]

Another unsung effort was the massive construction work in I Corps accomplished by the Navy construction battalions (Seabees), civilian construction firms, and Marine engineer battalions. The Seabees

Marines during Operation Texas carry a wounded comrade to a waiting evacuation helicopter in March 1966. A wounded Marine, on the average, could expect to be at a medical facility within 30 minutes after the helicopter was requested.

Marine Corps Photo A186817

Navy Seabees are seen at work constructing hardback tents in the base area of the 3d Battalion, 9th Marines at Da Nang. Seabees and civilian construction firms were largely responsible for the building of the large base facilities in the Marine enclaves.

Marine engineers construct a pontoon bridge across the Da Nang River. The new bridge, together with the old permanent one, connects the Tiensha Peninsula with the main base at Da Nang.

and the civilian contractors were largely responsible for the building of the large base facilities at the various Marine enclaves and airfield construction including the extension of the Da Nang runway and 10,000-foot permanent airfield at Chu Lai.* They helped to modernize port facilities with the construction of three deepwater piers, all of which were operational by the beginning of 1967 and increased the Da Nang port capacity by 5,140 short tons per month.[39]

Marine engineers also made their contribution. By the end of 1966, five Marine engineer battalions were in Vietnam: the 1st and 3d Engineers supported the 1st and 3d Marine Divisions respectively, while the heavy engineer battalions, the 7th, 9th, and 11th, operated directly under III MAF.** During the year the engineers built 107 miles of new roads, improved 1,582 miles of existing roads, and erected 48 bridges of all types, ranging from foot treadways to Class-60 bridges capable of supporting Marine M-48 tanks. They assisted the Seabees and

---

*During 1966, nearly 1,295,000 square feet of storage and maintenance facilities were built. Colonel Fred J. Frazer, the 1st MAW G-4, observed that although most of the construction was under Navy control, "III MAF and the Wing were extremely active in the planning and the allocation of construction resources." Col Fred J. Frazer, Comments on draft MS, dtd 16Jun78 (Vietnam Comment File). At least one Marine officer, Colonel Drew J. Barrett, Jr., who served both as Commanding Officer, 9th Marines and III MAF G-3, had his reservations about the extent of the base buildup in Vietnam: "The theatres, big messes, supermarket PX's, pools, bowling alleys, and the like merely created targets for the enemy, and additionally built up a fixed-base attitude in the minds of everyone except frontline troops. For what these installations cost us we could have provided three or four R&R's [Rest and Recuperation] for everyone and retained a lean and mean attitude." Col Drew J. Barrett, Jr., Comments on draft MS, dtd 5May78 (Vietnam Comment File).

**The 3d and 7th battalions were in Vietnam at the beginning of the year. The 1st Engineer Battalion arrived with the 1st Division in March. The 9th Engineers deployed to Vietnam in May and assumed responsibility for the larger engineering tasks at Chu Lai while the 7th operated in the Da Nang area. The 11th did not arrive until November 1966 and moved to Dong Ha, where it reinforced the hard-pressed 3d Engineer Battalion in the struggle along the DMZ.

Marine Corps Photo A187722

A Marine sweeps a road with a mine detector while the rest of the squad follows him. The men are students at the mine warfare school established by the 3d Engineer Battalion at Da Nang to reduce mine casualties.

private firms in base construction at Chu Lai and Da Nang. At Dong Ha and Khe Sanh, they assisted in the improvement of base areas, as well as the improvement of the airfield facilities at both locations. Moreover, Marine engineers provided combat support to the infantry by conducting daily road sweeps, and mine clearing, and destroying enemy tunnels.* Perhaps the best summation of the entire I Corps support effort, including that of the engineers, in 1966, is contained in the following excerpt from a 1st MAW report: "Much was accomplished, much more remains to be done."[40]

---

*Lieutenant Colonel Conway J. Smith recalled that through June 1966, "the young Marines of the 3d Engineer Battalion performed daily mine sweeps over more than 20 miles of tactical roads. These same Marines also provided demolition support during most infantry operations. They also constructed more than 600 weapons bunkers and built up an additional 48 miles of tactical roads and 60 pioneer bridges. In addition to this, a cadre of engineer mine warfare NCOs conducted a mine warfare school which instructed and indoctrinated more than 4,500 Marine (and some Army) personnel in the technicalities of Viet Cong mines and booby traps." LtCol Conway J. Smith, Comments on draft MS, dtd 9Jun78 (Vietnam Comment File).

PART VIII
THE SLF, ADVISORS, OTHER MARINE ACTIVITIES, AND A FINAL LOOK AT 1966

CHAPTER 19
The SLF of the Seventh Fleet

The SLF, Double Eagle, and Doctrinal Debates — The Okinawa Conference — Changes in Command and Composition — Further Operations and Changes in Commands and Units — The May Conference — The SLF to the End of the Year

The SLF, Double Eagle, and Doctrinal Debates

With the commitment of most Okinawa-based Marine forces to Vietnam by the end of 1965, the Seventh Fleet's Special Landing Force (SLF) was the Pacific command's only strategic reserve for all of the Far East.* It consisted of a SLF Marine command and staff, approximating the organization of an infantry regimental staff; a Marine battalion landing team, consisting of a Marine infantry battalion reinforced by artillery and other support elements; and a Marine helicopter squadron. The Marine SLF commander reported directly to the Navy amphibious ready group commander. Although under the overall operational control of the Seventh Fleet, the SLF was readily available to General Westmoreland for specific operations in Vietnam.

At the beginning of 1966, Colonel John R. Burnett was the SLF commander; his headquarters was on board the USS *Valley Forge* (LPH 8). Lieutenant Colonel William K. Horn's BLT 2/3 and Lieutenant Colonel Mervin B. Porter's HMM-261 made up the ground and aviation components. On 5 January, Lieutenant Colonel James Aldworth's HMM-362 replaced HMM-261. Burnett moved his headquarters from the *Valley Forge* to the attack transport *Paul Revere* (APA 248) on the same

Marine Corps Photo A422636
LtCol James Aldworth, Commanding Officer, HMM-362, is seen talking to LtCol Mervin B. Porter, Commanding Officer, HMM-261, on board the USS Valley Forge *(LPH 8). HMM-362 relieved HMM-261 as the helicopter squadron of the SLF on 5 January 1966.*

date.** From 5-26 January 1966, Burnett's staff was occupied with the planning effort for Operation Double Eagle.

Double Eagle, which began on 28 January and terminated on 1 March 1966, was the largest amphibious operation yet held in the Vietnam war. Task Force Delta, which included the SLF as well as III MAF units, landed first in Quang Ngai Province and then moved into the Que Son Valley further north. Despite extensive preparation and the lengthy duration of Double Eagle, the Marines failed to engage any large NVA or VC main force unit.

Double Eagle brought to a head some of the basic differences between III MAF and the SLF concerning

---

*Vice Admiral Edwin B. Hooper, who had commanded Amphibious Group 1 in the Far East in 1962, observed that "under Commander Seventh Fleet, the Western Pacific Amphibious Force and, except for units committed to Vietnam, Fleet Marine Force had to be prepared on little or no notice to conduct operations anywhere in the Far East and Western Pacific. This was especially true in the case of the Amphibious Ready Group and Special Landing Force." VAdm Edwin B. Hooper, Comments on draft MS, n.d. [May78] (Vietnam Comment File).

**The other ships of the amphibious task force were the attack transport ship USS *Montrose* (APA 212) and the landing ship dock USS *Monticello* (LSD 35).

its employment. According to amphibious doctrine, the amphibious task force commander, always a Navy officer, was to have operational control of all forces, including aviation, in the amphibious objective area until the amphibious portion of the operation was over.* He was to exercise control of the ground forces through his deputy, the landing force commander, either a Marine or an Army officer, depending on the composition of the landing force. As the landing force commander for Double Eagle, Colonel Burnett was to turn over command of the ground forces to General Platt, the Task Force Delta commander, once the landing was completed. Since bad weather delayed the completion of the amphibious portion of the operation, an awkward command relationship resulted. According to Colonel Burnett:

> The command relationship . . . in effect created a dual command structure for the period D thru D plus 3. Although the Landing Force Commander had responsibility and ostensibly command, this command was diluted . . . . When Task Force Delta did not assume OpCon [operation control] of Landing Force elements on D-Day as expected, but rather the Commander Landing Force retained OpCon, Task Force Delta in order to execute its original plan was forced to transmit its desires to the Commander Landing Force.[1]

Burnett claimed that "Although this did not adversely affect the operation, it caused some delay and confusion which in other situations . . . might have been disastrous." Furthermore, the SLF commander maintained: "Command and responsibility are inseparable and the person designated as Commander Landing Force with his commensurate responsibilities must have the requisite authority and control of all forces to execute the plan."[2]

III MAF Marine officers had another perspective of the situation. Although they recognized the SLF commander's desire to maintain autonomous command and control, many members of the III MAF staff believed that:

> . . . once the battalion is committed, let's commit it under the regimental commander who has that sector and the division commander who has that sector . . . terminate the amphibious [portion of the] operation more rapidly then we normally do. In fact, terminate them almost as soon as you get them ashore, so that we can then have one maneuver commander . . . to wit, Platt, [the in-country commander] in Double Eagle.[3]**

General Krulak's FMFPac Headquarters supported the amphibious commander's point of view. The FMFPac commander was less worried about III MAF commanders assuming control of amphibious forces, than the fact that the Double Eagle example would set a precedent for other corps areas in South Vietnam. General Krulak was also perturbed about the lengthy period that the SLF had been committed to Double Eagle. He did not want the SLF to be considered an "in-country" organization. According to FMFPac, the integrity and independence of the SLF, as distinct from Marine units assigned to III MAF, had to be safeguarded.[4]

It was obvious before the end of Double Eagle that some of these questions had to be resolved. On 15 February, answering a request from Admiral Roy L. Johnson's Pacific Fleet Headquarters for a Seventh Fleet and FMFPac review of the effectiveness of the past amphibious operations, General Krulak proposed that he host a conference at Okinawa later in the month. Admiral Johnson concurred in the recommendation and ordered Krulak to proceed. General Krulak's motives for holding the conference were obvious. As he explained to General McCutcheon, acting CG III MAF at the time, the purpose was "to get everyone talking the same language."[5] The FMFPac commander wanted to smooth the internal Navy/Marine relationship, cut down planning and reaction time, and make SLF operations more effec-

---

*Departments of the Navy and the Army, *Doctrine for Amphibious Operations* (Washington: July 1962) was published by the Navy as Naval Warfare Publication 22A, by the Marine Corps as Landing Force Manual 01, and by the Army as FM31-11. The Air Force was not a party to any agreement upon amphibious operations at this time.

**Lieutenant General Hugh M. Elwood, who served as both assistant wing commander and III MAF chief of staff in 1966, stated the III MAF point of view as follows: "The basic points were that the SLF was badly needed by CGIIIMAF. Yet under another command, they landed frequently where they weren't really needed, where the enemy mostly wasn't and, on occasion, required the shore-based Marines to move in order to make room for them." LtGen Hugh M. Elwood, Comments on draft MS, dtd 4Jun78 (Vietnam Comment File).

tive. Colonel Chaisson, the III MAF representative to the Okinawa conference, recalled:

> I think we were trying to get our ducks in order with regard to how the SLF would be used in-country . . . [and] what sort of an agreement should be entered into between PacFleet and MACV with regard to the routine employment or the abnormal employment of the SLF.⁶

The Okinawa Conference

The conference was held during the period 25 February - 1 March 1966, attended by representatives from the major Pacific Fleet and Marine commands in the Western Pacific. The conferees were able to resolve most of the differences that had arisen. The representatives reaffirmed the validity of the Navy-Marine amphibious doctrine, as outlined in NWP 22(A), but in their report the conferees noted that in the area of command relationships the fundamental doctrine required detailed exposition "so that all concerned will conduct planning and operations uniformly and in strict conformance . . . ."⁷

In its study of command relationships, the conference report observed that there were four types of amphibious situations which the Marines would face in South Vietnam:

> 1. The landing force is the SLF and the amphibious operation though independent is a supporting operation of a larger operation. [The Dagger Thrust operations of 1965 were cited since they supported the overall MACV campaign].
> 2. The landing force is the SLF and the amphibious operation is an integral part of "a specific in-country operation in which in-country forces ashore are also employed, but are not embarked. . . ."
> 3. The landing force is the SLF and in-country forces are usually elements of III MAF.
> 4. The landing force is composed entirely of III MAF forces.⁸

The Committee on Command Relations, headed by Colonel Chaisson, examined each of the four situations.* It recommended to the conference that whichever commander had the predominance of forces normally should have overall authority. It also reaffirmed the authority of the commander of the landing force, whether he be from III MAF or from the SLF, in the amphibious objective area (AOA) during the amphibious phase of the operation. The conferees emphasized that the amphibious phase should be terminated as "expeditiously as practicable, and the Landing Force passes soonest to the operational control of the commander of the forces ashore."⁹ Even in the AOA, the Chaisson committee recognized that the authority of the landing force commander was limited because of the presence of South Vietnamese forces in the area. The landing force commander had no operational control of allied units although, obviously, he should attempt to secure coordinating authority. In fact, the entire emphasis of the conference report, which incorporated the committee's recommendations, was the necessity of effective liaison and preplanning between the involved command echelons to avoid any possible misunderstanding about command and control.¹⁰

The conference arrived at several broad recommendations for consideration by the senior U.S. commanders in the Pacific. The representatives of the CinCPacFlt components agreed that amphibious operations were a vital element in the war and they emphasized compliance with amphibious doctrine, the acquisition of timely intelligence, early and detailed concurrent planning, and improved reaction time. The conferees proposed bolder exploitation of the helicopter by conducting deeper inland operations. Most importantly, the conference recommended that portions of its report should be developed as "Fleet Policy," to be given wide distribution, most particularly to include CinCPac and ComUSMACV.¹¹

Changes in Command and Composition

At the time the Okinawa conference was ending its deliberations, important changes were occurring in the Marine chain of command relative to the SLF. Until the end of February, the 1st Marine Division Headquarters on Okinawa had administrative control of the SLF. With the pending departure of the division headquarters for Vietnam, a new parent had to be found for Marine forces remaining on Okinawa and afloat with the Seventh Fleet. On 1 March,

---

*The other members of this committee were Captain William Stroud, USN, representing Navy Task Force 76; Colonel Joseph E. Loprete, representing the Seventh Fleet; Colonel Robert H. Barrow, representing FMFPac; Lieutenant Colonel Thomas E. Gleason, representing the SLF; and Major Peter L. Hilgartner, representing CinCPacFlt.

General Krulak activated the 9th Marine Amphibious Brigade under the command of Colonel Herman Hansen, Jr., a World War II flying ace and holder of the Navy Cross and two Silver Stars. The new command assumed operational control of most Marine units on Okinawa and, as Navy Task Force 79, administrative control of the SLF.*

In early March, the question arose whether the SLF should continue to be embarked at Okinawa or be formed in Vietnam and embarked there. On 4 March, Admiral Sharp, CinCPac, while on an inspection tour of Vietnam, spoke to General McCutcheon, acting CG III MAF, about using III MAF battalions for the SLF and Da Nang and Chu Lai as SLF embarkation ports. McCutcheon answered that although the proposal was feasible, he was under the impression that plans called for Okinawa to serve as the rotation base for Marine units and for the SLF. After Sharp's departure, General McCutcheon reported the details of the conversation to General Krulak. General Krulak agreed with McCutcheon that the SLF battalions should be home-based on Okinawa. The short flurry of concern about SLF basing came to an end in mid-March when General Westmoreland advised Sharp that he supported the Marine position.[12]

By this time, the SLF had a change in composition. After Double Eagle, Lieutenant Colonel Horn's 2d Battalion, 3d Marines reverted to its parent regiment's control at Da Nang. Lieutenant Colonel Harold L. Coffman's BLT 1/5, which had arrived at Subic Bay on 28 February from Camp Pendleton, California, became the new SLF battalion. The battalion had sailed in west-coast-based amphibious shipping which included the USS *Princeton* (LPH 5), USS *Pickaway* (APA 222), and USS *Alamo* (LSD 33). Colonel Burnett, his staff, and Lieutenant Colonel Aldworth's squadron on board the *Valley Forge* joined the amphibious task force in the Philippines. On 5 March, both the SLF headquarters and the squadron transferred from the *Valley Forge* to the *Princeton*. After a short amphibious exercise on the island of Mindoro in the Philippines, the SLF was ready for the next amphibious landing in South Vietnam.

---

*General Fields established the 1st Marine Division Headquarters at Chu Lai in March. Until 1 March, General Fields had also been Commander, Navy Task Force 79, the naval designation for Marine forces with the Seventh Fleet.

Further Operations and Changes in Commands and Units

The site for the operation was the Rung Sat Special Zone south of Saigon. Taking advantage of the protection of the swampy mangrove jungle of this region, VC gunners fired on ships using the main river channel to the Vietnamese capital. On 27 February, the enemy attacked a Panamanian ship, causing serious damage, and, again on 3 March, a South Vietnamese oil barge. To prevent the interdiction of Saigon's vital waterborne supply route, General Westmoreland requested authority to use the SLF to clear the Rung Sat. The request was granted and the result was Operation Jackstay, lasting from 26 March until 6 April 1966.

Complications concerning command and control arose during the planning phase. After preliminary

Marines of BLT 1/5 hurry to waiting helicopters to begin Operation Jackstay. The operation took place in the Rung Sat sector south of Saigon to prevent the VC from closing the river route to the Vietnamese capital.

Marine Corps Photo A413986

plans had already been completed, the South Vietnamese Government told General Westmoreland that it wanted two battalions of South Vietnamese Marines to participate in Jackstay with the U.S. forces. General Westmoreland agreed to the request, and U.S. and South Vietnamese Marine liaison officers met on board the command ship to assist in developing coordinating instructions. The Vietnamese Marine battalions were not to enter the operation until April and were assigned operational areas in the northwest sector of the Rung Sat, an area distinct and separate from the Marine battalion's operating area. In a sense, Jackstay was a combined operation because the South Vietnamese 4th and 5th Marine Battalions were under the *de facto* operational control of the commander of the amphibious task force.

On 22 March just before Jackstay began, General Westmoreland radioed Vice Admiral John J. Hyland, commander of the Seventh Fleet, indicating that he had reservations about the way in which the operation was being organized, and asked Hyland to meet him in Saigon. He told the Seventh Fleet commander that he had promised the South Vietnamese General Staff that he would review and concur in the plan and stated that unless certain modifications were made in it, he would have to ask for a postponement of the operation.[13]

The two commanders met on 26 March. After listening to a briefing on the Jackstay plan, General Westmoreland expressed concern about the fact that he did not have direct control over the operation. He pointed out that a Navy captain, the amphibious task force commander, and a Marine colonel, the landing force commander, not under his command, were going to be conducting an operation for which he personally would be accountable. General Westmoreland suggested that Admiral Ward, the senior MACV naval advisor, be made the commander of the amphibious task force. Admiral Hyland replied that this procedure would not be in accordance with published amphibious doctrine. On the other hand, the Seventh Fleet commander proposed that he assign Rear Admiral Don P. Wulzen, Commander, Task Force 76, as commander of the amphibious task force.* General Westmoreland finally agreed to this arrangement, but only after receiving Admiral Wulzen's assurance that he would be responsive to advice from MACV and that the operation would be terminated whenever MACV desired. The MACV liaison officers on the ships of the amphibious task force were to report directly to Admiral Ward, designated MACV senior liaison officer for the operation.[14] Although the question of command and control had been resolved for the time being, the subject was sure to come up again.

Jackstay was only partially successful in its attempt to eliminate the Viet Cong forces in the Rung Sat. Operating waist-deep in water with few suitable helicopter sites, the Marines would have been literally stuck in the mud, but for the availability of Navy boats and landing craft. The Viet Cong always seemed to be one step ahead and chose not to make a stand. Despite these handicaps, Lieutenant Colonel Coffman's troops did find and destroy enemy

Marine helicopters take off from the deck of the USS Princeton *(LPH 5) during Operation Jackstay. With few available helicopter landing zones, the Marines had limited mobility in the swampy mangrove jungles of the Rung Sat, often operating waist-deep in water.*

Marine Corps Photo A704376

---

*The amphibious ready group, the Navy task group that carried the Marine SLF, was assigned the Navy designation TG 76.5, and thus was a subordinate command to TF 76 in the Seventh Fleet chain of command.

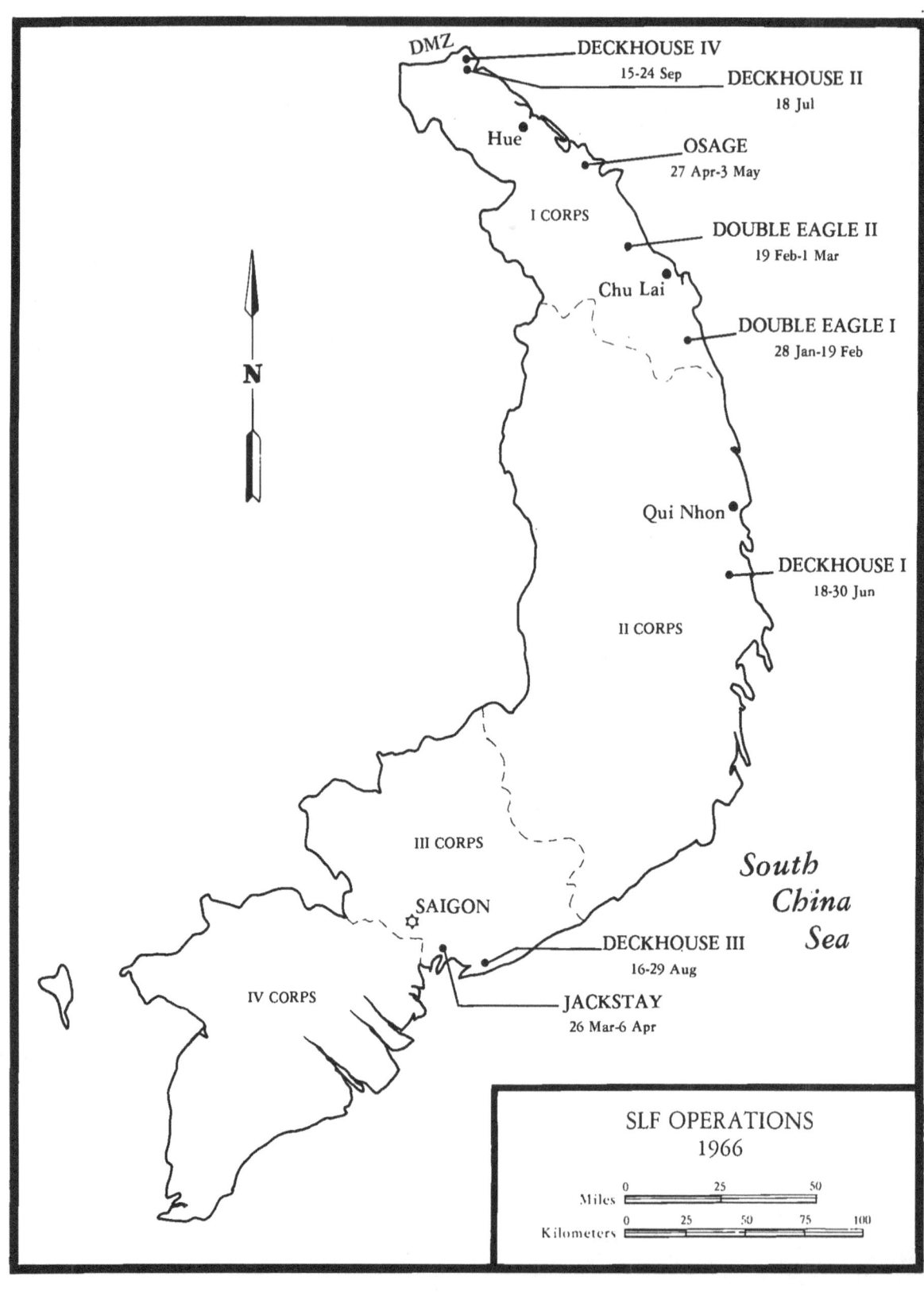

workshops, bunkers, food stocks, clothing supplies, and weapons. During the course of the operation, the Marines were able to experiment with riverine techniques such as mounting an Ontos on a LCM for fire support. Although the enemy main body of troops withdrew, small groups of Viet Cong remained to provide some resistance to the Marine advance. The SLF claimed to have killed at least 63 of the enemy, while suffering 5 killed, 2 missing in action, and 25 wounded. For the time being, the shipping channel to Saigon was clear.[15]

After Jackstay, the commanders and composition of both 9th MAB and the SLF were changed. Colonel Richard A. Brenneman relieved Colonel Burnett as SLF commander on 7 April 1966. Two days later, Lieutenant Colonel Daniel A. Somerville's HMM-364 flew on board the *Princeton* replacing HMM-362. In the meantime, Brigadier General William A. Stiles, the assistant 1st Marine division commander, had arrived on Okinawa from Camp Pendleton and assumed command of the 9th MAB from Colonel Hansen on 20 March. When General Stiles left for Chu Lai, he relinquished command of the MAB to Brigadier General Michael P. Ryan. General Ryan's command included both Colonel Harper's MAG-13 at Iwakuni and Colonel Widdecke's 5th Marines Headquarters and its 3d Battalion on Okinawa.* The newly organized 26th Marines was slated to relieve the 5th Marines as the RLT headquarters for the MAB.

In late April, after the command and unit changes had been accomplished, the SLF conducted an amphibious operation, codenamed Osage, in the Phu Loc District of Thua Thien Province. The Marine BLT was assigned the mission of destroying a VC main force battalion and elements of a NVA regiment reported to be operating in the coastal region. With the exception of delaying and harassing tactics, the enemy again chose not to fight. During Osage, which lasted from 27 April until 2 May, the Marines killed eight enemy while suffering casualties of eight dead and nine wounded.

The May Conference

By this time, both MACV and the Navy desired to reexamine the SLF employment in Vietnam. On 10 May, General Westmoreland radioed Admiral Sharp suggesting that the changing nature of the war in Vietnam made the original SLF mission, conducting amphibious raids to disrupt the buildup of enemy forces in the coastal regions, too narrow in scope. In General Westmoreland's opinion, the growth of U.S. forces in Vietnam and their expanded operations, combined with the Navy's Market Time campaign, had severely restricted enemy sea infiltration and the freedom of movement of Communist main force units. The MACV commander stated that he realized that enemy troop concentrations in coastal areas would continue to occur, but he wanted to develop, in concert with the Seventh Fleet, a more responsive procedure to destroy these forces. Admiral Johnson, CinCPacFlt, who had received an information copy of the MACV message, agreed that a more definite determination had to be made of the role of the SLF. He asked Admiral Sharp for authorization, which he readily obtained, to establish direct liaison with MACV. In a 17 May message to MACV, Admiral Johnson agreed with General Westmoreland that improvement should be made in SLF responsiveness, but pointed out that the basic concept of the SLF, as worked out the previous year, was still valid, but needed some modification. Johnson proposed holding a conference on Okinawa during which the two commands could determine the best means of SLF employment.[16]**

---

*The 9th MAB controlled FMFPac's major ground and air components in the Western Pacific outside Vietnam. Exceptions were the 3d Force Service Regiment and Marine Wing Service Group 17. The 2d Battalion, 5th Marines sailed from Okinawa for Chu Lai on 7 April.

**Colonel Francis F. Parry, a member of the MACV staff at the time, recalled in 1982 that he had initiated the Westmoreland message. He learned from his immediate superior, Brigadier General William K. Jones, who headed the MACV Combat Operations Center, that General Westmoreland was "grumbling about the Seventh Fleet. . . ." Parry told Jones that he "thought Westy was needlessly concerned. I had known of Johnny [Vice Admiral John J.] Hyland in the Pentagon and he had a reputation for being smart and easy to get along with. I suggested that I could straighten the emerging difficulties out in a hurry if I could deal directly at the staff level. Westy agreed to our proposing a MACV-PacFlt meeting in Okinawa and to my heading the MACV contingent. An Army colonel from FFI [I Field Force, Vietnam] was included to keep an eye on me." Col Francis F. Parry, Comments on draft MS, dtd 23Feb82 (Vietnam Comment File), hereafter Parry Comments.

MACV concurred and the conference took place from 25-28 May; officers representing components of both MACV and CinCPacFlt attended. With Captain Herman J. Trum, the senior CinCPacFlt representative as chairman, the conferees were organized into four committees to study the problems and arrive at a new agreement concerning amphibious relations for the signature of both General Westmoreland and Admiral Johnson.

The conference completed its work on 28 May and forwarded its proposed joint agreement to CinCPacFlt and to ComUSMACV. Its main provisions called for the:

> 1. Proper application of the time-tested Army-Navy-Marine Corps approved doctrine contained in NWP-22(A).
>
> 2. Early CinCPac approval for the conduct of these amphibious supporting operations.
>
> 3. Early concurrent and parallel planning at the Commander, Amphibious Task Force and Commander, Landing Force level, in accordance with decisions mutually agreed to by ComUSMACV and CinCPacFlt.
>
> 4. The acquisition of timely, detailed and accurate intelligence, requiring close coordination between the fleet and in-country intelligence agencies in accordance with procedures agreed upon by ComUSMACV and CinCPacFlt.
>
> 5. Improving amphibious reaction by streamlining procedures in order to improve the responsiveness of the ARG/SLF to ComUSMACV operations in RVN.[17]*

The MACV commander had one major objection to the original draft agreement. He believed that the requirement for CinCPac approval prior to committing the SLF was too restrictive for rapid reaction. This provision was modified, and a few editorial changes were made. The final signed agreement was almost identical to the one concluded by the conferees. General Westmoreland concurred in the joint agreement on 24 August 1966. Both Admiral Johnson and General Westmoreland had reason to be satisfied. The agreement furnished Westmoreland with more flexibility when calling for the SLF, while Admiral Johnson received assurance that the command relationship contained in NWP-22(A) would pertain to all amphibious operations in Vietnam as much as possible.**

The SLF to the End of the Year

An outgrowth of the May amphibious conference was the decision to initiate a broader type of amphibious operation, codenamed Deckhouse. The Deckhouse operations were designed to complement allied operations against enemy units. The first of the new series, Deckhouse I, took place in II Corps from 18-30 June 1966, in support of the U.S. 1st Cavalry Division's operation Nathan Hale. Although the Marines encountered only scattered resistance, Nathan Hale developed into a nine-battalion operation during which the allied forces killed over 400 of the enemy. Lieutenant Colonel Edward J. Bronars' BLT 3/5, which had replaced BLT 1/5 on 7 May, was the landing force for the operation.

---

*Colonel Parry remembered that when he arrived on Okinawa he found the Navy and FMFPac representatives "loaded for bear . . . [and] decided to . . . defuse the situation." He recommended that the conference break into committees to address each of the issues. While he and the senior Fleet and FMFPac representatives "repaired to the Kadena Golf Course . . . the ltcols and majors types worked[ed] things out. I'm sure our hours on the golf course over the next two days did more to ensure the success of the conference than anything else. . . . When we briefed Westy upon return to Saigon I believe he was not a little surprised at the degree of cooperation. Years of Navy-Marine hard-iron teamwork paid off!" Parry Comments

**A revised edition of the *Doctrine for Amphibious Operations* was published in 1967 as NWP-22(B). Most of the modifications from the older version were of a technical nature and beyond the scope of this history. The major importance of the new edition lay in the fact that NWP-22(B) was also published as an Air Force Manual as well as a Marine, Navy, and Army publication. The new NWP did not alter the agreement reached by General Westmoreland and Admiral Johnson, which was approved by CinCPac in November 1966. The issue over control, despite the agreement, remained a sensitive issue between MACV and the Navy. Admiral John J. Hyland, the Seventh Fleet commander, remarked that "the Army never ceased trying to obtain operational control of the SLF and the other assets of the Seventh Fleet which were operating in support of MACV. . . . The Army never liked the concept of the Navy 'operating in support,' because of the fear that the Navy might pull out at any time it felt that a threat outside the MACV area was greater than the threat inside that area. Actually, of course, the Navy would never pull out unless the highest authorities in Washington believed it was needed more in another area." Adm John J. Hyland, Comments on draft MS, dtd 6Jun78 (Vietnam Comment File). For a further discussion of the impact of the Vietnam War on amphibious doctrine, see LtCol Peter L. Hilgartner, "Amphibious Doctrine in Vietnam," *Marine Corps Gazette*, v. 53, No. 1 (Jan 1969), pp. 28-31.

Marine Corps Photo A704379

Two medium landing craft lay-to near the USS Thomaston (LSD 28) during Deckhouse IV. In this operation, the SLF battalion, BLT 1/26, landed near the DMZ and participated in Operation Prairie.

During the two months following Deckhouse I, the SLF once more rotated helicopter and infantry units. On 4 July, Lieutenant Colonel James D. McGough's HMM-363 relieved Lieutenant Colonel Somerville's HMM-364. Both Bronars' battalion and McGough's squadron participated in Deckhouse II during Operation Hastings.* On 4 August, Lieutenant Colonel Anthony A. Monti's BLT 1/26, newly arrived from the United States, became the SLF battalion. After a brief training phase in the Philippines, the newly constituted SLF conducted Deckhouse III on the Vung Tau Peninsula 60 miles southwest of Saigon, in conjunction with the U.S. Army's 173d Airborne Brigade. The results were disappointing; only two enemy were killed at the cost of four Marine dead and 21 wounded.

During the rest of the year, Seventh Fleet SLF forces focused on the northern battle zone. As an adjunct to Operation Prairie, which followed Hastings, the SLF once more landed below the DMZ in Operation Deckhouse IV.** Although the SLF ended its active participation in Operation Prairie on 24 September, the amphibious forces maintained an anxious eye on the DMZ. From October through November, a Marine BLT remained afloat off the northern coast to reinforce III MAF if the NVA renewed the offensive.

Concern about the DMZ caused a brief period of reinforcement of Seventh Fleet Marine amphibious units. Following Deckhouse IV, Lieutenant Colonel Garland T. Beyerle's BLT 3/26 replaced BLT 1/26 and Lieutenant Colonel Marshall B. Armstrong's HMM-362 relieved HMM-363. The reconstituted SLF was slated for an amphibious exercise in the Philippines. General Westmoreland, fearing that a major enemy thrust could occur in the DMZ during this time, asked Admiral Sharp to provide another contingency force to be stationed off the northern coast of South Vietnam. Approval was granted and

---

*See Chapter 10 for a detailed description of Deckhouse II.

**See Chapter 11 for a detailed description of Deckhouse IV.

Marine Corps Photo A187883

Marines from BLT 1/26 return to their quarters on board the USS Iwo Jima *(LPH 2) after the completion of Deckhouse IV. Although accounting for about 200 of the enemy, the battalion sustained 203 casualties, including 36 killed.*

General Ryan's 9th MAB on Okinawa was ordered to provide the force. Colonel John J. Padley, the commanding officer of the 26th Marines, which had arrived on Okinawa in August, embarked his headquarters and assumed the additional designation Commander, Task Group 79.2. The Task Group consisted of BLT 3/3, under Lieutenant Colonel Earl R. "Pappy" Delong, and HMM-163, under Lieutenant Colonel Rocco D. Bianchi. Padley's units remained off northern I Corps until 1 November. At that time, it was relieved by the regular SLF, TG 79.5, now under Colonel Harry D. Wortman. Task Group 79.2 was dissolved on 8 November and two days later TG 79.5 resumed its normal operations. With the easing of the fighting on the northern front, the special alert for the SLF was over.

In December, one more change occurred in SLF composition when Major James L. Day's BLT 1/9 relieved BLT 3/26 as the landing force battalion. Colonel Wortman and his staff immediately began planning for Deckhouse V which was to take place in the Mekong Delta in early 1967.

With few exceptions, SLF operations, to that point, had little resemblance to classical amphibious warfare. For the most part, Marine amphibious operations in Vietnam were either administrative landings, exploitations of an already existing battle situation, or amphibious raids. Marine landing forces were not assaulting hostile shores; they were landing where large U.S. and allied ground and air forces were already present. Colonel Chaisson later observed that the SLF operations "by and large were sort of contrived. It was almost a concept looking for a home."[18]

CHAPTER 20
Other Marine Activities

Staff and Security in Saigon — Marine Advisors to the VNMC — Rung Sat Marines — Marine I Corps Advisors — Air and Naval Gunfire Liaison

Staff and Security in Saigon

The composition of the MACV staff reflected the predominance of U.S. Army forces in Vietnam. Despite the fact that over two-thirds of the nearly 3,000 members of the joint MACV staff were Army personnel, General Westmoreland maintained a reputation of impartiality in dealing with the U.S. component commands in Vietnam. Brigadier General William K. Jones, the senior Marine on the MACV staff, observed that the Army officers who filled key staff positions took pains to ascertain the viewpoints of other services and "tried to develop a teamwork that was necessary to run the command."[1]

Brigadier General Jones had arrived in December 1965 for the express purpose of organizing the MACV Combat Operations Center. According to Jones, who had held a similar billet as Chief of the General Operations Division in the office of the Joint Chiefs of Staff during 1961-62, "It was a brand new proposition in which I was given plenty of leeway by both General Rosson and General DePuy to set up the overall operation."[2]*

The MACV Combat Operations Center eventually developed into a smaller version of the National Military Command Center in Washington, performing the same nerve-center function for Westmoreland as the latter did for the Joint Chiefs. The operations center had direct radio and teletype connections with Admiral Sharp's headquarters in Honolulu and the National Military Command

Marine Corps Photo A187971
LtGen Walt, Commanding General, III MAF (left), and BGen Jonas M. Platt, III MAF Chief of Staff (right), pin on the "stars" of newly promoted BGen John R. Chaisson, the III MAF operations officer. As a general officer, Chaisson relieved BGen William K. Jones as Director of the MACV Combat Operations Center.

Center. General Jones remained in command of the center until November 1966, when he was relieved by Marine Brigadier General John R. Chaisson, just promoted to his new rank after completing his tour as III MAF's G-3.*

The number of Marines on the staff at MACV Headquarters in Saigon grew from less than 80 in December 1965 to 185 by the end of 1966. In addition to Generals Jones and Chaisson, Colonel Francis F. "Fox" Parry, Lieutenant Colonel Paul B.

---

*General Jones had earned the Navy Cross and Silver Star in World War II. His assignment prior to his arrival in Vietnam was Commanding General, Force Troops, FMFPac. Major General William B. Rosson, USA, was the MACV Chief of Staff while Major General William E. DePuy was the MACV J-3. The latter was relieved by Major General John C. Tillson III in March 1966.

*Colonel Francis F. Parry, who was Jones' deputy, recalled that before General DePuy departed, he insisted that the operations center have an Army deputy as well as a Marine. Parry recommended to Generals Jones and Tillson "that the two deputies divide up their duties with the Marine having responsibility for activity in I Corps, II Corps, and air and naval matters; the Army taking III Corps, IV Corps, and Special Forces operations both in and out of country. This retained a Marine hand directly involved in those areas of most interest to us." Parry Comments.

Haigwood, and Lieutenant Colonel Heman J. Redfield III served in the Combat Operations Center. Other Marines were scattered throughout the MACV staff. Administratively, the Marines in Saigon were carried on the rolls of Headquarters Marine Corps in Washington. General Jones later commented that a separate administrative subunit in Saigon should have been established for these Marines declaring "having to go clear to [HQMC] . . . didn't make any damned sense at all."[3]

The Marine Security Detachment at the American Embassy, which was charged with protecting other U.S. civilian buildings as well as the Embassy, also increased in number during the year because of the proliferation of U.S. Government agencies in the South Vietnamese capital. Reflecting the augmented size and larger security responsibility of the detachment, 1st Lieutenant Phillip E. Tucker assumed command in April from Gunnery Sergeant Jerry N. Lorelli. By the end of 1966, the detachment had reached a strength of 68 Marines.

Marine Advisors to the VNMC

From the beginning of the Vietnamese Marine Corps in 1954, U.S. Marines, starting with Lieutenant Colonel Victor J. Croizat, served as advisors with its units. By January 1966, the U.S. Marine Advisory Unit, headed by Colonel John A. MacNeil, consisted of 25 officers and five enlisted men. The Marine Advisory Unit was part of the U.S. Naval Advisory Group; Colonel MacNeil as the senior advisor reported directly to Rear Admiral Norvell G. Ward, Chief of the U.S. Naval Advisory Group, who, in turn, was responsible to General Westmoreland.

The senior Marine advisor and his staff advised the Commandant of the Vietnamese Marine Corps in all matters pertaining to the organization and employment of the South Vietnamese Marines. Complementary to this function was the senior Marine advisor's responsibility for coordinating the planning for the projected growth of the Vietnamese Marine Corps with Admiral Ward and the South Vietnamese.

Although all of the senior Marine advisors had worked toward the development of a larger independent, self-sufficient Vietnamese Marine Corps, the exigencies of the war forestalled many necessary but ancillary activities. For example, the continuous need for infantry advisors in late 1965 and early 1966 prevented the assignment of the U.S. Marine operations and training advisor to his primary staff function until March 1966.

In the spring of 1966, Colonel MacNeil undertook a long delayed review of South Vietnamese Marine mission, organization, and objectives. In June, he submitted a Force Structure Plan for the Vietnamese Marine Corps to Admiral Ward. The plan was eventually incorporated into the MACV Joint Strategic Objectives Plan for 1972 (JSOP).* MacNeil visualized the expansion of the Vietnamese Marine Corps from a brigade to a division. Specifically, the plan called for the growth of the Vietnamese Marine Corps from a strength of approximately 7,000 men organized into five infantry battalions and support elements in 1966 to a strength of approximately 11,700 men organized into nine infantry battalions and support units by 1970.

In addition to adding to the number of infantry battalions, the Force Structure Plan restructured the Vietnamese headquarters and support elements. In 1968, a headquarters battalion was to be established containing a brigade/division headquarters, a headquarters and service company, a signal company, a reconnaissance company, and a military police company. The amphibious support battalion, which provided most of these services in 1966, was to be dissolved, while two new support battalions, a service battalion and a medical battalion, were to be established. The artillery battalion was to remain basically the same, with the exception of the addition of a 105mm battery by 1968 or 1969; then Vietnamese Marine artillery would consist of three 105mm batteries and two 75mm pack howitzer batteries.[4]

In 1966, the Vietnamese Marine Corps operated as an element of the general strategic reserve and, in effect, as a sort of "fire brigade" whenever trouble erupted. Its highly respected Commandant, Lieu-

---

*JSOP is a mid-range objectives plan which translated United States national objectives and policies for the time frame five to eight years into the future, into terms of military objectives and strategic concepts and defined basic undertakings for cold, limited, and general war which might be accomplished with the projected force levels. The MACV JSOP was for five years, thus the fiscal year 1972 JSOP was prepared in 1966.

South Vietnamese Marines cross a fast-rushing stream in Kontum Province using a make-shift bamboo bridge. The Vietnamese Marines were part of the RVN strategic reserve and used as a "fire brigade" wherever needed.

tenant General Le Nguyen Khang, not only headed the Marine Corps, but was the military governor of Saigon as well. In May, he assumed yet another duty when he became the commanding general of the South Vietnamese III Corps, which included those provinces of South Vietnam in the vicinity of the capital city. Khang's additional assignments caused no diminishment of the effectiveness of the Marine brigade. For the day-to-day administrative duties, he relied heavily upon his efficient and scholarly chief of staff, Colonel Bui The Lan. At least one Marine battalion remained in the Saigon area, while the other battalions, in task force organizations, were deployed throughout Vietnam wherever the need was greatest.

In the spring of 1966, the government sent two battalions of Marines, without their U.S. advisors, to put down the insurrections in Da Nang and Hue.* During the rest of the year, a Vietnamese Marine task force continued to operate in I Corps. During Operation Hastings, two Vietnamese Marine battalions were the I Corps reserve, but were never committed. In August, Vietnamese Marines participated with the 5th Marines during Operation Colorado in the Que Son Valley northwest of Tam Ky and, dur-

---

*See Chapters 5 and 6. U.S. advisors were excluded for obvious reasons.

Marine Corps Photo A332793 (Col Nels E. Anderson)
Commandant of the Vietnamese Marine Corps, LtGen Le Nguyen Khang (right), accompanied by Col Nels E. Anderson, the senior U.S. Marine advisor to the VNMC, reviews his troops. All U.S. Marine advisors to the Vietnamese Marine Corps wore the South Vietnamese Marine uniforms.

ing Prairie, the Vietnamese Marines supported ARVN 1st Division operations in Quang Tri Province.

The Vietnamese Marines spent nearly 90 percent of the time in the field during 1966. With the activation of a sixth infantry battalion in September, the Vietnamese Marine Brigade's battalion rotation system for refitting and retraining achieved more flexibility. Thereafter, one battalion could be held at its base camp. Despite constant hardships, the Vietnamese Marines maintained a six to one kill ratio over enemy forces. Colonel Nels E. Anderson, Colonel MacNeil's successor, described the readiness and effectiveness of the Vietnamese Marines at the end of the year in the following terms:

> At the present time, although the Vietnamese Marine Brigade comprises a little over one percent of the total RVNAF personnel structure, it contributes a great deal more than that in combat against the insurgents. The South Vietnamese Marine Corps at present returns more mileage for the money in the terms of devoted service, combat efficiency, and combat readiness.[5]

Rung Sat Marines

The Naval Advisory Group contained another group of Marine advisors; those operating under the U.S. senior advisor of the Rung Sat Special Zone Advisory Detachment, a Navy commander. The Rung Sat, which literally translated means Forest of Assassins, is a dense mangrove swamp southeast of Saigon in Quang Xuyen and Can Gio Districts of Bien Hoa Province. Roughly circular in shape and about 20 miles in diameter, it covers more than 400 square miles. Its major importance lies in the fact that it encompasses much of the Long Tao River, the main shipping channel from the sea to Saigon. No road net exists in the Rung Sat and most movement was along the streams which are narrow, shallow, and winding. The Vietnamese Navy was responsible for the administration and defense of the Rung Sat. A Vietnamese Army battalion, or occasionally a Vietnamese Marine battalion, normally operated in the Rung Sat area under the operational control of the Navy. The Rung Sat was traditionally a haven for fugitives from the law, and the Viet Cong took advantage of its physical characteristics to elude government forces while harassing shipping. Major McLendon G. Morris, the senior Marine, and two other officers and four enlisted Marines, served as infantry, psychological warfare, and intelligence advisors to the Vietnamese ground units in the Rung Sat. Several years later, Major Morris remembered the frequent Rung Sat search and destroy operations, "conducted in the unforgettable gray mud, up to hip-depth, which sucked one's energy away with every step, especially non-Vietnamese, who tended to sink more deeply with each step than did their counterparts."[6]

Marine I Corps Advisors

The largest number of Marines serving as advisors to the Vietnamese were assigned to the MACV I Corps advisory organization. General Walt, as senior advisor for I Corps, had overall responsibility for the U.S. advisory program in the five northern provinces. The advisory effort was entirely separated from III MAF and, in fact, was administered by the I Corps deputy advisor, an Army colonel. Colonel Howard B. St. Clair, St Clair served in this capacity until relieved on 1 March 1966 by Colonel Archelaus

L. Hamblen, Jr. During the year, the number of U.S. advisors was reduced for fear that too many advisors could stifle South Vietnamese initiative. The number of I Corps advisors was cut in January 1966 from 700 (65 of whom were Marines) to 630 (49 of whom were Marines) by the end of the year. The spring political crisis hampered the advisory effort to the 1st ARVN Division, but by December, the South Vietnamese unit was well on its way toward regaining its reputation as one of the best divisions of the Vietnamese Army. The 2d Division, which had not participated in the Struggle Movement, continued to improve throughout the year.

Air and Naval Gunfire Liaison

Subunit-1 of the 1st ANGLICO (Air and Naval Gunfire Liaison Company), Force Troops, FMFPac, although not in the normal III MAF chain of command and small in size, was vital to the successful use of all available supporting arms. The ANGLICO organization is specifically designed to support allied and U.S. Army forces in the employment of Marine close air support and naval gunfire.

Subunit-1, under Major Richard E. Romine, had been in South Vietnam since 1965. By January 1966, Major Romine, headquartered in Saigon, had a force of 55 men divided into 11 teams stationed throughout South Vietnam. In February, Lieutenant Colonel Carrol B. Burch assumed command of the detachment from Major Romine. Although nominally under III MAF, the subunit acted as an independent command under MACV. In September, formal operational control was transferred to General Westmoreland's headquarters. By December, the subunit had grown to a strength of 146 men, divided into 13 detachments. The largest detachment was attached to the Korean Marines at Binh Son, Quang Ngai Province. During the year,

Marine Corps Photo A188080

PFC Bennie C. Belton, a member of Subunit-1, 1st ANGLICO, assists a South Korean officer to call in Marine close air support near Binh Son in Quang Ngai Province. ANGLICO is an acronym standing for Air and Naval Gunfire Liaison Company, a unit made up of Marine and Navy personnel and specifically designed to provide support to U.S. Army and allied forces.

the subunit controlled more than 5,000 naval gunfire missions in support of U.S. and allied forces and was credited with killing 3,000 NVA/VC and destroying over 20,000 enemy structures.*

---

*Records do not indicate the number of airstrikes controlled by the subunit; only the detachment with the Koreans performed the air-liaison function in Vietnam.

CHAPTER 21
At the End of the Year

Plans for Reinforcing the Marines in I Corps — Planning the Barrier — Conclusion

---

Plans for Reinforcing the Marines in I Corps

Ironically, just when MACV and the South Vietnamese began emphasizing pacification, the Marines in I Corps found their personnel reserves available for that purpose stretched almost to the breaking point. III MAF was in the difficult position of pursuing an antiguerrilla campaign in its southern TAORs while at the same time containing a North Vietnamese incursion in the north.

The American command could only speculate about the reasons behind the North Vietnamese offensive in the summer of 1966. General Westmoreland expressed the belief that the enemy wanted to divert allied forces from the populated area around Saigon and suspected that the North Vietnamese had hoped to exploit the recent political crisis by establishing a "liberation government" in the northern two provinces.[1] Generals Krulak and Walt thought that the Communist leaders wanted to draw the Marine battalions out of the populated I Corps coastal plain into a campaign of attrition in the almost uninhabited rugged interior of northern Quang Tri Province. Much later, in 1967, General Krulak quoted a leading member of the North Vietnamese Government, Nguyen Van Mai, to support this argument:

> The National Liberation Front will entice the Americans close to the North Vietnamese border and will bleed them without mercy. In South Vietnam, the pacification program will be destroyed.[2]

Whatever their estimates of North Vietnamese reasons for opening the new front, Generals Westmoreland and Walt were in total agreement that the enemy forces had to be thrown back. The MACV commander compared his position to the stance of a boxer, who jabs with his left to keep the enemy off balance, while holding his right to protect vital areas.[3] In a sense, Operations Hastings and, later, Prairie were launched as jabs to counter the enemy offensive. As Prairie continued, the 3d Marine Division was deployed to the two northern provinces and an Army infantry battalion was moved in to reinforce the Marines at Da Nang. The enemy had expanded the war; the allied commands had little choice but to respond.

The realignment of forces was not a spontaneous decision. Early in 1966, the MACV and III MAF staffs prepared contingency plans for countering a North Vietnamese invasion through the Demilitarized Zone. With the beginning of Operation Hastings, the contingency planning effort took on an air of urgency. During a visit to General Walt on 12 July, Westmoreland discussed the long-range implications. The MACV commander believed that the NVA were preparing for a sustained drive in Quang Tri Province and asked Walt to prepare for it. The next day, General Westmoreland ordered III MAF to develop a plan for the employment of a Marine division in northern I Corps, based on two different sets of assumptions. According to the first, labeled Phase I, General Walt was to stop other operations, maintain defense of the base areas, and move a division north to counter the enemy offensive. During this phase, he would not receive reinforcements. Under Phase II assumptions, III MAF was to develop plans for the use of a three-battalion Army brigade to be placed under the operational control of the Marine command. The Army troops were to come from either I Field Force or II Field Force. On 16 July, MACV notified General Larsen, Commanding General, I Field Force, to prepare a plan for the movement of the 1st Brigade, 101st Airborne Division to I Corps. The entire contingency planning effort was given the designation South Carolina.[4]

During the summer and fall of 1966, General Westmoreland and his subordinate commanders continued to prepare contingency plans which presumed the reinforcement of III MAF by Army units. By the end of September, the American command had produced three planning directives which addressed this subject, codenamed South Carolina, North Carolina and Tennessee. All three plans were designed to cope with the manpower drain on III MAF as a result of a North Vietnamese drive in the north. If South Carolina were implemented, the 1st Brigade, 101st Airborne Division in II Corps was to reinforce III MAF in northern I Corps. In the North Carolina plan, the 173d Airborne Brigade in III Corps reinforced Da Nang, while the 3d Marine Division moved north and concentrated in Quang Tri and Thua Thien Provinces. According to the Tennessee plan, a brigade from the Army's 1st Cavalry Division was to move from II Corps to Chu Lai if more Marines were required in the northern two provinces.[5]

While this contingency planning was continuing, General Westmoreland was studying other alternatives. On 25 July, he stated that he was considering the establishment of a blocking force to prevent the enemy from moving through the DMZ. Westmoreland believed that there might be some merit in making this an international force, including Korean and Australian troops. Under his concept, observation posts would be established on the hills and mountains just south of the DMZ, while the blocking units would be inserted in the valleys.[6] At the meeting of the U.S. Mission Council the following week, General Westmoreland brought up the subject again. He stated that:

> The organization would be known as the KANZUS Force from its national components: Korean, Australian, New Zealand, and U.S. As presently visualized, the organization would be brigade-size, with two U.S. Marine and one ROK battalion as the combat elements. Individual battalions would retain their national identity. Formation of the command headquarters supporting structure would provide a place for incorporating token remaining national contributions from Australia and New Zealand and others such as the Philippines, should this become suitable. . . . The organization, commanded by a USMC Marine officer, possibly a brigadier general, would operate in the U.S. tactical chain of command in close coordination with and in support of the ARVN.[7]

The proposal received a favorable response from most of the participants at the meeting. Ambassador Lodge notified the State Department that such a force might provide the U.S. with a basis for the eventual creation of an international force under:

> UN or Asian regional sponsorship which would inherit the anti-infiltration role of KANZUS. An eventual successor would function obviously as a political and psychological cordon sanitaire, and not of course, as a military Maginot Line.[8]

At the same time, General Westmoreland forwarded his concept to the Joint Chiefs through Admiral Sharp's headquarters in Hawaii. According to the MACV historians, the American Ambassadors to Australia, New Zealand, and Korea all thought the idea had merit and concurred in the project.[9]

By 18 August, the MACV staff had completed its planning directive entitled "Operation Short Stop," which outlined the necessary actions to discover and disrupt the infiltration of enemy units through and around the DMZ into northern Quang Tri Province. Operation Short Stop required the improvement of Route 9 to Thon Son Lam and the stationing of the brigade-sized KANZUS force on the Dong Ha-Cam Lo-Thon Son Lam axis. The KANZUS brigade was to have a surveillance reaction mission under the operational control of III MAF. According to the timetable, road work and the positioning of the brigade would have to be accomplished before the onset of the northeast monsoon.[10]

Time was of the essence for General Westmoreland. On 21 August, he asked both the State and Defense Departments to furnish approval and guidance for the KANZUS project. He noted that base camps had to be erected, lines of communication opened, and supply points stocked by 1 October, or no sizeable force could operate in northern Quang Tri during the rainy season. The general then stated that there was also a minimum amount of time "for the assembly and shakedown of components of the force."[11]

In spite of MACV's sense of urgency, the international ramifications of the KANZUS proposal caused Washington authorities to take a long deliberate look at the concept. Several complications arose which had to be solved before troops could be deployed. Some exception even was taken to the designation KANZUS on the grounds that it was too restrictive and precluded additional nations from joining the force. Admiral Sharp noted that the ground rules for operations in the DMZ had to be reconsidered. He recommended that the KANZUS force should have the authority to move into the South Vietnamese portion of the DMZ to prevent the North Vietnamese from using the area as a sanctuary. It was feared that the establishment of KANZUS could pose legal problems with the International Control Commission, which was charged by the 1954 agreements with supervision of the DMZ.[12]

The uppermost question was whether KANZUS would require more manpower. General Westmoreland was able to furnish a breakdown of his estimate of the required force on 19 September. At that time, he told Admiral Sharp that the KANZUS force would consist of two Marine infantry battalions and either a Korean Marine or Army battalion. Supplementing these units would be two firing batteries, one Korean and one New Zealander, and an Australian reconnaissance company. All of these components were then in South Vietnam; no further augmentation was required. The complicating factor was whether the allied nations would release these troops for the DMZ mission; a definite answer to this critical question could not be determined until the KANZUS project was accepted by Washington. As far as U.S. forces were concerned, the only additional reinforcements not yet in Vietnam that were required were a helicopter company or squadron and additional headquarters personnel. The needed additional headquarters personnel included a Marine brigadier general to be the brigade commander and 10 other officers. A Marine regimental headquarters company was to form the nucleus of the brigade staff; the other allied units represented in KANZUS were to provide liaison personnel to the brigade headquarters.[13]

Despite all of the detailed planning, KANZUS became a moot point. It soon was obvious that approval would not come before 1 October, the date that General Westmoreland had set as the deadline for deployment before the monsoon rains. As fighting intensified in late September during Operation Prairie, the question also arose whether a brigade-size force would be adequate to meet the threat in the north. Subsequent events made the implementation of the KANZUS plan impractical.

On 6 October, Generals Westmoreland and Walt activated part of the North Carolina plan. The 3d Marine Division was moved into the two northern provinces, while the 1st Marine Division assumed the responsibility for both the Da Nang and Chu Lai TAORs. General Westmoreland dispatched the 4th Battalion, 503d Infantry, 173d Airborne Brigade from Bien Hoa to I Corps, with supporting artillery.

General Westmoreland anticipated that if it were necessary to implement the rest of North Carolina and the other contingency plans, the sequence would be North Carolina, South Carolina, and then Tennessee, realizing that circumstances could cause change to this order of events. The MACV commander considered the possibility of reinforcing Chu Lai before sending an Army brigade to the DMZ area, or even executing both options simultaneously. Westmoreland also thought that he could integrate RLT 26 into this sequence, either to reinforce the Army troops or even as a reinforcing regiment in lieu of them. All Marine and Army forces that might be introduced into I Corps under these contingencies were to be under III MAF operational control.[14]

After action in the DMZ area tapered off and forces were redeployed in early October, the threat of an all-out enemy offensive in the north receded. In November, General Westmoreland ordered the return of the Army infantry battalion to III Corps; it left the next month. During December, the 3d Division pulled the 4th Marines Headquarters away from the border region and reassigned it to Thua Thien Province to conduct Operation Chinook. By the end of the year, General Walt had reduced his DMZ forces to five battalions.

Despite the limited standoff in the northern area at the end of the year, the enemy could still reactivate this front at any time and the American command had to take this fact into consideration. As a countermeasure during December, the MACV and III MAF staffs completed operation plans Georgia I and Georgia II, the deployment of the Army's 9th Division to reinforce the Marines in I Corps. III MAF was extended from Chu Lai to the DMZ, which development had a drastic effect on Marine operations, especially on pacification. There was little doubt that if the enemy renewed the offensive along the northern boundary, U.S. Army units would have to beef up allied strength in I Corps.

Planning the Barrier

Secretary McNamara was interested in an entirely different alternative to meet the DMZ threat. During early 1966, the Defense Department began to look seriously at the possibility of establishing a physical barrier across the DMZ and the Laotian panhandle to stop North Vietnamese infiltration into South Vietnam. In April, the Secretary directed that a special study group composed of leading U.S. scientists examine the technical feasibility of such a

U.S. Secretary of Defense Robert S. McNamara (left) is greeted on one of his early trips to Vietnam by South Vietnamese General Nguyen Huu Co (right) and former U.S. Deputy Ambassador to Vietnam, U. Alexis Johnson (right). Secretary McNamara in 1966 directed that the U.S. study the feasibility of establishing a physical barrier across the DMZ.

barrier. Under the aegis of a private consulting organization, the Institute for Defense Analyses, 67 scholars took part in the study. Reporting on 30 August, the study group concluded that an air-supported barrier, not manned by ground troops, could be operational in approximately one year after the decision was made. The proposed barrier was to consist of two parts, one antipedestrian and the other antivehicular; the foot barrier was to extend along the southern edge of the DMZ into Laos while the antivehicular system would be located further to the west. According to the study, the barrier system was to include a series of minefields positioned at strategic points within the entire barrier region. These minefields were to be augmented by electronic acoustic and seismic sensors which would indicate attempted penetration. Patrolling on a 24-hour basis, U.S. Air Force monitoring aircraft would analyze sensor signals and call in air strikes against any suspicious movement.[15]

On 8 September, the Joint Chiefs forwarded the study group's conclusions to Admiral Sharp for his comments. In his reply, one week later, Sharp expressed his doubt about the practicality of the entire venture. He contended:

> ... that a barrier system must be tended. If not, it could be breached with ease, while the flow of men and material to the VC/NVA continued. An aerial delivered obstacle would not be expected to support the need for soldiers on the ground, and the time, effort, and resources of men and material required to establish a ground barrier would be tremendous.[16]

The Joint Chiefs, although concerned that the barrier would require funding from current service resources, agreed with Secretary McNamara that the program should receive further study. On 15 September, the Secretary appointed Lieutenant General Alfred Starbird, USA, to head Joint Task Force 728 within the Department of Defense to determine the feasibility of the barrier. General Starbird asked General Westmoreland to provide him with an estimate of what countermeasures the North Vietnamese might take. While not commenting on the practicality of the concept, General Westmoreland, in his reply, made it clear that any barrier project would present problems. He declared:

> . . . whether the enemy attempted to go over, through, or under the barrier it must be expected that these operations will be accompanied by coordinating harassing and diversionary operations elsewhere. With forces available in NVN and SVN, the enemy will be able to harass a fixed barrier at selected times and places both during and after the construction phase. Work will be hampered by sniper, AW [automatic weapon] and mortar fire and by equipment sabotage. Small units and working parties will be vulnerable to surprise attacks in superior strength. The enemy will make full use of the "bait and trap" technique in attempts to lure friendly elements into prepared ambushes. Extensive harassment, aimed at producing attrition of friendly forces and facilitating infiltration, could be directed not only at the barrier but simultaneously against our lines of communication. . . . Our enemy is self-confident, determined, ingenious and uses terrain and weather to his advantage. His solutions to problems are usually elemental, simple and practical from his view point.[17]

Despite his reservations about barriers, on 3 October, General Westmoreland ordered his own staff to prepare a study of the various defensive options in the DMZ area. The MACV planning group briefed the general on its preliminary findings six days later. It suggested the best defense would be a mobile one conducted behind a major barrier system. A 30-kilometer-long linear barrier system could be constructed in the coastal and piedmont regions south of the DMZ, envisioned as 1,000 meters wide and containing barbed wire, a minefield, remote sensor devices, bunkers for outpost forces, watch towers at periodic intervals, and an extensive communications network. A mobile force with good organic firepower, supported by artillery and air, was to conduct screening and delaying actions both in front of and behind the barrier. The planning group suggested that an ARVN armored cavalry regiment would provide depth to the defense. III MAF would continue normal operations in the northern provinces, but would be prepared to block, counterattack, or eliminate any enemy intrusion.

West of the linear barrier, the MACV planners proposed a strongpoint type of defense. The idea was to establish strongly fortified outposts at strategic positions in the mountainous terrain, forcing the enemy into the narrow defiles. There the enemy would be subjected to allied air and supporting arms. The MACV Staff proposed 20 outposts, extending from the western end of the linear barrier to the Laotian border. To man this strongpoint system, they recommended the deployment of at least an infantry division, possibly Korean, since the terrain in the area resembled that of the Korean Armistice Line. If the frontage to be covered proved too great for a single division, or if enemy deployments in and south of the DMZ or west of the outpost line posed a major threat, the staff suggested that the Koreans could be reinforced with a U.S. Marine regiment.

In its conclusions, the MACV planning group noted that the terrain in the coastal plain and foothills in the eastern DMZ favored the allied defensive measures, but the rugged mountains in the western region provided significant advantages to the infiltration tactics of the North Vietnamese. Considering these two factors, the planners stated that the defensive trace, which they had outlined in the body of the report, was the most advantageous of the various options studied. The group, however, made clear that if a barrier system were to be built, it would be a massive undertaking. In addition to an armored cavalry regiment and a ROK infantry division, the barrier would require a supporting artillery group and the equivalent of an Army aviation battalion for helicopter support. The greatest obstacle would be the building of the barrier itself and the subsidiary tasks of upgrading and constructing roads and logistic facilities to support the barrier and its defending forces. The MACV group finally warned that the North Vietnamese still would have the capability of outflanking the defenses by moving through Laos, posing a major threat to the integrity of the barrier. Despite all of the difficulties, the planning group proposed that its outline concept for the barrier be approved for guidance to MACV staff agencies in their preparation of detailed supporting plans.[18]

After discussing the various barrier projects with General Starbird, General Westmoreland met with Secretary McNamara on 10 October in Vietnam. At this meeting, the MACV commander presented his alternative conventional barrier and strongpoint system for the Secretary's consideration in lieu of the Washington proposal. During his visit, Secretary McNamara flew over the DMZ and apparently was impressed by the difficulties that the northwestern terrain would pose for the construction of a barrier. In any event, he indicated to General Westmoreland that he was receptive to Westmoreland's strongpoint system in this portion of the DMZ area.[19]

On his return to Washington, McNamara continued to advocate the building of some sort of barrier in this area of South Vietnam in spite of the difficulties. In a memorandum to President Johnson proposing the installation of the barrier near the 17th Parallel, he stated:

> The barrier may not be fully effective at first, but I believe that it can be made effective in time and that even the threat of its becoming effective can substantially change to our advantage the character of the war. It would hinder enemy efforts, would permit more efficient use of the limited number of friendly troops, and would be persuasive evidence both that our sole aim is to protect the South from the North and that we intend to see the job through.[20]

In his conversation with General Westmoreland the Secretary left no doubt that the MACV planning for the barrier should continue. He also declared that General Starbird's Washington group would continue to function. It would be charged with obtaining and delivering munitions and sensors to support the barrier. At the same time General Westmoreland was to determine his requirements for forces and material to support his concept. The MACV barrier planning effort would be designated Practice Nine.[21]

Shortly after the Secretary's visit, General Westmoreland ordered his subordinate commands to study the concept that his staff had prepared. The Seventh Air Force was tasked with the development of the air barrier, while III MAF, in conjunction with the MACV Combat Operations Center, was to provide the concept for the conduct of a "Mobile Defense/Conventional Barrier."[22]

General Walt ordered the 3d Marine Division to prepare the Marine version. He told General Kyle, the division commander, that a statement should be made at the outset that III MAF disagreed with the barrier concept.[23] In a letter to Walt, General Kyle noted that he, also, had serious reservations about the entire program. He believed that the proposed linear barrier in the east would require at least a division for monitoring and defense, rather than an armored cavalry regiment; this division would be in addition to the 1st ARVN and 3d Marine Divisions. He argued that the MACV proposal to use the latter two units to provide depth to the barrier defense nullified the only possible advantage of the plan. Instead of freeing these two divisions for operations in southern Quang Tri and Thua Thien Provinces, it would confine them to the border region. General Kyle also objected to positioning a Marine regiment in the western strongpoint area. He reiterated that the barrier defense system "should *free* Marine forces for operations elsewhere—*not freeze* such forces in a barrier watching defensive role."[24]

General Kyle presented a counterproposal to the MACV plan. He declared that it was obvious that whether there was a defensive barrier or not, at least two divisions would be needed to halt enemy infiltration through the DMZ. The 3d Marine Division commander stated that a two-division mobile defense force could accomplish the same mission as a barrier without tying down more forces to fixed positions, and this course of action would have the additional advantage of requiring a much less extensive engineering effort.[25]

Nevertheless, General Kyle's mobile two-division defense plan did require a great deal of engineering construction. The general pointed out five tasks which would have to be accomplished, irrespective of which plan was ultimately adopted. They were: (1) the upgrading of Route 9 to a two-lane paved road from Dong Ha to Khe Sanh; (2) widening Route 1 from Phu Bai to the vicinity of Gio Linh; (3) constructing two alternate roads from Route 1 eastward to the Cua Viet, one road emanating from Dong Ha and the other from Quang Tri City; (4) constructing a road from Quang Tri City through the Ba Long Valley to join Route 9 to Ca Lu; and (5) finally, the upgrading of the dock facilities at both Dong Ha and at Cua Viet to the level of a major port. General Kyle reemphasized his contention that this preliminary road construction and port development, combined with the insertion of a mobile two-

Marine Corps Photo A188167

Gen William C. Westmoreland, ComUSMACV (left) is seen on a visit to the 3d Marine Division Headquarters at Phu Bai together with MajGen Wood B. Kyle, Commanding General, 3d Marine Division (right), and LtGen Lewis W. Walt, Commanding General, III MAF (following behind). Generals Kyle and Walt both objected to any linear barrier in the DMZ sector.

division force, were all that was required to secure the northern area.[26]

Although General Walt agreed with his subordinate commander, neither he nor General Kyle had any choice in the matter. As General Walt later wrote to HQMC, he had commented to MACV that if he had the additional forces projected by the barrier planners, "a far better job of sealing the DMZ could be accomplished without the barrier itself." He also had recommended to MACV that any additional forces for manning the barrier should not come from III MAF; "we are already too short of troops to divert any of them to a function of this nature." Walt observed, however, that his "position has so far not prevailed."[27]

By the end of the year, the MACV and III MAF planners nearly had completed the first phase of their barrier planning. MACV had presented its Practice Nine Requirement Plan on 26 November and III MAF submitted its formal operation plan at the end of December. The concept envisioned the completion of the construction and the manning of the eastern portion of the barrier by 1 August 1967. According to the concept of operation, the 3d Marine Division would conduct a series of clearing operations in the vicinity of the strongpoint/barrier locations. Work would also be started on the improvement on the lines of communication in the area to include the dredging of the Cua Viet. On 1 August 1967, a South Korean division would take over responsibility of the western sector, which included all of the area west of Dong Ha Mountain. An ARVN regiment would man the 34 kilometers of the eastern linear barrier extending from Dong Ha Mountain to the South China Sea. The 3d Marine Division would then be free of the immediate responsibility for barrier defense.[28]

In January 1967, General Westmoreland made some modifications in the barrier plans, but the basic concept remained the same. There were also some changes in semantics. The term "anti-infiltration system" was substituted for "barrier," because the latter word connoted an impregnable defense. More substantially, the deadlines for the building and manning of both the eastern and western defense systems were pushed back. In its Practice Nine Requirements Plan of 26 January 1967, MACV now called for the completion of the eastern portion by 1 November 1967 instead of 1 August. In the western sector, logistic considerations caused the MACV planners to postpone the introduction of large forces in the area until November, although the Marine unit at Khe Sanh was to construct a strongpoint. While the original plan had envisioned the complete installation of the western strongpoint system by November, the new plan only stated that "the remainder of the system in this area will be completed subsequent to 1 November 1967." No provision was made for the construction of a base camp for the Korean division. This version of the barrier concept, according to its originators, reduced the costs by a third and cut down the number of troops required to man the defenses during the initial period. General Westmoreland submitted the new plan to Admiral Sharp and the Joint Chiefs for consideration. The barrier concept, even after the decision was made to implement part of the MACV plan in March 1967, was to be the subject of a great deal of controversy throughout that year.[29]

The Marine Corps was consistent in its opposition to the entire concept of a defensive barrier. Colonel Chaisson, the III MAF G-3, represented the feeling of most of his fellow officers when he declared in November 1966:

> All of the barrier plans are fantastic, absolutely impractical, and III MAF is opposed to all because of engineer requirements . . . and the installations must tie down troops to protect the barrier.[30]

General Walt even went further and declared that the entire barrier discussion placed undue emphasis on the infiltration problem. He believed that the primary enemy remained the guerrilla, and that the infiltrator, who came from the north, could only support the local forces, but not replace them. Walt observed:

> . . . the mass of infiltrators must be considered as NVA or main force VC types. As the record shows, we beat these units handily each time we encounter them. In my mind, therefore, we should not fall into the trap of expending troops unduly seeking to prevent the entry of individuals and units who pose the lesser threat to our ultimate objective, which remains the people of South Vietnam.[31]

As a 3d Marine Division briefing officer stated in January 1967:

> To sum it all up, we're not enthusiastic over any barrier defense approach to the infiltration problem—if there is such a problem in our area. We believe that a mobile defense by an adequate force—say one division give or take a battalion—would be a much more flexible and economical approach to the problem.[32]

Conclusion

During 1966, the III Marine Amphibious Force doubled in size. The 40,000, Marine manpower base in January had been expanded during the year and was rapidly approaching the 70,000 mark by the end of December. At the end of the year, General Walt's command consisted of the reinforced 1st and 3d Marine Divisions, the reinforced 1st Marine Aircraft Wing, and the Force Logistic Command.

Despite the rapid buildup of Marine forces, III MAF's high hopes for pacifying and unifying its three enclaves during 1966 had been dashed. The political upheaval caused by the removal of the powerful and popular Nguyen Chanh Thi, the I Corps commander, brought Marine pacification efforts to a complete standstill in the spring. At the same time, Marine units at Phu Bai and Chu Lai found themselves confronted by North Vietnamese and VC main force battalions and regiments in Thua Thien Province and southern I Corps. The North Vietnamese threat grew during the summer when an enemy division crossed into northern I Corps through the DMZ. In October, the 3d Marine Division deployed north of the Hai Van Pass to counter a new NVA offensive, while the 1st Marine Division assumed responsibility for Da Nang and Chu Lai. Although by the end of the year, the Marines had parried successfully the NVA thrust in the north, the pacification effort in the southern enclaves suffered.

At the end of 1966, the two Marine divisions of III MAF were fighting two separate wars: the 3d Marine Division conducting a more or less conventional campaign in northern I Corps, while the 1st Marine Division continued the combination of large unit and counterguerrilla operations south of the Hai Van Pass. Although General Walt wanted to reduce the size of his forces along the DMZ,[33] this pattern of warfare would continue into 1967.

Notes

PART I
The Marine Base Areas in Early 1966

CHAPTER 1

A LARGER FORCE FOR A GROWING WAR
III MAF IN JANUARY 1966

Unless otherwise noted the material in this chapter is derived from MilHistBr, Office of the Secretary, Joint Staff MACV, Command History, 1966, hereafter, MACV Comd Hist 1966; HqFMFPac, U.S. Marine Corps Forces in Vietnam, Mar65-Sep67, n.d., 2 vols., hereafter, FMFPac, "Marine Forces in Vietnam, Mar65-Sep67"; III MAF ComdCs Nov65-Feb66; Vietnam Comment File; Jack Shulimson and Major Charles Johnson, *U.S. Marines in Vietnam, 1965: The Landing and the Buildup* (Washington: Hist&MusDiv, 1978), hereafter Shulimson and Johnson, *Marines in Vietnam, 1965*; Dep of Defense, *United States Vietnam Relations*, 1945-67, 12 bks (Washington: GPO, 1971), hereafter *Pentagon Papers* with appropriate section title and book, volume or tab, and page numbers; Adm Ulysses S.G. Sharp, USN, CinCPac, and Gen William C. Westmoreland, USA, ComUSMACV, *Report on the War in Vietnam* (As of 30 Jun 1968) (Washington: GPO, 1968), hereafter Sharp and Westmoreland, *Report on the War*; Gen Louis W. Walt, *Strange War, Strange Strategy, A General's Report on Vietnam* (New York: Funk & Wagnalls, 1970), hereafter Walt, *Strange War, Strange Strategy*; BGen Edwin H. Simmons, "Marine Corps Operations in Vietnam, 1965-66," *Naval Review*, 1968 (Annapolis: U.S. Naval Institute, 1968), pp. 2-35, hereafter Simmons, "Marine Operations, Vietnam, 1965-66."

III MAF, I Corps, and the Three Marine TAORs

Additional sources for this section are: HqFMFPac, III MAF Operations, Jan 1966, n.d., hereafter III MAF Ops with specific month; III MAF ComdC, Jan66; Biographical Files (Historical Reference Section, History and Museums Division, Headquarters Marine Corps, Washington, D.C.), hereafter Biog Files (HRS).

1. Gen Lewis W. Walt biographic data in Biog Files (HRS). See also Walt, *Strange War, Strange Strategy*, p. 208.
2. See Gen Keith B. McCutcheon biographic data in Biog Files (HRS).

Command Relations

Additional source for this section is MajGen Lewis W. Walt, Address to Staff and Students, Marine Corps Schools, Quantico, Va, dtd 3Mar66 (No. 6010, OralHistColl, His&MusDiv, HQMC), hereafter Walt address to MCS, Mar66.

3. Office of Air Force History, Comments on draft MS, dtd 28Jul78 (Vietnam Comment File).
4. Gen William C. Westmoreland, USA, Comments on draft MS, dtd 27May78 (Vietnam Comment File), hereafter Westmoreland Comments, May 78.
5. Lester A. Sobel and Hal Kosut, eds., *South Vietnam: U.S. Communist Confrontation in Southeast Asia*, 1966-67 (New York: Facts on File, Inc., 1969), v. 2, p. 211.
6. Walt address to MCS, Mar66.
7. CGIIIMAF msg to CGFMFPac, dtd 15Jan66, encl 17, III MAF ComdC, Jan66.

Planned Deployment of the 1st Marine Division

8. "U.S. Ground Strategy and Force Deployments, 1965-67," *Pentagon Papers*, bk 5, v. I, p. 25 and FMFPac, "Marine Forces in Vietnam Mar65-Sep67," v. I, pp. 7-6, -7, -8.
9. Shulimson and Johnson, *Marines in Vietnam, 1965*, Chap. 8.
10. LtCol Roy E. Moss, Comments on draft MS, Capt Moyers S. Shore III, "Marines in Vietnam," pt III, dtd 10Dec69 (Vietnam Comment File).

The Enemy Buildup

11. MACV Comd Hist, 1966, p. 3.
12. Sharp and Westmoreland, *Report on the War*, p. 100.

The Marine Counterguerrilla War Versus the MACV Perspective

13. See FMFPac, "Marine Forces in Vietnam, Mar65-Sep67," v. I, p. 9-1, v. 2, p. 97 and III MAF Ops, Jan 66, p. 30.
14. Walt address to MCS, Mar66.
15. Col George W. Carrington, Jr., Comments on draft MS, dtd 15May78 (Vietnam Comment File).
16. LtGen Victor H. Krulak, Comments on draft MS, n.d. [May 78] (Vietnam Comment File), hereafter Krulak Comments, May 78.
17. CGFMFPac, "Pacific Operations," Tab F, HQMC, General Officers Symposium Book, 1967, pp. F6-F7.
18. Westmoreland Comments, May 78.
19. Ibid.
20. BGen William E. DePuy, ACS J-3, memo to Gen Westmoreland, dtd 15Nov65, Subj: The Situation in I Corps (Gen William E. DePuy Papers, Military History Institute, Carlisle Barracks, Carlisle, Pa.).
21. Gen William C. Westmoreland, *A Soldier Reports* (Garden City, N.Y.: Doubleday & Co, Inc., 1976), pp. 165-66, hereafter

Westmoreland, *A Soldier Reports*.

22. HistDiv, Memo for the Record, dtd 9Mar72, Subj: Conference with BGen Edwin H. Simmons, Director of Marine Corps History and Museums (Vietnam Comment File), hereafter Simmons Conference. For a further discussion of the Marine Corps and Army strategy see Simmons, "Marine Operations, Vietnam, 1965-66," p. 23 and Shulimson and Johnson, *Marines in Vietnam, 1965*, Chap 8.

23. Krulak Comments, May 78.

24. Gen Wallace M. Greene, Jr., Comments on draft MS, dtd 5 May 78 (Vietnam Comment File), hereafter Greene Comments, May 78.

Marine Mission and Future Plans

25. ComUSMACV ltr to CG III MAF, dtd 21Nov65, Subj: Letter of Instruction (LOI-4), encl 2, III MAF ComdC, Nov65.

26. MACV Comd Hist, 1966, p. 340.

27. HqIIIMAF, G-3 Section, "Presentation for LtGen Krulak," dtd 1Feb66, encl 18, III MAF ComdC, Feb 66, hereafter Krulak Presentation, Feb66.

28. Ibid.

CHAPTER 2

EXPANDING WAR IN SOUTHERN I CORPS

Unless otherwise noted the material in this chapter is derived from: MACV Comd Hist 1966; III MAF Ops, Jan-Feb66; III MAF ComdCs, Jan-Feb66; 3d MarDiv ComdCs, Jan-Feb66; 1st MAW ComdCs, Jan-Feb66; Vietnam Comment File; Capt Moyers S. Shore III, "Marines in Vietnam, Jan-Jun 1966," pt III of LtCol Ralph F. Moody et al., "Marines in Vietnam," MS (HistDiv, HQMC), hereafter Shore, "Marines in Vietnam, Jan-Jun66, pt III;" Shulimson and Johnson, *Marines in Vietnam, 1965*; Sharp and Westmoreland, *Report on the War*; Simmons, "Marine Operations, Vietnam, 1965-66."

The Chu Lai TAOR

Additional sources for this section are: 4th Mar ComdC, Jan66; 7th Mar ComdC, Jan66, 1st Mar ComdC, Jan66.

1. 7th Mar ComdC, Jan66.

2. 4th Mar ComdC, Jan66; 1/4 ComdC, Jan66.

3. LtCol Ralph E. Sullivan, Comments on draft MS, dtd 9May78, (Vietnam Comment File).

4. 7th Mar ComdC, Jan66. See 7th Mar FragO 1-66, dtd 18Jan66, encl 3, 7th Mar ComdC, Jan66.

5. 1st Mar ComdC, Jan66; 1/4 ComdC, Jan66.

Operation Double Eagle

Additional sources for this section are: TF Delta AAR Double Eagle I and II, 28Jan-1Mar66, dtd 15Mar66, hereafter TF Delta AAR Double Eagle; MAG-36 AAR Double Eagle I and II, 28Jan-28Feb66, dtd 20Mar66, encl to MAG-36 ComdC, Mar66, hereafter MAG-36 AAR Double Eagle; III MAF Jnl File, Opn Double Eagle, Dec65-4Feb66, hereafter III MAF Double Eagle Jnl File; CTF 79.5 AAR, Operation Double Eagle I and II, dtd 17Mar66, Tab F, TG 79.5 ComdC, Jan-May66, hereafter CTF 79.5 AAR Double Eagle.

6. MACV Comd Hist, 1966, p. 359.

7. Col Oscar F. Peatross, Comments on Shore, "Marines in Vietnam, Jan-Jun66, pt III," dtd 1Dec69, (Vietnam Comment File), hereafter Peatross Comments, Shore MS.

8. See Walt address to MCS, Mar66 and MajGen Oscar F. Peatross intvw by Oral HistU, HistDiv, HQMC, dtd 12Apr73 (OralHistColl, Hist&MusDiv, HQMC), pp. 38-39, hereafter Peatross Intvw, 73.

9. Walt address to MCS, Mar66.

10. CTF 79.5 AAR Double Eagle; III MAF, Summary of Significant Events in Planning Operation Double Eagle, n.d., encl 8, III MAF ComdC, Jan66, hereafter III MAF Planning Summary, Double Eagle.

11. III MAF, Memo for the Record, dtd 13Jan66, Subj: I Corps/II Corps Conference, I Corps Headquarters, 0930-1130, 13 January 1966, encl 7, III MAF ComdC, Jan66, hereafter, III MAF M/R, I Corps/II Corps Conference.

12. III MAF OpO 307-66, dtd 15Jan66; G-3, HQMC, Point Paper, dtd 19Jan66, Subj: Status Report of all USMC units and replacements now deploying or ordered to deploy (HQMC, G-3 Div, Point Papers-West Pac, Jan-Jun66).

13. See TF Delta, OpO 1-66, dtd 24Jan66; III MAF Planning Summary, Double Eagle; Col William G. Johnson, Comments on Shore, "Marines in Vietnam, Jan-Jun66, pt III," dtd 9Dec69 (Vietnam Comment File), hereafter Johnson Comments.

14. See "Concept of Operations," in TF Delta AAR Double Eagle, pp. 10-12 and TF Delta OpO 1-66, Operation Double Eagle, dtd 24Jan66.

15. See 3d MarDiv ComdC, Jan 66; 3d MarDiv FragO 359-66, Operation Birdwatcher II, dtd 7Jan66, encl to 3d MarDiv ComdC, Jan66; 1st MAW Sit Reps, Jan66; 1st Force Recon Co, OpO 2-66, dtd 12Jan66, encl 64, 3d Recon Bn ComdC, Jan66.

16. Hateful Patrol AAR, dtd 23Jan66, encl to 1st Force Recon Co ComdC, 20Jan-Feb66.

17. LtCol Ernest L. Defazio, Comments on Shore, "Marines in Vietnam, Jan-Jun66, pt III," *circa* 1969 (Vietnam Comment File).

18. Col Nicholas J. Dennis, Comments on draft MS, n.d. [Jun78] (Vietnam Comment File).

19. CTG 75.5 AAR Double Eagle; Rpt on Double Eagle, D-Day in III MAF Double Eagle Jnl File.

20. Col Robert J. Zitnik, Comments on draft MS, dtd 6Jun78 (Vietnam Comment File).

21. Ibid.

22. Rept on Double Eagle, D plus 1 in III MAF Double Eagle Jnl File.

23. Col William G. Johnson intvw by FMFPac, dtd 13Sep66 (No. 202, OralHistColl, Hist&MusDiv, HQMC), hereafter Johnson Intvw.

24. Johnson Comments.

25. Capt James R. Hardin intvw by HQMC, dtd 17Jan67 (No. 292, OralHistColl, Hist&MusDiv, HQMC).

26. 3dBrig, AirCavDiv, CAAR, Opn Masher/White Wing, dtd 10Mar66 (CMH).

27. TF Delta AAR Double Eagle; BGen Jonas M. Platt intvw by III MAF, dtd 6Dec66 (No. 268, OralHistColl, Hist&MusDiv, HQMC), hereafter Platt Intvw.

28. Ibid.

29. TF Delta AAR Double Eagle and MAG-36 AAR Double Eagle.
30. TF Delta AAR Double Eagle.
31. 1st Force Recon Co ComdC, 20Jan-Feb66.
32. SMA, MACV, 2dInfDiv, AAR Lien Ket-22, 29Jan-12Feb66, dtd 16Feb66 (SMA, MACV AARs 1966).
33. TF Delta AAR Double Eagle.
34. Ibid.
35. Maj Alex Lee, Comments on Shore, "Marines in Vietnam, Jan-Jun66, pt III," dtd 28Nov69, (Vietnam Comment File).
36. Capt Edwin W. Besch, Comments on draft MS, dtd 12Jun78 (Vietnam Comment File).
37. Col Glen E. Martin, Comments on draft MS, dtd 5Jun78 (Vietnam Comment File).
38. LtCol Alex Lee, Comments on draft MS, dtd 26May78 (Vietnam Comment File).
39. TF Delta AAR Double Eagle.
40. Platt Intvw.
41. LtGen Victor H. Krulak, Comments on draft MS, n.d. [May78](Vietnam Comment File).
42. 1/4 Sit Rep No. 266, dtd 27Jan66 in 1/4 ComdC, Jan66.
43. 7th Mar ComdC, Feb66.

CHAPTER 3

THE WAR IN CENTRAL I CORPS

Unless otherwise noted the material in this chapter is derived from: MACV Comd Hist 1966; III MAF ComdCs, Jan-Mar66; 3d MarDiv ComdC, Jan-Jun66; 1st MAW ComdCs, Jan-Mar66; Vietnam Comment File; Shore, "Marines in Vietnam, Jan-Jun66, pt III"; Sharp and Westmoreland, *Report on the War;* Walt, *Strange War, Strange Strategy;* Simmons, "Marine Operations, Vietnam 1965-66."

The Da Nang TAOR

Additional sources for this section are: 9th Mar ComdCs, Jan66; 3d Mar ComdC Jan66; MAG-16 ComdC, Jan66; 12th Mar ComdC, Jan66; MajGen Donald M. Weller, Unprocessed Working Papers on Pacification, hereafter, Weller Working Papers; Shulimson and Johnson, *Marines in Vietnam, 1965.*

1. Reports on Quang Nam Pacification Program, Nov 1965-Feb66 in Weller Working Papers.
2. Ibid. See Shulimson and Johnson, *Marines in Vietnam, 1965,* Chap 8 and Simmons, "Marines Operations, Vietnam, 1965-66," pp. 23 and 25.
3. See Walt, *Strange War, Strange Strategy,* pp. 86-88 and Simmons, "Marine Operations, Vietnam, 1965-66," p. 31.
4. BGen Edwin H. Simmons, Comments on draft chapter, dtd 27Dec71 (Vietnam Comment File).
5. 3d Mar AAR, Operation Mallard, dtd 6Feb66, encl 41, 3d Mar ComdC, Jan66.
6. *Sea Tiger,* dtd 26Jan66, pp. 1 and 8.
7. III MAF ComdC, Jan66, p. 2.
8. Report on Refugees at Dai Loc District Headquarters Resulting from Operation Mallard, encl 4, 3d Mar AAR, Operation Mallard, dtd 6Feb66. See also 3/7 AAR, Operation Mallard, dtd 22Jan66 in 3/7 ComdC, Jan 66 for a further descripion of the operation.
9. Walt, *Strange War, Strange Strategy,* p. 88.

Honolulu and the Reemphasis on Pacification

Additional sources for this section are: 9th Mar ComdC, Feb66; 3d Mar ComdC, Feb66; MAG-16 ComdC, Feb66; Weller Working Papers; BGen Edwin H. Simmons, 9th Marines Notebook, hereafter 9th Marines Notebook; Pentagon Papers; Lyndon B. Johnson, *The Vantage Point* (New York: Rinehart, Holt & Winston, 1971), hereafter Johnson, *The Vantage Point.*

10. "Re-emphasis on Pacification, 1965-67," *Pentagon Papers,* bk 6, Sec. IV-C-8, p. 27 and MACV Comd Hist, 1966, p. 504.
11. "Declaration of Honolulu," *The Department of State Bulletin,* v. LIV, no. 1392 (28Feb66), pp. 305-06.
12. Johnson, *The Vantage Point,* p. 243.
13. Westmoreland Comments, May 78. See also Memorandum entitled "1966 Program to Increase the Effectiveness of Military Operations and Anticipated Results thereof," *circa* 8Feb66, encl, Westmoreland Comments, May 78, and Westmoreland, *A Soldier Reports,* pp. 160-1.
14. MACV Comd Hist, 1966, pp. 504-506.
15. Quang Nam Priority Area in Weller Working Papers.
16. Simmons, "Marine Operations, Vietnam 1965-66," p. 28.
17. 1/9 ComdC, Feb66. See Shulimson and Johnson, *Marines in Vietnam, 1965,* Chap 8 for the background of the Combined Action Program.
18. Quoted in 9th Marines, Brief Narrative of Activities, Mar65-Jun66, dtd 4Jul66, p. 2. See also 9th Mar ComdC, Feb66; 3/3 ComdC, Feb66; and 9th Mar Sit Reps for 23-25Feb66.
19. Notes for Battalion Commander's Conference, dtd 27Feb66 in 9th Marines Notebook.
20. G-3 Section, Hq, III MAF, Agenda Memo, dtd 19Feb66, Subj: Operation Sparrow Hawk, encl 17, III MAF ComdC, Feb66.
21. 9th Mar Sit Rep No. 56, dtd 25Feb66, 9th Mar ComdC, Feb66.
22. See 9th Marines Casualty Chart in 9th Marines Notebook and 9th Mar ComdC, Feb66.
23. Col Joshua W. Dorsey III, Comments on draft MS, dtd 24Jul78 (Vietnam Comment Files). See also 9th Mar ComdC, Feb66.
24. Col Nicholas J. Dennis, Comments on draft MS, n.d. [Jun78] (Vietnam Comment Files). See also 9th Mar ComdC, Feb66.
25. 3d Mar ComdC, Feb66.

CHAPTER 4

A NEW THREAT IN NORTHERN I CORPS

Unless otherwise noted the material in this chapter is derived from: MACV Comd Hist, 1966; FMFPac, III MAF Ops, Jan-Mar66; FMFPac Sit Reps, Jan-Mar66; III MAF ComdCs, Jan-Mar66; III MAF Jnl & Msg File, Feb-Mar66; 3d MarDiv ComdCs, Jan-Mar66; DOD, Current News (daily extract of newspaper and magazine clippings as well as TV/Radio news transcripts), hereafter "Current News"; Vietnam Comment File; Gen William

C. Westmoreland Papers (CMH), hereafter Westmoreland Papers (CMH); Shore, "Marines in Vietnam, Jan-Jun66, pt III."

The Buildup at Phu Bai

Additional sources for this section are: HQMC Msg File; 1/1 ComdCs, Feb-Mar66; 2/1 ComdCs, Jan-Mar66; 4/12 ComdCs, Jan-Mar66.

1. 2/1 ComdC, Jan66
2. Krulak Presentation, Feb66.
3. Ibid.
4. 3d Mar ComdC, Feb66.
5. Ibid. See also CGFMFPac Sit Reps for 16-28Feb66.
6. 3d MarDiv OPlan 375-66, dtd 24Feb66, encl 7, and 3d MarDiv OPlan 376-66, dtd 23Feb66, encl 8, 3d MarDiv ComdC, Feb66.
7. 2/1 msg to 3d MarDiv, dtd 28Feb66, encl 5, 2/1 ComdC, Feb66, hereafter 2/1 msg, 28 Feb66.
8. 2/1 AAR, Opn New York, Pho Lai Village and Phu Thu Peninsula, dtd 6Mar66, encl 4, 2/1 ComdC, Feb66, hereafter 2/1 AAR, Opn New York.
9. Ibid. and Col Edwin M. Rudzis, Comments on draft MS, dtd 26 May78 (Vietnam Comment File), hereafter Rudzis Comments.
10. 2/1 msg, 28Feb66.
11. 2/1 AAR, Opn New York.
12. Passim., III MAF Jnl & Msg File, 28Feb-2Mar66.
13. 1/1 ComdC, Mar66. See also III MAF COC, report of Phone Msg, dtd 2Mar66 and CG3dMarDiv msg to IIIMAFCOC, dtd 1Mar66 (III MAF Jnl & Msg File).
14. 1/1 AAR 4-66, Opn Troy, dtd 21 Mar 66, Tab C, 1/1 ComdC, Mar66.
15. HQMC, G-3 Div, Point Paper, dtd 8Mar66 in G-3 Div, HQMC Point Papers 1966; CGFMFPac Sit Rep No. 340, dtd 5Mar66 (FMFPac Sit Reps 1966); 3dMarDiv SitRep No. 302, dtd 4Mar66 (III MAF Jnl & Msg File); 3d Mar msg to TG Foxtrot, dtd 4Mar66, encl 1, 3d Mar ComdC; CG3dMarDiv msg to CGIIIMAF, dtd 2Mar66 and 3dMarDiv msg to COC III MAF, dtd 3Mar66 (III MAF Jnl & Msg File). See also Rudzis Comments.
16. CGIIIMAF msg to CGFMFPac, dtd 4Mar66 (HQMC Msg File).
17. Ibid.
18. ComUSMACV, Memo for the Record, dtd 10Mar66, Subj: MACV Commanders's Conference, 20Feb66 (Westmoreland Papers, CMH).
19. CGFMFPac msg to CMC, dtd 4 Mar66 (HQMC Msg File).
20. CGIIIMAF msg to CGFMFPac, dtd 23Feb66 (HQMC Msg File).
21. CGFMFPAC msg to CMC, dtd 9Mar66 (HQMC Msg File).

The Fall of A Shau

Additional sources for this section are: U.S. Army 5th Special Forces Group (Abn) 2-12 Command Reporting Files, 1965-66, Box 14, Accession No. 69A729 (WFRC), hereafter, 5th SFG 2-12, 14 (69A729 WFRC); III MAF, A Shau Incident Jnl, 9-12 Mar66, hereafter III MAF, A Shau Incident; Col Francis J. Kelly *U.S. Army Special Forces—Vietnam Studies* (Washington: Dept of the Army, 1973), hereafter Kelly, *Special Forces*.

22. FMFPac Sit Rep No. 353, dtd 18Mar66 (FMFPac Sit Reps, 1966).
23. III MAF G-2 msg to 3d MarDiv G-2, dtd 5Mar66 (III MAF Jnl & Msg File). See also A Shau Analysis in 5th Special Forces Miscellaneous Report, 5th SFG 2-12, 14 (69A729 WFRC), hereafter A Shau Analysis.
24. Kelly, *U.S. Army Special Forces,* p. 92. See also Det C-1, 5th SFG, AAR, Battle for A Shau, dtd 28Mar66, 5thSFG 2-12, 14 (69A729 WFRC), hereater 5th SFG, Battle for A Shau.
25. A Shau Analysis and 5th SFG, Battle for A Shau
26. Shore, "Marines in Vietnam, Jan-Jun66, pt III," p. 11-3.
27. Det C-1, 5th SFG, Jnls, 9-12 Mar66 in 5th Special Forces Miscellaneous Report, 5th SFG 2-12, 14 (69A729 WFRC), hereafter 5th SFG, Jnls.
28. III MAF COC, Resume of tele con w/ C/S I Corps, dtd 9Mar66 (III MAF Msg & Jnl File); entry for 9Mar66, 1/1 Jnl, Tab P, 1/1 ComdC, Mar66.
29. BGen Marion E. Carl, Comments on Shore, "Marines in Vietnam, Jan-Jun66, pt III," dtd 5Dec69 (Vietnam Comment File), hereafter Carl Comments, 69.
30. LtCol Charles A. House, Comments on draft MS, n.d. [Jun 78] (Vietnam Comment File), hereafter House Comments.
31. Transcript of MajGen Marion E. Carl intvw by Hist & Mus Div, 1973 (Oral HistColl, Hist&MusDiv, HQMC), pp. 31-32, hereafter Carl Transcript.
32. IIIMAFCOC msg to MACVCOC, dtd 9Mar66 (III MAF Jnl & Msg File).
33. 5th SFG, Battle for A Shau.
34. BGen Leslie E. Brown, Comments on Shore, "Marines in Vietnam, Jan-Jun66, pt III," dtd 4Dec69, (Vietnam Comment File).
35. Entries for 10Mar66, 5th SFG, Jnls.
36. MajGen Marion E. Carl, Comments on draft MS, n.d. [Jun 78] (Vietnam Comment File), hereafter Carl Comments, 78. See also Carl Comments, 69.
37. Col Roy C. Gray, Jr., Comments on draft MS, dtd 20Jul78 (Vietnam Comment File), hereafter Gray Comments.
38. 5th SFG, Battle for A Shau.
39. Entries for 10Mar66, 5th SFG, Jnls.
40. Col Thomas J. O'Connor, Comments on draft MS, dtd 10Jun78 (Vietnam Comment File), hereafter O'Connor Comments.
41. "TV Defense Dialogue, Broadcast of 14Mar66," Current News, dtd 15 Mar66, p.4, hereafter "TV Defense Dialogue, 14Mar66." See also 5th SFG, Battle for A Shau and ComUSMACV msg to SecDef, (OASD P/A), dtd 16 Mar66 (III MAF Jul & Msg File), hereafter MACV msg to SecDef, 16 Mar66.
42. 5th SFG, Battle for A Shau and 1st MAW Sit Rep No. 297, dtd 10Mar66 (III MAF Jnl & Msg File).
43. "Radio-TV Defense Dialogue, 14Mar66," Current News.
44. MACV msg to SecDef, 16Mar66.
45. Notes on Personnel Rescued at A Shau, dtd 12Mar66 (III MAF Jnl & Msg File).
46. MACV msg to SecDef, 16Mar66.
47. House Comments. See also MAG-16 ComdC, Mar66.
48. MACVCOC msg to NMCC, dtd 15Mar66 (III MAF Jnl & Msg File).
49. Carl Transcript, p. 31. See also Carl Comments, 78 and House Comments.
50. O'Connor Comments.
51. Gray Comments.

NOTES

52. 5th SFG, Battle for A Shau, and Notes on Helicopter Sorties, n.d., in III MAF, A Shau Incident.
53. G-3, 3d MarDiv msg to COCIIIMAF, dtd 10Mar66 (III MAF Jnl & Msg File).
54. Passim., III MAF Jnl & Msg File, 10-13Mar66; 1/1 ComdC, Mar66; FMFPac Sit Rep No. 349, dtd 14Mar66 (FMFPac Sit Reps, 1966).
55. CGICorps msg to JGS, dtd 15Mar66 (III MAF Jnl & Msg File).
56. LtCol Raph E. Sullivan, Comments on draft MS, dtd 9May78 (Vietnam Comment File). See also MajGen Harold A. Hatch, Comments on draft MS, dtd 5May78 (Vietnam Comment File).
57. SA, 1st Inf Div, Hue msg to ComICorps Adv Gp, Da Nang, dtd 16Mar66 (III MAF Jnl & Msg File).
58. III MAF ComdC, Mar66 and Delta Team Reports, 17-29Mar66 (III MAF Jnl & Msg File). For organization of Delta Teams, see Kelly, *Special Forces,* passim.

Continuing Reinforcement of Phu Bai and Operation Oregon

Additional sources for this section are: 4th Mar ComdC, Mar66; 1/1 ComdC, Mar66; 2/1 ComdC, Mar66; 1/4 ComdC, 28-31 Mar66; 3/4 ComdC, Mar66; 3/12 ComdC Mar66; 4/12 ComdC, Mar66; TG Foxtrot AAR, Opn Oregon, dtd 10Apr66, hereafter TG Foxtrot AAR Opn Oregon; 1/4 AAR, Opn Oregon, dtd 14 Apr66, encl, 1/4 ComdC, 28-31Mar66, hereafter 1/4 AAR Opn Oregon.
59. CGIIIMAF msg to CGFMFPac, dtd 13Mar66 (HQMC Msg File).
60. 4th Mar ComdC, Mar66 and CGFMFPac Sit Rep. No. 352, dtd 17Mar66 (FMFPac Sit Reps, 1966)
61. G-3, III MAF note, Task Group Foxtrot Opn for 19 Mar 66, dtd 19 Mar 66 (III MAF Jnl & Msg File). See also III MAF Jnl & Msg File, passim., 19-23Mar66.
62. TG Foxtrot AAR Opn Oregon and 1/4 AAR Opn Oregon.
63. Ibid. and III MAF COC, Opn Oregon Rept, dtd 20Mar66 (III MAF Jnl & Msg File).
64. 1/4 AAR Opn Oregon. See also passim., III MAF Jnl & Msg File, 19-20Mar66.
65. TG Foxtrot AAR Opn Oregon and 1/4 AAR Opn Oregon.
66. Ibid. See also IIIMAFCOC msg to MACV, dtd 21Mar66 (III MAF Jnl & Msg File).
67. 1/4 AAR Opn Oregon and TG Foxtrot AAR Opn Oregon.
68. Rudzis Comments.
69. TG Foxtrot AAR Opn Oregon.
70. 1/4 AAR Opn Oregon and TG Foxtrot AAR Opn Oregon.
71. G-3 Div, HQMC, Point Paper, Subj: Distribution of Personnel in Vietnam as of 28Mar66, dtd 28Mar66 (G-3, HQMC, Point Papers, 1966); 4th Mar ComdC, Mar66; 4/12 ComdC, Mar66; 3/12 ComdC, Mar66; Provisional Recon Group Bravo, 3d Recon Bn ComdC, 28-31Mar66; 3d Recon Bn ComdC, Mar66.
72. 4th Mar ComdC, Mar66 and 1/4 ComdC, 28-31Mar66. See also 3d MarDiv OpO 378-66, dtd 26Mar66, encl 25, 3d MarDiv ComdC, Mar66.
73. CGIIIMAF msg to CGFMFPac, dtd 13Mar66 (HQMC Msg File).
74. MACV, AC/S J-2, report, n.d. [24?Mar66] Subj: The Threat in Northern I Corps (Westmoreland Papers (CMH)).
75. ComUSMACV, Memo for the Record, n.d. [24?Mar66], Subj: Meeting at Chu Lai on 24Mar66 (Westmoreland Papers [CMH]).

PART II
Crisis and War in Central I Corps, Spring 1966

CHAPTER 5

A TROUBLED SPRING

Unless otherwise noted the material in this chapter is derived from: MACV Comd Hist, 1966; III MAF Ops, Mar-Jun66; III MAF ComdCs, Mar-Jun66; Shore, "Marines in Vietnam Jan-Jun66, pt III"; Sharp and Westmoreland, *Report on the War;* Westmoreland, *A Soldier Reports,* Walt, *Strange War, Strange Strategy;* Simmons, "Marine Operations, Vietnam, 1965-66."

The Beginnings of the Political Crisis

Additional sources for this section are: MCCC, Chronology of Political Unrest in I Corps, 9Mar-23Jun66, covering ltr dtd 24Jun66, hereafter MCCC Chronology of Political Unrest; and Facts on File Inc., *South Vietnam; U.S. Communist Confrontation in Southeast Asia, 1966-67* (New York: 1969), v. 2, hereafter Facts on File, *South Vietnam 1966-67.*
1. *Washington Post and Times Herald,* 11Mar66, p.1.

Restructuring the Command

Additional sources for this section are: FMFPac ComdC, Jan-Jun66; 1st MarDiv ComdCs Jan-Jun66; 3d MarDiv ComdC, Mar66; FLC ComdC, Mar66.
2. CinCPacFlt, CinCPacFlt Inst 5440.11, Status, Responsibilities, and Tasks of Commander U.S. Naval Forces, Vietnam, n.d. [Mar 66], App 1, U.S. Naval Forces Vietnam, Historical Summary, Apr66 (OAB, NHD).
3. ComUSMACV ltr to CGIIIMAF, dtd 30Mar66, Subj: Letter of Instruction in MACV Historical Records, 69A702, Box 5, File VA (Marine).

The Beginnings of the Da Nang Offensive

Additional sources for this section are: III MAF Opn Kings Jnl File; 1st MAW ComdC, Mar 66; 3d MarDiv ComdCs, MarApr66; 3d Mar ComdC, Mar 66; 9th Mar ComdCs, Mar-Apr66; Col Edwin H. Simmons, Presentation to HQMC, Washington, D.C., Jul66 (Oral Hist Coll, Hist and Mus Div, HQMC), hereafter Simmons Presentation; Simmons, 9th Marines Notebook.
4. 1/3 OpO 302-66, dtd 14Mar66 in 1/3 ComdC, Mar66.
5. 2/3 ComdC, Mar66.
6. Simmons Presentation.
7. Ibid. and Status Rept for LtGen Walt, n.d. (Mar66) in Simmons, 9th Marines Notebook.

8. Col Joshua W. Dorsey III, Comments on draft MS, dtd 24Jul78 (Vietnam Comment File), hereafter Dorsey Comments.

9. 3/9 AAR for 4-5 Mar66, dtd 14Mar66, encl 19, 3/9 ComdC, Mar66.

10. Quoted in 3d MarDiv ComdC, Mar66, p. 19

11. 3/3 and 3/9 ComdCs, Mar66.

12. 3d MarDiv OpO 382-66, dtd 18Mar66 in III MAF Opn Kings Jnl File.

13. LtCol William F. Donahue, Jr., Comments on draft MS, dtd 6Jun78 (Vietnam Comment File), hereafter Donahue Comments. See also Dorsey Comments.

14. 2/9 AAR, Opn Kings, dtd 28Mar66 in 2/9 ComdC, Mar66.

15. 9th Mar ComdC, Mar66, pp. 2-7-2.8

16. Ibid., p. 2-13.

17. 1st MAW Sit Rep 312, dtd 26Mar66 in 1st MAW ComdC, Mar66.

18. 3/3 ComdC, Mar66 and 9th Mar ComdC, Mar66, p. 3-2.

19. Simmons Presentation.

20. 9th Mar ComdC, Mar66, p. 2-9.

21. Ibid., Apr66.

22. Mr. Paul Hare, Summary Notes on Pacification as contained in Regl Dir I Corps USAID, Da Nang memo to Dir USAID/Vietnam, USAID, Saigon, dtd 14Apr66, Subj: Ngu Hanh Son Campaign in Weller Pacification Material.

"Keep Out . . . Da Nang Has Troubles"

23. CO TG Foxtrot msg to CGIIIMAF, dtd 26Mar66 (III MAF Jnl Files).

24. Ibid.

25. Ibid.

26. MACV msg to NMCC, dtd 27Mar66 (III MAF Jnl Files).

27. Quoted in Shore, "Marines in Vietnam, Jan-Jun66, pt III," p. 10-9.

28. Facts on File, *South Vietnam, 1966-67*, pp. 214-216.

29. Walt, *Strange War, Strange Strategy*, p. 117-19.

30. 9th Mar Sit Rep 99, dtd 9Apr66 in 9th Mar ComdC, Apr66.

31. Chaisson Intvw, Mar69.

32. Donahue Comments.

33. 9th Mar Sit Rep 99, op.cit.

34. MCCC Chronology Of Political Crisis.

35. See various msgs between MACV and III MAF for 15May66 in III MAF Political Crisis Folder.

36. See Col Williams msg to Col Weyl, dtd 15May66 and III MAF C/S msg to Col Laverge, dtd 15May66 in Ibid.

37. Chaisson Intvw, Mar69. See also Walt, *Strange War, Strange Strategy*, pp. 125-30.

38. Gen Lewis W. Walt, Comments on draft MS, dtd 13May78 (Vietnam Comment File), hereafter Walt Comments.

39. Chaisson Intvw, Mar69.

40. III MAF COC msg to MACV COC, dtd 18May66 in III MAF Political Crisis Folder.

41. MACV msg to NMCC, dtd 18May66 in Ibid.

42. Walt Comment. See also LtGen Hugh M. Elwood, Comments on draft MS, dtd 4Jun78 (Vietnam Comment File).

43. Ltcol Paul X. Kelley intvw by HistDiv, HQMC, dtd 16Aug69 (No. 6145, OralHistColl, Hist and MusDiv, HQMC).

44. Shore, "Marines in Vietnam, Jan-Jun66, pt III," p.10-13.

45. Copy of Westmoreland msg to Sharp, dtd 27May66 in v. 6 (24Apr-28Apr66), Tab D/25, Westmoreland Papers (CMH).

46. Chaisson Intvw, Mar69.

47. Ibid.

CHAPTER 6

THE ADVANCE TO THE KY LAM

Unless otherwise noted the material in this chapter is derived from: III MAF Ops, Apr-Jun66; III MAF ComdCs, Apr-Jun66; 3d MarDiv ComdCs, Apr-Jun66; 1st MAW ComdCs, Apr-Jun66; 9th Mar ComdCs, Apr-Jun66; Simmons Presentation; Shore, "Marines in Vietnam, Jan-Jun66, pt III"; Simmons, "Marine Operations, 1965-66."

April Actions and Operation Georgia

Additional sources for this section are: III MAF Jnl File, Opn Georgia; 3/9 ComdCs, Apr-May66; 3/9 AAR, Opn Georgia, 20Apr-10May66, dtd 14May66, hereafter 3/9 AAR Opn Georgia.

1. Simmons Presentation.

2. 2/9 AAR for Company H engagement, dtd 16Apr66, encl to 9th Mar Sit Rep 106-66, dtd 16Apr66, Tab B, Sit Reps, 9th Mar ComdC, Apr66.

3. Ibid.

4. Ibid.

5. Ibid.

6. See 3d MarDiv OpO 369-66 (Georgia), dtd 1Apr66, encl 3, 3d MarDiv ComdC, Apr66 and 9th Mar OpO 111-66, dtd 14Apr66, Tab H, 9th Mar ComdC, Apr66.

7. 3/9 AAR Opn Georgia, pp. 2-7–2-8.

8. Artillery Supplement, encl 1, 3/9 AAR Opn Georgia.

9. Reconnaissance Supplement, encl 5, 3/9 AAR Opn Georgia.

10. Col Paul C. Trammell, Comments on draft MS, dtd 12Jun78 (Vietnam Comment File).

11. Amphibian Howitzer Supplement, encl 4, 3/9 AAR Opn Georgia.

The May Ky Lam Campaign

Additional sources for this section are: 1/9 ComdC, May66; 2/9 ComdC, May66; 2/4 ComdC, May66.

12. 9th Mar ComdC, May66, p. 3-1.

13. 9th Mar OPlan 118-66 Ky Lam, dtd 4May66, Tab H, 9th Mar ComdC, May66.

14. 9th Mar ComdC, May66, p. 3-1.

15. Simmons Presentation.

16. 1/9 AAR for unnamed opn 9-15 May66, dtd 19May66, Tab 4, 1/9 ComdC, May66. The description of the 1/9 action below Dai Loc in the following paragraphs is taken from this account as supplemented by the 9th Mar S-3 Jnl and Sit Reps. All quotations are from the 1/9 AAR.

17. 3d MarDiv ComdC, May66, p. 7.

18. 9th Mar ComdC, May66, p. 2-10.

19. Ibid., p. 3-2. The comparative figures for Marine and VC casualties for the month are found on pp. 1-1 and 2-11 respectively.

Operation Liberty

Additional sources for this section are: 3d Mar ComdC, Jun66; 1st Mar ComdC, Jun66.

20. 9th Mar FragO 153-66, dtd 2Jun66, Tab C, FragOs, 9th Mar ComdC, Jun66.
21. 3d MarDiv OpO 399-66, dtd 5Jun66, encl 4, 3d MarDiv ComdC, Jun66.
22. See 9th Mar FragO 157A-66, dtd 6Jun66, Tab C, FragOs and 9th Mar OPlan 118A-66 Ky Lam, Jun66, Tab G, 9th Mar ComdC, Jun66.
23. Col Van D. Bell, Jr., Comments on draft MS, dtd 15Jun78 (Vietnam Comment File) and III MAF ComdC, Jun66.
24. 9th Mar ComdC, Jun66, p. 9-1
25. 9th Mar Sit Rep 162-66, dtd 11Jun66, Tab B, 9th Mar ComdC, Jun66.
26. 9th Mar ComdC, Jun66, p. 2-4.

PART III
Spring Fighting in Southern I Corps

CHAPTER 7

"THEY'RE NOT SUPERMEN," MEETING THE NVA IN OPERATION UTAH, MARCH 1966

Unless otherwise noted, the material in this chapter is derived from: III MAF Ops, Mar66; III MAF ComdC, Mar66; III MAF Jnl File, Operation Utah, 4Mar-7Mar66, hereafter Utah Jnl File; 3d MarDiv ComdC, Mar66; 1st MAW ComdC, Mar66; 1st MAW Sit Reps, Mar66; MAG-36 ComdC, Mar66; TF Delta AAR 3-66, Operation Utah, dtd 7Apr66, encl 6, 7th Mar ComdC, Mar66, hereafter TF Delta AAR Opn Utah; 1/7 AAR Opn Utah, dtd 15Mar66, Tab 9, 1/7 ComdC, Mar66, hereafter 1/7 AAR Opn Utah; 2/7 AAR Opn Utah, dtd 12Mar66, App A-1, 2/7 ComdC, Mar66, hereafter 2/7 AAR Opn Utah; 2/4 AAR, Opn Utah, dtd 9Mar66, Tab G-1, 2/4 ComdC, Mar66, hereafter 2/4 AAR Opn Utah; 3/1 AAR Opn Utah, dtd 11Mar66, encl 3, 3/1 ComdC Mar66, hereafter 3/1 AAROpn Utah; Vietnam Comment File; Shore, "Marines in Vietnam, Jan-Jun66, pt III"; BGen Oscar F. Peatross and Col William G. Johnson, "Operation Utah," *Marine Corps Gazette*, v. 50, no. 10 (Oct66), pp. 20-27, hereafter Peatross and Johnson, "Operation Utah"; Simmons, "Marine Operations, Vietnam 1965-66."

First Contact with the NVA

1. Maj Alex Lee, Comments on Shore, "Marines in Vietnam, Jan-Jun66, pt III," dtd 28Nov69 (Vietnam Comment File), hereafter Lee Comments. See also Col Robert J. Zitnik, Comments on draft MS, dtd 6Jun78 (Vietnam Comment File), hereafter Zitnik Comments; TF Delta AAR, Opn Utah; Platt Intvw; and Peatross and Johnson, "Operation Utah," pp. 20-21 for further detail concerning the preparation for the operation.
2. MAG-36 ComdC, Mar66; 1st MAW Sit Rep No. 291, dtd 4Mar66; Zitnik Comments; LtCol Elmer N. Synder, Comments on Shore, "Marines in Vietnam, Jan-Jun66, pt III," dtd 22Dec69 (Vietnam Comment File), hereafter Snyder Comments and Peatross and Johnson, "Operation Utah," p. 22.
3. Johnson Intvw.
4. Peatross Comments, Shore MS; MajGen Oscar F. Peatross, Comments on draft MS, dtd 1Jun78 (Vietnam Comment File); Zitnik Comments; Snyder Comments.
5. Platt Intvw and LtGen Keith B. McCutcheon, Comments on Shore, "Marines in Vietnam, Jan-Jun66, pt III," dtd 20 Nov69 (Vietnam Comment File).
6. Col Leon N. Utter, Comments on Shore, "Marines in Vietnam, Jan-Jun66, pt III," dtd 2Mar70 (Vietnam Comment File), hereafter Utter Comments, Shore MS.
7. 2/7 AAR Opn Utah.
8. LtCol Jerry D. Lindauer, Comments on draft MS, dtd 12Jun78 (Vietnam Comment File).
9. Utter Comments, Shore MS.
10. Ibid.
11. LtCol Martin E. O'Connor, Comments on draft MS, dtd 24May78 (Vietnam Comment File).
12. 2/7 AAR Opn Utah.
13. Utter Comments, Shore MS.
14. Copy of Capt Jerry D. Lindauer ltr to LtCol Leon N. Utter, dtd 16Mar66, encl to Maj Jerry D. Lindauer, Comments on Shore, "Marines in Vietnam, Jan-Jun66, pt III," dtd 4Dec69 (Vietnam Comment File).
15. Ibid.
16. Utter Comments, Shore MS.
17. Ibid. See also Lee Comments.
18. Utter Comments, Shore MS; 2/7 AAR Opn Utah.
19. Snyder Comments; TF Delta AAR Opn Utah.
20. Utter Comments, Shore MS.
21. Brown Intvw. See also 1st MAW Sit Rep No. 292, dtd 5Mar66.
22. Snyder Comments; 3/11 ComdC, Mar66.

Operation Utah Expands

23. TF Delta AAR Opn Utah; Utah Jnl File.
24. Snyder Comments; MAG-36 ComdC, Mar66.
25. 2/4 AAR Opn Utah.
26. 3/1 AAR Opn Utah. See also MGySgt J. J. McDowell and LtCol Timothy B. Lecky, Comments on draft MS, dtd 23Mar79 (Vietnam Comment File).
27. LtCol Paul X. Kelley, Comments on Shore, "Marines In Vietnam, Jan-Jun66, pt III," n.d. (Vietnam Comment File), hereafter Kelley Comments; 2/4 AAR Opn Utah.
28. Snyder Comments.
29. Ibid. See also Company B, 1/7 Special CAAR, n.d., encl to 1/7 AAR Opn Utah.
30. TF Delta AAR Opn Utah; 3/1 AAR Opn Utah; 2/7 AAR Opn Utah. See also Utah Jnl File.
31. Utter Comments, Shore MS.

CHAPTER 8

FURTHER FIGHTING AND AN EXPANDING BASE OF OPERATIONS, CHU LAI, MARCH-JUNE 1966

Unless otherwise noted the material in this chapter is derived from: III MAF ComdCs, Mar-Jun66; Vietnam Comment File; Shore, "Marines in Vietnam, Jan-Jun66, pt III"; Simmons, "Marine Operations, Vietnam, 1965-66."

A Bloody March

Additional sources for this section are: III MAF Jnl File, Opn Texas, hereafter Texas Jnl File; 3d MarDiv ComdC, Mar66; 1st MAW ComdC, Mar66; 1st MAW Sit Reps, Mar66; TF Delta AAR Opn Texas, dtd 10Apr66, encl 8, 7th Mar ComdC, Mar66, hereafter TF Delta AAR Opn Texas; 7th Mar ComdC, Mar66; MAG-36 ComdC, Mar66; 3/1 AAR Opn Texas, encl 4, 3/1 ComdC, Mar66, hereafter 3/1 AAR Opn Texas; 2/4 AAR Opn Texas, dtd 29Mar66, Tab G, 2/4 ComdC, Mar66, hereafter 2/4 AAR Opn Texas; 3/7 AAR Opn Texas, dtd 31Mar66, App F, 3/7 ComdC, Mar66, hereafter 3/7 AAR Opn Texas; Artillery AAR Opn Texas, dtd 31Mar66, Tab b, 3/11 ComdC, Mar66, hereafter Arty AAR Opn Texas.

1. MAG-36 ComdC, Mar66; 1st MAW Sit Rep No. 305, dtd 19Mar66; various msgs and entries for 19Mar66 in Texas Jnl File.
2. See Texas Jnl File for 19Mar66 and TF Delta AAR Opn Texas.
3. Kelley Comments.
4. Ibid.
5. Ibid., and Zitnik Comments.
6. Zitnik Comments.
7. Texas Jnl File for 20-21 Mar66.
8. Kelley Comments.
9. Ibid.
10. Ibid., and 2/4 AAR Opn Texas.
11. Arty AAR Opn Texas; III MAF COC Spot Report to MACV COC, dtd 21Mar66 in Texas Jnl File; Zitnik Comments.
12. Kelley Comments.
13. CGIIIMAF Operational Summary to CGFMFPac, dtd 21Mar66 in Texas Jnl File, hereafter IIIMAF Op Sum, 21Mar66; 3/7 AAR Opn Texas.
14. Zitnik Comments.
15. TF Delta AAR Opn Texas; 3/1 AAR Opn Texas; MAG-36 ComdC, Mar66.
16. 3/1 AAR Opn Texas and III MAF Op Sum, 21Mar66.
17. For ARVN action see 7th Mar (Fwd) msg to CG3dMarDiv, dtd 21Mar66 in Texas Jnl File.
18. MajGen Oscar F. Peatross, Comments on draft MS, dtd 1Jun78 (Vietnam Comment File), hereafter Peatross Comments, Jun78 and III MAF Op Sum, 21Mar66.
19. III MAF Op Sum, 21Mar66.
20. TF Delta AAR Opn Texas.
21. LtCol R. A. Savage, informal rept to CG 1st MAW, dtd 25Mar66, Doc 15, Miscellaneous Documents, Operation Texas, 1st MAW Sit Reps, Mar66. This miscellaneous file will hereafter be referred to as 1st MAW Sit Rep Miscellaneous File, Opn Texas.
22. 3/7 AAR, Opn Texas.
23. TF Delta AAR Opn Texas and Texas Jnl File.
24. 2/4 AAR Opn Texas.
25. Quoted in CGIIIMAF msg to 3d MarDiv, dtd 25Mar66, Doc No. 12, 1st MAW Sit Rep Miscellaneous File, Opn Texas.
26. For Operation Indiana, see account in III MAF Ops, Mar66 and 7th Mar AAR 1-66, Operation Indiana, dtd 7Apr66, encl 7, 7th Mar ComdC, Mar66.
27. Peatross Comments, Jun78.

Expansion at Chu Lai

Additional sources for this section are 1st MarDiv ComdCs, Mar-Jun66; 1st Mar ComdCs, Apr-Jun66; 5th Mar ComdCs, May-Jun66; 7th Mar ComdCs, Apr-Jun66.

28. CGFMFPac msg to CG 1st MarDiv, dtd 26Mar66, encl 14-35, 1st MarDiv ComdC, Mar66.
29. Col Glen E. Martin, Comments on draft MS, dtd 5Jun78 (Vietnam Comment File).
30. LtGen Lewis J. Fields, Comments on draft MS, dtd 15Jun78 (Vietnam Comment File).
31. For comparison, see III MAF Ops for Apr and Jun66 respectively.

Operation Kansas

Additional sources for this section are III MAF Jnl File, Opn Kansas, hereafter Kansas Jnl File; 1st MarDiv ComdC, Jun66; Task Force X-Ray ComdC, 1-26Jun66, hereafter TF X-Ray ComdC, Jun66; 1st Recon Bn CAAR Opn Kansas, dtd 28Jun66, encl 15, 1st Recon Bn, ComdC, Jun66, herefter 1st Recon Bn AAR Opn Kansas; 11th Mar AAR Opn Kansas, dtd 1Jul66, Tab 8, 11th Mar ComdC, Jun66 hereafter 11th Marines AAR, Opn Kansas; Staff Sergeant Jimmie L. Howard intvws by 1stMarDiv and MCRD, San Diego, dtd 6Feb67 and 24Apr67 (No. 367 and 677, OralHistColl, Hist&MusDiv, HQMC), hereafter Howard Tapes; Capt Francis J. West, *Small Unit Action in Vietnam, Summer 1966* (Washington: HistDiv, HQMC, 1967), hereafter West, *Small Unit Action*.

32. Task Force X-Ray ComdC, Jun66: CGIIIMAF msg to CGFMFPac, dtd 16Jun66 in Kansas Jnl File.
33. FMFPac, "Marine Forces in Vietnam, Mar65-Sep67," v. 1, p. 4-49.
34. Task Force X-Ray ComdC, Jun66; CG1stMarDiv msgs to CGIIIMAF, dtd 13-15Jun66 in Kansas Jnl File.
35. Ibid.
36. CGIIIMAF msg to CMC, dtd 18Jun78 in Kansas Jnl File.
37. The account of Howard's patrol on Nui Vu is drawn from the following sources: West, *Small Unit Action*, pp. 15-30; Howard Tapes; various msgs in Kansas Jnl File; 1st Recon Bn AAR Opn Kansas.
38. Quotations are from West, *Small Unit Action*, pp.18-19.
39. Zitnik Comments.
40. Quote is from West, *Small Unit Action*, p. 25. See Also Capt Marshall B. Darling, Comments on Shore, MS, "Marines in Vietnam, Jan-Jun66, pt III," dtd 22Jan70 (Vietnam Comment File).
41. TF X-Ray ComdC, Jun66, and CGIIIMAF msg to MACV, dtd 16Jun66 in Kansas Jnl File.

NOTES

42. 11th Mar AAR Opn Kansas; 3/1 ComdC Jun66.
43. CGIIIMAF msg to CGFMFPac, dtd 17Jun66 in Opn Kansas Jnl File.
44. 11th Mar AAR Opn Kansas.
45. 1st Recon Bn AAR Opn Kansas.
46. TF X-Ray ComdC, Jun66. See also CGIIIMAF msg to MACV, dtd 22Jun66 in Kansas Jnl File.
47. 11th Mar AAR Opn Kansas and 1st Recon Bn AAR Opn Kansas.
48. 1st Recon Bn AAR Opn Kansas.
49. III MAF Ops, Jun66, p.27.

PART IV
The DMZ War

CHAPTER 9

THE ENEMY BUILDUP IN THE NORTH

Unless otherwise noted the material in this chapter is derived from: MACV Comd Hist, 1966; III MAF ComdCs, Apr-Jul66; III MAF Jnl & Msg File, Apr-Jun66; 3d MarDiv ComdCs, Apr-Jun66; 1st MAW ComdCs, Apr-Jun66; 4th Mar ComdCs, Apr-Jun66; HQMC Msg Files; Vietnam Comment File; Westmoreland Papers (CMH).

Speculation about the Enemy's Intentions

Additional sources for this section are: Sharp and Westmoreland, *Report on the War*, and Westmoreland, *A Soldier Reports*.

1. Westmoreland, *A Soldier Reports*, p. 168; Sharp and Westmoreland, *Report on the War*, pp. 115-16; General Westmoreland's Historical Briefing, dtd 17Jun66, v. 7, Tab F, Westmoreland Papers (CMH); MACV Comd Hist, 1966, p. 33.
2. Westmoreland, *A Soldier Reports*, p. 168; MACV Comd Hist, 1966, pp 21, 25, 33; Notes on MACV Commanders' Conference, dtd 24Apr66, v. 6, Tab A, encl 2, Westmoreland Papers (CMH); George McGerrigle, "Shift to the North," draft MS (CMH), pp 5, 10; MACV, AC/S J-2 Report, n.d., Subj: The Threat in Northern I Corps, [24?Mar66], v. 5, Tab B, encl 3, Westmoreland Papers (CMH), hereafter, MACV, The Threat in Northern I Corps.
3. III MAF ComdC, Apr66.
4. Col Donald W. Sherman intvw by FMFPac, dtd 6Aug66 (No. 199, OralHistColl, Hist&MusDiv, HQMC).
5. Notes on MACV Commanders' Conference, dtd 24Apr66, loc. cit.
6. Quoted in CGIIIMAF msg to CGFMFPac, dtd 22Apr66 (HQMC Msg File).
7. Transcript of LtGen John R. Chaisson intvw by Hist&MusDiv, dtd 3Apr72 (OralHistColl, Hist&MusDiv, HQMC), p. 376, hereafter, Chaisson Intvw, 1972.

Reconnaissance at Khe Sanh, Operation Virginia

Additional sources for this section are: HQMC G-3, Point Papers, 1966; 1/1 ComdC, Apr66; 1/1 CAAR 5-66, Operation Virginia, dtd 5May66, Tab E, 1/1 ComdC, Apr66, hereafter, 1/1 AAR Opn Virginia; Opn Virginia Jnl File in III MAF Jnl & Msg File, hereafter, Virginia Jnl File.

8. Westmoreland, *A Soldier Reports*, p. 336.
9. ComUSMACV, Memo for the Record, n.d. [24Mar66], Subj: Meeting at Chu Lai on 24Mar66, v. 5, Tab B, encl 1, Westmoreland Papers (CMH). See also, MACV Comd Hist, 1966, p. 33; MACV, The Threat in Northern I Corps; Virginia Jnl File, 13-20Mar66.
10. Col Van D. Bell, Jr., Comments on draft MS, dtd 15Jun78 (Vietnam Comment File), hereafter, Bell Comments. See also, 3dMarDiv OpO 374-66, dtd 27Mar66, encl 28, 3dMarDiv ComdC, Mar66.
11. 1/1 AAR Opn Virginia; 1/1 OpO 8-66 (Opn Virginia), dtd 3Apr66, Tab C, 1/1 ComdC, Apr66; HQMC G-3, Point Paper, dtd 20Apr66.
12. Col George W. Carrington, Jr., Comments on draft MS, dtd 15May78 (Vietnam Comment File).
13. Chaisson Intvw, 1972, p. 371-72.
14. 1/1 AAR Opn Virginia. See also Bell Comments.
15. 1/1 AAR Opn Virginia.

Marine Operations in Thua Thien, April-May 1966

16. Col Francis F. Parry intvw by FMFPac, dtd 15Aug66 (No. 198, OralHistColl, Hist&MusDiv, HQMC), hereafter, Parry Intvw.
17. ComUSMACV, Historical Briefing, dtd 10May66, v. 6, Tab B, Westmoreland Papers (CMH).
18. LtCol Ralph E. Sullivan, Comments on draft MS, dtd 9May78 (Vietnam Comment File). See also 4th Mar ComdC, May66 and III MAF Jnl Files.

Contingency Planning and Reconnaissance at Dong Ha

19. Minutes of MACV Commanders' Conference, dtd 24Apr66, v. 6, Tab A, encl 2, Westmoreland Papers (CMH).
20. Quoted in CGFMFPac msg to CMC, dtd 1Apr66 (HQMC Msg File).
21. Quotes are from CGIIIMAF msg to CGFMFPac and CMC, dtd 22Apr66 (HQMC Msg File). See also Parry Intvw and CGFMFPac msg to CMC, dtd 4Jun66 (HQMC Msg File).
22. III MAF ComdC, May66 and III MAF Jnl and Msg File, 19-22May66.
23. LtGen Krulak msg to Gen Greene, dtd 27May66 (HQMC Msg File); CGIIIMAF msg to CG1stMAW and CG3dMarDiv, dtd 28May66 and ICorps TOC telecon with IIIMAFCOC, dtd 29 May66 (III MAF Jnl and Msg File); 4th Mar FragO 212-66, Opn Reno, dtd 30May66, encl 7, 4th Mar ComdC, May66; 4th Mar ComdC, May66, p. IV-5.
24. MACV msg to NMCC, dtd 5Jun66 and COC 3dMarDiv msg to COCIIIMAF, dtd 8Jun66 (III MAF Jnl and Msg File).
25. III MAF ComdCs, May-Jun66.

Politics and War

Additional source for this section is: 4th Mar AAR, Operation Florida, dtd 25Jun66, hereafter, Florida AAR.

26. III MAF ComdCs, May-Jun66; CGIIIMAF msg to ComUSMACV, dtd 1Jun66, v. 7, Tab A, encl 10 and MACV msg to NMCC, dtd 2Jun66, v. 7, Tab A, encl 16, Westmoreland Papers (CMH); IIIMAFCOC msg to ComUSMACV, dtd 3Jun66 (III MAF Jnl and Msg File).

27. III MAF ComdC, Jun66.

28. 4th Mar ComdC, Jun66, p. IV-1; Florida AAR.

29. Col Boston telecon to IIIMAFCOC, dtd 7Jun66, and 3dMarDiv COC msg to IIIMAFCOC, dtd 8Jun66 (III MAF Jnl and Msg File).

30. IIIMAFCOC, Note on Political Situation, dtd 8Jun66, and Col Wegley telecon to Col Quanti, dtd 8Jun66 (III MAF Jnl and Msg File).

31. Florida AAR.

32. Ibid.

33. General Westmoreland's Historical Briefing, dtd 22Jun66, v. 7, Tab C, Westmoreland Papers (CMH).

34. DepSAICorps telecon to IIIMAF, dtd 17Jun66; IIIMAFCOC, Notes, Political Events, dtd 19Jun66; IIIMAFCOC msg to MACVCOC, dtd 18Jun66 (III MAF Jnl and Msg File).

35. III MAF ComdC, Jun66 and III MAF Jnl and Msg Files, 20-23Jun66.

Heavy Fighting in Thua Thien Province

Other sources for this section are: 4th Mar AAR, Opn Jay, 25Jun-2Jul66, dtd 19Aug66, 10 encls, hereafter, Jay AAR; Capt Thomas E. Campbell, MAU, NAGMACV, AAR, Ambush of 29Jun66, dtd 19Jul66 (SMA, MACV, AARs, 1966), hereafter, Campbell AAR.

36. III MAF and 4th Mar ComdCs, Jun66.

37. CGIIIMAF msg to CG3dMarDiv, dtd 1Jun66, encl 2, 3dMarDiv ComdC, Jun66.

38. Ibid.

39. CG3dMarDiv msg to CGIIIMAF, dtd 10Jun66, encl 10, 3dMarDiv ComdC, Jun 66.

40. CG3dMarDiv msg to CO4thMar, dtd 11Jun66, encl 12, and CGIIIMAF msg to CG3dMarDiv, dtd 13Jun66, encl 16, 3dMarDiv ComdC, Jun66.

41. CG3dMarDiv msg to CGIIIMAF, dtd 19Jun66, encl 34, 3dMarDiv ComdC, Jun66.

42. III MAF and 3d MarDiv ComdCs, Jun66.

43. Jay AAR.

44. 4th Mar FragO 4-66, Opn Jay, dtd 24Jun66, Tab 14, 4th Mar ComdC, Jun66.

45. Jay AAR. See also sections on Air Support and Naval Gunfire, encls 1 and 3; 3/12 AAR Opn Jay, dtd 9Jul66, encl 2; 2/1 AAR, Opn Jay, dtd 8Jul66, encl 9; 2/4 AAR Opn Jay, dtd 8Jul66, encl 10, Jay AAR, hereafter, name of unit, Jay AAR.

46. Jay AAR.

47. 3d MarDiv ComdC, Jun66.

48. 3/12 Jay AAR.

49. Jay AAR.

50. 2/4 Jay AAR.

51. Jay AAR.

52. CG3dMarDiv msg to CO4thMar, dtd 28Jun66 (III MAF Jnl and Msg File).

53. Jay AAR and 3/12 Jay AAR.

54. 3/12 Jay AAR.

55. Jay AAR.

56. Campbell AAR.

57. Ibid.

58. Ibid.

59. Jay AAR and 3/12 Jay AAR. See also Campbell AAR; Capt Edwin W. Besch, Comments on draft MS, dtd 12Jun78 (Vietnam Comment File), hereafter, Besch Comments; IIIMAFCOC msg to MACVCOC, dtd 29Jun66 (III MAF Jnl and Msg File), hereafter, IIIMAFCOC 29Jun msg.

60. Jay AAR and IIIMAFCOC 29Jun msg.

61. Besch Comments. See also, Jay AAR and Campbell AAR.

62. Besch Comments; Jay AAR; Campbell AAR; IIIMAFCOC 29Jun msg; SMA NAG, SitRep, 24-30Jun66, dtd 1Jul66 (SMA, NAG, MACV, SitReps, 1966).

63. Campbell AAR.

64. Jay AAR and ICorps G-2 AdvGp 1st ARVN Div msg to IIIMAFCOC, dtd 30Jun66 (III MAF Jnl and Msg File).

65. Col Samuel M. Morrow, Comments on draft MS, dtd 23May78 (Vietnam Comment File). See also 4th Mar msg to CG3dMarDiv, dtd 30Jun66, Tab 13, 4th Mar ComdC, Jun66 and III MAF ComdC, Jul66.

Further Reconnaissance in the North

66. III MAF ComdC, Jun66.

67. HqUSMACV, Memo for the Record, dtd 20Jun66, Subj: MACV Commanders' Conference, 5Jun66, v. 7, Tab B, encl 1, Westmoreland Papers (CMH), hereafter, MACV Commanders' Conference 5Jun66.

68. Quoted in Robert Shaplen, *The Road from War, Vietnam, 1965-1970* (New York: Harper & Row, 1970), p. 98.

69. MACV Commanders' Conference 5Jun66; 3d MarDiv msg to IIIMAF, dtd 20Jun66, encl 35, and 3d MarDiv FragO 405-66, dtd 20Jun66, encl 36, 3d MarDiv ComdC, Jun66.

70. 3d Recon Bn, Prov Group Bravo ComdC, 28Mar-27Apr66; Company B, 3d Recon Bn ComdC, 28Apr-May66; Company B, 3d Recon Bn ComdC, Jun66; 1st Force Recon Co ComdCs, Apr-Jun66; CGIIIMAF msg to CGFMFPac, dtd 8Jun66 (III MAF Jnl and Msg File).

71. 4th Mar ComdC, Jun66, pp. IV-3, IV-4 and Task Unit Charlie OpO 1-66, dtd 23Jun66, encl 12, 1st Force Recon Co ComdC, Jun66.

72. Ibid.

73. LtCol Dwain A. Colby, Comments on draft MS, dtd 2Jun78 (Vietnam Comment File).

CHAPTER 10

MARINES TURN NORTH, OPERATION HASTINGS

Unless otherwise noted the material in this chapter is derived from MACV Comd Hist, 1966; III MAF ComdC, Jul66; 3dMarDiv ComdC, Jul66; 1st MAW ComdC, Jul66; Task Force Delta AAR Opn Hastings, dtd 17Sep66, hereafter TF Delta AAR; III MAF Jnl File, Opn Hastings, 22Jun-7Aug66, hereafter Hastings Jnl File; MajGen Lowell E. English, Personal Notes, Operation Hastings, n.d., hereafter English Personal Notes; Vietnam Comment File; Westmoreland Papers; Sharp and Westmoreland,

Report on the War; Westmoreland, *A Soldier Reports*; Walt, *Strange War, Strange Strategy*; Simmons, "Marine Operations, Vietnam, 1965-66"; Robert Shaplen, *The Road from War, Vietnam, 1965-1970* (New York: Harper & Row, 1970), hereafter Shaplen, *Road from War*; Robert Shaplen, "A Reporter at Large, Hastings and Prairie," *The New Yorker*, v. XLII, no. 43 (Dec 17, 1966), pp. 129-93, hereafter Shaplen, "Hastings and Prairie."

Finding the Enemy

1. LtCol Dwain A. Colby, Comments on draft MS, dtd 12Jun78 (Vietnam Comment File) and 2/1 ComdC, Jul66.
2. Maj Ernest L. DeFazio intvw by MCB, Camp Lejeune, dtd 8Mar67 (No. 466, OralHistColl, Hist&MusDiv, HQMC).
3. TF Delta AAR.
4. Ibid.
5. Transcript of MajGen Wood B. Kyle intvw by HistDiv, dtd 9, 12, and 16Jun69 (OralHistColl, Hist&MusDiv, HQMC), p. 185.
6. TF Delta AAR and 4th Mar msg to CG3dMarDiv, dtd 11Jul66 (Hastings Jnl File).
7. CG3dMarDiv msg to 4th Mar, dtd 11Jul66 (Hastings Jnl File).
8. Gen Westmoreland's Historical Briefing, dtd 17Jul66, v. 7, Tab F, Westmoreland Papers (CMH). See also Westmoreland, *A Soldier Reports*, p. 197 and Shaplen, *Road From War*, p. 100.

Reactivation of Task Force Delta and Heavy Fighting Along the DMZ, 12-25 July 1966

9. Shaplen, "Hastings and Prairie," p. 157 and BGen Lowell E. English, Comments on draft MS, dtd 12Jun78 (Vietnam Comment File). See also TF Delta AAR.
10. CGTFDelta FragO 1, dtd 12Jul66 (Hastings Jnl File) and TF Delta AAR. See also Col Sumner A. Vale, Comments on draft MS, dtd 12Jul78 (Vietnam Comment File), hereafter Vale Comments.
11. TF Delta AAR and various msgs in Hastings Jnl File, 12-15Jul66.
12. TF Delta AAR. See BGen Edward J. Doyle, Comments on draft MS, n.d. [Jun 78] (Vietnam Comment File) relating to air-ground coordination.
13. 3/4 AAR Operation Hastings, encl 5, TF Delta AAR, hereafter 3/4 AAR; MAG-16 ComdC, Jul66; Shaplen, *Road From War*, p. 104.
14. 3/4 AAR.
15. Shaplen, *Road From War*, p. 104.
16. LtCol John J. W. Hilgers, Comments on draft MS, dtd 6Sep78 (Vietnam Comment File), hereafter Hilgers Comments.
17. Shaplen, *Road From War*, p. 105. See also TF Delta and 3/4 AARs.
18. Col Arnold E. Bench, Comments on draft MS, dtd 20Jul78 (Vietnam Comment File), hereafter Bench Comments. See also Shaplen, "Hastings and Prairie," p. 158.
19. TF Delta AAR.
20. Ibid., and 3/4 AAR.
21. Bench Comments.
22. 2/4 AAR, encl 4, TF Delta AAR, hereafter 2/4 AAR.
23. Detailed AAR on 15-18Jul66 by Company Commander, Company K, encl 3, 3/4 AAR, hereafter Company K AAR.

24. III MAF SitRep, Opn Hastings, No. 12, dtd 17Jul66 (Hastings Jnl File). See also III MAF SitRep No. 9, dtd 16Jul66 and COC 3dMarDiv msg to COC III MAF, dtd 16Jul66 (Ibid).
25. English Personal Notes, p. 3. See also III MAF COC msg to MACV COC, dtd 18Jul66 (Hastings Jnl File).
26. BLT 3/5 AAR Opn Hastings, encl 6, TF Delta AAR, hereafter BLT 3/5 AAR.
27. Bench Comments and Hilgers Comments. See also 2/4 AAR.
28. Vale Comments.
29. Shaplen, *Road From War*, p. 109.
30. Ibid., p. 110.
31. Vale Comments.
32. Company K AAR.
33. III MAF COC msg to MACV COC, dtd 19Jul66 (Hastings Jnl File).
34. Quoted in Shaplen, *Road From War*, p. 110.
35. TF Delta msg to CG3dMarDiv, dtd 18Jul66 (Hastings Jnl File).
36. English Personal Notes. See also 2/4 AAR.
37. Hilgers Comments.
38. BLT 3/5 AAR.
39. 2/1 AAR Opn Hastings, dtd 7Aug66, encl 2, TF Delta AAR.
40. *Washington Post*, 26Jul66, pp. 1 and 3; FMFPacISO msg to IIIMAFISO, dtd 28Jul66 (Hastings Jnl File). See also BLT 3/5 AAR; English Personal Notes; HM2 Victor R. Marget intvw by Hist Sec, III MAF, dtd 22Mar67 (No. 742, OralHistColl, Hist&MusDiv, HQMC), hereafter Marget Tape.
41. Marget Tape.
42. BLT 3/5 AAR.
43. Ibid.
44. Ibid. and English Personal Notes.
45. FMFPacISO msg op. cit.; see also Marget Tape and BLT 3/5 AAR.
46. BLT 3/5 AAR; Hastings Jnl File; English Personal Notes.
47. CG3dMarDiv msg to TF Delta, dtd 25Jul66 (Hastings Jnl File).

Hastings Comes to an End, 26 July-3 August 1966

48. TF Delta AAR.
49. Shaplen, "Hastings and Prairie," p. 169. See also Bench Comments and Hilgers Comments.
50. 2/4 AAR.
51. Bench Comments.
52. Hilgers Comments.
53. West, *Small Unit Action*, p. 59.
54. TF Delta AAR; 3/12 AAR Opn Hastings, encl 7, TF Delta AAR; West, *Small Unit Action*, p. 74.
55. Capt Francis J. West, "Sting Ray 70," *USNI Proceedings*, v. 95, no. 11, (Nov69), pp. 26-37.
56. 1st Force Recon Co AAR, Operation Hastings, encl 14, TF Delta AAR.
57. English Personal Notes and TF Delta AAR.
58. MAG-16 ComdC, Jul66; HMM-164 ComdC, Jul66; HMM-165 ComdC, Jul66; English Personal Notes. See Chapter 16 for a further discussion of the CH-46A problem.
59. As quoted in Shaplen, *Road From War*, p. 111.

60. TF Delta AAR.
61. Walt, *Strange War, Strange Strategy*, p. 141.

CHAPTER 11

THE DMZ WAR CONTINUES, OPERATION PRAIRIE

Unless otherwise noted the material in this chapter is derived from: MACV Comd Hist, 1966; FMFPac, III MAF Ops, Jul66-Jan67; III MAF ComdCs, Jul66-Jan67; 3dMarDiv ComdCs, Jul66-Jan67; 1st MAW ComdCs, Jul66-Jan67; III MAF Jnl File, Opn Prairie; HQMC Msg File; Vietnam Comment File; LtCol Ralph F. Moody and Maj Thomas E. Donnelly, "Introduction of North Vietnamese Regulars," pt IV of LtCol Ralph F. Moody et. al., "Marines in Vietnam," MS (HistDiv, HQMC), hereafter Moody and Donnelly, "Introduction of North Vietnamese Regulars"; Sharp and Westmoreland, *Report on the War*; Westmoreland, *A Soldier Reports*; Walt, *Strange War, Strange Strategy*; Shaplen, *Road from War*; Shaplen, "Hastings and Prairie"; Simmons, "Marine Operations, Vietnam, 1965-1966."

Reconnaissance in Force, 3Aug-13Sep66

Additional sources for this section are: CMC WestPac Trip Rpt, Aug66 in Gen Wallace M. Greene, Jr., Personal Official Files, hereafter CMC WestPac Trip, Aug66; CGFMFPac, Rpt of WestPac Trip, 29Aug-7Sep66, n.d., hereafter CGFMFPac Trip Rpt 29Aug66-Sep66; 4th Mar AAR Operation Prairie, 31Aug-30Sep66, n.d., and enclosures, hereafter 4th Mar AAR; Col Alexander D. Cereghino intvw by FMFPac, n.d. (No.450, OralHistColl, Hist&MusDiv, HQMC), hereafter Cereghino Intvw; LtCol Arnold E. Bench et. al. intvw by III MAF, n.d. (No. 1083, OralHistColl), hereafter Bench et. al. Intvw; LtCol Jack Westerman intvw by III MAF, n.d. (No. 269, Oral Hist Coll, Hist&MusDiv, HQMC), hereafter Westerman Intvw.

1. CGFMFPac msg to III MAF, dtd 22Jul66 (HQMC Msg File); HQMC AO2C Brief, dtd 28Jul66, Subj: Enemy Threat Capabilities in ICTZ in HQMC Staff Briefs Suitable for Discussion with CinCPac and ComUSMACV (CMC WestPac Trip Aug66, Bk. I); MACV Comd Hist, 1966, p. 26; Westmoreland, *A Soldier Reports*, p. 198.
2. 2/4 AAR Opn Prairie, dtd 28Sep66, encl 5, 4th Mar AAR, hereafter 2/4 AAR 28Sep66.
3. Bench et. al. Intvw.
4. 2/4 Special Operation Debriefing Rpt, dtd 13Aug66 in 2/4 AAR 28Sep66.
5. Ibid. and Bench et. al. Intvw. See also Col Vincil W. Hazelbaker, Comments on draft MS, n.d. [Aug78] (Vietnam Comment File), hereafter Hazelbaker Comments.
6. LtCol Howard V. Lee, Comments on draft MS, dtd 14Jun78 (Vietnam Comment File).
7. Hazelbaker Comments.
8. Bench et. al. Intvw.
9. See Special Operation Debriefing Rpt, op. cit.; Bench et. al. Intvw; Shaplen, "Hastings and Prairie"; MAG-16 ComdC, Aug66; VMO-2 ComdC, Aug66 for detailed account of action.
10. Cereghino Intvw.
11. LtCol John J.W. Hilgers, Comments on draft MS, dtd 6Sep78 (Vietnam Comment File), hereafter Hilgers Comments, 6Sep78.
12. 2/4 Special Operation AAR No. 2, dtd 5Oct66 in 2/4AAR, 28Sep66, hereafter 2/4 Special AAR No. 2.
13. Ibid. and Hilgers Comments, 6Sep78.
14. 2/4 Special AAR No. 2 and Capt Edwin W. Besch, Comments on draft MS, dtd 12Jun78 (Vietnam Comment File), hereafter Besch Comments.
15. LtCol John J.W. Hilgers, Comments on draft MS, dtd 2Sep78 (Vietnam Comment File), hereafter Hilgers Comments, 2Sep78.
16. Ibid.
17. Besch Comments.
18. Ibid.
19. Ibid.
20. Ibid.
21. 2/4 Special AAR No. 2.
22. Hilgers Comments, 2Sep78 and Col Arnold E. Bench, Comments on draft MS, dtd 20Jul78 (Vietnam Comment File).
23. Hilgers Comments, 2Sep78.
24. 2/4 Special AAR No. 2.
25. Statement of Capt John J.W. Hilgers concerning recommendation for award, case of Second Lieutenant Stephen Snyder, n.d., encl to LtCol John J.W. Hilgers, Comments on draft MS, dtd 14Aug78 (Vietnam Comment File).
26. Besch Comments.
27. LtCol Arnold E. Bench, Comments on draft MS, Moody and Donnelly, "Introduction of North Vietnamese Regulars," dtd 12Sep69 (Vietnam Comment File); 3/12 AAR, dtd 5Jan67, encl 2, 4th Mar AAR.
28. Westerman Intvw.
29. Col Alexander D. Cereghino, Comments on draft MS, dtd 17Aug78 (Vietnam Comment File), hereafter Cereghino Comments.
30. Ibid.
31. Westerman Intvw.

Assault from the Sea, Deckhouse IV

Additional sources for this section are: CAF Seventh Flt, Hist of Amphib Ops; MCOAG, Study on SLF Opns; 1/26 ComdC, Aug-Sep66; 1/26 AAR Opn Prairie, 19-23Sep66, dtd 16Nov66, hereafter 1/26 AAR; TG79.5 ComdC, Sep66.

32. CGIIIMAF msg to ComUSMACV, dtd 2Sep66, encl 2, 3dMarDiv ComdC, Sep66.
33. MCOAG, Study on SLF Opns, pp. A-21-A-22.

The Continued Fighting for Nui Cay Tre (Mutter) Ridge and the Razorback

Additional sources for this section are: 3dMarDiv AAR Opn Prairie I, Oct66-Jan67, dtd 28Apr67, hereafter 3dMarDiv AAR; 4th Mar AAR; 3/4 AAR Opn Prairie, 17-30Sep66, dtd 7Jan67, encl 6, 4thMar AAR, hereafter 3/4 AAR, Sep66; 3/4 AAR Opn Prairie, 1Oct66-24Dec66, dtd 29Jan67, encl 13, 3dMarDiv AAR.

34. Westerman Intvw.
35. 2/7 AAR, dtd 5Oct66, encl 8, 4th Mar AAR, hereafter 2/7 AAR.

36. 1stLt Robert T. Willis intvw by 1stMarDiv, dtd 16Jun67 (No. 1084, Oral HistColl, Hist&MusDiv, HQMC).
37. 2/7 AAR.
38. Shaplen, "Hastings and Prairie," p. 184.
39. Quoted in Ibid.
40. Ibid., pp. 184-5.
41. Ibid.
42. Quoted in Ibid., p. 186.
43. 3/4 AAR, Sep66.
44. Maj Robert G. Handrahan, Comments on draft MS, dtd 12Jun78 (Vietnam Comment File).
45. Ibid.
46. Ibid.
47. Quoted in Shaplen, "Hastings and Prairie," p. 188.

The Opening of Khe Sanh and the 3d Marine Division Moves North

Additional sources for this section are: 3dMarDiv AAR; 1/3 ComdCs, Sep66-Jan67.

48. CGFMFPac Trip Rpt, 29Aug-7Sep66, p. 5.
49. BGen Lowell E. English intvw by FMFPac, n.d. (No. 402, OralHistColl, Hist&MusDiv, HQMC).
50. MACV Comd Hist, 1966, p. 36.
51. Transcript of intvw with Col John R. Chaisson by FMFPac, dtd Nov66 (No. 327, OralHistColl, Hist&MusDiv, HQMC), pp. 4-5, hereafter Chaisson Intvw, Nov66.
52. 1/3 AAR, dtd 7Feb67, encl 4, 3dMarDiv AAR.
53. Chaisson Intvw, Nov66, p. 5.
54. ComUSMACV msg to CinCPac, dtd 29 Sep66 in III MAF Jnl File, Opn Prairie.
55. Cereghino Comments.

PART V
The Unrelenting War in Central and Southern I Corps, July-December 1966

CHAPTER 12

THE STRUGGLE FOR AN HOA, OPERATION MACON

Unless otherwise noted the material for this chapter is derived from: MACV Comd Hist, 1966; III MAF ComdCs, Jul-Oct66; 3d MarDiv ComdCs, Jul-Oct66; 1st MAW ComdCs, Jul-Oct66; 9th Mar ComdCs, Jul-Oct66; 3d Mar ComdCs, Jul66; 12th Mar ComdCs, Jul-Oct66; MAG-16 ComdCs, Jul-Oct66; III MAF Opn Macon Jnl File, 5Jul-28Oct66, hereafter Opn Macon Jnl File; HQMC Msg File; Moody and Donnelly, "Introduction of North Vietnamese Regulars."

The First Clash

1. 9th Mar ComdC, Jul66, p. 2-2.
2. 9th Mar Int Sum No. 182, dtd 2Jul66 in 9th Mar Int Sums, Jul66.
3. Ibid.
4. 1st MAW Op Rep 5-004, dtd 4Jul66 in 1st MAW Daily Op Reps, App 16, 1st MAW ComdC, Jul66; 9th Mar ComdC, Jul66, pp. 2-3; 9th Mar Int Sum No. 185, dtd 5Jul66 in 9th Mar Int Sums, Jul66.
5. 9th Mar Sit Rep No. 186, dtd 5Jul66 in 9th Mar Sit Reps, Jul66.

The Operation Expands

6. IIIMAF msg to MACVCOC, dtd 5Jul66 in Opn Macon Jnl File.
7. 3d MarDiv, FragO 408-66, Opn Macon, dtd 5Jul66, encl 10, 3d MarDiv ComdC, Jul66.
8. 9th Mar FragO 186-66, Operation Macon, dtd 5Jul66 in 9th Mar FragOs, Jul66.
9. 3d MarDiv FragO, Opn Macon, op.cit.
10. CGIIIMAF msg to CGFMFPac, dtd 6Jul66 in Opn Macon Jnl File.
11. 1st MAW Op Rep 5-006, dtd 6Jul66 in 1st MAW Daily OpReps, App 16, 1st MAW ComdC, Jul66; 9th Mar Sit Rep No. 187, dtd 6Jul66 in 9th Mar Sit Reps, Jul66; 3d MarDiv ComdC, Jul66, p. 13.
12. 3/3 AAR, Opn Macon, dtd 19Jul66, encl 88, 3d Mar ComdC, Jul66.
13. See 9th Mar Sit Reps and FragOs for period 6-8Jul66.
14. 9th Mar Special Sit Rep No. 17, Opn Macon, dtd 10Jul66 in 9th Mar Sit Reps, Jul66.
15. 9th Mar FragO 191-66, dtd 10Jul66 in 9th Mar FragOs, Jul66.
16. 1/3 AAR, dtd 24Jul66, encl 1, 1/3 ComdC, Jul66, p. 1.
17. CG3dMarDiv msg to CO9thMar, dtd 13Jul66 in Opn Macon Jnl File.
18. 9th Mar, Special Sit Rep No. 32, Opn Macon, dtd 15Jul66 in 9th Mar Sit Reps, Jul66.

Macon Continues

19. IIIMAF msg to MACVCOC, dtd 14Jul66 and CG3dMarDiv msg to CO9thMar, dtd 14Jul66 in Opn Macon Jnl File.
20. CG3dMarDiv msg dtd 14Jul66 cited in Opn Macon Jnl File.
21. IIIMAF msg to MACVCOC, dtd 15Jul66 in Opn Macon Jnl File.
22. CO9th Mar memo to CG3dMarDiv, dtd 28Jul66, Subj: Visit of General Westmoreland to An Hoa, in Opn Macon Jnl File.
23. 3/9 ComdC, Jul66, p. 2.
24. 3/9 AAR, Opn Swannee, encl 6, 3/9 ComdC, Aug66.
25. LtCol Fred D. MacLean, Jr., Comments on draft MS, dtd 25April78 (Vietnam Comment File). See also 3/9 ComdC, Aug66.
26. 12th Mar S-3 Jnl in 12th Mar ComdC, Sep66.
27. 3d MarDiv Sit Rep No. 245, Opn Macon, dtd 6Sep66 in Opn Macon Jnl File.
28. 9th Mar ComdC, Sep66, p. 3-1 and III MAF COC, Record of Telephone Call, dtd 6Sep66 in Opn Macon Jnl File.
29. 9th Mar ComdC, Sep66, p. 2-5.
30. 3/9 ComdC, Sep66, p. 2.

Macon Ends but Little Changes

31. 9th Mar ComdC, Oct66, p. 3-1.

CHAPTER 13

THE CONTINUING WAR

Unless otherwise noted, the material in this chapter is derived from: MACV Comd Hist, 1966; III MAF ComdCs, Jul-Dec66; 1st MarDiv ComdCs, Jul-Dec66; 3d MarDiv ComdCs, Jul-Dec66; 1st MAW ComdCs, Jul-Dec66; FMFPac, III MAF Ops, Jul-Dec66; HQMC Msg File; III MAF Jnl and Msg Files; Moody and Donnelly, "Introduction of North Vietnamese Regulars"; Vietnam Comment File; Simmons, "Marine Operations, Vietnam, 1965-1966."

Operations Washington and Colorado

Additional material for this section include: 1st Recon Bn, AAR, Opn Washington, dtd 23Jul66, encl 19, 1st Recon Bn ComdC, Jul66, hereafter 1st Recon Bn, AAR, Opn Washington; Miscellaneous Messages, Operation Washington, in 1st MAW Daily SitReps, 1st MAW ComdC, Jul66, hereafter Miscellaneous Messages, Opn Washington, III MAF Op Washington Jnl and Msg File, hereafter Washington Jnl File; 5th Mar AAR, Opn Colorado, 6-22Aug66, dtd 5Sep66, hereafter 5th Mar AAR Colorado; SMA, MACV AAR Lien Ket-52, 6-14Aug66, n.d. in SMA, MACV AARs, 1966, hereafter SMA AAR Lien Ket 52; III MAF Opn Colorado Jnl and Msg File, hereafter Colorado Jnl File; West, *Small Unit Action*.

1. CG1stMarDiv msg to CGIII MAF, dtd 4Jul66 and CG1stMarDiv OpO 308-66, dtd 4Jul66 in Miscellaneous Messages, Opn Washington.
2. MACV msg to CinCPac, dtd 8Jul66, v. 7, Tab E, encl 1, Westmoreland Papers (CMH).
3. 1st Tactical Area msg to III MAF G-3, dtd 6Jul66 in Washington Jnl File.
4. 1st Recon Bn AAR Opn Washington and 2/11 ComdC, Jul66.
5. 1st MarDiv PerIntRep No. 2, Anx C, dtd 22Jul66, encl 83, 1st MarDiv ComdC, Jul66. See also 1st MarDiv Special SitRep No. 13, dtd 10Jul66 in Washington Jnl File and 1st Recon Bn AAR, Opn Washington.
6. 1st Recon Bn AAR Opn Washington.
7. Minutes of MACV Commanders' Conference, 24Jul66, dtd 17Aug66, v. 8, Tab B, encl 1, Westmoreland Papers (CMH).
8. 1st MarDiv PerIntRep No. 2, dtd 22Jul66 and No. 3, dtd 28 Jul66, encl 83 and 101, 1st MarDiv ComdC, Jul66.
9. CG1stMarDiv msg to CGIIIMAF, dtd 18Jul66, encl 75, 1st MarDiv ComdC, Jul66.
10. CG 1st MarDiv Planning Directive Opn Colorado, dtd 30Jul66, encl 1, 5th Mar AAR Colorado.
11. See the various messages pertaining to planning and orders in Colorado Jnl File.
12. III MAF msg to MACVCOC, dtd 4Aug66 in Ibid.
13. 1st MAW SitRep No. 444, dtd 6Aug66 in 1st MAW SitReps, App. 9, 1st MAW ComdC, Aug66.
14. See LtCol Alexander S. Ruggiero, USMC, memo to G-3, III MAF, dtd 6Aug66 Subj: Resume of Flight to Tam Ky and Que Son, in Colorado Jnl File and SMA AAR Lien Ket-52, pp. 3-4 for a detailed description of the VNMC action.
15. SMA AAR Lien Ket-52, p. 4.
16. West, *Small Unit Action*, p. 91.
17. Ibid., p. 119.
18. SMA AAR Lien Ket-52, p. 8.
19. Ibid.
20. 2/5 AAR, Opn Colorado, dtd 26Aug66, encl 6, 5th Mar AAR Colorado.

The September Election

Additional material for this section includes: 9th Mar ComdC, Sep66; 3d Mar ComdC, Sep66; Weller Pacification Material; MACV Historical Records, 69A702.

21. 3d MarDiv ComdC, Jul66, p. 18.
22. CGIIIMAF msg to subordinate units, dtd 26Aug66 in Folder No. VA(1)(7), Impact of Political Developments on Operations (MACV Historical Records, 69A702).
23. III MAF ComdC, Aug66, p. 11.
24. 9th Mar ComdC, Aug66, p. 2-6.
25. 1st Mar ComdC, Sep66.
26. 9th Mar ComdC, Sep66, p. 2-6.

The Marine TAORs, July-December 1966

Additional material for this section include: TF X-Ray ComdCs, Oct-Dec66; 9th Mar ComdCs, Oct-Dec66; 4th Mar ComdCs, Oct-Dec66; 5th Mar ComdCs, Oct-Dec66; 7th Mar ComdCs, Oct-Dec66; 1st Mar ComdCs, Oct-Dec66; 4th Mar AAR Opn Chinook I, 25Dec66-20Jan67, dtd 12Mar67, hereafter 4th Mar AAR Opn Chinook; MACV Historical Records 69A702; Weller Pacification Material; CGFMFPac Trip Rept, 29Oct-3Nov66, n.d., hereafter FMFPac Trip Rep, Oct-Nov66; LtGen Herman Nickerson, Jr. intvw by Hist Div, HQMC, dtd 10Jan73 (OralHistColl, Hist&Mus Div, HQMC), hereafter Nickerson Intvw; Col Donald L. Evans, Jr. intvw by Hist Div, HQMC, dtd 18Feb72 (Vietnam Comment File), hereafter Evans Intvw.

27. IIIMAFCOC msg to MACVCOC, dtd 5Sep66 in III MAF Jnl and msg File. The message was drafted by Col Chaisson.
28. LtCol Emerson A. Walker, Comments on draft MS, n.d. [Jun78] (Vietnam Comment File); CO MAG-16 rept to CG 1st MAW, dtd 24Jul66 Subj: Viet Cong Attack on Marble Mountain, 23Jul66, App. B, MAG-16 ComdC, Jul66.
29. III MAF and 1st MarDiv ComdCs, Aug66.
30. Nickerson Intvw.
31. LtCol Warren P. Kitterman, Comments on draft MS, dtd 16Jun78 (Vietnam Comment File).
32. 3d MarDiv ComdCs, Oct-Dec66.
33. Ibid., Dec66 and 3/26 AAR, Opn Chinook I, dtd 26Feb67, encl 2, 4th Mar AAR, Opn Chinook.
34. 4th Mar AAR, Opn Chinook; 3d MarDiv ComdC, Dec66. See also Col Alexander D. Cereghino, Comments on draft MS, dtd 30May78 (Vietnam Comment File).
35. FMFPac Trip Rep, Oct-Nov66, p. D-71.
36. Col Edward L. Bale, Jr., Comments on draft MS, dtd 14Jun78 (Vietnam Comment File).
37. CGIIIMAF msg to ComUSMACV, dtd 9Oct66 in Folder No. VA(1) Marine (MACV Historical Records, 69A702).
38. FMFPac Trip Rep, Oct-Nov66, p. D-71.
39. Evans Intvw.
40. III MAF ComdC, Dec66.
41. Ibid., p. 42. See also III MAF Campaign Plan 1-67, dtd 26Dec66, encl 3, III MAF ComdC, Dec66.

42. BGen Lowell E. English intvw by FMFPac, n.d. (No. 402, OralHistColl, Hist&MusDiv, HQMC).

PART VI
Pacification: The Elusive Goal

CHAPTER 14

MARINE CORPS PACIFICATION

County Fair and Golden Fleece

Additional material for this section is derived from: 9th Marines ComdC, Jan-Apr66; 1st Mar ComdC, Jul66; 3d Marines ComdC, Jul66; 7th Mar ComdC, Sep66; 1/7 AAR Golden Fleece 7-1, 17-27 Sep66, dtd 28Sep66, hereafter 1/7 AAR Golden Fleece 7-1; LtCol Littleton W.T. Waller, II, Comments on Moody and Donnelly draft MS, "Marines in Vietnam," pt IV (Vietnam Comment File), hereafter Waller Comments; Simmons, 9th Marines Notebook; U.S. Marine Corps, *Small Wars Manual* (Washington: 1940), hereafter *Small Wars Manual*.

1. Walt, *Strange War, Strange Strategy*, p. 29.
2. For a detailed description of the background of the *Small Wars Manual*, see LtCol Kenneth E. Clifford, *Progress and Purpose: A Developmental History of the U.S. Marine Corps 1900-1970* (Washington, D.C.: Hist&MusDiv, HQMC, 1973), pp. 36-37 and Ronald Schaffer, "The 1940 Small War Manual and the Lessons of History," *Military Affairs*, Apr 72, v. 36, no. 2, pp. 46-51.
3. *Small Wars Manual*, p. II-32.
4. See Shulimson and Johnson, *Marines in Vietnam, 1965*, pp. 141-142, and Simmons, "Marine Operations, Vietnam, 1965-66," pp. 28-29.
5. See 9th Marines OpO 117-66 (County Fair), dtd 4May66 in Folder no. VA (1) Marine, Box 5 (MACV Historical Records, 69A702).
6. 9th Marines ComdC and SitReps, April 66.
7. FMFPac, III MAF Ops, Apr, May, Jun, Jul 66; Westmoreland, *Report on the War*, p. 121.
8. ComUSMACV ltr to CGIIIMAF, dtd 4Jul66. Subj: Military Support for Revolutionary Development, encl 9, 3d MarDiv ComdC, Jul66.
9. Ibid.
10. ComUSMACV msg to CGIIIMAF, dtd 10Jul66, in Folder No. VA (1) (8) Tactical Innovations, Box 6 (MACV Historical Records, 69A702).
11. 1st Marines ComdC, Jul66.
12. 1/3 AAR County Fair 3-14, dtd 30Jul66 in 1/3 ComdC, Jul66.
13. CGFMFPac, WestPac Trip Report, 29Aug-7Sep66, n.d. p. 4.
14. FMFPac, III MAF Ops, Dec 1966, pp. 54-55.
15. See Shulimson and Johnson, *Marines in Vietnam, 1965*, pp. 138-141.
16. III MAF ComdC, Sep66, p. 30.
17. 1/7 AAR; Waller Comments; 1st MarDiv ComdC, Sep66, pp. 15-16.
18. Waller Comments.
19. 1/7 AAR Operation Golden Fleece 7-1, p. 8.
20. Ibid., p. 8.
21. Ibid., p. 22.
22. Ibid., p. 18.
23. Ibid.
24. Waller Comments.
25. Moody, "Marines in Vietnam," pt V, pp. 13-14 – 13-25 and Waller Comments.
26. CGFMFPac Trip Rpt, Oct-Nov66, p. 5.

Combined Action

Additional material is derived from: FMFPac, The Marine Combined Action Program, Vietnam, Aug65-Jan67, n.d., hereafter FMFPac, " The Marine Combined Action Program"; Capt John J. Mullen, Jr., "Modification to the III MAF Combined Action Program in the Republic of Vietnam," Student Staff Study, Class 1-69, Amphibious Warfare School, Ed Center, MCDEC, Quantico, hereafter Mullen, "III MAF Combined Action Program"; Francis J. West, Jr., *The Village*; (N.Y.: Harper & Row, 1972), hereafter West, *The Village*; Capt Francis J. West, Jr., "Fast Rifles," *Marine Corps Gazette*, v. 51, no. 10 (Oct67), pp. 38-44, hereafter West, "Fast Rifles"; Capt Francis J. West, Jr., "Something of Significance," unpublished MS (Vietnam Reference Material), hereafter West, "Something of Significance."

27. See Shulimson and Johnson, *Marines in Vietnam, 1965*, pp. 132-138 and Mullen, III MAF "Combined Action Program" for the formation of the Combined Action Program in 1965.
28. FMFPac, "The Marine Combined Action Program," p. 22.
29. Ibid., p. 14.
30. See Mullen, "III MAF Combined Action Program."
31. West, *The Village*, p. 9.
32. Quoted in Ibid., pp. 46-47.
33. See West, "Fast Rifles," p. 40.
34. Ibid., p. 42.
35. West, "Something of Significance," p. 3.
36. HQMC, General Officers Symposium, 1967, pp. F-18 and F-32.

Personal Response

Additional material for this section is derived from John J. O'Connor, "Cross Cultural Interaction: An Evaluation of some Conceptual Approaches" (Unpublished PhD dissertation, Georgetown University, 1970), hereafter O'Connor, "Cross Cultural Interaction."

37. Quoted in O'Connor, "Cross Cultural Interaction," p. 189. Most of the material in the preceding paragraphs pertaining to Personal Response is derived from the O'Connor dissertation. One should consult this source for the full ramifications of the Personal Response Project and for the sociological implications that cannot be covered in this monograph on Marine operations.
38. CGIIIMAF msg to CG 1st MarDiv, CG 1st MAW, CG 3d MarDiv and CG ForLogCom, dtd 27Nov66 (HQMC Msg File).

Kit Carson

39. BGen Edwin H. Simmons, remarks to Kit Carson Scout Graduation, dtd 21Aug70 (Vietnam Comment File).

40. See Parker, *Civil Affairs*, p. 70 and Nickerson Interview.
41. Parker, *Civil Affairs*, p. 82.
42. 1st MarDiv ComdC, Dec 1966, p. 8. For a detailed history of the Kit Carson Program through February 1967 see "Returnee Exploitation, the Kit Carson Scout Program Development," encl 9, III MAF ComdC, Feb67.

Psychological Warfare

43. HqIIIMAF, ForceO 5401.2, dtd 5Sep66, Subj: Establishment of the Psychological Operations Section, attached to Anx E, Pt II, Sec IX, III MAF ComdC, Feb67. See also Col Robert R. Read, Comments on draft MS, dtd 7Jun78 (Vietnam Comment File), hereafter Read Comments.
44. Read Comments. See also PsyOps Section ComdC, 1Jul66-31Dec66, Anx E, Pt II, Sec IX, III MAF ComdC, Feb67.

Civic Action

45. MajGen Jonas M. Platt, "Military Civic Action," *Marine Corps Gazette*, v. 54. no. 9 (Sep70) pp. 20-26.
46. Ibid.
47. 3d TankBn ComdC, Dec66.
48. FMFPac, III MAF Ops, Dec 1966, pp. 51-52.
49. Lt Marion Lee "Sandy" Kempner, "Letters from Sandy," *American Jewish Archives*, v. 31, no. 1 (Apr79) pp. 7-34, p. 16.

The I Corps Joint Coordinating Council

Additional material for this section is derived from the I Corps Joint Coordinating Council Minutes Folder, 1965-66, hereafter ICJCC Minutes Folder.
50. ICJCC Minutes Folder, 2Aug66.

CHAPTER 15

PACIFICATION, THE LARGER PERSPECTIVE

Unless otherwise noted, material for this chapter is derived from: MACV Comd Hist, 1966; FMFPac, III MAF Ops, Jan-Dec66; III MAF ComdCs, Jan-Dec66; MACV Historical Records, 69A702; HQMC Msg File; Weller Pacification Materials; Sharp and Westmoreland, *Report on the War*; Walt, *Strange War, Strange Strategy*; Westmoreland, *A Soldier Reports*; *Pentagon Papers*; Parker, *Civil Affairs*; Stolfi, *Marine Corps Civic Action*; Simmons, "Marine Operations, Vietnam, 1965-66."

Pacification Receives Priority

1. Sharp and Westmoreland, *Report on the War*, p. 116.
2. See Parker, *Civil Affairs*, the bottom of pp. 63-64 for the listing of the Honolulu goals.
3. Quoted in "Re-Emphasis on Pacification 1965-67," *Pentagon Papers*, bk 6, sec IV-C-8, p. 80.
4. Ibid., p. 8.
5. See Ibid. pp. 83-87 for detailed analysis of the "Roles and Missions" Report.
6. Tillson Briefing, encl to Minutes of the Mission Council Meeting of 8 Aug 66, dtd 10 Aug 66 in Mission Council Memo Folder (MACV Historical Records, 69A702).
7. ComUSMACV msg to CinCPac, dtd 26Aug66 in Folder VA (1) (1) Guidance from ComUSMACV (MACV Historical Records, 69A703), hereafter ComUSMACV msg to CinCPac, 26Aug66. Part of this document is reprinted in "Re-Emphasis on Pacification," op. cit., p. 90.
8. Ibid.
9. Quoted in "Re-Emphasis on Pacification," op. cit., p. 90.
10. See ComUSMACV msg to CinCPac, dtd Oct66 in Folder VA (1) (1) Guidance from ComUSMACV, Box 1 (MACV Historical Records, 69A703).
11. See also MACV J-3, Historical Summaries Files, Box 2 (MACV Historical Records, 69A703) and MACV, Combined Campaign Plan (Excerpts) in Weller Working Materials.

Reorganization and Support of Revolutionary Development

12. MACV msg to CinCPac, dtd 18Dec66 in Folder VIIIB Rural Construction, Box 6 (MACV Historical Records, 69A702), hereafter MACV msg to CinCPac, 18Dec66.
13. Ibid.
14. MACV Planning Directive 4-66, dtd 20Jul66, Subj: MACV Planning Cycle in Folder VA (1) (1), Guidance from ComUSMACV, Box 5 (MACV Historical Records, 69A702).
15. ComUSMACV msg to CinCPac, 26Aug66.
16. Ibid.
17. Ibid.
18. ComUSMACV msg to CinCPac, dtd 16Sep66 in Folder VA (1) (14) After Action/Lessons Learned, Box 6 (MACV Historical Records 69A702).
19. Minutes of the Mission Council Meeting of 19Sep66, dtd 22Sep66 in Mission Council Memo Folder (MACV Historical Records, 69A702).
20. ComUSMACV msg to CinCPac, dtd 13Oct66 in Folder VA (1) (1) Guidance from ComUSMACV, Box 1 (MACV Historical Records, 69A703).
21. ComUSMACV msg to CinCPac, dtd 18Dec66.
22. Quoted in "Re-Emphasis on Pacification," op.cit., p. 91.
23. Ibid., p. 108.
24. For the texts of the conference and the President's speech at Cam Ranh Bay, see: "President Johnson's Trip to Asia: Seven Nations Declare Unity at Manila Conference; President Johnson Visits American Troops at Cam Ranh Bay," *The Department of State Bulletin*, v. LV, no. 1429 (14Nov66), pp. 730-39.

Measurements of Progress

Additional sources for this section are: Col Albert C. Bole, Jr. (USA) and Col K. Kobata, (USA), "An Evaluation of the Measurements of the Hamlet Evaluation System," MS., Stu Monograph, Center for Advanced Research, U.S. Naval War College, Newport, R.I., 1975 (Copy in CMH), hereafter Bole and Kobata, "An Evaluation . . . of the Hamlet Evaluation System"; Reporting and Reporting Systems Folder, 1966 (CMH), hereafter CMH Reporting Systems Folder; Evans Interview.
25. Bole and Kobata, "An Evaluation . . . of the Hamlet Evaluation System," pp. 13-18; CMH Reporting Systems Folder; MACV Comd Hist, 1966, p. 543.

NOTES

26. For a chart depicting the detailed breakdown of the Marine reporting system, see Stolfi, *Marine Corps Civic Action*, p. 76.
27. Evans Interview; CMH Reporting Systems Folder; MACV Comd Hist, p. 546.
28. FMFPac, "Marine Forces in Vietnam, Mar65-Sep67," v.I, p. 5-36.
29. Hq3dMarDiv, Brochure for Briefing MajGen Robert E. Cushman, 17-22Apr67, encl to 3d MarDiv ComdC, Apr67, p. 2-4.
30. Bole and Kobata, "An Evaluation . . . of the Hamlet Evaluation System," pp. x-xi.
31. Simmons, "Marine Operations, Vietnam, 1965-66," p. 34.
32. LtCol Warren P. Kitterman, Comments on draft MS, dtd 23Jun78 (Vietnam Comment File).

PART VII
Supporting the Troops

CHAPTER 16

MARINE AVIATION IN 1966

Unless otherwise noted the material in this chapter is derived from: CinCPac Comd Hist 1966; MACV Comd Hist 1966; FMFPac, "Marine Forces in Vietnam, Mar65-Sep67"; FMFPac, III MAF Ops, Jan-Dec66; III MAF ComdCs, Jan-Dec66; 1st MAW ComdCs, Jan-Dec66; MAG-11 ComdCs, Jan-Dec66; MAG-12 ComdCs, Jan-Dec66; MAG-13 ComdCs, Sep-Dec66; MAG-16 ComdCs, Jan-Dec66; MAG-36 ComdCs, Jan-Dec66; HQMC Msg File; Vietnam Comment File; LtCol Ralph F. Moody, Maj Thomas E. Donnelly, and Capt Moyers S. Shore III, "Backing Up the Troops," pt VIII of Moody et. al., "Marines in Vietnam," hereafter Moody et. al., "Backing Up the Troops"; Sharp and Westmoreland, *Report on the War*; Westmoreland, *A Soldier Reports*; Shulimson and Johnson, *U.S. Marines in Vietnam, 1965*; LtCol William R. Fails, *Marines and Helicopters, 1962-1973* (Washington: Hist&MusDiv, HQMC, 1978), hereafter Fails, *Marines and Helicopters*; LtGen Keith B. McCutcheon, "Marine Aviation in Vietnam, 1962-70," *Naval Review 1971* (Annapolis: U.S. Naval Institute, 1971), pp. 122-55, hereafter McCutcheon, "Marine Aviation"; Simmons, "Marine Operations, Vietnam, 1965-66."

Wing Organization and Expansion

1. Col Harry W. Taylor, Comments on draft MS, dtd 12Jun78 (Vietnam Comment File).
2. G-3 Sec, Hq, III MAF memo, dtd 4Jan66, Subj: Fragmentation of Marine Air-Ground Team, encl 12, III MAF ComdC, Jan66.
3. McCutcheon, "Marine Aviation," p. 133.

The Pilot Shortage

4. FMFPac Trip Rept, Oct-Nov66, p. 6.
5. *Baltimore Sun*, 18Oct66, p. 1.
6. BGen Jonas M. Platt, ACS, G-1, Personnel Presentation, HQMC, General Officers Symposium, 1967, Tab G, p. 13.
7. Ibid.
8. MajGen Keith B. McCutcheon, DCS, Air, Aviation Presentation, Ibid., Tab H, p. 13. See also Gen Wallace M. Greene, Jr., Comments on draft MS, dtd 5May78 (Vietnam Comment File), hereafter Greene Comments.

Marine Aircraft: The New and the Old

9. McCutcheon, "Marine Aviation," p. 134.
10. Fails, *Marines and Helicopters*, pp. 101-102 and FMFPac, III MAF Ops, Dec66, p. 77.
11. FMFPac, "Marine Forces in Vietnam, Mar65-Sep67," v. I, p. 6-19.
12. LtGen Louis B. Robertshaw, Comments on draft MS, n.d. [Jun78] (Vietnam Comment File), hereafter Robertshaw Comments, 1978.
13. Col Robert J. Zitnik, Comments on draft MS, dtd 6Jun78 (Vietnam Comment File), hereafter Zitnik Comments.
14. Col Thomas J. O'Connor, Comments on draft MS, dtd 10Jun78 (Vietnam Comment File).
15. Col George W. Carrington, Jr., Comments on draft MS, dtd 15May78 (Vietnam Comment File).
16. H&MS-16 ComdCs, Sep-Dec66.
17. Zitnik Comments.

Relations with the Seventh Air Force

18. Shulimson and Johnson, *U.S. Marines in Vietnam, 1965*, p. 152.
19. McCutcheon, "Marine Aviation," p. 136.
20. Ibid.
21. Greene Comments.
22. LtGen Louis B. Robertshaw, Comments on draft MS, Moody et. al., "Backing Up the Troops," n.d. (Vietnam Comment File).

Marine Air Control Systems

23. FMFPac, "Marine Forces in Vietnam, Mar65-Sep67," v. I, p. 6-16.

Air Defense

Additional sources for this section are: 1st and 2d LAAM Bns, ComdCs, Jan-Dec66; AAM-6, Point Paper, n.d., Subj: LAAM Posture in RVN, DCS Air, HQMC, Point Papers, 1967, hereafter, "LAAM Posture in RVN."
24. FMFPac, III MAF Ops, Dec66, p. 62 and "LAAM Posture in RVN."
25. 1st and 2d LAAM Bns ComdCs, Jan-Dec66 and "LAAM Posture in RVN."
26. 1st LAAM Bn ComdCs, Aug-Sep66.
27. 2d LAAM Bn ComdC, Dec66.
28. 1st LAAM Bn ComdC, Jun66.
29. Ibid., Dec66.
30. "LAAM Posture in RVN."
31. 1st and 2d LAAM Bns ComdCs, Mar-Apr66.
32. Robertshaw Comments, 1978.

Air Operations

33. FMFPac, "Marine Forces in Vietnam, Mar65-Sep67," v. I, p. 6-20; FMFPac, III MAF Ops, Dec66, pp. 65, 67; MCCC, Status of Forces, Dec66.
34. 1st MAW ComdCs, Jan-Dec66 and MCCC, Status of Forces, Dec66.
35. Westmoreland, *A Soldier Reports*, p. 196; Office of Air Force History, Comments on draft MS, dtd 28Jul78 (Vietnam Comment File), hereafter Air Force History Comments.
36. 1st MAW ComdCs, Jan-Mar66.
37. Sharp and Westmoreland, *Report on the War*, p. 24; CinCPac Comd Hist, 1966, v. II, pp. 494 and 497; MACV Comd Hist, 1966, p. 428.
38. CGFMFPac msg to CMC, dtd 28Mar66 (HQMC Msg File).
39. CG1stMAW msg to CGFMFPac, dtd 7Apr66 (Ibid.)
40. CGIIIMAF msg to ComUSMACV, dtd 11Apr66 (Ibid.).
41. CGFMFPac msg to CGIIIMAF, dtd 11Jun66 (Ibid.).
42. Westmoreland, *A Soldier Reports*, p. 196; Gen Westmoreland's Historical Briefing, dtd 24Jul66, v. 8, Tab A, Westmoreland Papers (CMH); Air Force History Comments. For the statistics of Marine jet operations, see 1st MAW ComdCs, Jun-Jul66.
43. 1st MAW ComdCs, Aug-Dec66.
44. LtGen Hugh M. Elwood, Comments on draft MS, dtd 4Jun78 (Vietnam Comment File), hereafter Elwood Comments; VMCJ-1 ComdCs, Jan-Dec66.
45. VMGR-152 ComdCs, Jan-Dec66.
46. CG1stMAW ltr to SecNav, dtd 19Oct66, Subj: Recommendation for Navy Unit Commendation, App A, VMGR-152 ComdC, Jul-Dec66.
47. Elwood Comments.
48. *The Rotor Blade*, dtd 5Aug66, p. 5.
49. *Sea Tiger*, dtd 27Jul66, p. 5. See also Maj. Fritsch's debrief, dtd 15Jul66 in VMFA-323, Debriefing Reports, 6-31Jul66.

CHAPTER 17

ARTILLERY SUPPORT IN 1966

Unless otherwise noted the material in this chapter is derived from: MACV Comd Hist 1966; FMFPac "Marine Forces in Vietnam, Mar65-Sep67;" FMFPac, III MAF Ops, Jan-Dec66; III MAF ComdCs, Jan-Dec66; 1st MarDiv ComdCs, Jan-Dec66; 3d MarDiv ComdCs, Jan-Dec66; 11th Mar ComdCs, Jan-Dec66; 12th Mar ComdCs, Jan-Dec66; 1st FAG ComdCs, Nov-Dec66; HQMC msg File; Vietnam Comment File; Moody, et. al., "Backing Up the Troops"; MCCC, Status of Forces, Jan-Dec66; Shulimson and Johnson, *U.S. Marines in Vietnam, 1965*.

Organization and Employment, January-June 1966

1. Col Edwin M. Rudzis, Comments on draft MS, dtd 26May78 (Vietnam Comment File).
2. 3d MarDiv ComdC, Feb66, p. 21.
3. "Commander's Analysis, Techniques Utilized and Lessons Learned, Operation Double Eagle I and II," n.d., encl 32, 3d MarDiv ComdC, Apr66, p. 3.

The Guns Move North and Restructuring the Command, July-December 1966

4. Col Glenn E. Norris, intvw by FMFPac, dtd 3Jul67 (No. 1386 OralHistColl, Hist&MusDiv, HQMC).
5. CGFMFPac msg to CGIIIMAF, dtd 9Oct66 (HQMC msg File).
6. 1st FAG ComdC, Dec66.
7. Col David G. Jones, Comments on draft MS, dtd 4Jun78 (Vietnam Comment File).
8. CG1stMarDiv msg to CGIIIMAF, dtd 27Nov66, encl 70, 1st MarDiv ComdC, Nov66.
9. 1st MarDiv ComdC, Dec66, p. 6.
10. Quoted in Col Robert D. Heinl, Jr., *Dictionary of Military and Naval Quotations* (Annapolis: U.S. Naval Institute, 1966), p. 40.

CHAPTER 18

MEN AND MATERIAL

Unless otherwise noted the material in this chapter is derived from: MACV Comd Hist 1966; FMFPac, "Marine Forces in Vietnam, Mar65-Sep67"; FMFPac, III MAF Ops, Jan-Dec66; III MAF ComdCs, Jan-Dec66; 1st MarDiv ComdCs, Jan-Dec66; 3d MarDiv ComdCs, Jan-Dec66; 1st MAW ComdCs, Jan-Dec66; HQMC Msg File; Vietnam Comment File; Moody et. al., "Backing Up the Troops"; Shulimson and Johnson, *U.S. Marines in Vietnam, 1965*.

Manpower

Additional material for this section is derived from HQMC, General Officers Symposium, 1966; HQMC, General Officers Symposium, 1967; *Pentagon Papers*.

1. Clipping from *New York Times*, dtd 21Feb66 in Current News, dtd 21Feb66.
2. LtGen Leonard F. Chapman, Jr., "View from the Top—Assistant Commandant's Overview," HQMC, General Officers Symposium, 1967, Tab B, p. 1, hereafter Chapman, "View from the Top."
3. See entries for Jun, Jul, Aug, 1966 in Hist&MusDiv, HQMC, "Commandant's Chronology, 1954-71," MS.
4. See briefing for CMC in the respective 1st and 3d MarDiv ComdCs, Aug66.
5. Chaisson Intvw, Nov66.
6. FMFPac Trip Rpt, Oct-Nov66, p. C-26.
7. Supplement to General Officers Symposium, dtd 20Jan67, HQMC, General Officers Symposium, 1966, p. B-1.
8. BGen Lowell E. English intvw by FMFPac, n.d. (No. 402, OralHistColl, Hist&MusDiv, HQMC).
9. Chapman, "View from the Top," p. B-2.

NOTES

Logistics, Medical Support, and Construction

Additional sources for this section are: FLSG ComdCs, Jan-Mar66; FLC ComdCs, Mar-Dec66; 1st Med Bn ComdCs, Feb-Dec66; 3d Med Bn ComdCs, Jan-Dec66; 1st Engr Bn ComdCs, Mar-Dec66; 3d Engr Bn ComdCs, Jan-Dec66; 9th Engr Bn, ComdCs, May-Dec66; 11th Engr Bn, ComdCs, Nov-Dec66; Col George C. Axtell, Jr. intvw by FMFPac, dtd 5Oct66 (No. 219, OralHistColl, Hist&MusDiv, HQMC), hereafter Axtell Intvw; Hooper, *Mobility, Support, Endurance*.

10. Shulimson and Johnson, *Marines in Vietnam, 1965*, Ch 12.
11. LtGen Lewis W. Walt, Comments on draft MS, Moody et. al., "Backing Up the Troops," dtd 19Feb70 (Vietnam Comment File).
12. Hooper, *Mobility, Support, Endurance*, p. 85.
13. III MAF ComdCs, Jan and Feb66.
14. Hooper, *Mobility, Support, Endurance*, p. 85.
15. Shulimson and Johnson, *Marines in Vietnam, 1965*, pp. 184-5.
16. 3d MarDiv ComdC, Feb66.
17. III MAF ComdC, Mar66.
18. FMFPac, ComdC, Jan-Jun66, p. 26.
19. Ibid., p. 7, and Col Mauro J. Padalino, Comments on draft MS, Moody et. al., "Backing Up the Troops," dtd 10Mar70 (Vietnam Comment File), hereafter Padalino Comments.
20. III MAF ComdC, Mar66 and III MAF ForceO P40005, dtd 13Mar66, Subj: Standing Operating Procedures for Logistics, encl 8, III MAF ComdC, Mar66.
21. FLC ComdC, Mar66.
22. Padalino Comments.
23. FLC ComdC, Apr66.
24. Ibid., Jun66.
25. 3d MarDiv ComdC, Jul66.
26. CMFMFPac Trip Rpt, 29Aug-Sep66, p. 6.
27. Axtell Intvw.
28. Hooper, *Mobility, Support, Endurance*, p. 119.
29. See FLC ComdCs, Oct-Dec66.
30. Col Franklin C. Thomas, Jr., Comments on draft MS, dtd 19May78 (Vietnam Comment File).
31. Col James M. Callender, Comments on draft MS, dtd 1Jun78 (Vietnam Comment File).
32. Col Edward L. Bale, Jr. Comments on draft MS, dtd 12Jun78 (Vietnam Comment File).
33. Axtell Intvw.
34. FMFPac, III MAF Ops, Nov66, p. 51; FMFPac, "Marine Forces in Vietnam, Mar65-Sep67," v. 1, pp. 8-38—8-39; Hooper, *Mobility, Support, Endurance*, p. 77.
35. *Sea Tiger*, 21Dec66, pp. 1 and 11. See also 3d Med Bn ComdC, Dec66.
36. Moody et. al., "Backing Up the Troops," pp. 22-34—22-35.
37. FMFPac, "Marine Forces in Vietnam, Mar-Sep67, Statistics," v. 2, pp. 87-88.
38. Quoted in *Sea Tiger*, 18Jan67, p. 1.
39. FMFPac, "Marine Forces in Vietnam, Mar65-Sep67," v. 1, pp. 8-23—8-24.
40. 1st MAW G-5 Narrative Summary, App. 5, encl 2, 1st MAW ComdC, Aug66.

PART VIII
The SLF, Advisors, Other Marine Activities, and a Final Look at 1966

CHAPTER 19

THE SLF OF THE SEVENTH FLEET

Unless otherwise noted the material in this chapter is derived from: MACV Comd Hist, 1966; FMFPac, III MAF Ops, Jan-Dec66; TG 79.5 ComdCs, Jan-Dec66; FMFPac, Report of Amphibious Operations Conference held at direction of CinCPacFlt, 26Feb-1Mar66, n.d., hereafter FMFPac, Amphib Conference Rept; CinCPacFlt, Report of the CinCPacFlt-ComUSMACV Amphibious Conference Report, 25-28 May66, dtd 29Jun66 (OAB, NHD), hereafter CinCPacFlt-ComUSMACV Amphibious Conference Rept; HQMC Msg File; MACV Historical Records 69A702; LtCol Ralph F. Moody and Benis M. Frank, "SLF Operations in Vietnam," MS, Hist&MusDiv, HQMC; Chaisson Intvw, 1972.

The SLF, Double Eagle, and Doctrinal Debates

1. CTF 79.5 AAR Operation Double Eagle I and II, dtd 17Mar66, Tab F, TG 79.5 ComdC, Jan-May66.
2. Ibid.
3. Chaisson Intvw, 1972, pp. 380-81.
4. CGFMFPac msg to CGIIIMAF, dtd 18Feb66, (HQMC Msg File).
5. Ibid.
6. Chaisson Intvw, 1972, p. 379.

The Okinawa Conference

7. FMFPac, Amphib Conference Rept, p. I-6.
8. Ibid., pp. 2-1—2-2.
9. Ibid., p. 2-5.
10. Ibid., pp. 2-1—2-10.
11. Ibid., pp. 1-9—1-10.

Changes in Command and Composition

12. CGIIIMAF msg to CGFMFPac, dtd 4Mar66; CGFMFPac msg to CGIIIMAF, dtd 6Mar66; AdminOFMFPac to CGFMFPac, dtd 14Mar66 (HQMC Msg File).

Further Operations and Changes in Command and Units

13. ComUSMACV msg to ComSeventhFlt, dtd 22Mar66, File No. VA (1) (MACV Historical Records, 69A702).
14. CGFMFPac msg to CMC, dtd 26Mar66 (HQMC Msg File).
15. For a detailed description of Operation Jackstay, see LtCdr Robert E. Mumford, Jr., "Jackstay: New Dimensions in Amphibious Warfare," *Naval Review, 1968* (Annapolis: U.S. Naval Institute, 1968), pp. 68-87.

The May Conference

16. CinCPacFlt-ComUSMACV Amphibious Conference Rept and MACV Comd Hist, 1966, pp. 416-18.
17. CinCPacFlt-ComUSMACV Amphibious Conference, pp. I-1 and I-3.

The SLF to the End of the Year

18. Chaisson Intvw, 1972, p. 391.

CHAPTER 20

OTHER MARINE ACTIVITIES

Unless otherwise noted the material in this chapter is derived from: MACV Comd Hist 1966 and MACV Strength Reports, 1966.

Staff and Security in Saigon

Additional material from this section is derived from HQMC, Status of Forces, 1966; LtGen William K. Jones intvw by OralHistU, HistDiv, HQMC, dtd 23Apr73 (OralHistColl, Hist&MusDiv, HQMC), hereafter Jones Intvw.

1. Jones Intvw.
2. Ibid.
3. Ibid.

Marine Advisors to the VNMC

Additional material for this section is derived from MACV, NAG, Joint Tables of Distribution, 1966 (OAB, NHD); Senior Marine Advisor (SMA), NAG, Monthly Historical Summaries, 1966; SMA, NAG, AARs, 1966; SMA, NAG, ltr to CMC, dtd 13Jul66, Subj: Organization, Employment, and Support of the Vietnamese Marine Corps, (MacNeil Report), hereafter MacNeil Report.

4. Marine Advisory Unit, Naval Advisory Group, MACV, Force Structure Plan for Vietnamese Marine Corps, dtd 4Jun66, encl 1, MacNeil Report.
5. SMA, NAG, Monthly Historical Summary for Dec 1966, dtd 1Jan67.
6. LtCol McClendon G. Morris, Comments on draft MS, dtd 13Jun78 (Vietnam Comment File).

Air and Naval Gunfire Liaison

Additional material for this section is derived from 1st ANGLICO ComdCs, 1966.

CHAPTER 21

AT THE END OF THE YEAR

Unless otherwise noted, the material in this chapter is derived from: MACV Comd Hist, 1966; MACV Historical Records, 69A702; III MAF ComdCs, Oct66-Feb67; 3d MarDiv ComdCs, Oct66-Jan67; 1st MarDiv ComdCs, Oct-Dec66; Sharp and Westmoreland, *Report on the War*; HQMC, General Officers Symposium, 1967; *Pentagon Papers*.

Plans for Reinforcing the Marines in I Corps

1. Sharp and Westmoreland, *Report on the War*, p. 116.
2. Quoted in HQMC, General Officers Symposium Book, 1967, pp. F-6—F-7.
3. Sharp and Westmoreland, *Report on the War*, p. 190.
4. See ComUSMACV msg to CinCPac, dtd 12Jul66; ComUSMACV msg to CGIIIMAF, dtd 13Jul66; MACVJO3, Memo for the Record, dtd 13Jul66, Subj: Conference-Situation in I CTZ; CGIForceV msg to CG1stBde, 101st Abn Div, dtd 16Jul66. All four documents are in Box 5, File No. VA(1) Marine (MACV Historical Records, 69A702).
5. See MACV Comd Hist, 1966, p. 367, and planning directives attached to 3d MarDiv and 1st MarDiv ComdCs, Sep-Oct66 for further discussion of these plans.
6. Minutes of the Mission Council Meeting of 25Jul66, dtd 26Jul66, Box 5, Mission Council Action Memo Folder (MACV Historical Records, 69A702).
7. Quoted in "U.S. Ground Strategy and Force Deployments, 1965-1967," *Pentagon Papers*, bk 5, sec. IV-C-6, v. I, p. 64.
8. Ibid.
9. MACV Comd Hist, 1966, p. 85.
10. HqUSMACV Planning Directive 6-66, Operation Short Stop, dtd 18Aug66, Box 5, File No. VA (1) Guidance from MACV (MACV Historical Records, 69A702).
11. MACV Comd Hist, 1966, p. 85.
12. Ibid.
13. ComUSMACV msg to CinCPac, dtd 10Sep66, Box 5, File No. VA (1) Marine (MACV Historical Records, 69A702).
14. ComUSMACV msg to CinCPac, dtd 3Oct66, Box 5, File No. VA (1) Marine (MACV Historical Records, 69A702).

Planning the Barrier

Additional material for this section are III MAF OPlan 121-66, Practice Nine, dtd 26Dec66, hereafter III MAF OPlan 121-66; Chaisson Intvw, Nov 66; Chaisson Intvw, 1972; BGen Edwin H. Simmons, "Marine Corps Operations in Vietnam, 1967," *Naval Review, 1969* (Annapolis: U.S. Naval Institute, 1969), pp. 112-141, hereafter Simmons, "Marine Corps Operations, 1967."

15. See "Air War in the North, 1965-1968," *Pentagon Papers*, bk 6, sec. IV-C-7, v. I, pp. 156-59; "U.S. Ground Strategy and Force Deployments, 1965-1967," *Pentagon Papers*, bk 5, sec. IV-C-6, v. I, p. 65; Office of Air Force History, Comments on draft MS, dtd 28Jul78 (Vietnam Comment File).
16. Quoted in "U.S. Ground Strategy and Force Deployments, 1965-1967," *Pentagon Papers*, bk 5, sec. IV-C-6, v. I, p. 66.
17. ComUSMACV msg to DCPG Washington, dtd 25Sep66, Box 8, Barrier/Starbird Folder (MACV Historical Records 69A702).
18. The account in the previous three paragraphs is largely based on working papers attached to CG3dMarDiv ltr to CGIIIMAF, n.d., Subj: ComUSMACV Concept of Defensive Operations in

NOTES

the Vicinity of the DMZ, encl 2, 3d MarDiv ComdC, Oct66.
19. Ibid.
20. Quoted in "U.S. Ground Strategy and Force Deployments, 1965-1967," *Pentagon Papers*, bk 5, sec. IV-C-6, v. I, p. 83.
21. MACV Working Paper, dtd 18Oct66, Subj: Barrier Study Conference, attached to encl 2, 3d MarDiv ComdC, Oct66.
22. Ibid.
23. Chaisson Intvw, 1972.
24. CG3dMarDiv ltr to CGIIIMAF, n.d., op. cit.
25. Ibid.
26. Ibid.
27. LtGen Lewis W. Walt, CGIIIMAF ltr to LtGen H.W. Buse, Jr., Acting Chief of Staff, HQMC, dtd 29Dec66, covering ltr to III MAF OPlan 121-66, hereafter Walt ltr, 29Dec66.
28. See Briefing Paper, Practice Nine Requirement Plan of 26Nov66, encl 7, 3d MarDiv ComdC, Jan67.
29. See Briefing Paper, Practice Nine Requirement Plan of 26Jan67, encl 6, 3d MarDiv ComdC, Jan67; LtCol Lane Rogers and Major Gary L. Telfer, draft MS, "U.S. Marines in Vietnam, 1967," Ch 9; and Simmons, "Marine Corps Operations; Vietnam, 1966-1967," pp. 133-34.
30. Chaisson Intvw, Nov66.
31. Walt ltr, 29Dec66.
32. 3dMarDiv Practice Nine Briefing for UnderSecNav Baldwin, dtd 12Jan67, encl 3, 3d MarDiv ComdC, Jan67.

Conclusion

33. See Walt ltr, 29Dec66.

Appendix A
Marine Command and Staff List
January-December 1966

MARINE COMMAND AND STAFF LIST,
1 January - 31 December 1966*

Unless otherwise indicated, dates refer to the period a unit was in South Vietnam. With the exception of 3d Marine Division (Fwd) and Task Force X-Ray and Force Logistic Command, Marine organizations of battalion/squadron-size and above are listed below (For a complete listing of location and strength of Marine units in the Western Pacific, see Appendix G.).

III MAF Headquarters 1Jan-31Dec66

CG MajGen Lewis W. Walt	1Jan-9Feb66
MajGen Keith B. McCutcheon (Acting)	10Feb-8Mar66
LtGen Lewis W. Walt	9Mar-31Dec66
DepCG MajGen Keith B. McCutcheon (Additional Duty)	1Jan-28Mar66
MajGen Lewis J. Fields (Additional Duty)	29Mar-30Sep66
MajGen Herman Nickerson, Jr. (Additional Duty)	1Oct-31Dec66
C/S Col George C. Axtell, Jr.	1Jan-14Mar66
BGen Jonas M. Platt	15Mar-5Dec66
BGen Hugh M. Elwood	6Dec-31Dec66
G-1 Col Don W. Galbreaith	1Jan-7Jun66
Col John L. Mahon	8Jun-31Dec66
G-2 Col Leo J. Dulacki	1-24Jan66
LtCol Joseph T. Odenthal	25-31Jan66
Col John E. Gorman	1Feb-3May66
Col Thell H. Fisher	4May-31Jul66
Col Carl A. Sachs	1Aug-6Sep66
Col Roy H. Thompson	7Sep-31Dec66
G-3 Col Edwin H. Simmons	1Jan-12Feb66
Col John R. Chaisson	13Feb-8Nov66
Col Drew J. Barrett, Jr.	9Nov-31Dec66
G-4 Col Harold A. Hayes, Jr.	1Jan-19Feb66
Col Steve J. Cibik	20Feb-20May66
Col Joseph F. Quilty, Jr.	21May-31Dec66
G-5 Maj Charles J. Keever	1Jan-31Jan66
Col Eric S. Holmgrain	1Feb-31Dec66

1st Marine Division*

The 1st Marine Division was placed under the operational control of III MAF on 29Mar66. Individual units were in Vietnam at that time and many arrived later. The listing below reflects administrative rather than operational organization.

1st Marine Division Headquarters 29Mar-31Dec66

CG MajGen Lewis J. Fields	29Mar-30Sep66
MajGen Herman Nickerson, Jr.	1Oct-31Dec66
ADC BGen William A. Stiles	29Mar-31Dec66
C/S Col Gordon H. West	29Mar-9Sep66
Col Sidney J. Altman	10Sep-31Dec66
G-1 Col William F. Fry	29Mar-4Aug66
Col Charles C. Crossfield II	5Aug-31Dec66
G-2 Col John J. O'Donnell	29Mar-31Dec66
G-3 Col Louis H. Wilson, Jr.	29Mar-26Jun66
Col Herman Poggemeyer, Jr.	27Jun-31Dec66
G-4 Col William R. Bennett	1Jan-31Aug66
LtCol William E. Bonds	1Sep-1Oct66
Col Edward L. Bale, Jr.	2Oct-31Dec66
G-5 Maj James S. Ready	29Mar-5Apr66
Col Louie N. Casey	6Apr-30Sep66
Col Walter Moore	1Oct-31Dec66

Headquarters Battalion

CO Col James P. Treadwell	29Mar-31Mar66
LtCol Neil Dimond	1Apr-25Jul66
Col Warren A. Leitner	26Jul-31Dec66

Task Force X-Ray 10Oct-31Dec66*

TF X-Ray was established at Chu Lai on 10Oct66 when the 1st Marine Division Headquarters moved to Da Nang.

CG BGen William A. Stiles	10Oct-31Dec66
C/S Col Charles F. Widdecke	10Oct-25Dec66
Col Fred E. Haynes, Jr.	26Dec-31Dec66
G-1 LtCol Paul A. Lorentzen	10Oct-6Dec66
LtCol Roland L. McDaniel	7Dec-31Dec66
G-2 Maj Glenn K. Maxwell	10Oct-31Dec66
G-3 LtCol Robert E. Hunter, Jr.	10Oct-15Nov66
LtCol Edward J. Bronars	16Nov-31Dec66
G-4 LtCol William E. Bonds	10Oct-10Dec66
LtCol Louis A. Bonin	11Dec-31Dec66

COMMAND AND STAFF LISTS

G-5 Maj James S. Ready	10Oct-8Dec66	
Maj Joseph T. Smith	9Dec-31Dec66	

1st Marines*
The headquarters arrived in RVN on 16Jan66.

CO Col Bryan B. Mitchell	16Jan-18Aug66
Col Donald L. Mallory	19Aug-31Dec66

1st Battalion, 1st Marines

CO LtCol Harold A. Hatch	1Jan-31Mar66
LtCol Van D. Bell, Jr.	1Apr-31Dec66

2d Battalion, 1st Marines

CO LtCol Robert T. Hanifin, Jr.	1Jan-1Jul66
LtCol Jack D. Spaulding	2Jul-9Oct66
Maj William F. Hohmann	10Oct-16Oct66
LtCol Haig Donabedian	17Oct-31Dec66

3d Battalion, 1st Marines*
The battalion arrived in RVN on 16Jan66.

CO LtCol James R. Young	16Jan-10Jun66
LtCol Emerson A. Walker	11Jun-25Oct66
LtCol Hillmer F. Deatley	26Oct-31Dec66

5th Marines*
The regimental headquarters arrived in RVN on 22May66. With the establishment of TF X-Ray on 10Oct66, the 5th Marines became largely an administrative headquarters.

CO Col Charles F. Widdecke	22May-25Dec66
Col Fred E. Haynes, Jr.	26Dec-31Dec66

1st Battalion, 5th Marines*
The battalion arrived in RVN on 8May66.

CO LtCol Harold L. Coffman	8May-18Sep66
LtCol Edward R. Watson	19Sep-3Nov66
Maj Peter L. Hilgartner	4Nov-31Dec66

2d Battalion, 5th Marines*
The battalion arrived in RVN on 5Apr66.

CO LtCol Robert H. Uskurait	5Apr-23May66
LtCol Walter Moore	24May-30Sep66
Maj Leonard E. Wood	1Oct-2Oct66
LtCol William C. Airheart	3Oct-31Dec66

3d Battalion, 5th Marines*
The battalion was assigned to III MAF on 2Aug66.

CO LtCol Edward J. Bronars	2Aug-14Nov66
Maj Jim T. Elkins	15Nov-22Dec66
LtCol Dean E. Esslinger	23Dec-31Dec66

7th Marines

CO Col Oscar F. Peatross	1Jan-3Apr66
Col Eugene H. Haffey	4Apr-31Jul66
Col Lawrence F. Snoddy, Jr.	1Aug-31Dec66

1st Battalion, 7th Marines

CO LtCol James P. Kelly	1Jan-25Apr66
LtCol Frederick S. Wood	26Apr-3Sep66
Maj Littleton W. T. Waller, II	4Sep-21Oct66
LtCol Basile Lubka	22Oct-31Dec66

2d Battalion, 7th Marines

CO LtCol Leon N. Utter	1Jan-4Jun66
LtCol John J. Roothoff	5Jun-9Oct66
Maj Warren P. Kitterman	10Oct-31Dec66

3d Battalion, 7th Marines

CO LtCol Charles H. Bodley	1Jan-28May66
LtCol Birchard B. Dewitt	29May-31Aug66
LtCol Raymond J. O'Leary	1Sep-31Dec66

11th Marines*
The regimental headquarters arrived in RVN on 16Feb66.

CO Col Peter H. Hahn	16Feb-16Jun66
LtCol John B. Sullivan	17Jun-12Sep66
Col Glenn E. Norris	13Sep-31Dec66

1st Field Artillery Group*
The headquarters arrived in RVN on 30Nov66.

CO LtCol Joe B. Stribling	30Nov-31Dec66

1st Battalion, 11th Marines*
The battalion arrived in RVN on 16Jan66.

CO LtCol Willard C. Olsen	16Jan-29Mar66
LtCol James C. Gasser	30Mar-23Jun66
Maj Lee C. Reece	24Jun-28Dec66
LtCol Mark P. Fennessy	29Dec-31Dec66

2d Battalion, 11th Marines*
The headquarters arrived in RVN on 27May66.

CO LtCol Joe B. Stribling	27May-20Aug66
Maj Ivil L. Carver	21Aug-31Dec66

3d Battalion, 11th Marines

CO LtCol Paul B. Watson, Jr.	1Jan-29Mar66
LtCol John P. O'Connell	30Mar-13Aug66
LtCol Robert E. Young	14Aug-21Dec66
LtCol Alexander S. Ruggiero	22Dec-31Dec66

4th Battalion, 11th Marines*
The battalion arrived in RVN on 23Feb66.

CO LtCol John F. Crowley	23Feb-30Jun66
LtCol George R. Lamb	1Jul-31Dec66

1st Reconnaissance Battalion*
The battalion arrived in RVN on 22Mar66.

CO LtCol Arthur J. Sullivan	22Mar-7Aug66
LtCol Donald N. McKeon	8Aug-31Dec66

1st Anti-Tank Battalion*
The battalion arrived in RVN on 27Mar66.

CO LtCol Walter Moore	27Mar-22May66
Maj Robert E. Harris	23May-9Nov66
Maj Martin F. Manning, Jr.	10Nov66
Maj John J. Keefe	11Nov-31Dec66

1st Tank Battalion*
The battalion arrived in RVN on 28Mar66.
CO LtCol Albert W. Snell	28Mar-10Jun66
Maj Lowell R. Burnette, Jr.	11Jun-11Jul66
Maj Robert E. B. Palmer	12Jul-1Sep66
Maj John W. Clayborne	2Sep-31Dec66

1st Motor Transport Battalion*
The battalion arrived in RVN on 1Apr66.
CO LtCol John J. Roothoff	1Apr-3Jun66
Maj John H. Doering, Jr.	4Jun-7Sep66
Maj Russell E. Johnson	8Sep-22Dec66
Maj Jim T. Elkins	23Dec-31Dec66

1st Engineer Battalion*
The battalion arrived in RVN on 17Jan66.
CO LtCol James R. Aichele	17Jan-19Aug66
LtCol Charles O. Newton	20Aug-31Dec66

1st Medical Battalion*
The battalion arrived in RVN on 20Mar66.
CO Cdr Robert H. Mitchell (MC)USN	20Mar-31Dec66

1st Shore Party Battalion*
The battalion arrived in RVN on 20Mar66.
CO LTCol Roma T. Taylor, Jr.	20Mar-4Aug66
Maj Stanley G. Roberts, Jr.	5Aug-9Sep66
LtCol Edward H. Jones	10Sep-31Dec66

1st Amphibian Tractor Battalion
CO LtCol William D. Pomeroy	1Jan-5Aug66
Maj Walter W. Damewood, Jr.	6Aug-31Oct66
Maj Albert R. Bowman, II	1Nov-31Dec66

7th Motor Transport Battalion*
The battalion arrived in RVN on 6Mar66.
CO LtCol Louis A. Bonin	6Mar-27Jun66
Maj Arthur C. Stephens, Jr.	28Jun-8Sep66
Maj Sydney H. Batchelder, Jr.	9Sep-31Dec66

7th Communications Battalion*
The battalion arrived in RVN on 1Jul66.
CO Maj James H. Bird, Jr.	1Jul-24Nov66
LtCol William M. Clelland	25Nov-31Dec66

11th Motor Transport Battalion*
The battalion arrived in RVN on 29Dec66.
CO Maj Lee V. Barkley	29Dec-31Dec66

3d Marine Division
3d Marine Division Headquarters 1Jan-31Dec66
CG MajGen Lewis W. Walt	1Jan-9Feb66
BGen Lowell E. English (Acting)	10Feb-9Mar66
LtGen Lewis W. Walt	10Mar-18Mar66
MajGen Wood B. Kyle	19Mar-31Dec66
ADC BGen Lowell E. English	1Jan-31Dec66
BGen Jonas M. Platt	1Jan-14Mar66
C/S Col Donald W. Sherman	1Jan-23Jan66
Col Leo J. Dulacki	24Jan-1May66
Col John B. Sweeney	2May-31Dec66
G-1 Col Robert M. Port	1Jan-18May66
LtCol Karl T. Keller	19May-28May66
Col Glen E. Martin	29May-7Jul66
Col John P. Lanigan	8Jul-30Nov66
Col Robert M. Jenkins	1Dec-31Dec66
G-2 LtCol Richard J. Schriver	1Jan-3Jan66
Col George W. Carrington, Jr.	4Jan-30Jun66
Col Thomas M. Horne	1Jul-7Nov66
LtCol Jack L. Miles	8Nov-31Dec66
G-3 Col Don P. Wyckoff	1Jan-20Feb66
Col Frank R. Wilkinson, Jr.	21Feb-19May66
Col Noble L. Beck	20May-30Jul66
Col William F. Doehler	31Jul-12Dec66
Col Edward E. Hammerbeck	13Dec-31Dec66
G-4 Col Frank R. Wilkinson, Jr.	1Jan-6Feb66
Col James F. McClanahan	7Feb-11Jun66
LtCol Charles S. Wilder	12Jun-9Jul66
Col Robert M. Richards	10Jul-7Oct66
Col John F. Mentzer	8Oct-31Dec66
G-5 Maj John Colia	1Jan-28Feb66
LtCol Edward H. Mackel	1Mar-3Aug66
Col Edward R. McCarthy	4Aug-31Dec66

Headquarters Battalion
CO Maj John E. Watson, Jr.	1Jan-2Jan66
LtCol Robert J. Perrich	3Jan-4May66
Col Edwin G. Winstead	5May-24Jun66
Maj Herbert L. Fogarty	25Jun-9Jul66
Col Robert M. Jenkins	10Jul-30Nov66
LtCol Thomas J. Johnston, Jr.	1Dec-31Dec66

3d Marine Division (Fwd)*
Established at Dong Ha on 10Oct66.
CG BGen Lowell E. English	10Oct-31Dec66
C/S Col Alexander D. Cereghino	10Oct-24Oct66

3d Marines
CO Col Thell H. Fisher	1Jan-15Apr66
Col Harold A. Hayes, Jr.	16Apr-18Aug66
Col Edward E. Hammerbeck	19Aug-12Dec66
Col John P. Lanigan	13Dec-31Dec66

1st Battalion, 3d Marines
CO LtCol Robert R. Dickey III	1Jan-22Sep66
LtCol Peter A. Wickwire	23Sep-31Dec66

2d Battalion, 3d Marines*
The battalion arrived in RVN from duty as SLF Battalion on 28Feb66.
CO LtCol William K. Horn	28Feb-30Jun66
LtCol Fredric A. Green	1Jul-31Jul66
LtCol Victor Ohanesian	1Aug-31Dec66

COMMAND AND STAFF LIST

3d Battalion, 3d Marines*
The battalion departed RVN for Okinawa on 30Aug66 and returned to RVN on 29Oct66.

CO LtCol Joshua W. Dorsey III	1Jan-29Jun66
LtCol Earl R. DeLong	30Jun-31Dec66

4th Marines

CO Col James F. McClanahan	1Jan-23Jan66
Col Donald W. Sherman	24Jan-29Jul66
Col Alexander D. Cereghino	30Jul-31Dec66

1st Battalion, 4th Marines*
The battalion departed RVN for Okinawa on 16Dec66.

CO LtCol Ralph E. Sullivan	1Jan-26Jun66
LtCol Jack Westerman	27Jun-16Dec66

2d Battalion, 4th Marines*
The battalion departed RVN for Okinawa on 5Nov66.

CO LtCol Rodolfo L. Trevino	1Jan-21Feb66
LtCol Paul X. Kelley	22Feb-6Jul66
LtCol Arnold E. Bench	7Jul-5Nov66

3d Battalion, 4th Marines*
The battalion arrived in RVN from Okinawa on 18Mar66.

CO LtCol Sumner A. Vale	18Mar-27Jul66
LtCol William J. Masterpool	28Jul-31Dec66

9th Marines

CO Col John E. Gorman	1Jan-15Feb66
Col Edwin H. Simmons	16Feb-4Jul66
Col Drew J. Barrett, Jr.	5Jul-7Oct66
Col Robert M. Richards	8Oct-31Dec66

1st Battalion, 9th Marines*
The battalion departed RVN for Okinawa on 29Sep66.

CO LtCol Verle E. Ludwig	1Jan-5Jan66
LtCol William F. Doehler	6Jan-31May66
LtCol Richard E. Jones	1Jun-25Sep66
Maj James L. Day	26Sep-29Sep66

2d Battalion, 9th Marines

CO LtCol William F. Donahue, Jr.	1Jan-23Jun66
LtCol John J. Hess	24Jun-9Nov66
Maj John J. Peeler	10Nov-31Dec66

3d Battalion, 9th Marines

CO LtCol William W. Taylor	1Jan-7May66
LtCol Paul C. Trammell	8May-22Jun66
Maj George H. Grimes	23Jun-31Jul66
Maj Fred D. MacLean, Jr.	1Aug-4Dec66
LtCol Sherwood A. Brunnenmeyer	5Dec-31Dec66

12th Marines

CO Col James M. Callender	1Jan-30Jun66
Col Benjamin S. Read	1Jul-31Dec66

1st Battalion, 12th Marines

CO LtCol Warren E. McCain	1Jan-28Feb66
LtCol Adolph J. Honeycutt	1Mar-18Apr66
LtCol Thomas J. Johnston, Jr.	19Apr-4Nov66
LtCol Marshall S. Campbell	5Nov-30Dec66
LtCol Lavern W. Larson	31Dec66

2d Battalion, 12th Marines

CO LtCol Eugene O. Speckart	1Jan-28Feb66
LtCol Joris J. Snyder	1Mar-30Jun66
LtCol James R. Gallman, Jr.	1Jul-8Dec66
LtCol Willis L. Gore	9Dec-31Dec66

3d Battalion, 12th Marines

CO LtCol Leslie L. Page	1Jan-31May66
Maj Samuel M. Morrow	1Jun-30Aug66
LtCol Charles S. Kirchmann	31Aug-31Dec66

4th Battalion, 12th Marines

CO LtCol Edwin M. Rudzis	1Jan-30Apr66
Maj Paul E. Wilson	1May-31Jul66
LtCol David G. Jones	1Aug-31Dec66

3d Reconnaissance Battalion

CO LtCol Roy R. Van Cleve	1Jan-5May66
Maj Thomas R. Stuart	6May-4Jul66
LtCol Gary Wilder	5Jul-31Dec66

3d Anti-Tank Battalion

CO LtCol Bruce A. Heflin	1Jan-12Jul66
Maj Eddis R. Larson	13Jul-16Aug66
Maj Karl E. Sharff	17Aug66
Maj Donald E. Newton	18Aug-22Oct66
Maj Charles R. Stiffler	23Oct-31Dec66

3d Tank Battalion

CO LtCol Milton L. Raphael	1Jan-2Aug66
Maj James G. Doss, Jr.	3Aug-5Sep66
LtCol William R. Corson	6Sep-31Dec66

3d Motor Transport Battalion

CO Maj Freddie J. Baker	1Jan-5Aug66
LtCol Edwin W. Killian	6Aug-23Aug66
Maj Richard F. Armstrong	24Aug-31Dec66

3d Engineer Battalion

CO LtCol Nicholas J. Dennis	1Jan-31May66
Maj Conway J. Smith	1Jun-1Jul66
Maj Charles D. Wood	2Jul-30Sep66
LtCol Garry M. Pearce, Jr.	1Oct-31Dec66

3d Medical Battalion

CO Cdr Almon C. Wilson, MC, USN	1Jan-31May66
Cdr John T. Vincent, MC, USN	1Jun-31Dec66

3d Shore Party Battalion

CO Maj John M. Dean	1Jan-30Apr66
Maj Thomas W. Jones	1May-30Sep66
LtCol Donald E. Marchette	1Oct-31Dec66

3d Amphibian Tractor Battalion*
The battalion arrived in RVN on 3Mar66.

CO LtCol Leroy C. Harris, Jr.	3Mar-28Mar66
LtCol Richard E. Campbell	29Mar-5Jun66

Maj William J. Dinse	6Jun-30Sep66		
Maj Jack D. Rowley	1Oct-31Dec66		

9th Motor Transport Battalion

CO Maj Joseph F. Jones	1Jan-30Jun66
Maj Emmett R. Haley	1Jul-25Aug66
Maj Donald R. Tyer	26Aug-31Dec66

11th Engineer Battalion*

The battalion arrived in RVN on 30Nov66.

CO LtCol Ross L. Mulford	30Nov-31Dec66

5th Marine Division Units in RVN

1st Battalion, 26th Marines*

The battalion arrived in RVN from duty with the SLF on 27Sep66.

CO LtCol Anthony A. Monti	27Sep-23Oct66
LtCol Donald E. Newton	24Oct-31Dec66

2d Battalion, 26th Marines*

The battalion arrived in RVN on 27Aug66.

CO LtCol James J. Wilson	27Aug-14Sep66
Maj Walter S. Pullar, Jr.	15Sep-26Sep66
LtCol James M. Cummings	27Sep-31Dec66

3d Battalion, 26th Marines*

The battalion arrived in RVN from duty with the SLF on 11Dec66.

CO LtCol Garland T. Beyerle	11Dec-31Dec66

1st Marine Aircraft Wing

CG MajGen Keith B. McCutcheon	1Jan-15May66
MajGen Louis B. Robertshaw	16May-31Dec66
AWC BGen Marion E. Carl	1Jan-11Apr66
BGen Hugh M. Elwood	12Apr-30Nov66
BGen Robert G. Owens, Jr.	1Dec-31Dec66
C/S Col Thomas G. Bronleewe, Jr.	1Jan-18Apr66
Col Harry W. Taylor	19Apr-31Aug66
Col Edward J. Doyle	1Sep-31Dec66
G-1 Col Wilbur D. Wilcox	1Jan-15Jun66
LtCol Robert O. Carlock	16Jun-11Aug66
Col Dan H. Johnson	12Aug-31Dec66
G-2 LtCol Billy H. Barber	1Jan-1Aug66
Col George H. Dodenhoff	2Aug-31Dec66
G-3 Col Roy C. Gray, Jr.	1Jan-30Apr66
Col Edward J. Doyle	1May-31Aug66
Col Arnold A. Lund	1Sep-11Nov66
Col Guy M. Cloud	12Nov-31Dec66
G-4 Col Robert J. Lynch, Jr.	1Jan-6Jun66
Col Fred J. Frazer	7Jun-21Aug66
Col Herbert H. Long	22Aug-31Dec66
G-5 LtCol George W. King	1Jan-31Jan66
Col Fred J. Frazer	1Feb-6Jun66
LtCol Ernest J. Berger	7Jun-31Dec66

MWHG-1

CO Col Edward I. Lupton	1Jan-31May66
Col William L. Atwater, Jr.	1Jun-31Dec66

MAG-11

CO Col Emmett O. Anglin, Jr.	1Jan-6Jul66
Col Franklin C. Thomas, Jr.	7Jul-31Dec66

MAG-12

CO Col Leslie E. Brown	1Jan-7Jul66
Col Jay W. Hubbard	8Jul-31Dec66

MAG-13*

The group arrived in RVN on 25Sep66.

CO Col Douglas D. Petty, Jr.	25Sep-31Dec66

MAG-16

CO Col Thomas J. O'Connor	1Jan-26Mar66
Col Richard M. Hunt	27Mar-15Oct66
Col Kenneth L. Reusser	16Oct-21Nov66
Col Frank M. Hepler	22Nov-31Dec66

MAG-36

CO Col William G. Johnson	1Jan-23Aug66
Col Victor A. Armstrong	24Aug-31Dec66

MWSG-17*

The group arrived in RVN on 12Sep66.

CO Col Orlando S. Tosdal	12Sep-31Dec66

H&HS-1

CO Maj Chester A. Liddle, Jr.	1Jan-31Jan66
Maj Carl C. Foster	1Feb-31Dec66

H&MS-11

CO LtCol William H. Bortz, Jr.	1Jan-8Apr66
Maj Don A. Mickle	9Apr-9Jun66
LtCol Francis C. Opeka	10Jun-30Nov66
LtCol Raymond A. Cameron	1Dec-31Dec66

H&MS-12

CO Maj William E. Garman	1Jan-31Mar66
Maj Richard E. Hawes, Jr.	1Apr-20Aug66
LtCol Roger A. Morris	21Aug-5Dec66
LtCol Paul G. McMahon	6Dec-31Dec66

H&MS-13*

The squadron arrived in RVN on 26Sep66.

CO LtCol Walter E. Domina	24Sep-31Dec66

H&MS-16

CO LtCol Jerome L. Goebel	1Jan-19Mar66
LtCol Leslie L. Darbyshire	20May-14Oct66
LtCol Manning T. Jannell	15Oct-28Oct66
LtCol Lucius O. Davis	29Oct-31Dec66

H&MS-36

CO LtCol Thomas G. Mooney	1Jan-5Sep66
LtCol William C. Carlson	6Sep-31Dec66

COMMAND AND STAFF LIST

HMM-161*
The squadron arrived in RVN on 1Apr66 and departed 31Oct66.

CO LtCol William R. Quinn	1Apr-9Aug66
LtCol Samuel F. Martin	10Aug-4Oct66
LtCol Charles E. Wydner, Jr.	5Oct-31Oct66

HMM-163*
The squadron departed RVN on 1Aug66 and returned to RVN on 1Nov66.

CO LtCol Charles A. House	1Jan-11Aug66
LtCol Rocco D. Bianchi	12Aug-31Dec66

HMM-164*
The squadron arrived in RVN on 7Mar66.

CO LtCol Warren C. Watson	7Mar-31Dec66

HMM-165*
The squadron arrived in RVN on 1Oct66.

CO LtCol William W. Eldridge, Jr.	1Oct-31Dec66

HMM-261*
The squadron arrived in RVN on 6Jan66 and departed RVN on 26May66.

CO LtCol Mervin B. Porter	6Jan-26May66

HMM-262*
The squadron arrived in RVN on 4Dec66.

CO LtCol Ural W. Shadrick	4Dec-31Dec66

HMM-263*
The squadron departed RVN on 23May66 and returned to RVN on 1Aug66.

CO LtCol Truman Clark	1Jan-19Mar66
LtCol Jerome L. Goebel	20Mar-30Sep66
LtCol Manning T. Jannell	1Oct-14Oct66
LtCol Leslie L. Darbyshire	15Oct-31Dec66

HMM-265*
The squadron arrived in RVN on 22May66.

CO LtCol Herbert E. Mendenhall	22May-27Sep66
Maj Frank B. Ellis	28Sep-31Dec66

HMM-361*
The squadron departed RVN on 1Apr66 and returned to RVN on 26May66. It departed RVN again on 16Dec66.

CO LtCol Lloyd F. Childers	1Jan-9May66
LtCol McDonald D. Tweed	10May-15Dec66

HMM-362*
The squadron departed RVN on 8Jan66 and returned to RVN on 9Apr66. It departed RVN again on 28Sep66.

CO LtCol James Aldworth	1Jan-22Apr66
LtCol Alfred F. Garrotto	23Apr-31Aug66
LtCol Marshall B. Armstrong	1Sep-27Sep66

HMM-363*
The squadron departed RVN on 4Jul66 and returned to RVN on 28Sep66.

CO LtCol George D. Kew	1Jan-16Mar66
LtCol James D. McGough	17Mar-5Oct66
LtCol Kenneth E. Huntington	6Oct-31Dec66

HMM-364*
The squadron departed RVN on 9Apr66 and returned on 3Jul66. It departed RVN again on 1Nov66.

CO LtCol William R. Lucas	1Jan-22Mar66
LtCol Daniel A. Somerville	23Mar-31Oct66

MACS-7

CO LtCol Richard R. Miller	1Jan-18Jun66
LtCol Charles E. Showalter	19Jun-22Nov66
Maj Thomas K. Burk, Jr.	23Nov-31Dec66

MASS-2

CO LtCol Ralph L. Cunningham, Jr.	1Jan-10Jan66
LtCol Richard W. Sheppe	11Jan-20May66
LtCol Elwin M. Jones	21May-12Sep66
LtCol Harry Hunter, Jr.	13Sep-31Dec66

MASS-3*
The squadron arrived in RVN on 1Nov66.

CO Maj John C. Dixon	1Nov-14Nov66
LtCol Donald L. Fenton	15Nov-31Dec66

MABS-11

CO Maj Douglas A. McCaughey, Jr.	1Jan-30Jun66
Maj Clifton B. Andrews	1Jul-25Jul66
Maj Guy R. Campo	26Jul-31Dec66

MABS-12

CO Maj John W. Parchen	1Jan-28Feb66
LtCol Paul G. McMahon	1Mar-21May66
Maj George M. Lawrence, Jr.	22May-31Aug66
LtCol William G. McCool	1Sep-16Oct66
Maj William W. Campbell	17Oct-1Dec66
LtCol Ralph D. Wallace	2Dec-31Dec66

MABS-13*
The squadron arrived in RVN on 9Sep66.

CO LtCol Owen L. Owens	9Sep-31Dec66

MABS-16

CO Maj Lewis I. Zeigler	1Jan-20Apr66
LtCol William J. Webster	21Apr-18Jun66
Maj Lewis I. Zeigler	19Jun-25Jun66
LtCol Rodney D. McKitrick	26Jun-31Dec66

MABS-36

CO Maj Jack A. Kennedy	1Jan-30Mar66
LtCol McDonald D. Tweed	31Mar-9May66
Maj Gordon H. Buckner II	10May-5Jul66
LtCol Edward K. Kirby	6Jul-1Aug66
LtCol William C. Carlson	2Aug-5Sep66
LtCol Joseph A. Nelson	6Sep-31Dec66

VMFA-115*
The squadron departed RVN on 13Jan66 and returned to RVN on 11Apr66.

CO LtCol Clyde R. Jarrett	1Jan-23Feb66

LtCol Dean C. Macho	24Feb-7Aug66
Maj Larry R. Van Deusen	8Aug-31Dec66

VMA-121*
The squadron arrived in RVN on 1Dec66.

CO LtCol Donald R. Stiver	1Dec-31Dec66

VMA-211*
The squadron departed RVN on 14Jul66 and returned to RVN 1Oct66.

CO LtCol John W. Kirkland	1Jan-29May66
Maj Thomas J. Ayers	30May-16Oct66
LtCol William G. McCool	17Oct-31Dec66

VMA-214*
The squadron departed RVN on 16Feb66 and returned to RVN on 30Apr66.

CO LtCol Keith O'Keefe	1Jan-31Mar66
LtCol Dellwyn L. Davis	1Apr-8Jun66
Maj Ralph D. Wallace	9Jun-30Nov66
Maj Richard E. Hemmingway	1Dec-31Dec66

VMA-223*
The squadron departed RVN on 1Dec66.

CO LtCol Alexander Wilson	1Jan-1Apr66
LtCol Robert B. Sinclair	2Apr-26Nov66
LtCol Leonard C. Taft	27Nov-30Nov66

VMA-224*
The squadron departed RVN on 30Apr66 and returned to RVN on 14Jul66. It departed RVN again on 1Nov66.

CO LtCol Thomas E. Mulvihill	1Jan-31Mar66
LtCol John Browne	1Apr-1Nov66

VMF-(AW)-232*
The squadron arrived in RVN on 15Nov66.

CO LtCol Nicholas M. Trapnell, Jr.	15Nov-31Dec66

VMF-(AW)-235*
The squadron arrived in RVN on 1Feb66 and departed RVN on 15Nov66.

CO LtCol George A. Gibson	1Feb-1Jul66
Maj Don A. Mickle	2Jul-31Oct66
LtCol Edward R. Rogal	1Nov-15Nov66

VMA-(AW)-242*
The squadron arrived in RVN on 1Nov66.

CO LtCol Howard Wolf	1Nov-31Dec66

VMA-311*
The squadron arrived in RVN on 15Feb66.

CO LtCol Jack W. Harris	15Feb-20May66
LtCol Paul G. McMahon	21May-5Dec66
LtCol Roger A. Morris	6Dec-31Dec66

VMF-(AW)-312*
The squadron departed RVN on 2Feb66.

CO LtCol Richard B. Newport	1Jan-1Feb66

VMFA-314*
The squadron arrived in RVN on 15Jan66 and departed RVN on 14Apr66. It returned to RVN on 1Aug66.

CO Maj Charles A. Sewell	15Jan-4May66
LtCol Darrel E. Bjorklund	5May-18Nov66
Maj William H. Heintz	19Nov-31Dec66

VMFA-323*
The squadron departed RVN on 1Mar66 and returned on 5Jul66.

CO LtCol Andrew W. O'Donnell	1Jan-20Jul66
LtCol Aubrey W. Talbert, Jr.	21Jul-31Dec66

VMFA-542
The squadron arrived in RVN on 1Mar66 and departed RVN on 1Aug66. It returned to RVN on 10Oct66.

CO LtCol Eddie E. Pearcy	1Mar-22May66
Maj Paul S. Frappollo	23May-6Jul66
LtCol Donald L. May	7Jul-31Dec66

VMCJ-1

CO LtCol Francis C. Opeka	1Jan-9Jun66
Maj Robert W. Tucker, Jr	10Jun-28Oct66
LtCol William B. Fleming	29Oct-31Dec66

VMO-2

CO LtCol George F. Bauman	1Jan-8Apr66
LtCol Arnold W. Barden	9Apr-30Sep66
Maj Robert A. Plamondon	1Oct-30Nov66
LtCol William F. Harrell	1Dec-31Dec66

VMO-3*
The squadron arrived in RVN on 29Dec66.

CO Maj Kyle W. Townsend	29Dec-31Dec66

VMO-6

CO LtCol Robert J. Zitnik	1Jan-23Mar66
Maj Robert E. Presson	24Mar-10Jun66
Maj William J. Goodsell	11Jun-16Jun66
Maj Rawley M. Gregory	17Jun-23Jul66
Maj William R. Maloney	23Jul-31Dec66

1st LAAM Bn

CO LtCol Clyde L. Eyer	1Jan-1Oct66
Maj Thomas G. Davis	2Oct-10Dec66
LtCol Merton R. Ives	11Dec-31Dec66

2d LAAM Bn

CO Maj Edward F. Penico	1Jan-30Jul66
LtCol Thomas I. Gunning	31Jul-31Dec66

Force Logistic Command*
Activated on 15Mar66 from the Force Logistic Support Group (FLSG).

Force Logistic Command Headquarters

CO Col George C. Axtell, Jr	15Mar-2Oct66
BGen James E. Herbold, Jr	3Oct-31Dec66

COMMAND AND STAFF LIST

C/S* Col William H. Cowper 3Oct-31Dec66
*Billet established on 3Oct66.
G-1 Maj Harold J. Field, Jr. 15Mar-28Sep66
   Maj Leonard E. Fuchs 29Sep-10Oct66
   Maj Joe B. Noble 11Oct-31Dec66
G-2* LtCol Willard C. Olsen 1Jun-30Jun66
   Maj Herbert C. Sanford 1Jul-21Oct66
   LtCol Richard M. Taylor 22Oct-31Dec66
*Billet established on 1Jun66.
G-3 LtCol William L. Nelson 15Mar-31May66
   Col William H. Cowper 1Jun-22Jul66
   LtCol Raymond E. Roeder, Jr. 23Jul-29Oct66
   Col Lyle S. Stephenson 30Oct-31Dec66
G-4 LtCol Richard M. Cook 15Mar-14Jun66
   Maj Robert P. Chaney 15Jun-23Jun66
   Maj Gilbert C. Hazard 24Jun-31Dec66
G-5* Maj Leonard E. Fuchs 11Oct-31Dec66
*Billet established on 11Oct66.

Force Logistic Support Group A*

*The Force Logistic Support Group was redesignated FLSG A on 15Mar66.
CO Col Mauro J. Padalino 1Jan-31May66
   Col Robert R. Weir 1Jun-31Dec66

Force Logistic Group B*

*FLSG B was activated on 15Mar66 from the Logistic Support Unit at Chu Lai.
CO Col Mitchell O. Sadler 15Mar-24Aug66
   Col Kermit H. Shelly 25Aug-31Dec66

Force Logistic Support Unit-2*

*FLSU-2 was designated as a major subcommand of the Force Logistic Command on 1Dec66.
CO LtCol Rollin F. VanCantfort 1Dec-31Dec66

5th Communication Bn*

*The battalion was attached to the Force Logistic Command on 15Nov66 from the administrative control of III MAF.
CO LtCol Hercules R. Kelly, Jr. 1Jan-30May66
   LtCol Joseph Nastasi 31May-30Sep66
   LtCol Phillip K. Leeseberg 1Oct-31Dec66

Separate Units under III MAF

1st MP Battalion*

*The battalion arrived in RVN on 17Jun66.
   LtCol Paul G. Stavridis 17Jun-31Dec66

7th Engineer Bn

CO LtCol Ermine L. Meeker 1Jan-31Oct66
   LtCol Frank W. Harris III 1Nov-31Dec66

9th Engineer Bn*

*The battalion arrived in RVN on 6Jun66.
CO LtCol Richard W. Crispen 6Jun-31Dec66

Marine Operating Forces, Western Pacific

1st MAW (Rear)/TG 79.3* 1Jan-14Apr66

*1st MAW (Rear) was the controlling headquarters for most of the wing's units outside Vietnam until 14Apr66.
CO Col Harry W. Taylor 1Jan-14Apr66

MAG-13 (1Jan-14Feb66)
CO Col Odia E. Howe, Jr. 1Jan-10Apr66
CO Col Edwin A. Harper 11Apr-14Apr66

H&MS-13 (1Jan-14Apr66)
CO LtCol Lytton F. Blass 1Jan-23Mar66
   LtCol Kenneth G. Fiegener 24Mar-14Apr66

MABS-13 (1Jan-14Apr66)
CO Maj William E. Caslin 1Jan-14Apr66

VMA-311 (1Jan-14Feb66)
CO LtCol Jack W. Harris 1Jan-14Apr66

VMFA-314 (1Jan-14Jan66)
CO Maj Charles A. Sewell 1Jan-14Apr66

VMFA-542 (1Jan-28Feb66)
CO LtCol Eddie E. Pearcy 1Jan-28Feb66

VMFA-115 (15Jan-10Apr66)
CO LtCol Clyde R. Jarrett 15Jan-22Feb66
   LtCol Dean C. Macho 23Feb-10Apr66

VMA-214 (16Feb-14Apr66)
CO LtCol Keith O'Keefe 16Feb-31Mar66
   LtCol Dellwyn L. Davis 1Apr-14Apr66

VMFA-323 (2Mar-14Apr66)
CO LtCol Andrew W. O'Donnell 2Mar-14Apr66

HMM-161 (4Jan-31Mar66)
Co LtCol Rex C. Denny, Jr. 4Jan-31Mar66

HMM-361 (1Apr-14Apr66)
CO LtCol Lloyd F. Childers 1Apr-14Apr66

VMGR-152 (1Jan-14Apr66)
CO LtCol Dan C. Holland 1Jan-14Apr66

9th MAB/TF 79*

*The 9th MAB was established on 1Mar66 and assumed responsibility for TF 79 from the CG 1st MarDiv on that date. On 15Apr66 the MAB assumed responsibility for most Marine air and ground units in the Western Pacific outside of Vietnam.

9th MAB Headquarters

CO Col Herman Hansen, Jr	1Mar-29Mar66
BGen William A. Stiles	30Mar-14Apr66
BGen Michael P. Ryan	15Apr-31Dec66
C/S Col Herman Hansen, Jr	30Mar-23Sep66
Col Richard R. Amerine	24Sep-31Dec66
G-1 LtCol James M. Cummings	1Mar-21Sep66
LtCol Edward V. Easter	22Sep-31Dec66
G-2 Maj George J. Kleess	1Mar-14Sep66
Maj John H. Broujos	15Sep-4Oct66
Maj James C. Hitz	5Oct-31Dec66
G-3 Col Arnold L. Emils	1Mar-8Dec66
LtCol James G. Dionisopoulos	9Dec-31Dec66
G-4 Col Oscar B. Johnston	1Mar-3Oct66
Col Elton Mueller	4Oct-31Dec66

SLF 7th Fleet/TF 79.5

CO Col John R. Burnett	1Jan-6Apr66
Col Richard A. Brenneman	7Apr-31Aug66
Col Harry D. Wortman	1Sep-31Dec66

SLF Battalion Landing Teams

BLT 2/3 1Jan-27Feb66

CO LtCol William K. Horn	1Jan-27Feb66

BLT 1/5 28Feb-7May66

CO LtCol Harold L. Coffman	28Feb-7May66

BLT 3/5 14May-1Aug66

CO LtCol Edward J. Bronars	14May-1Aug66

BLT 1/26 2Aug-26Sep66

CO LtCol Anthony A. Monti	2Aug-26Sep66

BLT 3/26 4Oct-10Dec66

CO LtCol Garland T. Beyerle	4Oct-10Dec66

BLT 1/9 3Dec-31Dec66

CO Maj James L. Day	3Dec-31Dec66

SLF Helicopter Squadrons

HMM-261 1Jan-5Jan66

CO LtCol Mervin B. Porter	1Jan-5Jan66

HMM-362 6Jan-8Apr66

CO LtCol James Aldworth	6Jan-8Apr66

HMM-362 28Sep-31Dec66

CO LtCol Marshall B. Armstrong	28Sep-31Dec66

RLT 5/79.2 30Mar-4Apr66

CO Col Charles F. Widdecke	30Mar-26May66

BLT 2/5 30Mar-4Apr66

CO LtCol Robert H. Uskurait	30Mar-4Apr66

BLT 3/5 7May-13May66

CO LtCol Edward J. Bronars	7May-13May66

RLT 26 20Aug-31Dec66

CO Col John J. Padley	20Aug-31Dec66

BLT 3/3 6Sep-29Oct66

CO LtCol Earl R. DeLong	6Sep-29Oct66

BLT 1/9 5Oct-1Dec66

CO Maj James L. Day	5Oct-1Dec66

BLT 2/4 8Nov-31Dec66

CO LtCol Arnold E. Bench	8Nov-31Dec66

BLT 1/4 21Dec-31Dec66

CO LtCol Jack Westerman	21Dec-31Dec66

1st Battalion, 13th Marines 20Aug-31Dec66

CO LtCol Joseph M. Laney, Jr	20Aug-28Oct66
LtCol Robert L. Christian, Jr.	29Oct-31Dec66

TG 79.2 2Oct-7Nov66

CO Col John J. Padley	2Oct-7Nov66

BLT 3/3 2Oct-28Oct66

CO LtCol Earl R. DeLong	2Oct-28Oct66

HMM-163 2Oct-28Oct66

CO LtCol Rocco D. Bianchi	2Oct-28Oct66

MAG-13/TG 79.3* 15Apr-14Aug66

MAG-13 came under the operational control of the 9th MAB on 15Apr66.

CO Edwin A. Harper	15Apr-15Aug66
Col Douglas D. Petty, Jr.	16Aug-24Sep66

H&MS-13 15Apr-24Sep66

CO LtCol Kenneth G. Fiegener	15Apr-13Sep66
LtCol Owen L. Owens	26Aug-8Sep66

MABS-13 15Apr-9Sep66

CO LtCol William E. Caslin	15Apr-14Aug66

VMA-214 15Apr-29Apr66

CO LtCol Dellwyn L. Davis	15Apr-29Apr66

VMFA 323 15Apr-4Jul66

CO LtCol Andrew W. O'Donnell	15Apr-4Jul66

VMFA-314 15Apr-1Aug66

CO Maj Charles A. Sewell	15Apr-4May66
LtCol Darrel E. Bjorklund	5May-1Aug66

VMA-224 1May-6Jul66

CO LtCol John Browne	1May-6Jul66

VMA-211 14Jul-30Sep66

CO LtCol Thomas J. Ayers	14Jul-30Sep66

VMFA-542 1Aug-14Aug66

CO LtCol Donald L. May	1Aug-14Aug66

HMM-361 15Apr-26May66

CO LtCol Lloyd F. Childers	15Apr-9May66
LtCol McDonald D. Tweed	10May-26May66

COMMAND AND STAFF LIST

HMM-263 24May-31Jul66
CO LtCol Jerome L. Goebel — 24May-31Jul66

HMM-163 1Aug-14Aug66
CO LtCol Rocco D. Bianchi — 1Aug-14Aug66

MACS-6 15Apr-14Aug66
CO Maj Francis L. Delaney — 15Apr-14Aug66

VMGR-152 15Apr-14Aug66
CO LtCol Dan C. Holland — 15Apr-19May66
LtCol John Urell — 20May-14Aug66

MAG-15/TG 79.3 15Aug-31Dec66
CO Col Charles Kimak — 15Aug-31Dec66

H&MS-15 15Aug-31Dec66
CO LtCol James McDaniel — 15Aug-31Dec66

MABS-15 15Aug-31Dec66
CO LtCol George H. Albers — 15Aug-31Dec66

VMA-121 15Aug-30Nov66
CO LtCol Donald R. Stiver — 15Aug-30Nov66

VMF(AW)-232 2Sep-15Nov66
CO LtCol Nicholas M. Trapnell, Jr. — 2Sep-15Nov66

VMF(AW)-235 16Nov-31Dec66
CO LtCol Edward R. Rogal — 16Nov-31Dec66

VMA-223 1Dec-31Dec66
CO LtCol Leonard C. Taft — 1Dec-31Dec66

VMFA-542 15Aug-9Oct66
CO LtCol Donald L. May — 15Aug-9Oct66

HMM-163 15Aug-31Dec66
CO LtCol Rocco D. Bianchi — 15Aug-31Oct66

HMM-161 7Nov-17Dec66
CO LtCol Charles E. Wydner, Jr. — 7Nov-17Dec66

HMM-361 16Dec-31Dec66
CO LtCol McDonald D. Tweed — 16Dec-31Dec66

MACS-6 15Aug-31Dec66
CO Maj Francis L. Delaney — 15Aug-17Oct66
Maj Richard L. Hawley — 18Oct-1Nov66
Maj William K. Hutchings — 2Nov-31Dec66

VMGR-152 15Aug-31Dec66
CO LtCol John Urell — 15Aug-31Dec66

Appendix B
Glossary of Terms and Abbreviations

A-1E—Douglas Skyraider, a propeller-driven, single-engine, attack aircraft.

A-4—Douglas Skyhawk, a single-seat, light-attack jet bomber in service on board carriers of the U.S. Navy and with land-based Marine attack squadrons.

A-6A—Grumman Intruder, a twin-jet, low-level, attack bomber specifically designed to deliver weapons on targets completely obscured by weather or darkness.

AAR—After action report.

AC-47—Douglas C-47 Skytrain, fixed-wing transport modified with 7.62mm miniguns and used as a gunship.

ADC—Assistant division commander.

AdminO—Administrative officer.

Adv—Advanced.

AGC—Amphibious command ship.

AK-47—Russian-made Kalashnikov auotmatic rifle, gas operated, uses 7.62mm ammunition with an effective range of 400 meters. It was the standard rifle of the North Vietnamese Army.

AKA—Attack cargo ship, a naval ship designed to transport combat-loaded cargo in an assault landing.

ANGLICO—Air and naval gunfire liaison company, an organization composed of Marine and Navy personnel specially qualified for shore control of naval gunfire and close air support.

AOA—Amphibious objective area, a defined geographical area within which is located the area or areas to be captured by the amphibious task force.

APA—Attack transport ship a naval ship, designed for combat loading a battalion landing team.

APC—Armored personnel carrier.

Arc Light—The codename for B-52 bombing missions in South Vietnam.

ARG—Amphibious ready group.

Arty—Artillery.

ARVN—Army of the Republic of Vietnam (South Vietnam).

ASRT—Air support radar team, a subordinate operational component of a tactical air control system which provides ground controlled precision flight path guidance and weapons release.

B-3 Front—North Vietnamese military command established in the Central Highlands of South Vietnam to control military operations in Kontum, Dar Loc, and Pleiku Provinces.

B-52—Boeing Stratofortress, U.S. Air Force eight-engine, swept-wing, heavy jet bomber.

BGen—Brigadier general.

BLT—Battalion landing team.

Bn—Battalion.

Brig—Brigade.

C-117D—Douglas Skytrain, a twin-engine transport aircraft.

C-130—Lockheed Hercules, a four-engine turboprop transport aircraft.

CAAR—Combat after action report.

Capt—Captain.

CAS—Close air support.

CG—Commanding general.

CH-37—Sikorsky twin-engine, assault, heavy transport helicopter which carries three crew members and 36 passengers.

CH-46—Boeing Vertol Sea Knight, a twin-turbine, tandem-rotor transport helicopter, designed to carry a four-man crew and 17 combat-loaded troops.

CH-53—Sikorsky Sea Stallion, a single-rotor, heavy assault transport helicopter powered by two shaft-turbine engines with an average payload of 12,800 pounds. Carries crew of three and 38 combat-loaded troops.

CIDG—Civilian Irregular Defense Group, South Vietnamese paramilitary force, composed largely of Montagnards, the nomadic tribesmen who populate the South Vietnamese highlands, and advised by U.S. Army Special Forces troops.

CinCPac—Commander in Chief, Pacific.

CinCPacFlt—Commander in Chief, Pacific Fleet.

Class (I-V)—Categories of military supplies, e.g., Class I, rations; Class III, POL; Class V, Ammunition.

CMC—Commandant of the Marine Corps.

CMH—Center of Military History, Department of the Army.

CNO—Chief of Naval Operations.

CO—Commanding officer.

Col—Colonel.

Cdr—Commander.

Combined action program—A Marine pilot pacification program established at Phu Bai in August 1965 which integrated a Marine infantry squad with a South Vietnamese Popular Forces platoon.

ComdC—Command chronology.

ComUSMACV—Commander, U.S. Military Assistance Command, Vietnam.

COSVN—Central Office of South Vietnam, the Communist military and political headquarters in South Vietnam.

County Fair—A sophisticated cordon and search operation in a particular hamlet or village by South Vietnamese troops, police, local officials, and U.S. Marines in an attempt to screen and register the local inhabitants.

CP—Command post.

CRC—Control and reporting center, an element of the U.S. Air Force tactical air control system, subordinate to the Tactical Air Control Center, from which radar and warning operations are conducted.

CTZ—Corps Tactical Zone.

GLOSSARY

DASC—Direct air support center—A subordinate operational component of the Marine air control system designed for control and direction of close air support and other direct air support operations.

D-Day—Day scheduled for the beginning of an operation.

DD—Destroyer.

DMZ—Demilitarized Zone separating North and South Vietnam.

DRV—Democratic Repubic of Vietnam (North Vietnam).

Dtd—Dated.

Div—Division.

DOD—Department of Defense.

EA-6A—The electronic countermeasures version of the A-6A Intruder.

ECM—Electronic countermeasures, a major subdivision of electronic warfare involving actions taken to prevent or reduce the effectivness of enemy equipment and tactics employing or affected by electromagnetic radiations and to exploit the enemy's use of such radiations.

EF-10B—An ECM modified version of the Navy F-3D Skynight, a two-engine jet night-fighter.

ELINT—Electronic intelligence, the intelligence information product of activities engaged in the collection and processing, for subsequent intelligence purposes, of foreign, noncommunications, electromagnetic radiations emanating from other than nuclear detonations and radioactive sources.

Engr—Engineer.

F-4B—McDonnell Phantom II, a twin-engined, two-seat, long-range, all-weather jet interceptor and attack bomber.

FAC (A)—Forward air controller (Airborne).

FFV—Field Force, Vietnam I and II, U.S. Army commands in II and III Corps areas of South Vietnam.

FLC—Force Logistic Command.

FLSG—Force logistic support group.

FLSU—Force logistic support unit.

FMFPac—Fleet Marine Force, Pacific.

FO—Forward observer.

FSCC—Fire support coordination center, a single location in which were centralized communication facilities and personnel incident to the coordination of all forms of fire support.

FSR—Force service regiment.

Fwd—Forward.

G—Refers to staff positions on a general staff, e. g., G-1 would refer to the staff member responsible for personnel; G-2 intelligence; G-3 operations; G-4 logistics, etc.

Gen—General.

Golden Fleece—Marine rice harvest protection operation.

Grenade Launcher, M79—U.S. built, single-shot, break-open, breech-loaded shoulder weapon which fires 40mm projectiles and weighs approximately 6.5 pounds when loaded; it has a sustained rate of aimed fire of five-seven rounds per minute and an effective range of 375 meters.

Gun, 175mm, M107—U.S. built, self-propelled gun which weighs 62,000 pounds and fires a 147-pound projectile to a maximum range of 32,800 meters. Maximum rate of fire is one-half round per minute.

Gun, 155mm, M53—U.S. built, medium, self-propelled gun, with a 23,300 meter range, and weighing 96,000 pounds. It has a sustained rate of fire of one-half rounds per minute.

GVN—Government of Vietnam (South Vietnam).

H&I fires—Harassing and interdiction fires.

H&S Co—Headquarters and service company.

HAWK—A mobile, surface-to-air, guided missile, designed to defend against enemy aircraft flying at low altitudes and short-range missiles.

HE—High explosive.

H-Hour—In connection with planned operations, it is the specific hour the operation begins.

HistBr, G-3Div, HQMC—Historical Branch, G-3 Division, Headquarters, U.S. Marine Corps.

HLZ—Helicopter landing zone.

HMM—Marine medium helicopter squadron.

Howitzer, 8 inch (M55)—U.S. built, self-propelled heavy-artillery piece with a maximum range of 16,800 meters and a rate of fire of one-half rounds per minute.

Howitzer, 105mm, M101A1—U.S built, towed, general purpose light artillery piece with a maximum range of 11,000 meters and maximum rate of fire of four rounds per minute.

Howitzer, 155mm, M-114A towed and M-109 self-propelled—U.S. built medium artillery with a maximum range of 15,080 meters and a maximum rate of fire of 3 rounds per minute. Marines employed both models in Vietnam. The newer and heavier self-propelled M109 was largely road bound, while the lighter towed M114A could be moved either by truck or by helicopter.

Howtar—A 4.2-inch (107mm) mortar tube mounted on the frame of a 75mm pack howitzer.

"Huey"—Popular name for UH-1 series of helicopters.

ICC—International Control Commission established by the Geneva Accords of 1954 to supervise the truce ending the First Indochina War between the French and the Viet Minh and resulting in the partition of Vietnam at the 17th Parallel. The members of the Commission were from Canada, India, and Poland.

ICCC—I Corps Coordinating Council, consisting of U.S. and Vietnamese officials in I Corps and coordinated the civilian assistance program in I Corps.

I Corps—The military and administrative subdivision which includes the five northern provinces of South Vietnam.

J—The designations for members of a joint staff which includes members of several services comprising the command, e.g., J-1 would refer to the staff member responsible for personnel; J-2 intelligence; J-3 operations; J-4 logistic etc.

JCS—Joint Chiefs of Staff (U.S.).

JGS—Joint General Staff (South Vietnamese).

JTD—Joint table of distribution.

KANZUS—A proposed international brigade to man defenses along the DMZ; the acronym stands for Korean, Australian, New Zealand, and United States.

KC-130—The in-flight refueling tanker configuration of the C-130 Lockheed Hercules.

KIA—Killed-in-action.

Kit Carson Scout—Viet Cong defectors recruited by Marines to serve as scouts, interpreters, and intelligence agents.

L-Hour—In planned helicopter operations, it is the specific hour the helicopter land in the landing zone.
LAAM Bn—Light antiaircraft missile battalion.
LCM—Landing Craft mechanized, designed to land tanks, trucks, and trailers directly onto the beach.
LCVP—Landing craft vehicle personnel, the principal craft used to transport assault troops to the beach.
LOI—Letter of Instruction.
LPD—Amphibious transport, dock, a ship designed to transport and land troops, equipment, and supplies by means of embarked landing craft, amphibious vehicles, and helicopters.
LPH—Amphibious assault ship, a ship designed or modified to transport and land troops, equipment, and supplies by means of embarked helicopters.
LSA—Logistic support area.
LSD—Landing ship, dock, a landing ship designed to combat load, transport, and launch amphibious crafts or vehicles together with crews and embarked personnel, and to provide limited docking and repair services to small ships and crafts.
LST—Landing ship, tank, landing ship designed to transport heavy vehicles and to land them on a beach.
Lt—Lieutenant.
LtCol—Lieutenant colonel.
LtGen—Lieutenant general.
Ltr—letter.
LVTE—Amphibian vehicle, tracked engineer, a lightly armored amphibious vehicle designed for minefield and obstacle clearance.
LVTH—Amphibian vehicle, tracked howitzer, a lightly armored, self-propelled, amphibious 105mm howitzer.
LVTP—Landing vehicle, tracked personnel, an amphibian vehicle used to land and or transport personnel.
LZ—Landing zone.

MAB—Marine Amphibious Brigade.
Machine gun, .50 caliber—U.S. built, belt-fed, recoil-operated, air-cooled automatic weapon, which weighs approximately 80 pounds without mount or ammunition; it has a sustained rate of fire of 100 rounds per minute and an effective range of 1,450 meters.
Machine gun, M60—U.S. built, belt-fed, gas-operated, air-cooled, 7.62mm automatic weapon, which weighs approximately 20 pounds without mount or ammunition; it has a sustained rate of fire of 100 rounds per minute and an effective range of 1,000 meters.
MACS—Marine air control squadron, provides and operates ground facilities for the detection and interception of hostile aircraft and for the navigational direction of friendly aircraft in the conduct of support operations.
MACV—Military Assistance Command, Vietnam.
MAF—Marine amphibious force.
MAG—Marine aircraft group.
Main Force—Refers to organized Viet Cong battalions and regiments as opposed to local VC guerrilla groups.
Maj—Major.

MajGen—Major general.
MarDiv—Marine division.
—Marines—Designates a Marine regiment, e.g. 3d Marines.
MASS—Marine air support squadron, provides and operates facilties for the control of support aircraft operating in direct support of ground forces.
MAW—Marine aircraft wing.
MCAF—Marine Corps air facility.
MCAS—Marine Corps air station.
MCCC—Marine Corps Command Center.
MCOAG—Marine Corps Operations Analysis Group.
MedCap—Medical civilian assistance program.
MIA—Missing-in-action.
MilHistBr—Military History Branch.
Mortar, 4.2-inch, M30—U.S. built, rifled, muzzle-loaded, drop-fired weapon consisting of tube, base-plate and standard; weapon weighs 330 pounds and has a maximum range of 4,020 meters. Rate of fire is 20 rounds per minute.
Mortar, 60mm, M19—U.S. built, smooth-bore, muzzle-loaded, single-shot, high angle of fire weapon, which weighs 45.2 pounds when assembled; it has a maximum rate of fire of 30 rounds per minute and sustained rate of fire of 18 rounds per minute; the effective range is 2,000 meters.
Mortar, 81mm, M29—U.S. built, smooth-bore, muzzle-loaded, single-shot, high angle of fire weapon, which weighs approximately 115 pounds when assembled; it has a sustained rate of fire of two rounds per minute and an effective range of 2,300-3,650 meters, depending upon ammunition used.
Mortar, 82mm, Soviet-built, smooth-bore, muzzle-loaded, single-shot, high angle of fire weapon which weighs approximately 123 pounds; it has a maximum rate of fire of 25 rounds per minute and a maximum range of 3,040 meters.
Mortar, 120mm—Soviet or Chinese Communist built, smooth bore, drop or trigger fired, single-shot, high angle of fire weapon, which weighs approximately 600 pounds; it has a maximum rate of fire of 15 rounds per minute and a maximum range of 5,700 meters.
MR-5—Military Region 5, a Communist political and military sector in northern South Vietnam, including all of I Corps.
MS—Manuscript.
Msg—Message.

NAG—Naval Advisory Group.
NCC—Naval component commander.
NCO—Non-commissioned officer.
Ngu Hanh Son—The pilot pacification program begun south of Da Nang in 1965 and incorporated into the I Corps National Priority Area in 1966.
NLF—National Liberation Front, the political arm of the Communist-led insurgency against the South Vietnamese Government.
NMCB—Naval mobile construction battalion (Seabees).
NMCC—National Military Command Center.
NPA—National priority area, designated targeted area for pacification in South Vietnam.
Nui—Vietnamese word for hill or mountain.
Nung—A Vietnamese tribesman, of a separate ethnic group and probably of Chinese origin, trained for special operations and used as separate bodyguards.
NVA—North Vietnamese Army.

GLOSSARY

O-1B — Cessna, single-engine observation aircraft.

OAB, NHD — Operational Archives Branch, Naval History Division.

Ontos — U.S. built, lightly-armored tracked antitank vehicle armed with six coaxially mounted 106mm recoilless rifles.

OpCon — Operational control, the authority granted to a commander to direct forces assigned so that the commander may accomplish specific missions or tasks which are usually limited by function, time, or location.

OpO — Operation order, a directive issued by a commander to subordinate commanders for the purpose of effecting the coordinated execution of an operation.

OPlan — Operation plan, a plan for a single or series of connected operations to be carried out simultaneously or in succession; it is usually based upon stated assumptions and is the form of directive employed by higher authority to permit subordinate commanders to prepare supporting plans and orders.

OpSum — Operational summary.

OSJS (MACV) — Office of the Secretariat, Joint Staff (Military Assistance Command Vietnam).

PAVN — Peoples Army of Vietnam (North Vietnam).

PF — Popular Force, Vietnamese militia who were usually employed in the defense of their own communities.

POL — Petroleum, oil, and lubricants.

Practice Nine — The codename for the planning of the antiinfiltration barrier across the DMZ.

Project Delta — A special South Vietnamese reconnaissance group consisting of South Vietnamese Special Forces troops and U.S. Army Special Forces advisors.

Recoilless rifle, 106mm, M401A1 — U.S built, single-shot, recoilless, breech-loaded weapon which weighs 438 pounds when assembled and mounted for firing; it has a sustained rate of fire of six rounds per minute and an effective range of 1,365 meters.

RF — Regional Force, Vietnamese militia who were employed in a specific area.

RF-4B — Photo-reconnaissance model of the F4B Phantom II.

RF-8A — Reconnaissance verson of the F-8 Chance Vought Crusader.

Regt — Regiment.

Revolutionary Development — The South Vietnamese pacification program in 1966.

Revolutionary Development Teams — Especially trained Vietnamese political cadre who were assigned to individual hamlets and villages and conducted various pacification and civilian assistance tasks on a local level.

Rifle, M14 — Gas-operated, magazine-fed, air-cooled, semiautomatic, 7.62mm caliber shoulder weapon, which weighs 12 pounds with a full 20-round magazine; it has a sustained rate of fire of 30 rounds per minute and an effective range of 460 meters.

RLT — Regimental landing team.

ROK — Republic of Korea (South Korea)

Rolling Thunder — Codename for U.S. air operations over North Vietnam.

RRU — Radio Research Unit.

Rural Reconstruction — The predecessor pacification campaign to Revolutionary Development.

RVN — Republic of Vietnam (South Vietnam)

RVNAF — Republic of Vietnam Armed Forces.

S- — Refers to staff positions on regimental and battalion levels. S-1 would refer to the staff member responsible for personnel; S-2 intelligence; S-3, operations; S-4 logistics; etc.

SAR — Search and rescue.

SATS — Short airfield for tactical support, a minimal expeditionary airfield used by Marine Corps aviation elements providing tactical air support for the landing force; characterized by a portable runway surface, aircraft launching and recovery devices, and other essential expeditionary airfield components.

SEATO — Southeast Asia Treaty Organization.

2d AD — 2d Air Division, the major U.S. Air Force command in Vietnam prior to the establishment of the Seventh Air Force.

SecDef — Secretary of Defense.

SecState — Secretary of State.

Seventh AF — Seventh Air Force, the major U.S. Air Force command in Vietnam.

Seventh Flt — Seventh Fleet, the U.S. fleet assigned to the Pacific.

SitRep — Situation Report.

SLF — Special landing force.

Song — River in Vietnamese.

SOP — Standing operating procedure, set of instructions covering those features of operations which lend themselves to a definite or standardized procedure.

Sortie — An operational flight by one aircraft.

Steel Tiger — The codename for the air campaign over Laos.

Stingray — Special Marine reconnaissance missions in which small Marine reconnaissance teams call artillery and air attacks on targets of opportunity.

Strike Company — an elite company in a South Vietnamese infantry division, directly under the control of the division commander.

Struggle Forces — the coalition in I Corps which directed the protests against the central government after the removal of the I Corps commander Nguyen Chanh Thi in the spring of 1966. Also known as "Military and Civilian Struggle Committee for I Corps" and "Popular Forces to Struggle for the Revolution."

TAC (A) — Tactical air coordinator (Airborne), an officer, who coordinates from an airplane, the action of aircraft in close support operations.

TACC — Tactical air control center, the principal air operations installation from which all aircraft and air-warning functions of tactical air operations are controlled.

TADC — Tactical air direction center, an air operations installation under the overall control of the tactical air control center, from which is directed aircraft and aircraft warning functions of the tactical air center.

TAOC — Tactical air operations center, a subordinate operational component of the Marine air command and control system designed for direction and control of all en route air traffic and air defense operations.

TAFDS — Tactical airfield fuel dispensing system, the expeditionary storage and dispensing system of aviation fuel at tactical airfields. It uses 10,000 gallon fabric tanks to store the fuel.

Tally Ho—Bombing campaign under ComUSMACV begun in July 1966 of Route Package I in North Vietnam.

Tank, M48—U.S. built 50.7-ton tank with a crew of four; primary armament is turret-mounted 90mm gun with one .30 caliber and one .50 caliber machine gun. Maximum road speed of 32 miles per hour and an average range of 195 miles.

TAOR—Tactical area of responsibility, a defined area of land for which responsibility is specifically assigned to the commander of the area as a measure for control of assigned forces and coordination of support.

TE—Task element.

TG—Task Group.

Tiger Hound—Airstrikes in Laos directed by U.S. Air Force small fixed-wing observation aircraft, flying up to 12 miles in southeastern Laos.

TU—Task unit.

UH-1E-Bell "Huey"—A single-engine, light attack/transport helicopter noted for its maneuverability and firepower; carries a crew of three with seven combat troops; in its armored configuration it is armed with air-to-ground rocket packs and fuselage-mounted, electrically-fired machine guns.

UH-34D—Sikorsky Sea Horse, a single-engine medium transport helicopter with a crew of three, carries 16-18 combat soldiers.

USA—United States Army.

USAF—United States Air Force.

USAID—United States Agency for International Development.

USMC—United States Marine Corps.

U.S. Mission Council—Council, chaired by the U.S. Ambassador to South Vietnam and included ComUSMACV, which developed and coordinated U.S. policy within South Vietnam.

USN—United States Navy.

USOM—United States Operations Mission, the United States civilian organization in RVN including the U.S. Embassy, AID, etc.

VC—Viet Cong, a term used to refer to the Communist guerrilla in South Vietnam; a derogatory constraction of the Vietnamese phrase meaning "Vietnamese Communists."

Viet Minh—The Vietnamese contraction for Viet Nam Doc Lap Nong Minh Hoi, a Communist-led coalition of nationalist groups, which actively opposed the Japanese in World War II and the French in the first Indochina War.

VMA—Marine attack squadron.

VMF (AW)—Marine fighter squadron (all-weather).

VMFA—Marine fighter attack squadron.

VMCJ—Marine composite reconnaissance squadron.

VMGR—Marine refueller transport squadron.

VMO—Marine observation aircraft squadron.

VNAF—Vietnamese Air Force.

VNMB—Vietnamese Marine Brigade.

VNMC—Vietnamese Marine Corps.

VNN—Vietnamese Navy.

VT—Variable timed electronic fuze for an artillery shell which causes airburst over the target area.

WestPac—Western Pacific.

WIA—Wounded-in-action.

WFRC—Washngton Federal Records Center.

Appendix C
Chronology of Significant Events

4 Jan—The Special Forces camp at Khe Sanh reported 20 rounds of incoming 120mm mortar fire. This was the first comfirmed enemy use of 120mm mortars in RVN.

18 Jan—The 1st Marines Headquarters arrived at Chu Lai.

28 Jan-19 Feb—Operation Double Eagle I was conducted by Task Force Delta in southern Quang Ngai Province.

6-8 Feb—President Johnson together with senior military and civilian advisors met with South Vietnamese Premier Nguyen Cao Ky and Head of State Nguyen Van Thieu in Honolulu. The resulting "Declaration of Honolulu" outlined U.S. and South Vietnamese political and military policy.

19 Feb-1 Mar—Operation Double Eagle II was conducted 30 miles south of Da Nang.

23 Feb—A detachment of the 3d FSR; HQ, 11th Marines; a detachment of HQ Bn, 1st Marine Division; and 4/11 arrived RVN.

1 Mar—The 26th Marines was activated at Camp Pendleton, California, initiating the formation of the 5th Marine Division. The 9th Marine Amphibious Brigade was activated on Okinawa.

4-7 Mar—Task Force Delta conducted Operation Utah south of Chu Lai.

7 Mar—Secretary of Defense McNamara requested authorization for 278,184 Marines on active duty by 30 June 1967. This increase made the Marine Corps the only service to have a strength larger than its peak during the Korean War.

9-12 Mar—The *NVA 95th Regiment* overran the A Shau Special Forces Camp in western Thua Thien Province. HMM-163 assisted in the evacuation of the camp.

10 Mar—Prime Minister Ky removed LtGen Nguyen Chanh Thi from his position as ARVN commander, I Corps. As a result of this, protest demonstrations and strikes began in the Hue-Da Nang area and slowly spread to Saigon.

15 Mar—The Force Logistic Command (FLC) was established at Da Nang. The unit is made up of the 1st and 3d Service Battalions and the in-country elements of the 3d Force Service Regiment (FSR).

18 Mar—MajGen Wood B. Kyle assumed command of the 3d Marine Division from General Walt. General Walt continued as CG III MAF.

18 Mar—3d Battalion, 4th Marines arrived RVN.

20-25 Mar—Operation Texas was conducted south of Chu Lai by Task Force Delta.

26 Mar-6 Apr—The SLF Battalion, BLT 1/5, began Operation Jack Stay in the Rung Sat Special Zone about 27 miles SE of Saigon. This was the first operation by American troops in the Saigon River Delta.

29 Mar—MajGen Lewis J. Fields established the 1st Marine Division Headquarters at Chu Lai.

1 Apr—U. S. Naval Forces, MACV was established in Saigon and assumed control of the Naval Support Activity, Da Nang from III MAF. The 2d Air Division was redesignated the Seventh Air Force.

12 Apr—The 2d Battalion, 5th Marines arrived in RVN.

7 May—CG FMFPac assumed operational control of RLT-26.

8 May—1st Battalion, 5th Marines arrived RVN (formerly SLF).

15-31 May—The political unrest in I Corps flared up as Prime Minister Ky sent ARVN units, loyal to the Saigon government, into Da Nang to reestablish his authority. After several days, the "Struggle Forces" in Da Nang backed down but in Hue the situation was out of control until the end of the month.

16 May—MajGen Lewis B. Robertshaw relieved MajGen Keith B. McCutcheon as CG 1st MAW.

27 May—The 5th Marines Headquarters arrived at Chu Lai from Okinawa.

28 May—The 1st Military Police Battalion arrived at Da Nang from ConUS.

1-21 Jun—In Hue, militant Buddhist Thich Tri Quang began a hunger strike in protest against the government. The Buddhist leader was subsequently arrested and moved to Saigon where he was imprisoned.

Forces loyal to the South Vietnamese government seized the Buddhist-controlled cities of Hue and Quang Tri and the Buddhist Secular Affairs Institute Headquarters in Saigon.

Ten civilians, representing different religions and political factions, were added to South Vietnam's ruling junta on 6 June. In Saigon, the Unified Buddhist Church issued a manifesto disavowing Communism and recognizing the necessity of the temporary presence of American forces.

7 June-30 Jun—The 3d Marine Division conducted Operation Liberty, an extensive pacification sweep and clear operation in the Da Nang TAOR.

18-27 Jun—Deckhouse I was the first of a series of SLF amphibious attacks on Viet Cong coastal strongholds. This operation was in Phu Yen Province, 12 miles NW of Tuy Hoa in II CTZ. There were four operations in this series during 1966.

7 Jul-2 Aug—Operation Hastings, a search and destroy mission, 55 miles NW of Hue, was conducted under the command of Task Force Delta to counter the movement of the *NVA 324B Division* across the DMZ. In addition BLT 3/5 made an am-

phibious landing and conducted Deckhouse II in conjunction with Hastings.

1 Aug — The advance echelon of the 2d Korean Marine Brigade arrived in I Corps approximately three miles south of Chu Lai.

3 Aug — The Marines began Operation Prairie in the former Hastings Area of Operations. Prairie, which started as a one-battalion operation, soon expanded into a multi-battalion campaign and continued through the end of the year. The Marines encountered elements of two NVA divisions, the *324B* and the *341st*.

26 Aug — The campaign for election to South Vietnam's Constituent Assembly officially opened with 540 candidates running.

28 Aug — BLT 2/26 arrived at Da Nang.

11 Sep — Of the 718,024 eligible voters in the I Corps area, 87.4 percent voted in South Vietnam's Constituent Assembly election. Over 80 percent of those registered voted throughout South Vietnam.

15-18 Sep — Deckhouse IV amphibious search and destroy operation was conducted in conjunction with Prairie I, eight miles NE of Dong Ha in I CTZ.

19 Sep — The 2d Battalion of the 2d Brig, ROKMC arrived at Chu Lai from Cam Ranh Bay.

25 Sep — MAG-13 arrived at Chu Lai from Iwakuni.

27 Sep — Elements of BLT 3/26 arrived at Okinawa.

1 Oct — MajGen Herman Nickerson Jr., relieved MajGen Lewis J. Fields as CG 1st Marine Division.

2 Oct — Battery C, 6th Bn (175mm guns), 27th Arty, USA, came under the operational control of Task Force Delta.

8 Oct — The 4th Battalion, 503rd Abn Inf, 173rd Abn Brig, USA, arrived at Da Nang.

10 Oct — The 3d Marine Division was ordered to displace to Thua Thien and Quang Tri Provinces to conduct offensive operations as directed and continue current offensive operations in the Phu Bai TAOR. Task Force Delta was ordered deactivated and Task Force X-Ray was activated at Chu Lai under the 1st Marine Division. The 1st Division assumed responsibility for all three southern provinces.

17-18 Oct — The 1st Bn, 40th Field Arty Regt (105mm How [SP]), USA, arrived at Da Nang and the next day the 2d Bn, 94th Arty Regt (175mm gun), USA, arrived.

24-25 Oct — At a conference in Manila, President Johnson met with leaders of six other nations: South Vietnam, New Zealand, Australia, Korea, Thailand, and the Philippines. The conferees issued a four-point "Declaration of Peace," calling for the peaceful settlement of the Vietnam War.

23 Nov — The Office of Civil Operations was established in South Vietnam as a U.S. Embassy activity to direct U.S. civilian support of revolutionary development.

29 Nov — Headquarters Btry, 1st Field Arty Grp (FAG), arrived at Chu Lai.

3 Dec — The 4thBn, 503d Inf, USA, departed I CTZ for III CTZ. The battalion was relieved by 3/9.

6 Dec — The administration disclosed that 9 to 10 billion dollars more is needed to pay for the war in Vietnam in the current fiscal year.

31 Dec — III MAF strength at the end of the year was 65,789.

Appendix D
Medal of Honor Citations, 1966

The President of the United States in the name of The Congress takes pride in presenting the MEDAL OF HONOR posthumously to

STAFF SERGEANT PETER S. CONNOR
UNITED STATES MARINE CORPS

for service as set forth in the following

CITATION

For conspicuous gallantry and intrepidity in action against enemy Viet Cong forces at the risk of his life above and beyond the call of duty while serving as Platoon Sergeant of the Third Platoon, Company F, Second Battalion, Third Marines, First Marine Division (Reinforced), Fleet Marine Force, in Quang Ngai Province, Republic of Vietnam on 25 February 1966. Leading his platoon on a search and destroy operation in an area made particularly hazardous by extensive cave and tunnel complexes, Sergeant Connor maneuvered his unit aggressively forward under intermittent enemy small arms fire. Exhibiting particular alertness and keen observation, he spotted an enemy spider hole emplacement approximately fifteen meters to his front. He pulled the pin from a fragmentation grenade intending to charge the hole boldly and drop the missile into its depths. Upon pulling the pin he realized that the firing mechanism was faulty, and that even as he held the safety device firmly in place, the fuze charge was already activated. With only precious seconds to decide, he further realized that he could not cover the distance to the small opening of the spider hole in sufficient time, and that to hurl the deadly bomb in any direction would result in death or injury to some of his comrades tactically deployed near him. Manifesting extraordinary gallantry and with utter disregard for his personal safety, he chose to hold the grenade against his own body in order to absorb the terrific explosion and spare his comrades. His act of extreme valor and selflessness in the face of virtually certain death, although leaving him mortally wounded, spared many of his fellow Marines from death or injury. His gallant action in giving his life in the cause of freedom reflects the highest credit upon the Marine Corps and the Armed Forces of the United States.

The President of the United States in the name of The Congress takes pride in presenting the MEDAL OF HONOR to

GUNNERY SERGEANT JIMMIE E. HOWARD
UNITED STATES MARINE CORPS

for service as set forth in the following

CITATION

For conspicuous gallantry and intrepidity at the risk of his life above and beyond the call of duty while serving as a Platoon Leader, Company C, First Reconnaissance Battalion, First Marine Division, in the Republic of Vietnam. Gunnery Sergeant (then Staff Sergeant) Howard and his eighteen-man platoon were occupying an observation post deep within enemy-controlled territory. Shortly after midnight on 16 June 1966, a Viet Cong force of estimated battalion size approached the Marines' position and launched a vicious attack with small arms, automatic weapons, and mortar fire. Reacting swiftly and fearlessly in the face of the overwhelming odds, Gunnery Sergeant Howard skillfully organized his small but determined force into a tight perimeter defense and calmly moved from position to position to direct his men's fire. Throughout the night, during assault after assault, his courageous example and firm leadership inspired and motivated his men to withstand the unrelenting fury of the hostile fire in the seemingly hopeless situation. He constantly shouted encouragement to his men and exhibited imagination and resourcefulness in directing their return fire. When fragments of an exploding enemy grenade wounded him severely and prevented him from moving his legs, he distributed his ammunition to the remaining members of his platoon and proceeded to maintain radio communications and direct air strikes on the enemy with uncanny accuracy. At dawn, despite the fact that five men were killed and all but one wounded, his beleaguered platoon was still in command of its position. When evacuation helicopters approached his position, Gunnery Sergeant Howard warned them away and called for additional air strikes and directed devastating small arms fire and air strikes against enemy automatic weapons positions in order to make the landing zone as secure as possible. Through his extraordinary courage and resolute fighting spirit, Gunnery Sergeant Howard was largely responsible for preventing the loss of his entire platoon. His valiant leadership and courageous fighting spirit served to inspire the men of his platoon to heroic endeavor in the face of overwhelming odds, and reflect the highest credit upon Gunnery Sergeant Howard, the Marine Corps and the United States Naval Service.

The President of the United States in the name of The Congress takes pride in presenting the MEDAL OF HONOR to

SECOND LIEUTENANT JOHN J. MCGINTY III
UNITED STATES MARINE CORPS

for service as set forth in the following

CITATION

For conspicuous gallantry and intrepidity at the risk of his life above and beyond the call of duty as Acting Platoon Leader, First Platoon, Company K, Third Battalion, Fourth Marines, Third Marine Division, in the Republic of Vietnam on 18 July 1966, Second Lieutenant (then Staff Sergeant) McGinty's platoon, which was providing rear security to protect the withdrawal of the Battalion from a position which had been under attack for three days, came under heavy small arms, automatic weapons, and mortar fire from an estimated enemy regiment. With each successive human wave which assaulted his thirty-two-man platoon during the four-hour battle, Second Lieutenant McGinty rallied his men to beat off the enemy. In one bitter assault, two of the squads became separated from the remainder of the platoon. With complete disregard for his safety, Second Lieutenant McGinty charged through intense automatic weapons and mortar fire to their position. Finding twenty men wounded and the Medical Corpsman killed, he quickly reloaded ammunition magazines and weapons for the wounded men and directed their fire upon the enemy. Although he was painfully wounded as he moved to care for the disabled men, he continued to shout encouragement to his troops and to direct their fire so effectively that the attacking hordes were beaten off. When the enemy tried to out-flank his position, he killed five of them at point-blank range with his pistol. When they again seemed on the verge of overrunning the small force, he skillfully adjusted artillery and air strikes within fifty yards of his position. This destructive fire power routed the enemy, who left an estimated 500 bodies on the battlefield. Second Lieutenant McGinty's personal heroism, indomitable leadership, selfless devotion to duty, and bold fighting spirit inspired his men to resist the repeated attacks by a fanatical enemy, reflected great credit upon himself, and upheld the highest traditions of the Marine Corps and the United States Naval Service.

The President of the United States in the name of The Congress takes pride in presenting the MEDAL OF HONOR to

MAJOR ROBERT J. MODRZEJEWSKI
UNITED STATES MARINE CORPS

for service as set forth in the following

CITATION

For conspicuous gallantry and intrepidity at the risk of his life above and beyond the call of duty while serving as Commanding Officer, Company K, Third Battalion, Fourth Marines, Third Marine Division, in the Republic of Vietnam from 15 to 18 July 1966. On 15 July, during Operation Hastings, Company K was landed in an enemy infested jungle area to establish a blocking position at a major enemy trail network. Shortly after landing, the Company encountered a reinforced enemy platoon in a well organized, defensive position. Major (then Captain) Modrzejewski led his men in the successful seizure of the enemy redoubt, which contained large quantities of ammunition and supplies. That evening a numerically superior enemy force counterattacked in an effort to retake the vital supply area, thus setting the pattern of activity for the next two and one-half days. In the first series of attacks, the enemy assaulted repeatedly in overwhelming numbers but each time was repulsed by the gallant Marines. The second night the enemy struck in battalion strength, and Major Modrzejewski was wounded in this intensive action which was fought at close quarters. Although exposed to enemy fire, and despite his painful wounds, he crawled 200 meters to provide critically needed ammunition to an exposed element of his command and was constantly present wherever the fighting was heaviest. Despite numerous casualties, a dwindling supply of ammunition and the knowledge that they were surrounded, he skillfully directed artillery fire to within a few meters of his position and courageously inspired the efforts of his Company in repelling the aggressive enemy attack. On 18 July, Company K was attacked by a regimental size enemy force. Although his unit was vastly outnumbered and weakened by the previous fighting, Major Modrzejewski reorganized his men and calmly moved among them to encourage and direct their efforts to heroic limits as they fought to overcome the vicious enemy onslaught. Again he called in air and artillery strikes at close range with devastating effect on the enemy, which together with the bold and determined fighting of the men of Company K, repulsed the fanatical attack of the larger North Vietnamese force. His unparalleled personal heroism and indomitable leadership inspired his men to a significant victory over the enemy force and reflected great credit upon himself, the Marine Corps and the United States Naval Service.

The President of the United States in the name of The Congress takes pride in presenting the MEDAL OF HONOR to

MAJOR HOWARD V. LEE
UNITED STATES MARINE CORPS

for service as set forth in the following

CITATION

For conspicuous gallantry and intrepidity at the risk of his life above and beyond the call of duty as Commanding Officer, Company E, Fourth Marines, Third Marine Division near Cam Lo, Republic of Vietnam, on 8 and 9 August 1966. A platoon of Major (then Captain) Lee's company, while on an operation deep in enemy territory, was attacked and surrounded by a large Vietnamese force. Realizing that the unit had suffered numerous casualties, depriving it of effective leadership, and fully aware that the platoon was even then under heavy attack by the enemy, Major Lee took seven men and proceeded by helicopter to reinforce the beleaguered platoon. Major Lee disembarked from the helicopter with two of his men and, braving withering enemy fire, led them into the perimeter, where he fearlessly moved from position to position, directing and encouraging the overtaxed troops. The enemy then launched a massive attack with the full might of their forces. Although painfully wounded by fragments from an enemy grenade in several areas of his body, including his eye, Major Lee continued undauntedly throughout the night to direct the defense, coordinate supporting fires, and apprise higher headquarters of the plight of the platoon. The next morning he collapsed from his wounds and was forced to relinquish command. However, the small band of Marines had held their position and repeatedly fought off many vicious enemy attacks for a grueling six hours until their evacuation was effected the following morning. Major Lee's actions saved his men from capture, minimized the loss of lives, and dealt the enemy a severe defeat. His indomitable fighting spirit, superb leadership, and great personal valor in the face of tremendous odds, reflect great credit upon himself and are in keeping with the highest traditions of the Marine Corps and the United States Naval Service.

The President of the United States in the name of The Congress takes pride in presenting the MEDAL OF HONOR to

SERGEANT RICHARD A. PITTMAN
UNITED STATES MARINE CORPS

for service as set forth in the following

CITATION

For conspicuous gallantry and intrepidity at the risk of his life above and beyond the call of duty as a member of First Platoon, Company I, Third Battalion, Fifth Marines during combat operations near the Demilitarized Zone, Republic of Vietnam. On 24 July 1966, while Company I was conducting an operation along the axis of a narrow jungle trail, the leading company elements suffered numerous casualties when they suddenly came under heavy fire from a well concealed and numerically superior enemy force. Hearing the engaged Marines' calls for more firepower, Sergeant (then Lance Corporal) Pittman quickly exchanged his rifle for a machine gun and several belts of ammunition, left the relative safety of his platoon, and unhesitatingly rushed forward to aid his comrades. Taken under intense enemy small-arms fire at point blank range during his advance, he returned the fire, silencing the enemy positions. As Sergeant Pittman continued to forge forward to aid members of the leading platoon, he again came under heavy fire from two automatic weapons which he promptly destroyed. Learning that there were additional wounded Marines fifty yards further along the trail, he braved a withering hail of enemy mortar and small-arms fire to continue onward. As he reached the position where the leading Marines had fallen, he was suddenly confronted with a bold frontal attack by 30 to 40 enemy. Totally disregarding his own safety, he calmly established a position in the middle of the trail and raked the advancing enemy with devastating machine gun fire. His weapon rendered ineffective, he picked up a submachine gun and, together with a pistol seized from a fallen comrade, continued his lethal fire until the enemy force had withdrawn. Having exhausted his ammunition except for a grenade which he hurled at the enemy, he then rejoined his own platoon. Sergeant Pittman's daring initiative, bold fighting spirit and selfless devotion to duty inflicted many enemy casualties, disrupted the enemy attack and saved the lives of many of his wounded comrades. His personal valor at grave risk to himself reflects the highest credit upon himself, the Marine Corps and the United States Naval Service.

Appendix E
List of Reviewers

Marines

Gen Wallace M. Greene, Jr. (Ret)
Gen Lewis W. Walt (Ret)

LtGen Leslie E. Brown (Ret)
LtGen Leo J. Dulacki (Ret)
LtGen Hugh M. Elwood (Ret)
LtGen Lewis J. Fields (Ret)
LtGen Victor H. Krulak (Ret)
LtGen Herman Nickerson, Jr. (Ret)
LtGen Louis B. Robertshaw (Ret)
LtGen Lawrence F. Snowden (Ret)

MajGen Marion E. Carl (Ret)
MajGen Lowell E. English (Ret)
MajGen Harold A. Hatch
MajGen Wood B. Kyle (Ret)
MajGen Oscar F. Peatross (Ret)

BGen Edward J. Doyle (Ret)
BGen Roy E. Moss
BGen Edwin H. Simmons (Ret)
BGen William A. Stiles (Ret)

Col Sidney J. Altman (Ret)
Col Nels E. Anderson (Ret)
Col Emmett O. Anglin, Jr. (Ret)
Col Edward L. Bale, Jr. (Ret)
Col Drew J. Barrett, Jr. (Ret)
Col Noble L. Beck (Ret)
Col Van D. Bell, Jr. (Ret)
Col Arnold E. Bench (Ret)
Col Rocco D. Bianchi (Ret)
Col James M. Callender (Ret)

Col George W. Carrington, Jr. (Ret)
Col Bevan G. Cass (Ret)
Col Alexander D. Cereghino (Ret)
Col Steve J. Cibik (Ret)
Col James M. Cummings (Ret)
Col Clyde D. Dean
Col Earl R. Delong (Ret)

Col Nicholas J. Dennis (Ret)
Col Birchard B. DeWitt (Ret)
Col Haig Donabedian (Ret)

Col Joshua W. Dorsey, III (Ret)
Col Donald L. Evans, Jr. (Ret)
Col Fred J. Frazer (Ret)
Col William F. Fry (Ret)
Col Roy C. Gray, Jr. (Ret)
Col Edward E. Hammerbeck (Ret)
Col Harold A. Hayes, Jr. (Ret)
Col Vincil W. Hazelbaker
Col Peter L. Hilgartner (Ret)
Col William K. Horn (Ret)

Col Thomas M. Horne (Ret)
Col Robert M. Jenkins (Ret)
Col David G. Jones (Ret)
Col Charles J. Keever
Col Karl T. Keller (Ret)
Col James P. Kelly (Ret)
Col John P. Lanigan (Ret)
Col Edward R. McCarthy (Ret)
Col James F. McClanahan (Ret)
Col John L. Mahon (Ret)

Col Glen E. Martin (Ret)
Col William J. Masterpool
Col Herbert E. Mendenhall (Ret)
Col John F. Mentzer (Ret)
Col Anthony A. Monti
Col Samuel M. Morrow
Col Ross L. Mulford (Ret)
Col Michael J. Needham
Col Glenn E. Norris (Ret)
Col Thomas J. O'Connor (Ret)

Col Mauro J. Padalino (Ret)
Col Leslie L. Page (Ret)
Col Francis F. Parry (Ret)
Col Robert M. Port (Ret)
Col Walter S. Pullar, Jr.
Col Robert R. Read (Ret)
Col Edwin M. Rudzis (Ret)

Col Mitchell O. Sadler (Ret)
Col Richard A. Savage (Ret)

Col Donald W. Sherman (Ret)
Col Harry W. Taylor (Ret)
Col Frank C. Thomas (Ret)
Col Paul C. Trammell (Ret)
Col Leon N. Utter (Ret)
Col Sumner A. Vale (Ret)
Col Roy R. Van Cleve (Ret)
Col Paul B. Watson, Jr. (Ret)
Col E. Robert Watson (Ret)

Col Gordon H. West (Ret)
Col Frank R. Wilkinson, Jr. (Ret)
Col Paul E. Wilson (Ret)
Col Robert J. Zitnik (Ret)

LtCol James Aldworth (Ret)
LtCol Billy H. Barber (Ret)
LtCol Garland T. Beyerle (Ret)
LtCol John E. Clements
LtCol Dwain A. Colby (Ret)
LtCol Ernest L. De Fazio (Ret)
LtCol William F. Donahue, Jr. (Ret)
LtCol Robert J. Driver, Jr.
LtCol Jim T. Elkins (Ret)
LtCol Fredric A. Green (Ret)
LtCol George R. Griggs

LtCol John J. Hess (Ret)
LtCol John J. W. Hilgers
LtCol Charles A. House (Ret)
LtCol Richard E. Jones (Ret)
LtCol Warren P. Kitterman (Ret)
LtCol Timothy B. Lecky
LtCol Alex Lee
LtCol Howard V. Lee (Ret)
LtCol Jerry D. Lindauer (Ret)
LtCol Fred D. MacLean, Jr. (Ret)

LtCol Robert J. Modrzejewski

LtCol McLendon G. Morris
LtCol Martin E. O'Connor
LtCol Raymond J. O'Leary (Ret)
LtCol John J. Roothoff (Ret)
LtCol Conway J. Smith (Ret)
LtCol Daniel A. Somerville (Ret)
LtCol Ralph E. Sullivan (Ret)
LtCol Emerson A. Walker (Ret)

Maj James O. Black (Ret)
Maj Marshall B. Darling
Maj Charles L. George
Maj Robert G. Handrahan
Maj Richard E. Maresco
Maj Theard J. Terrebone, Jr.

Capt Edwin W. Besch (Ret)
Capt James J. Kirschke (Ret)

MGySgt J. J. McDowell

Others

Historical Division, Joint Secretariat, Joint Chiefs of Staff
Center of Military History, Department of the Army
Office of Air Force History, Department of the Air Force
Naval History Division, Department of the Navy

Adm John J. Hyland, USN (Ret)
Adm Ulysses S. Grant Sharp, USN (Ret)
Gen William C. Westmoreland, USA (Ret)
VAdm Edwin B. Hooper, USN (Ret)
Capt John H. Craven, USN (Ret)
Mr. V. Keith Fleming, Jr.
Mr. Francis J. West, Jr.

Appendix F
Distribution of Aircraft, Fleet Marine Force, Pacific*

UNIT	DA NANG	CHU LAI	PHU BAI	OKINAWA	JAPAN	HAWAII	EASTPAC	OTHER
MAG-11								
H&MS-11	3/UH-34D							
	4/TF-9J							
	1/C-117D							
VMCJ-1	9/EF-10B							
	1/RF-4B							
	4/EA-6A							
VMFA-115	11/F-4B							
VMF (AW)-232	15/F-8E							
VMA (AW)-242	12/A-6A							
MAG-12								
H&MS-12		1/C-117						
VMA-121		22/A-4E						
VMA-211		22/A-4E						
VMA-214		19/A-4C						
VMA-311		17/A-4E						
MAG-13								
H&MS-13		4/TF-9J						
		1/C-117						
VMFA-314		15/F-4B						
VMFA-323		13/F-4B						
VMFA-542		14/F-4B						
MAG-15								
H&MS-15					2/C-54			
					2/TF-9J			
					1/C-117D			
VMGR-152				12/KC-130F				
VMA-223					19/A-4E			
VMF (AW)-235					10/F-8E			
HMM-361				23/UH-34D				
HMM-362								24/UH-34D**
MAG-16								
H&MS-16	1/C-117D							
	9/O-1C							
	4/UH-34D							
	6/CH-37C							
VMO-2	27/UH-1E							
HMM-163			24/UH-34D					
HMM-164	20/CH-46A							2CH-46A**
HMM-263	22/UH-34D							
HMM-265	22/CH-46A							

UNIT	DA NANG	CHU LAI	PHU BAI	OKINAWA	JAPAN	HAWAII	EASTPAC	OTHER
MWSG-17								
H&MS-17	1/UC-45J							
	4/UH-34D							
	2/C-117D							
	2/US-2B							
MAG-36								
H&MS-36		3/UH-34D						
		1/C-117D						
VMO-6		21/UH-1E						
HMM-165		23/CH-46A						
HMM-262		24/CH-46A						
HMM-363		23/UH-34D						
MAG-33								
H&MS-33							3/T-1A	
							1/C-47H	
VMCJ-3							12/RF-4B	
							8/EF-10B	
VMF-334							15/F-8C	
VMFA-122							14/F-4B	
MWSG-37								
MAMS-37							4/T-1A	
							3/C-117D	
							1/C-54Q	
							1/C-47J	
VMGR-352				4/KC-130F			10/KC-130F	
HMM-364							6/UH-34D	
HMH-463							10/CH-53A	4/CH-53A***
VMO-3								12/UH-1E***
MHTG-30								
HMMT-301							24/UH-34D	
HMMT-302							16/UH-1E	
VMO-5							16/UH-1E	
1ST MAR BRIG								
H&MS						4UH-34D		
						1/VH-34D		
						1/T-1A		
VMF (AW)-212						14/F-8D		
TOTAL PAC AIRCRAFT								
Fixed Wing (338)	72	129		16	34	15	72	
Helicopters (364)	108	94	24	23		5	68	42

*From Status of Forces, dated 29 December 1966, with correction of obvious errors in addition
**Aircraft indicated in "Other" column with SLF, Seventh Fleet
***VMO-3(-) and Det, HMH-463, enroute to RVN, 4/UH-1E of number indicated with SLF, Seventh Fleet

Appendix G

Distribution of Personnel Fleet Marine Force, Pacific 22 December 1966

UNIT	NOTE	ASSIGNED STRENGTH USMC	ASSIGNED STRENGTH USN	STR RPT DATE	DANANG USMC	DANANG USN	CHU LAI USMC	CHU LAI USN	DONG HA PHU BAI USMC	DONG HA PHU BAI USN	OTHER RVN USMC	OTHER RVN USN	OKINAWA USMC	OKINAWA USN	JAPAN USMC	JAPAN USN	HAWAII USMC	HAWAII USN	EASTPAC USMC	EASTPAC USN	SLF OTHER USMC	SLF OTHER USN
HEADQUARTERS																						
HQ, FMF, PAC																						
H&SBN, FMF, PAC		972	28	3NOV66													972	28				
HQ, FMF, PAC (FWD)																						
SU#2, H&SBN, FMFPAC		47	1	17NOV66									47	1								
HQ, III MAF																						
H&S CO, III MAF		714	18	30NOV66	714	18																
HQ, V MAF	1																					
1ST CIV AFF GP (FMF)	1																					
HQ, 1ST MAR DIV																						
HQ BN, 1ST MAR DIV		1753	31	1DEC66	1183	24	570	7														
HQ, 3D MAR DIV																						
HQ BN, 3D MAR DIV		1570	114	1DEC66					1570	114												
HQ, 5TH MAR DIV	1																					
HQ BN, 5TH MAR DIV	1																					
HQ, FORTPS, FMF PAC																						
HQ CO, FORTPS		394	31	1DEC66															394	31		
HQ, 9TH MAB																						
HQ CO, 9TH MAB		327		30NOV66									327									
HQ, 1ST MAR BRIG																						
HQ CO, 1ST MAR BRIG		314	35	1DEC66													314	35				
INFANTRY																						
1ST MARINES																						
HQ CO, 1ST MAR		257	4	1DEC66	257	4																
1ST BN, 1ST MAR		1048	5	1DEC66	1048	5																
2D BN, 1ST MAR		1071	61	1DEC66	1071	61																
3D BN, 1ST MAR		1040	50	1DEC66	1040	50																
3D MARINES																						
HQ CO, 3D MAR	4	231	8	2DEC66					231	8												
1ST BN, 3D MAR	4	1059	53	1DEC66					1059	53												
2D BN, 3D MAR		1140	62	1DEC66					1140	62												
3D BN, 3D MAR		1068	63	1DEC66					1068	63												
4TH MARINES																						
HQ CO, 4TH MAR	4	253	6	1DEC66					253	6												
1ST BN, 4TH MAR		1032	56	1DEC66									1032	56								
2D BN, 4TH MAR		1132	45	8DEC66									1132	45								
3D BN, 4TH MAR	4	1128	71	8DEC66					1128	71												
5TH MARINES																						
HQ CO, 5TH MAR		229	5	1DEC66			229	5														
1ST BN, 5TH MAR		1025	50	1DEC66			1025	50														
2D BN, 5TH MAR	4	1170	53	1DEC66	1170	53																
3D BN, 5TH MAR		1044	56	8DEC66			1044	56														
7TH MARINES																						
HQ CO, 7TH MAR		258	5	1DEC66			258	5														
1ST BN, 7TH MAR		1077	61	1DEC66			1077	61														
2D BN, 7TH MAR		1096	61	1DEC66			1096	61														
3D BN, 7TH MAR	4	1141	56	1DEC66	1141	56																
9TH MARINES																						
HQ CO, 9TH MAR		195	4	1DEC66	195	4																
1ST BN, 9TH MAR	3	1674	95	2DEC66																	1674	95
2D BN, 9TH MAR		1029	54	11NOV66					1029	54												
3D BN, 9TH MAR		1086	60	8DEC66	1086	60																
26TH MARINES																						
HQ CO, 26TH MAR		400	14	30NOV66									400	14								
1ST BN, 26TH MAR		1035	69	8DEC66	1035	69																
2D BN, 26TH MAR		1037	60	2DEC66					1037	69												
3D BN, 26TH MAR	4	1694	97	24NOV66					1694	97												
27TH MARINES																						
HQ CO, 27TH MAR		70	2	15SEP66															70	2		
1ST BN, 27TH MAR		1156	39	1DEC66													1156	39				
2D BN, 27TH MAR																						
3D BN, 27TH MAR																						

UNIT	NOTE	ASSIGNED STRENGTH		STR RPT DATE	DANANG		CHU LAI		DONG HA PHU BAI		OTHER RVN		OKINAWA		JAPAN		HAWAII		EASTPAC		SLF OTHER	
		USMC	USN		USMC	USN	USMC	USN	USMC	USN	USMC	USN	USMC	USN	USMC	USN	USMC	USN	USMC	USN	USMC	USN
28TH MARINES																						
HQ CO, 28TH MAR	1																					
1ST BN, 28TH MAR	1																					
2D BN, 28TH MAR	1																					
3D BN, 28TH MAR	1																					
ARTILLERY																						
11TH MARINES																						
HQ BTRY, 11TH MAR		283	8	1DEC66					283	8												
1ST BN, 11TH MAR		537	15	1DEC66	537	15																
2D BN, 11TH MAR		498	15	1DEC66			498	15														
3D BN, 11TH MAR		555	15	10NOV66			555	15														
4TH BN, 11TH MAR		471	10	1DEC66					471	10												
12TH MARINES																						
HQ BTRY, 12TH MAR	4	234	8	1DEC66					234	8												
1ST BN, 12TH MAR	4	569	15	10NOV66					569	15												
2D BN, 12TH MAR		515	13	1DEC66	515	13																
3D BN, 12TH MAR		396	15	24NOV66					396	15												
4TH BN, 12TH MAR	4	330	7	2DEC66					330	7												
13TH MARINES	2																					
HQ BTRY, 13TH MAR	2	63	2	15SEP66															63	2		
1ST BN, 13TH MAR		330	9	1DEC66									330	9								
2D BN, 13TH MAR	2	19		15SEP66															19			
3D BN, 13TH MAR	1																					
4TH BN, 13TH MAR	2	122	2	15SEP66									122	2								
HQ BTRY, 1ST FAG		143	3	29NOV66			143	3														
HQ BTRY, 3D FAG	1																					
1ST 155MM GUN BTRY		118	2	10NOV66					118	2												
3D 155MM GUN BTRY		144	2	17NOV66			144	2														
5TH 155MM GUN BTRY		154	3	1DEC66															154	3		
7TH 155MM GUN BTRY	1																					
1ST 8" HOW BTRY		165	2	27OCT66	165	2																
3D 8" HOW BTRY		186	4	10NOV66					186	4												
5TH 8" HOW BTRY	1																					
1ST SEARCH LIGHT BTRY	1																					
RECONNAISSANCE																						
1ST RECON BN		615	38	1DEC66	615	38																
3D RECON BN	4	481	26	27OCT66			336	18	145	8												
5TH RECON BN	2	54		8DEC66									54									
1ST FORCE RECON CO		163	6	17NOV66	163	6																
3D FORCE RECON CO		74	1	1DEC66	15														59	1		
5TH FORCE RECON CO	1																					
ANTI-TANK																						
1ST AT BN		371	7	1DEC66	371	7																
3D AT BN		297	7	27OCT66	297	7																
5TH AT BN	2	62	1	1DEC66									62	1								
TANK																						
1ST TANK BN		568	10	10NOV66	568	10																
3D TANK BN	4	536	10	10NOV66	536	10																
5TH TANK BN	2	93	2	1DEC66									93	2								
AMTRAC																						
1ST AMTRAC BN		636	12	11NOV66	636	12																
3D AMTRAC BN		644	12	10NOV66			644	12														
5TH AMTRAC BN	2	159	2	1DEC66									159	2								
1ST ARM AMPHIB CO		274	3	28NOV66	274	3																
ENGINEER																						
1ST ENGR BN		571	1	1DEC66	571	1																
3D ENGR BN		690	15	8DEC66	690	15																
5TH ENGR BN	2	85		1DEC66									85									
7TH ENGR BN		916	20	11NOV66	916	20																
9TH ENGR BN		894	15	10NOV66			894	15														
11TH ENGR BN		1059	20	30NOV66					1059	20												
13TH ENGR BN	2	22		15SEP66													22					
1ST BRIDGE CO		139		11NOV66	139																	
3D BRIDGE CO		174		11NOV66	174																	
5TH BRIDGE CO	1																					
MOTOR TRANSPORT																						
1ST MT BN		268	7	1DEC66	68		200	8														
3D MT BN		259	7	20OCT66	259	7																
5TH MT BN	2	52	1	8DEC66									52	1								
7TH MT BN		334	8	10NOV66	187	6	147	2														
9TH MT BN	4	304	9	10NOV66					304	9												
11TH MT BN	6	383		1DEC66																	383	
13TH MT BN	2	21	9	15SEP66															21	9		
COMMUNICATION																						
1ST RADIO BN		456	3	1DEC66	171												285	3				
5TH COMM BN		591	7	10NOV66	591	7																
7TH COMM BN		690	12	10NOV66	188	1	455	11	47													
9TH COMM BN	2	183	1	24NOV66									183	1								
1ST ANGLICO	5	254	9	1DEC66							130	6					124	3				
SHORE PARTY																						
1ST SP BN		409	23	1DEC66	94	3	315	20														
3D SP BN		429	35	1DEC66	429	35																
5TH SP BN	2	32		5DEC66									32									

DISTRIBUTION OF PERSONNEL

UNIT	NOTE	ASSIGNED STRENGTH USMC	USN	STR RPT DATE	DANANG USMC	USN	CHU LAI USMC	USN	DONG HA PHU BAI USMC	USN	OTHER RVN USMC	USN	OKINAWA USMC	USN	JAPAN USMC	USN	HAWAII USMC	USN	EASTPAC USMC	USN	SLF OTHER USMC	USN
MILITARY POLICE																						
1ST MP BN		747		11NOV66	747																	
3D MP BN	2	51		15SEP66															51			
5TH MP BN	1																					
SERVICE/SUPPORT																						
1ST FSR																						
H&S BN		311	50	8DEC66															311	50		
SUPPLY BN		298	9	8DEC66															298	9		
MAINT BN		491		9DEC66															491			
3D FSR																						
H&S BN		950	59	1DEC66									950	59								
SUPPLY BN		1622	40	1DEC66									1622	40								
MAINT BN		1140		1DEC66									1140									
5TH FSR (-)	1																					
H&S BN	1																					
SUPPLY BN	1																					
MAINT BN	1																					
HQ, FLC, III MAF		6187	117	17NOV66	6187	117																
H&SCO, FLC																						
1ST SERV BN																						
3D SERV BN																						
PROV SERV BN, 9TH MAB		883	19	24NOV66									883	19								
5TH SERV BN																						
7TH SEP BULK FUEL CO	6	360		2DEC66																	360	
9TH SEP BULK FUEL CO	1																					
MEDICAL																						
1ST MED BN		127	323	1DEC66			127	323														
3D MED BN		150	327	1DEC66	150	326																
5TH MED BN	2	9	15	1DEC66	9	15																
1ST HOSP CO		31	59	3NOV66			31	59														
5TH HOSP CO	1																					
1ST DENT CO			71	1DEC66				71														
3D DENT CO			79	15SEP66		79																
5TH DENT CO	2	2	28	20OCT66													1	12	1	16		
11TH DENT CO			51	1DEC66		51																
13TH DENT CO			33	24NOV66																33		
15TH DENT CO	2		10	15SEP66									10									
17TH DENT CO																						
USMC		66,409			25,631		11,299		13,411		130		8,715		0		2,852		1,954		2,417	
USN		3,361			1,209		842		681		6		252		0		120		156		95	
GROUND TOTAL		69,770			26,840		12,141		14,092		136		8,967		0		2,972		2,110		2,512	

AVIATION UNITS

UNIT	NOTE	USMC	USN	STR RPT DATE	DANANG USMC	USN	CHU LAI USMC	USN	DONG HA PHU BAI USMC	USN	OTHER RVN USMC	USN	OKINAWA USMC	USN	JAPAN USMC	USN	HAWAII USMC	USN	EASTPAC USMC	USN	SLF OTHER USMC	USN
HQ SQDN, FMF, PAC		71		1DEC66															71			
1ST MAW																						
MWHG-1																						
H&HS-1		1087	61	1DEC66	1087	61																
MASS-2		230	2	1DEC66	230	2																
MACS-7		198	3	1DEC66			198	3														
1ST LAAM BN		472	17	1DEC66	472	17																
2D LAAM BN		462	14	1DEC66	462	14																
MASS-3		137	2	1DEC66	137	2																
MATCU-62		36		24NOV66	36																	
MAG-11																						
H&MS-11		441		1DEC66	441																	
MABS-11		496	32	1DEC66	496	32																
VMCJ-1		485	1	2DEC66	485	1																
VMFA-115		273	1	2DEC66	273	1																
VMF(AW)-232		189	1	1DEC66	189	1																
VMA(AW)-242		309	5	1DEC66	309	5																
MAG-12																						
H&MS-12		448	1	1DEC66			448	1														
MABS-12		621	32	1DEC66			621	32														
MATCU-67		93		1DEC66			93															
VMA-214		188	1	1DEC66			188	1														
VMA-121		215	5	1DEC66			215	5														
VMA-211		184	3	1DEC66			184	3														
VMA-311		187	2	30NOV66			187	2														
MAG-13																						
H&MS-13		364	3	30NOV66			364	3														
MABS-13		541	23	30NOV66			541	23														
VMFA-314		263	2	1DEC66			263	2														
VMFA-542		243	4	1DEC66			243	4														
VMFA-323		255	4	30NOV66			255	4														

UNIT	NOTE	ASSIGNED STRENGTH		STR RPT DATE	DANANG		CHU LAI		DONG HA PHU BAI		OTHER RVN		OKINAWA		JAPAN		HAWAII		EASTPAC		SLF OTHER	
		USMC	USN		USMC	USN	USMC	USN	USMC	USN	USMC	USN	USMC	USN	USMC	USN	USMC	USN	USMC	USN	USMC	USN
MAG-15																						
H&MS-15		363		8DEC66											363							
MABS-15		477	20	8DEC66											477	20						
NBC WPNS SEC-1		17		18NOV66									17									
MACS-6		232	3	8DEC66									232	3								
MATCU-60		67		8DEC66									67									
MATCU-66		54		30NOV66									54									
VMGR-152		560	9	1DEC66									467	9	93							
HMM-361		180		30NOV66									180									
VMA-223		183	5	8DEC66											183	5						
VMF(AW)-235		216	1	8DEC66											216	1						
H&MS, FUTENA		232	56	1DEC66									232	56								
H&MS, IWAKUNI		485	298	1DEC66											485	298						
HMM-362	3	220	4	3NOV66																	220	4
MAG-16																						
H&MS-16		460			460																	
MABS-16		585	14	1DEC66	585	14																
MACTU-68		72		30NOV66	72																	
VMO-2		182	4	1DEC66	182	4																
HMM-163		218	4	1DEC66					218	4												
HMM-164		219	5	1DEC66	219	5																
HMM-263		213	4	1DEC66	213	4																
HMM-265		218	3	1DEC66	218	3																
MWSG-17																						
H&MS-17		735	26	17NOV66	735	26																
WERS-17																						
MAG-36																						
H&MS-36		333		1DEC66			333															
MABS-36		443	40	17NOV66			443	40														
VMO-6		232	3	8DEC66			232	3														
HMM-165		239	1	1DEC66			239	1														
HMM-363		197	1	30NOV66			197	1														
HMM-262		147	2	24NOV66			147	2														
3D MAW																						
MWHG-3																						
H&HS-3		1040	7	8DEC66															1040	7		
NBC WPNS SEC-3		15		15SEP66															15			
5TH LAAM BN		442	12	1DEC66															442	12		
MACS-1		211		8DEC66															211			
MACS-4		250		8DEC66															250			
MATCU-65		46		8DEC66															46			
MASS-5	1	173		8DEC66															173			
MHTG-30																						
H&MS-30		482	3	8DEC66															482	3		
HMMT-301		242	1	8DEC66															242	1		
HMMT-302	2																					
VMO-5																						
MAG-33																						
H&MS-33		499	1	8DEC66															499	1		
MABS-33		487	2	8DEC66															487	2		
VMFA-122		313	1	19SEP66															313	1		
VMF-334		174	1	8DEC66															174	1		
VMCJ-3		223	1	8DEC66															223	1		
MWSG-37																						
H&MS-37		439		8DEC66															439			
MABS-37		702	133	8DEC66															702	133		
MWMS-37		401	1	8DEC66															401	1		
HMH-463		182	1	1DEC66															182	1		
HMH-364																						
HMH-462		8		8DEC66															8			
VMGR-352		362	4	8DEC66															362	4		
VMO-3	6	216	3	1DEC66																	216	3
1ST MAR BRIG AIR																						
H&MS, 1ST MAR BRIG		107		1DEC66													107					
MACS-2		184		8DEC66													184					
MATCU-70		30		18NOV66													30					
VMF(AW)-212		157		8DEC66													157					
USMC		23,943			6,230		6,462		218				1,017		2,049		549		6,982		436	
USN			893			159		163		4				12		380		0		168		7
AVIATION TOTAL		24,836			6,389		6,625		222				1,029		2,429		549		7,150		443	

DISTRIBUTION OF PERSONNEL

RECAPITULATION OF PERSONNEL DISTRIBUTION

		ASSIGNED STRENGTH	DANANG	CHU LAI	PHU BAI	OTHER RVN	OKINAWA	JAPAN	HAWAII	EASTPAC	OTHER
GROUND TOTAL	USMC	66,409	25,631	11,299	13,411	130	8,715	0	2,852	1,954	2,417
	USN	3,361	1,209	842	681	6	252	0	120	156	95
AVIATION TOTAL	USMC	23,943	6,230	6,625	218		1,017	2,049	549	6,982	436
	USN	893	159	163	4		12	380	0	168	7
GRAND TOTAL	USMC	90,352	31,861	17,761	13,629	130	9,732	2,049	3,401	8,936	2,853
	USN	4,254	1,368	1,005	685	6	264	380	120	324	102

NOTES:
1. NOT ACTIVATED
2. PARTIALLY ACTIVATED
3. FIGURES IN "OTHER" ASSIGNED TO SLF, TOTAL INCLUDES ALL ATTACHED UNITS
4. UNITS LOCATED AT DONG HA
5. FIGURE IN "OTHER RVN" AT VARIOUS RVN LOCATIONS
6. FIGURES IN "OTHER" ENROUTE TO RVN

UNLESS OTHERWISE NOTED, STRENGTHS AND LOCATIONS ARE THOSE REPORTED BY UNIT PERSONNEL STATUS REPORTS AND DO NOT REFLECT DAY-TO-DAY ADJUSTMENTS BETWEEN REPORTING PERIODS.

Index

A Loui, 56
A Shau Special Forces Camp, 56-65, 61n, 69, 139-40, 149-150, 275; illus., 59, 63
A Shau Valley, 56, 64
Ai Nghia River, 48
Air Force (U.S.), 7, 24, 28-29, 33n, 41, 58-59, 61, 74, 82, 93, 114, 134, 146-147, 155, 169, 179, 185, 214, 262, 268-271, 275, 298n, 304n, 315n; illus., 31, 263
  Air Force Commands and Units
    Strategic Air Command, 22
    Seventh Air Force, 74, 265, 268-272, 274, 317
    Seventh Air Force Tactical Air Command Center, 270
    2d Air Division, 7, 74, 268, 272
    1st Air Commando Squadron, 61
Air support radar team (ASRT), 58, 269
Aircraft
  Types
    Bell UH-1E (Huey), 24, 27-28, 33, 33n, 59, 61, 61n, 62, 99, 109-110, 121, 124, 134, 150, 173, 177, 179, 181-182, 202, 218, 237, 266, 267n, 271; illus., 266
    Boeing B-52 (Stratofortress), 22, 24, 28, 41, 136, 156, 169, 169n, 182, 214; illus., 31
    Boeing Vertol CH-46 (Sea Knight), 79, 80n, 135, 149-150, 164, 166, 166n, 168, 176-177, 179, 191, 202, 204, 211, 263-264, 264n; illus., 161, 165, 211, 263-264
    Cessna O-1C (Birddog), 267
    Chance-Vought F-8E (Crusader), 29, 83, 83n, 99, 164n, 175, 216, 265, 265n; illus., 265
    Chance-Vought RF-8A, 274
    Douglas A-1E (Skyraider), 61, 87-88; illus., 263
    Douglas A-4 (Skyhawk), 17, 25, 29, 33n, 61-62, 87, 99, 109, 114, 121, 164, 164n, 175, 202, 204, 216, 218, 266, 269; illus., 263, 266
    Douglas AC-47 ("Puff the Magic Dragon"), 58, 114, 179, 185-186
    Douglas C-117 (Skytrain), 179, 213, 263
    Douglas EF-10B, 274
    Douglas F3D, 274
    Fairchild C-123 (Provider), 61, 93
    Grumman A6A (Intruder), 264-266, 264n, 269
    Grumman EA6A, 264, 274
    Lockheed C-130 (Hercules), 28, 41
    Lockheed KC-130 (Hercules), 64, 141, 146, 161, 176, 196, 198, 261, 268-269, 274-275; illus., 146, 275
    McDonnell F-4B (Phantom II), 25, 29, 62, 99, 109, 120, 123, 155, 164, 164n, 175, 179, 188, 202, 216, 264, 265n, 266, 269, 275; illus., 267
    McDonnell RF-4B, 264, 274
    Sikorsky CH-3C, 24, 29, 33n; illus., 31

    Sikorsky UH-34 (Sea Horse), 24-25, 27-29, 33, 33n, 50, 58, 62-63, 110, 117, 120-121, 134, 168, 176, 179, 181, 191, 263n, 265; illus., 32, 35, 130, 216, 265, 268
    Sikorsky CH-37 (Mojave), 29, 176, 267; illus., 268
    Sikorsky CH-53 (Sea Stallion), 267; illus., 268
Airheart, LtCol William C., 197-198
Alamo (LSD 33), 300
Albany, Georgia, 290
Aldworth, LtCol James, 300; illus., 297
Allen, George, 257
Amphibious doctrine, 21, 299, 304n (See also *Doctrine for Amphibious Operations*)
Amphibious objective area, 299
An Hoa, 18, 40-41, 41n, 43, 92-93, 96-97, 104, 201-202, 204, 206-210, 213, 226; illus., 40, 44, 201-202, 206, 208-209, 227, 246, 277
An Hoa airstrip, 202, 204, 206, 206n, 207
An Hoa Basin, 120n, 204
An Hoa industrial complex, 40-41, 226-227; illus., 93, 227
An Hoa outpost, 120, 120n, 121
An Lao, 32
An Lao Bridge, 224
An Lao River Valley, 21
An Trach, 100
An Tuyet (1), 115, 118
Anderson, SSgt Gerald E., illus., 248
Anderson, Col Nels E., 310; illus., 310
Anglin, Col Emmett O., Jr., 37
Annamite Mountains, 3, 17, 40
Anti-infiltration systems, 318 (See also Barrier)
Ap Chinh An, 67, 69, 152, 154, 156
Ap Dai Phu, 67
Ap Phu An, 65
Ap Tay Hoang, 65
Arc Light, 24, 28-29, 136, 214
"Arizona Territory," 41, 208; illus., 40
Armed Forces (U.S.), 283
Armstrong, LtCol Marshall B., 305
Army FM31-11, 298n (See also *Doctrine for Amphibious Operations*)
Army (U.S.), 6, 33, 50, 74, 81, 86, 90n, 99, 143, 145, 155, 177, 197-198, 219, 231n, 233, 239, 241, 247, 266n, 267n, 270, 278, 280-281, 304, 304n, 305, 307, 307n, 312-314; illus., 311
  Center of Military History, U.S. Army, 256n
Army War College, 204
Army Commands and Units
  U.S. Army, Pacific, 145
  U.S. Army, Vietnam, 7
  Field Force, Vietnam, 6-7, 19, 21-22, 74, 261

INDEX

I Field Force, Vietnam, 74, 303n, 312
II Field Force, Vietnam, 74, 312
1st Cavalry Division (Airmobile), 9, 21, 25, 30, 33, 304, 313
    2d Brigade, 32
    3d Brigade, 30, 32
    30th Artillery, 1st Battalion, Battery B, 33
9th Division, 314
101st Airborne Division, 1st Brigade, 312-313
5th U. S. Special Forces Group (Airborne), 58
173d Airborne Brigade, 188n, 305, 313
    503d Airborne Infantry Regiment, 226n, 281
    4th Battalion, 197, 226, 314
40th Artillery, 1st Battalion, 198, 278
94th Artillery, 2d Battalion, 198, 278
    Battery A, 279
8th Radio Research Unit, 50
24th Psychological Operations Company, 247
29th Civil Affairs Company, 248-249
220th Aviation Company, 177
Special Forces, 21, 23, 56, 56n, 58, 58n, 59, 61-62, 62n, 63, 132, 141, 149, 196, 265, 307n; illus., 23, 63
Artillery Plateau, 198n, 278; illus., 193, 279, 281
Australia, 256, 313
Axtell, Col George C., Jr., 75, 288-290

B-3 Front, 11
Ba Long Valley, 318
Ba To Special Forces Camp, 21, 23-24, 33-34; illus., 23
Baldwin, Hanson, 283
Bale, Col Edward L., Jr., 226, 290
Barrett, Col Drew J., Jr., 204, 206-207, 221-222, 226, 244n, 292n
Barrier, 314-319 (See also antiinfiltration system and Practice Nine)
Barrow, Col Robert H., 299n
Barry (DD 933), 25, 25n
Barstow, California, 290 (See also Marine Supply Center, Barstow)
Batangan Peninsula, 223
"Battalion days in the field," 143
Bay, Ngo Van, 245
Beck, Col Noble L., 22n, 168n, 240n
Beebe, Cpl Robert A., 241-242
Bell, LtCol Van D., Jr., 104, 141-143, 145, 149, 163, 172, 174; illus., 141
Belton, PFC Bennie C., illus., 311
Ben Hai River, 3; illus., 157
Ben Van River, 17
Bench, LtCol Arnold E., 163, 166-169, 171, 171n, 174-175, 175n, 177, 179, 181-186, 186n, 187-188
Besch, Capt Edwin W., 35, 111n, 148n, 183-184, 186
Beyerle, LtCol Garland T., 305
Bianchi, LtCol Rocco D., 306
Bien Hoa Province, 310, 314
Binh Dinh Province, 10, 13, 21-22, 24-25, 30, 33
Binh Nghia, 241-243
Binh Son, 17, 19, 110, 114-115, 115n, 118, 120, 120n, 121, 125, 241; illus., 311
Binh Yen Noi, 241-243
Binh Yen Noi (3), 241
Bishko, Sgt Orest, 175

Black, Capt James O., 113, 120
Blair, Capt John D. IV, USA, 59, 62; illus., 63
Blue Beach, 22n, 168, 188
Bo River, 147, 224
Bodley, LtCol Charles H., 18, 41, 121, 125, 127
Boeing Vertol Corporation, 264
Bolster (ARS 38), 25n
Bong Son, 25, 32
Boston, Col Geoffrey H., USA, 81
Boxer Rebellion, 234n
Braun, Maj Richard, USA, 241
Brenneman, Col Richard A., 188n, 303
Bridge Cargo Facility, illus., 286
Bridge Class-60, 292
Bronars, LtCol Edward J., 168-169, 172-75, 214, 304-305
Brown, Col Leslie E., 17, 61, 115; illus., 266
Brust, 1stLt David E., 58
Buchanan, 1stLt William L., 33n
Buddha Hill, 111; illus., 111 (See also Nui Thien An)
Buddhist Institute, 84, 89-90
Burch, LtCol Carrol B., 311
Burnett, Col John R., 21, 26, 297-298, 300, 303
Butler buildings, 288

C-rations, 191; illus., 41, 209, 286
CBS, 63
Ca Lu, 142, 318
California, 246n
Callender, Col James M., 37, 276-278, 278n, 290
Cam Khe, 218-220; illus., 218-219
Cam Lo, 157-159, 161, 163-164, 174-175, 177, 179, 181-182, 184-188, 190, 195, 198, 278, 313; illus., 187
Cam Lo Combat Base, 164
Cam Lo River, 161, 163, 168, 181
Cam Lo River Valley, 174
Cam Ne, 78, 78n
Cam Ne (4), 78
Cam Ne (5), 78
Camp Carroll, 195, 198, 198n, 278; illus., 193, 279, 281
Camp Courtney, Okinawa, 9
Camp Pendleton, California, 9, 128, 128n, 284, 300, 303
Campaign Plan for 1966, US/GVN Combined, 15, 255
Campaign Plan for 1967, US/South Vietnamese Combined, 252, 254
Campaign Plan, Northeast Monsoon, 255
Campbell, Capt Thomas E., 155-156
Can Bo, 38, 38n, 45
Can, Le Thuc, 40-41, 43, 93, 227; illus., 93, 227
Can Bien River, 76
Can Gio District, 310
Cao, MajGen Huynh Van, 85-89
Cape Gloucester, 6
Caputo, Philip, 245n
Carl, BGen Marion E., 59, 61, 61n, 63, 274
Carrington, Col George W., Jr., 11, 41n, 76n, 100n, 142, 267
Carroll, Capt James J., 192, 194, 194n; illus., 193, 279
Carson, Kit, 246, 246n
Catamount (LSD 17), 24n
Cau Do River, 37, 78, 80, 102, 248 (See also Song Cau Do)

Cau Lau River, 97
Central Highlands, 9-11, 13, 157
Central Intelligence Agency, 256n, 257
Central Office of South Vietnam (COSVN), 11, illus., 11
Cereghino, Col Alexander D., 175, 177, 181-182, 186-187, 187n, 189-191, 197-198, 224; illus., 187
Chaisson, Col John R., 83, 86, 91, 142, 175, 196, 222, 285, 299, 306, 319; illus., 307
Chandler, LCdr James G., USN, 291
Charlemagne [Peralte], 231
Chau, Tam, 84, 90
Chau Nhai, 125
Chau Nhai (3), 117
Chau Nhai (4), 114-115
Chau Nhai (5), 109, 112
Chiem Son River, 204
Chieu Hoi, 245, 247
Cho River, 17
Chool, BGen Lee Bong, 223, 223n
Chu Lai, 3, 11, 14-15, 17, 17n, 18, 21, 24, 27, 34-36, 41, 48n, 51, 54, 64-65, 69, 75, 87-88, 88n, 104, 109-111, 114-115, 115n, 120, 126, 128-131, 128n, 135-136, 139-140, 177, 187, 191, 197-198, 210, 223n, 234, 239, 241, 258, 261-262, 262n, 266, 266n, 269-271, 276-277, 277n, 280-282, 284-285, 286n, 288-290, 292, 292n, 293, 300, 300n, 303, 303n, 313-314, 319; illus., 18, 129-130, 134, 211, 248, 258, 266, 270, 287-288
Chu Lai Airfield, 233; illus., 223, 262-263
Chu Lai Conference, 88-89
Chu Lai tactical area of responsibility (TAOR), 3, 6, 17-19, 75, 131, 135-136, 214, 220, 223, 241, 243n, 277-280; illus., 18
Chuan, BGen Nguyen Van, 51-52, 61, 64-65, 75, 82
Citadel, Hue, 90
Civic Action Program, 3n, 100, 247-249, 248n, 256, 291; illus., 248
Civil Operations and Revolutionary Development Support (CORDS), 257
Civilian Irregular Defense Group (CIDG), 56, 56n, 58, 58n, 59, 62, 62n, 63-64
Co Bi-Thanh Tan, 64, 69, 143, 145, 147-149, 198, 224, 226
Co, Gen Nguyen Huu, illus., 315
Coffman, LtCol Harold L., 214, 217-218, 300; illus., 217, 219
Colby, Maj Dwain A., 157-159, 163, 168, 175, 175n, 177
Combined Action Company, 47, 50, 239-244, 240n, 252; illus., 239, 241
Commandant of the Marine Corps (CMC), 8, 14n, 219, 248n, 253n, 267n, 269, 272, 283n, 285; illus., 14, 73 (See also Greene, Gen Wallace M., Jr.)
Committee on Command Relations (Okinawa Conference), 299
Compton, Capt James L., 33, 69
Con Thien, 145, 187-189, 198, 278
Constitutional Election (Vietnam), 236
Corps Tactical Zones
  I Corps Tactical Zone (I CTZ) or I Corps, 3, 7, 10-11, 13-15, 19, 21, 21n, 22, 25, 33, 43, 45, 58-59, 61, 63-64, 69, 73-75, 81-82, 84-88, 90-91, 106n, 109, 128, 131-132, 135-136, 139-140, 143, 145, 147, 161, 197, 198n, 201, 211, 221-223, 227, 234, 247, 249-250, 253, 257, 261, 269-272, 274, 280, 282, 285, 286n, 290-291, 293, 306, 307n, 310, 312, 314, 319; illus., 89, 279, 286
  I Corps Joint Coordinating Council (ICJCC), 8, 8n, 227, 231n, 249-250; illus., 249
  I Corps National Priority Area, 45, 80, 226, 234 (See also National Priority Area and National Priority Area I)

  II Corps Tactical Zone (II CTZ) or II Corps, 3, 6, 9-10, 15, 19, 21-22, 74, 253, 261, 304, 307n, 313
  III Corps Tactical Zone (III CTZ) or III Corps, 74, 188n, 253, 307n, 309, 313
  IV Corps Tactical Zone (IV CTZ) or IV Corps, 85, 253, 307n
Control and reporting center, 270
Corson, LtCol William R., 248
County Fair Operations, 47, 76, 78, 80, 93, 102, 231-234, 239, 247, 252; illus., 47, 232-233
Craven, Capt John, USN, 244, 244n
CritiPac, 287
Croizat, LtCol Victor, Jr., 308
Crowell, 1stLt Edward J., illus., 194
Cu Ban (1), 209
Cu De River, 49, 75, 85, 102
Cu De River Valley, 37
Cua Valley, 198
Cua Viet River, 161, 168, 188, 198, 289, 318
Cuong, LtCol Le Chi, 88
Cushman, MajGen Robert E., Jr., 284

Da Lat, 88-89
Da Nang (Tourane), 3, 5-6, 9, 11, 13-15, 17-18, 21, 24, 37, 40, 44, 47, 48n, 49-51, 54, 56, 58-9, 64-65, 69, 73-75, 75n, 76, 76n, 78, 80-81, 83, 83n, 84, 86-88, 90-93, 100, 102, 104, 106, 115n, 120n, 127n, 128, 130-131, 135-136, 139, 141n, 145, 145n, 161, 172, 176-177, 188, 196-198, 201, 209, 221, 223-224, 226, 231n, 232, 234, 239, 240n, 246-247, 250, 258, 263-264, 266, 266n, 268-272, 274, 276-282, 277n, 284, 284n, 285, 286n, 288-293, 292n, 300, 309, 312-314, 319; illus., 14, 43, 79, 84-85, 87, 89, 102, 129, 197, 208, 223, 226, 248, 277, 284, 286, 288, 291, 293
Da Nang Airbase, 28, 43, 74, 82, 84, 92, 102, 231; illus., 74
Da Nang Airfield, 3, 41, 276
Da Nang Harbor, 285, 287
Da Nang River, 37, 87; illus., 286, 292
Da Nang River Bridge, 86; illus., 87
Da Nang Soccer field, 84
Da Nang Special Sector, 82, 278 (See also Quang Da Special Sector)
Da Nang tactical area of responsibility (TAOR), 3, 5, 23, 37-43, 48, 48n, 49, 75-81, 102, 109, 131, 197, 222-223, 226-227, 277, 279, 281n; illus., 38, 109
Dai Giang River, 50
Dai Loc District, 43, 76, 97, 99, 106; illus., 102
Dac Cong, 236-237
Dagger Thrust operations, 299
Dai Dong, 217
Dawkins, Capt Peter, USA, 112, 113n
Dar Loc Province, 10-11
Darling, 1stLt Marshall B., 135, 219; illus., 219
Davis (DD 957), 152
Davis, Maj Thomas G., 270n
Day, Maj James L., 306
Dean, Col Clyde D., 240n

Deckhouse operations, 304
Defazio, Maj Ernest L., 25
Defense, Department of (U.S.), 262, 272, 284, 313-314, 316
Defense, Office of the Secretary of, 63
DeLong, LtCol Earl "Pappy" R., 205, 306
Demilitarized Zone (DMZ), 3, 7, 10, 15, 69, 139-140, 142, 145, 157-158, 160-161, 163, 168, 174, 174*n*, 175-177, 187-189, 195, 196*n*, 197-198, 214, 220-222, 269, 271, 274, 278, 281, 281*n*, 282, 285, 289, 292*n*, 305, 312-319; illus., 159-160, 181, 197, 280, 289, 305, 315-318
Dennis, LtCol Nicholas J., 26, 48; Col, 22*n*, 48*n*, 78*n*, 92*n*
DePlanche, Cpl Mark E., 41, 43
DePuy, BGen William E., USA, 13; MajGen, 307, 307*n*
Dewitt, Col Birchard B., 284*n*
Dickey, LtCol Robert R. III, 37, 41, 75-76, 163, 174-175, 205-206, 234
Diem, Ngo Dinh, 8, 40, 84-85
Dien Ban District, 45, 76, 83, 97, 227
Dien Binh River, 97
Dinh, Gen Ton That Dinh, 83-85
Direct air support center (DASC), 29, 164, 269, 277
Do Nam, 97, 99
Do Xa Region, 131-132, 311, 211*n*, 213; illus., 211
Doctrine for Amphibious Operations, 298*n*, 304*n* (See also Naval Warfare Publication 22A; Army Field Manual 31-11; and Marine Landing Force Manual-01)
Doehler, LtCol William F., 37, 47, 97, 99-100, 100*n*
Donahue, LtCol William F., Jr., 23, 28, 37, 47-48, 78, 83, 83*n*, 92-93, 106, 232
Donaldson, SSgt Billy M., 177, 179
Dong, BGen Du Quoc, 87
Dong Ha, 142, 145-148, 157-159, 161, 163-164, 166*n*, 168, 172, 174, 176-177, 179, 181, 186-189, 191, 195-198, 224, 267, 269, 275, 278-279, 289-290, 292*n*, 293, 313, 318; illus., 142, 160, 176, 181, 195, 289
Dong Ha Air Facility, 145-146, 161; illus., 146
Dong Ha Logistic Support Area (LSA), 289
Dong Ha Mountain, 318
Dorsey, LtCol Joshua W. III, 37, 47-48, 76, 78, 80, 97
Downey, Sgt Anthony, 192
Driver, Capt Robert J., Jr., 48, 79
Duc Pho, 21-22
Dung Quat Bay, 17
Duong Son (2), 78

Eastern Pacific, 283*n*
Egan, 1stLt James T., Jr., 24, 24*n*
Elkhorn (AOG 7), 25*n*
Elwood, BGen Hugh M., 274-275; LtGen, 7*n*, 298*n*
English, BGen Lowell E., 6, 34*n*, 51, 54, 75, 75*n*, 109, 125, 127, 127*n*, 147, 160, 163, 163*n*, 166, 166*n*, 168, 168*n*, 169, 172, 174-176, 176*n*, 195, 197, 197*n*, 198, 227; illus., 127, 163
Evans, LtCol Donald L., Jr., 227; Col, 231*n*,; illus., 249
Exercise Hill Top III, 24
Eyer, LtCol Clyde, L., 270, 270*n*

"Fake," The, 193
Far East, 297, 297*n*
Fields, MajGen Lewis J., 9, 75, 128, 130, 132, 211, 213-214, 223, 236, 300*n*; illus., 223

Fire Support Coordination Center (FSCC), 29, 269
Fisher, Maj Bernard F., USAF, 61
Fisher, Col Thell H., 37, 49, 51, 54, 64-65, 67, 69, 75, 81, 104
Fleming, Victor K., Jr., 223*n*
Fort Belvoir, Virginia, 48*n*
Fort Marion (LSD 22), 25*n*
Fort Page, 242-243
Frazer, Col Fred J., 292*n*
Fritsch, Maj Billy D., 275
Futema, Okinawa, 261, 261*n*

Galvin, 1stLt Gerald T., 186, 187*n*
Gardner, Capt Grady V., 48
Gary, Capt John H., 181
General Electric Corporation, 264
General Officers Symposium, USMC, 262
George, 1stLt Charles L., 166
Georgia I Plan, 314
Georgia II Plan, 314
Gettysburg (Battle of), 111; illus., 111
Giang Hoa (2), 208
Giao Ai outpost, 80
Giao Thuy, 100
Giao Thuy (2), 99
Giao Thuy (3), 99
Gillespie, Lt Archibald, 246*n*
Gio Linh, 145, 188-189, 318
Glaize, Capt Samuel S., 173
Gleason, LtCol Thomas E., 299*n*
Golden Fleece operations, 75-76, 78, 93, 143, 231, 234-239
Goodsell, Maj William J., 134
Gordon, Marcus, 249-250
Gorman, Col John E., 37, 45; illus., 45
Gray, Col Roy C., Jr., 58*n*, 61
Green, LtCol Fredric A., 196*n*, 197*n*
Greene, Gen Wallace M., Jr., 8, 14, 14*n*, 219, 248*n*, 253*n*, 267*n*, 269, 272, 283*n*, 285, 287; illus., 14, 73, 219 (See also Commandant of the Marine Corps [CMC])
Greenwood, Col John E., 283*n*
Gregory, 1stLt William J., 62
Griggs, Capt George R., 95, 201
Grimes, Maj George H., 204-206, 209; illus., 202
Grissett, LCpl Edwin R., 24, 24*n*
"Groucho Marx patrol," 177-181
Guadalcanal, 6, 264
Guam, 169n, 278*n*
Guay, Maj Robert P., 120
Gunning, LtCol Thomas I., 270*n*

Ha Thanh Special Forces Camp, 280
Ha Tinh, 139
Haffey, Col Eugene H., 129-130
Hahn, Col Peter H., 277*n*
Hai Van Pass, 102, 139, 143, 224, 226, 226*n*, 270, 278, 319
Haigwood, LtCol Paul B., 307
Haiti, 231
Hamblen, Col Archelaus L., Jr., USA, 86, 311
Hamlet Evaluation System (HES), 257-258
Hamlet Festival, 233
Hammerbeck, Col Edward E., 198, 198*n*

Handrahan, Capt Robert G., 193-194; Maj, 194n
Hanifin, LtCol Robert T., Jr., 50-52, 65, 67, 143, 147, 149, 154, 156, 158-159
Hanoi, 274; illus., 10
Hansen, Col Herman, Jr., 300, 303
Hardin, Capt James R., Jr., 30
Hare, Paul, 80
Harper, Col Edwin A., 261, 303
Hatch, LtCol Harold A., 37, 49, 54, 64, 141
Hau Duc, 211, 213
Hawaii, 313
HAWK missiles, 269-271, 270n; illus., 270
Hayes, Col Harold A., Jr., 104
Hazelbaker, Maj Vincil W., 179, 181
Healy, 1stLt William E., 166-168
Heintges, LtGen John A., USA, 61; illus., 30
"Helicopter Valley," 165, 168, 171-172, 174,; illus., 164, 167, 174 (See also Ngan Valley)
Henderson, BGen Melvin D., 75n
Henry, Maj Clark G., 171
Henry, Capt Norman E., 97, 99
Herbold, BGen James E., Jr., 290, 290n
Hess, LtCol John J., 175, 191, 204
Hiep Duc, 131-132, 136, 213-214, 217
Hiep Duc Valley, 214, 220 ((See also Que Son Valley)
Hieu Duc District, 45, 227
Highway 1, 85, 155, 188, 237 (See also Route 1)
Highway 9, 142 (See also Route 9)
Highway 578, 236 (See also Route 578)
Hilgartner, Maj Peter L., 299n
Hilgers, Capt John J. W., 166, 172, 183-185; 186n; illus., 185
Hill 23, 126
Hill 29, 135-136
Hill 42, 202, 204
Hill 50, 109-110, 112, 115, 117-119; illus., 117
Hill 54, 131
Hill 55, 48, 76, 78, 80, 100, 201, 270; illus., 49
Hill 65, 125
Hill 85, 109, 112
Hill 97, 109, 112
Hill 100, 169
Hill 141, 120-121, 271
Hill 163, 23, 27; illus., 25
Hill 200, 166
Hill 208, 163, 172; illus., 172
Hill 252, 181-182
Hill 327, 270
Hill 362, 173; illus., 174
Hill 400, 104, 191, 193
Hill 484, 191, 193-194; illus., 194
Hill 508, 29
Hill 555, 132
Hill 724, 270
Hill 726, 33, 33n
Hill 829, 24
Ho Chi Minh trail, 56, 140, 196n
Hoa, Capt, 81
Hoa Long, 47, 76
Hoa Nam, 99-100
Hoa Tay, 99

Hoa Tho, 248; illus., 248
Hoa Vang District, 38, 45, 81, 227
Hoa Xuan Island, 17, 19
Hoi An, 82-83, 97
Hoi An River, 97
Hoi Chanhs, 245-247; illus., 246
Honolulu Conference, 44-45, 56, 73, 139, 220, 251; illus., 45
Honolulu, Declaration of, 44
Hooper, VAdm Edwin B., USN, 7, 7n, 21n, 285, 286n, 287, 289, 297n (See also Service Force, Pacific Fleet)
Horn, LtCol William K., 29, 49, 76, 297, 300
Hotel Da Nang, illus., 83
House, LtCol Charles A., 50, 52, 59, 62, 62n, 63-64, 275; illus., 63
Howard, SSgt Jimmie L., 132, 134-135, 135n, 136, 175n, 213; illus., 134
"Howard's Hill," illus., 134 (See also Nui Vu)
Hubbard, Col Jay W., 266; illus., 266
Hue, 3, 5, 50-52, 56, 64-65, 69, 73-74, 81, 84-85, 89-90, 90n, 135, 139-140, 147-150, 155, 161, 163, 221, 224, 250, 309; illus., 139
Hue City LCU Ramp, 81
Hue City LST Ramp, 147
Hunt, Col Richard M., 164, 166n, 216
Hyland, VAdm John J., USN, 21, 303n

Ia Drang Valley, 9
Institute for Defense Analysis, 315
International Control Commission, 314
Intratheather squadron rations program, 261n
Ives, LtCol Merton R., 270n
Iwakuni, Japan, 261, 261n, 262n, 303
Iwo Jima, 176
Iwo Jima (LPH 2), 188-189; illus., 306

Jacobson, Col George D., USA, 252
Japan, 268
"Johnson City," 29, 32-33, 269
Johnson, President Lyndon B., 9, 44, 89, 139, 283, 317; illus., 45, 251
Johnson, Adm Roy L., 7, 298, 303-304, 304n (See also PacFlt)
Johnson, Deputy Ambassador to Vietnam U. Alexis, illus., 315
Johnson, Col William G., 17, 22, 22n, 29, 29n, 109-111, 120-122, 123, 134, 216
Joint Chiefs of Staff (U.S.), 13-14, 271-272, 307, 313, 315-316, 319
Joint Chiefs of Staff, General Operations Division, 307
Joint Task Force 728, 316
Jones, Col Bruce, USA, 109, 121
Jones, LtCol David G., 281
Jones, LtCol Richard E., 204
Jones, BGen William K., 65, 303n, 307, 307n, 308; illus., 307

Kadena Golf Course, Okinawa, 304n
Kane, LtCol Douglas T., 219
KANZUS, 314-314
Karch, BGen Frederick J., 17
Kelley, LtCol Paul X., 87-88, 93, 114-115, 117-118, 121, 123, 127, 145-147, 149-150, 152, 154; illus., 125

INDEX

Kelly, LtCol James P., 18, 115, 127-128
Kempner, 1stLt Marion (Sandy) L., 249
Kennedy, President John F., 13
Kenny, Capt James P., 117
Khang, LtGen Le Nguyen, 309; illus., 310
Khanh Hoa Province, 10
Khanh My (3), 125
Khe Gio River, 182 (See also Song Khe Gio)
Khe Sanh, 140-143, 195-196, 196n, 197-198, 278n, 289, 293, 318-319; illus., 196, 278
Khe Sanh Special Forces Camp, 43n, 69, 140-143; illus., 141-142
Khuong Nhon, 18
Kirchmann, LtCol Charles S., 191, 197
Kirschke, Capt James J., 173n
Kit Carson Scouts, 245-247; illus., 246
Kitterman, LtCol Warren P., 223, 239n, 258; illus., 258
Komer, Robert W., 256-257, 256n
Kontum Province, 10-11; illus., 309
Korea, 48, 181, 204, 256, 278n, 313 (See also South Korea)
Korean Armistice Line, 316
Korean War, 6
Kraft, 1stLt Noah M., 124
Krulak, LtGen Victor H., 7, 11, 13-14, 15n, 35-6, 48, 56, 128, 177, 234, 239, 243-244, 244n, 261-262, 272, 274, 280, 283n, 285, 287-290, 298, 300, 312; illus., 187, 239 (See also FMFPac)
Ky, Air Marshal Nguyen Cao, 8, 44, 64, 73-74, 81-82, 84-85, 87-88, 90, 90n, 91; illus., 45, 251, 253
Ky Ha Air Facility, 6, 19, 25, 134n, 217n, 266n
Ky Ha Peninsula, 17-18, 129
Ky Hoa Island, 18-19, 270
Ky Lam Campaign, 96-102
Ky Lam River, 3, 37, 47-48, 76, 78, 80, 92, 97, 102, 104, 106, 201, 204, 206n (See also Song Ky Lam)
Ky Long, 18
Ky Phu, 35, 217-218, 220; illus., 217
Ky Xuan Island, 18
Kyle, MajGen Wood B., 75, 78, 80, 82, 102, 104, 120, 140, 146, 149, 158, 160-161, 174, 174n, 195, 197-198, 205-207, 224, 281, 317-318; illus., 125, 163, 181, 187, 318

La Hoa (1), 106
La Tho River, 37, 47-48, 76, 78, 97, 102, 104
Lam Ap Thanh, 241-242
Lam, BGen Hoang Xuan, 21-22, 25, 34, 88, 90-91, 109, 111, 115, 117, 120-121, 125, 135-136, 147, 149, 157, 161, 227, 234, 236; illus., 89, 119, 127
Lambert, Sgt Enos S., Jr., illus., 248
Lam Loc (1), 127
Lan, Col Bui The, 309
Landing Zone Crow, 164, 166, 166n, 168, 171; illus., 164-165
Landing Zone Dixie, 205
Landing Zone Dove, 166
Landing Zone Duck, 67
Landing Zone Eagle, 65
Landing Zone Raven, 150, 152
Landing Zone Robin, 65, 67, 168
Landing Zone Savannah, 205
Landing Zone Shrike, 152
Laney, LtCol Joseph M., Jr., 280, 280n

Lanigan, Col John P., 283n
Laos, 3, 7, 139-140, 145, 149, 174n, 195, 196n, 198, 271, 274, 315, 317
Laotian panhandle, 272
Lap, LtCol, 45, 47, 81, 102
Larsen, MajGen Stanley R., USA, 22, 74; LtGen, 74, 312
Lathram, L. Wade, 256-257
Latting, Capt Charles W., 117
Lau, 1stLt James, 112
Laurence, John, 63
Lavoie, Sgt Leroy, illus., 227
Le My, 37, 44
Lee, Capt Alex, 35, 109, 113; LtCol, 88n
Lee, Capt Howard V., 179, 181, 183
Lee, Capt William F., 80, 86
Liberty Road, 201, 207, 209-210; illus., 208-209
Lieu, Mr., 238-239
Lindauer, Capt Jerry D., 112-113, 113n
Little Round Top, 111; illus., 111
Lo Bo Valley, 33n
Loan, Col Ngoc, 84, 87, 90
Loc Ban, 50
Loc Son, 135
Lodge, Ambassador Henry Cabot, Jr., 7, 44, 90, 254, 256, 313; illus., 253
Long, Maj Luther A., 275
Long Tao River, 310
Loprete, Col Joseph E., 299n
Lorelli, GySgt Jerry N., 308
Lucas, Jim, 63
Luckey, Capt Stephen A., 247
Ludwig, LtCol Verle E., 37
Ly Ly River, 216 (See also Song Ly Ly)
Ly Ly River Valley, 217 (See also Song Ly Ly Valley)

McCarthy, LtCol Edward R., 258
McClanahan, Col James F., 17, 22
MacLean, Maj Fred D., Jr., 209-210
McCutcheon, BGen Keith B., 6n; MajGen, 6, 34, 34n, 54, 56, 58, 109, 111, 118n, 126, 261-262, 268-269, 272, 298, 300; illus., 6, 45, 111
McGinty, SSgt John J., 171
McGonigal, LCdr Richard, USN, 244, 244n, 245
McGough, LtCol James D., 168, 188, 305
McMahon, Capt Daniel K., Jr., 189
McMinn, Capt Wilbur C., Jr., 63
McNamara, Secretary of Defense Robert S., 9, 44, 283-284, 314, 316-317; illus., 45, 315
MacNeil, Col John A., 308, 310
Maddocks, Capt William J., USN, 21, 26
Maginot Line, 313
Mai, Nguyen Van, 312
Mainland South East Asia Air Defense Regional Commander, 268, 270
Malaya, 8n
Mallory, Col Donald L., 226
Manila Conference, 256
Man, Dr. Nguyen Van, 73, 84, 88
Marble Mountain Air Facility, 6, 37, 47-49, 58, 76, 78, 87, 93, 104, 222, 263-264, 266n, 267; illus., 264

Maresco, Capt Richard E., 173
Marine Air Station, Iwakuni, 261
Marine Corps Landing Force Manual 01, 298n (See also *Doctrine for Amphibious Operations*)
Marine Corps Supply Activity, Philadelphia, 290n
Marine Corps Supply Center, Barstow, California, 287
Marine Corps Commands and Units
    Headquarters Marine Corps (HQMC), 75n, 175, 175n, 247, 265, 285, 308, 318
    Marine Corps Schools, Quantico, 118n, 223
    Marine Corps Development Center, Quantico, 231n
    Marine Security Detachment, Saigon, 308
    Fleet Marine Force, Pacific (FMFPac), 7, 7n, 9, 11, 14, 15n, 175n, 177, 240, 244n, 269, 272, 283n, 285, 287-288, 298, 299n, 303n, 304n, 307n; illus., 187 (See also Krulak, LtGen Victor H.)
    Marine Advisory Unit, Vietnam, 308
    Special Landing Force (SLF), 9, 21-22, 24, 27, 34, 49, 143, 161, 163, 168, 168n, 169, 174, 188, 188n, 189, 224, 261, 261n, 278n, 281n, 283n, 284-285, 297-306, 297n, 298n, 299n; illus., 28, 305 (See also Seventh Fleet)
    9th Marine Expeditionary Brigade (9th MEB), 3
    9th Marine Amphibious Brigade (9th MAB), 128n, 261, 261n, 268, 300, 303, 303n, 306
    III Marine Amphibious Force (III MAF), 3, 5-6, 6n, 7-9, 11, 13-15, 17, 19, 21, 21n, 22, 32, 34, 37, 41, 48, 51-52, 56, 58n, 59, 61, 63-65, 69, 75, 81-83, 83n, 84-88, 93, 109, 111, 120, 128, 131, 135, 140, 142-143, 145, 149-150, 157-158, 161, 175, 177, 186n, 188, 196-197, 197n, 198, 204, 207, 211, 213, 220-222, 226-227, 231, 231n, 233, 234, 239, 244, 247, 257, 261, 265, 268-269, 271-272, 274, 277, 282, 283n, 284-285, 287, 288n, 289-292, 292n, 297-300, 298n, 305, 311-313, 316-319; illus., 32, 45, 222, 287, 289, 307, 318
    III MAF Psychological Warfare Section, 247
    Chu Lai ADC Command Group, 22, 65, 129
    Chu Lai Artillery Group, 276
    Chu Lai Defense Command, 129
    Chu Lai Logistic Support Unit, 17, 29n
    Force Logistic Command (FLC), 75, 177, 226, 287-290, 290n, 319; illus., 287
    Force Logistic Support Group, 37, 287-288, 288n
    Force Logistic Support Group Alpha, 288, 290; illus., 288
    Force Logistic Support Group Bravo, 288-289; illus., 287-288
    Force Logistic Support Unit 2, 289
    Task Force Delta, 19, 22, 22n, 23-26, 28, 29n, 33, 33n, 34-35, 75, 111, 111n, 115, 118n, 125-127, 127n, 161-176, 163n, 197-198, 269, 278, 297-298; illus., 30, 34, 111, 117, 119, 127, 163
    Task Force X-Ray, 131-32, 135, 214n, 223, 280
    Task Group Foxtrot, 54, 56, 64-65, 67, 69, 75, 81
    Task Unit Charlie, 158-159
    Task Unit Hotel, 51, 52, 54
    1st Marine Division, 6, 9, 15, 19, 75, 128, 130-131, 197, 211, 213, 223, 226, 236, 246, 277-278, 281-284, 288n, 292, 292n, 299, 300n, 314, 319; illus., 129-130, 197, 223
    1st Marine Division Fire Support Coordinating Center (FSCC), 277
    3d Marine Division, 3, 5-7, 11, 22, 24, 34n, 51, 75, 78, 80, 100, 100n, 106, 109, 120, 125, 140, 142, 146-147, 149-150, 160-161, 195, 197-198, 204, 207, 210, 223-224, 240n, 258, 267, 269, 276-278, 283, 283n, 284-85, 288n, 289-290, 292, 312-319; illus., 5, 129, 163, 181, 187, 197-198, 289, 318
    3d Marine Division (Fwd), 198, 267
    3d Marine Division Drum and Bugle Corps, illus., 232
    3d Marine Division Fire Support Coordinating Center (FSCC), 277
    5th Marine Division, 278n, 284-285; illus., 284
    1st Marines, 9, 19, 104, 128, 130-131, 201, 222, 226-227, 234, 247, 277, 277n; illus., 226
    1st Battalion, 9, 37, 49, 54, 59, 64, 69, 104, 140-141, 143, 145, 145n, 149, 163, 168, 172, 174; illus., 141-142, 278
    Company A, 54, 81
    Company B, 141
    Company C, 54, 141
    Company D, 141n
    2d Battalion, 5, 9, 50-51, 65, 67, 69, 143, 145, 147, 149-150, 152, 154, 156, 158-159, 161, 163, 165n, 168, 172, 174, 276; illus., 52, 54
    Company E, 54, 67, 152, 158
    Company F, 51-52, 173
    Company G, 51-52, 152
    Company H, 152, 173
    3d Battalion, 19, 21-25, 30, 34, 114, 117, 119, 121, 124, 130, 135, 222, 284n
    Company I, 25, 115, 117-118
    Company L, 115, 117-118
    3d Platoon, 117
    Company M, 25, 115, 117-118; illus., 117
    3d Marines, 5, 18, 37, 41, 47-51, 54, 69, 75, 80, 86, 104, 141n, 198, 198n, 201, 204-205, 226, 234, 276-278; illus., 197
    1st Battalion, 37, 41, 75-76, 161, 163, 174-175, 196, 197n, 205-206, 226n, 234, 278n; illus., 196, 207
    2d Battalion, 9, 21-24, 29-30, 34, 37, 49, 75-76, 226n, 297, 300; illus., 28
    Company E, 27, 29
    Company F, 30
    3d Battalion, 37, 47-48, 76, 78-80, 86, 97, 102, 205, 240n, 284, 306; illus., 38, 49
    Company I, 48
    Company K, 51-52, 54, 80
    Company L, 80, 86
    Company M, 86
    4th Marines, 5, 17-19, 22, 22n, 65, 69, 111, 140, 143, 146-150, 154-158, 161, 169, 175, 177, 186n, 188-189, 198, 224, 276-277, 277n, 314; illus., 148, 152, 156, 187
    Headquarters Company, 148n
    1st Battalion, 17, 19, 36, 64-65, 90n, 143, 145, 152, 156, 181, 187, 189-190, 197n, 198, 224, 284n
    H&S Company, 184, 188
    Company A, 64-65, 67, 186-187
    Company B, 64-65, 67, 189
    Company D, 121, 123, 189
    2d Battalion, 18-19, 22-24, 26-27, 29, 34, 87-88, 93, 97, 104, 114-115, 117-118, 121, 123, 127, 130, 145-147, 149-150, 152, 154, 156-157, 161, 163, 166, 166n, 167-169, 172, 174-175, 177, 181-183, 185-186, 186n, 187-188, 197n, 224; illus., 18, 26, 30, 123, 125, 146, 172, 174, 184-185, 187, 279
    Company E, 25, 27, 29, 121, 150, 152, 154, 166, 171, 179, 181-186, 186n, 188; illus., 25, 181, 184
    Company F, 121, 150, 177, 181-182, 184-186, 186n, 188, 190

INDEX

Company G, 33, 33n, 117, 166-167, 171, 177, 182, 184-185, 188; illus., 167
Company H, 117, 150, 152, 166, 169, 172, 181, 185
  1st Platoon, 172
3d Battalion, 9, 47, 65, 69, 81, 90n, 142-143, 149-150, 156, 158, 161, 163-164, 166, 166n, 167-169, 171-172, 174, 191, 195, 197n; illus., 165, 167, 169, 195
Company I, 150, 154, 156, 166, 171, 192-193
Company K, 166-169, 171-172, 191; illus., 193-194, 279
  1st Platoon, 171
Company L, 154, 156, 166-168, 171, 191-192, 166
Company M, 192-4; illus., 192, 194
  1st Platoon, 193-194
  2d Platoon, 193-194
5th Marines, 6, 9, 128, 130, 135, 214, 214n, 216-217, 219-220, 223, 277, 277n, 280, 303, 309; illus., 214, 217
1st Battalion, 130-131, 143, 214, 217, 219, 300; illus., 217, 219, 300
Company A, 218
Company C, 134-135, 218-219; illus., 218-219
2d Battalion, 130, 197, 197n, 198, 214, 217, 220, 303n; illus., 216, 218
Company E, 136
3d Battalion, 130-131, 163, 168, 168n, 169, 171-175, 173n, 214, 284, 303; illus., 176
Company H, illus., 213
Company I, 168, 173, 173n; illus., 174
  1st Platoon, 173
  2d Platoon, 173
Company K, 168, 173
Company L, 168
Company M, 169
7th Marines, 5, 9, 17-19, 22, 29n, 36, 109, 111, 120-121, 125, 127-129, 131, 223, 223n, 236, 276-277, 280; illus., 111, 131
1st Battalion, 9, 18-19, 115, 127-128, 130, 234, 241, 243n; illus., 130, 236-238
Company A, 237-238
Company B, 117-118
Company C, 128, 242-243
2d Battalion, 9, 18-19, 34-35, 88n, 109-111, 114-115, 118-119, 128, 128n, 187, 189-191, 197n, 223, 239n, 258; illus., 111, 113, 187, 190, 258
Company E, 35, 88n, 110
Company F, 88n, 112-113, 191; illus., 110
  1st Platoon, 110
  2d Platoon, 112-113
Company G, 110, 112, 190-191
Company H, 110, 112-114
3d Battalion, 9, 18, 41, 120-121, 123, 125-126, 197n, 198, 284n; illus., 40
Company I, 121, 126
Company K, 126
Company L, 126
9th Marines, 5, 37-38, 40, 47-48, 54, 76, 78-80, 83, 87, 92-93, 97, 100, 102, 104, 106, 145n, 197, 201, 204-205, 207, 210, 221, 226-227, 231-232, 234, 244n, 277, 292n; illus., 45, 47, 49, 83
1st Battalion, 37, 47, 75, 97, 99-100, 104, 204, 208, 306; illus., 102
Company A, 97, 99-100

Company B, 97, 99; illus., 100
Company C, 100, 106
Company D, 99
2d Battalion, 23-24, 28, 34, 37, 47, 78, 83, 92, 104, 106, 172, 175, 191, 197n, 204, 224, 232; illus., 38
Company E, 48, 78-80, 83
Company F, 51, 54, 78, 83, 104
Company G, 41
Company H, 83, 92; illus., 79
  2d Platoon, 92
3d Battalion, 37, 47, 76, 78, 80, 93, 95, 97, 104, 202, 204-210; illus., 93, 95-96, 201-202, 291
Company I, 93, 202-204, 209-210
Company K, 202, 204, 206, 209-210
Company L, 93, 202, 204
Company M, 78-80, 95, 202, 204
11th Marines, 9, 128, 277, 277n, 278, 278n, 279
1st Battalion, 277, 279; illus., 248
Battery B, 50n
Battery D, 213
4.2-inch Mortar Battery, 50n, 128, 173, 214
2d Battalion, 277, 280
Battery D, 135
Battery E, 211
Battery F, 280
3d Battalion, 17, 115n, 118, 120, 123, 276-277, 280
Battery G, 236
Battery H, 26, 29, 224
4th Battalion, 135-136, 277, 279, 280n
Battery K, 115, 135
Battery M, 27, 110, 113, 115, 120

12th Marines, 5, 37, 96, 135, 198, 204, 276-278, 278n, 281, 281n, 290
1st Battalion, 37, 41, 276-278; illus., 277
Battery A, 206n
Battery B, 93, 147
Battery C, 56
2d Battalion, 37, 79, 99, 206n, 276-277, 279
Battery D, 206n, 209-210
Battery E, 206n
Battery F, 93, 206n
3d Battalion, 17, 69, 90n, 147, 150, 154-155, 161, 164, 168, 171, 181, 186-187, 224, 276-278, 281
Battery G, 177
Battery H, 24, 33, 158; illus., 279
Battery M, illus., 281
107mm Mortar Battery, 27
4th Battalion, 5, 50, 50n, 51, 69, 276-278, 281
Headquarters Battery, 50n
Battery K, 135, 277
Battery L, 206n, 277
Battery M, 50n
Provisional Battery Y (Yankee Battery), 50n, 67, 69, 135
13th Marines, 278n; illus., 280
Battery B, 278n
Battery D, illus., 280
15th Marines, 278n
26th Marines, 224n, 278n, 284-285, 303, 306, 314; illus., 280, 284

1st Battalion, 188, 188n, 284, 305; illus., 246, 280, 284, 305-306
  Company A, 188-189
  Company B, 189
  Company D, 189
2d Battalion, 224, 226n, 284
3d Battalion, 224, 285n, 305-306
  Company I, illus., 224
1st ANGLICO (Air and Naval Gunfire Liaison Company) Force Troops, FMFPac, 311
  Sub-Unit 1, 1st ANGLICO, 311; illus., 311
1st Amphibian Tractor Battalion, 48
  Company B, 93
1st Armored Amphibian Company, 281n
1st 8-inch Howitzer Battery (Self-Propelled) (-), 276, 279
  1st Platoon, 276
1st Engineer Battalion, 128, 292, 292n
1st Field Artillery Group (FAG), 280
1st Force Reconnaissance Company, 24, 33, 132, 135, 157-158, 168, 177, 181, 213
1st Force Service Battalion, 288, 288n
1st 155mm Gun Battery (SP), 277-78
1st Hospital Company, 290
1st LAAM Battalion, 270-71
  Headquarters Battery, 270
  Battery A, 270
  Battery B, 270
  Battery C, 270
1st Medical Battalion, 128, 290
1st MP Battalion, 102
1st Motor Transport Battalion, 128
1st Raider Battalion, 6
1st Reconnaissance Battalion, 132, 135-136, 211, 213
  Company A, 211
1st Shore Party Battalion, 128
1st Tank Battalion, 128
2d LAAM Battalion, 270; illus., 270
  Battery A, 270
  Battery B, 271
  Battery C, 271
3d Anti-Tank Battalion, 177
3d Engineer Battalion, 22n, 48, 48n, 92n, 177, 201, 292, 292n; illus., 293
  Company B, 26
3d Force Service Regiment, 261n, 288, 288n, 290, 303n
3d Medical Battalion, 290-291
3d 8-inch Howitzer Battery, 280n
3d 155mm Gun Battery, 27, 276, 280n
  3d Platoon, 276
3d Reconnaissance Battalion, 69, 93, 188
  Company A, 157-158
    3d Platoon, illus., 160
  Company B, 33, 69, 157
  Company D, 69
3d Shore Party Battalion, 286n
3d Tank Battalion, 177, 248; illus., 248
  Company C, 181-82, 188
7th Engineer Battalion, 292, 292n
9th Engineer Battalion, 292, 292n
11th Engineer Battalion, 292, 292n

Da Nang Base Defense Battalion, 37, 47, 97
Reconnaissance Group Bravo, 69, 157-58
  Detachment A, 159
1st Marine Aircraft Wing (1st MAW), 3, 5-6, 7n, 33, 34n, 58n, 61, 61n, 63, 123, 126, 150, 161, 219, 250, 261-275, 261n, 262n, 283, 292n, 293, 319; illus., 45, 249
1st Marine Aircraft Wing (Rear), 261
Marine Wing Headquarters Group (MWHG) 1, 270
Marine Wing Service Group (MWSG) 17, 261, 261n, 303n
Marine Aircraft Group (MAG) 11, 5, 25, 37, 80, 109, 126, 164, 164n, 171, 179, 188, 202, 216, 261, 266, 290
Marine Aircraft Group (MAG) 12, 5, 17, 25, 61, 80, 109, 114-115, 121, 126, 164, 164n, 171, 202, 204, 216, 218, 261, 266; illus., 266
Marine Aircraft Group (MAG) 13, 261, 262n, 266, 303; illus., 262
Marine Aircraft Group (MAG) 15, 262n
Marine Aircraft Group (MAG) 16, 6, 37, 41, 63, 83, 93, 110, 148, 150, 168, 173, 175-177, 179, 181, 188, 190-191, 204, 216, 261-262, 266
Marine Aircraft Group (MAG) 36, 6, 17, 22n, 24, 27-29, 29n, 109-110, 114-115, 120-121, 134, 176, 214, 216, 261-262, 264n
Marine Composite Reconnaissance Squadron (VMCJ) 1, 264, 274
Marine Air Support Squadron (MASS) 2, 29, 269
Marine Observation Squadron (VMO) 2, 62-63, 99, 150, 173, 177, 179, 185, 201-202, 266n
Marine Observation Squadron (VMO) 3, 266n
Marine Air Support Squadron (MASS) 3, 269
Marine Air Control Squadron (MACS) 6, 261
Marine Observation Squadron (VMO) 6, 3n, 27-28, 33, 33n, 109, 111, 120n, 121, 123-124, 134, 218, 264n, 266n
Marine Air Control Squadron (MACS) 7, 269
Headquarters and Maintenance Squadron (H&MS) 11, 267
Headquarters and Maintenance Squadron (H&MS) 12, 267
Headquarters and Maintenance Squadron (H&MS) 13, 267
Headquarters and Maintenance Squadron (H&MS) 16, 267
Headquarters and Maintenance Squadron (H&MS) 17, 267
Headquarters and Maintenance Squadron (H&MS) 36, 267
Marine Aerial Refueler Transport Squadron (VMGR) 152, 161, 176, 261, 268, 274-275
Marine Medium Helicopter Squadron (HMM) 161, 6, 152, 168, 179, 181
Marine Medium Helicopter Squadron (HMM) 163, 6, 50-52, 54, 59, 161-63, 67, 124, 147, 168, 275, 306; illus., 63
Marine Medium Helicopter Squadron (HMM) 164, 79, 150, 164, 166, 168, 204-205, 263; illus., 263
Marine Medium Helicopter Squadron (HMM) 165, 164, 166, 264
Marine Attack Squadron (VMA) 214, 99
Marine Fighter Squadron (VMF) 232 (All-Weather), 265; illus., 265
Marine Fighter Squadron (VMF) 235 (All-Weather), 99
Marine Fighter Squadron (VMF) 242 (All-Weather), 264
Marine Medium Helicopter Squadron (HMM) 261, 25, 110, 117, 120, 264, 297
Marine Medium Helicopter Squadron (HMM) 265, 177, 179, 202, 204-205, 263
Marine Aerial Refueler Transport Squadron (VMGR) 352, 176

Marine Medium Helicopter Squadron (HMM) 361, illus., 214
Marine Medium Helicopter Squadron (HMM) 362, 27, 29, 297, 305; illus., 297
Marine Medium Helicopter Squadron (HMM) 363, 6, 58, 110, 168, 188, 261, 305
Marine Medium Helicopter Squadron (HMM) 364, 110, 118, 303, 305,
Marine Fighter Attack Squadron (VMFA) 531, 109
Marine Fighter Attack Squadron (VMFA) 542, 99, 120
Market Time, 303
Martin, Col Glen E., 35, 129
Marton (DD 948), 106
Masterpool, LtCol William J., 191-193, 195
Mekong Delta, 253, 306
Mendenhall, LtCol Herbert E., 205
"Military and Civilian Struggle Committee for I Corps," 74 (See also "Struggle Force)
Military Region (MR-4), 11
Military Region 5 (MR-5), 10-11, 131, 211
Military Transport Management Terminal Service (MTMTS), 285
Mindoro, Philippines, 24, 300
Mitchell, Col Bryan B., 19, 104, 130, 226
Mixmaster Operation, 283*n*
Mo Duc, 234, 236, 238-239, 239*n*; illus., 236-238
Modrzejewski, Capt Robert J., 166-168, 171
Mole, Chaplain Robert L., USN, 244*n*
Monkey Mountain, 270
Monfort, Maj Robert A., 173*n*
Monsoon, Northwest, 198, 313; illus., 197
Montagnards, 56*n*; illus., 196
Monti, LtCol Anthony A., 188-189, 305
Monticello (LSD 35), 24*n*, 297*n*
Montrose (APA 212), 24*n*, 297*n*
Moore, Capt Brian D., 25, 27
Moore, Col Harold G., USA, 32
Moore, MajGen Joseph H., USAF, 268-269, 272
Moore, LtCol Walter, 214, 217, 220
Morrest, illus., 263
Morris, Maj McLendon G., 310
Morrow, Maj Samuel M., 93, 95, 164, 171, 174*n*, 176, 181, 187, 187*n*; Col, 90*n*
Morton (DD 948), 136
Moss, LtCol Roy E., 9
Museum Landing Ramp, illus., 286
Mutter Ridge, 189-194, 198; illus., 195, 279 (See also Nui Cay Tre)
My Hue, 241-242
My Loc (3), 202
My Loc (4), 202
My Phu, 152, 154, 156
Myers, Maj Dafford W., USAF, 61

Nam O Bridge, 85
National Junior Chamber of Commerce, 248*n*
National Military Command Center (U.S.), 307
National Priority Area, 227, 254
National Priority Area I (NPA I), 45 (See also I Corps National Priority Area under Corps)
Naval Academy (U.S.), 131, 226,
Naval gunfire, 33, 65, 106, 106*n*, 136, 150, 152, 156, 189, 236

Naval Warfare Publication 22A, 298*n*, 299, 304, 304*n* (See also Doctrine)
Navarro (APA 215), 25*n*
Navy, Secretary of the, 74
Navy, U.S., 7, 106*n*, 150, 175*n*, 181, 198, 208, 236, 241, 243, 249, 285, 286*n*, 289-291, 292*n*, 298, 298*n*, 303-304, 304*n*; illus., 248, 286, 311
Navy Commands and Units
  Naval Air Systems Command, 264
  Commander in Chief Pacific Command (CinCPac), 6-7, 13, 15*n*, 21*n*, 44, 84, 145, 161, 197*n*, 274, 299-300, 304, 304*n*; illus., 251 (See also Sharp, Adm Ulysses S.G.)
  Pacific Fleet (PacFlt), 7, 21*n*, 75, 298-299, 299*n*, 303, 303*n*, 304 (See also Johnson, Adm Roy L.)
  Service Force, Pacific Fleet, 7, 21*n*, 285 (See also Hooper, VAdm Edwin B.)
  Seventh Fleet, 9, 21, 21*n*, 22, 65, 143, 161, 168, 175, 188, 261, 261*n*, 274, 285, 297, 297*n*, 298-299, 300*n*, 303, 303*n*, 304*n*, 305
  Amphibious Group I, 297*n*
  Seventh Fleet Amphibious Ready Group, 21
  Task Force 76, 21*n*, 299*n*
  Task Force 79, 21*n*, 128*n*, 300, 300*n*
  Task Group 79.2, 306
  Task Group 79.5, 306
  U.S. Naval Forces, Vietnam, 74-75
  Naval Advisory Group, Vietnam, 8, 308, 310
  Naval Component Commander, Vietnam, 7-8, 75, 286
  30th Naval Construction Regiment (NCR), 288-289
  Naval Mobile Construction Battalions, 7 (See also Seabees)
  Naval Mobile Construction Battalion (NMCB) 4, 288
  Naval Support Activity, Da Nang, 7, 75, 286*n*, 289-90; illus., 286
  Rung Sat Special Zone Advisory Detachment, 310
Needham, Maj Michael J., 110
Nelson, LtCol William L., 29*n*
New Life Program, 257
New York Times, 283
New Yorker, 157
New Zealand, 256, 313-314
Ngan River, 172 (See also Song Ngan)
Ngan Valley, 163-165 (See also Song Ngan Valley and "Helicopter Valley")
Ngu Hanh Son, 38, 40, 43, 45
Nha Ngu River, 217
Nha Trang, 58-59
Nhat, Maj, 81
Nhuan, BGen Pham Xuan, 74, 85-86, 89-90, 147, 149
Nicaragua, 231
Nickerson, MajGen Herman, Jr., 223, 226, 246, 246*n*, 281-282; illus., 283
Nong River, 50
Nong Son, 40, 227
Noon, Sgt Patrick J., Jr., 185-186
Norris, Col Glenn E., 279-80
North Carolina Contingency Plan, 313-314
North Vietnam (Democratic Republic of Vietnam), 3, 7, 9, 11, 58, 139, 145, 195, 264-265, 271-272, 274, 316; illus., 157
North Vietnamese Army (NVA), 9-11, 15*n*, 21, 30, 32, 36, 61, 65, 69, 75, 88*n*, 109, 112, 113*n*, 114, 117-119, 131-132, 134,

136, 139, 140, 145, 147, 149, 152, 154, 157-160, 166, 167-169, 171-173, 175, 175n, 177, 179, 171-182, 184-185, 186n, 196n, 197n, 198, 216-219, 221, 253-255, 297, 303, 305, 312, 316, 319; illus., 117, 157, 190, 197 (See also People's Army of Vietnam)
North Vietnamese Army Units
  1st NVA Division, 10
  2d NVA Division, 10, 131 213-214, 220 (See also *620th NVA Division*)
  3d NVA Division, 10
  304th NVA Division, 177
  324B NVA Division, 139, 145, 157, 160-161, 163, 172, 175-177, 186-189, 198; illus., 172
  325th NVA Division, 58
  341st NVA Division, 177, 198
  620th NVA Division, 131 (See also *2d NVA Division*)
  1st NVA Regiment, 131
  3d NVA Regiment, 9, 131, 135, 213, 219
    1st Battalion, 216
  6th NVA Regiment, 140, 147, 149-150, 156, 224
  11th NVA Battalion, 127
  18th NVA Regiment, 10, 23, 30, 32-33
  21st NVA Regiment, 10, 109, 112, 115n, 121, 127, 131, 213; illus., 113
  22d NVA Regiment, 10
  32d NVA Regiment, 9-10
  33d NVA Regiment, 9-10
  66th NVA Regiment, 10
  90th NVA Regiment, 160, 163, 176, 188
  95th NVA Regiment, 23, 56, 58, 64, 69, 149-150; illus., 59
  409th NVA Battalion, 242
  803d NVA Regiment, 160, 176, 182, 186-187, 187n
  806th NVA Battalion, 150, 154, 156
  808th NVA Battalion, 149-150
  812th NVA Regiment, 160, 176, 187
    5th Battalion, 160
    6th Battalion, 174
  812th NVA Battalion, 150, 156
North Vietnam Government, 312
North Vietnamese National Defense Council, illus., 11
Northern Route Package Areas, 265
Nui Cay Tre, 177, 182, 189-194; illus., 192-195 (See also Mutter Ridge)
Nui Coi, 236
Nui Dau, 25
Nui Loc Son, 132
Nui Nham, 236
Nui Thien An, 111 (See Buddha Hill)
Nui Vu, 132, 134, 136, 213, 213n; illus., 134 (See also "Howard's Hill")
Nui Xuong Giong, 27
Nung, 111n, 141

O Lau River, 147, 150, 155, 224 (See also Song O Lau)
O'Connor, Capt Martin E., 113, 113n
O'Connor, Col Thomas J., 37, 63, 266
Office of Civil Operations (OCO), 256
Okinawa, 9, 65, 75, 128, 128n, 130, 145, 224, 224n, 261n, 264n, 268, 274, 278n, 280, 283n, 284-85, 288n, 289-290, 298-300, 303, 303n, 304n, 306; illus., 264

Okinawa Conference, 299
Oklahoma City (CLG 5), 25, 25n
Operations
  Athens, 143, 149, 156
  Beaver, 147
  Cherokee, 143, 224
  Chinook, 198, 224-226, 281, 314; illus., 224
  Colorado, 214-220, 214n, 309; illus., 213-214, 216-218, 220
  Cormorant, 231n
  County Fair 11, 232
  County Fair 4-11, 234
  Deckhouse I, 304-305
  Deckhouse II, 163, 168, 168n, 169, 305
  Deckhouse III, 188n, 305
  Deckhouse IV, 188-189, 305; illus., 305-6
  Deckhouse V, 306
  Doan Ket, 147-148
  Dodge, 149
  Double Eagle, 19-36, 22n, 47-48, 48n, 109, 114, 269, 278, 297-298, 300; illus., 23, 26, 28, 30-32, 34
  Double Eagle I, illus., 35
  Double Eagle II, 34-35, 49, 131; illus., 35, 213
  Florida, 147-49, 148n, 156, 224; illus., 148, 224
  Fresno, 234, 236, 243n
  Georgia, 93-96, 97, 202; illus., 93, 95
  Golden Fleece II, 75, 80
  Golden Fleece 7-1, 234-239, 239n, 243n; illus., 236-237
  Harvest Moon, 11, 19, 21, 22n, 34-35, 131, 217; illus., 213
  Hastings, 159-176, 164n, 168n, 169n, 177, 188n, 201, 214, 274-275, 289, 291, 305, 309, 312; illus., 161, 163, 211
  Holt, 156
  Hot Springs, 131; illus., 131
  Indiana, 127-28, 131
  Jackstay, 300; illus., 300
  Jay, 150-156; illus., 152, 156
  Kansas, 131-136, 211, 211n, 213; illus., 211, 213
  Kings, 78-80, 92-93, 96-97; illus., 79
  Lam Son-234, 51, 56
  Lam Son-235, 42, 52, 56
  Lam Son-236, 52, 56
  Lam Son-245, 65, 67
  Lam Son-283, 150
  Lam Son-284, 150, 154
  Lam Son-285, 155
  Lam Son-289, 161, 163, 176; illus., 161
  Liberty, 102-106, 201
  Lien Ket-22, 25, 34
  Lien Ket-52, 214-20
  Macon, 201-210, 206n; illus., 202, 205-207
  Mallard, 18, 41, 43, 93, 208; illus., 40-41, 43-44
  Masher, 25, 33
  Nathan Hale, 304
  New York, 51-53, 54, 56; illus., 52, 54
  Oregon, 65-69, 140, 150, 150n 152
  Osage, 143, 303
  Pawnee III, 224
  Prairie, 177-198, 197n, 201, 224, 274, 290-291, 305, 309, 312, 314; illus., 182, 197, 266, 280, 305
  Reno, 146-147, 157; illus., 146, 263, 279
  Sierra, 239n

Starlite, 11
Texas, 120-127, 131; illus., 123, 127, 291
Thang Phong II, 25
Troy, 54
Turner, 150
Utah, 109-119, 125, 131; illus., 110-111, 113-114, 119
Virginia, 140-143; illus., 141-142, 278
Washington, 211-213; illus., 211
Wayne, 143
White Wing, 33
Orsburn, Capt Lyndell M., 80

Pace, Sgt Robert L., 179
Pacific, illus., 284
"Pacification, Giving New Thrust to," 256
Padalino, Col Mauro J., 37, 287-288
Padley, Col John J., 306
Page, PFC Lawrence L., 242
Page, LtCol Leslie L., 23, 26, 32, 69, 276-277
Parker, 1stLt Richard F., Jr., 24
Parry, Col Francis F., 143, 303n, 304n, 307, 307n
Paul Revere (APA 248), 24n, 297
Paull, 1stLt Jerome T., 132
Pavlovskis, Capt Valdis V., 202, 204
Peace Corps, 249
Peatross, Col Oscar F., 18-19, 21, 75, 109, 111, 120, 120n, 121, 125, 127-128, 128n, 129; MajGen, 29n, 114n, 115n, 118n, 127n; illus., 111, 127
Peliliu, 6
Penico, Maj Edward F., 270, 270n
Pensacola Naval Air Station, 262
Pentagon, 143
Pentagon Papers, 256
People's Army of Vietnam (PAVN), 44, 112 (See also North Vietnamese Army)
Personal Response, 243-245, 244n
Pettengill, Capt Harold D., 169
Petty, Col Douglas D., Jr., 261; illus., 262
Phase Line Bravo, 152
Phase Line Brown, 97, 102
Phase Line Delta, 152
Phase Line Golf, 152
Phase Line Green, 102, 106
Philippine Insurrection, 234n
Philippine Islands, 9, 22, 24, 188n, 256, 268, 300, 305, 313
Pho Lai, 51-52
Phong Bac, 47, 248; illus., 47
Phong Dien District Town, 65, 67, 150, 155, 224
Phong Dien District, 52, 224
Phong Ho (2), 104
Phong Thu, 80, 92
Phu Bai, 5, 9, 14-15, 60-66, 59, 61, 61n, 62-65, 67, 69, 75, 81, 90n, 104, 136, 140-143, 145, 145n, 147-150, 156-158, 166, 176-177, 181, 191, 197-198, 223-224, 239, 269, 276-278, 281, 288-290, 318-319; illus., 54, 63, 129, 197, 275-276, 318
Phu Bai Airfield, 143, 148
Phu Bai tactical area of responsibility (TAOR), 5, 47, 51-52, 56, 166, 224, 277
Phu Bai Vital Area, 143, 145, 149
Phu Lac (6), 209

Phu Loc District, 54, 143, 224, 303
Phu Long (1), 95, 208
Phu Long (2), 208
Phu Tay (3), 80
Phu Thu Peninsula, 52, 54; illus., 52
Phuoc Loc, 125
Phuoc Loc (1), 126-127
Phuong Dinh (2), 121, 123-127; illus., 125-126
Pickaway, (APA 222), 300
Pierce, SSgt Charles W., illus., 206
Pineapple Forest, 220
Pittman, LCpl Richard A., 173, 173n
Planning Directive, Southwest Monsoon, 255
Platt, BGen Jonas M., 6, 17, 19, 21-24, 22n, 26-30, 32-35, 75, 85-86, 109, 111, 114-115, 117-118, 120, 247, 269, 276, 278, 298; MajGen, 262; illus., 30, 32, 111, 117, 119, 307
Pleiku, 61
Peliku Province, 10-11
Pleiku-Qui Nhon Axis, 13
Polk, President [James K.], 246n
Popular Force (PF), 40, 47, 52, 76, 81, 93, 111n, 154, 210, 227, 239-244, 252, 255; illus., 239
"Popular Forces to Struggle for the Revolution," 74 (See also "Struggle Force")
Porter, LtCol Mervin B., 117, 297; illus., 297
Porter, Deputy Ambassador William J., 44, 85, 251-252, 256
Powell, LCpl Raymond L., 173
Practice Nine Requirement Plan, 318 (See also Barrier)
Prewitt, Capt Robert C., 118
Princeton, (LPH 5), 175, 300, 303
Psychological Warfare, 247
Psychological Warfare Operations Center, 247
Pullar, Col Walter S., Jr., 226n

Quang, Thich Tri, 84, 89-90
Quang Da Special Sector, 102 (See also Quang Nam Special Sector)
Quang Dien District, 51, 150
Quang Nam Province, 3, 11, 34, 40, 64, 78, 92, 131, 213, 221
Quang Nam Special Sector, 40, 82 (See also Quang Da Special Sector),
Quang Ngai Airfield, 28-29, 110, 118, 120, 280
Quang Ngai City, 3, 10, 17, 22, 24-25, 28, 84, 109, 111, 115, 121, 280
Quang Ngai Drama Team, illus., 232
Quang Ngai Province, 3, 5, 7, 10, 15, 17-19, 21-22, 24, 33, 35, 58, 110-111, 120, 136, 223, 234, 236, 247, 282, 297, 311; illus., 34, 236, 311
Quang Tin Province, 3, 5, 10-11, 17, 34, 131, 136, 213
Quang Tri City, 52, 58, 64, 90, 145, 148-150, 318
Quang Tri Province, 3, 10-11, 15, 43n, 51-52, 58, 69, 139-140, 149-150, 157-158, 160-161, 163-164, 168, 189, 195, 197-198, 274, 280-281, 289, 310, 312-313, 317; illus., 197
Quang Xuyen District, 310
Quantico, Virginia, 231n
Que Son, 120, 213, 213n, 214, 216-217
Que Son Mountains, 40; illus., 201
Que Son Valley, 11, 34-35, 131-132, 135-136, 213, 220, 297, 309; illus., 35, 134, 213
Qui Nhon, 6, 9, 13, 25, 90, 261

Ram, Capt Cornelius H., 216
Rand Corporation, 10*n*
Razorback, 183-186, 189-191; illus., 183-185, 190-191
Read, Col Benjamin S., 198, 278, 278*n*
Read, Col Robert R., 247
Reckewell, Capt Carl A., 78, 83, 83*n*, 104
Red Ball, 287
Red Beach, 22, 22*n*, 23-27, 29-30, 288; illus., 26-27
Redfield, LtCol Heman J. III, 308
Reed, Cpl Paul M., 186*n*
Regional Force (RF), 40, 47, 52, 76, 81, 111, 210, 252, 255; illus., 207
Repose (AH 16), 291
Reserves (U.S.), 283, 283*n*, 284
Revolutionary Development, 227, 251-253, 253*n*, 254-256
Revolutionary Development Teams (Cadres), 45, 251-252
Richards, Col Robert M., 226
Richard B. Anderson (DD 786), 67
Richardson, 1stLt Terril J., 118
Roane, Capt Everette S., 92
Robertshaw, MajGen Louis B., 216, 250, 262, 265, 269, 271; illus., 249, 262
Rockpile, 159-160, 164, 168, 172, 174-175, 177, 179, 181-183, 186-187, 189-191, 195, 198, 275; illus., 159, 183-184, 187, 190
Roles & Missions, Jacobson Task Force on, 253
Rolling Thunder, 272, 274
Romine, Maj Richard E., 311
Roothoff, LtCol John J., 187, 190; illus., 187
Rosson, MajGen William B., USA, 34, 307, 307*n*
"Rough Rider" road convoys, 139, 176
Route 1, 17-18, 37-38, 50, 52, 54, 64-65, 82, 85, 97, 109, 121, 125, 131, 135, 139, 143, 145, 147-148, 150, 154, 161, 163, 168, 176, 189, 213, 217, 224, 232, 236-237, 318 (See also Highway 1)
Route 4, 76, 78-80, 92, 82*n*, 97, 100, 104, 201, 207
Route 9, 140, 142, 157, 163-164, 181-82, 185, 187, 196*n*, 313, 318; illus., 142, 182 (See also Highway 9)
Route 527, 109, 121, 125, 127
Route 534, 131
Route 535, 131
Route 537, 205, 209
Route 597, 65, 150, 152
Route Package 1 (RP-1), 271, 274
Royal Palace (Hue), illus., 139
Rudzis, LtCol Edwin M., 50, 56, 69, 276-277; Col, 50*n*
Rung Sat Special Zone, 300, 310; illus., 300
Rural Reconstruction, 38, 40, 44-45, 78
Rusk, Secretary of State Dean, 44; illus., 253
Ryan, BGen Michael P., 303, 306
Ryman, Capt Roger K., 192

Safeguard (ARS 25), 25*n*
Saigon, 13, 40, 73, 82, 84, 90, 115, 161, 195, 286*n*, 300, 307-310, 312; illus., 253, 286, 300
St. Clair, Col Howard B., USA, 310
Saint Paul (CA 73), 189
San Diego, California 188*n*
Sandino [Augusto], 231
Savage, LtCol Richard A., 126

Save-A-Plane, 277
Seabees, 7, 17, 37, 210, 270, 288, 291-292; illus., 292 (See also Navy Command and Units)
Seaman, LtGen Jonathan O., USA, 74
Senior U.S. Advisor for I Corps, 7
Sensor, electronic acoustic, 315
Sensor, seismic, 315
17th Parallel, 274, 317; illus., 275
Seymour, Capt William D., 112
Shakespeare [William], 282
Shaplen, Robert, 157, 186*n*
Sharp, Adm Ulysses S. Grant, 6-7, 13, 21, 21*n*, 44, 211, 253, 253*n*, 256, 268, 271-272, 300, 303, 305, 307, 313, 315, 319; illus., 251 (See also CinCPac)
Shaver, Capt William C., 24, 33
Sherman, Col Donald W., 22, 65, 69, 140, 147-150, 152, 154-156, 158, 161; illus., 148
Sherman, 2dtLt Andrew W., 179
Shylo, Cpl John J., illus., 241
Short airfield for tactical support (SATS), 17, 17*n*, 129, 262*n*, 263
Short Stop Contingency Plan, 313
Silverlance Exercise, 244*n*
Simmons, Col Edwin H., 14, 41, 41*n*, 45, 47, 76, 78, 82-83, 92, 96-97, 100, 102, 104, 202, 204, 245-246, 261; BGen, 58*n*, 83*n*; illus., 45
Single management of air, 269
Skagit, 25*n*
Small Wars Manual, 231
Smith, 1stLt Charles D., Jr., 275
Smith, LtCol Conway J., illus., 293
Snoddy, Col Lawrence F., Jr., 236, 236*n*, 243 (See also Snowden, LtGen Lawrence F.)
Snowden, LtGen Lawrence F., 236*n* (See also Snoddy, Col Lawrence F., Jr.)
Snyder, Maj Elmer N., 115, 117-118
Snyder, 2dLt Stephen F., 185, 186*n*
Somerville, LtCol Daniel A., 303, 305
Son Tinh, 120
Song Cau Do, illus., 248 (See also Cau Do River)
Song Khe Gio, 181 (See also Khe Gio River)
Song Ly Ly Valley, 214 (See also Ly Ly River Valley)
Song Ngan, 166-169, 172 (See also Ngan River)
Song Ngan Valley, 163 (See also Ngan Valley)
Song O Lau, 147 (See also O Lau River)
Song Tra Bong, 241 (See also Tra Bong River)
Song Tra Bong Valley, 271 (See Tra Bong Valley)
Song Thu Bon, 210 (See also Thu Bon River)
Song Tranh, 213
Song Ve, 29, 236-237
Song Ve Valley, 25, 27-29
South Carolina Contingency Plan, 312-314
South China Sea, 3, 17, 24, 102, 110, 161, 198, 318
South Korea (Republic of Korea) (ROK), 313
  ROK Army, 314, 317
  ROK Marine Brigade, 15, 51, 65, 131
  2d Korean Marine Brigade, 223; illus., 222
  ROK Marines, 223*n*, 280, 311, 314
South Vietnam (Republic of Vietnam) (RVN), 3, 75, 88*n*, 139, 145, 160, 176*n*, 196, 224*n*, 231, 248*n*, 250, 252, 254, 256-257, 261, 261*n*, 262, 264, 266, 268, 270-271, 275, 277*n*,

INDEX

283, 283n, 285, 287, 288, 288n, 292n, 297-300, 303n, 304-305, 307, 314, 316-317, 319; illus., 141, 157, 263, 280, 286, 309
South Vietnamese Air Force, 85, 87; illus., 263
South Vietnamese Armed Forces (RVNAF), 6-7, 253n, 254, 310
    Armed Forces Council, 90
South Vietnamese Army or Army of the Republic of Vietnam (ARVN), 3, 21-22, 25, 29n, 40-1, 41n, 49-50, 52, 56, 65, 76, 78, 81-90, 92, 92n, 93, 100, 102, 104, 109-110, 111n, 112, 113n, 115, 119-121, 124-128, 135, 141, 145-150, 154-156, 160-161, 164, 171, 176, 188, 196, 198, 210, 214, 219, 221, 223-224, 227, 231-232, 237, 239n, 240, 247, 252-254, 256, 272, 277-278, 280, 310, 313, 316, 318; illus., 119, 156, 161, 227
    ARVN Units
    1st ARVN Division, 3, 51-52, 56, 58, 64-65, 74, 81, 85, 89-90, 140, 143, 146-147, 149-150, 155-157, 160-161, 163, 163n, 310-311, 317
    2d ARVN Division, 3, 21-23, 25, 58, 88, 109, 111, 111n, 117-118, 120-121, 132, 135-136, 211, 214, 236-237, 311; illus., 89, 119, 127
        Reconnaissance Company, 24, 135
        Strike Company, 115, 115n, 124
    22d ARVN Division, 13, 22, 25
    ARVN Airborne Task Force Alfa, 115
    1st ARVN Airborne Battalion, 109-110, 115, 117
    2d ARVN Regiment, 2d Battalion, 145
    3d ARVN Regiment, 65
        1st Battalion, 52
    4th ARVN Regimental Task Force, 127
    4th ARVN Regiment, 23, 121
        3d Battalion, 2d Company, 25
    4th ARVN Armored Cavalry, 214
        2d Troop, 214
        3d Troop, 214
    5th ARVN Regiment, 1st Battalion, 118, 125
        2d Battalion, 121
        3d Battalion, 121, 127
    5th ARVN Airborne Battalion, 115, 117, 120-121, 125
    6th ARVN Regiment, 214, 219
        2d Battalion, 214
        4th Battalion, 214
    37th Ranger Battalion, 9, 115, 118
    39th Ranger Battalion, 80, 92
    51st ARVN Regiment, 3, 41, 45, 78, 80, 102, 205, 227, 234, 278; illus., 233
        2d Battalion, 207
            3d Company, 209
        3d Battalion, 232
    59th Regional Force Battalion, 40
    519th ARVN Ordnance Company, 87
    936th Regional Force (RF) Company, 120
South Vietnamese Government (GVN), 3, 38, 38n 40, 43, 47, 75, 80, 85, 89, 92, 102, 222, 227, 238, 247-248, 257
    Constituent Assembly, 221
    Directorate, 8, 73, 82, 85, 88, 90-91 (See also National Leadership Committee)
    Administration, Ministry of, 255
    Agriculture, Ministry of, 255
    Public Works, Ministry of, 255
    National Leadership Council (See also Directorate), 73-74, 255
    National Police, 84, 87, 90
    People-Army Council, 90
    Revolutionary Development Ministry, 255
South Vietnamese Joint General Staff, 8, 15, 64, 149, 161, 253-255
South Vietnamese Marine Corps (Vietnamese Marines), 82-84, 86, 88, 90, 92, 100, 135, 147, 148n, 149, 154-156, 214, 216, 219-220, 308-310; illus., 156, 309-310
    South Vietnamese Marine Corps Units
    Vietnamese Marine Brigade, 310
        Task Force Bravo, 25, 34
        1st Battalion, 216
        2d Battalion, 155, 156
            H&S Company, 155
            1st Company, 155
            2d Company, 155
            3d Company, 155
            4th Company, 155
South Vietnamese Navy, 310
South Vietnamese Special Forces, 64
    Mobile Strike Force, 58, 58n
    Project Delta, 64-65
    "Roadrunner" teams, 64
Southeast Asia, 271, 285
Southeast Asia Religious Research Project, 244n
Sparrow Hawk, 48, 48n, 100
Spaulding, LtCol Jack D., 163, 168, 172-173
Spurlock, Maj David A., 117
Starbird, LtGen Alfred, USA, 316-317
Steel Tiger, 271-272
Stiles, BGen William A., 9, 128n, 131-132, 135-136, 214n, 223, 303
Stringray Operations, 175, 175n, 177, 290; illus., 211
"Street Without Joy," 56
Stribling, LtCol Joe B., 214, 280, 280n
Stroud, Capt William, USN, 299n
"Struggle Forces", 74, 81-82, 84-88, 92, 102, 147, 149 (See also Military & Civilian Struggle Committee; Popular Forces to Struggle for the Revolution; Struggle Group; & Struggle Movement")
Struggle Group (See Struggle Forces), 149
Struggle Movement, 88, 98, 149, 221, 311; illus., 85
Subic Bay, Philippines, 9, 285, 300
Sullivan, LtCol Arthur J., 132, 134-136, 211, 213
Sullivan, LtCol John B., 277, 277n
Sullivan, Sgt Joseph, 242-243
Sullivan, LtCol Ralph E., 18-19, 64-65, 67, 69, 90n, 143, 145, 149, 284n
Suoi Co Ca River, 78

Ta Bat, 56
Ta Trach River, 50
Tactical Air Control Center (TACC), 29n, 123
Tactical Air Direction Center (TADC), 269
Tactical Air Fuel Dispensing System (TAFDS), 29
Tactical Air Operations Center (TAOC), 269
Taiwan, 279
Tally Ho, 272, 274

Tam Ky, 34, 131-132, 135-136, 213-214, 216-217, 217n, 220, 309; illus., 217
Tam Quan, 21
Tan Son Nhut Airfield, 270
Taylor, Col Harry W., 261
Taylor, LtCol William W., 37, 47, 76, 76n, 78, 80, 93, 95; illus., 93
Tennessee Contingency Plan, 313-314
Terrebone, 1stLt Theard J., Jr., 159; illus., 160
Tach An Noi, 124
Tach An Noi (1), 125, 126
Thach Thuong (3), 216
Thach Tru, 10, 22
Thailand, 256
Thang Binh, 135, 213-214, 219
Thang Binh-Hiep Duc Road, 214
Thang, Gen Nguyen Duc, 45, 254-255
Thanh, Capt Dinh Tan, 87-88
Thanh Quit, 232
Thanh Quit (3), 232
Thanh Quit Bridge, 83
Thanh Quit River, 37, 47, 76, 78, 97, 102, 232
Thi, LtGen Nguyen Chanh, 8, 21, 41, 64, 73-74, 80-81, 84, 88, 90, 90n, 132, 147, 319; illus., 73, 89
Thieu, Gen Nguyen Van, 8, 44, 84; illus., 45, 251
Thomas, Col Franklin C., Jr., 290
Thomaston, (LSD 28), illus., 305
Thon Hai (3), 217
Thon Son Lam, 187, 191, 313
Thu Bon River, 3, 37, 40, 47-48, 76, 78, 92-93, 95, 97, 99, 102, 201-202, 204, 206, 206n, 207-209 (See also Song Thu Bon)
Thu Duong, 50
Thua Thien Province, 3, 5, 11, 50-52, 54, 56, 58, 64, 89-90, 139-140, 143-145, 150, 156, 158, 160, 197, 281, 303, 313-314, 317, 319; illus., 59, 152, 197
Thuy Tan, 50
Tien Phuoc Special Forces Camp, 132, 135, 213
Tiensha Peninsula, 37, 83-84, 86-87, 270; illus., 87, 292
Tiger Hound, 271-272, 274
Tillson, MajGen John C. III, USA, 253, 307n
Tinh Hoi Pagoda, 87-88
Tioga County (LST 1158), 25n
Tom Green County (LST 1159), 25n
Ton Buu, 81
Topeka (CLG 8), 25n
Tra Bong River, 17, 19, 114-15, 120, 242-43 (See also Song Tra Bong)
Tra Cau River, 30
Tra Khuc River, 115, 126, 128
Trammell, Col Paul C., 83n, 95-96; illus., 202
Tranh, Gen Nguyen Chi, illus., 11
Tranh River, 132
Trevino, LtCol Rodolfo L., 18-19, 24, 26, 29
Tri-Thien-Hue Military Region, 11, 140
Troung River, 286n
Trum, Capt Herman J., USN, 304
Trung Luong (4), 78
Trung Phan Peninsula, 18
Truoi River, 54
Truoi River Bridge, 52, 54

Truong Giang River, 17
Truong, Col Ngo Quang, 149; Gen, 161, 163n
Tucker, 1stLt Phillip E., 308
Tuong, LtCol Le Trung, 40
Tweed, LtCol McDonald D., illus., 214
Typhoon Ora, 173

U.S. Agency for International Development (USAID), 227, 256, 256n; illus., 227
U.S. Embassy, Vietnam, 7, 44, 227, 257
U.S. Information Agency, 247, 256n
U.S. Information Service Building, 81, 147
U.S. Information Service Library, 89
U.S. Joint Agency Planning Group, 254
U.S. Military Assistance Command (USMACV), 6-9, 11, 13-15, 21, 21n, 28, 38n, 44, 51, 56, 59, 61, 62n, 63-64, 69, 74-75, 78, 82-85, 87, 90, 127, 131, 139-140, 143, 145, 157, 161, 177, 196n, 197, 197n, 211, 226, 233, 240, 247, 251-255, 257, 268-269, 272, 274, 283, 283n, 299, 303, 303n, 304, 304n, 307, 307n, 310-314, 316-319; illus., 30, 127, 163, 251, 318
MACV Aviation Directive 95-4, 268-269
MACV Combat Operations Center, 65, 303n, 307-308, 317; illus., 307
MACV enemy order of battle, 139
MACV Joint Strategic Objectives Plan for 1972 (SOP), 308, 308n
MACV Letter of Instruction, 21Nov65, 14
U.S. Mission Council, 7, 252, 254, 257, 313
U.S. Operation Mission (USOM), 8, 249
U.S. State Department, 313
U.S. Strike Command, 75n
Utter, LtCol Leon N., 18-19, 34-35, 90n, 109-110, 112-113, 113n, 114, 117, 119, 128; Col 128n

Vale, LtCol Sumner A., 65, 90n, 143, 149, 163-64, 166-169, 166n, 171, 171n, 174; Col, 8n, 165n
Valley Forge (LPH 8), 25n, 27, 29, 263, 297, 300; illus., 28
Van Ha (1), 237-238; illus., 237-238
Vancouver (LPD 2), 188
Vasdias, 1stLt Richard A., 58
Vichy French, 38n
Vien, Gen Cao Van, 161, 253-254
Viet Cong, 11, 13-15, 18-19, 21-22, 24, 28, 30, 34-37, 40-1, 41n, 43-44, 47-52, 56, 67, 69, 75-6, 78-80, 88n, 92, 92n, 93, 96-97, 99-100, 102, 104, 117, 121, 124, 126-128, 131, 143, 145, 147-148, 154-156, 160, 187, 201-202, 205-206, 208-211, 213, 217, 221-222, 224, 227, 231, 231n, 232-234, 236-239, 241-243, 243n, 244-247, 246n, 252-255, 257-258, 282, 297, 300, 303, 310, 316, 319; illus., 32, 38, 40, 79, 95-96, 100, 102, 207, 217, 232, 238, 246, 265, 300
Viet Cong Units
1st Viet Cong (VC) Regiment, 10, 34, 120, 127, 131, 213
1st Provisional VC Regiment, 51, 64
2d VC Regiment, 10, 23
5th VC Battalion, 41, 93
6th VC Regiment, 51
38th Independent Battalion, 23, 236
44th VC Battalion, 236
60th VC Battalion, 127
80th VC Battalion, 35

INDEX

90th VC Battalion, 127
800th VC Battalion, 147
802d VC Battalion, 64-65, 57, 154-156, 224; illus., 156
803d VC Battalion, 51
804th VC Battalion, 64-65, 143
806th VC Battalion, 56
808th VC Battalion, 56
810th VC Main Force Battalion, 50-52, 54, 56; illus., 52
VC R-20 (Doc Lap) Battalion, 41, 79-80, 92, 95, 97, 99-100, 201, 204, 207-209
   1st Company, 201
   Binh Son Transportation Battalion, 23
   VC A-19 Local Force Command, 19
   VC A-21 Local Force Company, 19
Viet Minh, 38n, 56, 241
Vinh Dien River, 232
Vinh Huy, 219
Vinh Loc (2), 128
Vinh Tuy Valley, 121, 123
Vu Gia River, 40-41, 93, 97, 208
Vu Gia River Valley, 270
Vung Tau Peninsula, 305
Vung Tau Training Center, 227

Walker, LtCol Emerson A., 222, 284n
Waller, MajGen Littleton W.T., 234n
Waller, Maj Littleton W. T. II, 234, 234n, 236-39
Walt, MajGen Lewis W., 3, 6-8, 11, 13-15, 17, 21, 21n, 22, 24, 34, 34n, 43, 47, 51, 58n; LtGen, 61, 64-65, 69, 75-76, 76n, 81-88, 90, 90n, 93, 109, 125, 127-128, 132, 135, 140, 142, 147, 149, 156-158, 160-161, 175-176, 188, 195-197, 197n, 204, 207, 210, 214, 220-222, 227, 231, 231n, 232-234, 239, 241, 243-245, 247, 249, 257, 268, 272, 274, 280-282, 285, 286n, 287-288, 310, 312, 314, 318-319; illus., MajGen, 6, 14, 30, 44; LtGen, 87, 89, 93, 227, 307, 318
"Walt's Ridge," 6
War Games Group, 231n
Ward, RAdm Norvell G., 8, 75, 308
Warrenton, Virginia, 44
Washington, D.C., 34, 88, 109, 140, 257, 304n, 307-308, 314, 317
Watson, LtCol Paul B., Jr., 123; Col, 115n
Watson, Col Robert B., 231n
Watson, LtCol Warren C., 80n, 205, 263
Weapons and Vehicles
   Armored car, M8, illus., 156
   Bomb, 250 pound, 33, 175, 290
   Bomb, 500 pound, 290
   Bomb, 750 pound, 290
   Bomb, 1000 pound, 290
   Bomb, 2000 pound, 266
   Cannon, 20mm, 61, 80, 87, 265
   Grenade Launcher M79, 99; illus., 110
   Gun, 8-inch, 189
   Gun, 90mm, 182; illus., 206
   Gun, 155mm, 23, 115, 206n, 210, 279
   Gun, 175mm, 278-280
   Howitzer, 8-inch, 83, 206n, 210, 279, 280n
   Howitzer, 105mm, 24, 41, 50, 50n, 56, 67, 123, 135, 142, 164, 211, 276, 278-279, 281n, 290; illus., 31, 277
   Howitzer, 155mm, 23, 50, 50n, 67, 82-83, 83n, 123, 135, 158, 164, 168, 177, 179, 182, 186, 206n, 276, 280, 280n, 281; illus., 276
   Howtar, 107mm, 50, 50n, 276
   LVTE-1, 48
   LVTH, 26, 93, 95, 281n
   LVTP, 202, 205
   Machine gun, 12.7mm., 119, 182-184, 201; illus., 199
   Machine gun, .30 caliber, 104n; illus., 131, 206
   Machine gun, .50 caliber, 184, 206, 219; illus., 131
   Machine gun, M60, 181, 266-267
   Man-pack line charges, 48, 48n
   Mini-gun, 7.62mm, 185
   Mortar, 4.2-inch, 23, 280
   Mortar, 60mm, 43, 78, 99, 114, 152, 154, 184, 201; illus., 30, 95
   Mortar, 61mm, 67
   Mortar, 80mm, 152
   Mortar, 81mm, 32, 78, 99, 112, 152, 165n, 179, 182, 201; illus., 31, 190
   Mortar, 82mm, 67, 190
   Mortar, 120mm, 19, 43, 43n, 140
   Napalm, 80, 109, 114, 127, 134, 164n, 171, 191, 206, 216, 275
   Ontos, 50, 83, 104, 104n, 154-156, 210, 303
   Radar, TPQ-10, 58, 269
   Radio, AN/PRC-25, 33
   Rifle, AK-47, 11n; illus., 124, 135
   Rifle, M14, 141n; illus., 96
   Rifle, recoilless, 57mm, 154, 210
   Rifle, recoilless, 75mm, 154, 156
   Rifle, recoilless, 106mm, 104n, 182-185; illus., 131, 185
   Rifle, .50 caliber spotting, 104n
   Rocket, 2.75-inch, 87, 266; illus., 266
   Rocket, 3.5-inch, illus., 192
   Sub-machine gun, Thompson, 111n
   Tank, M48, 88, 100, 179, 182, 185, 292; illus., 182, 206
Weaver, Maj Richard A., USA, 239
Weiss (APD 135), 25n
West, Capt Francis J., 175
West Point, 7, 112
Westchester County (LST 1170), 25n
Westerman, LtCol Jack, 181, 186, 189-190
Western Pacific (WestPac), 224n, 261, 261n, 283n, 285, 285n, 287, 297n, 299, 303n
Westmoreland, Gen William C., USA, 7, 7n, 8, 10, 13-14, 14n, 15, 15n, 19, 44, 51, 56, 58n, 61, 65, 69, 74-75, 84, 88, 90, 90n, 127, 139-140, 142-143, 145, 157, 160-161, 177, 188, 195, 196n, 197, 197n, 207, 211, 227, 233, 245, 251-253, 253n, 254-256, 256n, 257, 268-269, 271-272, 283, 289, 297, 300, 303, 303n, 304, 304n, 305, 307-308, 311-314, 316-319; illus., 127, 163, 227, 318
Whieley, Cpl Mark E., 173
White, Sgt James, 243
Wickwire, LtCol Peter A., 196, 198
Widdecke, Col Charles F., 130, 213-214, 218, 303; illus., 217
Willis, 1stLt Robert T., 190
Windham County (LST 1159), 25n
World War II, 6, 38n, 48, 181, 278n
Wortman, Col Harry D., 188n, 306
Wright, Cpl William F., 186n

Xavier, 1stLt Augusto M., 61
Xuan Hoa, 124-125

Yen River, 37, 48, 100, 104
Yeu, Col Dam Quang, 82-83, 83*n*, 102

Young, LtCol James R., 19, 25, 30, 34, 114-115, 117, 119, 121, 124-125

Zitnik, LtCol Robert J., 27-28, 111, 121, 123-124, 134, 216; Col, 3*n*, 22*n*, 29*n*, 33*n*, 48*n*, 120*n*, 134*n*, 217*n*, 264
Zone A, 50

The device reproduced on the back cover is the oldest military insignia in continuous use in the United States. It first appeared, as shown here, on Marine Corps buttons adopted in 1804. With the stars changed to five points this device has continued on Marine Corps buttons to the present day.

www.ingramcontent.com/pod-product-compliance
Lightning Source LLC
Chambersburg PA
CBHW082105230426
43671CB00015B/2608